Christmas 1969.

To Joy, w[...]

thoughts abou[...]

cooking experiments and

successes in

18 Greenside Place.

Affectionately. Carole.

1. Chicken Pie with Oysters, and Lemon Cream, Britain (pp.105, 114)

First Edition, June 1962
Second Revised Edition, 1969

Copyright Paul Hamlyn Ltd. 1962
Published by

SPRING BOOKS

Hamlyn House • The Centre • Feltham • Middlesex

Printed in Czechoslovakia by Svoboda, Prague
T 2052

ENCYCLOPEDIA of
EUROPEAN COOKING

edited by
MUSIA SOPER

SPRING BOOKS

LONDON

CONTENTS

ILLUSTRATIONS

LIST OF ILLUSTRATIONS

INTRODUCTION

In this jet and television age, with the world ever growing smaller and more familiar, and with customs becoming more alike, it is the differences we cherish more and more. It is these differences we seek, as well as the sun, as we travel ever further afield to find new customs, costumes, scenery and cooking. Sometimes, some of us may regard the unaccustomed food with suspicion and even dislike, feeling sure it will 'not agree with us', but once that prejudice is overcome, we can discover a whole field of fascinating new possibilities and delights, borrowing from all over the world those recipes we like best and preparing them in our own kitchens or trying them out in foreign restaurants, here or abroad. But we need to be adventurous. When confronted with a small, spider-like octopus on your plate of Fritto Misto Mare (mixed fried fish) it needs courage to eat it the first time, and probably the encouragement of a nice-looking Italian waiter to urge the signora to try it, at least, and prove how good it really is, otherwise he will be most hurt that this delicacy of Italy is disdained. Then, of course, there are things like the snails of France and the frogs' legs that taste like delicate chicken. However, let us not go to extremes at first. French Onion Soup, Italian Ravioli or Russian Beef Stroganoff will do very well to begin with. They are not difficult to prepare and, when met with anywhere, not to be feared as something exotic or too out of the way.

In the old days, before travelling became easy, each country's cooking was well defined, and it often took the conquest of one country by another to introduce new dishes. Even each region had its specialities as, for instance, in the counties or even towns of England, with their Banbury Cakes, Yorkshire Pudding, Cornish Pasties and so on. In Italy, the provinces have still retained their own tradition of cooking and many of their towns such as Florence, Venice and Bologna provide highly individual dishes. Many other countries make good use of their local produce.

In this book of European cooking, I have tried to include all the most typical and well known recipies of each country, laying the emphasis on the particular specialities of that country. For instance, the many dishes of Russia where smetana (sour cream) is used, the famous sausages of Germany, the pasta of Italy, the desserts and pastry of Austria, the Hungarian dishes cooked with paprika, the sauces of France and the variety of fish dishes of Scandinavia. Each country has a special dish particularly associated with it. Borshch, a red-coloured beetroot soup, immediately brings Russia to mind; Spaghetti Bolognese can only be from Italy; Poulet Marengo is one of the innumerable *pièces de résistance* of France; pastries with mountains of whipped cream are at home in Vienna. Then there is the infinite variety of hors-d'oeuvre which is the invention and glory of Scandinavian countries; the best fish and chips — where else but England, of course! Paella is the name of the golden-coloured rice dish filled with many delicacies which belongs to Spain. In Yugoslavia you are bound to eat Djuveč, a full-bodied meat stew and in Hungary their famous Chicken Goulash. Germany will offer you Frankfurters with Sauerkraut, the Czechs will fatten you on a variety of dumplings and the Turks will produce their famous Kebabs served on rice. Try the Greek Dolma, and for a convivial evening with your friends make some famous Swiss Fondue.

It is a matter of opinion where the best cooking is to be found. The Finns like their Blood Pancakes and the English prefer their Steak and Kidney Pie; Europeans in the South must have their garlic and wine cooking, but the general consensus of opinion has established France as the Queen of Cooking. It is true that like so many other things — art, ballet, music—the art of cooking has been influenced by Italy. Italian cooking was introduced into France at the time of the Renaissance; it was in the first part of the sixteenth century that Catherine de Medici brought her own Italian cook to France when she married Henry II. However, France soon made the art her own and has since not been surpassed. It is not that the French are greedier than anyone else or use better ingredients; on the contrary, they choose carefully what they eat and they are thrifty, but they have the imagination and wit to make the necessary function of eating delightful — a time to be spent not only in eating delicious, well cooked food, but in vivacious conversation on all subjects. Thus by the variety of their dishes and talk, they avoid monotony.

Climate gives Southern Europe some advantages over the North. It has more sun, warmth and colour as well as a wonderful variety of food. In the South, the dishes do not nearly all consist of garlic, oil and spices, as some people may suspect; fish, fruit of all kinds, olives, tomatoes, wine and cheese are abundant in most parts, and what could be better than these things for delicious, healthy eating? But the North has its good things too: rich soups, varieties of hors-d'oeuvre, game, poultry, meat dishes and an assortment of puddings.

Nowadays, professional cooks are mostly to be found only in hotels and restaurants. Very few people can afford cooks or to eat out all the time, so many more people do their own cooking — even quite a few men. For that reason no doubt, and because more people travel further afield, more and more interest has been shown of late in cooking and cookery books. Some people read cookery books just for the fun of it; some even take them to bed for soothing bedtime reading. When you are worried about money or love affairs going wrong, or the *faux pas* you made that morning, what could be more soothing and more likely to calm those jaded nerves than to murmur as you wait to fall asleep: '... Rose Petal Jam ... take fresh, pink rose petals, add sugar and rose-water', ... or ... 'For Gogol-Mogol, beat the egg yolks with sugar and heat gently...'

Cooking your way round Europe will lead you to a lot of discoveries if you are curious, not only about cooking but about the climate, habits and history of many places. You may want to find out why Turkish cooking has had so much influence on other countries; you will get to know that the Turks have been grilling pieces of meat on skewers over an open fire since time immemorial, and that their cooking is derived from the ancient Byzantine world. Dolma, which is a meat mixture wrapped in vine leaves, may remind you of the vineyards of Greece from where the leaves are obtained, and of the wine, maybe coming from Samos, one of the many islands of Greece. Perhaps you will be led to find out that in the vastness of Russia there are many nationalities, not only one, each with its own language, customs and ways of cooking. Because of the lack of transport in the past, over the long distances, regions remained isolated so they kept to their own ways for a long time. Food could not travel and there was no refrigeration, so when the milk and cream went sour, Yoghourt, cream cheese and smetana came into their own, with the smetana enhancing many a dish. Ways were found to preserve fish, fruit and vegetables with salt and by pickling.

You will find too that the exotic quality in the gypsy music of Hungary is reflected in their dancing, costumes and cooking. There appears to be no connection between colourful Hungary and the cold northern country of Finland, with its forests, reindeer and long, snowy winters; yet, we are told, there is an affinity between the Magyar language of Hungary and the language of Finland.

Many dishes were invented for economy, others were prepared specially for various festivals. Meat has nearly always been an expensive item everywhere, so it happened that in England, for example, the famous Yorkshire Pudding was originally made not to eat *with* Roast Beef but *before* it, so as to reduce appetites before the meat was served. Many dishes are prepared specially for the festival of Easter; Simnel Cake, Hot Cross Buns and Pancakes in England, Easter Lamb in Greece, Paskha, an elaborate cream cheese dish, in Russia, and many others. The Hungarians have Roast Sucking Pig for New Year and in Holland there are Letter Biscuits for St. Nicholas Day. There are many old customs in connection with eating which are linked with the history of the country.

Cooking the European way need not be difficult or expensive. After all, many of the dishes were invented to be cooked very simply over an open fire or in the simple kitchen of a peasant cottage. Bouillabaisse, the famous fish stew of Marseille, was first made and eaten by fishermen while on boats fishing in the Mediterranean. The Russian peasants made their beetroot and cabbage soups from what grew in the fields around them. The Greeks just grill or fry the red mullet of which they are so fond, the Portuguese can do wonders with cod and the Scandinavians with herring. Whatever has been near, handy and cheap has been used by the local people and turned into something good to eat. It is not so much what you cook as how you cook it and the imagination, time and patience you give to it. It is those little touches which count and give variety, like the well dressed woman we all hear about, with the simple well cut dress and *good*, attractive accessories. In cooking it is

9

the *soupçon* of garlic, the glass of wine, the dash of rum, the pinch of this and that, a good oil or fresh butter for frying and, sometimes, an unusual combination of ingredients which give a dish its individuality. Who would guess how good rabbit cooked with prunes could be, or chicken with nut sauce, or fish with olives, or potatoes browned with sugar, or aubergine made to resemble caviar, or grouse stuffed with grapes, and many other weird and wonderful combinations?

The general principles of good cooking are, after all, not so different anywhere. In Southern Europe, a good olive oil is mostly used, but a maize or corn oil is now generally considered to be healthier for cooking. The French use mostly butter for their cooking. No vegetables should be drowned in water and judicious use should be made of garlic, onions, and herbs. Wine is nearly always a great improvement on water for stews and sauces, and so is ale or cider. Sherry, Marsala, Madeira and brandy in small quantities are an excellent addition for flavouring sweet or savoury sauces and puddings. Smetana gives a unique flavour to some dishes, but remember to blend it with a little flour before adding it, otherwise it will disintegrate in cooking.

Most ingredients required for Continental cooking can be obtained from the food departments of large stores, delicatessen shops anywhere and the Soho area of London.

In the collection of recipes in this book, most are for four people, except where otherwise stated or obviously not practicable.

Remember, then, that cooking need not always be a chore; it can be fun and creative fun at that. It is like so many things, a question of overcoming prejudice, abandoning too fixed habits and getting rid of a few inhibitions. Remember, too, all those who are figure-conscious, that the larger the choice of food the less likely you are to pick on the fattening ones.

In this book you have such a wide choice of recipes that it is hoped that all of you will like some of them, and in any case, will get to know a great many dishes you may meet on your travels whether in fact, or in fancy from your armchair.

WEIGHTS AND MEASURES

English weights and measures have been used throughout this book. 3 teaspoons equal 1 tablespoon. The average English teacup is ¼ pint or 1 gill. The average English breakfast cup is ½ pint or 2 gills. When cups are mentioned in recipes they refer to a B.S.I. measuring cup which holds ½ pint or 10 fluid ounces. The B.S.I. standard tablespoon measures 1 fluid ounce.

In case it is wished to translate any of the weights and measures into their American, Canadian or French counterparts, the following tables give a comparison.

LIQUID MEASURE

The most important difference to be noted is that the American and Canadian pint holds 16 fluid ounces, as opposed to the British Imperial pint which is 20 fluid ounces. The American ½-pint measuring cup is therefore equivalent to two-fifths of a British pint.

ENGLISH	AMERICAN
1 lb. Butter or other fat	2 cups
1 lb. Flour	4 cups
1 lb. Granulated or Castor Sugar	2 cups
1 lb. Brown (moist) Sugar	2½ cups
1 lb. Icing or Confectioner's Sugar	3 cups
1 lb. Syrup or Treacle	1 cup
1 lb. Dried Fruit	2 cups
1 lb. Chopped Meat (finely packed)	2 cups
1 lb. Lentils or Split Peas	2 cups
1 lb. Coffee (unground)	2½ cups
1 lb. Breadcrumbs	4 cups
½ oz. Flour	1 level tablespoon
1 oz. Flour	1 heaped tablespoon
1 oz. Syrup or Treacle	1 tablespoon
1 oz. Sugar	1 level tablespoon
1 oz. Jam or Jelly	1 level tablespoon
½ oz. Butter	1 tablespoon smoothed off

FRENCH MEASURES

It is difficult to convert to French measurements with absolute accuracy, since 1 oz. is equivalent to 28.352 grammes. The table below is therefore very approximate.

Liquid Measure

Approximately 1¾ English pints may be regarded as equal to 1 litre. 1 demilitre is half a litre, and 1 decilitre is one-tenth of a litre.

Solid Measure

1 oz. is equal to approximately 30 grammes.
Approximately 2 lb. 3 oz. is equal to 1 kilogramme.

COOKING TEMPERATURES

Water
Simmering 180 °F.
Boiling   212 °F.

Oven Temperatures	Electricity °F.	Gas Regulo No.
COOL	225—250	0—½
VERY SLOW	250—275	½—1
SLOW	275—300	1—2
VERY MODERATE	300—350	2—3
MODERATE	350—375	4
MODERATELY HOT	375—400	5
HOT	400—450	6—7
VERY HOT	450—500	8—9

Note: This table is an approximate guide only. Different makes of cooker vary and if you are in any doubt about the setting it is as well to refer to the manufacturer's temperature chart.
To convert °F. to °C., subtract 32° and multiply by $\frac{5}{9}$.
To convert °C. to °F., multiply by $\frac{9}{5}$ and add 32°.

AUSTRIAN COOKING

Ann Knox

The Austrians cook in the same way as they dance and make music—light-heartedly, lavishly and enthusiastically. Even in their most economical dishes—and there are many of them—there is gaiety and imagination, a let's-have-a-party feeling that is irresistible.

Austria has had a long and chequered career at the cross-roads of Europe. Even the Romans campaigned from Vienna. Innumerable races—the Turks, the Hungarians, the Italians, the Germans—have been in and out of Vienna, and each left behind its legacy of cooking, which the Austrians immediately took and adapted in their own characteristic way. They added their own brilliance and lightness, their own sparkling flavouring to every dish they borrowed, even the great French ones.

When Vienna became a great capital in the seventeenth century, Austrian cooking really began to develop into an art. That was when the famous Viennese pastry began to be made. Food and ideas for cooking were imported from all over the continent, even from distant countries like Poland and Russia, and adapted to appreciative Austrian palates. The beloved sour cream came from the Slavs. The paprika which brightens so many Austrian dishes came from Hungary (Hungary got it from Turkey, and Turkey got it from India). The innumerable noodle dishes came from Italy. But everything, as soon as it reached Austria, became Austrian. The Austrian accent was quickly acquired!

Austrian cooking in its turn has a really universal appeal. It is substantial, not 'fussy', and very nourishing. Although some of the famous cakes and pastries are so wildly extravagant that they can only be used for special occasions (but well worth the indulgence!) most of the others are marvellously economical. The meat dishes, for instance, were ingeniously evolved because the Austrians were loth to kill bulls. They felt that it was wasteful to keep them and have to feed them all that time while they grew up and did no useful work. Therefore they kept only the cows, which had to work hard producing milk and calves, and were killed only when they were old and tough. So these mouth-watering dishes make brilliant use of old or tough or scraggy meat.

The many veal dishes, at which the Viennese are virtuosi, grew from the fact that so many baby bulls were killed. The celebrated Wiener Schnitzel is one result — a dish quite easy to master and very impressive to serve. The healthy down-to-earth soups, with their noodle and dumpling additions, are a brilliant way of supplying good filling food at little cost, or when supplies are scarce. And the sauces are so titillating that they can be like fairy godmothers to plain fish or cold meat.

You will find many unusual herbs called for, and it is well worth getting to know them. Many of them can be grown in your garden, some of them even in a window-box. Try chervil, chives, fennel, shallots, sorrel, mint, parsley, marjoram, thyme, garlic, bay leaves. Others you may have to buy dry, or order from a herb-farm. There are several of these farms which post fresh herbs to any address all through the year. You'll need basil, capers, juniper, tarragon, and of course caraway seeds. The Austrians adore caraway seeds and have added them to many of their borrowed dishes with characteristic dash. Buy your cinnamon in sticks, and your vanilla in pods if you want the truly subtle flavouring that the Austrians insist on in their sweet dishes.

You probably won't need any special equipment for any of these dishes, as you will have most of the things you will need on hand already. But you may need a larding needle.

A mould with a hollow centre isn't *absolutely* necessary, but it does give that gay Austrian look to your puddings, aspics and cakes. The Austrians use a great deal of art in the decoration of their dishes. For the same reason a piper for piping mayonnaise and icing would be a useful addition to your kitchen. You will certainly need lots of cake and bread tins, if you are to try all these tempting recipes. And you will need a deep fat-fryer. It will have lots of exciting new jobs to do!

A typical Austrian meal, especially in the good old days but even to-day, would be far too much for the average person's appetite—or capacity! You would begin with soup with noodles or dumplings, and fresh rolls or bread; or hors-d'oeuvre, if you hadn't had these as a snack before the meal. Then you would have a fish course with sauce and maybe potatoes; then meat; then chicken; with salad and or vegetables accompanying each. Then you would finish off with a sweet and cakes, coffee and liqueurs. There would be different wines throughout the meal.

But you cannot make the acquaintance of Austrian food without catching the spirit of it. You will find yourself improvising in a typically Austrian way. You will find yourself getting inspired ideas for out-of-the-ordinary meals. And it's a pretty sure guess that no matter how conservative your family may be about food, they won't take long to become enthusiasts about Austrian food.

There's something about Austrian cooking that makes food seem more fun!

ANCHOVY SHELLS

Sardellen in Muscheln

6 SERVINGS

8 oz. butter	2 tablespoons grated	6 scallop shells
5 eggs	Parmesan cheese	1 tablespoon fine
6 anchovy fillets	2 teaspoons chopped	breadcrumbs
	chives	

Cream the butter and add slowly the yolks of 5 eggs. Mix well, then add the anchovy fillets which have been carefully pounded beforehand. Stir well together. Now stir in the grated Parmesan cheese and the chives. Beat the egg whites until they are frothy, then fold them into the creamed mixture.

Fill the scallop shells with this mixture, sprinkle with breadcrumbs and cook in a hot oven for 10 or 15 minutes.

CHICKEN PANCAKES

Hühnerpalatschinken

egg-batter pancake
  mixture (see p. 26)
1 lb. cooked diced
  chicken
4 oz. chopped
  mushrooms

juice ½ lemon
2 tablespoons butter
  or margarine
1 teaspoon chopped
  chives
2 tablespoons cream

½ tablespoon flour
pinch cayenne pepper
salt and pepper
1 tablespoon grated
  Parmesan cheese

Melt 1½ tablespoons butter over a very low flame and stir in juice
of lemon. Add the chopped chicken meat, stir, cover and cook gently
for a few minutes. Add the mushrooms, chives, salt, pepper and cayenne
pepper, mix, cover, and cook for a another few minutes. Cream ½ tablespoon flour and ½ tablespoon butter together, add to the chicken mixture
together with the cream, cover and continue cooking very gently for
5 minutes. Make 4 pancakes with the egg-batter pancake mixture.
Spread these out and fill each with 4 tablespoons of the chicken and
mushroom mixture. Fold them over and place them in a fireproof
dish. Pour the remainder of the chicken and mushroom mixture over
them, sprinkle with Parmesan cheese and brown in a hot oven. *(Illustrated
in Plate 2.)*

GOOSE LIVERS

Gänseleber

4 goose livers
3 oz. butter
4 oz. mushrooms

4 tablespoons dry
  white wine

4 tablespoons sour
  cream
salt and pepper

Get the butter sizzling hot in a frying pan. Chop up the livers and fry
them in the butter for 3 or 4 minutes, stirring them constantly. Chop
up the mushroom caps, unpeeled, and add them to the frying pan.
Sprinkle with salt and pepper. Reduce the heat to low. Pour on the
wine. Stir. Cook very gently for about 10 minutes or until the livers
are quite tender, then add the cream. Serve on thin slices of toast.

HAM SLICES

Schinkenschnitten

6 TO 8 SERVINGS

1 lb. minced ham
4 oz. butter
½ pint thin cream

4 oz. grated cheese
2 oz. fine
  breadcrumbs
7 eggs

1 teaspoon chopped
  parsley
salt and black pepper

2. Chicken Pancakes, Austria (p.16)

3. Pork Chops in Fruit Aspic, Britain (p.95)

4. Blanquette de Veau, France (p.226)

Cream the butter. Add the egg yolks slowly, beating well as you add them. Then stir in the ham, cheese, cream and a good pinch of salt and black pepper. Beat the egg whites until stiff, then fold them into the mixture. Add the breadcrumbs and parsley lightly to the mixture. Line a shallow baking dish with greaseproof paper, fill it with the mixture, and cook in a moderate oven for twenty minutes. Serve in slices either hot or cold.

LIVER MEAT CAKE

Leberkuchen

6 SERVINGS OR MORE IF SMALL

1 lb. chopped livers (veal or goose)	½ pint cream	salt and pepper
	4 oz. butter	1 teaspoon parsley
	8 oz. breadcrumbs	2 teaspoons flour
6 eggs	1 gill milk	little mayonnaise

This hors-d'oeuvre should be made some time before you want it. Put the breadcrumbs to soak in the milk. Put the chopped livers in a pan in which you have first melted the butter, and cook them for about 10 minutes, with the lid on the pan, on a low heat. Then remove the livers and mince them into a bowl. Stir the milky breadcrumbs into the minced livers. Add the finely chopped parsley, the cream, the well beaten eggs, salt, and pepper. Melt a little butter and brush a jelly-mould (preferably one with a hollow centre) with it. Then sprinkle a little flour over the butter. Now fill it with the liver mixture and put it to steam for 1½ hours. Remove it from the steamer. Let it cool slightly. Turn it out on a serving dish. Slice it very thinly, and dab it all over with blobs of mayonnaise.

SPRING CHEESE

Frühlingskäse

4 thick slices black bread	8 oz. cream cheese	2 teaspoons paprika
8 stuffed olives	2 tablespoons butter or thick cream	2 teaspoons parsley
1 pickled cucumber	2 teaspoons salt	2 teaspoons chives
		few caraway seeds

Mix the cheese, butter or cream together well with the salt and paprika and caraway seeds. Chop the parsley and chives very, very fine and add them, mixing in well. Pile each slice of bread thickly with this mixture. Slice the olives and cucumber and arrange them over the top of each.

BEETROOT SALAD

Rote Rüben in Essig

1 large or 2 medium beetroots	1 teaspoon caraway seeds 1 pint vinegar	1 tablespoon grated horseradish

Wash the beetroots but do not remove either end. Boil until tender and meantime boil the vinegar with the caraway seeds. When the beetroots have cooled, skin them and cut into thin slices. Lay the slices in a dish with the grated horseradish sprinkled between, then pour the boiling caraway vinegar over and leave to get cold.

HERRING SALAD

Heringssalat

3 filleted salt herrings	1 lb. diced cooked potato	3 tablespoons white wine
2 slices cold pork	1½ gills olive oil	1 chopped onion
1 pickled cucumber	2 tablespoons vinegar	½ teaspoon sugar
2 gherkins	1 teaspoon strong mustard	½ teaspoon salt
3 apples		pinch white pepper
8 oz. diced beetroot		

Chop the salted herrings and pork slices into fairly large pieces. Slice the cucumber and gherkins. Dice the peeled and cored apples. Put all these with the diced beetroot and potatoes into a deep salad bowl. Mix olive oil, vinegar, mustard, wine, finely chopped onion, sugar, salt and pepper. Pour this mixture over the ingredients in the salad bowl, mix gently and serve cold.

DANDELION LEAVES IN SOUR CREAM

Rohsalat in saurem Rahm

1 lb. dandelion leaves	salt and pepper 1 gill sour cream	½ teaspoon paprika

Wash the dandelion leaves well. Put them in a bowl and pour boiling water over them. Drain well. Boil 3 tablespoons salted water and put the leaves in it, cover the pan and cook for 10 minutes, shaking the pan 2 or 3 times during cooking. Drain off all the water. Chop up the leaves coarsely. In a small thick-bottomed saucepan heat the sour cream. Add salt and pepper and stir the chopped leaves into it. Reduce the heat and let the cream begin to show tiny bubbles but not quite to boil. Pour into a serving dish and sprinkle with paprika.

BEGGARMAN'S SOUP

Bettelmannssuppe

4 slices rye bread	sufficient butter to	1 quart stock
4 eggs	spread	chopped parsley

While we may feel that a beggar would not have four eggs, the hostess beggared of time will be glad of this appetizing soup.

Toast the rye bread, and butter generously. Cut into snippets and place in 4 soup plates. While the stock is coming rapidly to a fast simmer, break an egg on to the toast in each plate and sprinkle with parsley. Share the stock equally over each plate and serve immediately.

TYROLEAN CLEAR SOUP WITH SLICED PANCAKES

Tiroler Fridattensuppe

6 SERVINGS

2 pints veal or beef stock	4 unsweetened pancakes (see p. 26)	salt and pepper

Heat the stock. Cut up the pancakes into narrow strips. Drop them in the stock. Simmer gently for 10 minutes and then serve.

VIENNESE BEEF SOUP

Wiener Kraftsuppe

6 TO 8 SERVINGS

2 lb. beef pieces	8 oz. shredded	3 pieces stale bread
8 oz. chopped	cabbage	1 onion
cauliflower	1 quart strong beef	4 oz. mushrooms
2 tablespoons butter	stock	salt and pepper

In a large saucepan, put the butter to melt. Add to it the chopped cauliflower, shredded cabbage, the onion peeled and finely chopped, the mushrooms also chopped, stalks and all, and the beef. Mix them all together, cover the pan and let them cook very slowly for about 7 to 10 minutes, shaking the pan occasionally. Heat the stock to boiling point and pour over the vegetables. Let it simmer for a few minutes removing any scum which forms. Add salt and pepper. Make croûtons with bread. Cut off crusts and dice the bread into about 1-inch cubes. Fry them in hot butter or fat and sprinkle them on top of the soup.

CHICKEN GIBLET SOUP WITH LIVER DUMPLINGS

Suppe mit Leberknödeln

8 oz. chicken livers	4 oz. + 1 heaped	salt and pepper
1 lb. chicken giblets	tablespoon flour	1 tablespoon parsley
2 or 3 chicken legs,	1 large carrot	1 egg
if possible	1 medium sized	2 tablespoons sour
3 oz. butter	parsnip	cream

Put the giblets in 2 pints of salted cold water and bring to the boil. Reduce the heat and simmer for 1 hour. Chop up the carrot and parsnip finely. Put the butter in a thick saucepan and when it has melted, add the carrots and parsnips, sprinkle with salt and pepper, and cook gently over a low heat, with the cover on the saucepan, for 15 minutes, shaking the pan every few minutes. Be sure the heat is very low, or the vegetables will burn. Now add the tablespoon of flour. Blend it well in and then slowly add the water in which the giblets have been cooking. Take the giblets themselves, mince them, and add them to the soup. When the soup comes to the boil, lessen the heat, so that it is barely simmering. Now make the dumplings: put remainder of flour in a big bowl. Beat up the egg in a little water and stir it into the flour. Add more water until you have added about a gill altogether. You should have a fairly thick dough. Chop up the chicken livers very small, and fry them for 3 minutes in 1 tablespoon hot butter. Add salt and pepper. Add the livers to the dough, blending them well in. Raise the heat under the soup and when it begins to bubble take the dough, a teaspoonful at a time, and push each down into the soup. Boil gently for 3 or 4 minutes, not fast, only the gentlest of bubbles. By that time all the little dumplings should be bobbing about on top of the soup. Remove the soup from the fire. Add 2 tablespoons sour cream, and chopped parsley.

VIENNESE CABBAGE SOUP

Wiener Kohlsuppe

6 SERVINGS

1 large cabbage	6 sausages (skinless	1 tablespoon butter
1 quart stock	pork)	salt
1 tablespoon flour		black pepper

Clean the cabbage and remove the soiled and biggest tough outside leaves. Shred it up finely. Melt the butter in a large saucepan and put the cabbage in it until it begins to brown, stirring it about so that all sides get slightly cooked. Sprinkle on the flour, mixing it in well, and cook until the flour also starts to brown. In another saucepan, heat the stock to boiling point, then slowly pour it over the cabbage, stirring all the time. Season with salt and pepper. Reduce heat. Simmer gently for 1 hour. Fry the sausages lightly. Slice them. Add them to the soup just before dishing it up.

CHICKEN AND VEAL BROTH

Lichte Kraftsuppe

5 OR 6 SERVINGS

8 oz. chicken, with skin	1 small pigeon or partridge	top of celery stick
8 oz. veal	2½ pints water	1 teaspoon parsley
8 oz. beef	1 small carrot	white pepper
chicken bones		salt
		1 small onion

Choose a large saucepan, big enough to hold 2 quarts of water. Chop up the raw meat and chicken and pigeon and put them, together with the bones, in the saucepan. Pour in 2½ pints of cold water. Bring to the boil. Remove the scum as it rises. Lower the heat until the water is just gently simmering, and simmer for 4 hours. Scrub the carrot and cut off its discoloured parts and add it whole to the soup. Peel the onion and add it with the celery top. Simmer for another 45 minutes.

Add salt and white pepper. Then strain the soup into a big tureen or individual bowls and garnish with chopped parsley. If you prefer the soup clear, as the Viennese do, add 3 or 4 eggshells, with a bit of white sticking to them, to the soup about 15 minutes before you take it off the stove. Remove the shells, of course, before you strain it. Serve the soup with dumplings (see p. 24).

CUCUMBER SOUP

Gurkensuppe

1 lb. chopped cucumber	1½ oz. butter	½ pint cream
1 chopped onion (rather small)	1 teaspoon chopped parsley	2 oz. white flour
	1½ pints stock	salt and white pepper to taste

Toss the cucumber, onion and parsley in the butter over a low heat until tender. Do not allow to brown. Add the flour, stirring carefully to avoid lumps. Remove from heat. When slightly cooled, add the cream (this way it will not curdle). Add the stock, which should be very hot, gradually. Season to taste and serve with noodles, dumplings or bread.

BREAD SOUP WITH HARD-BOILED EGGS

Brotsuppe mit Eiern

6 slices stale bread	a little butter	8 oz. smoked meat or
1½ pints veal stock	1 tablespoon chopped	sausages
3 eggs	parsley	salt and pepper

Use the end crusts of bread, if possible, but anyhow make sure the bread is quite dry. If necessary, crisp it in the oven. Warm the stock, but do not boil it. Break each piece of bread into about six pieces, and put them all in a large saucepan. Pour the stock over them. Leave for 15 minutes before putting them on the stove, then bring the stock to the boil. Add salt and pepper. Reduce the heat until the soup is barely simmering. Simmer for 30 minutes. With a potato masher or large wooden spoon, mash any bits of bread still intact. Break the yolk of 1 egg into a basin and whip it for 1 or 2 minutes. Take a little stock from the soup and blend it well into the egg. Remove the saucepan of soup from the fire. Wait 1 minute, then carefully stir in the egg and stock mixture. Put in a warm place to keep hot, but on no account let it boil or the egg will curdle. Hard-boil 2 eggs. Remove the shells by first plunging them into cold water. If you are using sausages, fry them lightly now. Fry the chopped parsley in a little butter for 2 or 3 minutes. Slice the hard-boiled eggs and add them, with the sliced sausages or smoked meat, to the soup. Leave for 2 minutes. Sprinkle on the parsley, and serve.

VIENNESE CREAMED LIVER SOUP

Lebersuppe mit Rahm

6 SERVINGS

1 lb. calf's liver	1 large onion	2 tablespoons flour
6 tablespoons sour	1 tablespoon cooking	salt and pepper
cream	fat	2 bay leaves
	2 pints meat stock	

Heat the fat until it is really hot in a large saucepan. Chop up the liver coarsely into pieces about 2 inches square. Peel and chop up the onion very small. Put both liver and onion to fry lightly in the fat, stirring all the time. Gently stir in the flour, little by little. After 2 minutes slowly begin to add the stock, stirring all the time until it is all added. Season with salt and pepper and add the bay leaves. Cover the pan. Simmer for 30 minutes. Remove the pieces of liver, mince them, and put them back in the soup, stirring them well around as you do so. Bring the soup just to the boil. Serve in individual bowls with a tablespoon of sour cream on top of each.

APRICOT SOUP

Marillensuppe

8 oz. fresh apricots	1 lemon	1 tablespoon cornflour
1 quart water	2 tablespoons sugar	

Wash and stone the apricots. Put 1 quart of water in a saucepan. Add the apricots and sugar, and bring to the boil. Reduce the heat and simmer gently for 45 minutes. Then pour the soup through a sieve, pressing the apricots through as much as possible. Return the sieved soup to the saucepan. Mix the cornflour to a smooth runny paste with a little cold water and stir it gradually into the soup. Squeeze the juice of a lemon into it as well, and serve at once.

HOT APPLE SOUP

Apfelsuppe

6 SERVINGS

1 lb. sour or cooking apples	8 oz. sultanas	1 tablespoon butter
	8 oz. currants	1 gill white wine
2 tablespoons sugar	1 or 2 tablespoons cornflour	1 lemon
4 pints water		

Cut up the apples, skin, core, and all, into small pieces and put them into a pan with the wine. Grate lemon rind over. Cook them slowly until the apples are soft. Then press them through a sieve into a bowl and return to the saucepan. Add 4 pints water, the sugar, currants, and sultanas. Simmer gently for 30 minutes. Now melt the butter in a small thick saucepan. Slowly stir the cornflour into it and then add this mixture to the soup gradually, stirring all the time. Simmer for another 10 minutes and then serve. In Austria, larger quantities of sugar and butter are generally used. Try experimenting with more of each and see if you like it the richer way.

FARFERL DOUGH

Farferlteig

4 oz. flour	1 egg white	½ teaspoon salt
1 whole egg		2 tablespoons water

Put the flour into a bowl. Beat the egg, egg white, water and salt together. Pour into the flour until the mixture forms small lumps or crumbs. Place them on a dry tea-towel and leave to dry. Drop the crumbs in boiling salted water. Remove with a draining spoon. Serve with soups and stews.

BREAD DUMPLINGS

Semmelknödel

6 SERVINGS

4 oz. breadcrumbs	1 egg yolk	teaspoon chopped
2 tablespoons melted	a little milk	parsley
butter	2 tablespoons flour	1 pinch marjoram
1 whole egg		½ teaspoon salt

Fry the chopped parsley in a little butter. Damp the breadcrumbs with a little milk. Add the fried parsley to the rest of the melted butter. Beat the whole egg and egg yolk together. Gradually add the egg, salt, marjoram and melted butter mixture to the breadcrumbs. Mix well and make into small dumplings with floured hands. Boil in stock or soup for 20 minutes. Serve with soup.

BUTTER DUMPLINGS

Buttermehlnockerln

3 oz. flour	1 dessertspoon melted	1 egg yolk
1 gill milk	butter	¼ teaspoon salt
1 whole egg		pinch pepper

Beat the whole egg and the egg yolk together. Add salt and pepper to the melted butter. Work all together until well mixed. Gradually add the flour and milk until a soft dough is obtained. These should be made just before the soup is ready to be served. Drop them from a small teaspoon into the boiling soup and do not allow them to cook more than 10 minutes. They will break up if left too long. Serve as a garnish for soup, and always cook them in soup or stock.

SNOW DUMPLINGS

Schneenockerln

6 SERVINGS

3 tablespoons	3 egg whites	¾ teaspoon mixed
semolina		salt and pepper

Beat the egg whites to a very stiff froth. Stir in the semolina and pepper and salt very gradually. Leave for nearly an hour. Use a small teaspoon and drop into boiling clear soup. They should take about 15 minutes. These are best served with white soups or any bouillon.

KIDNEY DUMPLINGS

Nierenknödel

calf's kidney	salt and pepper	1 tablespoon butter
4 oz. white bread- crumbs	1 tablespoon beef marrow	1 tablespoon flour
		3 egg yolks

Chop the kidney finely. Melt the butter in a pan and cook the chopped kidney. Simmer the beef marrow in a very little water for about 10 minutes. Put the cooked kidney in a basin. Add the marrow, bread-crumbs, flour and seasoning. Mix well. Beat the yolks of eggs and bind the mixture with these. The mixture should be firm. If needed, add a little more flour. Make into very tiny balls, about the size of a hazel nut. Drop into the simmering soup, stock or sauce about 10 minutes before the meal is to be served. Serve with soup or goulash.

LIVER DUMPLINGS

Leberknödel

ABOUT 18 DUMPLINGS

1½ lb. liver	pinch marjoram	2 eggs
6 oz. breadcrumbs	4 tablespoons butter	1 teaspoon salt
¾ pint water	1 tablespoon parsley	½ teaspoon ground
1 medium sized onion		pepper

Any liver can be used, ox, calf, chicken or turkey, but it must be free from skin or gristle. Chop it very finely. Chop the onion and the parsley. Melt the butter and cook the onion and the parsley for a few minutes. Add the liver, salt, pepper and marjoram and cook for another 5 minutes. Moisten the breadcrumbs with water and heat for a few minutes until it becomes like a paste. Add to the liver mixture. Beat the eggs well and stir into the dumpling mixture. Leave for about 30 minutes. Add more breadcrumbs if the mixture is too soft. Shape into medium-sized dumplings. It is always better to have dumplings on the small side. First of all they swell a lot and secondly they are much more attractive if small. Drop into salted boiling water and cook for about 30 minutes. They can also be cooked in the sauce or soup if desired.

TYROLEAN DUMPLINGS

Tirolerknödel

16 TO 18 DUMPLINGS

10 oz. flour	3 eggs	1¼ teaspoon pepper
8 oz. chopped ham (lean)	4 oz. breadcrumbs	½ pint milk
		½ teaspoon salt

Sieve the flour and put in a bowl. Add the salt and pepper. Make a well in the centre. Break in the eggs one at a time and stir alternately with the milk, making a nice creamy batter. Put in a cool place and leave it for 30 minutes. Heat the chopped ham in a saucepan and stir in the breadcrumbs. Allow to get cool and stir into the batter. Cover and leave for a further hour. Have the water boiling and salted and drop in the batter from a spoon. Cook for about 20 minutes. These can also be cooked in soup or sauce.

POTATO DUMPLINGS

Kartoffelknödel

1 tablespoon melted butter	4 large cooked potatoes	2 egg yolks
8 oz. rice	fat for frying	½ teaspoon chopped parsley
2 heaped tablespoons ham (lean)	2 tablespoons flour	salt and pepper

Cook the rice so that it is dry and separated. Boil the potatoes and put them through a masher. Add the rice, cooked minced ham, and potatoes to the melted butter, together with the parsley and the seasoning. Bind with egg yolks. Form into small balls with floured hands. Fry in deep hot fat. Serve with soup. If desired as main dish this quantity will serve 3.

PANCAKES FOR SOUPS

Fridatten

6 SERVINGS

½ pint milk	3 oz. flour	1 tablespoon butter
	2 eggs	

This recipe is given with dumplings, as it is served with soup in exactly the same way as dumplings. Make a smooth batter of the flour, eggs and milk. Allow to stand for at least 1 hour. Melt the butter and keep beside you in a cup. Use a very small omelette pan. Pour a very little of the butter in and quickly add a small quantity of the batter, just enough to cover the pan when tilted. Brown and toss or turn with a palette knife. Do the other side the same. Set aside on a close-meshed wire tray. Continue like this until all the batter is used up. Let the pancakes get cold and cut into thin strips almost like vermicelli. Add to soup just before serving.

STUFFED EGGS WITH CRAYFISH BUTTER

Eier mit Krebsbutter

4 eggs, hard-boiled	2 egg yolks	salt and pepper
1 teaspoon chopped	butter	2 oz. ragoût of veal
parsley	2 oz. crayfish butter	or chicken
2 tablespoons milk	(see p. 51)	2 oz. breadcrumbs

Cut the hard-boiled eggs in half and carefully remove the yolks. Take cooked and raw egg-yolks, breadcrumbs, a little milk, crayfish butter and parsley, and make a stuffing to fill the hollow of the eggs. Season with salt and pepper. Take 4 small baking dishes and butter them. Place the stuffed eggs in the dishes, two stuffed eggs to each dish, and surround with ragoût. Bake in a fairly hot oven for 15 minutes. Serve in the individual baking dishes. This is equally good hot or cold.

EGGS TYROLEAN STYLE

Tiroler Eierspeise

4 hard-boiled eggs	4 anchovies	1 tablespoon butter
1 gill fresh cream	½ teaspoon chopped	potatoes
salt and pepper	parsley	2 oz. breadcrumbs

Cook the potatoes and cut them into thin slices. Place a layer of these on the bottom of a well buttered dish. Over the potatoes place a layer of sliced hard-boiled eggs and chopped anchovy and so on until the ingredients have been used up layer by layer. Mix the cream with the chopped parsley, salt and pepper, and pour over the dish. Sprinkle with breadcrumbs and bake in a moderate to hot oven for 30 minutes. If the breadcrumbs fail to brown in the oven, the dish can be finished off under the grill.

AUSTRIAN EGGS

Österreichischer Eier

4 eggs	salt and pepper	2 teaspoons olive oil
1 slice cooked ham	2 anchovies	2 mushrooms
	2 teaspoons vinegar	

Hard-boil the eggs. Remove the yolks carefully, cutting the whites in half. Put the yolks in a dish. Poach the mushrooms until tender and chop them finely. Mix with the egg yolks. Chop the ham and add to this mixture. Chop the anchovies and mix with the oil, vinegar, salt and pepper. Blend all these ingredients together into a nice paste. Stuff the halves of egg white. Serve on little dishes, with some of the mixture surrounding them.

FISH WITH CAPER SAUCE

Fisch mit Kapernsauce

1 heaped tablespoon	1 lemon	salt
capers	1 gill sour cream	black pepper
1½ lb. any white fish	1 tablespoon parsley	1 tablespoon butter
	2 onions	

Clean and skin and fillet the fish (saving skin, heads, and tails for soup or stock). Cut it up into small pieces. Melt the butter. Peel and chop up the onions finely, and fry them in the butter. Add the fish to the onions. Add salt and pepper. Gradually stir in the sour cream. Add the capers, the parsley, well chopped, and the juice of the lemon. Grate a little of the rind in, too. Stir all gently together until everything is well blended, then turn it all into a buttered oven dish, and bake for 20 minutes in a moderate oven.

LARDED FISH

Gespickter Fisch

1 large turbot or cod	4 onions	salt and pepper
1 large piece larding	4 oz. mushrooms	little butter
bacon		8 oz. cauliflower

Clean and scale the fish but leave it whole. Butter a large baking tin. Peel and slice the onions and lay them over the bottom of the tin. Put the fish on top of them. Slice up the bacon into thin strips and arrange them all over the fish so that it is entirely covered with them. Dot with butter. Season with salt and pepper. Bake slowly in a moderate oven, basting every 5 minutes, until the fish is tender. The time needed depends on the size of the fish. While it is cooking, break the cauliflower into little flowerets and cook them in a little rapidly boiling salted water for 7 minutes, keeping the lid tightly on the pan. Drain. Fry the mushroom caps, unpeeled and whole, in a little butter, very lightly. When the fish is done, put it in a serving-dish, previously warmed, arrange the cauliflower and mushrooms in alternate heaps around it, and serve.

BLUE TROUT

Blaugesottene Forellen

| 4 *very* fresh trout | 1 dessertspoon salt | big bowl ice-water |
| | 1 pint vinegar | |

Do make sure that the trout are absolutely fresh. Get your fishmonger to draw them. Handle them as little as possible. Wash them gently 1 hour before you want to eat them and sew the head of each fish to its own tail with string. Put the vinegar in a large saucepan and bring it to the boil. Pick up each fish by the string you have sewn it with and dip it into the boiling vinegar. Leave for 1 minute. Then plunge it into the bowl of ice-water and then place it on a serving dish. See that each fish is separate from the other fish. Leave for 45 minutes. Get a large saucepan of salted water boiling. Slide the fish very gently into it, trying not to touch them except by the string. Lower the heat and cook for 10 minutes in water that is just *below* boiling point. Remove carefully and serve at once with melted butter poured over them. Or, alternatively, chill and serve with a dressing of 3 parts olive oil to 1 part vinegar.

BÜCKLINGE HERRINGS WITH EGG

Bücklinge mit Ei

4 herrings, preferably	1 tablespoon butter	8 eggs
Bücklinge ones		salt and pepper
which your fish-		
monger can		
probably supply		

Fillet the herrings and spread the fillets in a large well buttered oven dish, as far apart from each other as possible. Break the eggs into the dish around the herrings, taking care to keep the yolks intact. Sprinkle salt and pepper on the eggs. Dot the herrings with butter. Bake in a moderate oven until the whites of the eggs are firm and white.

29

CARP WITH HORSERADISH

Karpfen mit Kren

1 carp, about 3 lb.	pinch of thyme	2 pints vinegar
1 onion, 1 carrot,	dusting of powdered	1½ pints water
1 potato, 1 small	horseradish or	salt and pepper
turnip (all chopped	horseradish cream	1 bay leaf
fine)		

Scale and clean carp. Remove the head and put with vegetables, thyme, seasoning, vinegar and water into a thick pan. Boil for 20 minutes. Cut the carp, lengthways and then across, into fairly large pieces. Add them to the pan and simmer gently for 15 minutes. Serve the carp with strained vegetables and some of the liquid, sprinkled with a little powdered horseradish. Serve in a hot covered dish.

BAKED PERCH

Gebackener Barsch

2 large perch	1 tablespoon chopped	grated lemon peel
2 tablespoons capers	parsley	salt and pepper
4 anchovy fillets		1½ tablespoons butter

Buy the perch already filleted, unless, of course, it is a present from a family fisherman! Wash and dry the fillets, and cut them into chunky pieces. Thickly butter four individual earthenware dishes with lids. Butter the lids as well. Pack the fish pieces tightly in each dish, and dot capers over them. Sprinkle on salt and pepper and a grating of lemon peel. Cut the anchovy fillets into slender strips and lay a few across each dish of fish. Put the covers on the dishes and bake them in a hot oven for 15 minutes. Remove from the oven, take off the lids. Sprinkle with finely chopped fresh parsley, and serve. This is a very good way of cooking smelts, too.

CREAMED HERRINGS WITH ANCHOVIES

Heringe in Rahmsauce

4 fresh herrings,	4 small anchovies	breadcrumbs
filleted	in oil	salt and pepper
2 tablespoons butter		1 gill sour cream

Butter an oven dish. Put in the fillets of herring. Cover with sour cream. Sprinkle thickly with breadcrumbs. Season with salt and pepper. Slice up the anchovies into narrow strips and lay along the top of each herring. Dot with butter all over. Bake in a moderate oven for 30 minutes.

TYROLEAN TROUT

2 lb. filleted trout	1 dessertspoon	2 dill cucumbers
4 oz. butter	chopped parsley	2 tablespoons capers
salt and pepper	flour	1 pint mayonnaise
2 lemons	1 dessertspoon	sauce (see p. 263)
	chopped chives	

For this delicious quick way of doing trout, you should make the sauce a bit beforehand so that it is ready and waiting for the fish, which should be eaten the minute it is done. For this sauce, chop up the parsley, chives, and cucumbers very small and mix them thoroughly, with the capers, into a thick mayonnaise sauce. Leave to chill. After you have washed the trout fillets, rub each with salt, sprinkle it with pepper, and roll it in a plate of flour. Get the butter melted and beginning to sizzle in the frying pan. Put in the fillets and fry them quickly on both sides. They should be an even golden colour. Put them on a warm serving dish and surround them with thin slices of the lemon. Serve at once with the cold sauce in a sauceboat.

EELS IN WINE

Aal mit Wein

1 eel	1 teaspoon sugar	1 tablespoon butter
1 tablespoon chopped	2 lemons	1 teaspoon made
parsley	2 eggs	mustard
¾ pint dry white wine	½ pint stock	salt and pepper
	1 tablespoon vinegar	

4 hours before the meal, chop up the eel into 2-inch pieces and put these in a jug. Sprinkle them well with salt, and leave them in a cold place for 3½ hours. Then remove them and put them in a saucepan, so that they are tightly packed together. Pour the wine over them. Chop the parsley finely and lay it on top of the eels. Put a tight lid on the saucepan. Bring the wine to just under boiling point. Reduce the heat, and leave to simmer gently until the eels are tender. In the meantime, hard-boil 2 eggs, and remove the yolks from them into a bowl. With a fork mash up the egg yolks smoothly. Melt the butter and stir it into the yolks. Warm the stock and then gradually add it to the egg and butter mixture, Add salt, pepper, made mustard and 1 teaspoon of sugar. Slowly add the vinegar. Put this sauce into a saucepan and bring it just to boiling point but do not let it boil. Remove the eels and put them in a serving dish. Slice the two lemons and arrange them around the eel pieces, and serve, accompanied by the sauce in a sauceboat.

31

MUSSELS IN WINE

Muscheln Wein

2 quarts mussels	3 tablespoons butter	2 egg yolks
1 teaspoon black	2 lemons	1 tablespoon flour
peppercorns	1 pint dry white wine	½ pint sour cream
pinch salt		

Make quite sure that all the mussels are tightly closed when you buy them. Scrub them well, and rinse them 3 or 4 times. Crush the peppercorns. Put them in a large stewing saucepan, with salt and 2 tablespoons butter. Add the wine, the juice from the lemons, and the mussels. Bring to boiling point. Boil for 1 minute. Then lower the heat and simmer gently until every mussel has opened. Take out any half shells with no fish on them. Move the saucepan of mussels to the back of the stove to keep hot. In a small thick saucepan, melt 1 tablespoon butter. Blend in 1 tablespoon flour, stirring all the time. Beat up the egg yolks. Remove the saucepan from the fire, and gradually add the egg yolks to the contents. Add the sour cream also, very slowly, and stir well. Put the saucepan back on the fire, stirring all the time, and gradually add about a cup of the liquid from the saucepan of mussels, blending it in very slowly and carefully. When it is smooth and thickening, pour this sauce into a warm sauceboat. Put the mussels, including the rest of the liquid in which they were cooked, into a fairly deep serving dish, and serve, passing the sauce separately.

LARDING

In Austria and Hungary this is a very important part of their cooking, for poultry, game and meat. It is necessary to have a larding-needle. It is rather like our packing or carpet needle. It must have a very large eye.

The bacon is cut into strips about an inch or 1¼ inches long. Thread it through the eye of the needle and push through the skin of the bird or meat which you are cooking. Make the incisions small enough, so that a little bit of the fat bacon sticks out each end.

LEG OF VEAL LARDED

Gespickter Kalbschlegel

8 TO 10 SERVINGS

4 to 5 lb. leg of veal	½ teaspoon ground	1 onion
1 lb. good bacon or	pepper	1 pint white wine
uncooked ham	2 tablespoons capers	1 gill cream
12 anchovies		4 oz. butter

5. Christmas Dinner in Britain

6. Vol-au-Vent, France (p.200)

7. Streusel Cake, Austria (p.72)

Do not bone the leg of veal. Make a number of holes in the surface with a skewer or ice pick. Cut the bacon into little chunky bits about 1 inch long. Into each hole push a piece of bacon and a bit of anchovy. Seal the holes over with butter. Slice the onion. Melt the butter in a roasting-pan and put the leg of veal and the onion in it. Pour the wine over. Cover the pan and cook very slowly for about 2 hours, depending on the size of the joint. Allow 25 minutes per pound and 25 minutes over. Now add the capers and the pepper and cook for another 15 minutes. Place the joint on a serving-dish and pour the sauce into another saucepan. Pour in the cream and reheat but do not allow to boil. Serve separately. Serve with salad and rice or noodles.

STUFFED LOIN OF VEAL

Gewickelter Nierenbraten

6 TO 8 SERVINGS

loin of veal	4 mushrooms	4 anchovy fillets
4 oz. fine white	grated rind of lemon	½ pint stock
breadcrumbs	juice 1 lemon	1 egg yolk
1 dessertspoon	12 oz. fat bacon	salt and pepper
chopped parsley		4 oz. melted butter

Remove the bones and skin from the loin. Rub over with lemon juice. Chop the mushrooms and bacon and mash the anchovies. Mix together with the breadcrumbs, parsley and grated rind of lemon. Season with pepper and salt and moisten with the egg yolk. If this is not enough, add a little milk. Stuff the loin and roll up. Tie with string or skewer it together. Brown in a large casserole in the melted butter, turning to get it all brown. Pour over the stock and roast in a moderate oven until tender. Do not cover. It should take 25 minutes to the pound. Turn it several times. Serve the sauce separately.

MEAT IN VINEGAR

Sauerbraten

ABOUT 8 SERVINGS

4 lb. lean beef without	1 pint wine vinegar	2 bay leaves
bone	6 peppercorns, black	butter and suet
5 pints water	and white	for roasting

Wash the meat and place in a basin. Cover it with the water, vinegar, peppercorns and bay leaves. The water should be boiling. Leave overnight. Next day, wash the meat and roast as usual. Use half suet and half butter. Roast in a moderate oven and allow 15 minutes to the pound.

VIENNESE HAMBURGERS

Klops

6 SERVINGS

1 lb. minced beef	3 tablespoons chopped	½ teaspoon ground
1 lb. minced pork	onion	pepper
1 egg	2 tablespoons chopped	4 oz. breadcrumbs
grated rind of ½ lemon	parsley	juice ½ lemon
2 oz. butter for	2 tablespoons butter	1 gill white wine
frying	for patties	little milk

Separate the egg. Cream 2 tablespoons butter and add the egg yolk. Add the minced meats, lemon rind, seasoning and the breadcrumbs, soaked in milk. Last of all fold in the white of egg stiffly beaten. Divide into patties about ¾ inch thick. Let stand for 30 minutes. Melt butter in a frying-pan. Add the parsley and onions and fry golden brown. Raise the heat. Put the patties in and brown them quickly on both sides. Turn down the heat and add the lemon juice and wine. Allow to cook for 20 minutes over a low heat. Serve the patties on a hot serving-dish with the sauce in a separate bowl.

PAPRIKA VEAL

Paprika Kalbsschnitzel

1 lb. thin slices fillet	1 tablespoon paprika	2 tablespoons flour
veal	lemon juice	salt and pepper
½ pint sour cream	1 gill stock	butter
	5 onions	

Marinate the slices of veal in lemon juice for 1 hour. Slice the onions and fry in butter until just turning brown. Sprinkle with paprika. Dip slices of veal in flour, brown them in butter, in a separate pan. Lay browned slices of meat on top of the onions. Cover the pan and cook over a low heat for 5 or 6 minutes. Meanwhile mix a tablespoon of the flour with the sour cream and stock. Add salt and pepper. Pour over the meat and cook for another 5 minutes. Serve piping hot. Serve with very small dumplings (p. 347) or Tyrolean dumplings (p. 26). Veal chops or steaks can be used in this recipe. Follow the same instructions but allow longer for cooking.

HUNTSMAN'S BEEFSTEAKS

8 SERVINGS

8 slices of beef steak each weighing about 8 oz.	2 to 3 tablespoons flour	4 finely chopped anchovies
4 oz. bacon cut into dice	1 large finely chopped onion	1 large pickled gherkin
3 tablespoons butter for frying	1 tablespoon capers	1 gill sour cream salt

Wash the meat and beat until very thin but not broken. Fry the onion in butter. When cool add the anchovies. Spread this mixture on the pieces of meat. Add the gherkin cut into long thin slices, the diced bacon and capers. Now roll up the meat. Tie with string and fry slowly in butter on all sides. Should the butter get too brown add a little water. Now cover the frying-pan or pot and let the meat cook slowly for 3 hours. Baste frequently. During the last 30 minutes add the sour cream, little by little. Lastly pour the sauce through a fine sieve, add the flour and salt, boil slowly for 5 minutes. Remove the string and serve the meat separately from the sauce.

STUFFED LEG OF PORK

Faschierter Schweinschlegel

8 TO 10 SERVINGS

leg of pork	4 small onions	grated Parmesan cheese
1 carrot	6 anchovies	salt and pepper
1 parsnip	1 egg	$\frac{1}{2}$ pint brown soup or stock
1 celery stalk	2 oz. breadcrumbs	
2 tablespoons capers	little fat	

Take the bone out of the leg of pork. Wipe with a damp cloth. Rub salt and pepper inside and out. Chop the onions, anchovies and capers finely. Mix with the breadcrumbs and bind with a well beaten egg. Stuff the leg with this. Fold over and tie with string. Slice the vegetables and place in a roasting-pan with a little fat. Set the stuffed leg on the bed of vegetables and cover. Roast in a moderate oven, allowing 35 minutes to the pound. Turn from time to time. When nearly cooked pour over a cupful of good brown soup and continue until quite cooked. Take the lid off and sprinkle the meat with grated Parmesan cheese. Allow to get golden brown. Lift the meat out and serve on a hot dish surrounded by the vegetables, strained. Serve the gravy separately. Boiled rice, noodles or macaroni can be served with this dish.

STEWED MUTTON

Gekochtes Schöpsenfleisch

6 SERVINGS

2 lb. mutton pieces
1½ pints water
½ pint vinegar

1 dessertspoon
  paprika
1 tablespoon parsley
  (chopped)

salt and ground black
  pepper
4 onions

Chop the onions. Put them with the mutton pieces into the water and vinegar. Add the salt, ground black pepper and paprika. Bring to the boil and simmer slowly for about 1½ to 2 hours, or until the meat is tender. Serve very hot with the chopped parsley sprinkled over the top. Dumplings or potato balls (see pp. 26, 51) are usually served with this dish.

VIENNESE STEWED BEEF

Wiener Saftbraten

8 TO 10 SERVINGS

6 lb. lean beef
4 onions
4 carrots
2 turnips

1½ pints white wine
1 pint brown stock
4 oz. brown bread-
  crumbs
3 green figs

pinch mace
2 oz. butter
salt and pepper
1 oz. flour

Grease a large heavy casserole with butter, including the lid. Chop the onions, carrots, turnips and figs. Melt some butter and put in the casserole. Put all the chopped vegetables and the meat, which has been dusted with salt and pepper, in the casserole. Roast in a moderate oven for 1 hour. Baste occasionally. Pour off any excess fat, add flour, cover meat and vegetables with brown stock. Return to the oven and simmer until the meat is tender. Stir in the breadcrumbs, the pinch of mace and any other seasoning you may like. Lastly stir in the white wine. Serve in the casserole with potatoes.

STUFFED VEAL

Gefüllter Kalbsbraten

6 TO 8 SERVINGS

1 leg veal
4 onions
1 calf's kidney

salt and pepper
4 oz. breadcrumbs

2 egg yolks
fat and butter
sour cream

Remove the bone from the leg and flatten out the meat. Chop the onions and calf's kidney small. Brown in a little fat. Add the breadcrumbs, salt and pepper. Bind with the yolks of eggs, well beaten. Place on the veal. Roll up and tie with string. Roast in butter in a moderate oven. Allow 25 minutes to the pound and an extra 25 minutes if necessary. Do not serve underdone. When finished pour the hot sour cream over and serve with salad.

LAMB COOKED WITH MUSHROOMS

Lammfleisch mit Pilzen

2 TO 3 SERVINGS

8 slices of lamb	2 oz. mushrooms	butter sauce
1 teaspoon chopped	1 dessertspoon flour	(see p. 53)
parsley		2 oz. butter

Soak the slices of meat in hot water. Cook the mushrooms and parsley in the butter. Remove the slices of meat from the water and dust them with the flour. Add these to the cooked mushrooms and butter. Stir them together. Place on a hot deep dish and pour over the butter sauce.

BOILED BEEF

Gesottenes Rindfleisch

8 TO 10 SERVINGS

4 lb. beef (rump or brisket)	1 large onion, unpeeled	3 carrots
2 lb. chicken giblets, or rough parts, such as neck, legs etc.	1 bay leaf	2 small onions
	6 celery stalks	4 sprigs parsley
		2 pimentos
		6 peppercorns

Put chicken parts and vegetables except the large onion, cut in large pieces in a pan. Add peppercorns, pimentos, parsley and bay leaf. Cover well with water and bring to the boil. Now let simmer for about 2 hours. The beef should be in a neat piece, not too fat. Bake the large onion in its skin in the oven for about 30 minutes. Place the meat in a large deep heavy pot with the baked onion. Strain the stock and cover the meat with it. Bring to the boil and then lower the heat. Simmer for 2 to 2½ hours. Test the meat from time to time as the length of cooking depends on the thickness and age of the beef. This should be served with horseradish cream and noodles.

FILLET STEAK LARDED

Lungenbraten Filets

4 fillets of steak	fat bacon for larding	2 lamb's kidneys
several slices	salt and pepper	few truffles
smoked tongue	8 mushrooms	4—6 oz. butter

Have the steaks about ½ inch thick. Cut the bacon and smoked tongue into very thin inch lengths. With a larding needle lace the steaks with alternate strips of bacon and tongue. Season with salt and pepper. Cook very lightly in 3 oz. melted butter. The inside should be underdone. Slice the kidneys and truffles. Cook these together with the mushrooms in melted butter. Serve the steaks very hot, garnished with the mushrooms, sliced kidneys and truffles. Pour a little melted butter over them.

ROAST VEAL WITH KIDNEYS AND PAPRIKA

Kalbsnierenbraten mit Paprika

8 TO 10 SERVINGS

5 or 6 lb. leg of veal	2 oz. butter	2 tablespoons water
2 veal kidneys	2 tablespoons cream	1 tablespoon paprika

Bone the leg of veal. Sprinkle kidneys, on which the fat has been left, liberally with paprika. Put the kidneys in the bone cavity in the leg. Tie neatly with string in 3 places. Melt the butter in a roasting-pan. Put the joint in this. Pour the mixed cream and water over all. Roast uncovered and baste frequently, in a moderate oven. Time 25 minutes to the pound and 25 minutes extra. Thicken the sauce with flour and serve separately. Garnish with cucumber and serve with green salad and sauté potatoes.

VIENNA SCHNITZEL NO. 1

Wiener Schnitzel

5 TO 6 SERVINGS

2 lb. veal slices	fine white	salt and pepper
2 egg yolks	breadcrumbs	4 oz. butter
	flour	1 lemon

The veal for this should be cut from the leg of veal, which has been boned, or the fillet. The slices should be beaten out until they are almost wafer thin and the fibres broken. Any good butcher knows how to do this. If they are too thick you must do it yourself. Dip the slices in flour, then in the beaten yolks of egg, to which salt and pepper has been added, and finally in the fine breadcrumbs. Cook the slices in hot butter until a golden brown. Turn over and do both sides. It only takes a few minutes. Place on a hot dish and serve immediately, garnished with slices of lemon.

VIENNA SCHNITZEL NO. 2

Wiener Schnitzel

5 TO 6 SERVINGS

2 lb. veal slices, prepared	12 anchovy fillets	2 egg yolks
	salt and pepper	flour
juice of 2 or 3 lemons	4 oz. fine white	1 teaspoon paprika
8 oz. butter	breadcrumbs	lemon, stoned olives

Marinate the slices of veal in the lemon juice for 1 hour. Roll them in flour, to which salt and pepper has been added. Dip them in the beaten yolks of egg and finally in the fine white breadcrumbs. Before cooking prepare the sauce. Melt half of the butter and add the mashed anchovies and the paprika. Mix well and keep hot. In the remainder of the melted butter cook the schnitzels until golden brown on each side. They should be firm and dry. Serve on a hot dish. Pour the sauce over and garnish with slices of lemon, arranged alternately with olives.

STUFFED SADDLE OF LAMB

Gefüllter Schöpsenrücken

8 TO 10 SERVINGS

saddle of young lamb	4 oz. breadcrumbs	salt and pepper
6 shallots	1 teaspoon chopped	fat for roasting
1 onion	parsley	stock and flour for
2 eggs	8 oz. lean ham	gravy
4 oz. beef marrow	brown stock	1 tablespoon butter

Remove the bones and as much fat as possible from the saddle. Trim neatly and rub all over with the onion (or a clove of garlic), salt and pepper. Let it stand overnight in a cool place. Chop the ham, parsley, shallots and marrow very finely. Cook until golden in the butter. Season with salt and pepper. Add the breadcrumbs and bind together with the 2 eggs, well beaten. Stuff the saddle with this. Roll and tie with string. Roast in a moderate oven for about 1 to 1½ hours, depending on the size of the saddle. Baste frequently. Pour off some of the fat, leaving about 2 tablespoons liquid. Thicken this with flour and add brown stock for gravy. This dish is served with the gravy poured over.

TYROLEAN BEEF

Tiroler Speckbraten

ABOUT 8 SERVINGS

3 to 4 lb. lean beef	4 oz. melted butter	pepper and salt
fat bacon for larding		chopped onions

Dust the joint with pepper and salt. Lard the beef with the strips of bacon. Use a thick roasting-pot. Add some chopped onion. Pour the melted butter over and cover tightly with the lid. Cook slowly until tender, probably 2 hours. Serve with horseradish relish (see p. 53).

TONGUE WITH CAPER SAUCE

Zunge mit Kapernsauce

6 TO 8 SERVINGS

1 ox tongue	1 gill white wine	2 tablespoons flour
½ pint sour cream	½ pint brown stock	juice 1 lemon
2 small onions	or soup	4 oz. finely chopped
1 teaspoon chopped	1 tablespoon capers	liver
parsley		4 oz. butter

Cook the tongue as following recipe. Cook the onions, chopped finely, together with the parsley and liver in a thick saucepan in half the butter. When golden brown add the stock and the wine and simmer. With the flour and the rest of the melted butter make a paste and add the lemon juice. Stir this into the sauce but do not let it boil. Lastly add the cream and the capers. Serve the tongue whole and pour the sauce over it on the serving dish.

OX TONGUE WITH HORSERADISH

Ochsenzunge mit Kren

6 TO 8 SERVINGS

1 ox tongue	little mustard and	4 tablespoons cream
2 tablespoons grated	vinegar	1 tablespoon white
horseradish	1 tablespoon melted	breadcrumbs
½ pint stock	butter	salt and pepper
	2 egg yolks	

Boil the tongue in salted water for 2 hours. Remove from the pot and peel the skin off. Return to the pot and cook until tender. It will take 3 to 4 hours according to size. When it is nearly cooked make the horseradish sauce. Grate the horseradish finely. Put it in the stock and simmer for about 20 minutes. Remove from the heat and mix in the tablespoon of melted butter and the cream, also the breadcrumbs. Return to the heat and stir until the mixture thickens. Strain the sauce and stir in the beaten yolks of 2 eggs. Season with salt and pepper and a little mustard made with vinegar. Slice the tongue, put the slices on a hot serving dish and pour the sauce over.

CHICKEN WITH GREEN SAUCE

Hühner mit grüner Sauce

6 SERVINGS

1 roasting chicken	4 oz. button mush-	flour
1 celery stalk	rooms	salt and pepper
1 onion	1 pint chicken soup	green sauce
2 tablespoons butter		(see p. 52)

Chop the onion and celery, and cook together with the mushrooms in the butter. Add a pinch of salt and a shake of pepper. Use a thick deep pan. Cut the chicken into portions, making 6 good helpings. Add salt and pepper to the flour and roll the chicken pieces in this. Place the chicken on the vegetables. Pour the soup over, simmer gently for 1 hour. Serve with green sauce.

STUFFED CHICKEN

Gefülltes Huhn

6 SERVINGS

1 young chicken	2 tablespoons boiled	3—4 mushrooms
4 slices fat bacon	green peas	yolk 1 egg
8 oz. cooked rice	1 tablespoon melted	salt and pepper
	butter	

Cut the bacon fat into small strips about 1 inch long. Lard the breast with a larding needle. In a basin mix the cooked rice, the peas, and the mushrooms cut in pieces, and the melted butter. Bind together with the yolk of egg. Season with salt and pepper. Stuff the chicken and roast, basting frequently. Serve with tomato sauce and any green vegetable.

CHICKEN IN WINE PASTRY

Hühner in Weinteig

6 SERVINGS

6 portions of cold cooked chicken	wine pastry (see p. 61)	deep fat for frying lemon
salt and pepper		flour

Roll the chicken portions in flour which has been peppered and salted. Roll out wine pastry and cut into 6 pieces, large enough to enclose chicken pieces. Fry in fat. Garnish with slices of lemon.

CASSEROLE OF CHICKEN

Gedünstete Hühner

1 small chicken	1 onion, chopped	juice ½ lemon
4 tablespoons breadcrumbs	salt and pepper	6 anchovies
2 tablespoons butter	1 teaspoon chopped parsley	chicken stock
		1 tablespoon flour

Boil the chicken for 1 hour. Cut about 1 lb. of meat off the bones and dice it. Save the stock. Put the butter in a thick pan. Melt it and fry the onion a pale brown. Add the breadcrumbs, parsley, lemon juice and anchovies. Cook for a few minutes. Stir in the diced chicken. Sprinkle a tablespoon of sieved flour on top. Add salt and pepper. Stir all together. Cover with the stock and allow to simmer for a few minutes. Pour into a warmed casserole and bake in the oven for 1 hour at a moderate heat. Very small dumplings or Tyrolean dumplings go very well with this (see pp. 347, 26).

SACHER CHICKEN

Sacher Huhn

6 SERVINGS

1 roasting chicken	2 tablespoons butter	salt and pepper
1 lb. sausage meat	2 or 3 lamb's sweet-	3 tablespoons
1 goose's liver	breads	Madeira wine

Mince the goose's liver and mix it with the sausage meat. Season with salt and pepper. Have some melted butter ready. Chop the sweetbreads small and add to the sausage mixture. Cook in the melted butter. When nearly ready add Madeira wine. Stuff the breast of the chicken and roast for about 1 hour, basting frequently. Serve this dish with a garnish of young vegetables—young peas, baby carrots, asparagus and new potatoes.

ROAST GOOSE AND APPLE STUFFING

Gebratene Gans

1 young goose	2 springs marjoram	salt and pepper
4 sweet apples	8 lumps sugar	redcurrant jelly

Goose liver stuffing may be used instead (see below). The cooking in each case is practically the same. It is best to set a goose on a grid in a roasting pan, as the bird has enough fat of its own for basting. If you wish the skin on the breast to be crisp, do not cover the roasting-pan, but if you wish it to be soft, then put the lid on. When uncovered it is as well to baste it once or twice. Rub the bird well with salt and pepper and rub the inside with the sprigs of marjoram. Peel and core the apples and put two lumps of sugar inside each apple. Stuff the inside of the goose with these and leave the back end open. Roast the goose, allowing 20 minutes to the pound and a little over. Serve with redcurrant jelly.

GOOSE LIVER STUFFING

1 goose liver	1 tablespoon butter	1 tablespoon dry
4 oz. mushrooms	4 oz. fine breadcrumbs	white wine
4 oz. chopped bacon	1 egg	salt and pepper

Chop the liver and cook it with the bacon in the butter. Chop the mushrooms and cook together for another few minutes. Mix together with the breadcrumbs. Add the wine and bind together with the egg, well beaten. Salt and pepper to taste. This stuffing can be used as a filling for vol-au-vent cases (see p. 200). In this case omit the breadcrumbs and the egg but pour butter sauce (see p. 53) over liver mixture.

ROAST TURKEY AND STUFFING NO. 1

1 turkey	4 oz. white bread-	1½ lb. finely minced
bacon fat for larding	crumbs	veal pieces
greased paper or foil	salt and pepper	2 tablespoons butter
		1 egg

Lard the breast of the bird (see p. 32). See that plenty of breast skin has been left to cover and hold in the stuffing. Cook the veal pieces in the butter for a very few minutes. Add the breadcrumbs. Mix well and add salt and pepper to taste. Beat the egg and bind the stuffing mixture together with this. Stuff the breast of the bird with it. As a well-stuffed breast is inclined to cook too quickly, place sheets of foil or greased paper over the bird, if possible fastening them underneath so that the turkey is entirely wrapped up. With the larding of the breast and the steam enclosed in the paper it should be self-basting. Allow 20 minutes to the pound when cooking and 20 over.

TURKEY STUFFING NO. 2

18 oysters
1 teaspoon chopped
  parsley

grated rind lemon
1 tablespoon dry
  white wine
4 oz. breadcrumbs

salt and pepper
2 tablespoons butter
1 egg

Beard the oysters and cut in pieces. Simmer the beards in the oyster liquor and then strain. Mix together the breadcrumbs, parsley, lemon rind, and salt and pepper. Melt the butter and add it alternately with the wine to the breadcrumb mixture. Stir in the oysters. Add the lightly beaten egg and enough of the oyster liquor to make a soft stuffing. Stuff the breast with this.

TURKEY STUFFING NO. 3

1 lb. minced chicken
8 oz. minced ham

4 oz. white bread-
  crumbs

2 eggs
salt and pepper

Mix the chicken, ham and breadcrumbs together. Add the seasoning. Bind together with the eggs, lightly beaten. If preferred use only the yolks of the eggs.

TURKEY STUFFING NO. 4

10 oz. truffles
1 teaspoon chopped
  shallot

1 teaspoon chopped
  parsley
6 oz. breadcrumbs
4 oz. melted butter

2 eggs
nutmeg
salt and pepper

Cook truffles in butter, take out and leave to get cold. Fry shallot lightly in butter. Add to truffles the salt, pepper, pinch nutmeg and parsley. Mix well. Add the shallot and the breadcrumbs. Bind all together with the two eggs, well beaten.

ROAST PIGEON NO. 1

Gebratene Tauben

2 TO 3 SERVINGS

2 or 3 pigeons
bacon fat for larding
4 oz. chopped calves'
  liver

1 gill red wine
1 large anchovy
  (boned)

1 onion
4 oz. butter
salt and pepper
¼ teaspoon thyme

Lard the breasts (see p. 32). Melt a little of the butter in a pan and put in the chopped calves' liver, chopped anchovy and chopped onion. Add the thyme, salt and pepper and the red wine. Cook well and allow to cool a little. Stuff the pigeons with this mixture, and roast the birds in the remainder of the butter. Sour cream can be poured over them if liked before serving. Serve with white breadcrumbs, fried in butter. Green salad or fruit compote is a very nice addition.

ROAST PIGEON NO. 2

Gebratene Tauben

2 to 4 pigeons. Allow	fat bacon for larding	fresh parsley
1 pigeon to a person	fat for roasting	

Lard the breasts (see page 32). Always salt and flour the breasts before larding. Stuff the insides of the birds with fresh parsley. Roast in fat in a moderate oven for about 30 minutes.

ROAST SNIPE

Gebratene Schnepfe

2 TO 3 SERVINGS

3 or 4 snipe, with	parsley	1 egg yolk
hearts and livers	2 or 3 shallots	bread slices
fat bacon for covering	butter	stewed pineapple
1 tablespoon chopped	little stock	little sour cream
lemon peel	1 gill red wine	watercress
brown breadcrumbs		

Remove the insides of the birds but do not cut the heads off. Cover each bird with a slice of fat bacon and tie with string. The long beak is tucked underneath. Roast in a quick oven in butter and stock. They should take about 20 minutes. Chop the livers and hearts. Mix with the chopped shallots, chopped parsley, brown breadcrumbs, and lemon peel. Mix with egg yolk and a little of the wine. Cook in butter until the liver and heart are well cooked. Fry the rounds of bread in butter. Before the snipe are quite cooked, add the remainder of the wine and the sour cream to the roasting pan. Allow to get quite hot. Remove the birds to a serving dish. Place the fried bread round the birds, piled with the liver mixture. Put a few sprigs of watercress to garnish and serve with stewed pineapple.

GUINEAFOWL

Perlhuhn

1 guineafowl	4 oz. butter	1 gill milk
fat bacon for larding	slices bread	1 onion
1 gill sour cream	8 oz. calves' brains	salt

Clean the guineafowl and lard the breast (see page 32). The flesh is very dry and lean, so this is essential. Sprinkle it with salt. Roast in a moderately hot oven in butter. Slice the onion into the butter. Baste frequently. Time about 45 minutes, depending on the size of the bird. Pour in the sour cream. Stew the calves' brains in milk until well cooked. Fry the slices of bread in butter. Take the bird out of its sauce. Place on a serving dish, surrounded by the slices of fried bread, on which the calves' brains, well drained, have been heaped. Garnish with watercress, and serve with baked potatoes, blackcurrant jelly and salad. Put the gravy in a gravy-boat.

SAUERKRAUT WITH APPLES

Apfelkraut aus Sauerkraut

1 lb. sauerkraut	½ pint stock	2 teaspoons flour
4 rashers bacon	4 large apples	1 large onion

Chop the bacon and fry it gently until nearly crisp. Peel and chop the onion and add it to the bacon. Let them cook slowly until they are soft. Put bacon and onion in a large saucepan with the sauerkraut. Pour on the stock. Cover the pan. Simmer for 10 minutes. Peel and core the apples and cut them up into quarters. Put them in the saucepan. Add salt and continue to cook until the apples are very soft. Stir in the flour and mix well. Increase the heat and remove the saucepan lid. Cook for 7 minutes, stirring once or twice. Serve hot.

VIENNESE CABBAGE

Kraut auf Wiener Art

6 TO 8 SERVINGS

1 white or red cabbage	3 tablespoons wine	1 desertspoon flour
2 tablespoons sugar	vinegar	a little water
2 tablespoons butter		1 dessertspoon butter

Chop up the cabbage into small pieces. In a big saucepan put 2 tablespoons butter. Add the sugar and let it cook, stirring occasionally, until it is brown. Then put the cabbage in the saucepan, tossing it about until it is well coated. Reduce the heat and keep stirring all the time for 2 or 3 minutes. Now add 2 tablespoons water and 3 tablespoons wine vinegar. Heat 1 dessertspoon butter in a frying pan and stir into it 1 dessertspoon flour. When it is brown, pour a little of the liquid from the cabbage into it. Stir well and return all to the cabbage saucepan. Cook, stirring, for 10 minutes, then serve.

RED CABBAGE WITH CHESTNUTS

Blauer Kohl

1 big red cabbage	1 pint stock	8 oz. chestnuts
½ pint cream		1 dessertspoon sugar

A delicious accompaniment to pork or sausages. Boil the chestnuts and peel them. Wash the cabbage and remove any soiled or too tough outer leaves. Boil a large saucepan of salted water. Place the cabbage in it. Cover tightly. Cook for 10 minutes. Remove the cabbage from the water and take out its heart, disturbing the outer leaves as little as you can. (Save the heart for another dish, of course.) Chop up the chestnuts and mix them with the sugar, and stuff the cabbage with them. Place the cabbage in an oven-dish and pour hot stock over it. Cook in a moderate oven for 20 minutes. The stock should simmer but not boil fast while it is cooking. At the last moment pour the cream over the cabbage and serve.

VIENNESE POTATOES WITH LIVER STUFFING

Kartoffel mit Leberfasch

1 lb. liver, preferably calf's	2 tablespoons grated cheese	2 onions
4 large potatoes	4 tablespoons sour cream	3 tablespoons butter
		salt and black pepper

Scrub the potatoes and put them in a saucepan of boiling salted water. When they are soft but firm, drain off the water and carefully peel off the thin skin—being careful to keep the potato intact. Cut each in two, lengthwise, and scoop out the middle. Peel and chop up the onions and the liver into small pieces. Get the butter melted and beginning to sizzle. Fry the onions and liver pieces in it for 3 or 4 minutes, then put them through a mincer or Mouli-grater. Stir in salt and pepper and the scooped out centres of the potatoes. Arrange the potatoes that have been scooped out in a buttered oven-dish. Fill each one with the liver stuffing. Pour cream over them all and sprinkle with the grated cheese. Put in a hot oven until the cheese begins to brown.

VIENNESE BAKED TOMATOES

Gebackene Paradeisäpfel

6 SERVINGS

1½ lb. tomatoes	2 tablespoons	8 oz. Parmesan cheese
6 slices white bread	anchovy paste	salt and pepper
2 oz. butter	½ pint cream	4 pickled cucumbers

Plunge the tomatoes in a bowl of boiling water. Leave for 5 minutes, remove and skin them, which you will then find easy to do. Slice them as thinly as possible. Cut the crusts off the bread and cut each piece into 3, lengthwise. Fry the slices in butter, which you should first get very hot, until they are crisp and golden. Butter an oven dish. Put 3 pieces of fried bread in the bottom of the dish. Salt and pepper them. Now place a layer of tomatoes over them. Cover the tomatoes thickly with grated Parmesan cheese. Lay another layer of bread on top, this time spreading each piece with anchovy paste. Add another layer of tomatoes, salt and pepper, then grated cheese, and continue these layers in the same order, spreading anchovy paste on each bread slice, until the dish is full. Chop up the pickled cucumbers. Pour the fresh cream over them, and pour all this over the tomato dish. Bake for about 15 minutes in a warm but not too hot oven.

VIENNESE CAULIFLOWER

Karfiol auf Wiener Art

1 medium sized cauli-	2 tablespoons butter	1 tablespoon parsley
flower	1 lb. sweetbreads	2 tablespoons grated
2 egg yolks	¼ oz. flour	Parmesan cheese
4 tablespoons cream	6 pickled anchovies	3 tablespoons bread-
4 tablespoons milk	salt and pepper	crumbs

Put the anchovies to soak in water. Clean the sweetbreads. Wash the cauliflower, cut off the outside leaves, and make a few slashes in its base. Fill a large saucepan with water and bring it to the boil. Add 1 dessertspoon salt. Put in the cauliflower and cover the saucepan. Boil for 10 minutes. Remove from stove and drain, but keep it warm. Remove the anchovies from their water, take out all bones, and cut them up into tiny pieces. Melt a little of the butter in a frying-pan. Chop up the sweetbreads finely and put them in the butter to cook gently, shifting them about so that they do not burn or overcook. Cook for 2 or 3 minutes. Put remainder of butter in a small thick-bottomed saucepan. When it is melted stir in the flour. When it is blended, but before it begins to colour, slowly add the milk, stirring all the time. Remove from the fire while you beat up the egg yolks with the cream. Add this slowly to the white sauce. Now add the anchovies

8. Pancakes, Britain (p.114)

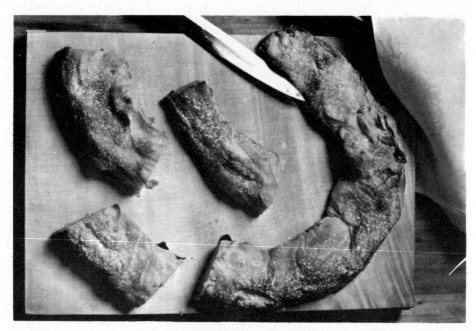

9. Apple Strudel, Austria (p.63)

10. Swiss Apple Flan (p.582)

and the sweetbreads, and put the saucepan back on the fire to cook gently for 1 minute, stirring all the time. Add the parsley, chopped fine. Butter a deep oven dish. Put the cauliflower in it. Pour the sauce over it and cover with cheese and breadcrumbs. Place little pieces of butter here and there on top and put in a hot oven for 10 minutes.

SWEET-SOUR GREEN BEANS

Süß-saure grüne Bohnen

1 lb. fresh string beans	1 bay leaf	1½ tablespoons
1½ gills water	1 tablespoon chopped	tarragon vinegar
1 clove garlic	parsley	2 cloves
1 small onion	salt and pepper	2 tablespoons butter
nutmeg, grated		1½ tablespoons sugar

String the beans and cut off heads and tails. Put the water in a large saucepan and bring it to the boil. Peel and slice the onion and add it with salt, pepper, bay leaf, peeled garlic clove and nutmeg to the water. Let these simmer for 10 or 15 minutes, then add the beans and cover the pan. Let them boil for 10 minutes. Pour off the water into a bowl and put the beans in a dish to keep hot. Put the liquid back into the saucepan and take out the garlic clove and the bay leaf. Add sugar, vinegar and cloves and bring to the boil. Boil until half the liquid has evaporated, then take out the cloves. Now stir in the butter. When it is melted add the beans. Chop up the parsley as small as possible and stir it in. Serve at once.

STEWED CUCUMBER

Gedünstete Gurke

3 cucumbers about	1 clove garlic	1 tablespoon flour
8 inches long	salt and pepper	½ pint stock
1 lemon	1 tablespoon butter	½ pint sour cream

Peel and slice the cucumbers. Melt the butter in a saucepan. Stir the flour into it. Stir, and let the flour cook until it is slightly brown. Slowly a little at a time, add the stock, constantly stirring. When it has all been added, slowly pour in the sour cream, the juice of the melon, the garlic clove chopped finely, salt and pepper. Add the cucumber slices. Cover the pan and simmer gently for 15 minutes. Then remove the cucumbers and put them in a hot serving dish. If the sauce is too thin, simmer it a little longer to reduce it and then pour it over the cucumbers and serve.

GREEN BEANS WITH FENNEL

Grüne Fisolen

1 lb. green beans	4 oz. chopped fennel	1 teaspoon lemon
2 oz. butter	1 tablespoon grated	juice
1 gill water	onion	salt
1 tablespoon flour		nutmeg

Boil a small amount of salted water in two separate saucepans. Put the beans in one and the fennel in the other. Cover both tightly, cook for 10 minutes, shaking the pans occasionally. Remove from fire, drain off water. Put beans in a warmed dish and lay the fennel on top of them. Keep warm while you make this butter sauce: melt half the butter in a saucepan, blend in the flour well. Gradually add cold water, a little at a time, always stirring constantly, until the sauce thickens. Add the rest of the butter, the lemon juice, a grating of nutmeg and the grated onion. Do not let the sauce boil, or it will curdle, and stir it all the time you are making it. Pour this sauce over the dish of beans and fennel and serve at once.

HOT SAUERKRAUT WITH ONIONS

Garniertes Kraut

2 lb. sauerkraut	2 onions	salt and pepper
	8 oz. butter	

Simmer the sauerkraut in salted water for 10 minutes. Pour off the water. Peel the onions and put them through a mincer. Melt the butter, stir onions in, season. Pour butter and onions over the sauerkraut and serve with frankfurters, chipolatas or other pork meat.

POTATOES IN MUSTARD SAUCE

Senkartoffeln

4 fairly large potatoes	1 tablespoon flour	½ pint stock
4 oz. German mustard	2 tablespoons butter	salt and pepper
	2 oz. breadcrumbs	

Peel the potatoes and cook them in boiling salted water until they are soft but still firm. Remove them and slice them and put them in an oven dish. Melt 1 tablespoon of the butter. Stir in the flour and when it is blended in slowly add the stock, stirring all the time. Add salt, pepper and mix in the mustard. Pour this sauce over the dish of potatoes. Sprinkle breadcrumbs all over the top and dot with little pieces of the remaining tablespoon of butter. Cook in the oven or under a grill until golden brown.

POTATO PANCAKES WITH SAUERKRAUT

Blatteln mit Kraut

1 lb. potatoes	1 lb. sauerkraut	½ pint brown sauce
1 tablespoon butter	1 dessertspoon salt	(see p. 258)
2 tablespoons flour	few caraway seeds	2 tablespoons fat

Peel the potatoes and cut them up coarsely. Cook them for 10 or 12 minutes in boiling salted water. Drain off the water and rub them through a sieve into a bowl. Add 1 dessertspoon salt, 1 tablespoon butter and the flour. Mix all well together into a dough. Add more flour if it is sticky. Roll into a ball and place on a floured board. Roll out with a floured rolling-pin about ¼ inch thick. Cut into 3-inch squares. Get the cooking fat really hot and fry each potato square until it is golden and crisp. Serve with hot sauerkraut heated in brown sauce and mixed with caraway seeds.

TYROLEAN POTATO BALLS

Erdäpfelnudeln

1 lb. potatoes	2 tablespoons butter	8 oz. fine bread-
1 dessertspoon salt	1—2 tablespoons flour	crumbs

Peel the potatoes and cut them up into fairly small pieces. Boil a saucepan of salted water rapidly and put the potatoes in. Cover and cook for 15 minutes. Drain and rub potatoes through a sieve into a large bowl. Add 1 tablespoon butter and 1 or 2 tablespoons flour. Work into a smooth dough and with floured hands make little balls about ½ inch in diameter. Boil a large saucepan of salted water and throw the balls into it. Cook for 5 or 6 minutes. Fry the breadcrumbs in the rest of the butter until they are golden and then lift each potato ball out with a perforated spoon and toss it in the breadcrumbs.

CRAYFISH BUTTER

Krebsbutter

6 SERVINGS

crayfish—about 1 lb.   dash cayenne pepper   1 lb. butter

If you would rather, use 2 cans of crayfish instead. Otherwise, wash the crayfish in several waters, and then put into boiling salted water and cook for 10 minutes. Remove from the water, shell and pound the meat. Soften the butter by leaving it in a warm place or over boiling water, and mix it well into the crayfish, pounding all together. Add pepper. Put in an earthenware pot. Chill and serve.

POTATO AND CHEESE TURNOVERS

Zillertaler Krapfen

8 oz. oatmeal flour	8 oz. fat or butter	1 tablespoon chives
3 potatoes	boiling salted water	1 small onion
8 oz. cream cheese	salt	1 gill milk

Put the flour in a bowl. Little by little stir into it boiling salted water until you have a firm but not sticky paste. Knead it well and with floured hands roll it out into a large roll about 1½ inches thick. Cut this roll into pieces about 1 inch long. Take these little cubes and roll each one out flat. Sprinkle flour on each and leave ready to fill. Peel, cut up and cook the potatoes until they are soft. Pour off the water and mash them up well. Add salt to taste and the cream cheese, chopped chives and milk. Peel and chop the onion very finely and add it too. Put a spoonful of mixture on each flat piece of dough, fold the dough over and press it together so that no filling can escape. Get the pan of deep fat smoking hot and cook the turnovers quickly in it until they are golden brown. Serve with sour milk, cream or yoghourt. These turnovers are often made using spinach as a filling instead of potato. They are also made with jam, prunes, apricots, etc.

GREEN SAUCE

Grüne Sauce

2 tablespoons chervil	2 oz. butter	1 gill white stock
2 tablespoons parsley	2 tablespoons white	1 gill cream
2 tablespoons sorrel	flour	salt and pepper

The herbs should be fresh and green. If chervil and sorrel are unobtainable, 2 tablespoons of chives can be used. Chop very finely. A rolling cutter is good for this, as it chops finely and at the same time squeezes out the juice. Save this juice. Melt the butter and stir in the flour until quite smooth. Add the stock and cream gradually and stir until the sauce is thick and creamy. Mix in the chopped herbs and juice. Salt and pepper to taste. The finished sauce should be a bright green.

WATERCRESS SAUCE

Brunnenkressensauce

big bunch watercress	3 tablespoons vinegar	6 tablespoons butter
½ pint stock	2 tablespoons flour	3 tablespoons toasted
½ pint white wine	salt	breadcrumbs

Place the butter in a small but heavy saucepan or in a double boiler. Sprinkle in, when the butter has melted, the toasted breadcrumbs, stirring all the time. Cook them on a low heat in the butter until they are golden-brown. Then stir in the flour. Blend well. Heat the stock and then add it gradually to the butter, crumb, and flour mixture, stirring as you pour it. Season with salt. Add the wine and vinegar. Increase the heat and bring the sauce almost to boiling point. Add the finely chopped watercress and remove at once from the stove. Serve hot or cold.

BUTTER SAUCE

Buttersauce

1 tablespoon butter	salt and pepper	2 tablespoons fine
¾ pint white stock		white flour
(see p. 88)		

Melt the butter in a saucepan. Before it boils, blend in the flour. If necessary, remove from the heat and stir until quite smooth. Gradually add the stock and stir until the whole is a smooth, fairly thick, creamy sauce. Salt and pepper to taste.

HORSERADISH RELISH

Essigkren

6 TO 8 SERVINGS

4 oz. horseradish	2 tablespoons vinegar	4 tablespoons clear
½ pint cream	2 tablespoons chives	stock
2 tablespoons olive oil	1 teaspoon paprika	salt and pepper

Put the stock in a saucepan on the stove and bring it just to the boil. Chop the chives up finely and add them, with the grated horseradish, to the stock. Boil for 5 minutes. Remove from the stove. In a bowl, put the olive oil, vinegar, salt, pepper, and paprika, and whisk them all fiercely together. Then slowly add the cream, stirring gently. Add this mixture to the horseradish and stock. Beat vigorously. Pour into a jug. Set to chill. When it is cold your relish is ready.

SORREL SAUCE

Sauerampfersauce

1½ tablespoons butter	salt and pepper	big handful fresh
2 tablespoons flour	1 gill sour cream	sorrel leaves
	1¼ pints clear stock	

Cut off the stalks of the small leaves. Use hot water for washing the leaves. Dry them well in a cloth, then put them through a mincer or chop them very finely. Cook them for 5 minutes in 2 teaspoons hot butter in a small saucepan. Then melt 1 tablespoon butter in a big saucepan. Blend in the flour until it is smooth. Pour on gradually the stock, which should be quite hot. Season with salt and pepper. Add the sorrel leaves. Remove from the fire and slowly stir in the sour cream. Use hot or cold.

53

OLIVE SAUCE

Olivensauce

8 green olives	4 anchovy fillets	1 pint clear stock
1 tablespoon olive oil	1 tablespoon flour	salt and pepper
	few grains cayenne	

Heat the olive oil in a thick large saucepan, and slowly stir the flour into it. Heat the stock to just below boiling point (in another saucepan) and then slowly add it to the flour and oil. Cook slowly, stirring all the time, for three or four minutes. Stone the olives and chop them up. Add them to the sauce. Chop the anchovies and add them too. Sprinkle with cayenne pepper. Taste, and add salt and white pepper if necessary. Stir again, and serve hot. Very good with hot or cold mutton and with plain fish dishes.

SCHNITZEL SAUCE

4 oz. butter	12 anchovy fillets, pounded	1 tablespoon paprika

Blend and heat the ingredients and pour them over the hot cooked schnitzel.

ALMOND PANCAKES

Mandelschmarren

1½ gills milk	2 tablespoons ground almonds	2 drops of almond essence
6 eggs		
1½ tablespoons sugar		1½ tablespoons butter

Separate the eggs and whip the whites. Mix up the milk, the egg yolks, the butter, the sugar, almond essence and ground almonds. Last of all beat in the whipped whites of the eggs. Beat all together well. Butter well a baking dish and pour in the mixture. Bake in a hot oven for 45 minutes, then divide roughly into pieces and serve with a sprinkling of sugar.

EMPEROR'S PUDDING

Kaiser Koch

2 oz. rice	1 drop almond essence	4 eggs
1 gill milk	2 oz. ground almonds	4 oz. sugar
	1 oz. butter	

Cook the rice in the milk, slowly, over a gentle heat, until a thick mixture is obtained. Now stir in the butter and set mixture aside to cool. Separate the eggs and beat the yolks with the sugar. Mix this into the rice, add the almonds and almond essence. Pour this into a buttered oven dish and pre-heat the oven to Hot. Whip the egg whites stiffly and fold them in to the yolk mixture just before putting it into the oven. Bake for about 45 minutes.

VIENNESE LEMON FOAM

Wiener Luft

1 dessertspoon gelatine	2 tablespoons maraschino liqueur 1 lemon	2 eggs 4 oz. vanilla sugar

Separate the egg yolks from the whites. Into the yolks slowly stir the sugar, mixing thoroughly. Add the lemon juice and stir it in well. Wet the gelatine with cold water, and then add a little boiling water, stirring until the gelatine is dissolved. When it has cooled add it to the bowl of egg and sugar. Stir well. Put the bowl in a cold place to get thoroughly chilled. Then beat the mixture until it starts to thicken. Add the maraschino and continue to beat until all is frothy. Separately beat up the egg whites until stiff and then fold them into the mixture. Wet a jelly mould with cold water. Pour the mixture into it and put it in a cold place to set.

RADETZKY RICE

Radetzky-Reis

4 oz. sugar	drop vanilla essence	1 tablespoon lemon
2 tablespoons butter	2 pints milk	juice
12 oz. rice	4 teaspoons rum	1 tablespoon orange
3 egg whites	strawberry jam	juice
2 tablespoons sugar		apple sauce

Boil the rice in milk until it is tender. Then strain. Put the butter, sugar, orange juice and lemon juice in a heavy pan and cook together. Add this mixture to the rice, mix well and set aside to cool. Then stir in the rum. Put a layer of this mixture on the bottom of a baking-dish which has been buttered. Over it put a layer of jam and then apple sauce. Repeat layers of rice, jam and apple sauce, until the dish is full. Beat the egg whites, fold in 2 tablespoons sugar with the vanilla essence and spread over the top of the pudding. Bake in a hot oven for 15 minutes and serve hot.

RED WINE PUDDING

Burgunder Koch

½ pint red wine	seedless raisins	3 egg yolks
apricot jam	slices bread	chopped blanched
1 tablespoon butter	2 oz. sugar	almonds
grated lemon peel	1 clove	chopped candied peel

Remove the crusts from the bread and bake for a short time in the oven. Put jam between the slices of bread and place in the bottom of a buttered baking-dish. Sprinkle over these candied peel, raisins, and almonds. Mix the clove, lemon peel, wine and sugar and cook together. Set aside to cool. Add the beaten yolks of the eggs to this mixture and pour over the contents of the baking-dish. Bake in a hot oven for 30 minutes.

BILBERRY FRITTERS

Heidelbeertascherln

4 oz. flour	1 lb. bilberries (or	2 tablespoons butter
½ pint white wine	raspberries, etc.)	pinch salt
	8 oz. castor sugar	

Put the flour in a bowl, mix in the salt. Slowly stir in the wine until you have a smooth batter. Then mix in the bilberries. Get the butter very hot in a frying pan. Drop spoonfuls of the batter in it and fry crisp on both sides. Drain on a piece of crumpled brown paper. Toss quickly in a plateful of castor sugar and serve, thickly coated with the sugar.

VIENNESE BEGGARMAN'S PUDDING

Bettelmann

2 eggs	3 tablespoons seedless	2 tablespoons
3 oz. stale bread-	raisins (or seeded)	almonds
crumbs		1 pint apple sauce

1½ hours before the meal, set the raisins to soak in water. After 1 hour drain them. Make the breadcrumbs by grating any stale left-over bread, either white, or brown or rye, or a mixture of all or any of them. In a bowl, mix the apple sauce with the breadcrumbs, and raisins. Chop the almonds finely and add them to the breadcrumbs. Beat the eggs well and add them too. Pour this mixture into a buttered oven dish and bake in a moderate oven for 35 minutes, or until it is golden-brown on top.

LOCKSMITH'S APPRENTICES

12 large prunes	8 oz. flour	Garnish:
12 blanched almonds	1 oz. sugar	2 oz. castor sugar
white wine or cider to	1 egg yolk	2 oz. plain chocolate,
mix	salt	grated

Soak the prunes overnight. Stew until tender. Replace each prune stone with an almond. Make a paste with the flour, salt, and egg yolk and wine. Roll out thin, cut into 12 rounds and wrap one prune in each. Bake on a very well buttered baking sheet in a moderate oven for 10—15 minutes, turning at half-time to brown both sides. Serve hot, rolled in sugar and chocolate.

COFFEE AND CHOCOLATE JELLY

Magda

½ pint strong clear	4 teaspoons chocolate	pinch of salt
coffee	powder	whipped cream to
1 level teaspoon	sugar to taste	garnish
granulated gelatine		little vanilla

Heat the coffee and the salt. Dissolve the gelatine in it. Add the chocolate powder, sugar and vanilla. Cook for a few minutes, until it is smooth and the chocolate is completely melted. Cool it, stirring from time to time. Pour into glasses when it is on the point of setting. Chill thoroughly. Top with whipped cream just before serving. Serve with sweet biscuits or sponge fingers.

MELONS WITH CREAM
AND STRAWBERRIES

Gefüllte Melonen mit Rahm und Erdbeeren

2 ripe cantaloup	2 oz. vanilla sugar	1 gill thick cream
melons	(see p. 73)	
	4 oz. strawberries	
	or more	

Cut the melons in two and scoop out the seeds. Carefully cut out the remaining melon in small neat pieces, taking care not to damage the rind. Put these pieces in a refrigerator or a very cold place for about an hour. Beat up the cream, adding the vanilla sugar little by little as the cream begins to thicken. Mix the melon pieces with the cream and fill each melon-shell full. Decorate the top of each with a few strawberries, and serve.

EMPEROR'S SCHMARREN

4 oz. flour	1 oz. castor sugar	1 oz. butter
¼ pint cream	1 oz. raisins, stoned	salt
	2 eggs, separated	

Beat together the egg yolks and cream, stir these into the flour, raisins, salt and sugar. Fold in the stiffly beaten egg whites. Melt the butter in a shallow baking pan, pour in the batter and bake in a hot oven for 10 minutes or until brown underneath. Turn the batter over and brown the other side, then tear into small pieces with two forks, return to the oven for a further 3 or 4 minutes. Serve hot with vanilla custard (see p. 267).

COFFEE CREAM JELLY

Kaffeecreme-Gelee

| 4 teaspoons instant coffee | 1 tablespoon gelatine | 4 tablespoons plain sugar |
| 1 pint thick cream | 2 tablespoons vanilla sugar (see p. 73) | ½ pint boiling water |

Pour 1 gill of boiling water over the instant coffee in a bowl, stirring all the time. Add the plain sugar and stir again. Pour a gill of water which is just off the boil on to the gelatine in another bowl, stirring as you do so. Mix the coffee and gelatine mixtures together thoroughly and put in a cold place. Whip the cream and when it begins to thicken add the vanilla sugar to it. When the coffee and gelatine mixture is just beginning to set, whip it up well with a whisk or rotary beater until it is frothy. Then stir it into the whipped cream. Wet a jelly mould and sprinkle it with coarse white sugar or coloured coffee-sugar crystals. Pour the pudding mixture into it and leave in a very cold place for 3 or 4 hours.

SOUR CREAM MOULD

Gefrorener sauer Rahm

| ½ pint sour cream | 2 tablespoons milk chocolate | 2 oz. vanilla sugar (see p. 73) |
| 2 tablespoons crushed macaroons | | 1 tablespoon rum |

Break up the chocolate into tiny pieces with a rolling pin. Whip the sour cream with an egg-whisk or rotary beater. When it begins to thicken, add the crushed chocolate, crushed macaroons, sugar and rum, and mix all well together. Pour the mixture into a cold wet jelly mould and put in a refrigerator until it is frozen.

BUTTER ICING

5 oz. icing sugar	1 drop almond essence	¾ pint thick cream
2 tablespoons water		4 egg yolks

Melt the sugar in the water until quite clear. Do not overheat. When cool, beat in the egg yolks and the almond essence. Whip the cream and fold lastly into the mixture. It is now ready for use and should be of the consistency of butter.

SALT ROLLS

Salzstangerln

ABOUT 24

12 oz. flour	caraway seeds	1 tablespoon beef suet
1 teaspoon sugar	½ pint milk	or lard
½ teaspoon salt	1 oz. yeast	water

A savoury roll to serve with dinner or savoury snacks. Boil the milk and reduce to blood heat. Dissolve the yeast in this. Add the sugar and salt. Stir and let stand for 5 minutes. Melt the fat and work in alternately with the flour. Knead for a few minutes in the bowl and then turn on to a floured board. Knead well until smooth and elastic. Put back in warmed bowl, cover with warm cloth and let rise until the bulk is doubled. Roll the dough out to about ¼ inch thickness. Cut into lengths about 1 inch by 6. Place on a greased baking-tin, cover again with cloth and let stand until the bulk has considerably increased. Brush with water, sprinkle with salt and caraway seeds (if liked). Bake in a hot oven for about 20 minutes.

BISHOP'S BREAD

Bischofsbrot

4 oz. butter	8 oz. chopped lemon	5 egg whites
4 oz. sugar	peel, sultanas,	4 oz. flour
5 egg yolks	orange peel and	rind and juice 1 lemon
	cooking chocolate	
	(in little lumps, not	
	grated)	

Beat the butter and sugar to a cream. Add the egg yolks well beaten, one at a time. Beat very well and add the lemon juice. Mix all the dry ingredients together. Beat the egg whites to a stiff froth. Fold the flour mixture and the whites of eggs into the butter mixture alternately. It should be a nice creamy batter. Pour into a well greased deep cake-tin with a loose base. Bake for 1 hour in a moderate oven.

PLAITED BREAD

Striezel

1 TO 2 LOAVES DEPENDING ON SIZE REQUIRED

1¼ lb. flour	4 oz. butter	1 extra egg yolk
5 tablespoons sugar	½ pint milk	2 oz. yeast
½ teaspoon salt		1 egg

Melt the butter and cool to blood heat. Dissolve the yeast in milk, which has been brought to nearly boiling point and then allowed to cool to blood heat. Add the sugar and salt. Stir until these are dissolved. Allow to stand for 5 minutes. Now add the egg and egg yolk, beaten together. Add about a cupful of flour and beat until it is a batter. Add the butter and remainder of the flour alternately until the mixture has become a fairly stiff dough. Turn on to a floured board and knead well. The dough should be elastic and not tough. Place in a warm place in a greased bowl and allow to rise for 30 minutes. Divide into 2 parts. Divide one half into 4 parts. Make this into a plait. Divide the second half into 3 parts. Knead together 2 of these parts, and divide this into 3 parts. Make these 3 parts into a plait. Roll the remaining piece into a twist, having divided it in 2 pieces. Brush the largest plait with milk and place the next plait on top. Brush this with milk and place the twist on top. Press these plaits into an oval shape and leave to rise to double their size. Brush the tops of these striezel with the white of egg, left from the yolk used in the recipe, mixed with milk. Bake in hot oven for 10 minutes, then reduce the temperature to moderate and bake for about 40 minutes to an hour.

MILK ROLLS

Milchrollen

4 GOOD-SIZED ROLLS

1 lb. flour	about ½ pint milk	2 oz. of butter
½ teaspoon salt	½ oz. yeast	egg to glaze

Bring the milk to the boil and allow to cool to blood heat. Dissolve the yeast in most of this. Warm the flour, add the salt and rub the butter into it. Make a hole in the centre of this and add the liquid yeast. Mix to a soft dough and add more milk if required. Knead well. Put in a warm bowl and cover with cloth. Leave for 1 hour until the size is at least doubled. Turn on to a floured board and knead well again. Shape into rolls, ovals or twists. Place on a warmed, greased tin and leave for another 10 to 20 minutes. Glaze with beaten egg and bake in a hot oven for 15 to 30 minutes. These should be golden-brown and very light.

CHEESE BREAD

Käsebrot

1 GOOD-SIZED LOAF

8 oz. flour
¾ teaspoon salt
1 tablespoon sugar

3 tablespoons hot
water
1 tablespoon tepid
water

1 egg
½ oz. yeast
4 oz. grated cheese

Dissolve the salt, and sugar in the hot water and leave to cool. To this add the yeast dissolved in the tepid water. Stir in the beaten egg and the grated cheese. Add a little flour and stir. Turn on to a floured board and knead. Add the remaining flour as required, but do not allow the dough to become tough. Shape into a loaf and place in a greased tin. Cover with a clean cloth and allow to rise for about 1 hour, or until it is twice the size. Have a moderate oven and bake for 45 minutes. When cooked, brush with melted butter and allow to cool.

HONEY BREAD

Honigbrot

1 GOOD-SIZED LOAF

8 oz. flour
1 teaspoon baking
  powder

1 teaspoon cinnamon
½ teaspoon salt
4 oz. sugar

1 tablespoon butter
½ pint milk
4 oz. honey

When baking this bread remember that it is easily burned, so watch it carefully. Mix all the dry ingredients together in a bowl, except the baking powder. Put the milk, butter and honey into a pan. Warm and stir all the time until they are well blended. Now into this, stir the baking powder. Pour this into the flour mixture. Stir well. This bread is not kneaded. Put into a floured bread tin and bake in a moderate oven for 1 hour. This can be iced or castor sugar may be dusted on top.

WINE PASTRY

Weinteig

4 oz. white flour
4 whites of eggs

1 gill white wine
pinch salt

1 teaspoon hot oil

Mix the flour and salt. Stir in the hot oil and wine. Cut and mix with a palette knife until the dough is smooth. Fold in the stiffly beaten whites of eggs. Use this pastry for rolling fruits in, such as bananas or slices of apple. Fry in deep fat or oil. It should be a golden brown. Dust with castor sugar.

POPPY-SEED ROLL

Mohnkipfel

1 TO 2 DEPENDING ON SIZE

8 oz. flour	½ oz. yeast	1 gill milk
1 tablespoon sugar	1 egg	poppy seeds
½ teaspoon salt		1 tablespoon butter

Boil the milk and allow to cool to blood heat. Dissolve the yeast in it. Add the sugar and salt and let it stand for 5 minutes. Melt the butter and let it cool to the same heat as the milk. Add the butter and milk alternately to flour and work in. Knead in the bowl with the hand until the dough is smooth and elastic. Leave for a few minutes and then knead again. Cover with a warm cloth and allow to stand for about 30 minutes. Divide the dough into three parts and plait it. Mould it gently so that each end is pointed. Brush with a little beaten egg mixed with water. Sprinkle well with poppy seeds. Bake in a moderate oven for about 30 minutes.

STRUDEL DOUGH

Strudelteig

8 oz. flour	1 tablespoon melted	1½ gills lukewarm
1 egg	butter	water
	salt	

Strudel dough is rather like a noodle dough, and should not be rolled out on a board in the usual way. It should be stretched by hand on a clean floured linen cloth. It is intended always to have a filling, such as apples, cheese, chocolate, cherries and so on. It is important to remember to have your filling ready, before you stretch the dough, which should always be paper thin when ready. As you pull and one part gets thin enough, leave it and go to work on another section. It should be possible to get it all of an even thickness. Put the flour on a board. Beat the eggs well. Mix the egg, water and melted butter. Make a well in the flour. Pour in the egg-and-butter mixture and add the salt. Stir gently so that the flour falls down from the sides into the well. It will be sticky at first. Flour the hands and knead. Rub the first sticky dough off your hands and flour again. Knead until it becomes smooth and elastic. Toss once or twice. Stretch once and knead again. Leave it covered in a warm place for about 1 hour. Cover the table with a linen cloth and dust with flour. Put the dough in the middle and roll out slightly. Now stretch by hand and follow the instructions given above. The filling should be placed on the dough while it is still on the cloth. It can then be rolled up and got into shape by lifting the cloth. Pinch the edges together to seal the contents. Do not fill right to the edges.

APPLE STRUDEL

Apfelstrudel

(Use strudel dough recipe. See p. 62)

3 large apples	4 oz. chopped walnuts	grated rind ½ lemon
4 oz. raisins (seedless)	6 oz. sugar	4 oz. melted butter
	icing sugar	

Core and peel the apples. Slice very thinly. Mix with all the other ingredients and spread over the strudel dough. Make it whatever size you wish. The larger it is the better flavour it seems to have. Pour some of the melted butter on top. With the assistance of the linen cloth, on which the dough is lying, roll the strudel up. Pinch the ends together. Do not fill right to the edges. Brush the edges with a wet brush and seal. Place the sealed side down on the baking sheet. Brush the top with the melted butter. Bake for 45 minutes in a moderate oven. When cold dust with icing sugar. *(Illustrated in Plate 9.)*

CHERRY STRUDEL

Kirchenstrudel

(Use strudel dough recipe. See p. 62)

Make in exactly the same way as Apple Strudel, but substitute 1 lb. cherries, stoned and sliced.

CREAM CHEESE STRUDEL

Strudel mit Topfen

(Use strudel dough recipe. See p. 62)

8 oz. cream cheese	½ teaspoon ground	4 whole eggs
½ pint cream	cinnamon	8 oz. seedless raisins
2 tablespoons butter	grated rind 1 small	(small)
6 oz. fine sugar	lemon	icing sugar

Beat the eggs well. Cream the butter and sugar. Put the cream cheese through a sieve. To the creamed butter mixture add the cheese, cream, cinnamon, lemon rind, and the beaten eggs. Lastly add seedless raisins. Spread this filling over the strudel dough. Wet the edges of the dough. Roll up as in Apple Strudel. Seal the edges. Turn the sealed side downward. Cut small slits in the top and bake in a moderate oven for about 1 hour. Allow to cool and then dust with icing sugar.

CREAM STRUDEL

Rahmstrudel

(Use strudel dough recipe. See p. 62)

4 oz. butter	1 tablespoons warmed	grated rind 1 small
6 eggs, separated	butter	lemon
4 oz. sugar	8 oz. sultanas	1½ pints sour cream
	(plumped)	

Cream the butter and sugar. Add the beaten egg yolks one by one. Add the cream and the lemon rind. Stir in the sultanas. Have the egg whites beaten stiffly. Now fold these into the mixture. This should be enough for two or three strudeln. Spread the mixture on the dough. Wet the edges with a pastry brush. Roll up and seal. Make a few cuts on the top. This is to allow the steam to escape so that the dough will not burst. Bake in a moderate oven for about 1 hour. Every 10 minutes brush the top with melted butter.

RUM DOUGHNUTS

4 oz. flour	2 tablespoons rum	2 oz. castor sugar
2 oz. butter	1 teaspoon powdered	deep fat for frying
½ pint water	cinnamon	salt
	3 eggs	

Boil water and butter, add flour and salt and beat over low heat until it forms a smooth ball of paste which will leave the sides of the pan clean. Chill slightly, add slightly beaten eggs. Beat these in gradually, making mixture smooth after each addition. When cool stir in the rum. Using an icing bag with a ½-inch nozzle, force 3-inch strips of the paste into the hot fat. Fry golden on both sides keeping the lid on the pan during the cooking of the first side. Drain on soft paper, serve hot, dusted with sugar and cinnamon.

YEAST DOUGH

Germteig

1 lb. flour	5 egg yolks	½ teaspoon vanilla
pinch salt	3 whole eggs	essence
2 oz. sugar	4 oz. butter	1 gill warm milk
	1 oz. yeast	

This is a fine light dough and can be used for making a variety of rolls and pastries, usually with fillings such as jam, fruit, almonds or cream cheese mixture. If these quantities are used several of the recipes given can be made and so a variety of delicious cakes and breads provided.

11. Linzer Torte, Austria (p.69)

12. Scotch Eggs, Britain (p.106)

13. Danish Liver Pâté (p.481)

Warm the milk and the butter and allow them to remain at blood heat. Work the yeast and the sugar together and stir this into the warm milk. Beat the butter, egg yolks, whole eggs and salt to a cream and add the yeast mixture. Mix well together. Work the flour and the vanilla essence in gradually. Mix with a knife until the knife comes clean. Cover the dough with a warm cloth and set to rise in a warm place until the size is doubled. This is now ready for use in the various recipes suggested. It can be rolled out and used as directed.

WINE STRUDEL

Weinstrudel

(Use strudel dough recipe. See p. 62)

8 oz. breadcrumbs	3 tablespoons butter	½ bottle white wine
	4 oz. white sugar	

Fry the breadcrumbs in the butter until a golden brown. Add the sugar and half of the wine. Mix well. Fill the strudel dough as directed in the other strudeln. Roll and seal. Bake in a hot oven for about 10 minutes. Pour over the remainder of the wine and bake in a moderate oven for about 30 minutes more. It should be a nice golden brown. Dredge well with castor sugar.

BUCHTELN

(Use yeast dough recipe. See p. 64)

Nut filling:

4 oz. grated hazelnuts	1 tablespoon butter	1 teaspoon vanilla
2 tablespoons breadcrumbs	1 gill cream or top milk	essence
	4 oz. Brazil nuts	8 oz. sugar

Work all together forming a paste. Keep cool.

Almond filling:

8 oz. ground almonds	4 egg whites	2 drops almond
2 tablespoons bread-crumbs	4 oz. castor sugar	essence

Work all the ingredients together to form a stiff paste. The dough, which has already risen to twice its size, is now ready for rolling out. Roll out on a floured board to a thickness of about ¼—½ inch. Cut into small squares, about 2 to 3 inches. Spread with the mixtures. Roll up from side to side. Do not pinch. Place on a buttered tin if possible not touching. Brush the tops and sides with melted butter. Leave in a warm place to rise until they are twice the size. Bake in a moderate oven for 45 minutes to 1 hour.

YEAST STRUDEL

(Use yeast dough recipe. See p. 64)

Almond filling:

8 oz. ground almonds	4 oz. castor sugar	chopped seeded raisins
2 tablespoons white breadcrumbs	2 drops almond essence	as required
		4 egg whites

Work all the ingredients together smoothly. When the dough has risen, roll out very thinly, if possible less than ¼ inch thick. Spread the almond filling over the complete surface. Sprinkle the raisins over this. Brush the edges of the dough with water. Roll up neatly and brush with melted butter. Sprinkle castor sugar over the top. Bake in a moderate oven for about 45 minutes. Allow to cool and cut in slices.

SACHER TORTE

8 oz. plain chocolate	12 oz. butter	chocolate icing
12 oz. fine white sugar	5 eggs	(see p. 67)
6 oz. flour	raspberry jam	2 tablespoons rum

This takes its name from the owner of a famous hotel in Vienna, in the time of the Emperor Franz Joseph. She was a rather tough, jovial, cigar-smoking lady, whom one would certainly not associate with anything as delicate as the Sacher Torte. Cream the butter and sugar. Beat well. Separate the eggs and beat the whites to a stiff froth. Add the yolks to the creamed butter and sugar and beat again. Fold in the whites of egg and the flour alternately and mix well. Melt the chocolate in a saucepan with a little rum and allow to cool. Add this to the mixture. Butter and flour 2 cake tins or torte tins. Divide the mixture between them and bake in a moderate oven for about 45 minutes to 1 hour. Allow the cakes to cool. Cover one half with raspberry jam and place the other on top. Cover this with chocolate icing.

CHOCOLATE TORTE

Schokoladentorte

6 eggs	4 oz. plain chocolate	6 oz. sugar
2 oz. butter		6 oz. ground almonds

Cream the butter and sugar together until light. Separate the yolks and whites of 5 of the eggs. Beat the egg yolks and 1 whole egg together. Stir into the butter and cream mixture. Melt the chocolate, add the almonds. Mix and stir into the mixture. Beat the egg whites until stiff but not too stiff. Fold into the mixture as it is now. Pour the mixture into a greased, deep flan-tin and bake in a moderate oven for 1 hour. Let cool and brush the top with jam sauce, then ice with chocolate icing.

Jam Sauce:

Any jam. Warm the jam. Add a little wine. Allow to cool and brush the top of the cake.

Chocolate Icing:

4 oz. plain chocolate	4 tablespoons icing sugar	6 tablespoons water

Melt the chocolate in the water. Add the sugar and cook slowly for about 10 minutes. To test it, dip clean scissors in, remove and open the blades. If it spins a thread between the two, then it is ready. Let it cool, but keep stirring. Spread at once on the cake and smooth with a palette knife. Serve with whipped cream.

ORANGE TORTE

Orangentorte

grated rind and juice 1 orange	8 oz. sugar	orange butter (see p. 75)
4 oz. fine white flour	4 oz. butter	
	4 eggs, separated	

Cream the butter and sugar. Add the beaten egg yolks and flour alternately. Stir in the orange rind and juice. Whip the egg whites stiffly and fold into the mixture. Put in a buttered and floured deep cake-tin with a loose base. Bake in a moderate oven for 45 minutes to 1 hour. Cover with orange butter.

NUT TORTE

Nußtorte

8 oz. sugar	12 oz. of grated nuts	¼ teaspoon grated
6 eggs	(can be walnuts, or	lemon peel
1 oz. flour	hazelnuts)	1 tablespoon rum

Separate the yolks and whites of the eggs. Beat the yolks and sugar together until creamy. Add the nuts and mix well together. Beat the egg whites to a stiff froth. Fold in the flour and egg whites alternately, adding the rum and grated lemon peel. Mix smoothly. Put in large sandwich or cake tin. Bake in a moderate oven for 40 to 45 minutes. When cold, split in half and spread bottom half with raspberry jam and whipped cream. This can also be iced with rum frosting (see p. 76). Decorate with a few roughly chopped nuts.

PUNCH TORTE

Punschtorte

| 8 oz. fine white self-raising flour | 9 eggs
10 oz. sugar | juice and grated rind 1 lemon |

Separate the yolks and whites of 7 eggs. Beat the 7 egg yolks and the remaining 2 eggs together until they are creamy. Add the sugar gradually. Beat again until it is very light and creamy. Add the lemon rind and juice. Fold in the flour, a little at a time. Beat the egg whites very stiffly. Fold into the mixture. Grease and flour 2 fairly deep cake-tins. Divide the batter between the two. Bake in a moderate oven for 30 to 35 minutes.

Syrup for flavouring:

| 1 gill water | 1 tablespoon sugar | 3 tablespoons rum |

Mix these ingredients together and moisten both pieces of cake, when cool. Spread both layers with raspberry or strawberry jam. Turn the two jam sides together and glaze with rum frosting (see p. 76).

MACAROON TORTE

Makronentorte

| 2 oz. fine, dry, white breadcrumbs | 10 oz. ground almonds
7 egg whites
12 oz. castor sugar | few drops almond extract |

Beat the whites to a stiff froth. Gradually add the sugar and beat continuously until the mixture is very stiff (as for meringue). Add the ground almonds and the breadcrumbs alternately, until it is all mixed well. Finally beat in the almond extract. Grease a cake tin and sprinkle with breadcrumbs. Pour the mixture into the tin. Bake in a slow oven for 45 minutes to 1 hour. Decorate with small macaroons, and serve with whipped cream.

POPPY-SEED TORTE

Mohntorte

| 1 lb. sugar
½ teaspoon ground cloves
rum | 1 gill rum
grated rind ½ lemon
1 teaspoon ground cinnamon
cream | 6 oz. raisins
2 oz. poppy seeds
10 eggs
breadcrumbs |

Plump the raisins in the rum. Drain well. Separate the egg yolks and whites. Grind the poppy seeds as finely as possible. (This can be done with a pestle and mortar if no grinding machine is available.) Beat the egg yolks and sugar until creamy. Add the raisins, cinnamon, cloves, lemon rind and the poppy seeds. Mix well. Fold in the egg whites, beaten to a light but not too stiff froth. Grease two 9-inch cake-tins and sprinkle with fine breadcrumbs. Divide the mixture in two and bake in a moderate oven for about 1 hour. Use tins with separate bottoms. Remove from tins and allow to cool. Brush rum over the top of the bottom layer, and the bottom of the top layer. Place one on top of the other. Pile whipped cream on top of the torte. (Whipped cream can also be spread between the layers if liked.)

VIENNA TORTE

Wiener Torte

4 whole eggs	10 oz. flour	apricot jam
12 oz. white sugar	1 teaspoon grated	fondant icing
8 oz. butter	lemon rind	(see p. 76)
4 egg yolks	cherries	cream
	angelica	

Beat the egg yolks and the whole eggs together. Add the butter and sugar. Beat well until the mixture is creamy. Fold in the flour and the grated lemon rind. Butter 4 large deep sandwich tins. Spread the mixture equally in these 4 tins. Bake in a hot oven for 30 minutes. Allow to cool in the tins. Turn out very carefully on a flat surface. Spread each layer with apricot jam, and place on top of each other. Ice with fondant icing and decorate with cherries and angelica. Serve with whipped cream.

LINZER TORTE

6 oz. flour	1 lb. jam, raspberry,	1 teaspoon powdered
8 oz. sugar	or strawberry	cinnamon
8 oz. butter	2 oz. ground almonds	grated rind and juice
2 egg yolks	castor sugar	1 lemon

This must have come from the city of Linz, in upper Austria. Nevertheless it has been associated with Vienna for so long that it has come to be thought completely Viennese. Sieve the flour and mix in all the dry ingredients, sugar, almonds, cinnamon and grated lemon rind. Work the butter and egg yolks together until smooth. Add these to the flour mixture together with the juice of the lemon. Mix well. Remove the paste to a floured board and roll out to $\frac{1}{4}$ inch thickness. Line a greased flan or sandwich tin with the paste. Roll out what is left over again, and cut in long strips about $\frac{3}{4}$ inch wide. Fill the flan with jam and cover the top with criss-cross strips. Sprinkle with castor sugar. Bake in a hot oven for about 35 minutes. When cool put more fresh jam in between the lattice work. This paste should be kept very cool until the time of cooking. Serve with whipped cream. *(Illustrated in Plate 11.)*

RADETZKY CHESTNUT TORTE

Radetzky-Kastanientorte

12 oz. castor sugar	1 lb. chestnuts,	1 saltspoon dry coffee
8 oz. butter	shelled, and boiled	14 egg yolks

Mash the chestnuts as finely as possible. Cream the butter and sugar and add the dry coffee. Now add the mashed chestnuts and egg yolks alternately. Work into a paste. Spread this on two large tins, well greased and floured. Bake for about 45 minutes in a moderate oven. Allow to cool in the tins before removing.

Filling:

6 oz. chestnuts,	2 egg whites	2 tablespoons rum
mashed	4 oz. castor sugar	

Mix all these together until they are a creamy paste. Spread on the lower round. Place the other round on top. Ice the top with nut icing (see p. 76).

APPLE TORTE

Apfeltorte

8 oz. butter	2 egg yolks	few drops lemon juice
10 oz. flour	4 tablespoons sour	pinch salt
	milk or cream	

Cut the butter into the flour. Beat the egg yolks and add, together with the salt. Add the sour cream gradually, until the dough is soft, also the drops of lemon juice. Roll it up and let it get cold; 10 minutes in the refrigerator will do. Roll out about $\frac{3}{8}$ inch thick. Place in a large flan-dish, rather deep, for the apples are bulky. Leave to get cold again while you prepare the rest.

Apple Filling:

8 apples	$\frac{1}{2}$ pint water	$\frac{1}{2}$ lemon peel, grated
4 oz. sugar	$\frac{1}{2}$ pint white wine	small stick cinnamon

Peel, core and quarter apples. Mix wine, water and sugar, and bring slowly to the boil. Add the lemon peel and cinnamon. Pour this over the apples, being careful not to break up the quarters. Cook very slowly until the apples are half cooked, still keeping their shape. Drain all liquid off. Place on the cold pastry after they are cool. Leave some space between each quarter for the next filling to be poured over.

Orange Filling:

3 whole eggs and 3 egg yolks	grated rind of 1 orange grated rind of 1 lemon 12 oz. castor sugar	6 oz. ground almonds juice of 1 lemon

Beat the whole eggs, the egg yolks and the sugar together until creamy and light yellow. Add the ground almonds, the grated rinds of orange and lemon, also the lemon juice. Mix all together. Pour over the apples. Bake in a moderate oven for 45 minutes to an hour until the filling is set and yellow in colour.

SNOW TORTE

Schneetorte

12 oz. castor sugar 2 tablespoons cornflour	1 teaspoon vanilla essence breadcrumbs	6 large egg whites 2 oz. fine white flour 4 oz. melted butter

Sieve the cornflour, sugar, and flour together. Beat egg whites to a light froth, not too stiff. Add vanilla essence. Fold into the flour mixture. When well mixed stir in the melted butter. Mix again, until the whole is smooth and creamy. Grease a cake-tin and dust with fine dry breadcrumbs. Pour the mixture in and bake in a moderate oven for about 1 hour. When cake is cold, coat with lemon icing (see below) and decorate with candied fruits.

Lemon Icing:

1 tablespoon lemon juice	4 oz. icing sugar	grated rind ½ lemon 1 tablespoon water

Add all together and stir until quite smooth. If necessary add more water. Spread on the cake as soon as prepared.

COFFEE CREAM CAKE

Mokkatorte

4 oz. flour 6 oz. ground almonds	6 oz. sugar 4 eggs	1 tablespoon strong black coffee (mocha)

Separate the egg yolks and whites. Beat the yolks and sugar together until creamy. Add the ground almonds and the tablespoon of coffee. Beat the whites to a stiff froth. Fold this in alternately with the flour, until the whole is stiff but quite light. Grease 2 cake tins and dust with flour. Bake in a moderate oven for about 30 minutes. Fill and cover with mocha cream (see p. 73).

STREUSEL CAKE

Streuselkuchen

3 oz. plain flour	1 level teaspoon	2 oz. butter
3 oz. fine semolina	each cinnamon	1 beaten egg
3 level teaspoons	and ginger	milk
baking powder	3 oz. castor	pinch salt
	sugar	

Filling and Topping Mixture:

1 oz. flour	1½ oz. butter	2 level teaspoons
1 oz. fine semolina	1½ oz. chopped nuts	cinnamon
	2 oz. Demerara sugar	

To make filling and topping mixture, sift together flour, semolina and cinnamon and stir in sugar and chopped nuts. Melt butter and stir into other ingredients. Set aside to cool whilst making up cake.

Sift together flour, semolina, baking powder, salt, spices and sugar. Rub in butter till fine. Stir in beaten egg and enough milk for a very soft dropping consistency. Have ready a shallow, 7-inch square cake tin, greased and lined at the bottom with greased paper. Spread half the cake mixture in the tin and scatter a layer of filling over. Cover with remaining cake mixture. Level off. Scatter the rest of the topping mixture over the surface. Bake in a moderately hot oven about 25—30 minutes. Leave to cool in the tin, about 10 minutes, before carefully turning out. Serve warm. A little icing sugar may be scattered over the top. (*Illustrated in Plate 7.*)

VIENNA GUGELHUPF

Wiener Gugelhupf

12 oz. flour	½ pint milk	12 sweet almonds
4 oz. butter	4 oz. stoned raisins	1 tablespoon yeast
2 oz. castor sugar	and currants	3 eggs

Dissolve the yeast in a little warm milk. Put the flour in a warmed bowl. Melt the butter. Put the eggs in a hole in the centre of the flour. Add the melted butter, the sugar and the dissolved yeast. Mix all very well together until very smooth. Finally stir in the raisins and currants. Have cylindrical moulds well greased. This mixture would fill at least three. Blanch and slice the almonds very finely and strew on the buttered sides of the moulds. Pour the mixture in on this, filling only three quarters full. Put the moulds in a warm place. Cover and leave to rise until the moulds are full. Place on a thick baking tin and bake for about 1 hour. This, of course, depends on the size of the mould. They will turn out easily when sufficiently baked. Place on a wire tray and dust with castor sugar.

FRIED STRAWS

Gebackenes Stroh

6 OR 8 SERVINGS WITH MAIN DISH

3 egg yolks	deep fat for frying	1 tablespoon butter
1 whole egg	1 gill creamy milk	(melted)
1 tablespoon sugar	½ teaspoon salt	1 tablespoon yeast
	8 oz. flour	

Beat the egg yolks and the whole egg separately. Blend the yeast with the creamy milk. Beat in the egg yolks and the whole egg. Warm a bowl and mix together the flour, sugar and salt. Pour the yeast mixture into the flour and add the melted butter. Work the whole into a dough, until it does not stick to the spoon. Cover with a warm cloth and leave to rise to twice the size. Knead again and cut into thin strips. Fry in deep fat until golden brown. Drain on greaseproof paper. Sprinkle with sugar or cheese (Parmesan), according to what you are going to garnish. They can be served with sweet puddings or stews and savouries.

VANILLA SUGAR

Vanillezucker

3 lb. sugar   1 vanilla pod

This is something every Austrian household has on hand, and it is much more flavoursome than vanilla extract. You cut the vanilla pod into small pieces and mix it with the sugar and put it in a jar. The sugar will not be properly flavoured for 3 days. When you use some sugar, add a bit more, mixing it well together with what is already there. Once a month take out the vanilla pieces and put in new ones. If you are using very little of this sugar, a new vanilla pod every 2 or 3 months is enough.

MOCHA CREAM

6 oz. sugar	3 egg yolks	1 gill strong black
4 oz. butter		mocha coffee

Beat the egg yolks with the sugar. Add the coffee and stir well. Put in a double boiler and cook until the mixture is like a creamy custard. Allow to cool. Beat the butter to a cream. Mix this in with the custard. Spread the cream on top of the lower half of the torte. Place the other half on top. Cover the top and sides with the remainder. If you can get little imitation coffee beans in chocolate or sweets, they make a nice decoration.

VIENNESE WHIPPED CREAM

Wiener Schlagobers

1 pint whipping cream   2 tablespoons vanilla
                                   sugar

Chill the cream for 4 hours. Get a bowl ice-cold. The cream will whip better if it and the bowl are left in the refrigerator for a while. Whip the cream with a whisk or rotary eggbeater, and add the sugar gradually, as soon as the cream begins to stiffen. This whipped cream is used for numerous puddings, on top of coffee and chocolate, or fruit, and in many other ways.

VANILLA CREAM

½ pint milk   2 oz. castor sugar   1 vanilla pod cut into
1 large egg   1 oz. cornflour   4 or 5 pieces

Mix the cornflour, sugar and egg yolk to a paste with little of the milk. Heat the remainder of the milk with the vanilla pod in a double saucepan. Pour the hot milk over the other ingredients, stirring all the time. When blended, return to the double saucepan, cook and stir until thick.

CHESTNUT SOUFFLÉ

Kastanienkoch

3½ tablespoons butter   3 tablespoons vanilla   6 eggs
1 lb. chestnut purée   sugar (see p. 73)

Mix 3 tablespoons butter with 3 tablespoons vanilla sugar and beat well, adding the beaten yolks of the eggs which have been separated. Add also the chestnut purée. Brush a soufflé dish with the remaining butter. Whip the egg whites and fold into the mixture and pour into the dish. Bake for 45 minutes in hot oven. Serve immediately.

NUT FILLING

Nußfüllung

8 oz. grated mixed   1 gill cream   2 tablespoons brown
  nuts   1 tablespoon butter   breadcrumbs
4 oz. sugar   vanilla essence

Work all together until a fairly stiff paste has been formed. Allow to get very cold and use as directed.

CHESTNUT FILLING

1 lb. chestnuts, mashed and sieved	5 eggs, separated ½ pint milk	2 oz. butter 4 oz. sugar

After the chestnuts have been boiled soft and peeled, before mashing, cover with the milk and cook slowly until they are very soft. They will then sieve easily. Cream the butter, add the sugar and egg yolks alternately. Beat well. Beat the whites very stiffly. Add the chestnut mixture to the egg yolk mixture and lastly fold in the whites. It is now ready to use.

ALMOND FILLING

Mandelfüllung

8 oz. ground almonds 4 oz. castor sugar	2 drops almond essence 4 egg whites	2 tablespoons white breadcrumbs

Mix the almonds and sugar together. Add the breadcrumbs and the almond essence. Stir in the stiffly beaten egg whites. Work all together and use as directed.

COFFEE CREAM

Kaffeecreme

4 oz. sugar 2 tablespoons butter	2 tablespoons strong coffee	2 egg yolks

Melt the butter and sugar together in a saucepan. Add the coffee over a gentle heat. When the sugar is quite dissolved beat in the egg yolks. Remove the saucepan from the heat, and beat thoroughly until the mixture becomes like a cream. Fill the tartlets and squeeze a pyramid of whipped cream on top.

ORANGE BUTTER

1 pint thick cream 6 oz. icing sugar	4 egg yolks	grated rind 1 orange 2 tablespoons water

Melt the icing sugar in the water on a gentle heat until it becomes quite clear. Cool and beat in the egg yolks and the grated orange rind. Whip the cream stiffly and fold into the mixture. It is now ready for use.

75

LEMON ICING

9 oz. icing sugar	grated rind 1 lemon	2 tablespoons lemon
1½ tablespoons water		juice

Mix all together with a palette knife until it is quite smooth. Spread with the same knife.

RUM FROSTING

6 oz. icing sugar	1½ tablespoons rum	1 tablespoon water

Dissolve sugar in the water over a gentle heat. Add the rum, drop by drop. Keep stirring, until the mixture coats the spoon. Allow to cool, then use immediately as directed.

BURNT SUGAR ICING

Gebrannter Zucker

1 oz. white sugar	2 tablespoons water

Cook the sugar and water in a saucepan until it turns a golden brown. While still warm brush over the cake top, or use as directed.

FONDANT ICING

1 lb. fine white sugar	1 gill water	pinch cream of tartar

Put the sugar and water into the top part of a double saucepan. Melt gently but do not overheat. Add the cream of tartar. When the icing sticks to the back of a spoon it is ready. If it gets too thick add a few drops more water or lemon juice. As soon as the icing is the right consistency spread it on top of the cake.

NUT ICING

4 oz. icing sugar	5 egg whites	2 tablespoons grated
		nuts

Beat the egg whites to a stiff froth. Then beat the sugar lightly in and add the grated nuts. Spread on top of the torte. Dust with sifted icing sugar, and place in a cool oven. This will set the icing. Remove from the oven and allow to get quite cool before turning out.

76

BELGIAN COOKING

Musia Soper

The Belgians have the same live interest in good food as the French. Just ask any taxi driver in Brussels where you ought to take your next meal, and you'll be lucky to get away in half an hour. He will give long dissertations on the relative value of various establishment, he will make detailed enquiries of your special preference. You will realise that this problem of a meal cannot be treated light-heartedly. It is a big enough problem to give it your whole mind, because good food is IMPORTANT.

To prepare a Belgian Chicken Pâté you must be at leisure, and furthermore of a generous nature to be willing to sacrifice 2 glasses of brandy for a truly royal pâté. It is not an everyday routine dish — but something to be prepared lovingly for special occasions.

Braised Chicory is one of the internationally known Belgian dishes— ideal for a luncheon party, served with a fresh salad.

Chicken Waterzoie is the oldest national Belgian dish and once you include it in your repertoire it will always stay in it. It is obviously a hearty country dish and has to be served in man-sized soup plates, which are big enough to hold the portions of chicken as well as the vegetables.

Neither rabbits nor prunes will ever send anyone into gastronomic raptures—so we can salute the Belgians for combining the two into an exquisite dish of Rabbit and Prunes—even if you do have to use half a bottle of wine when preparing it. Both the Rabbit dish and the Meat Rolls are perfect for the cook-hostess who wants to finish all the work in the kitchen well before the guests arrive.

LE PÂTÉ BRUXELLES

Brussels Pâté

1 small cooked chicken	½ teaspoon allspice	1—2 sprigs thyme
1 lb. fat bacon	3 tablespoons brandy	melted pork fat
1 lb. lean pork	1—2 bay leaves	salt and pepper
	12 rashers fat bacon	

Slice off the fillets of breast from the chicken and pass the remaining chicken meat with the fat bacon, and pork twice through a mincer. Add the allspice, brandy, salt and pepper and rub through a sieve. Then work the mixture with a wooden spoon until it is smooth and well blended. Line a deep, fireproof dish with rashers of fat bacon, put in the bay leaves, thyme, and then half the minced mixture. Place the slices of chicken breast on top, cover with rashers of bacon and put in the remaining minced mixture. Cover with the remaining bacon rashers, press down firmly, put on a lid and stand the dish in a pan with water. Put into a slow oven for 2 hours, adding water to the pan when necessary. When done, remove the lid, cover the pâté with a cloth and put a weight on it to press it down for about 12 hours. Then cover with an inch layer of melted pork fat and leave in a cold place until required.

POTAGE AUX HERBES

Sorrel Soup

4 oz. sorrel	6 tablespoons of tiny	1 heaped tablespoon
1 tablespoon lard	fried croûtons	chervil
1 tablespoon butter	1 small heart of	2 egg yolks
2½ pints stock	lettuce	1 teaspoon sugar

Cut the sorrel and lettuce into narrow strips. Chop the chervil. Melt the lard in a saucepan and add the sorrel, lettuce, chervil. Simmer them uncovered for 10 minutes, stirring frequently with a wooden spoon. Sprinkle with the sugar, add the stock, cover the saucepan and boil for 30 minutes. Mix the egg yolks carefully with a little cold stock. Remove the soup from the fire. Add 1 cupful of the warm soup very gradually to the egg mixture. Then add the egg mixture to the pot of soup. Cut the butter into very small pieces and sprinkle them on the soup. Reheat gently, and serve with the fried croûtons on a separate dish.

POTAGE DE FLANDRES

Flanders Soup

4 potatoes	2 small onions	pinch thyme
2 sticks celery	clove garlic	a little chervil
1 small can tomato	1 tablespoon butter	salt and pepper
purée	croûtons	about 1½ quarts water

Chop up the potatoes (peeled), celery, onions, garlic, and put them in a big saucepan of water with the tomato purée well stirred into it. Add the thyme, salt and pepper. Bring them to the boil. Then put them over a very low heat and let them simmer for about 3 hours, giving them an occasional stir with a wooden spoon. Strain off all the liquid gently into a bowl. Place the vegetables in another bowl and mash them to a smooth pulp. Then add gradually enough of the soup liquid to them to make a thick, creamy mixture. Reheat. Add the butter and chopped chervil and diced fried bread just before serving.

OEUFS MEULEMEESTER

Eggs in the Old Bruges Style

6 SERVINGS

6 eggs	1 dessertspoon	1 dessertspoon French
1 tablespoon butter	chopped chervil	mustard
1 tablespoon	6 prawns	salt and pepper
chopped parsley	½ pint cream	1 oz. grated cheese

Hard-boil the eggs. Plunge them in cold water. Shell them, cut them into shreds and put them in a bowl, together with the prawns cut in small pieces, the chervil, parsley, French mustard, cream, salt, pepper and butter, which should be melted. Mix well together. Butter an oven-proof dish. Pour the mixture in. Sprinkle the grated cheese on top and dot with a little butter. Brown in a hot oven.

MAQUEREAUX À LA FLAMANDE

Flemish Mackerel

2 mackerel	sprig thyme	8 peppercorns
2 pints water	10 sprigs parsley	½ pint white sauce
½ pint vinegar	3 chopped shallots	(see p. 257)
3 chopped carrots	1 heaped teaspoon	1 tablespoon French
1 chopped onion	kitchen salt	mustard
	bay leaf	

Make a *court-bouillon* by boiling in an uncovered saucepan 2 pints water, ½ pint vinegar, 3 chopped carrots, 1 chopped onion, 3 chopped shallots, bay leaf, sprig of thyme and parsley and heaped teaspoon of coarse kitchen salt. Boil gently for 50 minutes then add the peppercorns and continue to boil for another 10 minutes. Strain and allow the liquid to cool. Fillet the mackerel and place it in the tepid *court-bouillon*, bring to the boil then simmer until the fish is cooked (about 10 minutes). Make white sauce with liquid from *court-bouillon*, flavour with French mustard and serve with the mackerel.

L'ANGUILLE AU VERT

Eel Stewed with Fresh Herbs

2 lb. eel	mint	sorrel
2 oz. butter	chervil	juice 2 lemons
2 gills white wine	parsley	salt and pepper
	2 egg yolks	

14. A Fish Stall In Paris

15. Canard à l'Orange, France (p.240)

16. Potato Salad, Sweden (p.483)

Cut the eel into 2-inch lengths. Stew in the butter with the chopped herbs for 15 minutes. Add the wine and enough water to cover the fish. Simmer for 10 minutes. Put the fish in a shallow earthenware dish. Mix the egg yolks and lemon juice together, add gradually to the stock, season with salt and pepper. Pour over the fish. Leave to cool.

CROQUETTES AUX CREVETTES

Shrimp Rissoles

8 oz. cooked shrimps	1 teaspoon lemon juice	1 egg
2 oz. butter	1 tablespoon grated	breadcrumbs
3 oz. flour	cheese	fat for frying
salt, pepper	1 gill milk	

Melt the butter and blend with 2 oz. of flour and the milk. Add the cheese, salt and pepper and the lemon juice. Put in the shrimps, mix well and leave in a cold place until firm. Then shape the mixture into 8 long-shaped rissoles, cover with the remaining flour, dip in a beaten egg and roll in breadcrumbs. Fry in hot fat until brown all round. Serve hot or cold.

HOCHEPOT

Hot-Pot

12 TO 16 SERVINGS

2 lb. brisket of beef	12 chipolata sausages	12 onions
1 lb. pig's feet	3 sprigs parsley	3 leeks
8 oz. pig's ears	2 sprigs thyme	3 sticks celery
1½ lb. shoulder of veal	1 bay leaf	1 turnip
1 lb. shoulder of	1 cabbage	salt and pepper
mutton		3 carrots

Chop all the different pieces of meat, put them in a saucepan and cover with water. Bring to the boil and remove any scum that rises to the top. Repeat this skimming twice, then add the vegetables, whole if they are small, coarsely chopped if they are large; the cabbage is quartered. Season with salt and pepper, add the parsley, thyme and bay leaf. Cover the saucepan and simmer for 3 hours. Add the chipolata sausages and simmer for another hour. Remove meat, sausages and vegetables, place them in a hot casserole with a little of the stock in which they have cooked and serve. The stock may be served as a soup.

ENTRECÔTE AU LARD

Steak with Bacon

8 thin slices rump steak	1 oz. lard	1 gill red wine
8 rashers streaky bacon	1 large onion	chopped parsley
	½ pint stock	salt and pepper

Lay a rasher of bacon on each slice of beef. Season with salt, pepper and chopped parsley. Roll and secure with cocktail sticks. Fry in the lard until all sides are lightly browned. Transfer to a shallow fireproof dish. Fry the chopped onion until golden. Add it to the meat. Add the stock and the wine, cover the dish and cook in a moderate oven for 1 hour. Season the sauce with salt and pepper and reduce it if necessary.

CARBONNADE À LA FLAMANDE

Flemish Carbonnade

6 TO 8 SERVINGS

3 lb. lean stewing steak	1 tablespoon flour	1 teaspoon French mustard
1 sliced onion	sprig thyme	salt and black pepper
2 oz. butter	½ pint beer	1 lump sugar
	bay leaf	

Cut the beef into 1-inch cubes. Fry the sliced onion golden brown, with 2 oz. butter, in a heavy saucepan. Add the meat cubes, and brown them on all sides. Now add a lump of sugar, a teaspoon of French mustard, thyme, and bay leaf. Season with salt and pepper. Sprinkle with 1 tablespoon flour, and cover with a good ½ pint pale ale. Bring to the boil and stir. Cover and simmer for 2 hours. Serve with boiled potatoes. This stew is equally good, if not better, when reheated.

LES CHOESELS

Meat and Sweetbreads

1 oxtail	1 lb. mushrooms	mixed herbs
1 lb. mutton	4 fricadelles	2 cloves
1 lb. veal	(see p. 83)	grated nutmeg
4 sheep's trotters	1 pint beer	salt and pepper
4 sweetbreads	1 gill Madeira	2 oz. butter
4 oz. ox kidney		1 lb. onions

Chop the onions and fry in the butter until golden brown. Put into a large pan with the oxtail, cut into sections, and add herbs, cloves, a little grated nutmeg, 1 teaspoon of salt and ¼ teaspoon pepper. Cover with the beer, bring to the boil then put on a lid and simmer for 1 hour. Then add the mutton, cut into cubes, and simmer for another 30 minutes. In the meantime, split the sheep's feet into 4 parts, blanch and then boil until nearly done. Add these to the saucepan with the meat, together with the veal cut into cubes, sliced ox kidney and the sweetbreads and simmer for another hour. Finally add cooked fricadelles, the mushrooms, more seasoning to taste, and the Madeira, and cook for a further 15 minutes. Serve very hot.

LES FRICADELLES

Minced Meat Balls

2 lb. minced pork	1 gill white wine	1 pint stock
2 small onions, sliced	2 eggs	*bouquet garni*
2 slices bread	2 oz. lard	4 medium potatoes
1 gill milk	flour, extra lard	salt and pepper

Fry the onions lightly in 1 oz. lard. Mix with the meat. Add the bread, previously soaked in a little milk, the wine and the egg yolks. Season with salt and pepper. Beat well together and fold in the stiffly beaten egg whites. Shape into balls, roll in flour and fry in the lard until brown. Poach the meat balls in the stock with the *bouquet garni* and quartered potatoes for 30 minutes. Remove the *bouquet*. Serve the balls in their sauce, sprinkled with parsley.

ROGNONS DE VEAU À LA LIÉGEOISE

Veal Kidney with Juniper Berries

4 veal kidneys	½ gill white wine	salt and pepper
4 oz. butter		12 juniper berries

Sprinkle the kidneys with salt and pepper. Brown on both sides in half the butter. Cover the pan and cook slowly for 2 minutes. Add the wine, the crushed juniper berries and the rest of the butter cut into small pieces. Continue to cook slowly until the kidneys are tender.

CHICKEN WATERZOIE

1 boiling fowl	3 leeks sliced	*bouquet garni*
2 onions stuck with	1 carrot sliced	salt and pepper
cloves	½ bottle white wine	water
3 sticks celery, chopped	1 lemon	parsley

Rub the chicken with lemon. Simmer with the vegetables in just enough water to cover. When the water boils add the *bouquet garni* and the white wine. Season with salt and pepper. Continue simmering for 1½ hours. Cut the chicken into pieces, remove the *bouquet garni*, serve the chicken in the stock with the vegetables, garnished with chopped parsley.

POULET À LA WALLONNE

Chicken à la Wallonne

6 TO 8 SERVINGS

1 young chicken	salt and pepper	4 tablespoons cream
1 lb. knuckle of veal	1 onion stuck with a	4 egg yolks
1 calf's sweetbreads	clove	1 pint chicken stock
3 carrots	1 *bouquet garni*	1 liqueur glass white
3 sticks celery	4 tablespoons butter	wine
1 leek		4 tablespoons flour

Put the knuckle of veal in a casserole, cover with cold water, bring to the boil, skim. Add the carrots, celery and leek, all chopped, season with salt and pepper. Add also the *bouquet garni* and onion. Simmer for 45 minutes. Plunge the sweetbreads in boiling water for 5 minutes. Add chicken and sweetbreads to veal stock, bring to the boil and simmer for 45 minutes or longer if the bird is not very young. Melt the butter in a separate pan, add the flour and stir, without allowing the flour to colour, for 3 or 4 minutes. Add 1 pint of the stock in which the chicken has cooked, slowly stirring all the while. Mix the egg yolks, cream and wine in a bowl. Add a little of the sauce to them, then add to the sauce. Beat well until it comes to the boil. Cut the sweetbreads into cubes, joint the chicken and place them in a deep serving dish. Pour the sauce over them and serve.

OIE DE VISE

Belgian Style Goose

6 TO 8 SERVINGS

1 goose	3 carrots	½ pint cream
1½ pints milk	3 onions	3 cloves
4 cloves garlic	6 egg yolks	6 sprigs parsley
bouquet garni	4 rusks	salt
	4 peppercorns	

Clean the goose and put it, with the giblets, into a saucepan. Cover with water, bring to the boil and skim. Now add sliced carrots and onions, the cloves, peppercorns, *bouquet garni* and a good pinch of salt. Cover and simmer for 1½ hour. Skin the garlic cloves and simmer them in milk until they are quite tender. Remove the garlic cloves and add the quartered rusks to the milk. Continue to simmer, stirring a little, until the rusks are quite dissolved. Season with a little salt. Beat the egg yolks, stir the cream into them and add a little of the milk sauce and stir while simmering very gently for 2 minutes. Place the goose on a hot serving dish. Pour the sauce over it, decorate with the parsley sprigs, and serve.

LAPIN AUX PRUNEAUX

Rabbit with Prunes

1 rabbit, jointed	2 bay leaves	1 lb. prunes
½ bottle red wine	thyme	salt and pepper
2 tablespoons vinegar	2 oz. butter	1 tablespoon
4 peppercorns	2 oz. flour	redcurrant jelly

Marinate the rabbit in the wine and vinegar with the peppercorns and herbs for 24 hours. Drain and fry lightly on all sides in the butter. Stir in the flour. Add enough water to cover. Season with salt and pepper. Add the prunes, soaked if necessary, cover the pan and simmer for 1 hour or until tender. Stir in the redcurrant jelly before serving. *(Illustrated in Plate 75.)*

ENDIVES BRAISÉES

Braised Chicory

1½ lb. chicory	juice of ½ lemon	salt
2 oz. butter	(about tablespoon)	3 tablespoons water

Wash the chicory well and separate the leaves. Use only the tender ones, not the coarse outer ones. Choose a heavy-bottomed saucepan or earthenware oven dish. Sprinkle salt on the bottom of it, add the butter, water and lemon juice. Add the chicory, turning it about to mix it thoroughly with the other ingredients. Put a tight lid on the saucepan and let it simmer very slowly for 1—1½ hours. Or, if you are using an earthenware oven dish, cook in a slow oven. When done, lift chicory on to a hot dish. Reduce the liquid slightly and pour it over the chicory.

CHOUX DE BRUXELLES SAUTÉS

Sauté Brussels Sprouts

8 oz. Brussels sprouts	salt	pinch pepper
	1½ tablespoons butter	

Clean the Brussels sprouts, cut off the outer leaves and the stems. Plunge them into a saucepan of boiling salted water, and boil for 15 minutes. Remove, and drain them well. Heat 1 tablespoon of butter in a large frying pan and add the sprouts. Fry them on a hot fire for about 9 minutes, shaking the pan to avoid sticking. By then most of the water in the sprouts will have vaporized and they will be faintly browned. Put them in a serving dish with a pinch of pepper and ½ tablespoon of butter cut into tiny pieces.

BEIGNETS DE CHOUX-FLEURS

Cauliflower Butter-Balls

6 SERVINGS

1 cauliflower	½ pint milk	½ pint cheese sauce
1 egg	salt	(see p. 257)
4½ oz. flour	6 sprigs parsley	a pan of deep fat

Get a pint of water rapidly boiling in a saucepan. Add a teaspoon of salt. Break the cauliflower into tiny flowerets and put them in the water, stem side down. Cover the saucepan and let them boil for 7 minutes then test them; if a fork goes in they are done—they must not be soft. If they still seem hard give them another 3 minutes then remove them and let them drain in a colander. In a bowl beat up the yolk of an egg, add the flour the milk and a little salt and blend into a smooth creamy batter. Beat the egg white to a froth separately and add to the batter. Get the fat in your deep fat frying pan really hot. Then dip the sprigs of cauliflower in the batter and cook them in the deep fat until they are golden brown. Lift them out and let them drain on tissue paper for a minute then put them in a hot dish in the warming oven until all the cauliflower sprigs have been cooked in the same way. Serve them garnished with parsley and accompanied by a sauce-boat of hot cheese sauce.

GAUFRES À LA FLAMANDE

Flemish Waffles

1 lb. plain flour	½ pint cream	sugar
½ oz. yeast	2 oz. butter	pinch salt
8 eggs		3 tablespoons brandy

Dissolve the yeast in a little warm water, then mix well with 4 oz. flour. Leave for 1 hour and when risen add the rest of the flour, pinch of salt and sugar, the beaten eggs, cream, melted butter and brandy. Work all well together and leave for another 2 hours. Cook in waffle irons until golden brown on both sides. Serve hot sprinkled with sugar.

CAFÉ LIÉGEOIS

2 tablespoons vanilla or coffee ice cream	1 gill sweetened strong black coffee	1 teaspoon crushed ice (optional)
	thick cream	

The above ingredients are sufficient for 1 person. Put all the ingredients, except the cream into a glass and stir until the mixture is thick and creamy. Top generously with whipped cream.

BRITISH COOKING

Elizabeth Campbell and Musia Soper

Recently, when I opened the chapter on England, Wales and Northern Ireland in a round-the-world cook book, I read with quite a shock the following sentence: 'For their own protection, visitors to England should understand British food habits.' Come, come, it is not as bad as all that. The main trouble is the British attitude to food—not its inferior quality. I mean the attitude of 'I eat because I have to live, not because I enjoy my food'. But even this attitude is only characteristic of a small section of the British people and is changing from day to day. In fact I am not at all alone in thinking that British cooking can be exceptionally good, especially the dishes which hail from the North. A really light Yorkshire pudding can be served to gourmets from all over the world and win praise. The West of England has given us a recipe which should make a regular appearance in every household: Cornish Pasty. Jugged Hare, Irish Stew, Welsh Rarebit and Lancashire Hot Pot are all solid foundations to any kitchen. To say nothing of a nice joint of sirloin for the traditional English Roast Beef—a dinner which you can put before the choosiest Frenchman and feel sure that he will enjoy. Puddings and pies are a notable feature of British cooking, and Steak and Kidney Pudding has at last taken its rightful place on the menus of large hotels and restaurants.

You will also find a number of traditional Scottish recipes in this section which are well worth trying. They include the famous Cock-a-Leekie Soup, Scotch Eggs, Scotch Shortbread, Cream-Crowdie, an excellent Dundee cake, Musselburgh Pie made with steak and oysters, and of course a recipe for haggis. The traditional haggis involves a tremendous amount of preparation and you must obtain the large stomach bag of a sheep—but we have given a pot version which anyone can make without difficulty and which will look and taste every bit as authentic as the real haggis which is piped in at a Burns Supper.

CREAM OF TOMATO SOUP

1 lb. tomatoes, canned or fresh	1 turnip	salt and pepper
	2 celery stalks	few drops
1 oz. butter	1 teaspoon sugar	red colouring
1 oz. flour	½ oz. peppercorns	water
2 lb. knuckle of veal	mixed herbs	1 tablespoon lemon
3 onions		juice

Make the white stock by simmering the bones in 3 pints of water for 2 hours, then adding sliced turnip, celery and 2 onions, peppercorns and 1 teaspoon salt, and simmering for another hour. Strain the stock into a saucepan and add the tomatoes, 1 onion and herbs and simmer for 40 minutes. Then pass the soup through a sieve and thicken with butter and flour, blended with a little cold water. Add sugar, lemon juice, salt and pepper to taste and colouring, if desired, and heat gently, stirring until the soup is creamy.

COCK-A-LEEKIE SOUP

Scotland

1 small fowl	3 oz. butter	few sprigs of thyme
6 leeks	2½ quarts stock or	and parsley tied
2 tablespoons rice	water	together
(optional)		salt and pepper

Joint the fowl. Wash the leeks thoroughly and chop finely. Heat the butter in a large saucepan and add the pieces of fowl lightly seasoned with salt and pepper. Fry gently on all sides till brown, add the leeks and fry for a further 3 minutes. Pour on the stock, add the thyme and parsley, bring to the boil, skim if necessary, and simmer for 2 hours, or until the bird is tender. Remove the pieces of fowl, take out any bones and chop the meat, return to the soup, remove the thyme and parsley. If rice is used add after 1 hour's cooking. Add more salt and pepper to taste. This soup is better if made 24 hours before eating and re-heated when wanted.

OXTAIL SOUP

½ oxtail, cut into joints	2 oz. butter	1 teaspoon redcurrant
2 carrots	3 oz. flour	jelly
1 onion	1 teaspoon tomato	½ gill sherry
bouquet garni	purée	salt and pepper
	2 quarts water	

Slice carrots and onion and place in a saucepan with the oxtail, *bouquet garni* and water. Bring to the boil, remove scum from top and simmer for 2 hours. Take out the oxtail and strain stock. Cut off the meat from the oxtail. Melt butter and stir in flour, then stir in the stock. Bring to the boil, simmer for 5 minutes then add tomato purée, redcurrant jelly, sherry, chopped meat, salt and pepper. Simmer together very gently for a further 5 minutes.

SCOTCH BROTH

1 lb. neck of mutton	1 celery stalk	3 pints water
2 oz. pearl barley	1 small turnip	salt and pepper
1 onion	2 carrots	2 oz. peas or shredded
1 leek	1 tablespoon chopped	cabbage
	parsley	

Trim the meat, cut into small pieces and put into cold water. Add the barley, a teaspoon of salt and bring to the boil. Simmer gently for 1 hour. Remove scum, add 1 diced carrot and turnip, chopped leek, celery and onion, and simmer for another 2 hours. Add peas, if in season, or shredded cabbage, a grated carrot and salt and pepper to taste. Simmer for another 20 minutes and serve very hot with the parsley.

KIPPERS

Kippers are herrings which have been smoked in a special way and they are very much an English heritage. They are eaten for breakfast or supper and can be cooked very simply in the following ways:

In a pan of boiling water with the lid on for about 10 minutes.

Fried in a lightly greased pan for 5 minutes on each side.

Grilled, the side with the skin underneath, for about 8 minutes without turning. *(Illustrated in Plate 56.)*

FINNAN HADDOCK

Scotland

2 lb. smoked haddock	2—3 tablespoons	1 teaspoon cornflour
½ pint milk	butter	¼ teaspoon pepper

Remove the skin from the haddock and cut the fish into pieces. Melt the butter in a large pan, put in the fish, sprinkle with pepper, cover and cook gently for 5 minutes. Blend the cornflour with a little of the milk then add the rest of the milk to make a smooth mixture and pour it over the fish and cook gently for another 5 minutes. Serve with the sauce poured over the haddock. Pats of cold, fresh butter may be added, if desired.

SOUSED MACKEREL

4 cleaned mackerel, heads and tails removed	1 carrot, finely sliced	½ teaspoon salt
	1 teaspoon olive oil	enough cold water
	pinch dried thyme	mixed with 1 tea-
1 large onion, cut in thin rings	1 cut up bay leaf	spoon vinegar to
	¼ teaspoon black pepper	cover

Put the fish in a shallow fireproof dish, add all the other ingredients. Bake in a cool oven until the vegetables are tender, basting frequently. Leave to cool in the liquor if eaten cold, but they are good eaten hot. White wine and a good squeeze of lemon juice may be used instead of the vinegar and water.

GRILLED HALIBUT

4 slices halibut—1½ lb.	salt and pepper	1 lemon
	2 tablespoons butter	

Brush the fish with melted butter, sprinkle with salt and pepper and grill for 15 minutes. Turn the slices of fish twice during the grilling. Serve with slices of lemon.

WHITEBAIT

1½ lb. whitebait	1 lemon	brown bread and
flour	1 teaspoon salt	butter
corn oil or cooking fat	cayenne pepper	ice

Wash the whitebait and leave in a bowl of ice for a while. Then dry the fish, toss in flour seasoned with salt and place in a frying basket. Shake out the surplus flour and plunge the basket into deep, hot fat. Fry for 3—4 minutes, drain well and turn out on to greaseproof paper. Do not crowd too much fish into the basket at one time, but see that the white-bait are kept fairly separate. Serve very hot with cayenne pepper, slices of lemon and brown bread and butter.

BOILED MACKEREL WITH GOOSEBERRY SAUCE

4 fresh cleaned mackerel, heads and tails removed	boiling water ¼ teaspoon salt	gooseberry sauce (see p. 110)

Have enough boiling water to cover the fish, add the salt. Make several incisions in the back of each fish, put into the boiling water, simmer very gently for 15 minutes. Drain and serve with the hot gooseberry sauce.

JELLIED EELS

1 lb. eel	juice 1 lemon	water
1 bay leaf		1 teaspoon salt

Buy cleaned eel cut into 1 inch lengths. Put into a saucepan with the bay leaf, lemon juice, salt and enough water to cover the eel. Put on a lid and cook very gently for about 45 minutes. Then turn into a bowl and leave in a cool place to set into a jelly.

BOILED SCOTCH SALMON

4 salmon steaks — about 6 oz. each	1 lemon 1 small cucumber	salt water

Place the fish into just enough boiling water to cover, add salt to taste and simmer gently for 10—15 minutes or until the fish separates easily from the bone. Remove the salmon carefully from the pan with a fish slice and allow to drain. If the steaks are rather thin and therefore liable to break when being taken out of the pan, they can be sprinkled with a little salt and lemon juice, wrapped in buttered greaseproof paper and then boiled. Serve garnished with slices of lemon and accom-panied by sliced cucumber. If served cold accompany with salad and mayonnaise (see p. 263).

FISH AND CHIPS

2 lb. filleted fish (plaice, cod, haddock, etc.)	frying oil or fat 4 oz. flour 1 egg (optional) 1½ lb. potatoes	1 gill milk salt and pepper lemon parsley

Sift 3 oz. flour with a pinch of salt into a basin and mix with the egg. Add the milk gradually and beat the batter until it is smooth. Dry the fish, cover lightly with seasoned flour, then dip into the batter. Drain for a moment, using a skewer or fork, then lower into hot, deep fat, slightly smoking. Fry the fish until brown, take out with a perforated spoon, then drain on kitchen paper. Keep hot while preparing the chips. Peel the potatoes and slice into finger shapes. Dry well, then put into a frying-basket to about a third full and lower into hot fat. Cook for 3 minutes then drain. When all the potatoes have been done this way, fry them again in hot fat, until crisp and golden brown. More chips may be put into the frying-basket than for the first frying. Garnish with parsley. *(Illustrated in Plate 29.)*

FRIED SPRATS

1½ lb. sprats 1 tablespoon butter or margarine	2 tablespoons flour salt and pepper	brown bread and butter 1 lemon

Wash and dry the sprats, removing the heads if desired. Dip into flour seasoned with salt and pepper, and fry in hot fat on both sides until the fish is crisp and light brown. Serve very hot garnished with slices of lemon and accompanied by brown bread and butter.

STUFFED HERRING

4 herring 8 oz. rolled oats	2 tablespoons butter 1 teaspoon chopped parsley	salt and pepper 1 egg

Split the fish, clean and remove roe and backbone. Parboil roe then mix with egg, oats, parsley, 1 tablespoon of butter, salt and pepper. Stuff the fish with the mixture, place on a buttered oven dish, cover with greaseproof paper or foil and bake in a moderate oven for 30 minutes. *(Illustrated in Plate 117.)*

HERRINGS WITH MUSTARD SAUCE

| 4 herrings | salt and pepper | mustard sauce |
| | | (see p. 108) |

Prepare the herrings by cuting off the heads, cleaning the fish and drying them. Cut two or three deep gashes on both sides, sprinkle with salt and pepper and grill for 10—15 minutes. Turn the fish over to cook on both sides. Serve with hot mustard sauce. *(Illustrated in Plate 31.)*

FRIED TROUT

Scotland

| 4 trout | ½ pint milk | salt and pepper |
| 8 oz. coarse oatmeal | 2 oz. lard | 1 lemon |

Cut the trout open and remove the bone. Wipe the fish, dip in milk, season, cover with oatmeal. Heat fat and fry the fish on both sides until brown. Serve with slices of lemon.

GALANTINE OF VEAL

3 lb. breast of veal	1 tablespoon gelatine	1 carrot
1 lb. sausage meat	few sprigs parsley	1 bay leaf
6 oz. gammon	1 onion	salt and pepper
2 hard-boiled eggs	1 turnip	water

Bone the veal and put the bones into a saucepan with the vegetables, the bay leaf, seasoning and enough water to cover. Bring to the boil and allow to simmer. In the meantime, cut the gammon into very small cubes and mix with the sausage meat. Flatten out the veal and spread half the sausage mixture over it. Place sliced hard-boiled eggs on top, sprinkle with salt and pepper, cover with the rest of the sausage meat and roll up. Tie tightly in a cloth, put into the stock, brought to the boil, and simmer for 2½—3 hours. Take out the meat, tighten the cloth and leave pressed between two heavy dishes until cold. Then remove the cloth and lay the galantine on a dish. Dissolve the gelatine in 1 pint of stock, boil quickly until reduced to ½ pint, then brush the liquid glaze over the galantine. Serve garnished with sprigs of parsley.

TOAD-IN-THE-HOLE

1 lb. skinned sausages	4 oz. flour	½ pint milk
1 tablespoon cooking	1 egg	¼ teaspoon salt
fat		

Make a batter with the flour, salt, egg and milk and leave to stand for 30 minutes. Heat the fat in a shallow baking tin, put in the sausages and fry for 5 minutes, then pour the batter over them. Put into a hot oven and bake for about 30 minutes. *(Illustrated in Plate 94.)*

POT HAGGIS

Scotland

8 oz. sheep's liver	2 onions	salt and pepper
4 oz. beef suet	water	10 oz. oatmeal

Cover the liver with water and boil for 40 minutes. Drain and keep the liquid. Mince the liver finely. Parboil the onions, then chop small with the suet. Brown the oatmeal by tossing quickly in a thick pan over the fire. Now combine the minced liver, suet, onions and oatmeal and season with salt and pepper. Moisten with the liquor in which the liver was boiled. Turn into a greased bowl, cover with greaseproof paper and steam for 2 hours.

LIVER AND BACON

1 lb. liver	½ pint water	tomatoes and
4 rashers bacon	salt and pepper	mushrooms
	2 tablespoons flour	sweet corn

Trim, wash and dry the liver and cut into slices ½ inch thick. Remove the rind from the bacon, fry the rashers and keep hot. Dip the liver in seasoned flour and fry in the bacon fat for a few minutes on both sides. Remove the liver, sprinkle the remainder of the flour into the pan, blend with water, add a little salt and pepper and cook for a few minutes. Serve the liver with the bacon accompanied by fried tomatoes, sweet corn and mushrooms. *(Illustrated in Plate 37.)*

SCOTCH COLLOPS

1½—2 lb. veal or	1 teaspoon lemon	1—2 tablespoons
stewing steak	juice	mushroom ketchup
2 oz. butter or fat	2—3 sprigs parsley	salt and pepper
stock	1 tablespoon flour	

Cut the meat into small cubes and dip in seasoned flour. Heat the fat and fry the collops until slightly brown. Add the stock, bring to the boil, then cover with a lid and simmer gently for 45 minutes. Add the lemon juice, mushroom ketchup and more salt and pepper, if desired, and simmer for a further 15 minutes. Serve garnished with chopped parsley.

TRIPE AND ONIONS

1 lb. tripe	½ pint milk	salt and pepper
2 onions	1 tablespoon flour	croûtons
1 oz. butter		½ pint water

Plunge the tripe into boiling water to blanch. Drain, then remove any superfluous fat and cut into neat pieces. Put into a saucepan with the milk and water. Season with salt and pepper and bring to the boil. Add chopped onions and simmer very gently for about 2 hours. Then take a little of the liquid, mix with the flour to a smooth paste, stir into the tripe, bring to the boil. Add butter and a little more seasoning, mix well, simmer for another 10 minutes and serve on a hot dish. Garnish with fried bread croûtons.

PORK CHOPS IN FRUIT ASPIC

4 cooked pork chops
½ pint pineapple or other fruit juice

1 teaspoon meat extract
½ oz. gelatine

stuffed olives, cucumber and gherkins to garnish

Dissolve the gelatine in fruit juice and flavour with meat extract. When nearly on setting point, coat both sides of the chops and allow to set. Slice the olives and arrange in a flower design on the chops. Cut a stem and leaves from cucumber rind and gherkins and coat again with the jelly. Arrange on a bed of lettuce and chicory. *(Illustrated in Plate 3.)*

ROAST STUFFED SHOULDER OF MUTTON

4 lb. shoulder of mutton
1½ lb. potatoes
2 oz. dripping
onion sauce (p. 108)

Stuffing:
3 oz. breadcrumbs
1 finely chopped small onion

4 oz. finely chopped mushrooms
egg
salt and pepper

Ask your butcher to bone the shoulder. Mix all the stuffing ingredients together and stuff the meat. Skewer or tie into a neat shape. Peel and cut the potatoes in halves, if too big. Arrange the potatoes round the joint in the roasting tin, add the dripping and roast in a moderate-to-hot oven for 1½ hours. Serve with onion sauce.

BOILED SILVERSIDE AND DUMPLINGS

3 to 4 lb. silverside
2 lb. medium onions

1 lb. carrots
1 lb. parsnips

1 bay leaf
cold water

Put the meat in a large saucepan, add the prepared vegetables and bay leaf, cover with cold water. Bring to the boil gradually, skim if necessary, cover the pan and simmer gently for 2½ to 3 hours. Serve with hot dumplings (see p. 102). *(Illustrated in Plate 22.)*

IRISH STEW

2 lb. best end neck of   8 oz. onions   salt and pepper
   mutton   1 pint stock or water   few sprigs parsley
                        2 lb. potatoes

Cut the meat into cutlets and trim, removing as much fat as possible.
Lay in a large saucepan and cover with rings of onions and half the
potatoes, peeled and sliced. Season. Add stock or water and simmer
gently for about 1½ hours. Put the rest of the potatoes, peeled and sliced,
on top and cook for another 40 minutes. Serve the meat with the potatoes
ringed around, the liquid poured over and the whole sprinkled with
chopped parsley.

MUTTON STUFFED WITH OYSTERS

1 boned leg of mutton   1 hard-boiled egg   oyster sauce
8 oysters   1 pint vegetable stock   (see p. 108)
1 tablespoon   1 small onion   1 teaspoon chopped
   breadcrumbs   salt, pepper   parsley

Remove the oysters from their shells and plunge them into boiling water
to blanch. Strain the oysters, chop and mix with the breadcrumbs,
parsley, grated onion and chopped hard-boiled egg. Add salt and pepper
and moisten with a little oyster liquid. Fill the cavity in the leg of mutton
with the mixture, tie the meat so that the stuffing cannot escape and
put into a saucepan with the vegetable stock. Cover and simmer gently
for 2½ hours. Serve with oyster sauce.

CROWN ROAST OF LAMB

2 best end of   dripping   sage and onion
   neck joints   parsley   stuffing (see page 108)

Get the butcher to chop the bones at the thick end of joints, and to chop
through the projecting bony structure; this is called 'chining'. Use a
sharp knife to cut part of the way through the ends of the cutlets, to
separate them slightly. Cut the flesh straight across on skin side, then
remove fatty ends and trim bones, scraping them free of flesh. Join
at one end of the two joints, using thick needle and thin string. Bend
the joints round, skin side inwards and sew to join, making a 'crown'
shape. Twist a piece of foil or greaseproof paper round the bony ends to
check charring whilst roasting. Fill the centre with stuffing and roast in
very little dripping for 20 minutes per lb., plus an additional 20 minutes.
When cooked garnish with parsley, top bones with cutlet frills and
serve with carrots and creamed potatoes. (Illustrated in Plate 89.)

17. Apple Dumplings, Britain (p.112)

18. Flapjacks, Britain (p.126)

19. Ingredients for Coq au Vin, France (p.238)

LANCASHIRE HOT POT

2 lb. neck of mutton	3 sheep's kidneys	12 oysters (optional)
2 lb. potatoes	1 pint meat stock	little cornflour
3 large onions	2 oz. butter	salt and pepper
	8 oz. mushrooms	

Cut the meat into cutlets and remove excess fat. Peel and slice the potatoes fairly thickly, slice the onions thinly. Wash, but do not peel, the mushrooms and cut in two. Skin and core the kidneys, cut in halves. Take a deep casserole and place in each ingredient in layers, finishing with a ring of potatoes. Season each layer with salt and pepper, pour in the melted butter and the stock thickened with a little cornflour. Cover the casserole tightly and cook very slowly for 3 hours. *(Illustrated in Plate 105.)*

ROAST BEEF AND YORKSHIRE PUDDING

1 sirloin or middle rib	horseradish sauce	4 oz. flour
1½ lb. potatoes	Yorkshire Pudding	2 eggs
dripping	(see below)	½ teaspoon salt
½ pint water	1 pint milk	1 oz. dripping
	salt and pepper	

Sprinkle the joint all over with salt and pepper and rub well in. If the joint has not much fat put 2 oz. dripping on the fat side. Make the oven very hot, stand the joint in a roasting dish or on the oven bars with the pan underneath and cook for 20 minutes. Reduce to a moderate heat and cook; for underdone beef 15 minutes to the pound, 22 minutes for medium and an even 30 minutes for those who like it overdone. Peel the potatoes, cut into suitable sizes and put round the joint to roast until soft inside. To make the gravy, pour off the fat from the roasting dish, add water, flour and a pinch salt to the sediment and bring to the boil.

To Make the Yorkshire Pudding: Sift the flour and salt, add the milk gradually, stirring all the time till quite smooth, then stir in the beaten eggs. Always make this batter at least an hour before it is to be cooked. Melt the dripping in a shallow baking tin in the oven; when smoking hot, stir the mixture and pour in the batter. Cook in a moderate to hot oven for 30 minutes. A most delicious way of cooking this batter is to place the tin in which it is to be cooked under the meat which is roasting on the oven shelf. The essence of the meat drips into the pan and the batter is put in the tin 30 minutes before the meat is fully cooked. This however means a roast with no separately served meat gravy. Serve the beef and Yorkshire Pudding with the roast potatoes, and horseradish sauce.

STEAK AND CHIPS

1½ lb. rump steak	4 onions	salt and pepper
1½ lb. potatoes		3 tablespoons butter

Heat the grill and brush the steak with a little melted butter. Make little cuts round the edges of the meat to prevent curling while cooking. Place the meat on the grill, about 3 inches from the flame, for 10 minutes or until well browned, then sprinkle with salt and pepper and turn it, grill the other side and season. Slice the onions and fry in 2 tablespoons butter until light brown. Serve with the onions and chips (see p. 92).

DEVONSHIRE BACON IN CIDER

1—1½ lb. piece of collar	6 peppercorns	1 tablespoon flour
	1 bay leaf	1 tablespoon butter
1 onion	dry cider	pinch pepper

Soak the bacon for 2—3 hours in cold water. Place in a saucepan and pour in enough cider to cover. Add bay leaf, onion cut in quarters and crushed peppercorns. Put on the lid and simmer for 40 or 50 minutes according to the size of the ham. Blend flour and butter over a low heat, add pepper and dilute with the stock from the ham, when it has finished cooking. Serve the ham hot with the sauce poured over it and accompanied by mashed turnips or swedes. (*Illustrated in Plate 23.*)

BAKED HAM

1 ham	brown sugar	water
flour		cloves

Soak the ham in cold water for about 8 hours. Wipe the meat and cover with a thick mixture of flour and water. Place on a rack in a hot oven for about 15 minutes then reduce the heat to very moderate. Calculate 25 minutes to the pound for cooking, then take out of the oven 45 minutes before it is done. Remove the covering crust and skin, cut small gashes in the fat and insert cloves. Cover the whole ham with brown sugar and return to a hot oven for 45 minutes to finish cooking and to give a crisp golden brown covering.

ROAST CHICKEN WITH BREAD SAUCE

1 roasting chicken about 3 lb.	8 oz. bread sauce (see p. 107)	4 rashers streaky bacon
½ pint water or stock	salt and pepper	1 tablespoon fat

Place prepared and trussed chicken into a roasting pan, greased with fat, and the bacon in rolls. Put into a moderate oven for 1½ hours when the chicken should be tender. If it browns too quickly, cover with grease-proof paper. To make the gravy, pour off excess fat, pour stock or water into the pan, add salt and pepper to taste, and boil for a few minutes. Serve the chicken surrounded by bacon rolls, small baked onions and accompanied by the gravy and bread sauce. *(Illustrated in Plate 91).*

ROAST GROUSE

(Scottish way)

2 young grouse	toast	cranberry jelly
3 oz. butter	salt, white pepper	(see p. 110)
4 rashers of bacon	cayenne pepper	watercress

All grouse for roasting should be hung at least 3 to 4 days. Pluck and draw the grouse, wipe with a damp cloth and truss like a fowl. Sprinkle the insides with salt and pepper and put 1 oz. of butter into each one. Wrap the birds well in rashers of fat bacon. Put into a hot oven then reduce to moderately hot and roast altogether for about 30 minutes. Meanwhile, boil the liver from the grouse for 10 minutes then mince them and mix with 1 oz. of butter and a pinch of salt and cayenne. Spread the liver on 4 large slices of toast. Five minutes before the end of cooking the grouse, drain off the fat and remove the rashers of bacon. Cut the birds in half and place each portion on a slice of toast. Put back into a hot oven for a few minutes for the birds to finish roasting on the toast, and to get brown. Serve garnished with watercress and accompanied by cranberry jelly.

ROAST TURKEY

turkey	1 teaspoon chopped	bacon rolls
rasher of fat bacon	parsley	sausages
Chestnut Stuffing:	1 oz. butter	gravy
1 lb. chestnuts	1 egg	salt and pepper
2 oz. bacon	½ pint stock	bread sauce
3 oz. breadcrumbs	grated rind of ½ lemon	(see p. 107)

Prepare chestnut stuffing as follows: Slit skins of nuts and boil in water for 10—15 minutes. Skin, then place in a pan with the stock and simmer gently until they are tender. Mash well. Pound with chopped bacon, breadcrumbs, parsley, lemon rind and butter, season with salt and pepper and bind with beaten egg. Stuff the turkey—but not too full as this stuffing will swell during cooking. Extra stuffing can be made into balls and roasted with the bird. Cover the breast with the rasher of fat bacon and roast in a moderately hot oven for about 3 hours for a 12-lb. bird. When breast is brown, cover with foil or greaseproof paper. Serve turkey with sausages, bacon rolls, gravy and bread sauce (see p. 107).

ROAST DUCK

1 duck	1 tablespoon flour	apple sauce
sage and onion	½ pint stock	(see p. 110)
stuffing (see p. 108)		salt and pepper

Wipe the cleaned duck, fill with the sage and onion stuffing and truss. Sprinkle with salt and pepper, place in a greased roasting pan and put into a hot oven. After 15 minutes reduce the heat to moderate. Roast about 1½ hours, basting frequently. To make the gravy, pour off the fat from the pan, sprinkle the flour into the sediment and brown it. Blend with stock and boil for a few minutes. Serve the duck accompanied by gravy and apple sauce.

JUGGED HARE

1 hare, well hung	2 oz. butter	4 sprigs of parsley
salt and pepper	1 tablespoon lemon	1 sprig thyme, or
¼ pint red wine,	juice	marjoram
preferably port	1½ tablespoons flour	¼ teaspoon nutmeg
1 pint meat stock	1½ tablespoons butter	powder
or water	*Tied in Muslin:*	¼ teaspoon cinnamon
2 oz. bacon, chopped	4 cloves	powder
small	4 bay leaves	12 peppercorns

Ask your butcher to skin, clean and cut up the hare in pieces the size of an egg. Dust these with salt and pepper. Fry these with bacon in butter till browned. Put the pieces in a jar or deep casserole and pour over the wine. Cover tightly and cook in a moderate oven for 30 minutes. Now add the lemon juice, stock and herbs. Stand the jar or casserole in a pan of water, cover and cook in a moderate to cool oven for 3 hours or simmer very gently on top of the stove. Strain the gravy. Mix the butter with the flour, pour on the hot gravy, bring to the boil, stirring all the time, pour over the hare and serve hot.

SHORT PASTRY

8 oz. flour	mixture of half lard	pinch salt
4 oz. fat—lard *or*	and half butter or	water
cooking fat *or*	margarine	

Sift the flour and salt into a basin. Cut the fat into small pieces and rub into the flour with the fingertips until the mixture looks like breadcrumbs. Add enough water to make a stiff dough, using a knife for mixing. Turn out on to a lightly floured board and roll out the pastry with light, quick rolls. If possible, leave in a cool place for a while before using. Bake in a hot oven, and then reduce the heat to moderate when the pastry begins to brown.

ROUGH PUFF PASTRY

1 lb. flour	12 oz. butter or	juice of 1 lemon
1 egg yolk	margarine	1 gill cold water

Ingredients, utensils and hands must be cold. Sieve the flour into a basin. Beat the egg. Cut the butter into small dice and with the fingertips mix with the flour, but do not rub it in. Add the beaten egg, water and lemon juice spoon by spoon, mix quickly and lightly until the dough leaves the sides of the basin. Turn on to a floured board and roll quickly all over into an oblong, rolling with quick short pushing strokes away from you. Fold the pastry in three, top edge a third down, and bottom edge over the two thicknesses, making three thicknesses. Turn the pastry round on the board, folded edges at the sides, and repeat the process of rolling. Repeat twice more, four times in all. Put into a very cold place and leave for at least an hour before using.

FLAKY PASTRY

8 oz. flour	6 oz. fat or butter and	pinch salt
½ teaspoon lemon juice	lard mixed or	cold water
	margarine	

Mix salt with the flour and sift into a bowl. Divide the fat into four parts and rub one quarter into the flour. Add the lemon juice and enough water to mix to an elastic dough. Roll into a long strip on a lightly floured board. Spread another quarter of the fat, cut into small pieces down two-thirds of the way of the pastry. Fold the pastry into three parts, starting from the end portion without the sprinkling of fat. Press the edges of the pastry together and roll out lightly. Repeat the process twice with the remaining two portions of fat then leave in a cold place for about an hour. Finally, roll out to the required shape and use. Flaky pastry should be brushed with a beaten egg then put into a very hot oven for about 10 minutes, then the heat should be reduced to moderate.

SUET CRUST

8 oz. flour	1 level teaspoon	½ level teaspoon salt
4 oz. chopped suet	baking powder	cold water

Sift the flour, salt and baking powder, add the suet and mix well. Add a little cold water gradually and mix well until the paste forms a soft dough. When it leaves the sides of basin cleanly, it is ready to roll out.

101

SAUSAGE ROLLS

8 oz. sausages or sausage meat	flaky or short pastry using 4 oz. flour, etc. (see pp. 100, 101)	1 egg flour

Roll out the pastry to $\frac{1}{4}$-inch thick and cut into 8 strips, about $2\frac{1}{2}$ inches by 3 inches. Divide the sausage meat or skinned sausages into 8 finger-shaped pieces and cover lightly in flour. Place one sausage portion in the centre of each strip of pastry, roll up and press the edges together evenly, leaving the ends of the sausage rolls open. Slash the edges all along with the back of a knife and make 3 parallel gashes across the top of each roll. Brush the tops with beaten egg and put the rolls, sealed side under, not too close together, on to a greased baking tin. Put into a hot oven to bake for 25—30 minutes. Reduce the heat to moderate as soon as the pastry begins to brown.

DUMPLINGS

4 oz. flour	2 oz. chopped suet	$\frac{1}{4}$ teaspoon pepper
$\frac{1}{4}$ teaspoon baking powder	1 teaspoon finely chopped parsley	cold water to mix plenty of boiling
1 teaspoon salt	1 medium finely chopped onion	water or stock

Mix all the ingredients except boiling stock, add a little cold water, teaspoon by teaspoon to make a soft but firm dough: when it comes cleanly away from the sides of the basin it is right. Roll into 12 small balls. Have the water or meat stock boiling; put in the dumplings and cook, uncovered, for 20 to 30 minutes till dry inside and nicely swollen in size.

CORNISH PASTIES

6 SERVINGS

1 lb. short pastry (see page 100)	8 oz. potatoes or a mixture of onions,	4 oz. kidney 1 beaten egg
8 oz. raw steak	turnips and potatoes	salt and pepper

Cut the steak, kidney and peeled potatoes, etc., into $\frac{1}{2}$-inch dice, season with salt and pepper. Roll out the pastry and cut in six rounds the size of a saucer. Place a sixth of the mixture on each round, moisten the edges with cold water, fold over and seal tightly. Brush with the beaten egg. Cook on a baking sheet in a hot oven for 15 minutes, lower the heat to moderate and cook for a further 40 minutes. (*Illustrated in Plate 87.*)

PORK AND CRANBERRY PATTIES

1 lb. cooked chopped pork	12 oz. self raising flour	2 onions
salt and pepper	1 small can cranberry jelly	4 oz. lard
		$\frac{1}{4}$ pint water
		1 egg

Melt the lard in pan and add the water. Sieve the flour, salt and pepper into a warmed basin and stir in the hot fat mixture to make a pliable dough. Knead well and divide into five. Cut each portion in two. Line patty tins or small saucers with one half and roll out the other half for the lids.

For the Filling:

The pork (shoulder or belly) should be cooked in a very little liquid with onions and seasoning in a casserole. When cooked, drain and chop meat finely, mix with the cranberry jelly. Place the filling in the lined patty tins and brush round edges with egg. Seal on prepared lids, pierce holes in centre of each. Brush top with egg and decorate with pastry. Bake in hot oven for 15 minutes. Serve cold. *(Illustrated in Plate 74.)*

HUNTER'S PIE

Ireland

6 mutton chops	2 oz. butter	water
1½ lb. potatoes	1 lb. onions, sliced	salt and pepper

Brown the chops in a little butter, take out and add water to the pan to make a gravy. Peel the potatoes and place the chops in a casserole with the potatoes and onions. Season and pour over the gravy. Cover and bake in a moderate oven for 2 hours. Garnish with chopped parsley.

STEAK AND KIDNEY PUDDING

suet crust (see p. 101)	½ pint meat stock	2 oz. flour
1½ lb. rump steak	1 clove garlic	1 teaspoon salt
8 oz. kidney	(optional)	1 teaspoon pepper
	8 oz. mushrooms	

Cut the steak into thin slices, 4 × 3 inches. Cut the kidney in ½-inch squares. Slice the mushrooms. Mix the flour, salt and pepper together, and roll the steak, kidney and mushrooms in it. Wrap a piece of kidney and mushroom in a slice of meat. If using garlic, cut it in two and rub the inside of the basin well with it. Roll out the suet crust, line the basin with it, sides and bottom and cut a round for the top. Pack the steak rolls in the lined basin, add any extra pieces of kidney or mushroom, pour over the stock, cover with the round of pastry, damp the edges and seal tightly. Tie foil or double greased paper tightly over top. Steam for 4 hours. *(Illustrated in Plate 20.)*

SQUAB PIE

Devonshire

2 lb. neck of mutton	2 teaspoons brown	stock or water
2 lb. apples	sugar	pinch mixed spice
salt and pepper	8 oz. onions	

Cut the neck of mutton into chops, trim and lay half in a pie-dish. Sprinkle with salt and pepper. Peel and core the apples, slice and lay half over the meat. Sprinkle with some of the sugar and a pinch of spice. Put in a layer of chopped onions, then the rest of the meat. Add a little more salt and pepper, and cover with a final layer of apple, sprinkled with the rest of the sugar. Half fill with stock or water. Cover tightly with greaseproof paper of foil, bake in a moderate oven for 1½ hours.

VEAL AND HAM PIE

2 lb. veal	enough meat stock to	2 oz. lard
4 oz. ham	cover the meat, etc.	⅜ pint hot milk
2 hard-boiled eggs	6 oz. flour	salt and pepper
	pinch mixed herbs	

Cut the veal into slices 1 × 2 inches, also the ham. Slice the eggs. Arrange these ingredients in layers in a pie-dish, season with salt, pepper and a sprinkling of herbs. Pour over the stock. Make the pastry by melting the lard in the warmed milk, stir slowly into the sieved flour and salt, mix to a soft dough. Turn on to a floured board, roll out fairly thinly, cover the pie-dish, moisten and seal the edges. Decorate with any left-over pastry, make a hole in the middle and bake in a moderate to hot oven for 1 hour.

STAR GAZY PIE

Cornwall

8 herring or mackerel	3 eggs	1 tablespoon butter
flaky or short crust	1 tablespoon tarragon	2 tablespoons fine
pastry using 8 oz.	vinegar or 2 oz.	breadcrumbs
flour, etc. (see pp.	cream	salt and pepper
101, 100)		8 sprigs parsley

Clean and bone the fish, leaving the heads on, and season with salt and pepper. Butter a pie-dish, sprinkle with a thick layer of breadcrumbs and put in the fish so that the heads point upwards. Beat the eggs with the tarragon vinegar or cream and pour into the pie-dish. Cover the dish with pastry, making slits for the fish heads to gaze out of the top. Put into a very hot oven then reduce after 10 minutes to very moderate and bake until the crust is golden brown. Serve hot with a sprig of parsley in the mouth of each fish.

CHICKEN PIE WITH OYSTERS

1 tender chicken— approx. 3 lb.	juice of ½ lemon	breadcrumbs
½ onion	salt and pepper	2 eggs, hard-boiled
2 tablespoons flour	finely chopped parsley	short crust pastry
4 oz. butter	½ clove garlic, finely chopped	(see p. 100)
½ pint water	24 small oysters	¼ pint cream
		1 teaspoon cornflour

Bone chicken and simmer the wings, feet, neck and bones with finely chopped onion in ½ pint seasoned water to make a light stock.

Re-form the boned pieces of chicken; roll them lightly in flour and sauté them in 2 oz. butter until they are a light golden colour on all sides. Season well with lemon juice, salt and freshly ground black pepper, cover the pan and cook over a low flame for 20 minutes, turning occasionally.

Place chicken pieces in a deep pie dish, sprinkle with finely chopped parsley and finely chopped garlic and surround with 12 oysters, rolled in breadcrumbs and seasoned to taste with salt and pepper, and quartered hard-boiled eggs. Stir 6 tablespoons of chicken stock into the pan in which the chicken was cooked, blending it well with the butter and remaining juices. Pour this over the contents of the pie dish and cover with a top layer of pastry. Moisten the edges of pastry with water, pinch them together, cut five slits in crust to let steam escape and decorate to taste. Bake in a moderate oven (Gas Mark 4—350 °F.) for 30 minutes or until done.

To make oyster sauce, pour remainder of chicken stock into a saucepan, with liquid from oysters. Stir in 2 tablespoons butter and the cream, to which 1 teaspoon of cornflour has been added. Simmer a few minutes, add oysters and a squeeze of lemon, correct the seasoning and serve with the pie. *(Illustrated in Plate 19.)*

MELTON MOWBRAY PIE

8 oz. flour	bones	1 gill milk
3 oz. lard	½ teaspoon mixed	1 egg
1 lb. pork	herbs	water
1 small onion		salt and pepper

Sift flour and ½ teaspoon of salt into a bowl. Heat lard and milk together gradually bring to the boil and then add to the flour. Stir in the yolk of an egg, knead until smooth, then set aside for about 15 minutes. Meanwhile, put the bones, chopped onion, salt and pepper into a saucepan with a pint of water and simmer gently for about 2 hours, reducing the liquid to ½ pint. The stock when cold will form a jelly. Line a pie-dish with some of the pastry, put in diced pork, season with salt, pepper and herbs, add a little of the stock and cover with a lid of pastry. Decorate the edges with leaf shapes with the remaining pastry, make a ventilation hole and brush with milk or egg. Put into a hot oven for about 10 minutes then reduce the heat to very moderate and bake for 2 hours. When the pie is cool, pour in the stock through the hole in the pastry and leave to set. Serve cold.

DEVILLED KIDNEYS

4 pieces toast	1 tablespoon dry	1 dessertspoon
8 sheep's kidneys	mustard	Worcester sauce
salt and pepper		(see p. 108)
		2 oz. butter

Skin the kidneys, cut them in half and core them. Mix the sauce and the mustard together. Heat the butter in a saucepan, add the kidneys, season with salt and pepper, brown quickly for 2 minutes, lower the heat and cook very gently for 6 minutes with the pan covered, add the mustard mixture, stir well and cook slowly for 2 minutes more. Stir and serve on the hot toast. Garnish with mushrooms. *(Illustrated in Plate 21.)*

WELSH RAREBIT

4 slices of thick toast	2 oz. butter	1 teaspoon mustard
(crusts removed)	¼ pint beer or milk	2 beaten egg yolks
8 oz. grated cheese		½ teaspoon paprika

Make the toast, keep warm. Melt the butter in a double-boiler or over a very low heat, add the cheese, stir, then add the beer or stout slowly, stirring till smooth, now the mustard, paprika and the eggs. Keep stirring till warm throughout, pour over the toast and serve. Never let this mixture boil or bubble; if you do it will become 'stringy' and lumpy.

SCOTCH EGGS

4 hard-boiled eggs	1 egg	fat for deep frying
12 oz. sausage meat	breadcrumbs	salt and pepper

Shell the hard-boiled eggs and, when cold, enclose each in seasoned sausage meat. Coat with beaten egg and breadcrumbs and fry in deep, hot fat until golden brown. Drain and cut the eggs in half. Serve hot or cold. *(Illustrated in Plate 12.)*

SCOTCH WOODCOCK

4 eggs	1 oz. butter	salt and pepper
4 slices of toast	anchovy butter	2 tablespoons milk
	(see p. 262)	

Put the eggs, milk, butter, salt and pepper into a double saucepan and stir over the heat until the sauce thickens. Spread the slices of hot toast with anchovy butter and pour the sauce over immediately. Serve hot.

BLOATER PASTE

| 4 herrings | ½ teaspoon anchovy | cayenne pepper |
| 1 oz. butter | essence | water |

Put cleaned herrings into boiling water, and cook for 10 minutes. Then cut off the heads and remove the skin and bones. Pound the fish with the butter, anchovy essence and a pinch of cayenne pepper until the paste is smooth. Put in small jars and cover.

GRILLED BACON CHOPS

Bacon chops are back rashers, but thick. One per person is enough, two is a feast. Trim off the rind, snip the fat and grill for about 7 minutes each side. See that fat is brown and crisp. Serve with sliced tomato, braised celery and sauté potatoes. *(Illustrated in Plate 101.)*

OMELETTE WITH HAM, POTATOES AND CHEESE

2 level teaspoons	1 tablespoon corn	2 oz. mixed diced
cornflour	oil	ham, potato, cheese
1 tablespoon water	1 oz. butter	4—5 eggs

Mix cornflour and water in a bowl. Beat eggs into this mixture. Heat corn oil in omelette pan and pour eggs and cornflour mixture into pan. After a few seconds of cooking reduce heat and loosen omelette around edges of pan with a fork or palette knife so that the uncooked mixture has a chance to cook. Continue shaking pan occasionally until the surface of omelette is just creamy. When omelette is done, dot with butter; fold in lightly sautéed, diced ham, potato and cheese, and serve immediately. *(Illustrated in Plate 108.)*

BREAD SAUCE

½ pint milk	1 blade mace or	½ oz. butter
1 small onion	a good pinch of	1 tablespoon cream
2 oz. white fresh	ground nutmeg	½ teaspoon salt
breadcrumbs	2 cloves	pinch pepper

In a double boiler heat the milk, add the onion stuck with the cloves and nutmeg or mace until just not boiling, for 30 minutes. Remove the mace, if used, add the breadcrumbs, stirring and beating with a fork, now the salt, pepper and half the butter. Cook gently, beating frequently, for 20 minutes. Remove the onion, add the other half of butter and the cream. Serve hot.

SAGE AND ONION STUFFING

1 lb. chopped onions	1 teaspoon finely	1 teaspoon salt
4 oz. breadcrumbs	chopped sage	pinch pepper
1 oz. butter		boiling water

Put the onions and salt in a small pan and just cover with boiling water, simmer for 8 to 10 minutes till tender, add the breadcrumbs, sage and pepper, and butter, stir to make a smooth 'dryish' mixture.

OYSTER SAUCE

6 oysters	½ pint béchamel sauce	½ lemon
1 pint water	(see p. 256)	salt and pepper

Remove the oysters from their shells, plunge them into boiling water then cover and simmer very gently for about 25 minutes. Strain the stock and use to make the béchamel sauce. Cut the oysters into quarters, put back into the sauce, season with salt and pepper and add the juice of half a lemon. Heat for a further 5 minutes, stirring well. Serve with fish or mutton stuffed with oysters.

MUSTARD SAUCE

2 oz. butter	1 gill milk	1 teaspoon dry
1 oz. flour	1 gill fish stock	mustard

Melt half the butter, add the flour gradually, mixing well, and dilute with fish stock. When well blended, add the milk and mustard and bring to the boil. Stir in the rest of the butter and serve the sauce hot.

WORCESTER SAUCE

1 pint malt vinegar	3 tablespoons walnut	2 tablespoons soy
2 tablespoons anchovy	ketchup	salt and pepper
essence		2 shallots

Chop the shallots very finely and put together with all the other ingredients into a large bottle. Cork tightly and leave for about 2 weeks. During that period, shake the bottle several times a day. Then strain the sauce into bottles, cork tightly and store in a cool place.

ONION SAUCE

8 oz. chopped onions	½ pint béchamel sauce	½ teaspoon ground
salt and pepper	(see p. 256)	nutmeg

Peel the onions, put into a saucepan with enough water to cover them and add salt and pepper to taste. Bring to the boil then simmer till tender. Drain and mix with the sauce, nutmeg and a little more salt, if required. Stir well and serve hot.

MINT SAUCE

2 level tablespoons finely chopped mint	3 oz. sugar	½ teaspoon salt
	¼ pint white wine vinegar	2 tablespoons water

Boil the sugar, vinegar, water and salt for 4 minutes, pour over the chopped mint, cover tightly while cooling. Stir well before serving, when quite cold.

CUMBERLAND SAUCE

1 lemon rind and juice	½ gill water	pinch salt
1 orange rind and juice	2 tablespoons red-currant jelly	pinch cayenne pepper
½ gill port wine (⅛ pint)	½ teaspoon made mustard	2 oz. glacé cherries, chopped
		2 tablespoons vinegar

Shred the lemon and orange rinds very finely, no white pith must be attached. Squeeze the juice of both fruits and strain. Boil the shredded rinds in the water for 5 minutes, strain and put the liquid back in the saucepan. Add the wine, redcurrant jelly, mustard, cayenne, salt, the fruit juice and the vinegar. Boil all together for 3 minutes. When cold, add the chopped cherries.

REDCURRANT JELLY

1 lb. sugar to 1 pint redcurrant juice

Pick the fruit off the stems and wash it. Put it in a large basin or casserole, stand this in a saucepan of simmering water and steam for several hours until all the juice has run out of the currants or leave in a cool oven; the length of time depends, naturally, on how many pounds of fruit you have. Pour the currants into a jelly bag — one made of thick flannel is best—and leave them to drain until they stop dripping. Measure the juice. For each pint take 1 lb. sugar. Put both in the preserving pan, bring to the boil and boil for 5 minutes, or until the jelly sets. Bottle at once in warm jars and seal.

RUM SAUCE

½ oz. cornflour   1 tablespoon sugar   1 tablespoon rum
½ pint water   ¼ teaspoon cinnamon   1 oz. butter

Mix cornflour with a little cold water, pour on the rest of the boiling water to make a sauce. Add sugar, cinnamon, rum and butter cut in pieces. Stir gently until boiling.

CRANBERRY JELLY or SAUCE

8 oz. cranberries   ½ pint water   4 oz. sugar

Boil the cranberries and water in a saucepan. Stir well and crush with a wooden spoon. When quite tender, rub through a sieve. Add the sugar and stir until dissolved. Pour into a mould and leave to set. If a hot sauce is required, add a little hot water to the sauce to make a purée.

GOOSEBERRY SAUCE

½ pint young green   cooked sorrel or   salt and pepper
    gooseberries   spinach leaves   ¼ teaspoon ground
1 oz. butter   ¼ pint water   nutmeg
    1 oz. sugar

Boil the gooseberries in the water for 4 or 5 minutes, till tender and mushy. Drain and sieve them. Add a tablespoon of sorrel leaves chopped finely, the butter, sugar, salt and pepper to taste and the nutmeg. Re-heat and serve with mackerel or other fish. If wished, this concentrated sauce may be mixed with ¼ pint béchamel sauce (see p. 256).

APPLE SAUCE

1 lb. apples   1 tablespoon sugar   2 teaspoons lemon
1 tablespoon butter   1 tablespoon water   juice

Peel, quarter and core the apples and put into a pan with the water. Simmer until the apples are quite soft, then beat until smooth. Add the butter, sugar and lemon juice, then heat for 5 minutes, stirring continuously. Serve with roast pork, goose or duck.

BRANDY BUTTER

4 oz. butter   1 oz. sugar   brandy

Work the sugar into the butter till smooth. Add sufficient brandy into the mixture, gradually stirring all the time until the mixture will absorb no more brandy, while remaining stiff.

CLOTTED CREAM

Devonshire

Put fresh, creamy milk into a fireproof dish and leave for 12 hours. Then, without disturbing the milk, heat very slowly until bubbles appear round the sides. Do not let it boil, but remove gently and let it stand in a cool place for 24 hours. The cream can then be skimmed from the surface.

CUMBERLAND RUM BUTTER

8 oz. best fresh butter
1 lb. dark brown soft
  sugar

¼ teaspoon grated
  nutmeg

1 sherry glass rum
icing sugar for dusting

Melt the butter very slowly, do not let it froth. Put the sugar in a bowl, add the nutmeg. Pour in the rum and mix well. Pour the melted butter over the sugar mixture and beat for 10 minutes until it begins to set. Turn into a pretty china bowl and sprinkle with icing sugar. Delicious with unsweetened biscuits and bread and butter at tea time.

SCOTS CREAM-CROWDIE

1 pint double cream
2 oz. coarse oatmeal

2 oz. castor sugar
1 tablespoon rum

4 oz. fresh raspberries
  or blackerries

Toss the oatmeal in a thick-bottomed saucepan over the fire for a few moments. Beat cream to a thick froth and stir in the oatmeal, sugar, rum and fresh fruit. Serve at once.

GUARDS PUDDING

4 oz. flour
4 oz. butter
4 oz. castor sugar
2 eggs
2 oz. white
  breadcrumbs

pinch of bicarbonate
  of soda
2 tablespoons sieved
  raspberry jam or
  raspberry jelly

Sauce:
3 tablespoons
  raspberry jam
3 tablespoons water
1 teaspoon lemon
  juice

Butter a soufflé dish and put a round of buttered paper on the bottom. Cut another round of paper to be over the top of the dish. Cream the butter and sugar till quite white and fluffy. Beat in 1 egg, half the flour and half the breadcrumbs, then the other egg and the rest of the flour and breadcrumbs and the bicarbonate. Add the sieved jam or jelly. Pour into the dish. Tie over the buttered paper. Steam for 1½ hours. When done leave cooling for 8 minutes before turning out. Make the sauce by heating all the ingredients mixed together. Sieve and serve separately.

APPLE DUMPLINGS

short crust pastry using 8 oz. flour, etc. (see p. 100)	4 cloves	1 tablespoon butter
	2 teaspoons grated lemon rind	milk
2 oz. brown sugar	4 medium-sized apples	castor sugar
		cream

Divide the short crust pastry into 4 rounds and peel and core the apples. Mix the sugar, grated lemon rind and ½ tablespoon of butter and fill the hollows inside the apples. Stick a clove into each centre and put an apple on each round of pastry. Draw up the pastry to cover the apples completely, moisten the edges with milk and press together firmly. Place the dumplings, sealed side under, on to a baking pan greased with the remaining butter, brush them with milk, dredge with castor sugar and put into a moderate oven to bake for about 30 minutes. Serve hot or cold with cream. *(Illustrated in Plate 17.)*

QUEEN OF PUDDINGS

4 oz. fine white breadcrumbs	1 whole egg, beaten	3 or 4 tablespoons raspberry jam
3 eggs, the yolks and whites separated	1 pint milk	3 tablespoons castor sugar

Beat the 3 yolks and the 1 egg add to the milk and mix well. Add the breadcrumbs. Pour the milk, egg and crumb custard into a pie dish and leave for 30 minutes. Bake in a cool oven for 1 hour, till set. Spread a layer of jam about ¼ inch thick over the set custard. Whip the whites very stiffly, add the sugar. Pile on top of the jam, sprinkle a little sugar on top and put back in the very cool oven till the meringue is set and delicately browned.

APPLE CHARLOTTE

1 lb. cooking apples, peeled and cored	8 oz. sugar	¼ teaspoon cinnamon
rind and juice of ½ lemon	2 oz. butter	2 oz. almonds, skinned
	3 tablespoons apricot jam	puff pastry (see p. 101)

Cut the apples in ½-inch dice, put in a saucepan, add the sugar, lemon rind and juice, butter, jam and cinnamon. Cook very slowly, stirring all the time until the apples are soft. Add the almonds. Line a pie-dish, preferably one with straight sides, with puff pastry. Pour in the mixture. Bake in a moderate oven for 45 minutes. Serve with cream.

20. Steak and Kidney Pudding, Britain (p.103)

21. Devilled Kidneys, Britain (p.106)

JAM ROLY-POLY

8 oz. flour
pinch salt

4 oz. suet
1 level teaspoon
   baking powder

cold water
2-3 tablespoons jam

Sift the flour, baking powder and salt into a basin. Shred and chop the suet finely and add to the flour. Mix with sufficient water to make an elastic but firm dough. Turn out on to a floured board and roll out into an oblong shape, about ¼ inch thick. Spread with jam to within ½-inch of the edge, damp the edges and roll up the strip. Seal the edges and wrap the pudding in a floured cloth. Tie the ends of the cloth and put into a pan of fast-boiling water. Simmer for 2 hours. Remove from the cloth and serve with jam.

GOOSEBERRY PUDDING

Cake Mixture:
4 oz. self-raising flour
¼ teaspoon salt
4 oz. castor sugar

4 oz. butter
2 eggs, beaten

Fruit Mixture:
12 oz. gooseberries
3 oz. butter
3 oz. soft brown sugar
1 oz. chopped nuts

Wash and prepare the fruit. Melt the 3 oz. butter, add the brown sugar, stir well, add the nuts. Butter a deep fireproof dish and pour in this mixture. Place the gooseberries in a layer on top. Sieve the flour and the salt. Cream the butter with the castor sugar, add the eggs and flour gradually, stirring well. Pour over the fruit and bake in a moderate oven for 35 minutes. When done turn the pudding on to a dish so that the gooseberries are on top.

BLACKBERRY FOAM TRIFLE

1 sponge round
3 tablespoons
  blackberry jam
8 oz. marshmallows

12 oz. ripe
  blackberries
1 small can
  evaporated milk
2 oz. sugar

1 teaspoon lemon
  juice
¼ pint double
  cream
water

Split sponge round and sandwich together with jam. Place in round trifle dish. Cut marshmallows into pieces and place in basin. Cook blackberries with sugar and a little water until tender. Strain 3 table-spoons boiling juice over marshmallows and stir until dissolved. Leave to cool. Strain remaining juice over sponge. Sieve blackberries. Whip evaporated milk with lemon juice until double its bulk. Whisk blackberry purée and dissolved marshmallows together. Add to whipped evaporated milk and whisk again. Pour foamy mixture over contents of dish. Chill. Decorate with whipped cream and fresh, ripe blackberries.
(Illustrated in Plate 68.)

SUET PUDDING

8 oz. flour	pinch salt	2 tablespoons lemon
3 oz. suet	4 tablespoons jam or	juice
1 teaspoon baking	treacle	water
powder		1 teaspoon cornflour

Sieve the flour, baking powder and salt into a basin and add finely chopped suet. Stir in enough cold water to make a stiff dough then turn it out on to a floured board. Shape the dough into a roll, tie up in a floured cloth, place in a pan of boiling water and boil for 2 hours. Add more water if necessary. To make the sauce, boil the jam or treacle with ½ pint of water, lemon juice and the cornflour blended with a little cold water. Serve the pudding hot with the sauce poured over it.

LEMON CREAM

grated rind and juice	¼ pint dry white	sugar to taste
of 2 lemons	wine	3 egg whites
	1 pint thick cream	

Add the grated lemon rind to 1 pint of thick cream and whisk until stiff. Stir in lemon juice and dry white wine. Add sugar to taste. Whisk egg whites until they form stiff peaks and fold into whipped cream mixture. Serve in a glass serving dish or in individual glasses. Serves 4—6. *(Illustrated in Plate 19.)*

PANCAKES

4 oz. flour	1 tablespoon fat	salt
½ pint milk	castor sugar	1 lemon
	1 egg	

Sift the flour and salt into a basin, make a hollow in the centre and put in the egg and half the milk. Start mixing from the centre and make into a smooth paste. Beat well, then add the rest of the milk and beat again. Pour into a jug and leave in a cool place to stand for at least 30 minutes. Heat a little fat in a small frying pan about 6 inches across, make sure it is evenly coated then pour off the surplus fat. Pour in enough batter to cover the bottom of the pan, tilt it over to make it even and fry for a few minutes until the pancake is light brown underneath. Shake the pan and free the edges of the pancake with a knife to prevent it sticking. Toss or turn the pancake on to the other side, finish cooking then turn out on to a sugared paper. Fold and keep hot until all the pancakes are cooked. Sprinkle the folded pancakes with more sugar and serve hot with cut lemon. Jam pancakes are made in the same way, the jam being spread over each one before folding them. *(Illustrated in Plate 8.)*

APPLE PIE

short crust pastry	4 oz. sugar	1 teaspoon grated
using 6 oz. flour,	2—3 cloves	lemon rind
etc. (see p. 100)	2 lb. apples	custard or cream

Peel, core and quarter the apples and put into a pie-dish. Add the sugar, cloves and lemon rind, and arrange the fruit so that it is piled high in the centre of the pie-dish. Line the brim of the pie-dish with a strip of pastry, and cover the whole pie-dish with pastry. Press the edges together lightly and trim with a knife. Put into a hot oven for 10 minutes, then reduce the heat to very moderate and bake for a further 30 minutes. Serve hot or cold, accompanied by custard or cream.

BREAD AND BUTTER PUDDING

4 slices of bread	3 tablespoons sugar	grated lemon rind to
2 oz. butter	4 eggs, well beaten	taste
2 oz. currants	1⅛ pints milk	½ teaspoon nutmeg
	2 oz. sultanas	

Remove the crusts and butter each slice of bread. Cover the bottom o a greased dish with slices, sprinkle over some of the fruit and 2 tablespoons sugar. Repeat until bread and fruit and sugar are finished. Mix the eggs well into the milk, add the lemon rind and pour into the dish. And, this is important, leave for 2 hours. Sprinkle 1 tablespoon sugar and nutmeg on top and bake in a very slow oven for 1 hour or till the custard is set.

LEMON MERINGUE PIE

6 oz. castor sugar	2 eggs	pinch salt
small tin evaporated	rind and juice 1 lemon	short pastry (see p. 100)
milk	1 oz. cornflour	¼ pint water

Mix 2 oz. sugar, pinch of salt and cornflour and blend with the milk. Gradually stir in ¼ pint boiling water. Bring to the boil over a gentle heat, and simmer for 5 minutes. Remove from heat, allow to cool a little then add beaten egg yolks. Cook gently for a further 2—3 minutes, stirring continuously. Add lemon juice and grated lemon rind, mix well, allow to cool and pour into an 8-inch plate lined with pastry. To make the meringue, whisk the egg whites until stiff then whisk in 2 teaspoons of sugar. Fold in the rest of the sugar and pile on top of the pie. Bake in the centre of a slow oven for 30—40 minutes. (Illustrated in Plate 110.)

BAKEWELL TART

short crust pastry (see p. 100) with 1 oz. sugar added

4 oz. flour

2 teaspoons baking powder

2½ oz. cooking fat or butter

3 oz. castor sugar

2 eggs

3 dessertspoons milk

½ tablespoon almond essence

raspberry jam

pinch salt

Roll out the pastry and line a 7-inch flan tin. Put a little jam in the bottom. Sift the flour, baking powder, salt and sugar in a bowl, then rub in the fat. Now add the eggs, the milk and almond essence. Stir until smooth and pour into pastry case. Bake for 30 minutes in a moderate oven.

NORFOLK PUDDING

Yorkshire pudding batter (see p. 97)

1 lb. cooking apples

1 oz. lard

2 oz. sugar

Peel and slice apples. Heat fat in a shallow baking tin and place the apples in it. Add sugar, then cover with the batter mixture and bake in a hot oven for 30 minutes.

SPOTTED DICK

8 oz. self-raising flour

4 oz. chopped suet

3 oz. sugar

4 oz. currants

milk

pinch salt

Add suet, sugar and currants to sieved flour and salt and mix with sufficient milk to make a soft dough. Grease and flour a pudding cloth and place the dough, moulded into a roll, on this. Roll up and tie at both ends, leaving room for the pudding to swell. Steam for 3 hours. Serve with custard.

TREACLE TART

8 oz. plain or self-raising flour

4 oz. margarine

5 tablespoons golden syrup

3 oz. breadcrumbs

3 tablespoons cold water

pinch salt

Sieve the flour and salt into a bowl. Rub in the margarine until the mixture resembles fine breadcrumbs. Add the water and mix to a firm dough. Roll out thinly on a lightly floured board. Line a 9-inch flan dish with the pastry and slash the edges with a fork. Mix syrup and breadcrumbs together and spread over pastry. Roll the remaining pastry into 4 strips; twist and place these on top of the filling forming a lattice pattern; stick ends with cold water. Bake near the top of a moderately hot oven for 35—40 minutes. Serve either hot or cold. *(Illustrated in Plate 59.)*

RHUBARB PUDDING

short crust pastry (see p. 100)
2 oz. flour

12 oz. rhubarb, finely chopped
4 oz. soft brown sugar

grated rind ½ lemon
3 tablespoons thick cream

Line a plate with pastry. Cover with the rhubarb mixed with the flour, cream, sugar and rind. Bake in a moderately hot oven for 10 minutes, lower the heat and cook until the mixture is firm, about 25 minutes. Serve with whipped cream if possible.

TRIFLE

3 small sponge cakes
6 macaroons
1 oz. ratafias
¼ pint medium sweet sherry

2 oz. blanched almonds, shredded
strawberry jam
crystallized fruits etc. to garnish

½ pint custard
¼ pint cream
¾ oz. sugar
1 white of egg
3 tablespoons brandy

Put the sponge cakes, macaroons and ratafias in a dish, pour over the brandy and sherry, keeping back 1 teaspoon, leave to soak for 10 minutes. Cover with a thick layer of strawberry jam. Pour over the cooled custard. Whisk the cream, sugar, egg white and 1 teaspoon sherry till fluffy, cover the cake and jam mixture. Scatter shredded almonds all over the cream mixture. Garnish with crystallized fruits. Serve cold.

STRAWBERRY SOUFFLÉ

1 packet strawberry jelly
1 dessertspoon gelatine

juice ½ lemon
½ large tin evaporated milk
2 eggs

1 lb. fresh straw-berries
angelica
water

Dissolve jelly in ½ pint boiling water. Soften gelatine in three tablespoons cold water for 5 minutes and stir into hot jelly liquid until dissolved. Rub 8 oz. strawberries through sieve (or chop, if preferred) saving the choicest for decoration later. Stir into jelly mixture. Chill evaporated milk, then whisk with lemon juice until thick. When strawberry mixture is cool and commencing to thicken, fold in whipped milk, then swiftly whisk whites of eggs. Pour into rinsed soufflé dish and chill. When required for serving, decorate with whipped cream, choice strawberries and angelica. (Illustrated in Plate 114.)

GOOSEBERRY FOOL

1 lb. gooseberries	½ pint cream or
4 oz. sugar	2 cartons of yoghourt
¼ pint water	(in which case use
	6 oz. sugar)

Stew the gooseberries in water and sugar till tender. Sieve them and add the whipped cream, or the yoghourt. Sponge fingers or digestive biscuits are good served with this.

CHRISTMAS PUDDING

10 oz. chopped suet	5 oz. chopped apples	grated rind and juice
10 oz. breadcrumbs	4 eggs	½ lemon
5 oz. flour	5 oz. candied peel	3 oz. brown sugar
8 oz. raisins, seedless	chopped small	¼ teaspoon salt
and washed	1 oz. chopped	1 sherry glass rum
10 oz. sultanas,	almonds	¼ sherry glass sherry
washed	½ teaspoon nutmeg	1 sherry glass stout

Soak the raisins and sultanas in the rum and sherry. Sieve the flour, add the breadcrumbs, suet, salt, sugar, lemon rind, almonds, nutmeg, peel, apples and the fruit and rum mixture. Beat the eggs, add to the stout and lemon juice, stir well. Add gradually to the flour mixture, stirring for a long time until completely mixed. Put the mixture into greased basins. Tie two layers of greaseproof paper firmly over the top of each basin and tie the whole in a cloth. Boil for 6 hours. This pudding will keep for months. Before using boil again for 3 hours. Serve with brandy butter (see p. 110). *(Illustrated in Plate 24.)*

CHRISTMAS CAKE

1 lb. seedless raisins	8 oz. butter	¼ teaspoon mixed
1 lb. currants	8 oz. soft brown sugar	spice, cinnamon,
2 oz. almonds,	1 tablespoon black	nutmeg and ginger
shredded	treacle	4 eggs
3 oz. glacé cherries,	grated rind of 1 orange	¼ pint brandy or
chopped	and 1 lemon	sherry
4 oz. mixed peel,	few drops of vanilla	almond paste
chopped	essence	royal icing
8 oz. flour		

Line an 8 inch cake tin with 1 layer of brown and 2 layers of greaseproof paper to come 2 inches higher than the tin. Wash and dry the fruit. Take a large basin, put in the fruit, almonds, cherries, peel and 1 tablespoon flour. Mix well. In another basin cream the butter and sugar, add treacle, orange and lemon rinds, essence and the spices. Beat well, then add the eggs, one by one, beating between each. Sieve the flour and add with the fruit mixture. Pour in 2 tablespoons of brandy or sherry and mix well. Pour into the tin, make a hollow in the middle, for a flat top result. Tie a band of newspaper round the tin and bake in a slow oven for 1½ hours, reduce the heat to very slow and cook for a further 4 hours. Test with a skewer or knife, which will come out clean if the cake is done. Leave the cake in the tin for 40 minutes, turn upside down, prick deeply with a skewer and pour over the remaining sherry or brandy and let it run into the cake. Cover with almond paste and royal icing (see p. 128).

MINCE PIES

short crust or flaky pastry
(see pp. 100, 101)
Mincemeat:
8 oz. seedless raisins
2 medium apples
2 oz. almonds

6 oz. candied peel
8 oz. beef suet
8 oz. brown sugar
grated nutmeg
grated rind and juice
of lemon

2 tablespoons rum
1 teaspoon allspice
1 teaspoon of mixed
ground ginger,
cinnamon and cloves
½ teaspoon salt
2 tablespoons brandy

Put almonds into boiling water to blanch, then chop finely. Mince the fruit and chop the suet finely. Mix all the ingredients together, stirring well and pack into jars. Cover and tie down. For making the pies, roll out the pastry to about ⅛-inch thick and cut half of it into rounds about 2½ inches in diameter. Cut the remaining pastry into 3-inch rounds and line patty tins with them. Put a tablespoon of mincemeat into each section, brush the edges with water and cover with the smaller rounds of pastry. Press the edges together. Brush the tops with milk, sprinkle with sugar and make 2 small cuts on each pie. Put into a hot oven for 25—30 minutes. Sprinkle with castor sugar and serve hot or cold.

ECCLES CAKES
Lancashire

1 lb. puff pastry
(see p. 101)
4 oz. jam

2 oz. butter
2 oz. chopped candied
peel
8 oz. currants

½ teaspoon mixed
spice
sugar to coat

Melt butter and add jam, washed dried currants, chopped peel and mixed spice. Heat gently in a saucepan. Roll out the pastry thinly, cut into squares and, when cool, place a spoonful of filling in the centre of each square. Pinch together edges of pastry over the filling to make a round flat cake. Brush with water, sprinkle with sugar and make two cuts in the top of each cake. Bake in a hot oven for 10—15 minutes.

SIMNEL CAKE

An Easter Cake

6 oz. flour	2 oz. chopped mixed	1 level teaspoon
4 oz. butter	peel	baking powder
4 oz. sugar	½ teaspoon mixed	almond paste
3 eggs	spice	(see p. 128)
4 oz. sultanas	1 tablespoon brandy	royal icing, using
2 oz. currants	or rum	4 oz. sugar, etc.
4 oz. seedless raisins	pinch salt	(see p. 128)

Cream sugar and butter, add 2 beaten eggs and flour sifted with the salt and baking powder. Stir in all the other ingredients except the remaining egg, almond paste and icing. If the mixture is too stiff, add a little milk. Line a 7-inch cake tin with greaseproof paper and put in half the cake mixture. Cover with a layer of about a third of the almond paste and put the rest of the cake mixture on top. Bake in a moderate oven for 30 minutes, then reduce oven to slow and bake for a further 2 hours. Take out the cake and leave on a wire cake-cooler. When quite cold, cover the top with the remaining almond paste, decorating the edge with egg-shaped pieces of almond paste. Brush all over with a beaten egg diluted with a little water and put into a hot oven for a few minutes to brown the top. When cool, pour the icing on to the centre of the cake and then decorate with yellow chicks, tiny nests of Easter eggs, angelica and anything else suitable. *(Illustrated in Plate 53.)*

YULE LOG

Swiss Roll:	*Glacé Icing:*	2 tablespoons hot
4 oz. margarine	8 oz. icing sugar	milk
4 oz. castor sugar	2—3 dessertspoons	8 oz. icing sugar
2 eggs	water	*Decorations:*
4 oz. self-raising	*Chocolate Icing:*	1 7-inch square cake
flour	2 rounded tablespoon	board
2 heaped tablespoons	cocoa	Christmas cake
warm lemon curd	3 oz. margarine	decorations

To make the Swiss roll, cream the margarine and sugar together until very light. Beat in the eggs one at a time, adding a little of the sieved flour with the second. Fold in the remaining flour. Spread evenly in a medium-sized Swiss roll tin, lined with greaseproof paper and brushed all round inside with margarine. Bake in a pre-heated moderately hot oven on second shelf from top for 10—12 minutes. Have ready a piece of greaseproof paper, a little larger than the Swiss roll tin and sprinkle with castor sugar. Turn the roll on to the paper, quickly strip off paper lining. Trim edges, spread lemon curd evenly over. Roll up using the sugared paper as a guide. Fold paper over and hold for a few seconds to set. Cool on a wire tray. To make the chocolate icing, blend the cocoa and milk together in a small bowl. Cream the margarine and half the icing sugar together in a mixing bowl until very light. Mix in the chocolate mixture and remaining icing sugar. Beat until the icing is smooth and creamy. To make the glacé icing, sieve the icing sugar into a mixing bowl. Add the water and beat until smooth and glossy. Place the roll on a cake board, cover completely with chocolate icing and mark with a fork to represent the bark of a tree. Using a small plain tube and paper icing bag, pipe the glacé icing in rings at the dens of roll, also pipe 'Merry Christmas' on the front. Spread the remaining glacé icing on cake board around the roll to represent snow. Decorate the log with any Christmas cake decorations. *(Illustrated in Plate 52.)*

SAFFRON CAKE

Cornwall

8 oz. flour	1 egg	3 oz. seedless raisins
3—4 oz. butter or margarine	1 gill warm water	¼ oz. yeast
6 oz. sugar	packet saffron	1 oz. candied peel
	pinch salt	

Work the yeast, warm water and part of the flour into a soft dough. Mix well, cover with cloth and leave in a warm place to rise. Sift the remaining flour into a basin with the salt. Cream butter and sugar, add the beaten egg and the saffron infused in a little warm water and combine with the yeast dough. Knead with the raisins and peel, put into a greased baking tin and leave to rise again. Put into a moderate oven and bake for 1—1½ hours.

BANBURY CAKES

6 oz. flaky pastry (see p. 101)	1 oz. breadcrumbs	castor sugar
1 oz. butter	1 oz. brown sugar	½ teaspoon mixture cinnamon and
4 oz. currants	1 tablespoon rum or brandy	grated nutmeg
1 oz. chopped candied peel		

Roll out the pastry to about ¼-inch thick and cut into rounds 3 inches in diameter. For the filling, melt the butter and stir in all the ingredients until well mixed. Place a spoonful on each round of pastry and fold up, pressing the edges together. Roll out into oval shapes and cut 3 parallel gashes in the centre of each one. Put on a greased baking tin, brush with water and bake in a hot oven for 20 minutes. Sprinkle with castor sugar and put back in the oven for a few minutes.

MAIDS OF HONOUR
Richmond, Surrey

puff pastry, using 4 oz. flour etc. (see p. 101)	2 teaspoons rennet	1 oz. ground almonds
	4 oz. butter	1 tablespoon orange flower water
	1 oz. castor sugar	
2 pints milk	1 egg	pinch salt

Warm the milk to blood heat—100 °F., add the rennet and a pinch of salt. Leave for about 10 minutes to set then turn out into a fine muslin cloth, shaped into a bag. Hang up and leave to drain until next day. Rub the curd through a sieve and blend with melted butter, a beaten egg and the sugar. Add the orange flower water and ground almonds and mix well. Line some patty pans with the puff pastry, half fill with the mixture and put into a moderately hot oven to bake until set and golden brown. The cooking time should be 25—30 minutes.

DUNDEE CAKE

10 oz. flour	2 oz. cherries	1 teaspoon mixed spice
8 oz. butter	2 oz. candied peel	
4 eggs	2 oz. chopped almonds	split almonds to decorate
8 oz. sugar		
1½ lb. mixed dried fruit	2 tablespoons milk	egg white to glaze

Cream butter and sugar, add beaten eggs. Sieve flour and spice and add to the mixture, with the milk. Flour the cherries, fruit and chopped peel and stir in with the chopped almonds. Pour the mixture into a greased and floured 8-inch cake tin and decorate the top with split almonds. Brush with beaten egg white. Bake in a very moderate oven for 3 — 3½ hours. *(Illustrated in Plate 116.)*

PARKIN
Yorkshire

1 lb. flour	8 oz. syrup	1 teaspoon ground ginger
12 oz. medium oatmeal	8 oz. treacle	
	½ teaspoon bicarbonate of soda	1 egg
4 oz. butter		1 teaspoon salt
2 oz. sugar		½ pint milk

Dissolve the soda in the milk. Melt the treacle, syrup and butter together. Beat the egg. Mix all the dry ingredients together, pour in the melted butter and treacle and syrup, stir well, add the egg, then the milk, stirring all well together. Bake in a flat square greased tin for 45 minutes in a moderate oven. Turn out of the tin when cold. Half these quantities may be used, as this makes a big cake, but it matures with keeping.

FAT RASCALS

Yorkshire

8 oz. self-raising flour	1 oz. soft brown	7 tablespoons milk
1 level teaspoon	sugar	milk and castor sugar
baking powder	2 oz. currants	to glaze
	4 oz. margarine	

Sieve the flour and baking powder together. Rub in the margarine until mixture resembles fine breadcrumbs. Stir in the brown sugar and currants. Add the milk and mix to a moderately soft dough. Turn out on a floured board. Roll out approximately ½—¾ inch thick. Cut into rounds with a 2-inch plain cutter. Place on a baking sheet brushed with melted margarine. Brush the tops with milk and sprinkle with castor sugar. Put into hot oven and bake on the second shelf from top for 10—15 minutes. *(Illustrated in Plate 106.)*

HOT CROSS BUNS

Norfolk

1 lb. flour	½—¾ pint lukewarm	2 oz. currants
1 oz. yeast	milk	pinch salt
3 teaspoons sugar	1 oz. candied peel	1 teaspoon mixed
2 oz. lard or margarine	2 oz. short crust pastry	spice

Warm flour, spice and salt. Cream yeast and sugar. Rub fat into flour, then add candied peel and currants. Make a well in the centre. Add yeast and liquid and mix to a soft dough, just firm enough to be shaped after it has risen. Knead dough well until it is smooth and elastic. Put to rise in a warm place until it is twice its size—this will take about 45 minutes. Knead and shape into buns. Flatten slightly, make a cross on top of each with narrow strips of pastry. Allow to rise again in a warm place for 15 minutes. Bake in a hot oven for 20 minutes, lowering the heat slightly after 5 minutes. Rub with butter to glaze. *(Illustrated in Plate 113.)*

WELSH GRIDDLE CAKES

3 oz. self-raising flour	½ oz. sugar	fat for frying
1 egg	4 tablespoons milk	pinch salt

Beat egg and add flour, milk, salt and sugar gradually to make a batter. Beat for 1 minute. Drop spoonfuls of the mixture either on to a greased hot-plate or into a lightly greased frying pan. Cook until bubbles appear on the surface, then turn and cook on the other side until golden brown. Keep the scones in a linen cloth as you cook them; this keeps in the steam and prevents their becoming dry.

CORNISH SPLITS

1½ lb. flour	1 oz. yeast	¼ pint milk
4 oz. butter	½ teaspoon sugar	cream
1 oz. lard	¼ pint warm water	jam

Put the yeast, sugar and 1 teaspoon flour in a basin, pour on the warm water, mix well and leave in a warm place for 15 minutes. Sieve the flour in a large basin and leave in a warm place. Heat the milk gently, add the lard and butter, leave to melt. Make a well in the middle of the flour and gradually pour in the yeast water and the warmed milk, and butter and lard, mixing all to a soft dough. Leave in a warm place for 1½ hours to rise. Knead for 4 minutes, roll out ½ inch thick. Cut in pieces and form small balls about the size and shape of a tangerine, or small rissole. Bake in a moderate oven for 20 to 30 minutes until golden brown. Serve cold, split in half, filled with Cornish cream and jam, specially raspberry.

CHELSEA BUNS

12 oz. flour	1 oz. sugar	castor sugar
2 oz. margarine	1½ oz. currants	milk or egg for glazing
½ oz. yeast		½ gill tepid milk

Rub the fat into the flour. Cream yeast with ½ oz. of sugar and blend with flour mixture and milk. Knead the dough well and leave to rise until double its size. Then knead again lightly and roll out into a square about ¼ inch thick. Sprinkle with the currants and remaining sugar and roll up. Cut into slices about 1½ inches thick, and place, flat side down, on to a greased baking tin, close enough together to join slightly when baking. Leave to prove, then brush with milk or egg and put into a hot oven to bake for about 20 minutes. When the buns are cold, separate them and sprinkle with castor sugar.

OATCAKES
Scotland

4 oz. rolled oats	¼ teaspoon salt	1 level tablespoon
pinch bicarbonate	water	bacon fat or
soda		dripping

Mix oats, bicarbonate of soda and salt. Melt the fat with 1 tablespoon of water and pour into centre of oats. Mix to a soft consistency, adding boiling water as required. Turn on to a floured board and knead lightly. Roll out thinly and cut into rounds with a 3-inch pastry cutter. Place on a floured tin and bake in a moderate oven for 20—30 minutes or until crisp and lightly browned. Serve for breakfast with kippers (see p. 90). *(Illustrated in Plate 56.)*

SWEET SCONES

8 oz. self-raising flour	1 egg	pinch salt
2 oz. lard or margarine	5 tablespoons sour milk	strawberries and cream
	1 oz. sugar	

Sieve the flour, salt and sugar into a bowl. Rub in the fat until the mixture resembles breadcrumbs. Add lightly beaten egg and the sour milk and mix to a soft dough. Turn out on a floured board, roll out to ½ inch thick and cut into rounds with a 2-inch fluted cutter. Place on a greased baking tin and put into a hot oven near the top, and bake for 12—15 minutes. Cool on a wire tray. Serve the scones cut in half with whipped cream and sliced strawberries between the two layers. *(Illustrated in Plate 32.)*

LARDY JOHNS

Sussex

4 oz. flour	2 tablespoons currants	2 oz. lard
½ teaspoon baking powder		pinch salt
		water

Rub lard into flour then add baking powder and salt. Mix to a stiff dough with water. Stir in the currants, turn out on to a floured board and roll out thinly. Cut out the pastry into 2-inch squares, put on to a greased pan and bake in a hot oven for 10 minutes.

SALLY LUNN

A tea cake which was originally made by Sally Lunn and sold at her teashop in Bath.

12 oz. flour	1 oz. yeast	½ gill tepid milk
1 teaspoon sugar	1 beaten egg	pinch salt
	2 oz. margarine	

Mix flour and salt and rub in the fat. Cream yeast with sugar and blend with milk and egg. Add to flour mixture and knead into a soft dough. Place in a greased baking tin, or 2 smaller ones, and leave to rise. Then put into a hot oven at 400 °F. to bake for about 30 minutes or until golden brown on top. Serve hot with butter.

SCOTCH SHORTBREAD

6 oz. flour	2 oz. castor sugar	pinch salt
	4 oz. butter	

Mix flour and salt and rub in butter and sugar. Knead to a dough, then roll out and form into a round cake. Crimp the edges, prick all over with a fork and mark into portions with a knife before baking. Place on a baking sheet lined with greased paper and bake in a slow oven for 1 hour. Dredge with castor sugar.

BANNOCKS
Scottish Soda Scones

8 oz. flour	¼ teaspoon tartaric	sour milk
½ teaspoon	acid	pinch salt
bicarbonate of soda		

Sift the flour, soda and tartaric acid into a bowl and add enough sour milk to mix to a soft dough. Roll out on to a floured board into a round shape ½-inch thick. Bake in a hot oven for 10—15 minutes. Serve cut across to make 6 scones.

FLAPJACKS

6 oz. butter or	6 oz. demerara sugar	pinch salt
margarine		8 oz. rolled oats

Melt the fat in a saucepan over a very gentle heat. Mix in the sugar, oats and salt. Stir well and turn the mixture into a greased baking tin and press lightly together. Smooth the surface with a knife and bake for 30—40 minutes in a moderately hot oven. When cooked, leave to stand in a tin for a few minutes, then cut across into 16 squares or fingers. Leave in the tin until quite cold before removing. *(Illustrated in Plate 18.)*

BRANDY SNAPS

2 oz. plain flour	2 oz. sugar	1 teaspoon ground
3 oz. butter or cooking	3 oz. golden syrup	ginger
fat		whipped cream

Melt syrup, sugar and fat in a pan, cool slightly then stir in flour and ginger. Mix well and place teaspoons of the mixture well apart on greased baking sheets. Bake in a moderate oven for 10—15 minutes. Remove with a palette knife when they are just beginning to get crisp, and roll up — an easy way to do this is round the greased handle of a wooden spoon. When cold, fill with whipped cream.

MUFFINS

1 lb. flour	1 egg (beaten)	½ pint warm milk
1 teaspoon salt	1 oz. melted butter	(slightly less)
	¾ oz. yeast	

Mix flour and salt. Put sugar and crumbled yeast in well in centre of flour, add about a third of the milk (warmed) over the yeast and leave to stand for ten minutes. Mix beaten egg and melted butter, adding half the remaining milk. When yeast has risen to top of liquid in bowl, mix and knead with the egg and butter liquid, adding remaining milk gradually until a fairly soft dough is formed. Leave the dough to rise in a warm place 50 minutes to 1 hour, then knock it down and re-roll it on a floured board to a ½ inch in thickness. Cut out with a pastry cutter into 3—3½ inch rounds. Place on a well floured baking sheet and dust tops liberally with flour. Leave to rise for 30 minutes in a warm place. Lightly grease a hot griddle or thick frying pan, transfer the muffins carefully from the baking sheet to the pan, using a thin fish slice, and bake them 2 or 3 at a time, 5 minutes on each side, until golden brown. Turn them 2 or 3 times to make sure they are baked through. Serve immediately, split and buttered, or if left till following day, toast them lightly. (Do not cut new muffins; snip them round with scissors and pull apart.) *(Illustrated in Plate 69.)*

MACAROONS

3 oz. ground almonds	½ teaspoon vanilla	rice paper
4 oz. castor sugar	essence	blanched almonds
2—3 egg whites		1 teaspoon rice flour

Whisk egg whites until stiff. Mix the ground almonds, sugar, vanilla essence and rice flour together and fold into the egg whites. Place the rice paper on a baking tin and put on rounds of the mixture, about 1½ inches in diameter. Decorate with almonds sliced in half and bake in a moderate oven for 20—30 minutes. *(Illustrated in Plate 120.)*

LEMON CURD OR CHEESE

| 6 oz. castor sugar | grated rind and juice | 2 oz. butter |
| 4 eggs yolks | of 1 large lemon | 1 egg white |

Whip the egg yolks and white very well. Melt the butter, sugar, lemon rind and juice in a saucepan, add the eggs, mix well and cook very slowly, stirring all the time till thick, for about 15 minutes preferably over boiling water in a double saucepan. If overheated or not stirred, the eggs will scramble and the curd be ruined. Pour into pots and seal thoroughly if not to be eaten at once.

ALMOND PASTE

2 eggs
4 oz. castor sugar
4 oz. icing sugar
8 oz. ground almonds

4 drops lemon juice
3 drops almond
essence

1 dessertspoon brandy
or sherry
2 tablespoons warm
apricot jam

Spread the warm jam on top of the cake. Beat the eggs with the sugars in a basin over hot water until light and fluffy. Cool, add the almonds, lemon juice, almond essence and brandy. Roll out to fit the top of the cake. These quantities are sufficient for an 8-inch diameter cake.

ROYAL ICING

8 oz. icing sugar
1 egg white

1 teaspoon lemon
juice

1—2 drops glycerine

Sieve the icing sugar, beat the egg white lightly until slightly stiffening. Add gradually to the sugar, beating all the time, also the lemon juice and glycerine. Beat for 20 minutes. Spread over the cake, smoothing on at the end with a stainless steel knife dipped in boiling water.

ORANGE MARMALADE

2 lb. Seville oranges

4 lb. sugar
1 lemon

4 pints water

Wash and shred the oranges and the lemon and leave in water overnight. Next day, put into a large saucepan and bring to the boil. Then simmer gently for about 1½ hours or until the peel is soft and the contents of the saucepan reduced to nearly half. Add the sugar, stir until dissolved, then boil quickly for about 15 minutes. Test for setting then allow the marmalade to cool a little. Pour into warm jars and seal.

STRAWBERRY JAM

5 lb. strawberries

5 lb. sugar

juice of 4 lemons

Cook fruit and juice until tender. Add sugar, dissolve and boil up for 15—20 minutes until it will set. Cool slightly, stir, and pour into jars.

RHUBARB AND GINGER JAM

4 lb. rhubarb
3 lb. sugar

2 teaspoons ground
ginger

1 teaspoon citric acid

Cut up rhubarb and arrange fruit and sugar in layers in a bowl. Leave to stand for 12 hours. Then place in a pan, add acid and ginger and boil for 10—15 minutes until the jam will set.

22. Boiled Silverside and Dumplings, Britain (p.95)

23. Devonshire Bacon in Cider, Britain (p.98)

24. Christmas Pudding, Britain (p.118)

CRANBERRY CHEESE

1 pint cranberries	½ pint water	12 oz. sugar
2 oz. seedless raisins, chopped	2 oz. walnuts, chopped	1 orange, peeled and thinly sliced

Cook the cranberries in the water till soft. Sieve them. Add the sugar, raisins and walnuts. Bring slowly to the boil, stirring all the time, add the orange. Simmer for 20 minutes. Pour into jars and seal.

RUM PUNCH

3 parts rum	1 part lemon juice	6 parts hot, not
2 parts brandy	sugar to taste	boiling, water

Mix the rum, brandy, lemon juice together. Heat the water, add the sugar, stir till dissolved and pour over the rum, etc.

RHUBARB WINE

5 lb. rhubarb	3 lb. loaf or	grated rind and juice
1 gallon water	preserving sugar	of 1 lemon
	⅜ oz. isinglass	

Wash the rhubarb and cut into ½ inch slices. Put into a large basin and press and pound them well, pour in the water. Cover the basin, leave for 10 days, stirring once a day. Strain it, add the sugar and stir until dissolved, with the lemon juice and rind. Add the isinglass, stir well and pour into the cask. Leave uncorked for 10 days, but cover the bung hole with a folded cloth. After 10 days cork tightly. Drink it after 12 months.

SYLLABUB

1 gill cream	1 gill milk	1 tablespoon sherry
2 egg whites, stiffly beaten	1 gill lemon or orange juice	(optional) sugar to sweeten

An old English rich frothy drink, originally made from the milk straight from the cow. This is a modern version:
Put the sweetened juice and sherry in a large bowl, add the cream and milk and whisk till fluffy, be careful not to over-whisk and make buttery. Add the egg whites, whisk again, chill and serve in glasses. This will keep in a cold place for several days.

SLOE GIN

sloes   white sugar   gin

Wash and prick the sloes. Mix with an equal weight of white sugar. Half fill the bottles with this and fill up with the gin. Cork tightly. Drink in 3 months' time.

MULLED CLARET

2 nutmegs, grated   12 cloves   1 pint boiling water
2 pints claret   ½ teaspoon ground   1 sherry glass curaçao
2 oranges   cinnamon   1 sherry glass brandy
                             12 sugar lumps

Slice one unpeeled orange finely, pare the rind thinly off the other. Add these to the claret in a saucepan, plus the sugar, cloves and cinnamon. Heat slowly to comfortable drinking temperature, add the boiling water just off the boil, stir well, add the curaçao and the brandy. Pour into glasses and sprinkle the nutmeg over each. Serve at once.

MEAD WINE

1 gallon water   ⅓ oz. root ginger   2 sprigs rosemary
2 pints honey   1 lb. white sugar   1 oz. yeast
4 cloves   2 lemons

Boil together the water, sugar and honey and skim off the scum. Stand in a basin and add the juice of both the lemons and the skin of one. Add the cloves, well bruised ginger and rosemary. When at blood temperature or less add the yeast. This will start the fermentation which should be allowed to go on for 6 days but the lemon peel should be taken out after 3. Then bottle and cork lightly.

PARSNIP WINE

5 lb. parsnips   white sugar   1 gallon water
                             1 oz. yeast

Put the washed, peeled and chopped parnips into the water and bring to the boil. Cook till tender, mashing and pulping at the same time. Strain and measure the juice. To every 4 pints add 1½ lb. sugar. When cool add the yeast. Leave for 12 days to work in the open then strain, bottle and cork lightly. Bottle again in 6 weeks. Best not drunk for a further 6 months or 1 year.

BULGARIAN COOKING

Gordana Žunič and Musia Soper

Very often, the first thought about Bulgaria is that this is the country where people eat a lot of yoghourt and because of that live a very long time. Yoghourt, of course, is also eaten in other parts of the world and now it can be obtained everywhere from dairies. Bulgaria is also the country where miles and miles of roses grow in a valley; and it is from these roses that the unique essence is obtained and sent everywhere to become the basis for the best perfumes.

Bulgaria, whose people are mostly of Slav origin, was conquered, as were so many other parts of the Balkans at that time or later, by the Turks in the fourteenth century. Some Turkish influence is left and it can be noticed in various ways, including the cooking.

The Bulgarians are not a maritime people, though they do some successful fishing in the Black Sea. They produce, amongst other things, maize, good meat and good wine. The Balkan slopes are covered with fruit trees, and plums grow wild. The fruit is mostly eaten cooked. There is also plenty of poultry and wild game. Much of the cooking has a good deal in common with Yugoslavia.

VILLAGE SOUP

Selska Chorba

1 lb. onions	1 egg yolk	salt
1 celery head	2 tablespoons oil	water

Cook the onions in water until soft, strain and make a purée. Add grated celery, oil and a little of the onion water and bring to the boil. Beat the yolk and use some of the soup to dilute it, then add it to the rest of the soup. Thickness will depend on individual taste. If required, lemon juice or vinegar can be added.

LAMB SOUP

Agneshka Chorba

1 lb. lamb	4 oz. rice	2 egg yolks
8 oz. spinach	10 peppercorns	½ teaspoon paprika
1 bunch spring onions	sprigs parsley	water
3 oz. butter		1 gill sour milk

Cut the lamb into slices and fry lightly in butter. Add chopped spinach and spring onions. Fry again, add paprika and enough water to cover the meat well. When the meat is almost cooked, put the rice and peppercorns in and leave to cook until the rice is soft. Before serving beat yolks and sour milk together and add to the soup, stirring continuously. Sprinkle each plate with a little chopped parsley.

YOGHOURT SOUP

Tarator

2 large cucumbers	2 tablespoons chopped	salt and pepper
1 pint yoghourt	walnuts	1 clove garlic

Peel cucumbers and cut into ¼-inch slices. Sprinkle with 2 teaspoons of salt and leave in a cool place. Put into a large bowl of yoghourt, crushed garlic and salt and pepper to taste and mix well. Drain the liquid off from the cucumbers and add them to the yoghourt. Serve very cold, each plate sprinkled with chopped walnuts.

FRESH CABBAGE SOUP WITH BACON

Zeleva Chorba sas Beton

1 small cabbage	1 onion	caraway seeds
6 oz. bacon	1 egg	black pepper
4 tablespoons sour	2 tablespoons oil	salt
milk	flour	water

Slice the cabbage finely and cook in salted water. Meanwhile, fry chopped onion and bacon cut into dice in a frying pan with oil, stirring in the flour gradually. Pour over cabbage and continue cooking until bacon and onion are soft. Remove from the stove and add black pepper, caraway seeds, a well beaten egg and the sour milk.

VEAL WITH AUBERGINES

Teleshko sas Sini Domati

2 lb. veal	2 tomatoes	1 tablespoon flour
1 large or 2 small	¼ pint oil	1 egg
aubergines	2 teaspoons chopped	½ teaspoon paprika
2 onions	parsley	salt and pepper

Cut veal into moderate sized pieces. Salt and fry in some of the oil on both sides until light brown. Remove. In the same pan, fry the chopped onions until a golden colour, then stir in flour and paprika. Add some water and put back the meat. Allow to simmer and when half cooked add peeled, sliced tomatoes. Peel the aubergines, cut into small pieces, season with salt and allow to stand for 30 minutes. Then dip in beaten egg, roll in flour and fry in remaining oil until a light gold. Drain on brown paper. Combine aubergines with veal and simmer for at least 20 minutes. Serve sprinkled with chopped parsley.

BAKED BREAM WITH SAUERKRAUT

Bela Riba sas Kiselo Zele

2 lb. bream	salt and pepper	1 teaspoon paprika
1 lb. sauerkraut	1 gill nut oil	

Clean the fish and leave for 30 minutes in some of the oil. Meanwhile chop the sauerkraut, fry lightly in hot oil then put into a baking dish. Place the bream on top and sprinkle with paprika, salt and pepper. Bake in a moderately hot oven for 15—20 minutes.

MUTTON TONGUES

Ovneshki Ezeek

2 mutton tongues	1½ lb. potatoes	oil
3 tablespoons white wine	1 carrot	salt and pepper
	1 onion	water

Cook mutton tongues in salted water until tender. Skin them and then fry in oil to a light golden colour. Add enough water to cover, chopped onion, wine, sliced carrot, salt and pepper. Cook for about 20 minutes. Place in a fireproof dish topped with sliced potatoes and bake in a moderately hot oven for 30 minutes.

CHICKEN WITH TOMATOES

Kokoshka sas Domati

1 medium sized chicken	2 lb. fresh tomatoes	salt and black pepper
		oil

Rub chicken with salt and sauté in oil. Peel tomatoes and cut into halves. Place chicken in a fireproof dish, arrange tomatoes round the bird and sprinkle with salt and pepper. Cook in a hot oven. Serve with potatoes or rice.

STUFFED CABBAGE

Sarmi sas Zele

1 large cabbage	4 oz. rice	salt and pepper
8 oz. minced meat	1 tablespoon butter	water
1 lb. smoked pork ribs		1 large onion

Put the cabbage into boiling water and leave for 10 minutes to soften the leaves. Chop the onion and fry lightly in butter. Add the minced meat, rice, salt and pepper and mix well. Separate the cabbage leaves, lay out flat and fill each one with meat mixture. Roll up and tuck in the sides, but leave enough room for the rice to swell in cooking. Pack the stuffed cabbage leaves close together in a saucepan, and pour in a cup of water. Lay the pork ribs over the top, sprinkle with salt and pepper, cover with a lid and simmer for 1½ hours.

RUNNER BEANS WITH EGGS

Zeln Fasul sas Yaitza

1 lb. runner beans	6 sprigs parsley	1 teaspoon flour
2—3 eggs	½ pint milk	½ teaspoon paprika
2 onions	3 tablespoons oil	salt

Chop the onions and fry lightly in 2 tablespoons of oil. Prepare the runner beans, slice, sprinkle with salt and fry with the onions until fairly soft. Brown the flour in the remaining oil and add paprika and chopped parsley. Combine with the runner beans, mix well and put into a fireproof dish. Beat the eggs with the milk, adding a pinch of salt, and pour over the runner beans. Cover and put into a moderate oven to cook for 15 minutes.

VEGETABLE PURÉE

Purée Zelenchuk

3 lb. green peppers	2 cloves garlic	1 tablespoon vinegar
2 small aubergines	2 tablespoons olive oil	½ tablespoon salt

Bake the peppers and aubergines in the oven until the skins are very dark brown. Then peel off the skins and remove the seeds from the peppers. Mince the vegetables, add salt, oil, vinegar and crushed garlic and mix well. This is very good served as an accompaniment to roast poultry.

LEEK SALAD

4 leeks	olives	water
olive oil	salt and pepper	½ lemon
	juice 1 lemon	

Cut leeks lengthwise and cook in moderately salted water. When cooked, leave them to cool in the same water. Then drain and place them in a salad bowl. Blend lemon juice, olive oil and a dash of black pepper and pour over the leeks. Garnish with olives and slices of lemon.

BAKED POTATOES WITH CHEESE

Kartofi Furna sas Sireme

1½ lb. potatoes	½ pint sour milk	3 oz. butter
8 oz. curd cheese		4 eggs

Parboil the potatoes and slice in rounds. Crumble the cheese and arrange alternate layers of potatoes and cheese, finishing off with potatoes. Cover with pats of butter and put into a hot oven. Bake until the potatoes are almost ready, then pour over them sour milk beaten with eggs and leave for another 15 minutes to complete cooking. Serve hot.

POTATO SALAD WITH SOUR MILK

Kartofi Salata sas Kiselo Mleko

1 lb. potatoes	1 tablespoon wine	salt
5 tablespoons sour	vinegar	water
milk (solidified)	1 tablespoon olive oil	¼ teaspoon black
1 onion		pepper

Cook the potatoes in their skins in salted water. When cooked, peel, and slice into rounds. Add pepper, salt if necessary, chopped onion, vinegar and oil. Mix well together and then add the sour milk.

RICE WITH ROSE PETAL JAM

Sutliash

8 oz. rice	few drops vanilla	3 tablespoons sugar
1 pint milk	essence	rose petal jam
½ pint sour cream		(see p. 588)

Cook the rice in the milk, adding 2 tablespoons of sugar and the vanilla essence. Drain off any liquid left, add the remaining sugar and leave the rice to get cold. Then blend with the sour cream and put into individual glass dishes. Serve well chilled with rose petal jam on top of each portion of rice.

CZECH COOKING

Joža Břízová

Translated by

Helen Watney

An early Czech chronicler tells how Čech, the forefather of the Czechs, led his people from afar until he came to the mountain Říp, in Bohemia, and there he decided to settle because it was a very fertile land and rich in game and fish.

The Czech lands, lying in the heart of Europe, were the crossroads of trade and travel routes. Different dishes slowly began to make their way on to the Czech table, at first merely from neighbouring states (Vienna, in particular, for a certain time had a great influence on Czech cooking) but later from further afield as relations with other countries improved. Today, we no longer know whether fried schnitzel, so popular in Czech cooking, was really learned in England, potato crisp in France, borshch in Russia and so on.

These recipes are for dishes made by Czech housewives today. We have chosen those which are typical of Czech cooking and are not common in the menus of other countries. For the same reason we have included more sweet than vegetable dishes because Czech cooking is famed for its many delicious cakes and puddings. The recipes have been worked out to serve four persons. Sometimes, however, a pudding or cake provides more helpings. We have given the exact ingredients and best method of preparation.

We have omitted a few special country dishes which are still sometimes prepared for different occasions, but which are not very practical today and are rapidly being forgotten. In the past Czech food has tended to suffer from an excess of carbohydrates—too many floury and sweet dishes, and from an immoderate use of animal fats. These are now giving way to more valuable foods, with the stress on proteins and vitamins.

We hope you will try a number of recipes, and they will not just remain an exotic addition to your menu but will soon become firm favourites. We feel justified in thinking this after the great success which Czech dishes, particularly ham, roast pork with dumplings and sauerkraut, beef with cream sauce etc. had at the World Exhibition in Brussels.

Mothers of the older generation, when passing on their culinary arts to their daughters, never forget to remind them of the Czech proverb, 'The way to a man's heart lies through the stomach!' Although the modern woman may not believe that the preparation of food plays quite such an important role in emotional relationships, we hope that this little collection of recipes will gain many friends for Czech cooking.

ROAST GOOSE LIVER

liver from fattened goose (about 1 lb.)	1 gill goose fat	1 oz. almonds salt

Blanch the almonds and cut them into tiny strips. Poke them into the liver, place it on a baking dish and pour over the fat. Roast it slowly for 30—40 minutes. Cut the hot liver into slices, season with salt and serve with mashed potatoes. An excellent spread is obtained by pouring a spoonful of goose fat over the cooked liver and allowing to cool.

PÂTÉ FROM GOOSE LIVER AND GIBLETS

giblets from 1 goose	1 tablespoon bread-	ginger
1 small goose liver	crumbs	thyme
8 oz. pork	*Seasoning:*	bay leaf
1 egg	pepper	salt
	allspice	

Clean the giblets and boil till nearly tender. Remove the meat from the bones, mince it together with the liver and pork. Add the egg and seasoning to the mixture and thicken it slightly with breadcrumbs. Pile the mixture into a pudding bowl and steam for about 1 hour.

LIVER SPREAD

1 lb. liver (pig's or	2 eggs	salt, pepper, mace,
goat's)	1 onion	lemon rind
6 small cooked	2 anchovies	clove garlic, crushed
potatoes	flour	3 oz. butter
	breadcrumbs	

Mince the liver, potatoes and onion, add the seasoning, eggs, lemon rind and garlic and a little flour or breadcrumbs to thicken. Pile into a pudding bowl and steam for 45 minutes. Then beat butter and boned anchovies and gradually add to the cold pâté. Spread on black bread and garnish with pickled cucumber.

STUFFED NECK OF GOOSE

1 neck of goose	2 tablespoons goose	4 tablespoons
½ small goose liver	fat	breadcrumbs
8 oz. pork	4 tablespoons milk	lemon rind
	salt	

Clean the neck well and singe off the hairs. Mince the pork and liver, add a pinch of grated lemon rind, goose fat and the breadcrumbs soaked in milk. The mixture must be thick. Carefully stuff it into the skin of the neck and secure at both ends. Boil in water for about 1 hour, or roast it together with the goose. When cool, cut the neck into slices and serve with bread or hot with potatoes and salad.

RABBIT PASTE

1 skinned rabbit	3 oz. carrot, celeriac	*Seasoning:*
(2—3 lb.)	and parsley root	pepper
4 oz. calves' liver	1 onion	thyme
3 oz. bacon	a little anchovy paste	bay leaf
3 oz. butter		ginger

Fry the chopped onion and bacon in butter till golden brown. Add the washed, chopped meat and vegetables and simmer till tender. Then remove the meat from the bones, mince finely together with the liver and add salt, seasoning and a little anchovy paste. Steam the mixture in a pudding bowl for about 1 hour.

MINCED HARE

1 front portion of hare	2 tablespoons dripping	2 teaspoons plain flour
(about 2 lb.)	or lard	1 onion
8 oz. fat pork	about 2 oz. bread-	pepper
2 eggs	crumbs	salt
	3 oz. bacon	

Boil the meat from the hare in water, remove from bones and mince finely with the pork. Lightly fry the chopped bacon, add the chopped onion and fry till golden brown. Add to the minced meat and eggs, season with salt and pepper and thicken with a teaspoon of plain flour and a few breadcrumbs. Form the mixture into a long roll, and cook in the oven together with the dripping for about 1 hour. Dredge the juice with 1 teaspoon flour and boil for a few minutes. Serve with boiled potatoes and cranberries. It can also be served cold with bread.

SEMOLINA SOUP

3 pints water	1 tablespoon butter	chopped parsley
2 oz. semolina		1 meat cube

Melt fat in pan, allow semolina to brown slightly in it and then pour on cold water. Add a meat cube, beat well and simmer for a few minutes. Before serving add chopped parsley.

CHEESE SOUP

2½ pints water	3 oz. grated Parmesan	chopped parsley
½ pint sour cream	cheese	salt
3 potatoes		1 oz. butter

Peel potatoes and cook in salted water. Pass through sieve and add grated cheese. Simmer for a few minutes, then add cream and fresh butter. Before serving add chopped parsley.

CAULIFLOWER SOUP WITH BREAD DUMPLINGS

3 pints water
1 cauliflower
2 oz. fat
2 oz. flour

salt, pinch of mace
Dumplings:
1 egg
3 oz. breadcrumbs

1 teaspoon butter
little milk
parsley

Boil cauliflower in salt water. When nearly soft remove from pot, thicken liquid with light roux made from fat and flour, add mace and cook for 20 minutes. Then boil dumplings in soup and finally add cauliflower fleurettes. To make dumplings, first, moisten breadcrumbs with milk. Cream butter, egg and salt, add breadcrumbs and parsley. Form dough into tiny dumplings and cook in soup for 3—5 minutes.

SOUR MILK SOUP

2 pints water
1 pint sour milk or
  cream

4 eggs
1 oz. flour

few caraway seeds
little salt
1 oz. butter

Make a light roux from flour and butter, dilute with cold water, whisk well and cook for about 20 minutes. Mix in sour cream or milk, caraway seeds and salt, break in one egg after another. Break eggs just above surface and allow to slip into boiling soup, carefully using fork to cover yolk with white, so that they remain whole. Serve with hot potatoes which have been boiled in their jackets and then peeled.

CARAWAY SOUP

1 heaped teaspoon
  caraway seeds

1½ tablespoons flour
3 pints boiling water
2 tablespoons butter

8 oz. macaroni
salt and pepper

Heat the butter in a large saucepan on the stove. When it is melted, blend in the flour smoothly, stirring all the time. When it is getting brown, stir in the caraway seeds. Boil the water separately, and slowly pour it into the butter and flour, always stirring. Simmer for 30 minutes. Get a saucepan of salted water boiling rapidly. Break the macaroni into small pieces and throw it into the boiling water. Cook for 10 minutes. Drain. Strain the soup through a fine strainer or sieve. Return it to the saucepan. Throw the macaroni into the soup. Bring to boiling point and serve at once. *(Illustrated in Plate 55.)*

OATMEAL SOUP

3 pints water or stock	2 tablespoons grated	pinch of mace
2 tablespoons root	cheese	salt
vegetables	4 tablespoons oatmeal	½ pint milk (optional)

Clean vegetables and cut into pieces. Cover oatmeal and vegetables with water and boil for about 30 minutes. Pass through a sieve and dilute with water to bring up to 3 pints again. Add salt and a pinch of mace. Serve with grated cheese. A cup of milk may be added to this soup.

PEA SOUP WITH FRANKFURTER

3 pints water	1 oz. fat	1 clove garlic
3 oz. dried peas or	1 oz. flour	pinch paprika
lentils	½ onion	salt
	1 frankfurter	

Soak peas overnight in unsalted water. Next day cook in the same water until soft enough to pass through a hair-sieve. Make a light roux from the fat and flour, pour the purée over, stir well and cook for 15 minutes. Then add grated onion, crushed garlic, salt and a pinch of red pepper. Before serving add frankfurter, cut into small rounds, or pieces of smoked sausage.

CREAMY BRAIN SOUP

3 pints water	2 oz. flour	3 oz. root vegetables
1 brain (calf)	½ onion	parsley
3 oz. butter	1 egg yolk	salt

Boil cleaned and diced vegetables in water, thicken with light roux of 2 oz. butter and flour, and cook for about 30 minutes. Lightly fry blanched and skinned brain in remaining butter with chopped onion. Add to sieved soup with beaten yolk, season with salt and spoonful of chopped parsley.

FRESH PORK SOUP

3 pints water	2 oz. root vegetables	1 oz. groats
8 oz. pig's head (fresh	handful of dried	salt
from kill)	mushrooms	drop of meat extract

Wash meat and boil in salt water together with vegetables and mushrooms until soft. Take out meat, remove from bone and cut into small pieces. Add meat to soup with groats and meat extract and boil for a few minutes. Serve with a slice of black bread.

QUICK SOUP FROM EGG ROUX

3 pints water	3 tablespoons grated	chopped parsley
2 eggs	root vegetables	salt
1 tablespoon plain flour	1 oz. fat	meat extract (optional)

Melt fat, add flour and make light roux. Add 2 beaten eggs and stir until the mixture curdles. Pour on cold water and beat well. Add grated vegetables, salt and cook for about 15 minutes. A teaspoon of meat extract may be added with finely chopped parsley.

CREAM OF VEAL SOUP WITH PEAS

3 pints water	8 oz. fresh or frozen	bread rolls
1 lb. neck of veal	green peas	fat for frying
2 oz. plain flour	2 oz. butter	salt

Simmer veal in salted water until soft. Remove sinews and gristle and cut into small pieces. Add a light roux made from the flour and butter to the liquid, whisk well and boil for a few minutes. Return meat to soup and add peas, again boiling for a few minutes. Serve with fried croûtons made from bread rolls.

BEEF SOUP WITH CABBAGE AND RICE

3 pints water	1 large cabbage	salt and pepper
1 lb. beef		2 oz. rice

Pour boiling water over beef and simmer for about 3 hours. Add only boiling water during cooking so that it does not go off the boil. Then strain soup, cut meat into small pieces and return to pan. Season and add finely shredded cabbage and rice. Boil for about 5 minutes uncovered to allow pungent cabbage smell to escape.

SMOKED MEAT SOUP

3 pints stock from ham or smoked meat	1 oz. lard about 4 oz. root vegetables	2 tablespoons semolina
1 oz. plain flour	parsley	1 frankfurter

Make light brown roux from fat removed from stock, lard and flour, pour over stock and whisk well. Add diced vegetables and boil for a short time. Then add semolina, small pieces of frankfurter or chopped smoked meat and finely chopped parsley. Do not salt soup as stock is salty enough.

YEAST SOUP

3 pints water   small pieces of carrot,   parsley
3 oz. baker's yeast   celeriac, parsley root   salt
2 oz. plain flour   and onion   2 oz. butter
   Pasta: 1 egg, 3 tablespoons milk, about 3 oz. fine semolina, salt

Fry onion and yeast in butter. When yeast begins to brown at edges, sprinkle on flour, mix and pour on water. Add finely chopped vegetables, season with salt, whisk well and cook for 20 minutes. Now prepare pasta. Beat egg in a little milk, add semolina, a little at a time and salt. Using a teaspoon drop small pieces of dough into soup and cook for about 5 minutes. This soup is rich in vitamin B2.

CREAMY SMOKED MEAT SOUP

3 pints stock from   1 oz. plain flour   2 slices bread
  smoked meat   1 gill sour cream   a little fat for frying
1 oz. lard   2 egg yolks   parsley

Make light roux from lard and flour, dilute with stock and cook for about 30 minutes. Then add cream mixed with yolks and warm in soup. Do not reboil. Cut bread into small strips or cubes and quickly fry in fat to make them crisp. Place a little on plates together with finely chopped parsley and pour hot soup over. Do not salt the soup—the stock is salty enough.

CREAMY MUSHROOM SOUP

Kulajda

2 pints sour cream   2 oz. plain flour   a few caraway seeds
1 pint water   8 oz. fresh mushrooms vinegar
4 large potatoes   1 tablespoon dill   salt
                2—3 eggs

Clean and cut up the mushrooms and simmer in water with caraway seeds. After about 10 minutes add flour, mixed with cream, and diced raw potatoes. Cook for about 15 minutes. Before serving add 2—3 well beaten eggs, salt, a few drops of vinegar and chopped dill. *Illustrated in Plate 28.)*

QUICK SOUP FROM MINCED MEAT

3 pints water   about 4 oz. root   parsley
8 oz. minced beef   vegetables   1 meat cube or few
handful of rice   salt   drops of meat extract

25. Potato Soup, Czechoslovakia (p.145)

26. Onion Soup, France (p.206)

27. Champignons Flambés, France (p.256)

Place cleaned and diced vegetables and minced meat in pot, cover with cold water and simmer for about 25 minutes. Add salt, meat cube and at last minute, finely chopped parsley. A handful of rice may be added before simmering.

POTATO SOUP

2 pints water	1 teaspoon butter	*Garnish:*
6 medium sized	chopped parsley	1 oz. flour
potatoes	1 egg yolk	1 egg
1 pint milk	salt	

First prepare the garnish. Work egg with flour and a little water to a stiff dough, then grate on to a clean towel and leave to dry. Boil potatoes in water, pass through sieve and add milk. Add salt to taste and throw in garnish. Boil about 5 minutes. Before serving whisk in fresh yolk, and add butter and parsley. Do not boil again. *(Illustrated in Plate 25.)*

SOUP FROM SPRING LEAVES

3 pints water	2 handfuls chopped	1 egg yolk
2 oz. plain flour	leaves (tansy, ground	1 bread roll
2 oz. fat	ivy, strawberry	fat for frying
salt	leaves, nettle)	

Make light roux from fat and flour and pour over water or stock, whisk well and boil for 15 minutes. Add chopped green leaves, season and allow to come to boil and then break in fresh yolk. Serve with fried croûtons. This soup is usually served early in spring, around Easter.

LETTUCE SALAD WITH BACON
(MORAVIAN STYLE)

2 lettuces	1 egg	vinegar and sugar to
salt	1 oz. bacon	taste
		water

Wash the lettuces, place in a bowl and pour on the marinade made from a little vinegar diluted with water, salt and sugar. Hard-boil the egg and when cold cut into slices. Dice the bacon and fry lightly. Serve the salad garnished with the slices of egg and the warm bacon (the latter should not be hot or the lettuce will go limp).

CUCUMBER SALAD

1 large cucumber	3 tablespoons oil	sugar to taste
salt	1 tablespoon vinegar	dill or garlic
	lemon juice	

Peel the cucumber, slice and pour on marinade made as follows. Mix the oil and vinegar or lemon juice. Season with salt and sweeten. Add a chopped garlic clove or finely chopped dill. Mix well together. A cup of thick sour cream may be used instead of the oil.

SIMPLE POTATO SALAD

2 lb. potatoes	1 paprika	1 tablespoon French
2 eggs		mustard
2 pickled gherkins	*Marinade:*	a little vinegar
1 large onion	4 tablespoons oil	pinch salt and sugar

Cook the potatoes in their skins, then peel and allow to cool. Cut into slices, mix with the chopped onion, gherkins, paprika and sweet-sour marinade. Arrange slices of hard-boiled eggs on the top of the salad.

BOHEMIAN EGGS

6 eggs	4 oz. onion skins	1½ teaspoons caraway
1½ tablespoons salt	1¼ pints water	seeds
	6 peppercorns	

Hard-boil the eggs. Place them under a running tap of cold water, then tap the shells firmly all over to crack them. Place the peeled eggs in a deep fireproof dish. Boil the water, salt, onion skins, peppercorns and caraway seeds together for 5 minutes. Pour over the eggs. Stand in a cold place overnight, and serve the eggs cut in quarters.

FRIED SOFT-BOILED EGGS

4 eggs	1 egg and 3 oz.	salt
4 oz. fat	breadcrumbs for	1 oz. flour
	coating	

Soft-boil the four eggs until the white is firm and then remove the shell. Allow to cool, then dip in seasoned flour, egg and breadcrumbs and fry till golden in hot fat. Serve with raw or cooked vegetable salad. The eggs may also be wrapped in slices of ham, salami or very thin fillets of meat and then dipped in flour, egg and breadcrumbs and fried.

146

LOST EGGS

4 eggs	2 oz. butter	½ pint Madeira
1 onion	1 oz. truffles	nutmeg
salt	½ oz. flour	parsley
3 oz. mushrooms	½ pint beef stock	3 tablespoons vinegar
1½ pints water		

Bring water with the vinegar to the boil. Then break one egg after another into a ladle and carefully add to the water which has been removed from the stove for a few minutes. Using a fork, scoop the white close up to the yolk and again place on the stove. The eggs are cooked in about 3 minutes. Chop the onion and truffles into small pieces and fry in the butter. When the onion begins to brown add the flour and then dilute with the stock. Whisk the sauce well and cook for a few minutes. Add the seasoning, Madeira, sliced fresh mushrooms and chopped parsley. Pour this sauce over the eggs and serve with potatoes, rice or pasta.

BATTER PUDDING FOR BEEF BOUILLON

3 egg whites	1 tablespoon fresh	fat for greasing
1 tablespoon butter	mushrooms	salt
3 tablespoons bread-	1 tablespoon chopped	
crumbs	parsley	

Melt butter and allow to cool, then add to whisked egg whites alternately with breadcrumbs. Finally add chopped mushrooms, which have been simmered for about 10 minutes, little salt and finely chopped parsley. Pour mixture into baking tin, which has been greased with unmelted fat and sprinkled with breadcrumbs, and bake in moderate oven until golden brown. Cut finished pudding into small cubes, place a little on each plate and pour on hot bouillon.

SHAGGY DUMPLINGS FROM RAW POTATOES

1½ lb. potatoes	8 oz. fine semolina	salt
1 egg		2 oz. lard or dripping

Peel the potatoes and grate them finely or pulp them in an emulsifier. Drain off part of the water. Mix the pulp with salt, beaten egg and the fine semolina to a soft dough. Using a spoon dipped in hot water cut out knobs of dough and throw them into boiling water, taking care that they do not stick to the bottom of the pot. Boil for about 8 minutes, remove from the water and lightly fry in the melted lard or dripping. Shaggy dumplings are served with pork or bacon and hot sauerkraut or with roast pork.

OMELETTE NOODLES FOR BEEF SOUP

2 oz. flour	1 egg	salt
1 gill milk		fat for frying

Beat egg into milk, slowly add to flour. Season. Fry thin omelettes in greased pan. Cut omelettes crosswise into thin strips. Add to beef bouillon. The strips can also be fried quickly again to make them crisp.

LIVER DUMPLINGS FOR BEEF SOUP

4 oz. calves' or ox liver	about 3 oz. bread-crumbs	1 clove garlic
1 tablespoon butter		salt, pinch of pepper
		1 egg

Beat together butter and salt, add egg, finely minced liver, crushed garlic, pinch of pepper and enough breadcrumbs to form small round dumplings. Boil them in beef soup or bouillon for about 5 minutes. If fewer breadcrumbs are added to the liver, the mixture can be pressed through a coarse-grained sieve to give liver rice.

CZECH BREAD DUMPLINGS

1 lb. coarse flour or	about 1 pint milk	2 egg yolks
8 oz. plain flour and	4 bread rolls (about	$\frac{1}{2}$ teaspoon salt
8 oz. fine semolina	7 oz.)	1 teaspoon butter

Weigh the flour into a deep mixing bowl, add the salt and milk mixed with the yolks. Beat the dough with a wooden spoon until it is soft and bubbly. Cut the rolls into cubes (rolls a day old are best), lightly fry them in a small piece of butter and add them to the dough. Flour a board, turn part of the dough on to it and form it into a roll. Throw the roll into boiling water in a large pot so that it has enough room to float. When the water again comes to the boil, add another roll. The dumplings should boil for about 30 minutes. Remove from the water and cut into slices. These bread dumplings are served, for example, with roast pork, goose, duck, chicken in paprika sauce and with all meat dishes having thick sauces, especially creamy sauces.

DUMPLINGS FROM COOKED POTATOES

1½ lb. potatoes	salt	8 oz. coarse flour or
2 eggs	2 tablespoons semolina	4 oz. plain flour and
2 tablespoons vinegar		4 oz. fine semolina

Use potatoes which have been boiled and peeled the day before. Grate them and add a little salt, the eggs and vinegar, semolina and flour. Knead the dough till it is firm. Do not leave it to stand or it will get too soft. Form the dough into four rolls and throw into boiling salted water. After a few minutes they should rise to the surface. Cook them for about 20 minutes, then carefully take them out of the water and cut into slices with a sharp knife. Serve with roast meat.

POTATO DUMPLINGS WITH SMOKED MEAT

1½ lb. potatoes	1 egg	3 oz. butter or
8 oz. smoked meat	8 oz. fine semolina	dripping
	salt	flour

Boil the potatoes, then peel them and mash them on a board. Add the egg, salt and semolina and knead into a stiff, elastic dough. Flour the board, roll out the dough and cut into small squares. Finely chop the cooked smoked meat and place a little on each piece of dough. Join up the corners of each square and form into a small dumpling. Cook in boiling water for about 10 minutes. Drain off the water, prick with a fork, place on a plate and pour over the melted butter or dripping. Serve with hot cabbage or a vegetable salad.

RICH DUMPLINGS

1 lb. coarse flour or	4 oz. butter	1 teaspoon fat for
8 oz. plain flour and	4 eggs	frying
8 oz. fine semolina	½ pint milk	½ teaspoon salt
	7 oz. bread rolls	

Cream the butter, salt and egg yolks then alternately add the flour and milk and beat the dough. Fry the diced rolls in the fat and when cold add to the dough. Finally fold in the stiffly whisked egg whites. Place the dough in a damp greased napkin, stand in a bowl while tying up to make it round. Then cook it in the napkin in a large pot for about 1 hour. The dumpling must be able to move freely in the water so that it can swell. When cooked, carefully turn on to a board and cut into slices.

SEMOLINA DUMPLINGS

8 oz. semolina	½ pint milk	salt
2 eggs		3 oz. bread rolls

Boil the semolina in milk seasoned with salt, stirring well. When the mixture thickens, remove from stove and allow to cool. Add the eggs and diced rolls. Turn the dough into a damp napkin and tie just above the dough. Cook in boiling water for about 45 minutes. Then carefully turn on to a board and cut into slices.

SHKUBÁNKY FRY

shkubánky dough from 2 lb. potatoes (see p. 176)	1 egg breadcrumbs	flour 5 oz. fat for frying

Form small cakes from the shkubánky dough, dip in flour, egg and breadcrumbs and fry till golden brown. These are a filling accompaniment to spinach or peas.

MARINATED EEL

1 eel (about 2 lb.)	3 tablespoons oil	lemon
¼ pint mayonnaise	2 tablespoons flour	salt and pepper

Skin the eel, season with salt and pepper, dredge with flour and fry quickly in the oil till golden brown. Then cut it into small portions and pour over the marinade made from the mayonnaise, the remains of the oil in which it has been fried and a little water. Add a little lemon juice and more salt if necessary. Leave the eel in the marinade in a cool place till the next day.

CARP WITH ANCHOVIES

4 portions carp (about 2 lb.)	2 anchovies	lemon
	1 teaspoon plain flour	pepper
3 oz. butter	1 gill white wine	salt

Fry the fish in part of the butter. Beat the rest of the butter with the finely chopped anchovies. Remove the fish from the pan, add the flour, anchovy butter, seasoning, a few drops lemon juice and the wine and cook for a few minutes. Return the fish to the piquant sauce and serve with potatoes.

DEVILLED CARP

A Christmas Dish

6 TO 8 SERVINGS

3 lb. carp	1 pint brown ale	1 tablespoon sugar
2 oz. butter	1 tablespoon	2 tablespoons vinegar
1 carrot	currant jelly or	1 bay leaf
piece of celeriac	handful of prunes	5 peppercorns
½ small parsley root	1 tablespoon chopped	pinch allspice
½ onion	almonds	pinch thyme
8 oz. grated gingerbread	1 tablespoon sultanas	lemon rind salt

Keep the blood from a freshly caught carp and dilute with the vinegar. Clean the fish, cut into portions and fry in the butter. Remove the fish and prepare the sauce. Fry the vegetables in the butter, add the herbs and seasoning, grated gingerbread, blood and vinegar, beer and lemon rind and cook all together till the sauce thickens. Pass it through a sieve, add the redcurrant jelly, sultanas and peeled and chopped almonds, and a little sugar, vinegar and salt to taste. Return the fish to this sweet-sour sauce to heat through. The best results are obtained if the fish and sauce are prepared the day before and then heated up.

ROAST PORK

2 lb. pork from neck or loin	salt water	1 teaspoon caraway seeds

Wipe the meat and if it is very fat, nick the skin slightly. Season all over with salt, place on a baking tin and sprinkle with caraway seeds. Add a little water at first to prevent the joint from getting too brown on the surface and too dry. When the fat begins to run, baste well so that it browns gently. Roast pork is traditionally served with dumplings and stewed cabbage (see pp. 148, 162). The meat may also be roasted with a clove of garlic (farm fashion) and then served with cabbage and potato dumplings.

PIG'S KIDNEYS

4 kidneys (1 lb.)	1 teaspoon plain flour	2 pinches caraway seeds
3 tablespoons oil	1 onion	
salt	water	pinch pepper

Cut each kidney lengthwise, remove fat and wash well to remove pungent smell. Then cut it into slices. Heat oil in a large iron frying pan, add kidneys, caraway seeds and pepper (do not salt) and dry quickly for about 8 minutes. Then stir in a teaspoon plain flour, a little water and cook. Season with salt before serving. Serve with rice, potatoes or a salted roll.

MUTTON RIBS WITH MUSTARD

4 mutton ribs	1 tablespoon French mustard	ground pepper
2 tablespoons oil		salt
	½ teaspoon plain flour	water

Cut the ribs at the edges and fry quickly on both sides in oil. Dredge with a little plain flour, add salt, pepper, mustard and a little water and allow to cook until the meat is tender. Pour the strained sauce over the ribs and serve with rice.

STUFFED BREAST OF PORK

2 lb. fat breast pork	1 gill milk	1 oz. breadcrumbs
Stuffing:	1 oz. fat	parsley
2 bread rolls (3 oz.)	3 eggs	salt

Wipe the meat, season with salt and make a cavity in it. Beat the fat with the egg yolks and salt, add diced rolls which have been soaked in milk, the finely chopped parsley and finally the stiffly whisked egg whites. If necessary, add a few breadcrumbs to make it stiffer. Fill the meat with the mixture, sew up and place on a baking tin with the stuffed side upwards. Cook in a moderate oven, adding a little hot water from time to time. The fat soon starts to flow from the meat which should be basted frequently with the fat and water mixture so that it browns well. Serve with boiled potatoes or dumplings and cabbage. Cold roast breast is served with potato salad.

MUTTON IN MARJORAM

2 lb. boned blade end of shoulder	3 oz. chopped carrot, celeriac	1 chopped onion
1 tablespoon plain flour	and parsley root water	1 teaspoon marjoram salt
		4 oz. butter

Wipe the meat, cut into large pieces and fry gently in butter together with vegetables. When the meat is nearly soft, allow the juice to evaporate, dredge with plain flour and add a little water. Mix well and cook for a few minutes. When the sauce is nearly ready, add the marjoram and season with salt. Serve with potatoes.

BRNO SCHNITZEL

4 slices veal	2 oz. butter	1 teaspoon fine
2 oz. ham	1 tablespoon plain	breadcrumbs
2 eggs	flour	salt
1 lb. green peas	1 tablespoon milk	4 oz. fat for frying

Clean the meat, beat lightly with a mallet and season with salt. Scramble one egg in a pan together with the milk, butter, green peas and chopped ham. Spread a little of the mixture on each slice of veal, fold the meat in half and secure with a small skewer. Then carefully dip the meat in flour, egg and breadcrumbs and fry in hot fat.

MINCED VEAL SCHNITZEL

1 lb. veal	1 tablespoon plain	1 tablespoon parsley
3 oz. butter	flour	salt
	pinch mace	2 tablespoons water

Make a roux from a tablespoon of butter and the flour, dilute with 2 tablespoons water and boil for a few minutes. The sauce should be very thick. Add the minced meat, season with salt, parsley and mace. With wet hands form the mixture into small flat cakes and fry quickly on both sides in remaining butter.

VEAL ROLLS

4 slices veal	1 tablespoon flour	lemon rind
2 oz. bacon	1 gill sour cream	salt
1 oz. fat	water	parsley

Wipe meat, beat lightly with mallet and season with salt. Finely chop the bacon, parsley and lemon rind and place on slices of meat. Roll up and secure with thread or skewer. Dip rolls in flour and quickly fry in fat, add a little water and simmer, When tender, pour cream mixed with flour over meat and allow to simmer for a few minutes. Serve with potatoes or dumplings.

FRIED BEEF CAKES

1 lb. minced beef	3 tablespoons plain	1 onion
2 oz. fat	flour	salt, pepper, French
8 slices black bread	1 tablespoon water	mustard

Mix the water and flour into the minced beef. Season with salt and pepper and leave for 1 hour. Then, using wet hands, form the mixture into small flat cakes, fry quickly in hot fat. Place the cakes on slices of black bread smeared with mustard and decorate with chopped raw onion.

ROAST MINCED MEAT

1 lb. beef	3 bread rolls (about	1 onion
8 oz. pork	4 oz.)	fat for frying
2 oz. bacon	breadcrumbs	salt and pepper
	2 eggs	water

Wipe beef and pork and mince finely. Chop onion and fry in a little fat until golden brown. Cut bacon into cubes and heat slightly until it has glassy effect. Put meat, onion and bacon into bowl, add beaten eggs, rolls which have been soaked in water, salt, pepper and enough breadcrumbs to form a firm roll. To prevent the roll burning at the bottom it may be placed on a grid. Smooth the surface with wet hands or brush with egg white. Cook in moderate oven for about 1 hour, adding a little water from time to time. Cut into slices and serve with potatoes and salad or compôte.

MEAT PUDDING

1 lb. meat	1 gill milk	ground pepper
3 eggs	breadcrumbs	lemon rind
2 oz. bacon	1 teaspoon brandy	salt
	2 oz. butter	

Any kind of minced meat can be used (beef, veal, poultry, lamb or mutton). Add the egg yolks, chopped bacon, salt, pepper and brandy and a little grated lemon rind. Mix well. If the mixture is too stiff add a little milk, if too soft add a few breadcrumbs. Finally fold in stiffly beaten whites. Turn into a greased and breadcrumbed pudding bowl and steam for about 1 hour. Turn out and cut into slices. Serve with hot vegetables or potatoes and a vegetable salad.

BEEF ROLLS

1 lb. beef (4 slices from leg)	1 tablespoon plain flour	French mustard salt and pepper
4 thin slices bacon (3 oz.)	2 pickled cucumbers	celeriac, carrot
	1 onion	(optional)
	2 oz. dripping	stock or water

Wipe the slices of meat, season with salt and pepper and lightly spread with mustard. On each slice place a thin piece of bacon, chopped cucumber and onion. Finely chopped celeriac and a small piece of carrot may also be added. Carefully roll up each piece and secure with thread or a small skewer. First fry each roll on all sides and then add a little and sprinkle a little flour on the fat. Add a little water or stock, stir well and boil for a few minutes. Serve with rice, potatoes or macaroni.

PORK CUTLETS WITH CARAWAY SEEDS

1 lb. pork (4 cutlets)	1 tablespoon plain flour	salt, water
1 oz. lard or dripping		caraway seeds

Wipe the cutlets, beat gently with a mallet, cut the edges to prevent curling, season with salt and fry quickly in dripping. Then add a little water, a few caraway seeds and simmer until tender. When soft, dredge with flour, add salt and a cup of water and cook for a few minutes. Serve with dumplings (see p. 148).

CUTLETS WITH TOMATOES

Prepare in the same way as for cutlets with caraway seeds (above) but add a few sliced tomatoes and paprikas when simmering.

CUTLETS WITH FRENCH MUSTARD

Prepare as for cutlets with caraway seeds but add 2 teaspoons of French mustard and some cream before serving.

BRAIN WITH EGGS

calves' or pigs' brains (about 6 oz.)	1 tablespoon butter	parsley
	1 onion	salt
	4 eggs	

Blanch the brains. Fry the chopped onion in fat until a golden brown, add brains and cook gently for about 10 minutes. Then add the beaten eggs, season with salt and stir until the eggs curdle. Serve with chopped parsley sprinkled on top.

OX TONGUE WITH ANCHOVIES

1 small ox tongue (8 oz.)	3 oz. butter	a little anchovy paste
2 oz. bacon	salt	1 teaspoon bread-crumbs

Wipe the tongue and cook in salted water till tender. Then skin it and cut into slices. Beat a little over half the butter with the anchovy paste and smear on each slice of tongue. Sprinkle with a few fine breadcrumbs, dot with butter and place in a greased fireproof dish or baking tin. Bake in a moderate oven until the surface turns slightly brown. Serve with potatoes.

SHELLED DEVILS

1 lb. veal	1 teaspoon plain flour	8 oz. grated cheese
1 calf's brain (5 oz.)	1 onion	8 oz. green peas
3 beaten eggs	1 teaspoon bread-crumbs	1 lemon
3 oz. butter		salt, water

Fry the finely chopped veal and onion very slowly in part of the fat till the meat is soft. Sprinkle with the flour, then pour on a little water and cook for a few minutes. Blanch the brain, fry gently in a little fat and add to the sauce. Season the mixture with salt, a little grated lemon rind and juice and add the eggs and cooked green peas. Grease some shells, or small fireproof dishes, and sprinkle with breadcrumbs. Place a little of the mixture on each, sprinkle with grated cheese and dot with fresh butter. Cook in a hot oven for about 10 minutes. Serve with a slice of lemon and white bread.

VEAL STEW WITH DUMPLINGS

1 lb. veal	a small piece each of	*Dumplings:*
2 oz. butter	carrot, celeriac and	2 egg yolks
2 tablespoons plain	parsley root	2 oz. butter
flour	lemon rind and juice	4 tablespoons milk
½ onion	a pinch of mace	8 oz. breadcrumbs
parsley	salt, water	salt

Clean and cut up the vegatables and fry in the fat. Add the meat, cut into small pieces and seasoned with salt, and simmer until tender. Then dredge with flour, add water and boil for a few minutes. Season this thick sauce with grated lemon rind and juice, mace and finely chopped parsley. Prepare the dumplings in a bowl. First beat the fat, yolks and salt and then add the crumbs soaked in milk. Form into little balls and throw into boiling salted water. Cook for about 5 minutes. Remove from water, allow to cool and then add to meat and sauce. Cooked cauliflower fleurettes may also be added.

MINCED BEEFSTEAKS WITH TOMATO SAUCE

1 lb. minced beef	2 oz. bacon	1 teaspoon flour
1 egg	2 oz. fat	breadcrumbs
1 onion	1 small can tomato	salt
	purée	water

Finely mince the meat and onion, season with salt, mix with the chopped bacon and the egg and thicken with a few breadcrumbs. Form into small flat rounds, fry quickly in fat, then add a little water and simmer for about 20 minutes. Then remove the beefsteaks, sprinkle the juice with flour, add the purée and a little water and cook well. Strain the sauce over the beefsteaks and serve with rice or potatoes.

ZNOJMO GOULASH

2 lb. beef (shin)	1 tablespoon plain	pinch pepper
2 oz. dripping or lard	flour	salt
1 onion	water	2 pickled cucumbers

Wipe meat, cut into small pieces and season with salt and pepper. Fry the finely chopped onion in the fat, add the meat and fry quickly. Then add a little water and simmer until tender. When the liquid evaporates, sprinkle on the flour, allow to brown slightly, then add a little water and cook well. Add the diced cucumbers to the sauce and serve with dumplings or potatoes. Chopped tomatoes and paprikas may be added instead of the cucumbers.

STEAKS IN CAPER SAUCE

1 lb. steak (4 steaks)
2 oz. bacon, chopped
1 oz. lard or dripping
water

2 tablespoons flour
1 gill sour cream
2 tablespoons capers
salt and pepper

2 tablespoons
French mustard
1 chopped onion

Wipe the steaks, remove all fat, nick the sides to prevent them curling and beat lightly with a mallet. Season with salt and pepper and sprinkle with half the flour. Fry quickly on both sides with onion and bacon. Add mustard, capers and a little water, cover and simmer till tender. Take the meat out of the sauce and allow the latter to brown, then add cream mixed with the flour and boil. Return steaks to sauce and serve with dumplings or potatoes.

PIQUANT BEEFSTEAK

1 lb. beefsteak
 (4 steaks)

2 tablespoons oil

salt
3 cloves garlic

Wash the steaks, remove all fat and skin, and beat lightly with a small mallet or the handle of a knife. Put back into shape, then rub the surface with crushed garlic and salt and fry quickly on both sides. Serve with fried potatoes or rice.

VEAL SCHNITZEL IN BATTER

4 slices veal
2 eggs
4 oz. fat for frying

2 tablespoons plain
flour

1 oz. grated cheese
parsley
salt

Wipe the slices of meat and beat lightly with a mallet. To prepare the batter, mix the beaten eggs with the flour, salt, finely chopped parsley and grated cheese. Dip the meat in the batter and quickly fry on both sides in hot fat. Serve with potatoes and vegetables or with potato salad.

BEEF ROULADE

2 lb. beef
1 lb. minced pork

1 tablespoon French
mustard
2 oz. dripping or lard

1 onion
salt

Buy a flat piece of topside, wipe and beat well with a mallet. Season with salt and spread with French mustard and minced pork, mixed with chopped onion. Roll and tie up. Brown quickly in fat and then put in oven and roast until tender, basting from time to time. Cut the meat crosswise into slices and serve with dumplings or potatoes.

PIG'S HEAD WITH HORSERADISH

2 lb. meat from pig's head, tongue and heart	piece horseradish French mustard	salt water

Boil a piece of pig's head, tongue and heart in salt water for about 2 hours until soft. Place on a plate, season well with salt and serve hot with mustard or horseradish. Use the stock for a soup.

BREAST OF FATTENED GOOSE WITH GARLIC

1 breast (about 1 lb.) goose	2 oz. dripping salt	2 cloves garlic

If the goose is too fat, the fat should be stripped off. A whole layer of fat and skin is thus obtained which can be rendered down. Remove the meat from the breast, rub with crushed garlic and salt, and place in the oven with some dripping. Cook until tender and serve with rice.

GOOSE GIBLETS WITH CAULIFLOWER

giblets from 1 goose 1 oz. plain flour salt	1 oz. butter 3 oz. vegetables (carrot, celeriac, parsley root)	1 cauliflower pinch mace lemon rind water

Clean the giblets and place in boiling water. Add the chopped vegetables and simmer till tender. Make a light roux in a pot, pour over the stock from the giblets, mix well and cook for about 20 minutes. Season with salt, a pinch of mace and lemon rind. Boil the cauliflower separately. Remove the meat from the bones, cut into small pieces and heat together with cauliflower fleurettes in the sauce. Serve with noodles or rice.

VENISON SCHNITZEL AU NATUREL

4 slices from haunch of venison (1 lb.) 1 tablespoon oil pepper salt	*Piquant butter:* 1 tablespoon butter ½ small onion 1 anchovy piece pickled cucumber Worcester sauce (see p. 108)	½ teaspoon capers parsley small piece lemon rind small piece garlic (optional)

Finely chop all the ingredients for the piquant butter and beat into the butter. Form the mixture into a long roll and leave in a cold place to harden. Beat the slices of venison with a mallet, wipe them with oil and secure with small skewers to prevent them curling during cooking. Season with salt and a little pepper and fry them quickly in oil on both sides. Place the hot schnitzels on a plate, decorate with a slice of piquant butter and serve very hot garnished with potatoes. The butter melts on the meat and gives it a piquant taste.

ROAST VENISON AU NATUREL

2 lb. haunch of venison	3 oz. butter	2 juniper berries
	flour	salt
2 oz. bacon	water	1 onion

Wash the meat and thread strips of bacon through the flesh. Fry rapidly in butter then add the chopped onion, salt and juniper berries and cook in the oven, adding a little water at intervals. Remove the meat when tender, dredge the liquid with flour and mix well. Cook for a few minutes. Serve with potatoes, rice or dumplings.

ROAST GOOSE OR DUCK

1 goose (about 6 lb.)	hot water	1 teaspoon caraway seeds
salt		

Remove all feathers and hairs, carefully clean and season all over with salt. Sprinkle with caraway seeds and place on a baking tin. Add a few spoons of hot water before putting in the oven so that the skin can steam and give off fat, particularly if the goose is very fat. Roast slowly and when basting prick the surface to let the fat flow out better. First roast with the back upwards and then turn over. When the goose is tender and a good golden colour, remove from the oven, cut into portions and serve with dumplings (see p. 148) and stewed cabbage (see p. 162). A young goose takes about 1 hour to roast, an older, fattened one 2 hours or more.

STUFFED ROAST KID

1 front portion of kid (4 lb.)	*Stuffing:* salt	2 bread rolls (3 oz.) 1 gill milk
5 oz. butter	3 egg whites	parsley
1 tablespoon bread-crumbs	2 egg yolks 1 oz. butter	salt

Clean the meat, rinse and wipe with a paper napkin. Carefully make a cavity for the stuffing. Cut the rolls into small pieces and sprinkle with milk. Cream the butter with the yolks and salt, add the moist rolls, finely chopped parsley and finally the stiffly whisked whites. Stuff the cavity and sew up with thread. Place the meat, stuffed side upwards, on melted butter, sprinkle with breadcrumbs, and cook in the oven, basting from time to time. Serve with potatoes or potato salad.

CARROTS STEWED WITH PORK

1 lb. carrots	½ onion salt	1 teaspoon plain flour for thickening water

Wash the meat and boil in salt water to which half an onion has been added. Clean the carrots, cut into small pieces about the size of thick matchsticks, place in a pan with two or three spoonfuls of stock from the meat and simmer till soft. Then dredge with flour, add a little water and simmer for a few minutes. Cut the meat into portions, add to the carrots and again simmer for a while. Serve with potatoes, potato dumplings or potato cakes.

POTATO ROLL WITH SMOKED MEAT

2 lb. potatoes	3 oz. dripping or lard	1 onion
8 oz. smoked meat	2 tablespoons bread-	3 oz. butter
1 lb. fine semolina	crumbs	salt
	1 egg	

Use potatoes boiled the previous day. Grate them on to a board, sprinkle with semolina and salt, add egg and work into a dough. Carefully roll out, sprinkle with fat, fried onion, finely chopped cooked meat and a few fried breadcrumbs. Carefully roll up, place on a wet serviette and tie up the ends. Place the roll in a large pot of boiling water and cook for 45 minutes. Then remove roll from serviette and cut into slices with a sharp knife or wire. Place a few slices on each plate, sprinkle with melted butter and fried onion. Serve with hot spinach or cabbage or with vegetable salad.

POTATO CRISPS

3 oz. dripping or butter	2 lb. potatoes	5 cloves garlic salt

Scrub the potatoes and cut them into thin slices. Arrange on a baking tin and bake in a moderate oven. When they are slightly browned on one side carefully turn them over and brown on the other side. Crush the garlic in a bowl together with some salt and dripping or butter. Add the potatoes and shake well. Serve hot with tea or as an accompaniment to vegetables.

POTATO PANCAKES

2 lb. potatoes	5 oz. lard for frying	1 clove garlic
1 egg	a little milk	salt
	4 oz. plain flour	

28. Creamy Mushroom Soup, Czechoslovakia (p.144)

29. Fish and Chips, Britain (p.92)

Peel the potatoes and grate them finely. Then season with salt, sprinkle on a little milk and add the egg and enough flour to make a thick batter. Ladle small amounts into hot lard, pat out into pancakes with a knife, and fry quickly on both sides till golden. Remove from pan and smear thinly with crushed garlic. Chopped chives or a pinch of marjoram are sometimes added to the batter.

POTATOES FILLED WITH EGGS

8 large potatoes	3 oz. breadcrumbs	anchovy paste
3 eggs	2 oz. butter	parsley

Bake the potatoes in their jackets, then carefully cut the tops open and remove the soft potato inside. Hard-boil the eggs, beat the yolks with the butter and a little anchovy paste, add the finely chopped whites, breadcrumbs, chopped parsley, and the mashed potato. Fill the jackets with the mixture, place in a greased fireproof dish, sprinkle the surface with fat and bake in the oven. Serve with vegetables or salad.

MUSHROOM PUDDING

3 eggs	½ pint milk	3 oz. butter
3 bread rolls (sliced)	8 oz. mushrooms	parsley
2 oz. semolina		salt

Beat the eggs into the milk, add the semolina, salt and slices of rolls and leave for about 1 hour. Then add the chopped and stewed mushrooms and chopped parsley. Melt the butter in a baking dish, pile in the mixture and bake slowly for 30 minutes. Cut into squares and serve with lettuce salad or green vegetables (spinach, peas, etc.).

MUSHROOMS AND NOODLES

Halushky

8 oz. short noodles	12 oz. mushrooms	onion, parsley
2 oz. fat	2 eggs	½ pint milk

Boil the noodles in salted water for 10 minutes till soft. Fry the onion in the fat, add chopped parsley and mushrooms cook gently for 3 minutes. Drain noodles, mix with the mushrooms, pile mixture into a greased pie-dish. Bake for a few minutes and then pour over a cup of milk with the beaten eggs. Return to the oven and bake till golden brown. Serve with green vegetables or salad.

MORAVIAN CABBAGE

1 white cabbage	1—2 oz. flour	4 lumps sugar
(about 1 lb.)	caraway seeds	3 tablespoons vinegar
3 oz. fat	1 onion	salt, water

Clean the cabbage and grate on a medium grater. Add a little hot water and simmer till soft. Fry the chopped onion in the fat, dredge with flour to make a golden roux and add the cabbage water. Stir well and add to the cabbage. Season with salt, add the sugar, caraway seeds and vinegar. Simmer again till the cabbage is mushy. A sour grated apple may also be added. Serve with meat or potato dishes.

PICKLED GHERKINS

6 pints water	6 lb. small gherkins	3 green paprikas
3 tablespoons salt	5 slices horseradish	strand of dill

Thoroughly wash the gherkins, place in an earthenware pot and pour over hot boiled water. Leave to cool, drain, then arrange in a clean pickling bottle with the dill, chopped paprikas and slices of horseradish. Cover with boiling water containing 3 heaped tablespoons salt. Cover immediately and leave in a cool place to ferment. After about 5 weeks the gherkins are ready for use. Serve with meat, chopped into sandwich spreads or for garnishing. Pickled gherkins are also excellent in sauces.

BILBERRY SAUCE

1 lb. bilberries	1 oz. butter	1 teaspoon potato
2 oz. sugar	½ pint milk	flour

Wash and pick over the bilberries. Place in a pot together with half the milk and the butter and sugar and boil till soft. Mix the potato flour with the rest of the milk and add to the bilberries. Simmer for a few minutes, stirring all the time. This sauce is used on pancakes, dumplings, and doughnuts or for pouring over puddings and soufflés.

COTTAGE CHEESE MAYONNAISE

4 oz. cottage cheese	1 teaspoon vinegar	pinch sugar
2 egg yolks	or lemon juice	salt and pepper
3—4 tablespoons oil	½ teaspoon French	pinch ground
milk	mustard	caraway seeds

Pass the cottage cheese through a fine sieve and mix with the yolks. Alternately add oil, drop by drop, and milk, thus making a thick sauce similar to mayonnaise. Season with salt and pepper, pinch ground caraway seeds, French mustard, sugar, vinegar or a little lemon juice. Serve with boiled meat or fish. It can also be used in vegetable salads.

PLUM 'KLEVERA'

6 lb. plums	1 gill rum	pinch benzoic acid
	1 lb. sugar	

Stone the plums and pass them through a meat mincer. Cook rapidly for about 30 minutes. Then add the sugar and boil again for about 15 minutes. Remove from stove, add some good rum in which a pinch of benzoic acid has been dissolved. Pour into pots and cover. Klevera is poured over fruit dumplings, spread on yeast pancakes and 'vdolky' doughnuts and served as a sauce with puddings.

COTTAGE CHEESE BREAD PUDDING

1 lb. white loaf	2 egg yolks	5 oz. sugar
1 lb. soft cottage	lemon rind	1 oz. sultanas
cheese	3 oz. fat	vanilla essence
	1½ pints milk	vanilla sugar
		(see p. 73)

Cream half the fat with the sugar, add a little vanilla essence, grated lemon rind, 1 egg yolk and the soft cottage cheese. Mix well together and if necessary add a little milk. Cut the loaf into slices and moisten with milk. Place a layer in a greased pie-dish, sprinkle with melted fat, spread on some of the cottage cheese and strew with sultanas. Continue making layers of bread and cheese, ending with a layer of bread. Beat the other yolk in a cup of milk and pour over the pudding. Bake in a moderate oven for 30—45 minutes. Serve sprinkled with vanilla sugar.

COTTAGE CHEESE SCRAMBLE

1 lb. cottage cheese	3—4 oz. plain flour	½ pint milk
1 oz. sugar	mixed with fine	1 oz. butter
pinch salt	semolina	2 oz. fat for greasing
lemon rind	4 eggs	tin

Cream the butter and sugar. Add the salt, yolks, lemon rind and, after mixing well, add the sieved cottage cheese and milk. Stiffly whisk the whites and add to the mixture alternately with the flour. Turn into a greased frying pan and fry like a thick omelette or place in hot fat in a baking tin and bake in the oven. When the underside is golden, tear it apart with a fork and turn it over. Serve sprinkled with sugar and with fruit juice or compote.

COTTAGE CHEESE CREAM

1 lb. cottage cheese	vanilla essence	8 oz. fruit in season
3 oz. butter	3 eggs	5 oz. sugar
½ pint whipped cream		3 tablespoons rum

Sieve the soft cottage cheese and add the butter, sugar, a little vanilla essence, 3 tablespoons whipped cream and the rum and whisk well together. Then add the egg yolks and stiffly whisked egg whites. Pile the cream and fruit into a bowl and decorate with whipped cream.

FRUIT DUMPLINGS MADE WITH COTTAGE CHEESE

8 z. mixed flour and fine semolina	3 oz. cottage cheese	*Garnish:*
1 egg	1 gill milk	2 oz. butter
1 oz. fat	pinch salt	2 oz. hard cheese
	4 oz. fruit in season	1 oz. sugar

If hard cottage cheese is used, it should be grated; soft cottage cheese is beaten with the fat, salt and egg. Add alternately the flour and milk and mix until a soft elastic dough is formed. Turn on to a floured board, lightly roll out and cut into squares. Place fruit on the squares, roll up into a ball and throw into boiling water. Cook for 5—8 minutes. Drain and serve sprinkled with sugar and grated, hard cheese (or grated perník, see p. 174) and melted butter.

FRUIT DUMPLINGS FROM YEAST DOUGH

1 lb. mixed flour and fine semolina	1 egg	*Garnish:*
½ pint milk	1 lb. fruit	2 oz. butter
¾ oz. baker's yeast	1 tablespoon sugar	2 oz. cottage cheese
	salt	2 oz. sugar

Mix the yeast with the sugar and a little warm milk. Leave to sponge and then add to the sieved flour and bind with the rest of the warm milk mixed with the salt and egg. Knead well, then leave for 1 hour in a warm place, sprinkled with flour. Form into a long roll and cut off small pieces. Wrap each piece around fruit (such as plums, apricots etc.) and leave on the board for another 15 minutes to prove. Throw into boiling water and cook for 5 minutes, turn over and cook for another 3—5 minutes. Remove from the water and prick with a fork to let the steam escape. Serve sprinkled with grated cottage cheese or grated perník (see p. 174), sugar and melted butter.

FRUIT DUMPLINGS FROM POTATO DOUGH

8 oz. mixed flour and
  fine semolina
1 egg
2 large potatoes

about 8 tablespoons
  milk
salt
fruit for filling

Garnish:
2 oz. butter
2 oz. cottage cheese
1 oz. sugar

Use potatoes cooked the day before. Grate them and mix with the flour and salt. Make a well in the middle and break in the egg and add the milk. Work into a stiff dough. Turn out on to a floured board, roll out fairly thinly and cut into squares. Place fruit in the middle of each square, roll up into a ball and throw into boiling water, slightly salted; cook for 5—7 minutes. Serve sprinkled with sugar, grated cottage cheese and melted butter.

BISCUITS WITH PARMESAN

1 egg yolk
2 oz. fat
5 oz. plain flour

2 oz. Parmesan cheese
1 oz. almonds

1—2 tablespoons milk
sugar
½ oz. baker's yeast

Mix the yeast with a little sugar, warm milk and flour and leave to sponge. Crumble fat into the flour, sprinkle in the grated Parmesan and a little salt, add the risen yeast and work into a stiffish dough. Leave in a warm place for 30 minutes to rise. Then roll out thinly and cut into various shapes. Brush with egg, sprinkle with chopped almonds and bake in a moderate oven.

BAKED PANCAKES WITH COTTAGE CHEESE

1 pint milk
2 eggs
1 oz. sugar
7 oz. flour
lemon rind
2 oz. fat for frying
1 oz. vanilla sugar (see p. 73)

Custard:
½ pint milk
1 dessertspoon sugar
1 egg

Filling:
1 lb. cottage cheese
2 eggs
3 oz. sugar
2 oz. butter
1 oz. sultanas

Beat the eggs in a little milk, add the sugar and grated lemon rind and gradually spoon in the flour and the rest of the milk. Ladle into hot fat and fry thin pancakes. Cream the cottage cheese, egg yolks and sugar, add the butter, sultanas and stiffly whisked egg whites. Spread the filling on the pancakes, roll them up and cut in half. Arrange in fireproof dish and bake for a few minutes in the oven. Then pour over custard—the milk mixed with the beaten egg and sugar. Return to the oven and bake for about 20 minutes. Serve sprinkled with vanilla sugar.

SALTY YEAST DOUGH FOR ROLLS OR SALT STICKS

1 egg	2 oz. fat	½ teaspoon salt
1 lb. plain flour	1 oz. baker's yeast	poppy-seeds or
½ teaspoon sugar	1 gill milk	caraway seeds

Mix the sugar and yeast and when it begins to soften add 1—2 table-spoons flour and 2—3 tablespoons warm milk. Leave for 5 minutes to sponge, then add it to the flour, egg and warm fat. Mix with the rest of the warm milk and salt until the dough leaves the sides of the bowl. Leave to rise for 1 hour. Then roll out into long sticks or form into long plaits. The dough can also be cut into triangles, which are then brushed with melted fat and rolled up from the broad side to the tip. Leave to prove and then sprinkle with poppy-seeds and salt, or caraway seeds and salt, and bake in a moderate oven.

SALT STICKS

1 lb. flour and fine	1 gill milk	1 teaspoon sugar
semolina mixed	2 oz. fat	caraway seeds
1 egg	1 oz. baker's yeast	salt
		beaten egg or milk

Sieve the flour, semolina and salt into a bowl, add the yeast which has been put to sponge with a little milk and sugar, the egg and melted fat. Mix into a stiff dough and leave for about 1 hour to rise. Roll out long thin sticks from the dough, brush with milk or egg and sprinkle with coarse salt and caraway seeds. Bake in a moderate oven till golden brown. This dough may also be used to make small plaited rolls, caraway trefoil rolls etc.

DOMAZHLICE CAKES
Domazhlicke Kolache

2 eggs yolks	3 oz. margarine or	½ pint milk
1 lb. plain flour	butter	lemon rind, vanilla
3 oz. sugar	salt	sugar (see p. 73)
1 oz. baker's yeast	beaten egg	or vanilla
		essence to flavour

Mix the yeast and a little sugar with 2 tablespoons flour and 4 table-spoons milk and leave to sponge. Add remaining sugar, flavouring, flour, warm fat and milk in which the eggs and salt have been beaten. Using a wooden spoon, work the mixture into a soft smooth dough and leave in a warm place to rise. Turn it over several times during the rising period so that it will be light. When the dough has risen to one and a half times its original size, turn it on to a board and divide into four or five large pieces. Form each piece into a round kolach, patting out the middle so that the edge is higher. Place different fillings on the kolach, either a different one to each quarter or rings of different fillings, working from the centre to the edge. Brush the edge with beaten egg and bake in a hottish oven for 40-50 minutes.

Damson cheese filling:
5 oz. damson cheese
water

2—3 oz. sugar
1 tablespoon rum
vanilla essence

cinnamon, lemon or
orange rind

Dilute the damson cheese with a little water, add the sugar, rum, pinch cinnamon, a little vanilla essence and grated lemon or orange rind.

Cottage cheese filling:
1 lb. cottage cheese
2 oz. butter

3 oz. sugar
2 eggs
vanilla essence
lemon rind

2 tablespoons cream
or milk
1 oz. sultanas

Sieve the cottage cheese and add to the cream, butter and sugar and egg yolks. Flavour with vanilla essence and grated lemon rind, add the sultanas and finally fold in the stiffly beaten egg whites.

KOLACH WITH JELLIED FRUIT

1 egg yolk
8 oz. plain flour
5 oz. butter
2 oz. sugar
lemon rind
2 tablespoons jam

1 lb. fruit (straw-
berries, redcurrants,
apricots etc.)
Jelly:
1 gill water
1 oz. gelatine

3 oz. sugar
Edging:
2½ oz. ground
almonds
5 oz. sugar
½ egg white

Sieve the flour and sugar and crumble in the fat. Add the egg yolk and mix into a light pastry. Roll out and place in a greased baking or cake tin. Bake in a hot oven and when cold spread with jam to prevent the jelly soaking in. Cover with a layer of fruit. Mix beaten egg white with the ground almonds and sugar to a thick mixture, form into a long roll and place round the edge of the kolach. Dissolve the sugar and gelatine in water and spoon on to the top of the fruit. Leave to set and then cut into pieces.

FRIED BREAD

Pavézky

7 oz. bread or rolls
1 egg

breadcrumbs
3 oz. fat for frying

1 cup milk
salt

Cut the bread or rolls into thin slices, moisten each with a little milk, dip in beaten egg and breadcrumbs and fry in fat till golden. Pavézky form a tasty accompaniment to vegetables.

BAKED BATTER BALLS

Rozpeky

2 lb. plain flour	1 teaspoon baker's	a little milk
1 egg yolk	yeast	pinch sugar
3 oz. fat		salt

Put the yeast to sponge with a little milk, sugar and flour. Add to the 2 lb. plain flour, together with a pinch of salt, an egg yolk and the melted fat and mix to a soft smooth dough. Leave to rise in a warm place. Then form into small doughnuts, place on a greased tin and again leave to rise for about 15 minutes. Bake in a hot oven. These rozpeky are sometimes served for tea but more frequently as an accompaniment to meat with a sauce, instead of dumplings (e. g. with tomato sauce).

LARGE KOLACHE

2 eggs	½ pint milk	3 oz. flour
1 lb. plain flour	pinch salt	stoned fruit or
1 oz. castor sugar	lemon rind	damson cheese or
2 oz. butter or	vanilla flavouring	poppy-seed or
margarine	*Topping:*	cottage cheese to
½ oz. baker's yeast	2 oz. sugar	decorate
	2 oz. butter	

Mix the yeast with a spoonful of sugar and flour, add 2 tablespoons warm milk and leave to sponge. Sieve flour, sugar and salt into a bowl, add the yolks beaten in the rest of the milk, a little grated lemon rind and the vanilla flavouring. Work into a softish dough. Leave for about 30 minutes to rise and then turn on to a greased baking tin, spreading the dough over the tin with wet hands, so that it is about half an inch thick. Decorate with stoned fruit—apricots, plums or sliced apples—or spread with damson cheese or a poppy-seed or cottage cheese filling (see pp. 169, 167). Brush edges of kolache with egg whites. Before baking sprinkle the kolache with the following topping: crumble the fresh butter into the flour and sugar so that the mixture resembles fine breadcrumbs. The sugar, fat and flour form a sweet layer over the kolache and give it an attractive appearance. Bake in a well heated oven for about 30 minutes. When cold cut into squares, rectangles or narrow slices.

FLAKY KOLACHE

3 eggs	1 oz. sugar	¼ oz. baker's yeast
1 lb. plain flour	8 oz. margarine	4 tablespoons milk
1 gill milk	or butter	salt

Mix the fat with about 3 oz. flour and leave in a cool place. Mix the yeast with milk and pour this into the rest of the flour and sugar. Add the eggs and work the mixture into a soft dough. Leave for about 1 hour in a warm place to rise. Then roll it out and place on it the rolled out fat. Fold over the edges like an envelope, press together and fold in half. Lightly roll out, fold into three, turn and fold into three again. Leave for 1 hour and then repeat the rolling and folding. Leave for about 15 minutes and then roll out to about ½ inch and cut into squares. Place some thick poppy-seed, apple or nut filling on each square and fold up the corners to the centre, pressing them well together to prevent them opening up during baking. Brush the tops with beaten egg and bake in a hot oven.

Poppy-seed filling:

5 oz. poppy-seeds	vanilla essence	pinch cinnamon
½ pint milk	1 oz. fat	chocolate, honey, jam
	lemon rind	(optional)
	3 oz. sugar	

Grind the poppy-seed and simmer with the milk till soft. If necessary, add a little water from time to time. Add the sugar and butter and simmer, for a little longer, stirring all the time. Flavour with grated lemon rind, vanilla essence and a pinch of cinnamon. A little grated chocolate, a tablespoon of honey or jam may also be added. The filling should be thick but not dry.

CHOCOLATE RIBBED LOAF

6 eggs	pinch cinnamon	jam
5 oz. sugar	1 bread roll	1 oz. almonds for
3 oz. chocolate or	a little wine	decorating
cocoa	5 oz. almonds	extra sugar
butter		split almonds

Beat the egg yolks and sugar till creamy. Add the melted chocolate or cocoa heated with a little butter and sugar, and crumbled bread roll which has been soaked in a little wine. Chop the almonds and add to the mixture together with the stiffly whisked egg whites. Three-quarters fill a greased and floured mould and bake in a slow oven for 30—40 minutes. Leave to stand for a while and then turn out. When cold, spread with a thin layer of jam and cover with chocolate or cocoa icing (see Indiánky, p. 173). Decorate with split almonds.

BUNS WITH FILLING

Bukhty

1 egg or 2 yolks	1 oz. baker's yeast	lemon rind
1 lb. plain flour	½ pint milk	3 oz. fat for greasing
2 oz. butter or	½ teaspoon salt	tin
margarine	vanilla flavouring	2 oz. sugar

Poppy-seed filling:
5 oz. ground poppy-	3 oz. vanilla sugar	lemon rind
seed	(see p. 73)	½ pint milk
	cinnamon	

Mix the yeast and sugar to a paste, add 2 tablespoons flour, 4 tablespoons warm milk, mix to a thick batter and leave in a warm place to sponge. Sieve the rest of flour, sugar and salt into a bowl, add a little grated lemon rind and vanilla flavouring, 1 whole egg or 2 yolks, the yeast mixture and the rest of the warm milk mixed with the melted butter or margarine. Using a large wooden spoon beat well until the dough is shiny and bubbles form. Cover the bowl with a clean cloth and leave in a warm place to rise. This takes about 45 minutes — 1 hour. When it has doubled its size, turn on to a floured board and divide into small pieces. Pat out with a floured hand and place a little filling or fruit (see below) in the centre of each, press the edges of the dough together and round off the bukhty in the hands. Place on a greased tin, not too close together as they rise during baking, and grease well in between each piece. Leave for 30 minutes to prove and then put into a well heated oven. After about 10 minutes reduce the heat and bake till golden. The bukhty take about 35 minutes to bake. Then turn them out on to a board and, while still hot, sprinkle with vanilla sugar and separate them. The above amounts make about 30 small or 25 large bukhty. For poppy-seed filling simmer the poppy-seeds with the milk until a thick mixture is obtained. Sweeten and add a little cinnamon and grated lemon rind. Fill the bukhty with the cold mixture.

Bukhty may also be filled with cottage cheese filling (see p. 167), cherries, plums, apple purré, damson cheese (see p. 167) or jam.

LOMNICE RINGS

5 oz. fat	½ oz. baker's yeast	8 oz. vanilla sugar
10 oz. flour	1 oz. almonds, chopped	(see p. 73)
2 tablespoons milk		½ pint rum and water

Crumble the fat into the flour and add almonds and milk in which the yeast has been dissolved. Mix into a stiff dough and leave to rise. Then form into a roll, cut off equal sized pieces, roll each into a long thin roll and join up the ends to form a ring. Bake in a hot oven till golden. Then dip in water mixed with rum and coat with vanilla sugar.

CHRISTMAS PLAIT

Vanochka

2 eggs	1 oz. baker's yeast	1 oz. sultanas
1 lb. plain flour	vanilla essence	1 oz. almonds
4 oz. sugar	½ pint milk	1 oz. lemon rind
4 oz. fat	extra sugar	½ teaspoon salt

Sieve the flour, salt and most of the sugar into a large bowl. Make a well in the centre and crumble in the yeast. Add remaining sugar and 4 tablespoons warm milk and work into a thin batter in the centre of the flour. Cover with a cloth and leave the yeast to sponge. Then add the rest of the warm milk in which the yolks have been beaten (the whites are used for brushing the top of the plait). Add the melted fat, vanilla essence and lemon rind. Knead into a stiff, elastic dough. Then add the sultanas and peeled, chopped almonds. Cover the dough and leave in a warm place to rise, turning over the dough once or twice during this period. It takes 1—2 hours to rise. Then divide it into eight equal parts and form each part into a long roll. The bottom of the vanochka is plaited from four rolls, starting from the middle. Place the plait on greased paper on a tin. The next plait is made from three rolls and placed on the first plait. Finally divide the last roll into two thin ones and twist together. Place on the other plaits and tuck the ends well under the vanochka. The vanochka should be held firmly with slithers of wood to prevent the top slipping. Leave to prove for about 15 minutes and then brush with the beaten whites, sprinkle with a few chopped almonds and bake in a well heated oven for 45 minutes — 1 hour. Sprinkle the top with sugar while it is still warm.

EASTER MAZANETZ

3 eggs yolks	1 oz. baker's yeast	2 oz. sultanas
1 lb. plain flour	vanilla essence	1 oz. almonds
3 oz. sugar	½ pint milk	1 oz. lemon rind
4 oz. butter	vanilla sugar (see p. 73)	½ teaspoon salt
	1 egg , beaten	

Mix the yeast with 1 tablespoon sugar, 1 tablespoon flour and 4 tablespoons warm milk, leave to sponge. Sieve the rest of the flour, sugar and salt into a bowl, add the yeast, yolks, melted butter, the rest of the warm milk, grated lemon rind and a little vanilla essence and knead into a stiff dough. Add the sultanas and peeled and chopped almonds. Leave for 2 hours in a warm place to rise. Form into a round loaf and place on well greased paper on a tin. Brush the surface with beaten egg and leave for another 10 minutes to prove. Cut a cross into the top and place in a well heated oven. Bake gently for 35 minutes. When cooked sprinkle liberally with vanilla sugar.

COUNTRY-WAKE KOLACHE

3—4 egg yolks
1 lb. plain flour
4 oz. sugar
5 oz. butter

1 oz. baker's yeast
½ teaspoon salt
½ pint milk

2 tablespoons rum
lemon rind
vanilla flavouring
beaten egg

Apple Filling:

1 lb. apples
5 oz. sugar
water

1 lemon
pinch cinnamon
breadcrumbs

1 teaspoon rum
(optional)

Mix the yeast and a little sugar in a large bowl, add 2 tablespoons flour and 3 tablespoons warm milk, cover and leave for 10 minutes to sponge. Add the rest of the sugar, flour and milk into which melted butter, eggs and salt have been beaten, rum, lemon rind and vanilla. Work the dough until it is shiny and smooth and leaves the sides of the bowl. Sprinkle lightly with flour, cover with a cloth and leave in a warm place to rise. The dough should not rise too quickly. If a very light and flaky dough is required it should be turned over once or twice during the rising period. The dough is ready when it has risen to one and a half times its original size. If pressed lightly with the fingertip it should rise again immediately and retain no impression. Divide the dough into small pieces, about 1—2 oz. in weight, roll into little balls and place on a greased tin. For the filling wash, peel and core the apples, and simmer with a little water till soft. Pass through a sieve, add the sugar, a little lemon rind and juice, a pinch of cinnamon and, if desired, 1 teaspoon rum. If necessary, thicken with a few breadcrumbs. Poppy-seed or cottage cheese filling may be used instead (see pp. 169, 167).

Using the fingers of both hands pat out the middle of each kolache and place a little filling on each. Brush the edges of each kolache with beaten egg. Bake in a moderate oven for 20—30 minutes depending on the size.

COTTAGE CHEESE KOLACHE

3 oz. soft cottage
    cheese
1 oz. sugar

3 oz. roasted walnuts
3 eggs
1—2 oz. breadcrumbs
3 oz. butter

jam, nuts, grated
chocolate to
decorate

Cream butter and sugar and add the egg yolks. Mix in the sieved cottage cheese and chopped nuts. Stiffly whisk the whites and fold into the dough alternately with the breadcrumbs. Pile into a well greased cake tin and bake in a moderate oven for about 20 minutes. Spread a little jam on the finished kolache and decorate with grated nuts and chocolate.

APPLE KOLACHE

4 eggs
6 oz. flour
7 oz. sugar
3 oz. butter

1 oz. butter
½ teaspoon baking
  powder
4 tablespoons milk

3 tablespoons
  cornflour
1 lb. apples
vanilla sugar
  (see p. 73)
melted butter

Cream butter and sugar and gradually add the egg yolks. Beat until light and creamy. Then add alternately the cold milk and sieved flour, cornflour and baking powder. Finally fold in the stiffly whisked egg whites. Place the dough in a well greased and breadcrumbed baking tin, cover with a layer of thinly sliced apples and sprinkle with melted butter. Bake in a moderate oven for about 30 minutes. Sprinkle with vanilla sugar when done.

BÁBOVKA WITH NUTS AND CHOCOLATE

6 eggs
1 lb. plain flour
8 oz. sugar

½ pint milk
½ oz. baking powder
6 oz. chopped nuts
8 oz. butter

3 tablespoons rum
5 oz. grated chocolate
  or cocoa
bread or sponge
  crumbs

Cream the butter and sugar and gradually add the egg yolks. Mix in the flour and baking powder, finely chopped nuts and milk with rum. Finally fold in the stiffly whisked egg whites. Divide the dough into two parts, and add the grated chocolate or cocoa to one of them. Grease a mould and sprinkle with fine breadcrumbs or finely crumbled sponge. Pile in layers of light and dark dough and bake in a moderate oven for 40—50 minutes.

INDIÁNKY

3 egg yolks
4 egg whites
3 oz. plain flour
2 oz. castor sugar
1 oz. butter (for
  greasing)

Filling:
1 pint whipped cream
2 tablespoons icing
  sugar
Icing:
3 oz. butter

3 oz. icing sugar
½ oz. cocoa
1 tablespoon milk
1 tablespoon
  cornflour

Stiffly whisk the egg whites and fold in about 1 oz. sugar. Beat the yolks, add the rest of the sugar and the flour and gradually add to the whites. Grease and flour a baking tin and pipe on blobs of sponge. Bake in a hot oven. Cut the sponges in half, place the bottoms in paper cups, pile on the whipped cream beaten together with the icing sugar, cover with the top halves and decorate with the icing. To make the icing mix the cornflour and milk over a low flame until it thickens, then add the creamed butter and sugar, and cocoa.

FILLED PERNÍK

10 oz. plain wheat or rye flour	*Pernik seasoning:* cinnamon	*Filling:* 5 tablespoons damson cheese (see p. 167)
8 oz. sugar	vanilla	
1 egg	pinch fennel	1 teaspoon grated lemon rind
2 tablespoons honey	lemon or orange rind	
2 tablespoons milk		7 tablespoons chopped walnuts
1 tablespoon rum	beaten egg for	
½ tablespoon baking powder	glazing	4 tablespoons chopped dates

Sieve the flour, sugar, baking powder and seasoning on to a board. Warm the honey, add the rum, milk and beaten egg and stir into the flour. Work into a stiffish dough. If it is too soft add a little more flour. Roll out strips 2 inches thick. Place the filling in the middle and press the long sides of the strips well together. Place the dough, joined side downwards, on a greased tin, brush the top with beaten egg and bake in a moderate oven for about 30 minutes. The above ingredients make 3 to 4 rolls. When cold cut the rolls into oblique slices. The perník remains moist for a long time. The filling is made from finely chopped fruit and nuts and lemon rind mixed with damson cheese.

SIMPLE PERNÍK

1 lb. plain flour	2 oz. butter	*Pernik seasoning:*
5 oz. sugar	1 gill milk or black coffee	¼ teaspoon each cinnamon,
10 tablespoons honey		clove, vanilla,
1 egg	½ oz. baking powder beaten egg	aniseed, allspice

Sieve the sugar, baking powder, flour and perník seasoning into a bowl. Warm honey and butter, add to the egg, milk or black coffee and pour into the flour. Work into a dough and leave for 1—2 hours to stand. If the dough becomes too stiff, put it in a warm place to soften. The seasoning and baking powder work on the flour and make the dough light. Grease a baking tin and sprinkle with flour. Pile in the mixture and brush the top with beaten egg or sweetened milk or coffee. Place in a well heated oven and after a few minutes reduce the heat. If the perník is baked too quickly a hard crust forms and the inside remains too soft; if baked too slowly it dries out and is hard. So first bake in a hot oven and reduce the temperature to slow. Keep the perník in a tin so that it does not dry out. It is best eaten a week after baking.

HONEY PERNÍK

3 eggs	½ teaspoon bicarbonate of soda	2 oz. almonds
1 lb. plain flour		¼ teaspoon each vanila and ground cloves
1 pint honey	4 oz. butter	
	2 oz. nuts	lemon rind

Warm the honey till it is liquid, melt the butter in it and add the egg yolks and lemon rind, stirring all the time. Pour into the sieved dry ingredients. Beat the dough well and then fold in the stiffly whisked whites. Grease a baking tin and sprinkle with flour. Carefully pour in the dough, sprinkle the top with chopped nuts and bake in a moderate oven for about 30 minutes, until the perník remains firm to the touch. When cold, cut into slices or squares.

ICED PERNÍK

2 eggs	2 tablespoons honey	*Perník seasoning:*
1 lb. plain flour	½ teaspoon bicarbo-	¼ teaspoon each
8 oz. sugar	nate of soda	clove, vanilla, aniseed,
1 tablespoon rum	lemon rind	allspice, cinnamon
	beaten egg	

Sieve the flour, add the sugar, bicarbonate of soda and seasoning. Warm the honey and mix with the beaten eggs, lemon rind and rum. Pour into the flour and work all together into a stiff dough. Leave to stand overnight. The next day roll out a thick layer and cut out figures or various shapes. Brush with beaten egg and bake in a hot oven until firm to the touch. Ice when cold with lemon icing or rum frosting (see p. 76).

HONEY WAFER CAKE

8 oz. plain flour	1 tablespoon honey	*Filling:*
1 egg	little vanilla essence	1 pint milk
3 oz. sugar	chopped nuts or	3 oz. sugar
1 oz. butter	chocolate to	1 tablespoon cocoa
1 teaspoon	decorate	2 oz. butter
bicarbonate of soda		1 oz. cornflour

Whisk honey, sugar, egg, vanilla, and butter to a thick cream over a saucepan of boiling water. Add the soda and after whisking for a little while longer remove from the stove and fold in the flour. When cool turn on to a floured board. Divide into five parts and roll out each to wafer thinness. Bake in a moderate oven in a greased tin. When golden remove from the oven and use a knife to take from the tin while still warm. Mix a little of the milk for the cream filling, with the cornflour. Bring the rest of the milk and the sugar to the boil, add the cornflour and stir. Boil for a few minutes, then remove from the stove. When cold add the butter and cocoa. Join the wafers with the cream filling, cover with a weight and leave for several hours in a cool place. Then decorate with the remaining cream, sprinkle the sides and top with roasted chopped nuts or grated chocolate.

POTATO CAKES WITH POPPY-SEED

Shkubánky

2 lb. potatoes	3 oz. lard	2 oz. sugar
5 oz. plain flour	2 oz. poppy-seeds	salt
boiling water	grated gingerbread	

Peel and quarter the potatoes, cover with boiling salted water and cook till nearly soft. Then drain off the water into a bowl. Mash the potatoes, and make several holes in the mash with the end of a wooden spoon. The holes should reach right to the bottom of the pot. Fill them with the flour and pour on about half of the water, which should be boiling. Leave covered on the edge of the stove for about 30 minutes. Then pour off the excess water and beat the mixture with a wooden spoon till smooth. The mixture should be very stiff. Using a spoon dipped in hot lard, place spoonfuls of the mixture on a plate. Sprinkle with ground poppy-seeds or grated gingerbread, sugar and lard. An alternative is to sprinkle the shkubánky with grated cottage cheese and melted butter. Shkubánky are also excellent fried (see p. 150).

GYPSY SLICES

1 egg yolk	1 tablespoon milk	5 oz. sugar
2 oz. sugar	lemon rind	5 oz. nuts, ground
3 oz. butter	*Filling:*	cinnamon
8 oz. flour	3 egg whites	

Sieve the flour, mix with the sugar and a little grated lemon rind and cut in butter. Make a well in the centre and pour in the milk with the egg yolk. Work into a dough and roll out. Beat the 3 eggs whites with the sugar and add the ground nuts and a pinch of cinnamon. Spread the filling on to the dough and cut into slices with a wetted knife. Bake on a greased tin in a hot oven.

CELESTIAL FAVOURS

1 egg	½ oz. butter	pinch salt
2 egg yolks	2 tablespoons sugar	lemon rind
8 oz. plain flour	2 tablespoons rum	5 oz. lard for frying
		vanilla sugar
		(see p. 73)

Sieve the flour, sugar and salt on to a board, crumble in the butter and add the beaten egg and yolks, rum and a little grated lemon rind. Work into an elastic dough. Roll out thinly, cut into squares or use a cutter to make different sized stars. Place in hot lard and fry quickly on both sides. Dust with vanilla sugar.

30. Tomatoes Stuffed with Mushrooms, Sweden (p.489)

31. Herrings with Mustard Sauce, Britain (p.93)

32. Sweet Scones, Britain (p.125)

RICH POTATO SLICES

7 oz. sugar	7 oz. potatoes	grated rind ½ lemon
2 eggs	3 oz. walnuts	pinch baking powder
1 oz. flour	vanilla essence	½ pint whipped cream

Beat the egg yolks and sugar till light and creamy. Add the finely chopped nuts and cold, cooked and finely grated potatoes. Add the grated lemon rind, flour, a little vanilla essence and baking powder. Mix well together and fold in the stiffly whisked egg whites. Bake on a greased tin in a moderate oven till golden. Leave to cool and then spread with whipped cream or a butter cream.

FRUIT BUBBLE CAKE

Bublanina

8 oz. plain flour	3 eggs	lemon rind
5—6 oz. sugar	¼ pint milk	vanilla essence
4 oz. butter	2 lb. fruit	vanilla sugar
		(see p. 73)

Warm butter slightly and then cream with the sugar. Add the egg yolks and continue beating until the mixture is thick and creamy. Add spoonfuls of flour and milk alternately with a little grated lemon rind and vanilla essence. Fold in the stiffly whisked egg whites. Pile into a baking tin so that the layer is about 1 inch thick. Dot with washed and stoned fruit (cherries are the most suitable). Bake in a slowish oven till the surface is a light golden colour. Before serving sprinkle with vanilla sugar.

POPPY-SEED ROLL

1 lb. plain flour	8 oz. butter or	pinch salt
2 eggs	margarine	poppy-seed filling
2 oz. sugar	¾ oz. baker's yeast	(see p. 169)
	4 tablespoon milk	

Work about 3 oz. flour into the fat and leave in a cool place. Sieve the rest of the flour into a bowl and mix with the yeast which has been put to sponge with the warm milk, a little sugar and 1 tablespoon flour. Add the salt, remaining sugar and yolks to the flour and work into an elastic dough. Leave in a warm place to rise. Then roll out, place the fat in the middle, fold the edges like an envelope and press well together and fold the whole in half. Lightly roll out and fold into three, turn and again fold. Leave for 1 hour and then roll out to ½ inch thick, strew with poppy-seed filling, roll up firmly, press the edge to the roll and place on a greased tin. Brush with beaten white and bake in a well heated oven for about 45 minutes. Then cut into slices.

TWO-COLOURED LAYER CAKE

Layer 1:	*Layer 2:*	*Cream*
5 eggs	5 eggs	1 egg yolk
5 oz. sugar	6 oz. sugar	5 oz. butter
1 oz. crumbled sponge	4 oz. flour	4 oz. sugar
1 oz. chopped nuts		
1 oz. chocolate or cocoa		
3 oz. flour		
butter		

Layer 1: Beat the egg yolks and sugar to a thick cream. Add the softened chocolate or cocoa, warmed with a small piece of butter, and beat for a few more minutes. Stiffly whisk the egg whites and mix with the nuts, crumbled sponge and flour. Add to yolk mixture, bake in a moderate oven in a cake tin. When cold cut in half.

Layer 2: Stiffly whisk the egg whites, fold in the sugar, egg yolks and flour. Place on a baking tin to form a layer about ½ inch thick and bake in a hot oven to prevent the edges drying out.

Cream: Cream the sugar, butter, and egg yolk.

Spread a little cream on layer 2 and cut it into strips about 1 inch wide. Spread some cream on the bottom half of layer 1 and place the strips from layer 2 spirally on it, starting from the centre, until the whole of layer 1 has been covered. Spread with some more cream and cover with the second half of layer 1. Decorate the top with a white or cocoa icing. If it is to be decorated with cream, twice the amount of cream filling must be made. The spirals may also be made as follows: Roll up the second layer while still hot; when cool, unroll, spread with cream and again roll up. Cut into slices about 1 inch thick. The slices must be the same thickness or the cake will look crooked. Place them close together on top of the first layer, cut side downwards, cover with cream and then add the top half of layer 1.

SPONGE BÁBOVKA

6 eggs	vanilla essence	1 oz. almonds, sulta-
8 oz. sugar	lemon rind	nas or cocoa
	7 oz. plain flour	1 oz. butter

Beat the eggs and sugar in a bowl standing in hot water until the mixture thickens. Remove from the fire and stir until it cools. Then add the flour, a spoonful at a time. Grease a bábovka mould with melted butter and when it hardens sprinkle with flour. Pile in the sponge so that the mould is two-thirds full and bake in a slowish oven for 30—40 minutes. Turn out on to a rack. Vanilla essence, lemon rind, chopped almonds or sultanas may be added to the dough, or half the dough may be coloured brown with cocoa and then layers of white and brown mixture piled into the mould.

DUTCH COOKING

Musia Soper

The interesting aspect of Dutch cookery is its very solid national Nether-lands background, overladen by a definite Indonesian spice-veneer. Historically, it is very easy to explain, because the Dutch have always possessed a traditional characteristic cuisine, but they also used to own the Dutch East Indies, the Spice Islands—an archipelago now called Indonesia. From there they acquired and brought back the taste for unusual condiments. The Dutch housewife, like the German one, has to cater for hearty appetites. So first of all she specialises in good filling soups — soups which could mean a whole meal for daintier ap-petites. Fish is plentiful and cheap in Holland and consequently they have quite a few good fish specialities. By grating a little nutmeg into their Fish Cakes, they add a special touch to the ordinary fish cake recipe — a tip well worth accepting. Veal Olives is another national dish which the Dutch housewife prepares with care and love. Most housewives could learn the art of dealing with veal from the Dutch —remember that beating the slices of veal is absolutely essential. A dish of Minced Meat Balls is one of the richest and tastiest one-course meals —the very thing for a career woman's dinner party, as it can be all prepared well beforehand and heated up when wanted.

BROWN BEAN SOUP

8 oz. brown beans	2 oz. flour	salt and pepper
1 onion	*bouquet garni*	croûtons
2 oz. dripping	2 pints water	nutmeg

Soak the beans for 12 hours. Simmer in 2 pints of water with the *bouquet garni* until tender. Fry the chopped onion in the dripping until tender, stir in the flour and cook for 1 minute. Add to the soup. Season with salt and pepper and grated nutmeg. Pass through a sieve. Serve with croûtons of fried bread.

FARMER'S SOUP

8 oz. sauerkraut	2 rashers bacon	1 gill cream
3 pints stock	2 small, cooked	1 tablespoon flour
3 potatoes	sausages	2 oz. dried mushrooms
2 bay leaves		

Cut potatoes, bacon and mushrooms into small pieces, put together with bay leaves into the stock and cook gently for 20 minutes. Rub through a sieve or use electric blender, cut sausages in slices, heat them and the sauerkraut in the soup, add cream, and flour to thicken, reheat and serve at once. *(Illustrated in Plate 33.)*

SPINACH SOUP

1 lb. spinach	1 gill cream	1 oz. cornflour
2 oz. butter	salt and pepper	nutmeg
	hot milk	croûtons

Cook the spinach in a little salted water until tender. Pass through a sieve. Melt the butter, cook the cornflour in it for 1 minute, gradually add spinach purée and a little hot milk if necessary. Season with salt, pepper and nutmeg. Stir in the cream before serving. Serve with croûtons of fried bread. *(Illustrated in Plate 90.)*

GOUDA ASPARAGUS ROLLS

4 small plaice or sole fillets	8 cooked asparagus tips	4 large tomatoes unsalted butter
4 oz. grated Gouda cheese	1 tablespoon breadcrumbs	salt and pepper 1 lb. cooked rice

Cut the tops off the tomatoes and scoop out the centres. Mix breadcrumbs with grated cheese, salt and pepper and press inside the tomatoes. Season the fillets, roll each one round two asparagus tips, and stuff these rolls into the tomatoes. Place a knob of butter on top and bake in a slow oven for 30 minutes. Serve hot with boiled rice. *(Illustrated in Plate 70.)*

SAUSAGE WITH CURLY KALE

2 lb. curly kale, cooked	8 oz. smoked sausage	2 oz. rolled oats
2 lb. potatoes, cooked	sliced or frankfurters	2 oz. butter
½ pint stock		salt and pepper

Put the curly kale and potatoes together in a saucepan with ½ pint stock. Add sausage and oats and simmer for 15 minutes without a lid; the stock should almost all have evaporated. Remove the sausage, mash the vegetables with the butter. Season with salt and pepper. Arrange on a flat dish, garnished with the sausages.

MINCED MEAT SCALLOPS

8 oz. minced beef, fresh or cooked	½ pint Spanish sauce (see p. 568) parsley	2 oz. breadcrumbs 1 oz. butter

Mix the meat with the sauce. Fill 4 scallop shells with the mixture. Sprinkle with breadcrumbs. Dot with butter. Bake in a moderate oven for 30 minutes. Garnish each one with a sprig of parsley.

NASI GORENG

This is a recipe brought from Indonesia to Holland, and it has now become a traditional Dutch dish.

1 lb. Patna rice	8 oz. onions	*Garnish:*
4 oz. unsalted butter	1 teaspoon curry	1 egg omelette
8 oz. diced pork	powder	cucumber
12 oz. mixed cooked	salt and pepper	tomatoes
vegetables, i. e.	soy sauce	pickles
peas, carrots, etc.	4 pints water	lettuce

Cook the rice in boiling water until tender; that is for about 12 minutes. Strain, rinse with cold water and leave to drain well. Cut the onions into rings and brown with the pork in 2 oz. of the butter for about 15 minutes. Add the remainder of the butter, half the rice, salt, pepper, curry powder and a sprinkling of soy sauce. Continue cooking slowly, stirring frequently, until the meat is tender. Then add the vegetables and the rest of the rice. Mix well, heat a little longer, then turn out on to a large, flat heated plate. Garnish with thin strips of dry omelette and surround with slices of tomatoes. Serve immediately, accompanied by lettuce, cucumber and pickles. *(Illustrated in Plate 85.)*

VEAL OLIVES

8 slices lean veal	2 oz. butter	1 lemon
(4 oz. each)	½ pint stock	salt and pepper

Beat the veal, season with salt and pepper. Roll and secure with string. Brown all over in the butter. Arrange in a shallow fireproof dish, put a slice of lemon on each roll. Pour the stock over. Cover and cook in a moderate oven for 1 hour. Remove the string before serving.

PORK CHOPS WITH CHESTNUTS AND RED CABBAGE

4 pork chops	½ pint chicken stock	16 chestnuts
2 oz. butter	½ small red cabbage	salt and pepper

Shred the cabbage and remove the hard stalks. Soak in cold water for 1 hour. Peel and cook the chestnuts until soft. Lightly fry the chops on both sides in the butter. Drain the cabbage and place at the bottom of a deep, casserole put the chestnuts on top of it and then the chops. Season with salt and pepper. Pour in the stock. Cover with a lid, bake in a moderate oven for 1½ hours.

DUTCH HOTPOT

Hutspot

1 lb. beef	8 oz. onions	salt
2 lb. carrots	1 tablespoon vinegar	1 pint water
	1 lb. potatoes	

Wash the meat, put into cold water, add salt and vinegar, bring to the boil and skim. Cover with a lid and simmer gently for 2 hours. Then peel the carrots, mince them and add to the meat. After 30 minutes further cooking, add peeled potatoes and chopped onions and simmer for another 30 minutes or until the vegetables are well cooked. Add more water during the cooking, if necessary, and seasoning to taste. But when the dish is ready, all the water should have been completely absorbed. Serve the meat surrounded by the vegetables.

MINCED MEAT BALLS

8 oz. minced beef	1 beaten egg	1 gill sour cream
8 oz. minced veal	lard for frying	½ pint stock
8 oz. minced pork	2 tablespoons con-	salt and pepper
1 large onion, minced	centrated tomato	2 oz. breadcrumbs
	purée	

Mix the minced meats with the onion and breadcrumbs. Bind with the egg. Season with salt and pepper. Form into small balls and fry quickly in the lard. Gradually add the tomato purée and the stock, simmer for 15 minutes. Leave to stand for several hours. Reheat and stir in the cream just before serving.

HUNTSMAN'S PIE

1 lb. minced meat,	2 onions, sliced very	½ pint stock
fresh or cooked	thinly	4 oz. breadcrumbs
2 lb. cooked potatoes,	2 large cooking apples,	2 oz. butter
diced	sliced	nutmeg
	salt and pepper	

Arrange alternate layers of potatoes, cooked meat, onion and apple in a deep casserole, beginning and ending with a layer of potato. Season the stock with salt, pepper and grated nutmeg. Pour this into the dish. Sprinkle with breadcrumbs. Dot with butter. Bake in a moderate oven for 1 hour.

STUFFED BREAD ROLLS

8 long bread rolls	½ pint stock	1 oz. flour
8 oz. cooled meat or ham, minced	1 oz. butter	salt and pepper parsley

Make a sauce with the butter, flour and stock. Mix the meat with it. Season with salt, pepper and chopped parsley. Scoop out the insides of the rolls and fill with the mixture, brush with melted butter. Replace the lid and bake for 10 minutes in the oven or under the grill.

GHERKINS IN BATTER

1 lb. gherkins	1 egg	pinch salt
2 tablespoons vegetable stock	4 oz. flour	fat for frying cream

Make a batter with the flour and salt blended with the egg and vegetable stock. Dip the gherkins in the batter and fry in deep, hot fat until golden brown. Serve with cream. *(Illustrated in Plate 65.)*

DUTCH FONDUE

Bier Kaas

1 lb. grated Gouda cheese	1 flat tablespoon cornflour	cayenne pepper salt
½ pint beer	1 small clove garlic butter	French bread

Butter a fireproof dish and put in the cheese and beer. Heat very gently until all the cheese has melted. Add the crushed garlic, salt and cayenne pepper to taste. Blend the cornflour with a little water or beer, and add to the mixture. Stir the mixture until it thickens. Keep hot over a spirit stove set on the table where everyone can dip a piece of French bread, on the end of a fork, into the hot cheese. *(Illustrated in Plate 76.)*

DUTCH PANCAKES

Flensjes

4 oz. flour	2—3 eggs	pinch salt
½ pint milk	3 oz. unsalted butter	brown sugar or jam

Break the eggs into a basin and beat slightly. Add the flour and salt and a little of the milk. Beat well until the batter is smooth then gradually add the rest of the milk. Melt the butter and pour about 4 tablespoons of it into the batter, making a thin mixture. Fry the pancakes in the remaining butter until golden brown on both sides. Serve hot with sugar or jam.

184

BOTERCAKE

8 oz. unsalted butter   8 oz. castor sugar   5 oz. dried fruit
8 oz. self-raising flour   4 eggs

Cream the butter and sugar well. Blend in beaten eggs, a little at a time, keeping the mixture stiff. Fold in sieved flour and the fruit. Spread mixture in a large buttered loaf tin and bake for 1—1½ hours in a cool oven, until golden brown.

STRAWBERRY SHORTCAKE

1 lb. self-raising flour   ½ pint milk   2 tablespoons red jam
4 oz. unsalted butter   1½ lb. strawberries   ½ pint whipped cream
                            4 oz. sugar

Rub the butter into the flour until mixture resembles fine breadcrumbs. Add 2 oz. of sugar and mix to a stiff dough with the milk. Divide the mixture into two 9-inch buttered tins and level the surfaces. Bake in a very hot oven for about 20 minutes, until well risen and firm. Allow to cool on a wire rack. Spread the top of one shortcake with the jam and arrange 1 lb. of halved strawberries attractively over it. Cover the surface of the second shortcake with 8 oz. strawberries crushed with 2 oz. of sugar and the cream. Lift the top cake gently and place on to the strawberry and cream mixture. *(Illustrated in Plate 102.)*

ST. NICHOLAS DAY LETTERS

Boter Letters

On St. Nicholas Day, December 5th, little children in Holland leave their shoes by the chimney to be filled with presents. Amongst them they will find the boter letters, a pastry formed into their initial.

flaky pastry, using   3 oz. castor sugar   few drops almond
  8 oz. flour, etc.   3 oz. icing sugar   essence
  (see p. 101)   juice ½ lemon   2 large eggs
                         6 oz. ground almonds

Prepare the flaky pastry and roll thinly into strips 3 inches long and 2 inches wide. Mix the ground almonds, both types of sugar, juice of ½ lemon, almond essence and 1 large egg, to make a smooth paste. Roll into sausage shapes and wrap the pastry round each shape. Seal the edges with beaten egg, bend into letters and seal the ends. Place on a greased baking tin, glaze with the rest of the beaten egg and put into a hot oven to bake for about 30 minutes. Cool on a wire cake-tray. *(Illustrated in Plate 60.)*

DUTCH RING CAKE

flaky pastry, using
  4 oz. flour, etc.
  (see p. 101)
5 oz. ground almonds
5 oz. sugar

grated rind 1 lemon
apricot jam
2 tablespoons icing
  sugar
1 tablespoon water
2 small eggs

1 teaspoon lemon
  juice
glacé cherries
angelica
milk

Roll out the pastry thinly to a strip 18—16 inches long and 4 inches wide. To make the filling, mix the ground almonds and sugar together then add 1 egg and the lemon rind. Knead well then roll into a long roll about 16 inches long and 1 inch in diameter. Place the almond mixture on top of the pastry, brush edge of the pastry with water and roll up loosely, making sure the seam comes underneath. Shape the roll to form a ring, joining the edges together firmly, and place in a greased baking tin. Brush the cake over with a mixture of egg and milk and prick with a fork. Bake in a hot oven near the top for 20—25 minutes. When the cake is ready, but still hot, brush over the top with warmed apricot jam. Mix sieved icing sugar with the water and lemon juice to make a thin icing and pour over the jam. Allow to cool a little in the baking tin, then remove and cool on a cake rack. Decorate with halved cherries and angelica. (Illustrated in Plate 111.)

HAARLEM CELEBRATION CAKE

Cake:
2 eggs
4 oz. castor sugar
4 oz. unsalted butter
grated rind of lemon
3 oz. melted plain
  chocolate

8 oz. self-raising flour
$\frac{1}{4}$ pint milk
$\frac{1}{2}$ teaspoon salt
Filling:
4 oz. unsalted butter
3 oz. icing sugar

1 oz. chocolate powder
$\frac{1}{2}$ teaspoon vanilla
  essence
Topping:
$\frac{3}{4}$ pint thick cream
shredded chocolate

Cream the butter and sugar well. Add the lemon rind and beaten eggs. Blend in sieved flour and salt, melted chocolate and milk. Turn into a 9-inch buttered tin and bake in a moderate oven for approximately 45—55 minutes. To make filling, cream the butter and icing sugar, add the chocolate powder and vanilla essence and fill the cake when cool. The cake can be made and filled in advance, but the topping should be left until just before the cake is needed. Spread the whole cake with whipped cream, or pipe the cream using a forcing bag and rose tube. Sprinkle the top with shredded chocolate. The best way to shred the chocolate is to scrape a strong knife over the back of the slab. (Illustrated in Plate 119.)

FINNISH COOKING

Musia Soper

Finland has a sea coast as well a many lakes, so there are plenty of fish available. The winters are long and cold and there is not much fruit grown, but reindeer and wild game are plentiful and the Finnish housewife knows well how to prepare a good, sustaining variety of food suitable for the northern climate. There are many types of cheese obtainable; much fish and other food is salted, pickled or smoked, and the usual drinks are milk and sour milk.

As in the Scandinavian countries, the smörgasbord—a variety of open sandwiches and cold and hot hors-d'oeuvre—are often served before the main meal, specially at the beginning of formal dinners.

FISH SOUP

Kalakeitto

2 lb. fish, pike or perch	2 lb. potatoes	8 peppercorns
2 large onions	2½ pints of milk	salt
	1 tablespoon butter	water
	2—3 sprigs parsley	

Peel the potatoes, dice them, put into a pan of salted water. Add sliced onions and cook until the potatoes are done. Drain off the water, pour in the milk and bring to the boil. Skin the fish, cut into neat pieces and put into the saucepan with the potatoes. Add peppercorns and a teaspoon of salt, cover with a lid and simmer gently until the fish is tender. Add the butter at the end of the cooking. Serve the fish soup sprinkled with chopped parsley.

HERRING CASSEROLE

Kallallaatiko

2 salted herrings	2 lb. potatoes	1 tablespoon flour
8 oz. fat pork	1 pint milk	butter
8 oz. onions	2 eggs	salt and pepper

Soak the herrings for about 6 hours and then cut into 4 long fillets. Peel the potatoes and cut into thin slices. Cut the onions into large rings. Grease the casserole with butter and put in a layer of potato then two herring fillets. Lay over that some onion rings and then half the pork cut into slices. Put on another layer of potatoes, then the remaining herring fillets, the remaining onions and the pork. Finish with a layer of potatoes. Dot with butter, put into a moderate oven to cook for 1 hour. Beat the milk with the eggs, blend with the flour, season with a little salt and pepper and pour into the casserole. Cook for another 30—40 minutes in a moderate oven.

SALT COD PUDDING

8 oz. salted cod	2 tablespoons butter	pepper
1½ lb. potatoes	1 tablespoon bread-	water
2 eggs	crumbs	tomato sauce
½ pint milk		(see p. 333)

Soak the cod in cold water for 24 hours, changing the water whenever possible. Then simmer gently in enough water to cover until the cod is tender. Strain the cod and shred it. Meanwhile, peel the potatoes, boil them until done, then mash. Mix the fish and potatoes, add well-beaten eggs, butter, milk and a little pepper. Blend well and when the mixture is smooth put into a buttered mould sprinkled inside with breadcrumbs, and bake in a moderate oven for 30 minutes. Serve with tomato sauce.

FISH PIE

Patakukko

2 lb. fish; most kinds	4 oz. flour	½ pint water
will do	4 oz. rye flour	1 gill milk
4 oz. fat pork		salt and pepper

Fillet the fish and put into a greased pie dish. Add diced pork, salt and pepper, and pour in the milk. To make the pastry, sift the flour with 1 teaspoon of salt and add a cup of cold water. Knead the dough then turn out on to a floured board and shape to suit the pie dish. Cover the pie dish with the pastry, pressing the edges down firmly, and bake in a slow oven for about 2 hours. When the crust is brown, cover with greaseproof paper or foil until the pie is ready.

FRIED BALTIC SPRATS

Silakkapihvit

2 lb. sprats	2 tablespoons	salt and pepper
3—4 tablespoons rye	chopped dill	butter or margarine
flour		for frying

Clean the sprats and remove the heads, backbones and tails. Lay out half the sprats, skin side under, sprinkle with salt and pepper, and place each remaining half on top, skin side upwards. Cover with the flour, seasoned with salt, and fry in hot butter on both sides until golden brown. Serve hot sprinkled with dill.

FISH WITH NEW POTATOES

2 lb. fish, perch, cod, halibut, etc.	1½ lb. new potatoes	2 tablespoons chopped dill
12 oz. butter	salt	1 gill water

Put the water into a saucepan, add 1 teaspoon of salt and bring to the boil. Add the butter and allow it to melt. Put in cleaned slices of fish and cook very gently until tender. Scrub the new potatoes and boil them in their skins. When they are cooked, drain, dry off and serve, liberally sprinkled with dill, to accompany the fish.

KARELIAN STEW

This dish is popular served after a sauna bath.

1 lb. stewing steak	8 oz. pork	salt
1 lb. shoulder of mutton	1 onion	water
		12 peppercorns

Cut all the meat into pieces about 1 inch square. Put all the meat into a large oven dish, the mutton first and the steak and pork on top. Cut the onion into rings and lay over the pork. Add the peppercorns, sprinkle with salt and pour in enough hot water to cover. Put into a moderate oven without a lid and cook for 1 hour. Lower the heat and cook very slowly for another 2—3 hours. Serve with swedes and potatoes boiled in their skins.

MINCED MEAT AND CABBAGE

Liha ja Kaalilaatikko

8 oz. minced meat	1 tablespoon butter	breadcrumbs
1 medium sized cabbage	2—3 eggs	pinch sugar
1 onion	1¼ pints milk	water
		salt and pepper

Chop the onion and fry lightly in the butter. Add the minced meat and seasoning and fry for a few minutes. Beat the eggs and milk together, adding a pinch of sugar, pour over the minced meat and mix well. Meanwhile, slice the cabbage, and cook it for 5 minutes in salted, boiling water. Drain the cabbage and lay it in a casserole. Pour over it the minced meat mixture, sprinkle the top with breadcrumbs and put into a moderate oven to bake for 1—1½ hours.

REINDEER MEAT

Poronliha

Reindeer meat is found only in Northern Finland where it sometimes takes the place of beef.

1½ lb. reindeer steak	salt and pepper	1 gill water
	8 oz. streaky bacon	

Fry the bacon for a few minutes then put into a saucepan. Lay slices of reindeer meat on top, sprinkle with salt and pepper and add water. Cover with a lid and simmer for 25—30 minutes.

LIVER PUDDING

Maksalaatikko

1 lb. liver	3 eggs	pinch marjoram
6 oz. rice or pearl barley	1 large onion	½ teaspoon pepper
	1 pint milk	water
4 oz. seedless raisins	butter or margarine	cranberry jelly
	4 tablespoons syrup	salt

Boil the rice or pearl barley in plenty of salted water until tender, then drain. Chop the onion finely and fry lightly in butter and add to the rice. Mince the liver, wash the raisins and also add the rice together with beaten eggs, marjoram, salt, syrup, pepper and milk. Mix well and pour into a casserole greased with butter. The mixture will be rather slack but will thicken during cooking. Dot the top with butter, leave uncovered and put into a moderate oven to bake for 30 minutes. Serve with cranberry jelly.

BLOOD PANCAKES

Veriohukaiset

½ pint calf's or sheep's blood	1 small onion	pinch mixed herbs
	4 tablespoons rye flour	2 teaspoons salt
1 gill beer or kalja (see p. 192)	4 tablespoons barley flour	cranberry jelly
		melted butter
1 egg		2 oz. pork fat for frying

Strain the blood into a bowl. Chop the onion finely, fry lightly and add to the blood with the beer or kalja, beaten egg, herbs, seasoning and flours. Stir well until the batter is smooth then leave to stand for about 30 minutes. Pour a thin layer of batter into a small, hot, greased pan and fry on both sides until done. When all the batter is used up, serve the pancakes hot with cranberry jelly and melted butter.

BLACK PUDDING
Veripalttu

Prepare the mixture in the same way as for blood pancakes. Then pour the batter into a greased baking dish and put into a moderate oven to cook until the top is brown. Serve the pudding hot.

RED WHORTLEBERRY PUDDING
Puolukkapuuro

8 oz. red whortle-berries (bilberries)	4 oz. semolina	1½ pints water
4 oz. sugar	few drops vanilla essence	cream

Stew the whortleberries in the water until soft, then strain off the juice into a saucepan. Add sugar to the juice, bring to the boil, then gradually add the semolina, stirring continuously. Simmer gently until the semolina is cooked. Mash the whortleberries, add to the semolina with vanilla essence and mix well. When the pudding is cold whip until it is frothy. Serve with whipped cream.

KALJA
A Home Brew

½ pint rye malt	8 oz. sugar	1 teaspoon yeast
	10 pints water	

Put the sugar and malt into a large earthenware jar and mix. Pour on boiling water, and when it is cool, add the yeast, dissolved in a little warm water. Cover the jar with a cloth and leave to ferment. After a day or two, strain the liquid into bottles, cork and store in a cool place.

RICE WINE
Rusiviini

3 lb. rice	1 lb. brown sugar	18 pints water
2 lb. seedless raisins	1 teaspoon yeast	1 orange
	7 lb. sugar	

Put the ingredients, except the yeast and water, into a large earthenware jar. The orange should be thinly sliced. Pour on boiling water, and when cool, add the yeast, first dissolved in a little warm water. Cover, but not too tightly, and leave to ferment for 2—3 weeks or until the wine has finished bubbling. During that time, the wine should be stirred every morning and evening. When ready, strain into bottles. If there is any sediment, strain into other bottles until the wine is clear. Cork and store in a cool place.

33. Farmer's Soup, Holland (p.180)

34. Preparing the Christmas Cake, Britain

FRENCH COOKING

Elizabeth Smart and Agnes Ryan

The French have won themselves an enviable reputation for being the best cooks in the world. In every civilized country dishes are glamorized by French names, even if they haven't a single French antecedent. And although it was the Italians who first brought cooking as an art into France, the French always seem to have had an innate love of good food. They have made the art of cooking so much their own that no one can think of France without thinking of food. There isn't a French country girl or small-town working woman who wouldn't think it an unnecessary and unforgivable crime to serve badly cooked food. French wives willingly spend hours lovingly preparing dishes and carefully and critically choosing their ingredients from the market.

None of the French dishes given here requires elaborate equipment or unusual gadgets. But it is well worth while getting a few very good pots and pans. They may seem expensive to buy at first, but they last far longer, and mean less waste of food through burning or too-quick cooking. The finest French chefs believe firmly that a copper saucepan is much the best, especially for making sauces. It is thick, so that it keeps in the heat, and the sauces do not stick to the bottom or burn. And incidentally, copper saucepans are just as easy to keep clean as any other kind. The only extra attention they need is a retinning about every six months. This only costs a few pence, and is quite easy to get done, and your copper saucepan will last you a lifetime. Anyhow, copper or not, you will need three or four saucepans, each a different size, and they must have good thick bottoms. It is best, also, to have a heavy iron frying pan, two if possible: one larger and one smaller one. The smaller one should be kept only for making omelettes and never washed, but just wiped out each time with clean tissue paper. You will find it well worthwhile to invest in a large earthenware or cast-iron casserole, because this is used in so many important French recipes. You can buy them almost anywhere in England now. The big brown ones, with handle and lid, are excellent, and besides being so efficient for slow oven cooking, look nice on the table and suggest the presence of really succulent food. The little individual versions of these casseroles would also be a valuable addition to any kitchen. Then you will need a whip or whisk (rotary or hand, whichever you prefer), a wooden salad bowl, one or two wooden spoons, baking tins including the muffin kind, and some mixing bowls. Also a deep fat fryer and basket. Most important of all are some really good very sharp knives.

It will make your cooking much simpler and less confusing if you master a few of the very basic French principles before you begin on any individual recipe. Every French household has an indispensable stockpot always on hand, which is the making of so many soups, sauces, and stews. It is quite easy and very economical to keep a stockpot going ready for use at any time, and with it you will also get into the habit of never wasting any food. All the odds and ends can go into it to enrich it.

Other important items that you should get familiar with as they are referred to again and again are the *court bouillon* or fish stock, the *bouquet garni*, or bunch of herbs in muslin the *maître d'hôtel* butter, how to marinate, how to make croûtons.

All the ingredients in these famous French dishes can be found in England. No country in the world has better fish or vegetables. Many things like Jerusalem and globe artichokes, garlic, shallots, celeriac, blanched dandelion, chicory (which the French call endive: what we call endive they call chicory), and other vegetables can all be grown very successfully in any little English garden. Vegetables like green and red peppers and aubergines are now imported in great quantities and are available in shops all over the country. One point to remember: the French believe in eating their vegetables when they are young and tender. There is no point in waiting until they are large and tough. You may have more of them, but they are that much less worth eating. Pick or buy your green beans when they are young and stringless. Use your baby marrows instead of waiting until they are large and elderly, and you will discover a new delight in marrows. Try cooking your cucumbers for a change.

The wine, sherry, olive oil, butter, and so on that you will find mentioned so often in these recipes are of course important to their flavour and quality. The French believe that food is so important that to skimp on it is illogical. So do be as generous as you can. In many cases, though, you can safely use substitutes. Margarine can be used instead of butter, especially when it is to be mixed with stronger flavours like onion. Salad oil can replace olive oil. When wine is called for in a stew or casserole or soup, and you do not feel you can afford the expense, use instead two tablespoons of wine vinegar to each half-pint of water. White wine vinegar is slightly more expensive than malt, but it is well worth having some on hand. Lemon juice is a very good substitute for vinegar, especially white wine vinegar. Most of the herbs can be grown, even in a window-box, without much trouble. There are English shops that supply fresh herbs by post all the year round. For emergencies, keep small quantities of dried herbs and hand, but never get large quantities, as they lose their flavour, and their flavour is, after all, their whole point. Saffron is expensive, but you need very little, and many good grocers stock the real saffron in tiny thimble containers.

The secret of the Frenchwoman's success in the kitchen is that she really enjoys cooking: it is creative and therefore refreshing to her. The planning of meals for a week, so that they are economical as well as delicious and filling, can be as much fun as a crossword puzzle and infinitely more satisfying. Lovingly prepared dishes cannot fail to be lovingly received. There is no doubt that a good cook goes a long way towards making a happy family. Balzac, the celebrated French novelist, even goes so far as to say that 'men become passionately attached to women who know how to cosset them with delicate titbits'. Even if you live alone and like it, there is nothing quite so helpful as a knowledge of how to enjoy and get the best out of food.

One other lesson to be learnt from the French is from their cleverness in using their regional specialities. If your locality or your garden produces something particularly well, make an asset of this in your cooking. See how many different dishes you can find or invent for it. If you live in a cider-making district, for instance, choose all those recipes where cider is particularly recommended. The great regional dishes of France were invented by ingenious housewives faced with a local glut.

Anyone who can learn even a little from the French way with food, and a few of the many wonderful dishes—not only for special occasions but for making ends meet delectably during the thin days of the week— will find a rich new excitement in everyday life. For it is not only what the French do with food itself, but the whole French attitude to food, that is so stimulating.

These recipes should serve to introduce some of the delights of French cooking into ordinary households, and to demonstrate how easy it is for anyone to enjoy many of the most celebrated dishes of all time.

TOMATES AUX CREVETTES

Tomatoes with Shrimps

| ½ pint mayonnaise (see p. 263) | 4 large tomatoes | 8 oz. shelled shrimps 4 lettuce leaves |

Cut the tops of the tomatoes, empty them with a spoon and stand them to drain for a few minutes. Mix the freshly cooked cold shrimps with the mayonnaise. Stuff the tomatoes with this mixture and serve each tomato on a lettuce leaf.

TOMATES FARCIES AU RIZ

Rice-stuffed Tomatoes

8 SERVINGS

| 8 tomatoes ½ pint mayonnaise (see p. 263) | 2 hard-boiled eggs 1 tablespoon chopped tarragon 4 oz. boiled rice | 1 tablespoon chopped chives salt |

Cut a lid off the top of each tomato and empty them of pips and fibres. Sprinkle them inside with salt, and set them to drain, cut side down. Mince the hard-boiled eggs and mix them with the cold boiled rice, mayonnaise sauce, and half the chopped chives and tarragon. Fill the tomatoes with this mixture. Sprinkle the tops with the remaining chives and tarragon. This is a very good way of using up rice which is left over from a previous meal.

TOMATES CHAMPIGNONS

Mushroom Tomatoes

2 tomatoes (large)	½ pint mayonnaise	4 lettuce leaves
4 hard-boiled eggs	(see p. 263)	4 tooth picks

Cut the tomatoes in two across their middles and empty them. Take 4 small hard-boiled eggs, cut slices off one end of each egg to enable it to stand upright, and stick a toothpick into the other end, allowing about a quarter of an inch to show. Impale the halved tomatoes, cut side downwards, on the tooth pick. Place the eggs and tomato halves on the lettuce leaves. With a pinhead, dot the tomato halves with tiny blobs of mayonnaise. Put a helping of mayonnaise sauce with each 'mushroom' and serve.

ARTICHAUTS À LA VINAIGRETTE

Artichokes with Vinaigrette Sauce

4 artichokes	vinaigrette sauce
	(see p. 425)

Wash the artichokes, cut off the stems and remove the first two outer layers of leaves. Plunge them into plenty of boiling water and let them boil for 35 to 45 minutes depending on their size. Drain them and serve them cold with a vinaigrette sauce. They are eaten by dipping each leaf into the sauce and eating the soft part, discarding the rest. When the heart is reached the grass-like choke is removed, and the heart has a little sauce poured over it and is eaten with a spoon.

FONDS D'ARTICHAUTS
AUX CHAMPIGNONS

Artichoke Hearts with Mushrooms

4 globe artichokes	grated cheese	8 oz. mushrooms
2 tablespoons butter	(preferably Gruyère)	

Boil the artichokes stems downwards in boiling salted water for about 25 minutes, drain. Peel off all the leaves and remove the choke, but do not break the hearts. Melt the butter in a frying pan and gently fry the hearts. Remove and keep them warm. Then fry the mushrooms, chopped finely, in the same butter. Fill the artichoke hearts with the mushrooms. Sprinkle liberally with grated cheese and heat under the grill until the cheese melts.

HORS-D'OEUVRE JARDINIÈRE

Garden Hors-d'Oeuvre

6 SERVINGS

½ pint mayonnaise
(see p. 263)
4 oz. diced cooked
potatoes
4 oz. cooked peas
1 lettuce

1 dessertspoon
chopped chervil
2 oz. breadcrumbs
6 tomatoes
6 oz. diced cooked
ham

3 eggs
8 chopped black
olives
2 green peppers
1 gill milk
salt and pepper

Take 6 large sized and regular tomatoes. Slice off the tops and scoop out the seeds and pulp with a spoon. Mix the diced cooked potatoes, the cooked peas and mayonnaise together and add the diced ham. Fill the tomatoes with this mixture. Hard-boil the eggs, take off the shells and slice in two. Remove the yolk from each half. Soak the breadcrumbs in milk and mash the egg yolks and the soaked breadcrumbs together. Add the chopped chervil and the chopped black olives. With this mixture stuff the white hollow halves of the eggs. Now place one of these stuffed half-eggs on top of each stuffed tomato as a lid (the sliced tomato lids will not be used). Take the lettuce (which should be fresh and crisp) and cut into strips. Similarly, cut the fleshy part of the green peppers into strips (you will have removed the seeds). With these strips mixed, make a nest on which each tomato will be served separately.

PÊCHES AUX CRABES

Peaches with Crab Meat

6 SERVINGS

6 peaches
8 oz. crab meat

1 gill cream
salt

salt and paprika
pepper

Chop a lid off the end each peach. Remove the stone and a little of the flesh with a spoon. Mince the crab meat and mix it with the cream and the peach flesh. Season with a pinch of salt and paprika. Stuff the peaches with this mixture and keep them in the refrigerator until wanted.

ASPERGES À L'HUILE

Asparagus with Olive Oil

3 SERVINGS

24 spears asparagus
salt and black pepper

4 tablespoons olive oil

1 tablespoon wine
vinegar

Put the asparagus in a saucepan with plenty of boiling salted water. They will be cooked 12 minutes after the water reboils. Strain and allow them to cool. Mix the olive oil, vinegar, a pinch of salt and black pepper, thoroughly. The asparagus is served cold accompanied by this sauce.

OEUFS FARCIS AUX SARDINES

Eggs with Sardine Stuffing

6 SERVINGS

6 hard-boiled eggs	7 sardines	1 gherkin
3 tablespoons butter	6 oblongs of bread	salt and pepper

Shell the eggs and cut off the caps just enough to uncover the yolks at one end of the egg. Scoop out the yolks with a little spoon, taking care not to break the white part. Mash these yolks very finely. Cream the butter and add the eggs to it. Bone the sardines and press them through a sieve. Add them to the eggs and butter, with a pinch of salt and pepper. Cream all well together. Now stuff the egg whites with this mixture. Cut some crustless bread slices into little oblongs, spread them with the remainder of the stuffing, and place the eggs cut side down on them. Decorate with tiny slices of gherkin.

CROÛTES AU JAMBON À LA MÉNAGÈRE

Fried Bread and Ham

6 SERVINGS

6 pieces bread	1 dessertspoon flour	2 beaten egg whites
4 oz. lean cooked ham	1 gill boiling milk	salt and pepper
	1 oz. butter	

Remove the crusts from the bread slices and halve them triangularly. Mince the lean ham. Heat the butter in a little saucepan, stir in the flour and cook, stirring gently, for 2 or 3 minutes but do not let it brown. Add the boiling milk a little at a time, stirring all the while with an egg beater until you have a thick sauce. Season with salt and pepper. Reduce by half, stirring all the while. Add the ham. Beat the egg whites thoroughly and add them to the sauce. Spread the pieces of bread with this mixture and fry them in a deep pan of very hot fat for 6 minutes. Serve.

VOL-AU-VENT

Pastry with Creamed Filling

1 lb. of either:	oysters,	½ pint milk or cream
cooked chicken,	any other left-overs	salt and pepper
veal, scallops,	4 oz. mushrooms	puff pastry cases
fish,	1½ tablespoons butter	(see p. 101)
sweetbreads,	1 tablespoon flour	

You can now quite easily buy ready made individual pastry cases, but if you prefer to make your own pastry make sure it is very light and flaky and use plenty of butter. For the filling: melt the butter in a saucepan. Fry the chopped mushrooms in it. Add the flour, stirring well, and gradually add the milk. Season with salt and pepper. Add your chosen filling, chopped small, stirring all the time until all is hot. Warm up the pastry, fill with stuffing, and put on the pastry lids. *(Illustrated in Plate 6.)*

PÂTÉ TERRINE DE FOIE GRAS

Liver Pâté

2 lb. liver	1 dessertspoon	flour and water pastry
8 oz. lard	chopped parsley	to seal
pinch ground cloves	salt and black pepper	3 tablespoons port
½ bay leaf	2 tablespoons water	wine

Chop the liver and fry it gently in a little lard until it is brown. Mince it and mix it with the cloves, parsley, salt, and black pepper. Moisten with the port wine and water, which should be just enough to hold it together. Put the mince in a terrine or earthenware dish. Press it down firmly. Place the terrine in a dish of water. Cover it with the lard in a thin layer, the bay leaf stuck on top, and the edges sealed with a paste of flour and water. Place it in a fairly hot oven and cook for 3½ hours. Serve cold.

ESCARGOTS

Snails

40 snails	4 oz. butter	large handful fennel
1½ pints Chablis or	2 cloves of garlic	½ teaspoon ground
1½ pints salt water	handful parsley, finely	nutmeg
1 small handful thyme	chopped	salt and pepper

Add the thyme and fennel to the wine or water, simmer the snails in this for 1 hour. Strain. Keep snails warm. Pound the garlic to a pulp in a mortar, remove any hard pieces that refuse to be pulped, add the butter and the parsley, salt, pepper and nutmeg. With a wooden spoon work thoroughly till everything is mixed well together. Put over the warm snails in the serving dish and let the garlic butter melt and run into the snails.

FROG'S LEGS À LA PROVENÇALE

2 lb. medium sized frog's legs	1 tablespoon chopped parsley	juice ½ lemon
8 oz. butter	2 cloves of garlic, finely chopped	1 teaspoon chopped chives
1 tablespoon olive oil	2 tablespoons flour	½ teaspoon salt
1 gill milk		pepper

Add salt and pepper to the milk, dip the legs in and roll in flour. Heat 2 oz. butter and the olive oil, add the floured legs, gently fry for 12 minutes, till browned. Add the lemon juice, parsley, chives and a pinch of pepper, stir and keep warm in the serving dish. Melt the remaining butter, add the garlic and brown quickly, pour over the dish. Slices of lemon may be used as a garnish.

SALADE DE FONDS D'ARTICHAUTS

Globe Artichoke Salad

8 globe artichokes	mayonnaise (see p. 263)	salt

Boil the artichokes in salted water for 30 minutes. Drain upside down for 20 minutes or longer. Pull off all the leaves and remove the chokes carefully without breaking the hearts. Put the hearts in a dish and cover thickly with mayonnaise.

SALADE D'ENDIVES

Chicory Salad

3 heads of chicory	1 tablespoon lemon	salt and black pepper
3 tablespoons olive oil	juice	1 clove garlic

Wash and separate the chicory leaves and break the larger ones in two. Crush the garlic with salt and pepper in a wooden salad bowl. Add the oil and lemon juice and stir well. Put in the chicory and turn it over and over until each is thoroughly coated with dressing.

SALADE DE PISSENLITS

Dandelion Salad

6 handfuls dandelion leaves	½ clove garlic	1 tablespoon vinegar
	3 tablespoons olive oil	salt and pepper

The French are very fond of young dandelion leaves. If you keep the young plants covered, they stay white and are even better to eat. Choose young tender leaves. Wash and drain them well. Toss them in a dressing of oil and vinegar, salt and pepper, in a wooden bowl which has had a halved garlic clove rubbed round it.

SALADE DE HARICOTS VERTS ET TOMATES

Green Bean and Tomato Salad

1 lb. French or runner
  beans
8 oz. tomatoes

3 tablespoons olive oil
salt and black pepper

1 tablespoon white
  wine vinegar
½ clove garlic

Top and tail the beans and remove strings, if any. Get three cupfuls
of water boiling fast in a saucepan, add salt. Cut up the beans into
1-inch pieces and boil them for 10 minutes with the lid on. Drain and
cool. Cut the tomatoes in quarters and quarter them again. Crush
the garlic with salt around a wooden salad bowl. Add the olive oil
and vinegar, pepper, and mix well. Put in the beans and tomatoes and
toss.

SALADE NIÇOISE

Salad from Nice

6 TO 8 SERVINGS

1½ lb. new potatoes
24 black olives
6 anchovy fillets
1 clove garlic

1 small onion
4 tablespoons olive oil
1½ tablespoons wine
  vinegar
½ teaspoon salt

1 teaspoon chopped
  parsley
¼ teaspoon black
  pepper

Wash the anchovy fillets under running water, and cut them in three.
Slice the onion finely. Stone the black olives. Rub a salad bowl with
a crushed garlic clove in a little salt until the clove is pulverized. Boil
and peel the potatoes. While still warm slice them and put them into
the salad bowl. Mix the olive oil, vinegar, parsley, salt, and pepper.
Pour this mixture over the warm potatoes. Mix lightly but thoroughly.
When cool, stir in the olives, anchovy pieces, and the sliced onion.
Chopped green peppers and tomatoes also look very pretty added to
this salad.

SALADE DE LAITUES

Lettuce Salad

1 lettuce
1 teaspoon chopped
  chives
½ clove garlic
pinch sugar

1 dessertspoon wine
  vinegar
pinch salt
black pepper

½ teaspoon chopped
  tarragon
1 saltspoon mustard
3 dessertspoons
  olive oil

Wash a fresh young lettuce, dicard the outer leaves. Dry it thoroughly
with a clean dish cloth and hang it in a salad basket to dry further.
Rub one half clove of garlic with a pinch of salt in the salad bowl.

Mix the oil, vinegar, tarragon, chives, mustard, black pepper and sugar. Put the dry crisp lettuce in the bowl, cover with the dressing, toss well with wooden salad spoon and fork. Toss again just before you serve it.

CONSOMMÉ

Clear Soup

8 TO 12 SERVINGS

3 lb. stewing beef	4 oz. diced celery	1 bay leaf
1 lb. marrow bone	4 oz. diced onion	4 cloves
3 lb. knuckle of veal	3 quarts water	2 tablespoons butter
2 pints chicken stock	1 teaspoon thyme	1 teaspoon
4 oz. diced carrots	1 spring marjoram	peppercorns
4 oz. diced turnips	2 sprigs parsley	1 teaspoon salt

Cut the beef and veal into small pieces. Brown half the beef in some of the marrow from the bone. Add the bones the rest of the meat and the cold water. Let it stand for 30 minutes. Bring slowly to boiling point. Simmer for 3 hours, removing the scum as it forms. Add the chicken stock, and simmer for another 2 hours. Cook carrots, turnips, celery, and onion for 4 minutes in the butter, then add them to the soup, with the spices, herbs and seasonings. Simmer for another 1½ hours. Strain. Cool. Remove fat carefully. Reheat, and serve.

LE POT-AU-FEU

The Stockpot

3 lb. lean beef	1 turnip	salt and black pepper
8 oz. marrow bones	½ parsnip	2 cloves
3 carrots	2 sticks celery	clove garlic
3 leeks	bouquet garni	4 quarts water
	3 onions	

Put all the above ingredients together in a large saucepan. The meat and vegetables are left whole. One of the onions is stuck with the cloves. A teaspoon of pepper and nearly as much salt is added. Bring the mixture very slowly to the boil. Skim off the white scum that rises to the top of the water, several times. Then cover and simmer for 4 hours. The meat and vegetables are removed and eaten separately with a piquant, tomato or caper sauce (see pp. 256, 333, 261). Remove the bones (the marrow is very good eaten salted on dried toast). Cool the liquid. Remove as much fat as possible from the top. Strain through a cold wet cheese-cloth. Keep this stock always on hand and make it the basis of your soups and stews. It is best kept in a cool part of the kitchen and boiled up once every day. The French cook it in great earthenware lidded pots called *marmites*.

POTAGE GRÉCY

Crécy Soup

1½ lb. young carrots	2½ pints cold stock	salt
1 oz. butter	or water	*bouquet garni*
2 oz. rice	1 large onion	little sugar

Put the butter in a heavy saucepan on the fire. When it has melted add the onion chopped in very small pieces. Grate the carrots and add them to the saucepan with the *bouquet garni*, salt and a little sugar. Put the lid on the pan, lower the heat and let them cook slowly until they are tender. Stir them and shake the pan every few minutes to keep them from sticking to it. While they are cooking put the rice in a saucepan of rapidly boiling salted water. When it is tender, drain it and mix it with a cup of the cold stock. Put the sieved vegetables into the saucepan, add the rice and the rest of the stock and bring to the boil. Boil for 5 minutes, stirring constantly. The amounts of rice and stock can be varied to suit yourself.

BOUILLON DE CHAMPIGNONS

Mushroom Broth

8 TO 10 SERVINGS

2 lb. mushrooms	2 sticks celery	2 sprigs thyme
4 pints water	2 oz. butter	½ bay leaf
3 carrots	2 sprigs parsley	salt and black pepper
	3 leeks	

Slice the carrots, leeks, and celery sticks. Put them in a saucepan with the melted butter and fry gently, without letting them brown, for 10 minutes. Add the 4 pints of water. Cut the mushrooms, stalks included, into narrow strips lengthwise, and add them with the parsley, thyme, and the half bay leaf, to the soup. Bring to the boil, then simmer for 1 hour with the lid on the saucepan. Remove the mushrooms, strain the soup, return the mushrooms to the soup, and serve.

PANADE

Bread and Butter Soup

6 SERVINGS

3 pints stock	2 leeks	3 oz. butter
loaf French bread	2 egg yolks	salt and pepper

Cut the white part of the leeks into thin rounds, and fry them gently, without allowing them to brown, in 1 oz. of butter for 10 minutes. Now add the bread in slices. Cover with the stock, season to taste, bring to boiling point, and then simmer for 10 minutes. Add the rest of the butter in tiny pieces. Mix the egg yolks in a bowl, add a little of the soup, then slowly stirring all the while, add a few more cupfuls. Pour the bowl of eggs and soup into saucepan, mix, and it is now ready to serve. Children particularly love this soup.

POTAGE PURÉE DE LÉGUMES

Cream of Vegetable Soup

6 TO 8 SERVINGS

3 pints stock	1 small turnip	½ bay leaf
3 leeks	1 onion	8 oz. green peas
2 sticks celery	2 sprigs parsley	3 oz. butter
3 carrots	1 sprig thyme	salt and pepper

Cut the vegetables into small cubes, melt the butter in a saucepan, add all the vegetables except the green peas, and cook very slowly with the saucepan covered until the vegetables are soft but not browned. Now add the stock, with the parsley, thyme, bay leaf, green peas, and a pinch of salt and pepper. Boil for 30 minutes. Put through a sieve, and the soup is ready to serve.

PETITE MARMITE

Soup in Individual Tureens

8 TO 10 SERVINGS

1 boiling fowl	grated cheese	salt and pepper
6 pints water	2 veal bones	8 oz. chopped
3 carrots	2 leeks	cabbage
3 onions	1 turnip	¼ bay leaf
1 stick celery	pinch thyme	2 cloves

Put the fowl and the veal bones into a saucepan containing 6 pints water, thyme, bay leaf, an onion (into which you have stuck two cloves), salt and pepper. Bring the water to the boil and simmer for 2 hours. Then remove the fowl. Cool, and take off the fat which will have formed on the top of the soup. Strain it. Cut some of the white meat from the fowl into cubes and keep the remainder for another dish. Chop all the vegetables into small pieces. Put them with the chopped chicken into the soup, and simmer until the vegetables are tender. Boil the cabbage apart, drain and add it to the soup. Warm some small earthenware tureens, fill them with the soup, chopped vegetables, and chicken, and serve with tiny pieces of toast and grated cheese.

SOUPE À L'OIGNON

Onion Soup

2 or 3 medium onions	2 tablespoons butter	4 rounds toasted
1½ pints water	4 oz. grated Gruyère	French bread
1 gill white wine	cheese	little sugar
1 meat cube		salt and pepper

Fry the sliced onions thoroughly in the butter, but do not let them brown. When they are well cooked, sprinkle them with a little sugar. Add the water and meat cube, and bring to the boil and boil gently for 20 minutes. Reduce the heat to a gentle simmer, add the white wine and cook for another 10 minutes. Divide the grated Gruyère into four portions, place the pieces of toast in four earthenware soup plates (rimless ones are best) or one large dish, place the cheese on the toast pieces, and fill each plate up with the soup. Now place the individual plates under the grill until the cheese becomes crisp and golden. Serve in the same earthenware plates. This soup is very good even without the white wine. *(Illustrated in Plate 26.)*

POTAGE SAINT-GERMAIN

Green Pea Soup

6 TO 8 SERVINGS

2 pints marrowfat	12 spinach leaves	4 teaspoons sugar
peas	2 leeks	4 oz. butter
8 oz. small new peas	sprig chervil	1 teaspoon chopped
2 pints water	2 teaspoons salt	chervil
	12 lettuce leaves	

Chop the green part of leeks and place them in a large saucepan with the marrowfat peas, the roughly chopped lettuce and spinach leaves, the chervil, 3 oz. of the butter, salt, sugar, and half a glass of cold water. Bring to a fast boil, then lower the heat, cover the saucepan with a soup plate of cold water for a lid, simmer for 40 minutes, then sieve it all. Now add the water, which should be lukewarm, stirring with a wooden spoon. Bring to the boil, remove from fire, sprinkle with butter and the new peas which have been boiled apart and drained and your soup is ready.

WINE SOUP

2 pints veal stock or	2 tablespoons sugar	cinnamon
chicken broth	2 cloves	½ pint red wine
2 egg yolks		nutmeg

A good pick-me-up for a cold day. Bring the stock to the boil, add the sugar, cloves and nutmeg and let it simmer for 10 minutes. Beat the egg yolks, blend in the cinnamon and add the wine to them. Get the soup very hot (not boiling) and pour it over the egg and wine mixture— serve at once.

GARBURE

Cabbage Soup

6 TO 8 SERVINGS

1 small cabbage	8 oz. salt pork	1 onion
3 leeks	8 oz. soaked haricot	sprig thyme
1 carrot	beans	6 oz. butter
1 turnip	2 potatoes	salt and pepper
2 celery sticks	1 clove garlic	croûtons

Cut the cabbage, leeks, carrot, turnip, celery, garlic, and onion into medium cubes. Melt the butter in a large saucepan. Fry the chopped vegetables very gently in the butter for 10 minutes. Do not allow them to brown. Cover with about 4 pints of water, bring to the boil, and season well. Add the pork, quartered potatoes, haricot beans, and sprig of thyme. Simmer for 1 hour. Remove the pork, which is served separately. Sieve the soup and serve it on large croûtons of fried bread. This soup can also be made without the salt pork.

CRÈME DE LAITUES

Cream of Lettuce Soup

6 TO 8 SERVINGS

2 large or 3 medium	1 oz. butter or	salt
lettuces	margarine	2 slices thin fried
2 pints béchamel	1½ gills milk	bread
sauce (see p. 256)	pinch sugar	little fresh chervil

When you have washed and separated the lettuce leaves, plunge them into a pan of boiling water for 1 minute. Remove and leave them to cool and drain in a colander. Put the butter or margarine in a saucepan over a low heat, cut up the lettuces rather coarsely and put them on top of the butter in the saucepan. Add a little salt and the pinch of sugar. Cover the saucepan with a tight lid. Shake the saucepan. Now add the béchamel sauce, made either with milk or with stock, and cook slowly with the lid on until the lettuce is tender. Watch it carefully, because it is important not to have to add any more liquid than stated. When ready, pass the whole mixture through a sieve and add the milk. Reheat gently but do not let it boil. Just before serving, add the chervil finely chopped up and the fried bread cut into tiny squares.

POTAGE PISTOU

French Bean Soup with Potatoes and Vermicelli

12 oz. French beans	½ tablespoon salt	2 tablespoons olive oil
3 medium potatoes	7 oz. vermicelli	3 oz. grated Gruyère cheese
4 tomatoes	2 cloves garlic	½ oz. basil
	1¾ pints water	

Choose beans with plump pods. Cut them up into small pieces. Peel and slice two of the tomatoes and the three potatoes. Add the salt to the boiling water, then the vegetables. Cook for 10 minutes, then add the vermicelli and lower the heat. Now cook very slowly until the vegetables and vermicelli are tender, but be careful that the soup does not stick to the bottom of the pan, as it will be very thick. Thoroughly crush the 2 cloves of garlic with the basil. Grill the 2 remaining tomatoes. Skin them. Drain them. Add them to the garlic and basil. Now, drop by drop, add the olive oil to the garlic and tomatoes and then pour on them a couple of spoonfuls of the hot soup, stirring as you do so. Pour the soup into a well warmed tureen and add the garlic and tomato mixture immediately, and finally the Gruyère cheese, fresh and finely grated, and serve.

CROÛTE AU POT

Black Bread Soup

6 thin slices rye bread	grated nutmeg	1 egg yolk
1 tablespoon butter	1 large onion	2 tablespoons thick cream
2 pints water or stock	2 cloves	
salt and pepper		1 gill red or white wine

Put a tablespoon of butter in a saucepan and, when it has melted, put the rye bread cut in thin strips into it and let them brown on both sides. Add about 2 pints water, salt, pepper, a little grated nutmeg, and a large peeled onion into which you have stuck the cloves. Cover the saucepan and put it over a low heat to simmer gently for 1½ hours. Then pour it all through a coarse sieve, return it to the saucepan and let it come to the boil, then add the wine. Beat the yolk and cream together and put them in a warm soup tureen. When the soup is really boiling take it and quickly pour it over the egg and cream in the tureen. Stir it thoroughly and serve at once.

SOUPE RUSTIQUE

Grated Bread Soup

2 pints vegetable stock	8 oz. grated bread-crumbs	1 gill cream
1 egg yolk		salt and pepper

35. Stuffed Eggs with Curry, Denmark (p.478)

36. Quiche Lorraine, France (p.264)

Take enough of the cold vegetable stock to make a smooth paste with the breadcrumbs. Heat the rest of the stock until it comes to the boil, then pour it over the paste, stirring thoroughly and keeping the mixture smooth. Return it all to the saucepan, season and bring to the boil. Beat the egg yolk and the cream and add them to the soup just before you take it off the stove. Serve immediately.

RIZ AU GRAS

Broth with Rice

6 SERVINGS

3 pints stock from pot-au-feu (see p. 203)	4½ tablespoons rice	1 leek and one carrot from pot-au-feu

Take the rice and wash it in warm water. Bring the 3 pints of stock to the boil and add the rice. Take the carrot from a pot-au-feu and the leek from same and crush them. Add to the rice and stock and simmer for 30 minutes. In the event of a pot-au-feu being unavailable, use a good meat stock and add the rice as above, omitting the crushed carrot or leek.

CRÈME DE PROVENCE

Provence Soup

4 TO 6 SERVINGS

1 lb. potatoes	4 oz. very small white onions	3 pints water or stock
1 lb. tomatoes	little butter	fresh thyme
1 large onion	2 cloves garlic	chopped chervii
4 slices toast		salt and pepper

Put the tomatoes in boiling water for 2 minutes. Remove them and peel off the skins. Peel and chop up the potatoes. Put potatoes and tomatoes in a heavy saucepan with water, salt and pepper, one of the cloves of garlic, chopped fine, a little thyme, fresh if possible, coarsely chopped, and the big onion, also chopped. Let everything come just to the boil. Then lower the heat and simmer for 2 or 3 hours. In the meantime, put the small white onions into a pan of boiling salted water and cook until just tender. Drain them but keep them warm while you pour off the liquid for the other vegetables into a bowl, then take the vegetables and put them through a coarse sieve into another bowl. Then add gradually enough of the liquid to the purée to make a thick but runny soup. Return it to the saucepan, add the little white onions and bring to the boil. Just before removing from the stove, add a walnut of butter. After it is poured into the tureen or individual bowls, add chopped chervil. Serve with unbuttered toast which has been lightly rubbed with a slice of garlic.

POTAGE PAYSANNE

Peasant Soup

6 SERVINGS

2 pints stock or vegetable water	2 leeks	4 oz. green peas
	1 stick celery	4 oz. chopped green
2 carrots	8 oz. chopped sabbage	beans
1 small turnip	2 small onions	2 oz. butter
1 medium potato	salt	pinch sugar

Chop the carrots, turnip, onions, celery, and leeks (of which you use only the white part) into fine rounds. Heat the butter in a heavy saucepan, add the vegetables including the chopped cabbage. Sprinkle with a little sugar and a pinch of salt. Place on a moderate heat and stir with a wooden spoon. Let it heat well, stirring occasionally, for 5 minutes. Cover the saucepan and cook on a gentle fire for 10 minutes, taking care that the vegetables do not stick to the pan or burn (move them about from time to time). Add one pint of stock. Bring to the boil. Add the chopped potato, the green peas and beans. Cover and simmer for 30 minutes. Add the remainder of the stock and boil for another 5 minutes. Serve with small rounds of toasted French bread. Vegetables may be added or subtracted from this soup according to the season, without spoiling the character, but should, when possible, be young and fresh. If you have no meat or vegetable stock, water may be used, in which case add a little butter before serving.

POTAGE À LA BISQUE D'HOMARD

Lobster Soup

1 lobster	2 oz. butter	4 slices stale white
1 pint cold water	1 gill Madeira or white	bread
1 onion	wine	salt and pepper
1 carrot	1½ pints stock	*bouquet garni*

Dice the vegetables, add the water, salt, pepper and *bouquet*. Bring to a fierce boil, put in the lobster, simmer for 15 minutes. Strain, but keep the liquid. Take the meat out of the lobster tail and put the shell through the mincer, then pound it to a paste. Put this paste into 1 pint of the liquid, simmer for 5 minutes. Strain once more. Now put in the bread (crusts removed) and mash with a wooden spoon till free of any lumps, pour on the stock, the wine and the rest of the liquid, bring to the boil stirring the whole time. Take off the heat, put in the butter and the tail meat. Serve immediately.

SOUPE JULIENNE

Julienne Soup

2 oz. butter	2 medium potatoes	4 oz. green peas (or
2½ pints stock	2 leeks	4 oz. French beans)
2 carrots	4 cabbage leaves	salt and pepper
	2 small turnips	

Cut all the vegetables into very thin strips about 1½ inches long, except of course the peas. Melt the butter in the soup pot and add the vegetables and fry for 4 minutes. Stir them about, gently. Pour in the stock and bring to the boil. Simmer for 15 minutes, add the peas (or beans) and simmer for a further 15 minutes. Add salt and pepper. The special character of this soup is the matchstick appearance of the vegetables.

SOUPE AUX MOULES

Mussel Soup

5 dozen mussels	pinch saffron	1 onion
6 oz. rice	1 tomato	2 bay leaves
2 pints water	1 leek	salt and pepper
	3 tablespoons olive oil	1 gill white wine
		(optional)

Chop the onion and place it with the mussels and bay leaves in a saucepan with the water and a pinch of salt and pepper. Cover, and boil until the mussel shells open (about 10 minutes). Remove and put the soup through a sieve. Take the mussels from their shells and put them on one side. Chop the white part of the leek, and fry it in a saucepan in the heated olive oil until it is brown. Then pour the soup over it. Add the tomato, rice, and saffron. Simmer until the rice is well cooked, then add the mussels, and cook another 2 minutes. A gill of dry white wine may be added at the same time as the mussels.

CONSOMMÉ MADRILÈNE

Beef Soup

2½ pints beef stock	3 oz. lean raw minced	1 egg white
4 tomatoes	beef	salt and pepper

Peel and slice the tomatoes, add to the minced beef, salt, pepper. Stir. Pour on the stock, add the well beaten egg white, stir again, and simmer for 1 hour. Strain and serve.

SOUPE AUX CONGRES

Eel Soup

8 SERVINGS

2½ lb. conger eel	1 teaspoon lemon juice	1 sprig thyme
4 potatoes	2 onions	1 small bay leaf
6 tomatoes	2 cloves garlic	2 oz. butter
salt and black pepper	4 pints water	8 sprigs parsley

Cut eel into 4-inch lengths, cover with salt and let them stand overnight. Then wash them well in fresh water, remove the skin, put them into a saucepan and let them cook gently in the butter for 10 minutes. Now chop up the vegetables and add them, with the herbs and the garlic, which should be well crushed first, to the saucepan. Cover with 4 pints of water, season with salt and pepper, bring to the boil, and simmer for 1 hour. Then add the lemon juice and cook for another 5 minutes. This soup can be served either as it is, with the bones of the eel in it, as the peasants do, or else sieved, and reheated, before serving.

BOUILLABAISSE

Provençal Fish Soup

8 SERVINGS

1 small lobster	8 oz. bream	pinch thyme
4 oz. turbot	1 gill olive oil	½ bay leaf
4 oz. brill	½ teaspoon saffron	sprig parsley
4 oz. whiting	2 onions	sprig fennel
4 oz. eel	3 tomatoes	8 pieces bread
4 oz. crab	4 cloves garlic	water

Clean the fish, bone it, and cut it into 2-inch lengths. Crush the garlic cloves, and place them in a saucepan with the finely chopped onions, and the skinned tomatoes in quarters. Add the olive oil and all the herbs. Now add the fish. Cover with boiling water and boil on a very hot fire for 10 minutes. Toast the bread and place in eight soup plates and cover them with the fish. Make sure that each plate has a full variety of fish. Pour the soup over the fish and serve at once.

POTAGE DE POTIRON

Pumpkin Soup

6 SERVINGS

2 lb. pumpkin	1 teaspoon sugar	salt
3 tomatoes	2 egg yolks	1 onion
2 pints boiling milk	croûtons	nut of butter
	rice	

Remove the skin from the pumpkin and cut it in 3-inch lengths. Cut the tomatoes in half and squeeze out the pips. Cut the onion into thin slices. Place all these in a heavy stewpan and cover them with a piece of greased paper, then put a tightly fitting lid on the pan. Place the pan in a medium oven for 1 hour, then take it out and pour the mixture, liquid included, through a sieve. Replace in the stewpan, add 2 pints of boiling milk, and let it all boil for 2 minutes, then season with salt and sugar, cover it, and place it at the side of the stove. Cut the butter into tiny pieces, place them at the bottom of a soup tureen, add the egg yolks, cream them together, then add the soup a very little at a time. Serve with croûtons or a few spoonfuls of boiled rice.

OEUFS NOYÉS

Egg Soup

2½ pints water	1 egg per person	thyme
4 small onions	1 slice bread per	salt and pepper
white parts of 4 leeks	person	saffron
1 clove garlic	fennel	1 tablespoon olive oil

A very nourishing and satisfying soup, and a good way of giving an exotic air to everyday ingredients. Chop up the onions and leeks and put them in 2½ pints of cold water. Add the garlic, well crushed, pinch of fennel, thyme, salt and pepper. Put the lid on the pan and boil for 20 minutes. Put in a pinch of saffron and a tablespoon of olive oil and allow it to boil for another 5 minutes. Carefully break each egg into this soup and let it poach, removing each, when it is done, into a warm place to wait. Fry each piece of bread crispy brown in olive oil. Choose deep wide soup plates, warm them, place a piece of bread in each, an egg on each piece of bread, and pour the soup over.

OEUFS SUR LE PLAT

Baked Eggs

1 SERVING

2 eggs	1 oz. butter	pinch salt

You need flat shallow dishes—one for each person—of earthenware or ovenproof glass for this favourite. French way of serving eggs and they must be warmed beforehand. When they are hot, put ½ oz. butter in each one, break the eggs in gently, sprinkle the whites only with salt and place in the middle of a fairly hot oven for 3 or 4 minutes. They should not be overcooked but left with the yolk runny and the whites just softly set.

OEUFS POCHÉS PARMENTIER

Eggs Poached in the Parmentier Way

4 eggs	4 thin slices cooked	½ pint béchamel sauce
4 large potatoes	ham	(see p. 256)

Bake the potatoes. Cut off their tops and scoop out half their insides. Lay a thin slice of ham in each and put them in an ovenproof dish. Poach the eggs and lay one on the ham in each potato. Pour béchamel sauce over all and heat in the oven for 5 or 10 minutes.

OEUFS MATELOTES

Egg Stew

6 SERVINGS

6 eggs	6 shallots	1 teaspoon castor
4 oz. mushrooms	½ clove garlic	sugar
3 oz. butter	*bouquet garni*	little chopped parsley
2 carrots	1 pint red wine	3 slices fried bread
1 onion	1 tablespoon flour	

Grate the carrots. Peel and chop up the onion and garlic and shallots, and the mushrooms, including the stalks. Melt 1½ oz. butter in a saucepan and put all the vegetables in it with a *bouquet garni*. Let them all fry gently for a few minutes, turning them over once or twice. Pour on the red wine and leave to simmer until half of it has evaporated. Put 1½ oz. butter in a bowl and cream 1 tablespoon flour and 1 teaspoon sugar into it, until it is quite smooth. Keep stirring it and pour some of the wine stew into it until it is absorbed, then return the whole to the saucepan. Let it simmer very, very gently. Boil 6 eggs for 5 minutes. Shell them and lay them in a dish. Pour the wine and vegetable sauce over them. Sprinkle with chopped parsley and fried bread cubes and serve.

OEUFS À LA BONNE FEMME

Good Wife's Eggs

5 eggs	4 slices toast	salt and pepper
1 tablespoon butter		3 lean rashers bacon

Toast golden brown some small squares of crustless bread, butter them and put them in a round oven dish just large enough to hold them. Mix the eggs in a bowl, season them with salt and pepper, grill the rashers lightly. Chop them, and add them to the eggs. Pour this mixture over the pieces of toast. Place the dish in a hot oven. As soon as the eggs have set to the consistency of soft scrambled eggs, remove and serve them in the oven dish.

OEUFS FARCIS

Stuffed Eggs

6 SERVINGS

6 eggs	salt and pepper	1 dessertspoon
4 shallots	nutmeg	chopped parsley
4 slices white bread	1 teaspoon thyme	1 tablespoon butter
	½ pint milk	

Hard-boil the eggs. Slice them lengthwise in half. Scoop out the yolks. Remove he crusts from the bread and soak it in the milk. Add the egg yolks to it, also the shallots finely chopped, the thyme, parsley, salt and pepper, grated nutmeg, and blend well together. Melt the butter in a saucepan, add the mixture to it and let it cook slowly over a gentle heat. Stir in a little milk until you have a rich, thick, but creamy consistency. Remove from the stove. Place the halves of egg white on a plate and stuff them full of the mixture. When they are full, put the saucepan with the remains of the mixture back on the stove, keep stirring it, add a little more milk until it is thin enough to pour over the eggs. Place the whole dish in the oven for 5 minutes to get thoroughly warm.

OEUFS À LA MIMOSA

Mimosa Eggs

6 SERVINGS

6 hard-boiled eggs	½ pint mayonnaise	1 dessertspoon
seasoning	(see p. 263)	chopped parsley

Cut the hard-boiled eggs in half lengthwise, and place them cut side down on a serving dish. Pour over them a cup of mayonnaise highly seasoned and less solid than usual (add a little water to it). Sprinkle the chopped parsley over all, and serve.

OMELETTE AUX FINES HERBES

Herb Omelette

6 eggs	1 tablespoon chopped	salt and black pepper
1 oz. butter	parsley	1 teaspoon water
4 sprigs fresh parsley	1 tablespoon chopped	
	chives	

It is important to have really fresh chives and parsley for this recipe. It is made in the same way as an ordinary omelette, except that the parsley and chives are added to the eggs with the salt, pepper and water. It should be served with sprigs of fresh parsley.

215

OEUFS EN COCOTTE

Individual Baked Eggs

1 SERVING

1 egg
1 tablespoon cream

pinch salt

1 teaspoon or less of
butter

To make this egg dish you must have, for each person, a little cocotte dish—which is sold in most stores. A cocotte dish is a round earthenware dish, just big enough for one serving, with a little handle on one side. Warm it in the oven while you are preparing the eggs. Put the cream in a small saucepan on the stove and heat it but don't let it boil. Put the hot cream into the cocotte dish, take the egg and carefully break it into the cream. Add the butter and salt. Put the cocotte dish in a pan of boiling water that covers just half-way up it, cover it and let it cook in a moderate oven for about 7 minutes. The water in the pan should simmer gently but not boil fully all the time. The egg should be lightly set like a poached egg. Lift the cocotte dish out of the water, wipe it dry and serve immediately.

OEUFS À LA BRETONNE

Brittany Eggs

4 eggs
béchamel sauce
  (see p. 256)

8 medium potatoes
1 tablespoon chopped
  shallots

1 oz. grated cheese
salt nad pepper

Peel the potatoes and put them on to boil. Hard-boil the eggs. Plunge in cold water. Remove and peel immediately and put in a warm place. Make a fairly thick béchamel sauce and add the shallots to it, and plenty of salt and pepper. Take the cooked potatoes, which should be tender but firm, and quarter them. Butter a fireproof dish. Lay the potatoes on the bottom alternating with the eggs, which should be cut lengthwise in two. Pour the béchamel sauce with the shallots over the egg and potatoes and sprinkle with the cheese. Place the dish in a medium oven for about 10 minutes, but watch to make sure that the sauce does not burn. The cheese should melt but not go crisp.

OEUFS À L'AIL

Garlic Eggs

6 SERVINGS

6 eggs
4 fat cloves garlic
2 anchovy fillets

1 tablespoon capers
3 tablespoons olive oil
little wine vinegar

freshly ground black
  pepper
salt

Boil the eggs for 10 minutes. Plunge in cold water. Remove and shell them and let them get cold. Chop up the garlic in a bowl with the anchovies and capers. Stir them all vigorously and crush them into a smooth blended mixture. Add the oil, vinegar, salt and pepper. Cut the eggs into 4 lengthwise pieces, arrange them on a plate and pour the sauce over them.

OEUFS EN CHIFFONNADE

*Scrambled Eggs with Lettuce
and Sorrel*

6 SERVINGS

6 eggs	1 lb. sorrel	salt and pepper
4 oz. cooked ham	2 tablespoons grated Parmesan cheese	1 small lettuce

Beat the eggs with salt and pepper and the ham, chopped into small cubes. Wash the sorrel and lettuce, separate the leaves and shred them up finely. Butter a glass oven dish and put a layer of shredded lettuce and sorrel in the bottom. Sprinkle with salt and pepper. Pour the beaten eggs and ham cubes into a thick-bottomed saucepan on the stove. Let them set for 1 minute, then keep stirring them gently. When they are cooked almost solid but still moist, take them off the stove and put a layer of them on top of the layer of sorrel and lettuce leaves in the dish. Add another layer of shreds, another of eggs and so on until the dish is full. Sprinkle grated Parmesan cheese over the top and brown under the grill.

OEUFS CRÉCY

Crécy Eggs

4 eggs	1 tablespoon flour	nutmeg
1 lb. young carrots	½ pint milk	3 tablespoons grated
2 oz. butter	salt and black pepper	cheese

Put the eggs in boiling water for 5 minutes exactly. Then plunge them immediately into cold water. Take them out and shell them carefully. Keep them warm. Wash and scrape the carrots and cut them into tiny rings. Put them in a saucepan with 1 pint boiling water and boil for 7 minutes. Drain and keep warm. Melt the butter in a saucepan. Blend in the flour slowly, stirring all the time. Add 2 tablespoons of the grated cheese. Little by little add the milk. Season with salt, black pepper and a grating of nutmeg. Take an ovenproof dish and place the carrots in the bottom. Next, lay the eggs in the carrots. Pour the sauce over all and sprinkle with the rest of the cheese. Put in a fairly hot oven for 15 minutes.

OEUFS À LA MORNAY

Eggs with Cheese Sauce

6 SERVINGS

cheese sauce
  (see p. 257)

6 hard-boiled eggs

finely chopped parsley
salt and pepper

Cut the eggs in half and lay, flat side down, in a dish and sprinkle with salt and pepper. Pour the sauce over them and put into a hot oven or under a grill for a few minutes. Serve sprinkled with parsley. *(Illustrated in Plate 40.)*

OMELETTE AUX CHAMPIGNONS

Mushroom Omelette

6 eggs
4 oz. mushrooms

1 oz. butter

1 teaspoon water
salt and pepper

Wipe the mushrooms clean, but do not peel them or let them soak up too much water. Chop off the stems not too near the cap. Slice them sideways in as thin slices as possible. Get the frying pan hot and let the butter melt. Cook the mushrooms for 10 minutes in the butter. Sprinkle in the salt and pepper. Remove the mushrooms and put them in a dish to cool, and put more butter in the frying pan on the stove. Then mix the eggs, water, and seasoning gently in a bowl, add the mushrooms to them and cook them as for plain omelette.

MAQUERAUX AU BEURRE NOIR

Mackerel with Black Butter

2 mackerel
1 tablespoon capers

black butter sauce
  (see p. 262)

1 tablespoon grated
Parmesan

Simmer the cleaned fish for 40 minutes in salted water. Drain and remove the back bone. Place in a hot dish. Sprinkle with the capers and grated cheese. Cover with the black butter sauce and serve with boiled potatoes.

MERLANS À LA BERCY

Whitings with Mushrooms

4 small whiting
4 chopped shallots
2 tablespoons parsley

2 tablespoons butter
1 gill dry white wine

1 bay leaf
salt and pepper
4 oz. mushrooms

Chop the parsley and mix half of it with half the finely chopped shallots and 1 tablespoon butter. Clean the whiting and stuff them with this butter mixture. Sprinkle a well buttered fireproof dish with the rest of the parsley and shallots and lay the whiting on top. Sprinkle on salt and pepper. Pour on the white wine. Melt ½ tablespoon butter in a frying pan and toss the mushrooms, chopped into smallish pieces, about in it for a few minutes. Then add them to the fish dish with a bay leaf. Add the remaining butter in small blobs here and there over everything. Leave the dish on top of the stove until the wine comes to the boil, then put it in a medium oven and let it cook for 20 minutes. Every 5 minutes, at least, pour some of the juice from the bottom of the dish over the fishes. Serve in the dish in which it is cooked.

MOULES À LA MARINIÈRE

Mussels

6 SERVINGS

5 pints mussels	6 sprigs parsley	½ bay leaf
½ pint water	pinch thyme	pinch white pepper
	1 finely sliced onion	

Scrub the mussels carefully to remove all sand and grit. Place them with all the ingredients listed above in a very large saucepan with a tightly fitting lid. Place the saucepan on a very hot stove; after 2 minutes shake the saucepan well; continue to shake it very minute until the mussels are cooked—about 6 minutes. When all the mussels have opened they are cooked. Drain and keep liquid in which the mussels have cooked. Keep the mussels in a warm place until the sauce is ready. *(Illustrated in Plate 118.)*

Sauce

¾ pint liquid from mussels	1 small chopped shallot	1 teaspoon chopped parsley
1 gill white wine	3 oz. butter	2 soupspoons soft breadcrumbs

Put the white wine and shallot in a large saucepan. Cook rapidly until the wine is reduced to half its quantity. Now add the liquid from the mussels, bring to the boil and remove from the fire. Sprinkle on the breadcrumbs and the butter cut into tiny pieces. Mix well, add the parsley. Now add the mussels, mix well with the sauce, warm on the side of the stove for a few seconds, serve in the saucepan accompanied by chips.

COQUILLES SAINT-JAQUES

Scallops Saint-Jacques

4 scallops	salt and pepper	4 mushrooms
nut of butter	1 teaspoon chopped	milk
1 onion	parsley	mashed potatoes to
	4 oz. breadcrumbs	garnish

Remove scallops from shells and discard yellowish beard. Put in a pan with salt, pepper and a little milk. Bring gently to boil and remove from heat. Strain, retain from heat. Cut scallops into small pieces. Fry onion and sliced mushrooms gently in butter until soft but not brown. Add scallops, parsley pepper and breadcrumbs. Stir in a little liquid in which the fish were cooked — enough to make a smooth mixture. Simmer for 15 minutes then fill scallop shells or small dishes with mixture, sprinkle with fine breadcrumbs, dot with butter, surround with mashed potatoes, and put under grill or in a hot oven until top is browned.

SOLE CAPRICE

Caprice Sole

8 sole fillets	large nut of butter	4 oz. breadcrumbs
2 bananas	salt and pepper	Robert sauce
melted butter		(see p. 260)

Dip the sole fillets in melted butter, then cover them with breadcrumbs and grill them. While they are grilling, cut the bananas lengthwise and then across so that you have eight narrow slices. Fry these in butter with a pinch of salt and pepper. Place the grilled fillets on a hot dish, cover each one with a slice of fried banana and serve with Robert sauce.

FILETS DE SOLE COLBERT

Fried Fillets of Sole

6 SERVINGS

6 fillets of sole	2 oz. fine bread-	flour
1 beaten egg	crumbs	salt
	3 tablespoons milk	deep fat

Split the fillets in two, having removed all skin. Roll them on to skewers. Dip them in milk and then roll in salted flour. Shake gently, then dip them in the beaten, egg, and cover with breadcrumbs. Fry in a deep pan of boiling fat for 5 minutes. Serve.

SOLE BONNE FEMME

		Sauce:
4 medium sole	1 chopped shallot	$\frac{1}{4}$ pint dry white wine
1 teaspoon chopped parsley	8 oz. mushrooms	4 tablespoons fish stock
4 oz. butter	$\frac{1}{2}$ teaspoon lemon juice	$\frac{1}{2}$ oz. butter
	2 egg yolks	$\frac{1}{2}$ oz. flour
	salt and pepper	

Chop the mushrooms very finely. Melt the butter in a small saucepan, add the mushrooms, shallot, parsley, lemon juice and cook, covered, very slowly for 10 minutes. Make a sauce with the wine, fish stock, butter and flour as you would white sauce, put the soles in a flat fireproof dish, pour in this sauce. Cover the dish and cook till the soles are tender, about 15 minutes. Remove fish and pour sauce over mushrooms, etc., boil for 3 minutes, remove from heat, add salt and pepper and beaten egg yolks. Return sole to the dish. Pour sauce again over the fish, put under a hot grill for 3 minutes. Serve.

HOMARD À LA COURT-BOUILLON
Boiled Lobster

2 TO 4 SERVINGS

1 large lobster	salt and pepper	$\frac{1}{2}$ bay leaf
2 carrots	$\frac{1}{4}$ pint of wine vinegar	3 sprigs parsley
1 onion	2 sprigs thyme	5 pints water

Put all the above ingredients, except the lobster, into a saucepan and simmer them for 1 hour. Strain. Bring the strained liquid to the boil and plunge in the live lobster. Continue boiling until the lobster is cooked (about 35 minutes for a 2 lb. lobster). Drain, and allow to cool, serve with mayonnaise or tartar sauce (see p. 263, 256). If sea water is available, the lobster is delicious simply boiled in the salt water.

SAUMON À LA BRETONNE
Breton Salmon

6 SERVINGS

2 lb. fresh salmon	4 tablespoons butter	1 tablespoon chopped parsley
6 small mushrooms	juice $\frac{1}{2}$ lemon	

Heat 2 tablespoons butter in a pan which can later be placed in the oven. Cut the raw salmon into small cubes, slice the unpeeled mushrooms lengthwise. Fry the salmon and mushrooms in the heated butter until they are half cooked then place the pan in a hot oven to finish cooking. Brown the remaining tablespoons of butter in a pan. Remove from the fire, add the chopped parsley and the juice of a $\frac{1}{2}$ lemon. Pour this sauce over the cooked salmon and mushrooms. Serve.

TRUITES À LA GRENOBLOISE

Grenoble Trout

4 trout	few capers	1 tablespoon flour
1½ tablespoons butter	1 lemon	salt and pepper

Clean the trout, leaving on heads and tails. Get the frying pan hot and melt the butter. Roll each trout in seasoned flour and fry it in the butter. Remove each fish as it is done and put it on to a hot plate or dish. Let the butter continue to cook until it goes brown and smells of nuts. Then pour it over the trout, adding a few capers. Decorate each trout with thin slices of lemon.

BARBUE À LA SAINT-GERMAIN

Brill Saint-Germain

1 medium brill	butter for frying	béarnaise sauce
1 egg	4 tomatoes	(see p. 255)
	4 oz. breadcrumbs	

Fillet the brill and remove all skin. Dip the fillets in the beaten egg and then in the breadcrumbs. Heat the butter well in the frying pan, fry the fillets. While they are frying, cut the tomatoes in two and grill them, placing a pat of butter on each cut half. When the fillets are nicely cooked and brown, serve them with the grilled tomatoes and a béarnaise sauce.

HOMARD À LA DIABLE

Lobster Devils

1½ lb. lobster	1 tablespoon chopped	2 egg yolks
1 teaspoon French	parsley	1 hard-boiled egg
mustard	5 soupspoons butter	salt and pepper
	1½ lemons	

Cook the lobster in boiling salted water, skin it and break into medium sized pieces. Keep these in a warm place while you prepare the sauce. Melt the butter in a bain-marie or in a small saucepan which can be held over a larger one of boiling water. When the butter has melted, add the parsley and the juice of ½ lemon, salt and pepper. Now thicken with 2 egg yolks. Put the mustard in a bowl, add the sauce slowly stirring all the time until you have a smooth creamy mixture. Keep it warm. Place the lobster on a hot serving dish, cover with the sauce and decorate with slices of lemon and hard-boiled egg. Serve. This recipe may be used with white fish.

LOBSTER THERMIDOR

2 small boiled lobster
8 oz. finely chopped
  mushrooms
1 tablespoon tomato
  purée

2 tablespoons grated
  Parmesan cheese
2 tablespoons butter
½ tablespoon finely
  chopped onion
salt

dash of cayenne
3 tablespoons dry
  white wine
½ pint béchamel sauce
  (see p. 256)

Pick the meat out of the claws, etc. Chop into dice, coral included, if any. Heat the butter in a saucepan, add the lobster meat, coral, onion, cayenne and wine. Simmer for 5 minutes, stirring constantly. Add the mushrooms, tomato purée, salt, if necessary, simmer for 5 minutes more. Fill the shells with this mixture and put in serving dish. Cover with the béchamel sauce, sprinkle on the cheese. Heat thoroughly in a hot oven, then put under a hot grill for 2 minutes. (*Illustrated in Plate 39.*)

ENTRECÔTE MINUTE

Minute Steak

4 thin slices fillet steak
black pepper

½ onion

1 dessertspoon olive
  oil

Have the fillet steaks cut in pieces about 6 inches in diameter and a quarter of an inch thick. Rub them with an onion which you have cut in two. Sprinkle them with some freshly ground black pepper. Heat the olive oil in a frying pan until it begins to smoke, place the steak in the frying pan and cook quickly for one minute on each side. Serve with spinach and sauté potatoes.

ENTRECÔTE MARCHAND DE VIN

Wine Merchant's Steak

2 SERVINGS

2 entrecôte steaks
1 shallot
2 oz. butter

½ pint red wine
1 tablespoon cream
drop of vinegar

pepper and salt
1 teaspoon chopped
  parsley

Melt the butter in a frying pan. When it is very hot add the steaks, and fry them 3 minutes on each side. Place them on a warm dish. Fry the chopped shallot in the frying pan from which you have just taken the steaks. When cooked, add red wine (Burgundy is best), seasoning and a drop of vinegar. Boil until the sauce is reduced by half. Add the fresh cream. Pour the sauce over the steaks, sprinkle with parsley, and serve.

ENTRECÔTE GRILLÉE

Grilled Rib Steak

entrecôte steak	1 dessertspoon olive	béarnaise sauce
black pepper	oil	(see p. 255)

Remove all fat from the steak. Give it a few blows with a wooden mallet. Cover it with olive oil, sprinkle with black pepper, and cook it under a very hot grill for 6 minutes, i.e. 3 minutes on each side. Serve with béarnaise sauce, grilled tomatoes, and sauté potatoes.

CHÂTEAUBRIAND

Porterhouse Steak

fillet or porterhouse	maître d'hôtel butter	3 tablespoons melted
steak	(see p. 261)	butter

Take a large steak, which must be at least 2 inches thick. Give it a few blows with a wooden mallet. Cover it with a little melted butter and grill it under a hot grill for 2 minutes on one side, and 3 minutes on the other. Now lower the heat of the grill to moderate, cover the steak with some more melted butter, and grill for 10 minutes on each side. Serve with maître d'hôtel butter and chips.

BOEUF À LA MODE

Beef à la Mode

8 TO 10 SERVINGS

4 lb. rump steak	2 pints water	2 sprigs thyme
small calf's foot	salt and black pepper	½ bay leaf
3 strips salt pork	3 tablespoons wine	2 dessertspoons butter
10 small onions	(red or white)	liqueur glass cooking
	3 sprigs parsley	brandy
	5 carrots	

Brown the beef on all sides in a pan in hot butter. Put beef in a casserole, and lard it with 3 strips of salt pork. Surround it with the onions and the carrots, which must be quartered if they are large. Add the calf's foot, the parsley, thyme, and bay leaf. Season with salt and pepper. Pour in the wine, brandy and water, cover the casserole and simmer in fairly hot oven for 5 hours. Remove the meat, place it on a hot serving plate, surround it with vegetables and sauce. Serve.

37. Liver and Bacon, Britain (p.94)

38. Garnishing the Poultry, France

BIFTECK À L'AMÉRICAINE

Steak Tartare

1 lb. good steak	1 dessertspoon capers	1 dessertspoon Wor-
1 chopped onion	2 dessertspoons	cester sauce
2 egg yolks	oil	(see page 108)
		salt and black pepper

Take 1 lb. good tender steak from which every bit of fat has been renoved. Put it through a meat grinder. Mix the 2 egg yolks in a bowl with a finely chopped onion, capers, olive oil, Worcester Sauce, and a pinch of salt and black pepper. Add the ground steak and mix it thoroughly with this sauce. Cut the meat into 4 portions, roll these into flat ball shapes, and serve without cooking. Chipped potatoes should accompany this dish.

CÔTES DE PORC CHARCUTIÈRE

Pork Chops Charcutière

6 SERVINGS

6 pork chops	salt and pepper	1 gill white wine
3 oz. lard	1 onion	½ pint stock
1 gherkin	1 teaspoon flour	4 peppercorns
	1 teaspoon mustard	

Chop the onion into thin slices, and fry to a golden brown in 1 oz. lard. Add 1 teaspoon flour, and stir a little with a spoon until the flour has coloured slightly. Then add the wine and stock, a little at a time, stirring as you add. Season with salt and pepper, and 4 peppercorns, then bring to the boil. Skim, then simmer for 30 minutes. Fry the pork chops in very hot lard for about 10 minutes on each side. Place the chops on a hot dish, spread a little mustard on top of each chop, pour the prepared sauce over them, and sprinkle with the gherkin, which has been chopped into tiny oblong pieces. Serve.

ALOYAU BRAISÉ

Braised Sirloin of Beef

2 lb. sirloin	2 slices fat bacon	2 sprigs thyme
6 small onions	1 gill dry white wine	salt and pepper
½ bay leaf		3 sprigs parsley

Lard the sirloin with the bacon. Tie it and place it in a casserole. Surround it with the onions, and sprinkle with salt and pepper. Add the thyme, parsley and bay leaf. Cover with water to about half-way up the sirloin, and add dry white wine. Cover the casserole and cook in a moderate oven for 2 hours.

225

BLANQUETTE DE VEAU

Veal Stew

6 SERVINGS

2½ lb. breast of veal	½ bay leaf	2 egg yolks
1 onion stuck with a clove	1 sprig thyme	8 mushrooms
	2 sprigs parsley	1 gill cream
1 carrot	10 button onions	juice ½ lemon
1 stick celery	3 oz. butter	1 teaspoon chopped parsley
2 pints water	1 tablespoon corn-flour	salt and pepper

Cut the veal into oblong pieces and place in a heavy saucepan. Cover with water, bring to the boil and remove any scum that rises to the top. Add the carrot and celery sliced, an onion stuck with a clove, bay leaf, thyme and parsley sprigs, season with salt and black pepper and boil for 1 hour in a covered saucepan. Remove the pieces of veal and place them in a clean saucepan. Peel the mushrooms, put the peelings aside to be used later on. Boil the mushrooms until tender. Fry the button onions a pale golden colour in 1 oz. butter. Melt 2 oz. butter in a saucepan, add 1 tablespoon cornflour, cook gently, stirring a little with a wooden spoon for about 7 minutes—do not allow the flour to brown. Add pint of the strained stock in which the veal has cooked. Add it very slowly, stirring all the while, then add the mushroom peelings and simmer 5 minutes. Mix the egg yolks in a basin with the juice of a ½ lemon. Add a little lukewarm sauce to them, mix well and fold into the sauce. Next fold in the fresh cream. Pour the sauce over the veal, add the prepared onions and mushrooms, cook very gently for a few minutes, sprinkle with parsley and serve. *(Illustrated in Plate 4.)*

CÔTELETTE DE VEAU EN PAPILLOTE

Veal Cutlets in Paper Cases

4 veal cutlets	4 slices lean ham	salt and pepper
4 oz. mushrooms	2 tablespoons butter	4 sheets plain paper
2 small onions		1 tablespoon olive oil

Fry the cutlets golden brown in a little butter. Chop the onions very finely and fry them in a mixture of oil and butter, about ½ tablespoon of each. When the onion begins to colour a little, add the sliced mushroom and continue frying until they are almost cooked. Cut some large pieces of paper into heart shapes, about 10 inches long at the middle and 16 inches across. Paint the insides of the paper hearts with olive oil. In the middle of one side of each heart place a slice of ham cut in the same shape as the cutlets. On top of each slice of ham place a veal cutlet. Season them with salt and pepper. Drain away the grease from the onion and mushroom mixture. Place some of this drained mixture on each cutlet. Fold the heart shaped pieces of paper in two, and fold over the open edges carefully. Crinkle the edges so that the cases will not come undone. Place in a very slow oven and cook for 10 or 15 minutes. Serve in their paper cases. A delicious dish and well worth the trouble.

RÔTI DE BOEUF JARDINIÈRE

Roast Beef Jardinière

6 TO 8 SERVINGS

2½ lb. roasting beef	1 lb. tomatoes	1 teaspoon bicarbo-
5 oz. butter	2 lb. French beans	nate of soda
8 oz. mushrooms		salt and black pepper

Roast the beef, having larded it with 2 oz. of the butter. Boil the young French beans in plenty of boiling water with a teaspoon of bicarbonate of soda and another of salt until they are tender. Slice the mushrooms lengthwise and fry them golden in a little butter. Remove the skins from the tomatoes (plunge them in a saucepan of boiling water and the skin will come off quite easily). Halve them and then grill them with butter and a pinch of salt and pepper. Slice the beef and place in a large warm serving dish. Surround it with bouquets of green beans, groups of golden mushrooms, and the halved and grilled tomatoes. Serve.

RÔTI DE VEAU AUX PETITS POIS

Roast Veal with New Peas

6 TO 8 SERVINGS

2½ lb. roasting veal	1 egg yolk	1 lettuce heart
4 oz. butter	2 lb. green peas	1 teaspoon sugar
water	3 dessertspoons thick cream	salt and pepper

Lard the piece of roasting veal with 1 oz. butter. Envelop it in foil or greased paper, place it in a hot oven. After 50 minutes remove the paper, add a few spoons of water to the roasting pan, return to the oven and cook for 15 minutes longer. Cook the green peas with the lettuce, 3 oz. butter, sugar, and ½ pint water, in a covered saucepan until they are tender. Mix the egg yolk with the cream and a pinch of salt and pepper. Fold this mixture into the peas, having first removed the lettuce. Serve with the roast veal.

BOEUF EN DAUBE

Beef Stew

6 TO 8 SERVINGS

2½ lb. chuck beef	1 gill stock	1 sprig thyme
4 onions	1 pint red wine	1 bay leaf
3 carrots	3 tomatoes	2 tablespoons olive oil
1 calf's foot	2 cloves garlic	5 cloves
4 oz. fat bacon	2 sprigs parsley	salt and black pepper

Cut the beef into 2-inch pieces, and clean and break the calf's foot in two. Slice the onions, carrots, garlic cloves, fat bacon, and tomatoes. Put them all in saucepan in which you have well heated 2 tablespoons of olive oil. When they begin to brown add the wine, stock, cloves, parsley, thyme, bay leaf and a pinch of salt, and black pepper. Bring to the boil. Then cover and simmer gently for 3 hours. This dish is equally good, eaten cold or hot.

TOURNEDOS À LA BÉARNAISE

Fillet of Steak with Sauce

2 lb. fillet steak	2 tablespoons butter	salt and pepper
4 slices bread (for croûtes)	½ pint béarnaise sauce (see p. 255)	

Trim the steak and cut into 4 rounds, 2 inches in diameter and 1 inch thick. Sprinkle with salt and pepper and grill on both sides. Fry the bread in the butter. Place the tournedos on the croûtes, and serve with the béarnaise sauce around the meat.

GIGOT À LA BRETONNE

1 small leg of mutton	5 oz. haricot beans	*bouquet garni*
1 clove garlic	1 large onion	salt and pepper
2 oz. butter or cooking fat	1 large tomato	water
		1 shallot

Soak the haricot beans overnight. Take the beans and the whole onion, add the *bouquet*, salt and pepper, cover with water and boil till soft, skimming frequently. Strain. Keep the beans and the onion warm. Slit the meat, press the garlic in next to the bone. Dust with salt and pepper and rub with 1 oz. fat. Roast the ordinary way, 20 minutes to the lb. Keep warm in the serving dish. Keep the gravy in the pan. Make a sauce by melting 1 oz. fat, salt and pepper, add the chopped shallot, tomato peeled and quartered, the chopped boiled onion. Cook till soft. Stir this mixture into the gravy left in the roasting pan, add the cooked beans and pour over the roast joint. *(Illustrated in Plate 43.)*

LENTILLES AU LARD

Bacon with Lentils

1½ lb. prime collar bacon	black pepper	*bouquet garni*
1 oz. dripping	1 lb. brown lentils	2—3 garlic cloves
12 small onions	1 stick celery	½ oz. butter
	2 carrots, water	parsley to garnish

Place bacon in a saucepan and cover with cold water, bringing it slowly up to boiling point, then strain and rinse in cold water.

Melt dripping in a deep casserole. Dry the bacon and put it in the casserole with onions and a seasoning of black pepper. When the onions begin to brown, add lentils, celery, carrots cut lengthwise, *bouquet garni* and 2 or 3 crushed cloves of garlic. Cover with cold water, and cook very slowly with the lid on for about 2 hours.

Test lentils to see if they are cooked. Take out carrots and herbs, strain the lentils. Stir in a lump of butter with the lentils, arrange them round a serving dish with carrots and onions, and after slicing the bacon, arrange the slices in the middle of the dish. Garnish with chopped parsley. Sufficient for 5—6 people. *(Illustrated in Plate 42.)*

TÊTE DE VEAU LYONNAISE

Calf's Head Lyonnaise

10 SERVINGS

½ calf's head	4 tablespoons vinegar	1 bay leaf
4 oz. flour	3 oz. butter	2 onions
1 onion stuck with clove	2 oz. beef dripping	4 dessertspoons breadcrumbs
6 peppercorns	3 sprigs parsley	salt
	3 sprigs thyme	5½ pints water

I am giving the recipe for half a calf's head as that seems more suitable to the normal household. If, however, you should want to cook a whole calf's head simply double the proportions given above. Soak the calf's head for 24 hours in winter, 12 in summer. Clean and bone it, put it in a saucepan with the onion which has been stuck with a clove, peppercorns, vinegar, parsley, thyme, bay leaf, flour, dripping and a good pinch of salt. Cover with about 5½ pints of water, bring to the boil and simmer fairly rapidly for 1½ hours. Slice onions: fry to a golden brown in 1 oz. butter. Place them on a heated oven dish and place the half calf's head in this bed of onions. Cover it with 2 oz. melted butter and sprinkle well with the breadcrumbs. Place in a hot oven until the crumbs are crisp and browned, serve very hot.

GIGOT RÔTI À L'AIL

Leg of Lamb with Garlic

6 TO 8 SERVINGS

3 lb. leg of lamb	salt and pepper	½ pint boiling water
4 oz. butter		2 cloves garlic

Insert the garlic cloves near the bone in a leg of lamb. Place the leg in a roasting dish. Lard with 4 oz. butter, and sprinkle with salt and pepper. Cook for 1 hour 20 minutes in a hot oven, basting frequently. Remove the grease from the sauce in the roasting pan, add the water. Boil for a few minutes, scraping the bottom of the pan with a wooden spoon. Pour this liquid into a sauce-boat, and serve with the leg of lamb.

TRIPES À LA MODE DE CAEN

Caen Tripe

6 TO 8 SERVINGS

2½ lb. tripe	4 peppercorns	1 sprig thyme
6 carrots	4 cloves	½ bay leaf
4 onions	2 sprigs parsley	salt, water

Slice the onions and carrots and line the bottom of a heavy saucepan with 2 sliced onions and 3 sliced carrots. Add the tripe, cut into thick slices, the peppercorns, cloves, parsley, thyme, bay leaf and salt. Cover with a layer of the remaining sliced onions and top with a layer of 3 sliced carrots. Cover with water and bring to the boil. Seal the saucepan with a piece of greased paper and a tightly fitting lid. Simmer gently for 3 hours. Remove the tripe and vegetables and place them in a hot casserole dish. Reduce the liquid in which they have cooked by half by boiling it rapidly, pour it over them and serve very hot.

ENTRECÔTES À LA BRETONNE

Breton Entrecôtes

2 SERVINGS

2 rib steaks	3 oz. butter	1 teaspoon chopped
1 tablespoons olive oil	1 chopped shallot	parsley
black pepper		creamed potatoes

Remove all fat from the steaks. Rub with olive oil and grill them for 2 minutes on each side. Cream the 3 oz. butter with the chopped shallot, parsley, and a pinch of black pepper. Spread this cream in the bottom of an oven dish, and lay the two steaks on it. Place the oven dish over a saucepan of boiling water. Cover the steaks with a plate and leave them for 6 minutes. Serve with the butter sauce and creamed ploatoes.

BOEUF BOURGUIGNONNE

Beef Stew

6 SERVINGS

2 lb. lean stewing beef	4 sprigs parsley	4 oz. button mush-
½ pint red wine	1 sprig thyme	rooms
¼ pint meat stock	½ bay leaf	salt and pepper
3 oz. butter	4 oz. lean rashers	1 tablespoon flour
1 sliced onion		12 button onions

Marinate—that is, let the beef stand—in the wine, seasoned with parsley, thyme and bay leaf, for 3 hours. Remove the beef and strain the wine. Melt 2 oz. butter in a heavy saucepan. Fry the sliced onion in it till golden. Add the beef and brown it all over. Remove the beef and onion, stir in 1 tablespoon flour. Let it brown. Add the stock—slowly stirring as you do so—then add the wine in which the beef has marinated. Replace the beef in this sauce and simmer, covered, for 3 hours. The beef may be served at once or, if you wish, with the following garnish. Slice mushrooms and rashers, and fry them with onions in 1 oz. butter until they are all golden brown. Place the beef on a hot dish, surround it with the pieces of mushroom and bacon and the button onions, and serve the sauce, in which the beef has cooked, in a sauce-boat.

NAVARIN

Navarin Mutton Stew

8 SERVINGS

3½ lb. boned shoulder or breast of mutton	2 lb. potatoes	2 sprigs parsley
3 pints boiling water	1 teaspoon sugar	2 sprigs thyme
2 dessertspoons tomato paste	2 oz. dripping	½ bay leaf
	1 oz. flour	salt and pepper
	1 clove garlic	10 button onions

Heat the 2 oz. dripping in a saucepan. When hot add the mutton cut into pieces of about 1½ inches and 1 teaspoon sugar. Brown them well, season with salt and pepper. Pour off most of the dripping, stir in 1 oz. flour. Continue stirring gently until the flour becomes brown, then add the boiling water slowly, stirring as you add it. Add a crushed clove of garlic, tomato paste, parsley, thyme and bay leaf. Bring to the boil, then simmer covered for 1 hour. Remove the pieces of mutton. Let the sauce cool, then remove the grease which will form at the top. Place the mutton pieces in a casserole and strain the sauce over them. Peel the potatoes, new ones if possible (if not they should be quartered). Put the potatoes in the casserole with the mutton. Fry the button onions whole in dripping. Drain them and add them to the casserole. Bring the stew to the boil, then cover it tightly and simmer in the oven for 1 hour. Serve in its casserole.

LA DAUBE PROVENÇALE

Provençal Stew

6 TO 8 SERVINGS

2 lb. stewing beef	salt and black pepper	1 onion
2 carrots	2 sprigs thyme	2 sprigs parsley
½ pint white wine	6 bacon rinds	½ bay leaf
2 cloves garlic	6 oz. fat bacon	2 dessertspoons olive
4 mushrooms	6 oz. black olives	oil or corn oil
3 tomatoes	chopped parsley	½ pint meat stock

Marinate the beef, which is chopped in 1-inch cubes, in white wine, with parsley, sprigs thyme, bay leaf, and oil. Let it stand in a cool place for 3 hours. Place the bacon rinds in the bottom of a casserole, cover with sliced carrots, season with salt and pepper and add the onion sliced in rounds. Then add the sliced mushrooms and chopped tomatoes. Remove the beef from the marinade, place on the tomatoes, sprinkle with finely chopped garlic and parsley, and a pinch of salt and black pepper. Cover with diced fat bacon and stoned olives. Pour in the wine in which the beef has been marinated, and meat stock. Cover the lid as tightly as possible, and simmer in a moderate oven for 6 hours. *(Illustrated in Plate 49.)*

LANGUE DE BOEUF AU GRATIN

Ox Tongue au Gratin

8 OR 10 SERVINGS

1 ox tongue	1 bay leaf	2 shallots
2 onions stuck with	salt and pepper	1 dessertspoon
2 cloves	nut of butter	chopped chives
4 peppercorns	1 gill stock	2 dessertspoons
4 sprigs parsley	2 gherkins	breadcrumbs
water	2 sprigs thyme	

Clean and scrub an ox tongue weighing about 4½ lb. Cover it in cold water and let it stand for 1 hour. Drain and place it in a saucepan with 2 onions stuck with cloves, 4 peppercorns, parsley, thyme, bay leaf and a pinch of salt. Cover with fresh water. Bring to the boil, then simmer covered for 3 hours. Remove and drain the ox tongue (keep the stock in which it has cooked for making soups etc.). Remove the outer skin from the ox tongue and cut it lengthwise. Slice these lengths into thin pieces, place them in an oven dish, and cover with the gherkins cut into tiny oblongs, the finely chopped shallots, and the chives. Cover with stock, sprinkle the surface with breadcrumbs and dot with butter. Place in a hot oven until well browned. Serve.

39. Lobster Thermidor, France (p.223)

40. Oeufs à la Mornay, France (p.218)

41. Poulet à l'Estragon, France (p.234)

42. Lentilles au Lard, France (p.229)

43. Gigot à la Bretonne, France (p.228)

RÔTI DE PORC À LA FAÇON

Roast Pork Old Style

6 TO 8 SERVINGS

3 lb. loin of pork	3 oz. butter	salt and pepper
2 lb. apples		1 lb. prunes

Soak prunes overnight. Drain them, cover with cold water and bring to the boil. Continue boiling for 7 minutes. Peel, core and slice apples finely. Place in a saucepan with 2 oz. butter, no water, and cook very gently for ½ hour. Take care that the apples do not stick or burn. Press through a sieve and keep warm. Roast the loin of pork for 1½ hours, in a moderate oven, with 1 oz. butter and a sprinkle of salt and pepper. Slice the cooked pork, place the slices on an oblong dish, surround with the prunes, and serve the apple sauce separately.

ROGNON AU VIN BLANC

Kidneys with White Wine

6 SERVINGS

6 lamb's kidneys	6 chipolata sausages	salt and pepper
3 oz. butter	1 teaspoon chopped	½ pint white wine
6 mushrooms	parsley	1 teaspoon arrowroot

Slice the mushrooms lengthwise, then slice the kidneys. Fry them golden brown in 2 oz. butter, drain and put in a warm place. Mix the arrowroot with the butter in the frying pan, add the white wine slowly, stirring all the while. Bring to the boil, add parsley and a pinch of salt and pepper, and simmer for 5 minutes. Grill the sausages and place them in the middle of a warm serving dish. Surround them with the kidneys and mushrooms. Stir 1 oz. butter into the sauce, pour it over the sausages and serve.

ROGNON FLAMBÉ AU PORTO

Kidneys with Port

6 SERVINGS

1½ lb. veal kidneys	½ pint port wine	black pepper
2 oz. butter	1 teaspoon chopped	1 teaspoon flour
	parsley	

Cut the kidneys into small narrow slices. Melt the butter in a saucepan, when hot add the kindeys. Season with black pepper and cook gently until they are browned. Stir in 1 teaspoon of flour, cook gently for 2 minutes, then add port wine slowly, stirring as you go. Add the chopped parsley, simmer for 4 minutes, and serve.

GIGOT À LA PROVENÇALE

1 leg mutton	1 oz. butter	3 chopped gherkins
1 clove garlic	3 anchovy fillets	salt and pepper

Slit the meat near the bone and push in the garlic about 1 inch down. Dust with salt and pepper and rub with the butter. Roast the meat, 20 minutes to the lb., plus 20 minutes. Keep the meat gravy, add anchovy fillets and the gherkins, all very finely chopped. Pour the gravy over the roast joint.

POULET À L'ESTRAGON
Tarragon Chicken

1 boiling chicken	1 carrot	salt and pepper
4 oz. rice (Patna)	fresh tarragon	white sauce
1 leek	3 pints stock (or	(see p. 257)
1 onion stuck with	water)	sprigs parsley
clove	3 tablespoons butter	

Chop a few fresh tarragon leaves and mix with the butter. Place inside the chicken and put it into a heavy saucepan. Add the stock, vegetables, salt and pepper and bring to the boil. Cover with a lid and simmer for $1\frac{1}{4}$ hours or until the chicken is tender. Boil the rice in the strained stock and prepare the white sauce. Serve the chicken with the sauce poured over it and surrounded by rice. Decorate with parsley and tarragon. *(Illustrated in Plate 41.)*

POULET À LA MARENGO
Chicken Marengo
5 SERVINGS

It is said that Napoleon always took his chef with him when he went to battles, and the chef always had chickens, ready cooked in various ways, day or night, in case Napoleon wanted to eat. This dish is said to have been invented after the famous battle of Marengo.

1 young chicken	1 gill white wine	1 teaspoon chopped
3 tablespoons olive oil	1 gill veal stock	parsley
2 large tomatoes	1 clove garlic	little butter
2 dessertspoons tomato	12 button mushrooms	salt and pepper
purée	20 black olives	1 teaspoon marjoram
	12 shallots	

Joint the chicken and fry it golden brown in the olive oil. Remove the chicken pieces and add crushed garlic clove and the tomato purée. When the purée darkens a little, add the stock, wine and the tomatoes, peeled and quartered. Season with salt, pepper and marjoram and mix well. Return the chicken pieces to the saucepan, bring to the boil, cover and then simmer gently for 45 minutes. Meanwhile, fry the mushrooms and onions gently in a little butter for 2 minutes and stone the olives. Add the mushrooms, onions and olives to the chicken and simmer for a further 25 minutes. Place in a deep serving dish and sprinkle with parsley.

POULET À LA NAVARESSA

Chicken Navaressa

4 TO 5 SERVINGS

1 young chicken	½ pint stock	3 carrots
4 oz. ham	salt and pepper	2 leeks
2 tablespoons chopped tarragon	1 tablespoon flour	4 oz. butter
	3 onions	small *bouquet garni*
	½ pint white wine	

Take 2 tablespoons of tarragon and mix it well with 2 oz. butter and a pinch of salt in a bowl. Prepare the chicken and stuff it with the butter and tarragon mixture. Cover its breast with some more butter and put it in a hot oven to roast for 20 minutes. Place the chicken in casserole, surround it with chopped onions, carrots, leeks and ham. Add a *bouquet garni*. Season with salt and pepper, cover with wine and stock, and simmer in the oven gently for 45 minutes. Mix 1 tablespoon flour with the fat at the bottom of the roasting pan. When the flour colours a little, add some of the liquid from the casserole slowly, stirring well. Boil for a few minutes and return this mixture to the casserole, stir well, and simmer a little while longer. Place the chicken on a hot dish, surround it with vegetables, ham and sauce. Serve with boiled Patna rice.

COQ À LA NORMANDE

Normandy Chicken

4 SERVINGS

1 young chicken	3 oz. butter	salt and pepper
¾ pint cider	4 oz. mushrooms	seasoned flour
	½ gill cream	

Joint a young chicken and roll the joints in seasoned flour. Shake them. Heat 2 oz. butter in a frying pan and fry the chicken pieces golden brown in it. Chop the mushrooms lengthwise and fry them in 1 oz. butter with a little salt and pepper. Boil cider until it is reduced by half. Pour the reduced cider into the frying pan in which the chicken was cooked, and stir with a wooden spoon scraping the bottom of the pan. Add cream and cook, mixing well, for a few minutes. Place the chicken pieces in the middle of a serving dish, surround them with a ring of fried mushrooms. Pour the cider sauce over all and serve.

FRICASSÉE DE POULET

Chicken Fricassée

5 SERVINGS

1 chicken	1 onion stuck with	2 egg yolks
2 oz. butter	cloves	1 gill thick cream
2 oz. flour	6 sprigs parsley	salt and pepper
	2 pints boiling water	

Joint the chicken. Heat the butter in a heavy saucepan, add the chicken and a little salt and white pepper. Cook the chicken pieces gently on a low fire for about 10 minutes without allowing them to brown. Sprinkle with flour, stir with a wooden spoon, and continue to cook for 2 minutes. Add boiling water slowly, stirring as you add. Add the onion, and the parsley sprigs tied in a little bundle. Bring to the boil, cover and simmer for 45 minutes. Remove onion and parsley.

Mix the yolks of 2 eggs and the cream in a basin, add a little of the stock from the saucepan to them, mix well. Add a little more stock, then fold this mixture into the saucepan with the chicken. Serve in a hot deep dish garnished with mushrooms and triangles of toast. (*Illustrated in Plate 47.*)

POULARDE CÔTE DU NORD

Chicken with Cider

4 TO 5 SERVINGS

1 chicken	2 onions	2 sprigs thyme
½ pint cider	3 fat bacon rashers	½ bay leaf
½ pint cream	4 oz. cooked pork	salt and pepper
½ pint water	3 sprigs parsley	1 lemon
	3 carrots	

At the bottom of a saucepan which has a tightly fitting lid, put a layer of cooked pork slices. Cover the breast of the chicken with 3 fat bacon rashers, place it on the pork. Chop the carrots and onions and place them around the chicken. Season with a pinch of salt and pepper, add parsley, thyme and bay leaf, and pour the juice of a lemon over the chicken. Add water, bring to the boil, then cover the saucepan with a layer of greased paper and its well fitting lid. Simmer very gently for about 45 minutes or until the chicken and vegetables are cooked. Remove the chicken, joint it and keep it warm. Strain the sauce through a piece of wet cheese cloth, put it in a saucepan and add cider. Reduce a little, add the cream and cook gently for a few minutes. Put the chicken pieces on a warm serving dish, pour the sauce over them and serve.

POULET À LA PROVENÇALE

Chicken with Garlic

6 SERVINGS

1 chicken	½ gill milk	salt and black pepper
5 cloves garlic	½ gill stock	2 oz. butter
1 shallot	3 tablespoons olive oil	1 teaspoon parsley
	4 oz. breadcrumbs	

Clean the chicken out and keep its liver aside for the stuffing. Put 3 cloves garlic inside the chicken, spread butter over its breast, and roast in a hot oven for 35 minutes. To make the stuffing, mix the chopped chicken liver with breadcrumbs, milk, the shallot, chopped garlic cloves, parsley, 1 tablespoon olive oil and stock. Stuff the chicken with this mixture, heat 2 tablespoon olive oil and roast the chicken in it fairly slowly for about 15 minutes. Serve with a salad.

POULET EN CASSEROLE

Chicken Casserole

1 chicken	3 tablespoons butter	1—2 carrots
1 oz. flour	or corn oil	1 pint stock
4 oz. streaky bacon	3—4 shallots	salt and pepper
	4 oz. mushrooms	

Joint the chicken, cover in flour and fry in the butter or oil until golden brown. Add the bacon, cut into small pieces, and fry for a few minutes. Put the chicken, bacon, carrot, shallots and mushrooms into a casserole, and pour in the stock. Season with salt and pepper and cover with a lid. Put into a moderate oven and cook until the chicken is tender. Serve in the casserole. *(Illustrated in Plate 1.)*

DINDE AUX CERISES

Turkey with Cherries

6 SERVINGS

2 lb. breast of turkey	2 lb. cherries	salt and pepper
1 gill Madeira	½ pint water	1 teaspoon white
	2 oz. butter	vinegar

Slice the turkey and fry the slices gently in butter. Add the Madeira wine and a little salt and pepper. Stone the cherries and cook them in a saucepan with ½ pint water and a teaspoon of white vinegar until they are soft. Drain them and press them through a sieve. Add the sauce in which the turkey slices have cooked to the cherry sauce. Put the sauce in the centre of a serving dish, surround it with slices of turkey and serve.

COQ AU VIN

Chicken in Red Wine

4 TO 6 SERVINGS

1 chicken	1 oz. butter	salt and black pepper
6 mushrooms	3 dessertspoons olive	3 cloves garlic
6 small onions	oil	bottle of red wine
2 fat rashers		1 tablespoon flour

Slice the mushromms and the fat rashers and fry them with the small onions in 1 oz. butter until they are lightly browned. Joint the chicken and fry it gently in the olive oil. Add the mushrooms, onions and bacon pieces to the chicken, mix. Strain all the fat into a saucepan, mix a tablespoon of flour with it and stir till brown. Add a bottle of red wine (Chambertin is very good for this dish) slowly, stirring as you add it. Put the chicken, mushrooms, onions, bacon, the chopped garlic cloves, salt and black pepper into this wine sauce. Stir well, bring to the boil, cover and simmer on top of stove or in a deep casserole in the oven for 1 hour.

CANARD AUX CERISES

Duck with Cherries

5 SERVINGS

1 duck	1 lb. cherries	salt and black pepper
2 oz. butter	boiling water	½ pint red wine

Empty and truss the duck. Cover it with butter and roast in a hot oven for 40 minutes, basting from time to time. During the basting add about 2 soupspoons of boiling water and a pinch of salt and pepper to the bottom of the dish. Cook the cherries (which must be stoned carefully so that they do not lose their shape) in red wine until they are soft. Stir the sauce from the oven dish into the cherries. Place the duck on a deep, warm serving dish. Surround it with the cherries and serve. A delicious and very colourful dish.

CANARD AUX POMMES

Duck with Apples

5 SERVINGS

1 duck	2 pints dry cider	2 lb. cooking apples
4 oz. butter	1 liqueur glass	1 gill cream
1 lemon	Calvados	salt and pepper

Empty and truss the duck. Butter the duck and an oven dish with 3 oz. butter. Put the duck in the oven dish, sprinkle with salt and pepper and cook in a hot oven for 40 minutes. Pour the Calvados over the duck and set it alight. Cover the duck, after 5 minutes, remove it from the oven dish, and pour away about half the grease from the bottom of the dish. Place the dish on top of the oven, pour in 2 pints of cider and bring to the boil. Scrape the bottom of the oven dish with a wooden spoon and continue boiling until the cider is reduced by one half. Add the fresh cream, season with salt and pepper. Reduce the sauce again, on a very gentle fire this time. Return the duck to the oven dish and continue cooking in the oven for 10 minutes. Peel and quarter the apples and fry them, until they are soft, in 1 oz. butter. Place the duck on a serving dish, surround it with the quartered apples and serve the cider sauce apart. If you have no Calvados, this recipe is also very good when simply cooked with the cider.

BÉCASSE RÔTIE

Roast Woodcock

2 TO 4 SERVINGS

2 woodcocks	2 slices salt pork	salt and pepper
	2 pieces bread	

Empty and clean the woodcocks, replace their livers with a pinch of salt inside them. Place them on a grill in a roasting pan with the pieces of pork over their breasts and the slices of bread underneath them on the bottom of the roasting pan. Roast them in a hot oven for 25 minutes, sprinkle with salt and pepper, serve.

CAILLES AU RIZ

Quails with Rice

4 quails	1 *bouquet garni*	1 pint stock
6 oz. rice	2 small onions	black pepper
3 oz. bacon		1 oz. lard

Melt the lard in a heavy saucepan. Add the cleaned quails, the bacon cut in strips, and the onions, and cook for about 7 minutes. Remove the quails. Add a good pint of stock, bring to the boil. Throw in the rice, stir until it comes to the boil again, add the *bouquet garni* and a good pinch of black pepper. Cover the saucepan and simmer gently for 15 minutes. Place the quails on top of the rice, cover and simmer (if possible in the oven) for about 12 more minutes, or until the rice has absorbed all the stock. Serve the rice on a dish surrounded by the quails.

239

CANARD À L'ORANGE

Duck with Orange Sauce

4 TO 5 SERVINGS

1 duck	2 sprigs thyme	1 liqueur glass cooking
3 carrots	½ bay leaf	brandy
3 oranges	1 gill white wine	small veal bone
1 oz. butter or	½ pint meat stock	salt and pepper
margarine	2 sprigs parsley	

Empty and truss the duck. Melt butter in an oven dish, and brown the duck all over. Remove the duck, pour brandy over it and set it alight. Return it to the oven dish. Chop the carrots and place them, together with the veal bone, parsley, thyme and bay leaf, around the duck. Pour white wine and stock over the duck and season with salt and pepper. Cover the oven dish. Place it in a fairly hot oven and cook for 1 hour. Strain the sauce in which the duck has cooked through a wet cheese cloth, add the juice of orange and a little of its peel finely chopped. Boil this sauce for 3 minutes. Slice the remaining 2 oranges and throw them into boiling water for 2 minutes. Put the duck on a warm serving dish, surround it with slices of orange, pour the sauce over it and serve. *(Illustrated in Plate 15.)*

PIGEONS À LA CRAPAUDINE

Pigeon Toads

2 young pigeons	sauce diable	1 tablespoons bread-
2 oz. butter	(see p. 261)	crumbs
	salt and pepper	

Cut the pigeons in two down the breast bone. Flatten out the sides as evenly as you can. Cover them with melted butter seasoned with salt and pepper, then coat them with breadcrumbs and grill them under a moderately hot grill for about 25 minutes—basting them from time to time with melted butter. Serve very hot with sauce diable, sauce rémoulade, or sauce piquante (see pp. 261, 263, 256).

PÂTÉ DE PIGEON

Pigeon Pie

2 pigeons	short pastry using	1 oz. butter
6 oz. minced pork	8 oz. flour, etc.	1 dessertspoon flour
4 oz. minced veal	(see p. 100)	4 dessertspoons stock
4 oz. mushrooms	2 hard-boiled eggs	salt and pepper
	½ pint red wine	

44. Charlotte Russe, France (p.270)

45. Chocolate Eclairs, France (p.270)

46. Meringues, France (p.272)

Soak the minced pork and veal in a little red wine, about a gill, for 1 hour. Line a deep pie dish with pastry, and spread half of the mixed minced meat on the bottom of the dish. Roast the pigeons in a hot oven for 5 minutes. Joint them and place the joints with quartered eggs and the mushrooms sliced lengthwise on top of the minced meat. Season with salt and pepper, cover with the remaining minced meat. Put on a pastry top, glaze and leave a fairly big opening in the middle. Cook in a medium oven for 40 minutes. Melt the butter and stir in the flour. Brown it. Add remaining red wine and the stock slowly, stirring all the while. Bring to the boil and cook for 2 minutes. Pour this sauce through the opening in top of the pastry. Return the pie to the oven for 10 minutes, then serve.

CAILLES AUX LAITUES

Quails Lettuce

2 TO 4 SERVINGS

4 quail	1 slice gammon	$\frac{3}{4}$ pint good stock
4 strips bacon fat	4 lettuces	salt and pepper

Plunge the lettuces into a saucepan of boiling water. After 3 minutes remove them and drain. Place the slice of gammon at the bottom of a saucepan; over it place the lettuces, cover them with stock, season with salt and pepper, bring to the boil, then simmer, covered, for 1½ hours. Clean and truss the quail, replacing their livers inside them after cleaning them out. Put strips of fat bacon over their breasts, then place them close together in a small oven dish. Pour in some stock so that it reaches about half-way up then season with salt and pepper. Bring to the boil then place greased paper or foil over the quail, cover the oven dish, and let them simmer gently in the oven for 25 minutes. Drain the lettuces thoroughly and arrange them on a serving dish. Remove the bacon strips from the quail and place them on the bed of lettuce. Drain the sauce in which the quail have cooked through a piece of wet cheese cloth, boil it for 2 minutes, pour it over the quail and serve.

FAISAN EN COCOTTE

Pheasant Casserole

1 pheasant	4 oz. butter	1 gill white wine
2 bacon rashers	½ pint veal stock	salt and pepper
	¼ bay leaf	

Melt the butter in a heavy lidded casserole, brown the pheasant slowly all over in the butter, season with salt and pepper, add the bay leaf and bacon rashers, cover with stock and white wine. Bring to the boil then simmer gently for 2 hours. Serve.

OIE À LA BONNE FEMME

Goose Bonne Femme

6 TO 8 SERVINGS

1 goose	4 peppercorns	4 oz. butter
3 carrots	salt and pepper	1 tablespoon flour
3 onions	3 tablespoons bread-	½ pint thick cream
bouquet garni	crumbs	1 clove garlic
2 cloves		(optional)
		egg

Put the cleaned goose with its giblets in a saucepan. Cover with cold water, bring to the boil and skim. Add chopped carrots, onions, *bouquet garni*, cloves, peppercorns and a good pinch of salt. Cover the saucepan and simmer for 1 hour. Remove the goose, cut meat into small cubes. Dip these cubes in beaten egg, cover with breadcrumbs and fry in 3 oz. melted butter. Melt remaining ounce of butter in a saucepan, stir in flour. Cook the flour, stirring with a wooden spoon for a few minutes—without allowing the flour to brown. Add a choppped clove of garlic if liked, and sprinkle with salt and pepper. Stir in the cream slowly until the sauce has become thick and creamy. Pour the sauce into a rather deep serving dish, put the pieces of goose in the sauce and serve.

PERDREAUX AUX CHOUX

Partridges with Cabbage

4 TO 6 SERVINGS

2 fat partridges	4 oz. carrots	*bouquet garni*
4 oz. lean gammon	5 strips fat bacon	1½ pints stock
4 oz. chipolata	1 onion stuck with	4 oz. lard
sausages	clove	pepper
	2 lb. green cabbage	

Plunge the cabbage into boiling water, boil for 5 minutes and drain. Melt the lard in a deep heavy oven dish, brown the partridges all over then remove them. Place the strips of fat bacon at the bottom of the dish. Over them place three-quarters of the cabbage. Lay the partridges on top of the cabbage surrounded by the gammon, sausages, carrots, onion and *bouquet garni*. Season with pepper. Place the remaining cabbage on top, cover with stock and bring to the boil. Lay a piece of greased paper on top, cover tightly and simmer in a moderate oven. If the partridges are young, remove them with the sausages and the piece of gammon after 40 minutes. Keep them in a warm place. If they are old partridges, continue cooking them with the cabbage for another 40 minutes. Drain the cabbage thoroughly, place it in the middle of a serving dish. Put the partridges on top and surround them with a circle of sliced sausages, carrots and gammon. Serve a little of the stock in which they have cooked as a sauce.

LAPIN À LA BRABANÇONNE

Rabbit in Beer

1 young rabbit	½ pint pale ale	*bouquet garni*
4 oz. streaky bacon	1 tablespoon vinegar	1 tablespoon butter
rashers	1 teaspoon French	2 lumps sugar
4 onions	mustard	salt and pepper
	1 tablespoon flour	

Slice the onions and chop the rashers. Fry them golden in the butter. Joint the rabbit (which has been soaked overnight in water and vinegar) and fry the joints golden in the pan. Empty the contents of the pan into an earthenware casserole or oven dish. Add the sugar lumps, *bouquet garni*, mustard, and a pinch of salt and pepper. Sprinkle with flour. Cover with the beer. Bring to the boil. Cover the casserole and cook in a slow oven for 2 hours. Serve in the casserole.

GIBELOTTE

Rabbit Stew

4 SERVINGS

1 young rabbit	*bouquet garni*	3 sliced carrots
1 oz. butter	salt and pepper	1 pint white wine
2 dessertspoons olive	15 small onions	¾ pint stock
oil	4 oz. mushrooms	1 tablespoon flour
	4 oz. lean gammon	

Joint the rabbit and fry to a golden brown in 1 oz. butter and 2 dessert-spoons olive oil in a saucepan. Remove the rabbit pieces, stir 1 table-spoon of flour into the saucepan. Stir until the flour browns a little, then add the stock and wine slowly, stirring all the while. Bring to the boil, then simmer. Season with salt and pepper, add the rabbit, carrots and the *bouquet garni*. Simmer for 30 minutes. Add the mushrooms and the onions whole and simmer for another 30 minutes. Place in a deep hot dish and serve with fried croûtons.

LIÈVRE EN CASSEROLE

Hare Casserole

6 SERVINGS

1 young hare	½ pint red wine	12 black olives
1 onion	¾ pints stock	salt and black pepper
1 clove garlic	3 peppers	1 dessertspoon
3 tablespoons olive oil	2 very small marrows	chopped parsley
	1 tablespoon flour	

Joint a young hare and fry it with a sliced onion and a sliced clove of garlic in 2 tablespoons olive oil with plenty of salt and pepper. When the hare is well browned, stir in some flour then add the wine and stock, slowly mixing well. Bring to the boil and cover, simmering gently for 2 hours. Slice the marrows and peppers and fry them in a tablespoon of olive oil. Soak the olives in lukewarm water, then stone them. Put the pieces of hare on a warm serving dish. Strain the sauce over them and decorate with slices of pepper, baby marrows and black olives.

LIÈVRE À LA TRENTINA

Hare Trentina

6 SERVINGS

1 young hare	salt and pepper	4 oz. butter
½ pint red wine	3 tablespoons raisins	1 teaspoon sugar
½ pint stock	2 strips lemon peel	*bouquet garni*
	pinch nutmeg	boiled rice

Clean the hare and joint it. Take the heart, liver and gizzard, chop them finely. Marinate them by placing them in a deep dish and covering them with the raisins, chopped lemon peel, sugar, nutmeg, *bouquet garni* and red wine. Let them stand for 2 hours. Brown the pieces of hare in a saucepan with the butter, add the stock and then the marinade. Season with salt and pepper. Simmer gently for 2 hours. Serve in a deep dish accompanied by boiled rice.

POMMES FRITES

Chips

6 SERVINGS

8 large potatoes	cooking oil	salt

Peel the potatoes and cut them into ¼-inch slices, then cut the slices into strips. Dry them carefully with a clean dish cloth. In a deep fat frying

244

pan which has a basket, heat some cooking oil. The oil should reach half-way up the pan. When a blue smoke begins to rise from the oil, put half the potatoes in the iron basket and plunge them into the oil. When they are golden and crisp, remove them and put them aside. Repeat this operation with the other half of the chips. Just before serving, replace all the chips in the iron basket and when a little blue smoke begins to rise from the oil, plunge them in once more. After a few seconds remove them, drain them on some kitchen or tissue paper, sprinkle them with salt and serve.

POMMES DE TERRE AU LARD

Potatoes with Gammon

6 SERVINGS

1¼ lb. potatoes	2 oz. chopped onion	1 teaspoon chopped
4 oz. lean gammon	½ pint stock	parsley
2 oz. butter or	6 tablespoons white	mixed herbs
cooking fat	wine	salt and pepper
	1 tablespoon plain flour	

Peel the potatoes, which should be medium sized and as similar as possible. Cut each potato into four pieces and let them dry well after they are washed. Plunge the gammon into boiling water and leave it for 3 minutes. Then cut it into very small pieces, having first dried it on a clean cloth. Fry the pieces in butter until they are slightly brown. Remove them from the pan and keep them in a warm place. Fry the chopped onion very slowly and gently in the butter in which you have fried the gammon. Do not let them brown, but when the are yellowish add flour, stirring constantly for 5 minutes. Then add the stock, white wine, herbs, and lastly the potatoes and gammon, and a little pepper and salt. When the liquid boils, cover the frying pan and simmer gently for 30 to 45 minutes. The potatoes should be tender but still firm. Remove the potatoes and put them in a hot dish. Arrange the gammon around them. Pour the sauce from the frying pan over them and serve.

POMMES DE TERRE SAUTÉES

Sauté Potatoes

6 medium potatoes	salt	black pepper
	4 oz. butter	

Boil the potatoes in their jackets in salted water. Remove them and, when they are cool enough, peel off the skins gently. Put the butter in a frying pan and when sizzling hot, put in the potatoes, cut into rounds about ¼ inch thick. Fry until they are golden but not brown. Sprinkle with salt and black pepper and serve.

POMMES DE TERRE À LA LYONNAISE
Lyonnaise Potatoes

8 oz. onions	4 tablespoons	parsley, preferably
2 lb. potatoes	butter	fresh
	salt and pepper	

Boil some salted water rapidly and put the well-scrubbed potatoes in their jackets to cook until they are just tender, but before they start to burst. When done, peel off the skins, being careful not to damage the shape of the potatoes. Cut them in their round slices. Put the butter in a frying pan to heat until it sizzles, add the potato slices and fry until golden. Remove from the heat. Cut the onions into very thin slices and fry them in butter until they are transparent but not brown. Then add the potatoes, salt, pepper and chopped parsley, and serve.

POMMES DE TERRE LIMOUSINE
Limousine Potatoes

4 large potatoes	1 tablespoon butter	salt and pepper
	2 rashers bacon	

Peel the potatoes. Cup up the rashers and put them in a frying pan with the butter. Grate the raw potatoes with a coarse grater into the frying pan. Add salt and pepper and mix them well with the butter and bacon. Press everything down well into a sort of thin cake, the thinner the better. Cover with a plate. When one side is brown, turn it all over in one whole piece and brown the other side. Potatoes are also very good done this way without the bacon.

PETITS POIS À LA FRANÇAISE
Sweet French Peas

6 SERVINGS

4 lb. green peas	2 oz. butter	*bouquet garni*
6 tiny white onions	2 teaspoons sugar	1 egg yolk
1 lettuce heart	1 tablespoon water	salt

Choose a heavy saucepan with a tight lid. Put the butter, the sugar, salt, and *bouquet garni* in the bottom, then the lettuce heart whole, and the onions peeled and also whole. Shell the peas and place them on top of the lettuce and onions. Place the saucepan, tightly covered, on a very low heat and leave for 1 hour. Shake the pan 2 or 3 times. Remove the *bouquet garni*. Beat an egg yolk with the water. Pour all the liquid from the saucepan into it. Put this in a saucepan to heat; do not let it come to the boil. Place the peas, lettuce and onions in a serving dish and pour the egg sauce over them.

ÉPINARDS AU BEURRE

Buttered Spinach

6 SERVINGS

2 lb. spinach	black pepper	salt
2 tablespoons butter		1 teaspoon lemon juice

Clean the spinach thoroughly in three waters. Put into a pan and cook gently, without adding water, until it is tender (from 10 — 15 minutes, depending on whether it is fresh and young or not). Press water out of the spinach, then chop it finely. Heat the butter, add the spinach, a pinch of salt and sprinkling of pepper. Heat, stirring, for 2 minutes. Then sprinkle with lemon juice and serve.

ÉPINARDS À LA CRÈME

Creamed Spinach

6 SERVINGS

2 lb. spinach	croûtons of fried bread	1 gill cream
4 tablespoons butter	1 tablespoon flour	pinch sugar
	pinch salt and pepper	

Cook the spinach and drain thoroughly, as in recipe above. Melt 3 table-spoons butter in a broad heavy saucepan, add the spinach and cook on a quick fire for 5 minutes. Add the salt, pepper, sugar and flour, mix well and cook for 2 minutes longer. Remove the saucepan from the fire and stir in the cream. Then replace it in the fire and bring to the boil, stirring all the while. Cover the saucepan and simmer for 5 minutes. Place the spinach in a hot vegetable dish, sprinkle with tiny pieces of butter, decorate with croûtons of fried bread and serve. The cream may be replaced by a ½ pint milk which is reduced by boiling to half its original volume.

ASPERGES AU BEURRE

Asparagus with Butter

24 sticks of asparagus	4 oz. butter	salt and pepper

Clean the asparagus and put them to cook in a large saucepan of boiling salted water. When the water begins to boil again, count 12 minutes for the asparagus to cook. Remove them, drain and serve hot with plenty of melted butter, seasoned with salt and pepper.

HARICOTS VERTS À LA LYONNAISE
Sauté French Beans

1 lb. French beans	1 small onion	black pepper
3 tablespoons butter		pinch salt

French beans should be small, young, and stringless. Break a little bit off each and of the beans, but if they are rather long, break them in two. Plunge them into boiling water which you have salted and boil them for about 10 or 15 minutes. Drain them. Heat the butter in a large frying pan and in it cook a small sliced onion until it is soft but not brown. Add the French beans. Sprinkle them with a good pinch of salt and a little black pepper. Cook them, stirring a little to prevent burning or sticking to the pan, until they begin to colour slightly. Then serve in a hot vegetable dish.

ENDIVES AU FOUR
Baked Chicory with Lemon

4 TO 6 SERVINGS

6 heads of chicory	4 tablespoon fresh	1 tablespoon sugar
1 tablespoon butter	lemon juice	salt

Leave the chicory whole, merely cutting off the discoloured part of the root and the damaged outer leaves. Take a large, preferably glass, oven dish and melt the butter in it. Lay the chicory in it, in layers, salting each one and sprinkling it with sugar before you lay the others on it. Then pour the lemon juice over all, and cover with foil or well-buttered paper and place in the oven. Look at the chicory from time to time to make sure that the lemon juice has not dried up. If it has, before the chicory is tender, add a very little water. Test with a fork. When golden, the chicory is ready to serve in the dish in which it has been cooked.

CÉLERI AU JUS
Stewed Celery

8 sticks celery	stock	1 tablespoon butter
1 onion	1½ tablespoons flour	*bouquet garni*
	1 carrot	

Place the cleaned celery sticks in an oblong casserole or oven dish, with an onion, a chopped carrot, and a *bouquet garni*. Just cover them with stock, bring to the boil, cover with a piece of greaseproof paper, and place in a moderate oven for 1½ hours. Remove and drain the celery and place it in an oven dish. Strain the liquid in which it has been cooked, take 1½ pints and boil until it has been reduced by one half.

Melt the butter in a saucepan, stir in the flour and continue stirring until the flour browns. Now add the stock a little at a time, stirring until the mixture comes to the boil. Simmer for 7 minutes, pour over celery and serve.

ARTICHAUTS FRITS

Fried Artichokes

4 small globe arti- chokes	4 oz. flour	pan of cooking fat for deep frying
1 egg	1 teaspoon olive oil	½ pint water
	salt	

Cut off the stems and the coarse outside leaves from the artichokes. Slice them in half and remove all the chokes. Then cut each half into 4 pieces. Put them into boiling, salted water and leave for 15 minutes. Remove and drain. Make a batter by beating the egg thoroughly, adding the flour gradually, then the water, ½ teaspoon salt and the olive oil. When this is creamy and smooth, dip each piece of artichoke in it and fry in very hot deep fat. When the batter is golden, remove, sprinkle with salt and eat at once.

CHOU FARCI

Stuffed Cabbage

4 TO 6 SERVINGS

1 large solid cabbage	1 carrot	1 large meatbone
2 oz. butter	8 oz. minced steak	chopped in two
1 pint stock	8 oz. sausage meat	2 tablespoons flour
1 onion		salt and pepper

You need a really big saucepan for this dish because the cabbage must fit into it with the lid on. Pull off any tough flopping outer leaves of the cabbage and carefully cut out the middle of it without breaking it up. Set it on the draining board and pour boiling water over it. Let the water drain off. Mix the steak, sausage meat, salt and pepper together. Place some of this mixture between each leaf of the cabbage and a little in the centre. Tie a string around the middle of the cabbage. Put the saucepan on the stove and melt butter in it. Blend in flour; slowly add stock (water could be used instead), stirring all the while to keep the mixture smooth. Slice the onion and carrot and add them, with the bone, to the water. Place the cabbage on top. Cover with a tight lid. Place over a low heat and simmer for 3 hours. Look at it from time to time to make sure there's enough liquid. If it has evaporated too much, add a little more. You will need a deep dish to serve this cabbage because it is very juicy. Don't forget to remove the string and the bone. Pour some of the remaining liquid over the cabbage when it is in the serving dish.

249

TOPINAMBOURS EN DAUBE

Jerusalem Artichoke Stew

6 SERVINGS

2 lb. Jerusalem arti-chokes	nutmeg	1 gill white wine
	1 large onion	*bouquet garni*
1½ pints stock	2 tablespoons butter	salt and pepper
	1 clove garlic	

Wash and peel the artichokes and cut them into quarters. Put a fairly large saucepan on the stove and melt the butter in it. Peel the onion and slice it up finely. Add it to the butter and let in cook until it begins to brown. Now put in the artichokes, sprinkle with salt and pepper, the garlic chopped very small, a grating of nutmeg and the *bouquet garni*. Pour on the stock and wine. Cover the saucepan and simmer gently for 20 minutes.

GRATIN DE COURGETTES

Baby Marrows with Cheese

6 SERVINGS

3 or 4 marrows, each about 6 inches long	1 egg	salt and pepper
	4 tablespoons cream	nut of butter
	3 oz. grated cheese	

Boil a very little salted water in a saucepan. Put the marrows, peeled and chopped, into the water and cook them gently, stirring all the while, until all the water has boiled away. Remove them and place them in a buttered fireproof dish. Put a nut of butter over them, cut up in small pieces. Beat the egg and cream together, add one third of the cheese and salt and pepper. Pour this mixture over the marrows, sprinkle the rest of the cheese over the top with a few dots of butter, and bake in a hot oven until the cheese on top begins to get brown.

ARTICHAUTS À LA BARIGOULE

Stuffed Artichokes

4 firm medium sized globe artichokes	1 small onion	2 oz. butter
8 oz. breadcrumbs	salt and pepper	1 tablespoon flour
4 oz. sausage meat	2 oz. chopped parsley	1 tablespoon olive oil
	4 oz. mushrooms	2 lemons
	1 tablespoon stock	

Fil a large saucepan with water, and add at least a tablespoon of salt. When the water is boiling fast, cut off the stems and tops of the artichokes (saving the tops for later) and plunge them stem first into the water.

Boil, uncovered, for 30 minutes. Remove the artichokes and let them drain well. Cut out the chokes carefully. In a bowl mix the bread-crumbs with the stock, sausage meat, mushrooms cut up into small pieces, chopped parsley, and chopped onion. Get the frying pan sizzling hot and melt the butter in it. Fry the sausage mixture in the butter until it is golden. Blend in the flour. Now fill the centre of each artichoke with the stuffing and put the artichoke tops back on them. Rub olive oil generously over an ovenproof dish, place the artichokes in it, and bake in a fairly hot oven for 30 minutes. When done, garnish with sliced lemon.

ASPERGES À LA PARMESANE

Asparagus with Parmesan Cheese

2 bundles asparagus   4 oz. Parmesan cheese   salt and pepper
2 tablespoons butter

Wash the asparagus gently and cut off the hard ends. Tie it in four bundles and boil in salted water, stems downward, for 15 minutes. Drain. Cut into pieces about 1 inch long. Butter an oven dish, preferably glass. Put a layer of the asparagus pieces on the bottom. Sprinkle with salt and pepper, grated cheese and tiny dots of butter. Then add another layer of asparagus and sprinkle them likewise. Repeat until you have used all the asparagus. Save a bigger amount of cheese and a little more butter for the top layer. Put into a medium-hot oven until the cheese on the top gets golden brown. Cheddar cheese may be used instead of Parmesan.

LAITUE AU JUS

Stewed Lettuce

4 lettuce with firm hearts   1 tablespoon flour   1 bay leaf
½ pint clear stock   1 tablespoon chopped parsley   1 tablespoon butter   salt and pepper
1 large onion

Wash the lettuces and be very careful to remove every bit of grit or earth. Boil a saucepan of water, slightly salted. Move it to a low heat, put the lettuces in, cover the pan, and let them simmer for 10 minutes. Then remove them, dip them quickly into cold water and out again. Let them drain thoroughly. Put the butter in a saucepan. When it has melted, gently blend in the flour, stirring all the time with a wooden spoon. Slowly and carefully pour in the stock, still stirring, until it thickens. Add salt and pepper to taste, the onion chopped as fine as possible, then the parsley and bay leaf. Lastly, put in the lettuces. Remove the saucepan to the side of the stove, cover it, and let the lettuces cook gently for ½ hour, stirring occasionally.

HARICOTS VERTS SAUTÉS

Sauté French Beans

1½ tablespoons butter	2 lb. young French green beans	salt and pepper

Fill a saucepan one third full of water and bring it to the boil. Add about a level tablespoon of salt. Put in the washed and trimmed young beans, cover the pan and cook for 10 minutes. Pour off the water. Heat the butter sizzling hot in a frying pan, add the boiled beans and keep tossing them about until they just begin to get brown. Add black pepper and more salt if needed.

RATATOUILLE

Provençal Mixed Vegetables

2 aubergines	2 large onions, sliced	1 clove garlic, finely
4 medium tomatoes, peeled and quartered	2 red or green peppers, sliced	chopped
	1 gill olive oil	salt and pepper

Slit the peppers and pull out seeds and core, wash thoroughly to remove every seed. Slice. Cut the aubergines into 1-inch squares. Warm the oil in a large frying pan, add the sliced onions and stew gently for 8 minutes. Now add sliced peppers and aubergines, stew gently for 10 minutes. Add garlic, salt and pepper, then the quartered tomatoes. Cover the pan and simmer gently for another 10 minutes, or until all the olive oil has been absorbed.

RAGOÛT DE TOMATES

Tomato Stew

4 TO 6 SERVINGS

8 small tomatoes	3 strips lean bacon	8 black olives
1 tablespoon olive oil	2 tablespoons white wine	1 tablespoon flour
3 small onions		1 oz. butter

Heat the olive oil in a frying pan and fry the chopped onions in it until they are golden. Add the chopped bacon. Cut up each tomato into four pieces, add to the frying pan and cook gently for 5 minutes or so. Slowly stir in 1 tablespoon flour, the white wine little by little and the black olives which you have first stoned and chopped coarsely. At the last moment, add the butter, stirring all the time. When it is blended, your ragoût is ready to serve.

CHAMPIGNONS FLAMBÉS

Mushrooms Flambé

1 lb. mushrooms	2 tablespoons cream	1 gill brandy
1 oz. butter	½ pint sherry	salt

Melt the butter in a chafing dish. Add salt liberally. Put in the mushroom caps and fry gently for 5 minutes. Pour the sherry over them and allow them to simmer until they become rather dry. Now add the half glass of brandy and set it alight. After the flame has gone out, add the cream. Serve. *(Illustrated in Plate 27.)*

CHAMPIGNONS DE PARIS

Paris Mushrooms

6 SERVINGS

8 oz. button mushrooms	juice 1½ lemons	1 teaspoon chopped parsley
2 tablespoons olive oil	1 teaspoon French mustard	salt and black pepper

Clean the mushrooms and put, whole, into an enamel saucepan, with the lemon juice, olive oil, and pinch of salt and black pepper. Cook on a fast heat for 10 minutes. Let the mushrooms cool in this sauce. When cold, remove them and place them on a serving plate. Stir the mustard into the sauce, pour it over the mushrooms, sprinkle the dish with parsley and serve.

CHAMPIGNONS BOURGEOIS

Mushrooms Bourgeois

6 TO 8 SERVINGS

1 lb. mushrooms	1 lemon	1 teaspoon chopped chives
1 teaspoon chopped parsley	6 or 8 slices bread	1 gill white wine
1 dessertspoon flour	4 oz. fat bacon	pepper
	fat for frying	

Cut the fat bacon into small pieces and place these, spread out, on the bottom of a saucepan so that it is more or less all covered. Cook slowly on a very low heat for 10 to 15 minutes. Take care it does not burn. Clean the mushrooms with a wet cloth and cut in two. Place the sliced mushrooms in the fat in the saucepan and season with pepper. Now add the chopped parsley and the chopped chives, and the spoonful of flour. Slowly add the white wine and cook until the liquid is well reduced. Now take the slices of bread and fry separately until crisp and brown. Pour the mushrooms over the bread, add a squeeze of lemon to each helping and serve.

CHAMPIGNONS FARCIS

Stuffed Mushrooms

6 SERVINGS

12 field mushrooms	1 clove garlic	1 teaspoon flour
1 onion	1 tablespoon olive oil	4 oz. breadcrumbs
1 shallot	1 gill stock	salt and black pepper
1 teaspoon chopped parsley	2 teaspoons tomato sauce (see p. 333)	1 oz. butter

Take 12 large mushrooms (cultivated mushrooms will do if they are big). Remove the stems. Put them hollow side down in an oven dish. Sprinkle them with olive oil and cook them in a fairly hot oven for 8 minutes. Remove them from the oven and turn them hollow side up in the oven dish. Chop the mushroom stalks, the onion, shallot, and the garlic clove. Fry them in butter quickly, until they are golden. Stir in flour. Add stock and tomato sauce. Season with salt and pepper. Simmer for 5 minutes. Stir in 2 oz. breadcrumbs and parsley. Fill mushroom caps with this mixture. Sprinkle remaining breadcrumbs over the stuffed mushrooms. Put a tiny piece of butter on top of each dome of stuffing, and cook in a medium oven (placing them near the top) for 15 minutes.

CHAMPIGNONS AU LARD

Baked Mushrooms

8 oz. mushrooms	1 tablespoon olive oil	salt and pepper
1 gill white wine	1 fat bacon rasher	juice ½ lemon

Clean the mushrooms by wiping with a wet cloth. Separate the stalks from the caps and place the caps in a frying pan with a tablespoon of olive oil. Cook gently for 2 or 3 minutes and then remove them to an oven dish. Take the stalks and chop finely. Also chop the bacon into tiny pieces. Fry in the pan, from which you have removed the caps for 3 to 4 minutes. Pour this mixture over the mushroom caps in the oven dish. Season with salt and pepper. Add the white wine and the lemon juice and cook in a slow oven for 30 minutes. Serve.

CHAMPIGNONS AU GRATIN

Cheese Mushrooms

1 lb. mushrooms	2 oz. butter	1 teaspoon chopped chives
1 tablespoon grated Parmesan cheese	1 teaspoon chopped parsley	salt and pepper
	fresh breadcrumbs	

Clean and trim the mushrooms, removing the stalks. Butter a baking dish well and in it place the mushroom caps, gills upwards. Over the caps sprinkle the breadcrumbs and the chopped parsley, together with the chopped chives. Lastly, sprinkle over this grated Parmesan cheese and season with salt and pepper. Pour a little melted butter over this and place in a moderate oven. Cook for 20 minutes.

SAUCE BÉARNAISE

Béarn Sauce

4 TO 6 SERVINGS

½ pint water (or white wine)
½ pint vinegar

1 teaspoon chopped parsley
2 egg yolks
2 chopped shallots

salt and pepper
pinch red pepper
nut of butter

Put the chopped shallots in a saucepan and add water or white wine if you have it. Add vinegar. Boil rapidly until the liquid is reduced almost by half. Beat the egg yolks. Cream butter, and add it to them, with the chopped parsley. Season with salt, pepper, and a pinch of red pepper. Add this mixture drop by drop to the sauce, which must no longer boil. Stir it all the time that you are adding the egg mixture. This sauce is a very good accompaniment to a grilled steak.

SAUCE CHASSEUR

Hunter's Sauce

6 SERVINGS

1 dessertspoon butter
1 dessertspoon flour
¾ pint meat stock
1 gill white wine

4 mushrooms
2 shallots
2 tablespoons olive oil
1 dessertspoon tomato paste

1 dessertspoon chervil
pinch chopped parsley
1 oz. butter
pinch black pepper

Melt the butter, add the flour, and gently stir with a wooden spoon until it becomes brown. Then add the meat stock, with the tomato paste and a pinch of black pepper. Stir, then simmer uncovered for 10 minutes. Thinly slice the mushrooms, add to the olive oil which is heated in a saucepan, and fry gently for 5 minutes. Add the chopped shallots and continue frying for another minute. Pour away the oil, add the white wine and boil until it is reduced by half. Pour the sauce of stock and tomato paste over the mushroom mixture, mix well and simmer gently for 6 minutes. Just before serving, add butter and the finely chopped parsley and chervil. Excellent with steaks or left-over beef or mutton.

SAUCE PIQUANTE

Piquant Sauce

6 SERVINGS

1 gill vinegar	½ pint brown sauce	2 dessertspoons butter
1 teaspoon chopped	(see p. 258)	2 gherkins
parsley	1 chopped shallot	salt and black pepper

Put the vinegar, a pinch of pepper, salt, shallot, parsley, and butter, in a saucepan. When the butter has melted, add brown sauce gradually. Mix well. Chop gherkins into tiny oblongs and add them to the sauce just before serving. This sauce is very good served with the meat from a pot-au-feu, or with cold pork.

SAUCE TARTARE

Tartar Sauce

6 SERVINGS

2 onions	1 teaspoon wine	½ teaspoon French
1 teaspoon chopped	vinegar	mustard
chervil	1 egg yolk	pinch salt and black
½ pint olive oil	1 teaspoon chopped	pepper
	tarragon	

Mix the salt, pepper, mustard, and egg yolk in a shallow bowl or soup plate. Add the olive oil, drop by drop, following the instructions for mayonnaise (see p. 263). When all the oil has been incorporated, add the very finely chopped onions, together with the vinegar, chervil, and tarragon. This sauce is a delicious addition to steaks.

SAUCE BÉCHAMEL

Béchamel Sauce

6 SERVINGS

2 oz. butter	½ pint milk	*bouquet garni*
2 tablespoons flour	salt and pepper	

Melt the butter in saucepan over a low flame. Add the flour and stir with a wooden spoon for 2—3 minutes. Do not allow the flour to become brown. Boil the milk and add it drop by drop to the flour, stirring slowly all the time. Add *bouquet garni*. Continue to cook gently, and to stir slowly until the sauce has thickened. Add salt and pepper. Continue to simmer sauce for about 30 minutes. Strain and serve.

47. Chicken Fricassée, France (p.236)

48. Ingredients for Bouillabaisse, France

SAUCE BLANCHE

White Sauce

2 oz. butter
1 oz. flour

½ pint hot milk
salt and pepper

Melt the butter on a low flame, add flour and cook, stirring with a wooden spoon, for 2 or 3 minutes. Do not allow the flour to brown. Add a little hot milk and stir well. Then add the rest of the milk, and simmer for a few minutes. Season with salt and pepper, and serve.

SAUCE MORNAY

Cheese Sauce

2 oz. butter
½ pint milk
bouquet garni

2 tablespoons grated
  cheese
2 tablespoons flour

1 tablespoon cream
salt and pepper

Make a béchamel sauce (see p. 256). Reduce it by one third of its volume by cooking it fairly quickly for a few minutes. Add grated cheese, preferably Gruyère. Cook slowly for another minute, stir in a spoonful of cream, and it is now ready to serve. Very good with vegetables such as cauliflower.

SAUCE POIVRADE

Game Sauce

10 SERVINGS

2 oz. butter
1 oz. flour
2½ pints meat stock
8 coarsely ground
  peppercorns

2 carrots
2 onions
pinch salt
1 small shallot
few sprigs parsley

sprig thyme
small bay leaf
1 gill olive oil
½ pint wine vinegar
pinch cayenne pepper

Heat the olive oil in a saucepan until it begins to smoke. Then add the shallot, carrots, onions, and parsley, all finely chopped, together with the thyme and bay leaf. Fry very gently, without letting the vegetables brown, for 10 minutes, then pour away the oil. Add the vinegar and boil until the liquid is reduced by half. Melt 1 oz. of the butter, add flour and stir until it browns. Add 2 pints meat stock. Stir. Add the vinegar and vegetables, bring to the boil and simmer gently for 50 minutes. Add coarsely ground peppercorns and simmer for 10 minutes more. Strain. Add rest of stock. Bring to the boil. Simmer for 30 minutes. Remove any scum. Boil rapidly until the sauce is reduced to 1½ pints. Season with salt and cayenne, add 1 oz. butter, and strain. Serve with venison or hare.

257

SAUCE À LA CRÈME

Cream Sauce

2 oz. butter
1 tablespoon flour

salt and pepper
1 tablespoon chopped
spring onion

pinch chopped parsley
½ pint cream

Melt the butter in a saucepan over a low heat, add the flour, and cook, stirring with a wooden spoon, for 2—3 minutes. Do not let the flour brown. Place the saucepan in a bain-marie or over a larger saucepan of boiling water. Stir slowly while adding cream drop by drop. Add a pinch of salt and pepper, the chopped green part of a spring onion and the chopped parsley. Stir until the sauce thickens.

SAUCE DUXELLES

Duxelles Sauce

1 gill white wine
2 oz. chopped stewed
mushrooms

1 gill brown sauce
(see below)
salt and pepper

1 shallot
1 tablespoons tomato
sauce (see p. 333)

Chop the shallot. Place it in a saucepan with the wine and the stewed mushrooms. Boil until the liquid is reduced by one half. Add it to brown sauce in another saucepan. Mix in tomato sauce. Season. Bring to the boil, and then simmer for 5 minutes. This sauce is good with nearly all meat dishes.

SAUCE HOLLANDAISE

Hollandaise Sauce

6 TO 8 SERVINGS

8 oz. butter
1 lemon

1 dessertspoon
vinegar

salt
3 egg yolks

Melt the butter in a bain-marie, or in a bowl which can be placed over a saucepan of boiling water. Add the vinegar, a pinch of salt, and the egg yolks. Stir well until the sauce thickens, do not let the ingredients boil. Add the juice of 1 lemon. Stir and serve. This sauce is perfect with boiled fish.

ROUX BRUN

Brown Sauce

2 oz. butter
1 tablespoon flour

½ pint stock

black pepper
salt

Melt the butter in a saucepan. Add the flour, and stir it with a wooden spoon until it becomes a light brown colour. Heat the stock and add it very slowly to the flour and butter, stirring all the time. Season with salt and black pepper, continue to cook, and stir it, until it becomes fairly thick. It is then ready to serve.

SAUCE SOUBISE

Soubise Sauce

2 onions	¾ pint cream sauce (see p. 258)	salt and black pepper

Make cream sauce, omitting the parsley and spring onion. Slice onions and boil them for 5 minutes. Drain and boil again until they are soft. Drain, press through a sieve, and fold into sauce. Mix well and season with salt and pepper. This sauce is excellent with lamb, mutton or pork chops.

SAUCE PÉRIGUEUX

Truffle Sauce

10 SERVINGS

1 pint brown sauce (see p. 258)	2 oz. lean bacon	pinch thyme
4 truffles and juice (canned)	1 teaspoon chopped shallot	1 oz. butter
		1½ gills Madeira
		tiny piece bay leaf

Chop the bacon and fry it gently in the butter. Add the shallot, thyme and bay leaf. Fry another minute, then add 1 gill Madeira and truffle juice. Boil very gently in an uncovered saucepan until it has reduced by one half, then strain it on to the truffles, peeled and chopped into tiny pieces. Cook in a bain-marie for 3 minutes. Strain brown sauce on to truffle mixture, and cook gently for 5 minutes. Remove from heat, add remaining wine and serve.

SAUCE MOUSSELINE

Mousseline Sauce

6 TO 8 SERVINGS

hollandaise sauce (see p. 258)	1 gill thick cream

Make a hollandaise sauce, using a little more vinegar and salt than usual. Whip the cream thoroughly, and at the last moment fold it into the hollandaise sauce. Serve with asparagus.

SAUCE ROBERT

Robert Sauce

6 SERVINGS

2 onions	1 tablespoon flour	½ pint white wine
3 oz. butter	½ pint stock	1 teaspoon mustard

Thinly slice the onions. Fry them very gently in a saucepan with the butter. This should take about 10 minutes and the onions should be quite soft but not brown, by that time. Add the flour and cook, stirring with a wooden spoon, for 5 minutes. Boil the white wine separately until it is reduced by half. Add it to the onions, then add the stock. Bring to the boil, and simmer for 25 minutes. Mix the mustard with a little of the sauce and at the last moment add it to the sauce proper. This sauce is excellent with left-over meat or fowl.

MIREPOIX

Mirepoix Sauce

2 onions	2 oz. butter	½ bay leaf
2 carrots	3 sprigs parsley	black pepper
4 oz. lean bacon		1 sprig thyme

The mirepoix is a sauce in itself, but it is also used as a basis for various soups, stews, and sauces. Cut the vegetables and the lean bacon into small narrow oblong pieces. Fry very gently in butter. Season with a pinch of black pepper. Add the parsley, thyme, and the bay leaf. Continue cooking for about 15 minutes. The vegetables should be quite soft by this time, but not browned. The ingredients must be stirred from time to time to prevent sticking. If the mirepoix is required as a sauce, pass it through a sieve.

SAUCE AUX OEUFS

Egg Sauce

6 SERVINGS

4 tablespoons butter	3 tablespoons flour	pinch pepper
2 hard-boiled eggs	½ teaspoon salt	½ lemon
	¾ pint hot fish stock or water	

Melt the butter in a saucepan. Add the flour. Cook gently for 1 minute without allowing the flour to brown. Add the hot stock (or water), drop by drop into the mixture. Stir gently all the while. Add the salt, pepper, and the lemon juice. Bring to the boil and then simmer for 8 minutes. Chop the hard-boiled eggs and add to the sauce just before serving. This sauce is delicious with boiled fish.

SAUCE AUX CÂPRES

Caper Sauce

6 SERVINGS

4 tablespoons butter	1 gill drained capers	1 teaspoon lemon
¾ pint meat stock	pinch pepper	juice
½ teaspoon salt		3 tablespoons flour

Make this sauce in the same way as the egg sauce, but add the capers instead of the hard-boiled eggs, and use meat instead of fish stock. Serve it with mutton.

SAUCE DIABLE

Devil's Sauce

6 SERVINGS

1 tablespoon flour	1 teaspoon chopped	1 gil white wine
1 tablespoon butter	chervil	1 gill wine vinegar
1 chopped shallot	¼ teaspoon red pepper	¾ pint meat stock

Put the shallot with the wine and vinegar in a little saucepan and boil until the liquid is reduced to a quarter of its original volume. Melt the butter in another saucepan. Add the flour to it. Stir a little with a wooden spoon until the flour begins to brown. Add the stock mixed with the reduced wine and vinegar. Add it slowly, stirring all the while, until the mixture comes to the boil. Then simmer gently for 5 minutes. Just before serving, stir in the red pepper and add the chopped chervil.

BEURRE À LA MAÎTRE D'HÔTEL

Maître d' Hôtel Butter

8 oz. butter	1 tablespoon lemon	1½ tablespoons
1 teaspoon salt	juice	chopped parsley
	pinch black pepper	

Cream the butter in a bowl. Season it with salt and pepper. Add the very finely chopped parsley. Mix well. Add the lemon juice very slowly, stirring all the time. This butter is used as a garnish for many dishes.

SAUCE MADÈRE

Madeira Sauce

8 SERVINGS

1 pint brown sauce (see p. 258)   1 gill Madeira

Bring the brown sauce to the boil. Remove it from the heat, add the Madeira, stir and serve at once.

BEURRE D'ANCHOIS

Anchovy Butter

8 oz. butter   6 anchovy fillets   pinch cayenne

Cream the butter. Pound the anchovy fillets and add them to the butter. Add the cayenne pepper. Mix well with a wooden spoon. Put into an earthenware pot and chill. Serve as a sauce or garnish. It is also very good on toast.

BEURRE NOIR

Black Butter

4 oz. butter   2½ tablespoons vinegar

Melt the butter in a saucepan and cook until it becomes a rather dark brown (not black, in spite of its name). Now pour it over the fish, or whatever else it is to accompany. Put the vinegar in the hot pan and boil it until it is reduced by half, and pour it over the butter.

MAYONNAISE VERTE

Green Mayonnaise

2 egg yolks   1 teaspoon chopped   1 teaspoon chopped
1 tablespoon wine   chervil   chives
  vinegar or lemon   ½ pint olive oil   salt and pepper
  juice

Put yolks in a soup plate, season with a pinch of salt and pepper and stir with a fork. Add olive oil drop by drop, stirring all the time. Gradually increase rate at which olive oil is added to a steady trickle, stirring throughout, until all the oil has been incorporated. Add wine vinegar, chives, chervil, and mix into sauce. This mayonnaise has a very attractive appearance and is particularly good with cold fish dishes.

BEURRE BLANC

Butter Sauce

4 oz. butter 1 shallot 2 tablespoons vinegar

Cut the shallot into thin slices, place in a saucepan with the vinegar and simmer until the vinegar is reduced by half. Add 3 oz. butter, and stir over a saucepan of boiling water until the sauce becomes frothy. Then add remaining butter in tiny pieces. Remove the pan from the fire and serve.

SAUCE RÉMOULADE

Mustard Mayonnaise

½ pint olive oil 1 tablespoon vinegar 1 tablespoon
2 hard-boiled eggs 1 egg yolk mustard

Take the yolks of the eggs and cream them with the raw egg yolk and mustard. Add olive oil, drop by drop, as for mayonnaise (see below). When all the oil has been added, stir wine vinegar into sauce. This is a very tasty sauce for salads and hors-d'oeuvre. In France it is very popular when celery or celeriac is chopped into tiny matchsticks and mixed with it.

SAUCE MAYONNAISE

Mayonnaise

1 tablespoon wine ½ pint olive oil salt and pepper
vinegar or 2 egg yolks
lemon juice

Put the yolks in a soup plate. Add a pinch of salt and pepper. Stir with a fork, adding the olive oil drop by drop. Keep stirring all the time. Increase the flow of the olive oil to a trickle and gradually add more quickly, making sure to keep stirring, until all the oil has been incorporated in the sauce. Now add a small tablespoon of wine vinegar, or lemon juice.

The secret of making mayonnaise sauce is to add the olive oil very, very slowly to begin with. Some people also find that they get better results by using an egg-beater instead of a fork for mixing. If the sauce should go wrong and the egg yolks and olive oil separate, instead of blending to form a thick creamy sauce, save your mayonnaise by taking a third egg yolk, placing it in another soup plate, and adding the spoilt mayonnaise to it slowly, stirring all the time.

GOUGÈRE BOURGUIGNONNE

Burgundian Cheese Loaf

6 eggs	4 oz. butter	salt
6¼ oz. Gruyère cheese	¾ pint milk	8 oz. flour

Put the butter in a thick saucepan with a pinch of salt. Pour on it half the milk and bring to the boil. Make a smooth paste with the flour and the rest of the milk and pour the boiling milk into it, stirring all the time. Return to the saucepan, stirring all the time. Break the eggs into the milk, one at a time, and add 6 oz. of the Gruyère cut up into small pieces. The mixture should be smooth and thick and creamy. Butter a deep pie dish. Pour the mixture in, sprinkle it with the remaining cheese and bake in a hot oven for 30 minutes. This dish is equally good eaten hot or cold.

PISSALADIÈRE

Onion Pie

6 onions	4 finely chopped	1 lb. flour
2 tablespoons olive oil	anchovies	1 egg
2 tomatoes	6 black olives	1 tablespoon butter
	½ oz. baker's yeast	

Make the yeast dough the night before; mix yeast, flour, well-beaten egg and melted butter. Roll out and form into a ball. The next day, roll it out again and line a flan case with it. Brown the chopped onions gently in olive oil. Add the tomatoes, chopped coarsely. Remove from the heat, cool. Add the anchovies, chopped very small. Fill the crust with this mixture. Halve and stone the olives and decorate the top of the pie with them. Bake in a hot oven for 15 to 20 minutes.

QUICHE LORRAINE

Cheese Custard and Bacon Tart

6 bacon rashers	8 oz. grated cheese,	6 oz. flour
8 oz. grated cheese,	Gruyère	2 oz. butter
Parmesan	2 eggs	1 oz. dripping
1 gill milk	water	salt and pepper

Make a pastry with the flour, butter, dripping, salt and water. Roll it 2 or 3 times, leave in a ball for 1 hour. Line a flan tin (6—8 inches in diameter) with the pastry. Dice the bacon, having taken off the rind, and fry for 1 minute. Spread over the bottom of the pastry. Mix the cheese with eggs, milk and pepper, pour over the bacon. Bake in a slow to moderate oven till brown, about 20 minutes. Serve with watercress salad, with French dressing. (Illustrated in Plate 36.)

BANANES AU RHUM

Bananas with Rum

6 large bananas	juice 1 lemon	1 nut butter
3 tablespoons	3 tablespoons water	cream to serve
Demerara sugar		1 sherry glass rum

Butter a shallow fireproof dish. Cut the bananas in half lengthways and arrange overlapping in the dish. Sprinkle the sugar over, add the lemon juice and water. Bake in a moderate oven for 20 minutes or till brown. Add the rum 5 minutes before the end. Serve with whipped cream, which also may be flavoured with rum.

CRÊPES SUZETTE

Pancakes Suzette

12 SERVINGS

10 oz. flour	1 tablespoon orange	*Sauce:*
3 eggs	juice	juice 2 oranges
1 teaspoon salt	1 dessertspoon olive oil	2 tablespoons sugar
1 pint milk	butter for cooking	3 tablespoons
½ pint water		Cointreau
		juice ½ lemon

Put the salt and flour in a bowl and stir in the milk, slowly stirring all the while. Add the eggs, water, orange juice and olive oil, beat well and leave to stand for 30 minutes. Melt a little butter in a frying pan. When it is very hot, pour in a little batter and turn the pan from side to side so that it spreads very thinly and evenly over the pan. When the bottom is done, turn the pancake and brown on the other side. Fold the pancake in four and place it in a warm, fairly deep dish and cover with a napkin. Continue this operation until all the batter has been used (you should have about 24 pancakes). Make the sauce by boiling the orange and lemon juices together with 2 tablespoon sugar until the sugar has dissolved. Then add the Cointreau. Pour this sauce over the pancakes, light with a match and carry flaming to the table.

MELON AU PORTO

Melons with Port

3 SERVING

1 melon	1 gill Marsala	icing sugar

Cut the melon lengthwise into three parts, and scoop out the pips and fibres. In the hollows thus formed, pour the Marsala. Stand in the refrigerator or ice-box until ready to use. Serve with icing sugar.

CRÈME CARAMEL
Caramel Custard

2 oz. lump sugar ½ gill water 10 drops vanilla
1 oz. castor sugar 4 egg yolks essence
 1 pint milk

Put water into a saucepan with the lumps of sugar and boil until it turns into a rich brown caramel mixture. Coat the bottom of a mould with this. Beat the yolks, castor sugar and vanilla essence, combine them with the warmed milk and pour into the mould. Stand in a tin of water and bake in a moderate oven until it sets, then turn out.

MOUSSE AU CHOCOLAT
Chocolate Mousse

4 oz. slab bitter 2 tablespoons water 5 eggs
  chocolate small liqueur glass 6 oz. castor sugar
 brandy

Heat chocolate in a bain-marie or double boiler. When chocolate has melted, add sugar, and water, stir until sugar has dissolved. Separate eggs. Add yolks one at a time to chocolate, beating all the time. Remove saucepan from heat, stir in brandy. Beat egg whites until stiff, fold into chocolate mixture. Put into dessert glasses and leave in a very cold place for about 2 hours before serving.

ST. ÉMILION AU CHOCOLAT
St. Émilion Chocolate

4 oz. butter 8 oz. chocolate 2 lb. macaroons
4 oz. sugar 1 tablespoon water (see p. 127)
1 egg ½ pint milk 1 liqueur glass rum

Soak the macaroons in the rum. Cream the butter and sugar. Scald the milk and when cool beat in the egg yolk. Melt the chocolate in the water over a low heat, stir in the milk and egg mixture, then the creamed butter and sugar. Stir till quite smooth. In a soufflé dish put a layer of rum-flavoured macaroons, then a layer of the chocolate cream; repeat until the dish is full, finishing with macaroons. Chill for 12 hours or more and serve.

COMPOTE DE CERISES AU VIN ROUGE
Cherries in Red Wine

1 lb. cherries ¾ pint red wine 1 gill water
8 oz. castor sugar 4 oz. ripe gooseberries

Put stoned cherries and gooseberries in a bowl with castor sugar. Mix them gently. Pour the wine and water over them. Place bowl over saucepan of boiling water, cover bowl, let it cook for 15 minutes. Serve cold with little cakes or biscuits.

PÊCHES FLAMBÉES

2 peaches	1 oz. sugar	4 tablespoons water
1 level teaspoon arrowroot	1 tablespoon lemon juice	2 tablespoons brandy or kirsch

Skin, halve and stone peaches. Boil sugar and water to make light syrup. Place peaches in syrup till just softened. Lift out the peaches. Thicken the syrup with arrowroot blended with lemon juice. Bring to the boil. Replace peaches. Finish off at table. Heat peaches through gently. Pour over warm brandy or kirsch. Set alight just before serving.

PÊCHES AUX FRAISES DE BOIS

Peaches with Wild Strawberries

6 SERVINGS

3 peaches	basket of wild strawberries	icing sugar

Halve the peaches and remove stones and a little of the flesh. Arrange the halves, cut side uppermost, in a circle on a serving dish. Fill and heap them with wild strawberries, sprinkle with icing sugar and serve.

CRÈME À LA VANILLE

Vanilla Custard

1 pint milk	3 egg yolks	1 teaspoon vanilla essence
8 oz. castor sugar		

Beat egg yolks and sugar together. Heat milk, allow to cool and when tepid, add to sugar and egg mixture, very slowly, stirring all the while. Place over saucepan of boiling water and continue to stir until sauce thickens. Remove from fire and stir in vanilla essence.

COMPOTE DE POIRES AU VIN ROUGE

Pears in Red Wine

10 pears	½ pint red wine	2 cloves
4 oz. sugar		1 pint water

Peel the pears carefully without removing their stems. Take a saucepan just big enough to hold the pears upright. Put the wine, water, sugar and cloves in the saucepan and bring to the boil. Place the pears upright in the syrup, cover the saucepan and simmer very gently for 45 minutes. Put the pears on a serving dish, boil the syrup until it is reduced by a third. Pour it over the pears and serve either hot or cold.

FRAISES AU PORTO

Strawberries in Port

1 lb. strawberries	3 tablespoons castor	1 cup **Crème Chan-**
1 gill Port	sugar	tilly (see p. 269)

Put the strawberries in a deep fruit dish and sprinkle with sugar. Pour the Port wine over them and leave in the refrigerator or in a very cold place for 30 minutes. Just before serving, pile the Crème Chantilly on top of them.

ANANAS AU KIRSCH

Pineapple with Kirsch

6 SERVINGS

1 wineglass kirsch	6 slices fresh	castor sugar
	pineapple	

Take 6 slices pineapple, cut away all the rough outer skin and put each one on a plate. Pour kirsch over and leave in a cool place for about an hour. About 15 minutes before serving, sprinkle a little castor sugar over each pineapple slice.

BABA AU RUM

Cake with Rum

6 SERVINGS

6 oz. flour	3 tablespoons warm	4 eggs
1 level tablespoon	milk	1½ tablespoons sugar
yeast	3 oz. butter	pinch salt
	2 tablespoons rum	¼ pint water

Sift the flour into a large warmed bowl. Make a well in the centre and in it put the yeast and half the warm milk. Mix it with the index finger, adding a little flour to the mixture. Cover this hollow gently with the flour, and let it stand for 6 minutes. Break the eggs in a bowl and add them to the flour. Mix with the tips of your fingers. Add the rest of the milk. Then knead for about 5 minutes with your fists. Cover the bowl and stand it away from all draughts for 30 minutes, by which time the dough should have nearly doubled its volume. Melt the butter and when it is lukewarm add the sugar and salt and pour it into the dough. Mix well in, shaping your hand like a spade for this operation. It should take about 5 minutes. When the dough can be lifted in one piece it is ready. Grease a turk's head mould with melted butter and fill it less than halfway with the dough. Place the mould away from draughts and wait until the dough has risen to the top. This should take between 30 and 60 minutes. Bake it in a moderate oven for 40 minutes. Take the cake from the mould before it cools. Dissolve the sugar in the water and boil for 2 minutes. Cool. Add the rum. Put the cake on a serving dish and pour the rum syrup over it.

CRÈME CHANTILLY

Whipped Cream

| ½ pint thick fresh cream | 2 tablespoons sugar | ½ teaspoon vanilla sugar (see page 73) or ½ teaspoon vanilla essence |

Keep cream in a coool place or in the refrigerator for 24 hours before using, if possible. Then beat it until it doubles in volume. At the last moment, add the sugar and vanilla sugar or essence.

This cream is delicious served with strawberries or raspberries or with cakes and trifles.

OMELETTE AU RHUM

Rum Omelette

3 SERVINGS

| 6 eggs
1 oz. butter | 4 dessertspoons castor sugar | 2 tablespoons rum
pinch salt |

Separate the eggs. Beat the whites until they are stiff. Beat the yolks until they become a pale lemon colour. Add the sugar and a pinch of salt, fold in the egg whites. Heat the butter in a large frying pan. When it is very hot pour in the egg mixture. Raise the sides of the omelette during the cooking so that the uncooked part runs under and is cooked. When the omelette is ready, fold it over and slide in on to a warm dish. Pour the rum over it, set the rum alight and bring it flaming to the table.

OEUFS À LA NEIGE

Snow Eggs

6 SERVINGS

6 eggs	1 teaspoon lemon	¼ teaspoon vanilla
¾ pint milk	juice	essence
5 oz. lump sugar		5 oz. castor sugar

Separate the eggs and beat the whites until they are very stiff. Add the castor sugar and continue beating for a while. Put the lump sugar, lemon juice, vanilla essence and milk in a saucepan and boil, stirring well until the sugar has dissolved. Take a soup spoon full of the beaten egg whites, level the top with a knife and place this 'egg' in the boiling milk. Continue this operation until all the egg white has been used. Leave these 'eggs' to cook for 2 minutes, turning them once during the cooking. Remove them carefully, and drain on a cheese-cloth. Sieve the boiled milk. Beat the yolks, add the milk slowly to the yolks, beating well. Return to the saucepan and cook, stirring until the mixture thickens. When this mixture is quite cold, pour it into a deep serving dish, place the 'eggs' on top and serve.

CHARLOTTE RUSSE

1 packet lemon jelly	sponge fingers	glacé cherries
½ pint cream or	2 teaspoons lemon	1 small can
1 large can evapor-	juice	mandarins
ated milk	2 teaspoons sugar	¾ pint hot water
	1 banana	

Dissolve the jelly in the hot water and pour enough into a 1½-pint mould to line it. Arrange glacé cherries, mandarins and slices of banana at the bottom of the mould. Whip the cream or canned milk with lemon juice and sugar until thick. When the remaining jelly is nearly set, beat until frothy and add to the whipped cream. Mix well, pour into the mould and leave to set. When cold, turn out on to a large dish and arrange the sponge fingers, cut in halves longwise, upright round the sides. Decorate with whipped cream or fruit in season. *(Illustrated in Plate 44.)*

CHOCOLATE ÉCLAIRS

6 SERVINGS

1 gill water	pinch salt	2½ tablespoons flour
4 oz. flour	chocolate or coffee	½ pint milk
2 oz. butter or	glacé icing (see p. 272)	6 oz. sugar
margarine	*For the Filling:*	drop of vanilla essence
1 dessertspoon sugar	4 eggs	pinch salt
4 eggs		

Put the water, salt and sugar, with the butter cut into tiny pieces, in a saucepan. Bring them to the boil, and when they begin to bubble, remove from the fire. Put the flour in a saucepan and add the first mixture to it slowly, beating well until smooth. Put the saucepan on over a medium heat, stirring constantly until mixture begins to dry and does not cling to the bottom of the saucepan. Remove from the heat, cool and stir the eggs well in, one at a time. Beat until the mixture is very light. Pipe this dough into fingers about 3½ inches in length, and place them on a floured baking tin. Brush them with a little beaten egg yolk. Cook in a moderate oven for 1 hour.

To make the filling: Boil the milk and add the vanilla essence to it. Mix the flour, sugar, salt, and eggs in a saucepan and add the milk, slowly, stirring well. Place the saucepan on the fire and stir well until the mixture comes to the boil. Continue stirring for 2 minutes, then remove from the fire and let it cool. Cut your cooked 'fingers' in half lengthwise and fill them with this cream. Crème Chantilly (see p. 269) may be used in place of the cream given above, if you prefer. Spread tops with chocolate glacé icing (see p. 272). *(Illustrated in Plate 45.)*

CHOUX À LA CRÈME

Cream Buns

These are made in the same way as the éclairs, except that the dough is placed on the baking tin in the shape of little balls, which when cooked are cut in half and filled with the cream given in the éclair recipe, or with Crème Chantilly (see p. 269).

MARRONS GLACÉS

Candied Chestnuts

| 2 lb. chestnuts | water | few drops vanilla |
| 3 lb. loaf sugar | | essence |

Make cuts in the chestnuts, put into warm water and bring to the boil. Simmer for about 10 minutes then drain and remove the shell and skin. Put the peeled nuts back into a pan of warm water and simmer until tender but not broken. Make a syrup with 1 lb. of the sugar and ½ pint of water and boil to 250° F. Put in the nuts and leave until cool. Then take out and drain.

Again make a syrup with 1 lb. of sugar and ½ pint of water, adding a few drops of vanilla essence. Put in the nuts, stirring gently so as not to break them and to get them well covered with syrup. Take out the nuts and drain. When they are cold give them a third coating with the remaining 1 lb. of sugar and ½ pint of water brought to the boil. Add a few more drops of vanilla essence and boil the nuts in the syrup for a few minutes. Remove and place in an oiled slab to cool. When set put the candied chestnuts into paper confectionery cases.

MERINGUES

12 SERVINGS

4 egg whites	blanched almonds	icing sugar
4 tablespoons castor sugar		Crème Chantilly (see p. 269)

Beat the whites, if possible in a copper basin. When they are stiff, add a spoonful of sugar and beat for a few seconds, then fold in the rest of the sugar slowly. Continue beating until the mixture, when lifted, stands in peaks. Butter a piece of greaseproof paper, sprinkle it with icing sugar, and place it on a baking sheet. Place spoonfuls of the mixture on a baking sheet. Sprinkle lightly with icing sugar and place them on the bottom shelf in a very low oven. (If your warming compartment has a fairly high temperature you could use it instead.) Leave them to cook for 1½—2 hours, depending on the temperature of the oven. Remove them, lifting them very gently, and crush the middle of the flat side carefully with your finger. Replace them in the oven for 10 minutes. Place a layer of Crème Chantilly on the crushed sides between two layers of meringue. Decorate with shredded almonds. *(Illustrated in Plate 46.)*

CHOCOLATE GLACÉ ICING

1½ oz. plain chocolate	1 tablespoon warm water	4 oz. icing sugar

Break the chocolate into small pieces, put into a bowl and leave to stand in hot water until the chocolate melts. Add sieved icing sugar and water and stir until well mixed and smooth.
For coffee icing, use ½ teaspoon of coffee essence instead of the chocolate and omit ½ teaspoon of water.

MADELEINES

Madeleine Tea Cakes

24 CAKES

5 oz. flour	1 dessertspoon lemon juice	2 eggs
10 oz. sugar		6 oz. butter
jam	desiccated coconut	glacé cherries

Beat egg yolks with sugar and butter (previously melted, and lukewarm when added). Beat until mixture is smooth, add lemon juice then sieved flour slowly, stirring all the time. Add egg whites, unbeaten. Take 24 dariole tins and butter them. Fill them with the cake mixture and cook them in a hot oven for 25 minutes. Brush the cakes with sieved, heated jam. Roll in coconut. Place a cherry on top.

49. La Daube Provençale, France (p.232)

50. Cooking with Wine in France

BRIOCHE

8 TO 12 SERVINGS

14 oz. flour	1 teaspoon salt	3 large eggs
1 oz. yeast	4 oz. melted butter	1 tablespoon sugar
1 gill water	2 tablespoons water	

Mix the yeast and 4 oz. of the flour with 1 gill warm water to form a ball. Gash the ball with a knife and put it in a warm place out of draughts. Leave it until it has swollen to twice its size. Break 3 eggs into remainder of flour and mix well together with your hands. If the dough is too dry to mix, add a very little warm water. Beat and stir it with your hands for 10 minutes. Now add the melted butter, salt, and sugar, and beat for 5 more minutes. Take the yeast and flour mixture and add it to the dough. Mix them quickly with your hands. Cover the basin and leave it to stand away from all draughts for about 5½ hours when the dough should have swollen to twice its original size. Knead it carefully. Then leave it in a cool place out of draughts overnight. Next day take the dough and place it in a round buttered mould. After 30 minutes place it in a very hot oven and bake it for 35 minutes, covering the top with buttered paper or foil to prevent burning.

BILLETS DOUX

Love Letters

12 SERVINGS

8 oz. flour	4 oz. sugar	1 tablespoon cream
5½ oz. butter	7 egg yolks	1 pint custard sauce

Mix sugar and butter in bowl. Add egg yolks and flour. Mix with cream to consistency of a shortbread dough. Let stand for 2 hours. Then roll and cut into 4-inch squares. Fill one side of each square with thick custard sauce (see p. 267), fold other side over it, seal edges and place little 'letters' on floured baking dish. Bake in very moderate oven for 30 minutes.

PETITS FOURS

Literally these are just 'little bakes', miniature editions of popular favourites:

1) *Petits choux* — tiny éclairs and choux buns (see pp. 270, 271).
2) *Almond Petits Fours* — smaller versions of Almond Macaroons (see p. 127). Decorate with a button of icing.
3) *Marrons Glacés* — (see p. 271).
   Coloured and flavoured to choice and decorated as desired.
4) *Meringues* — miniature versions of recipe on page 272.

SOME FRENCH MENUS WITH SUITABLE WINES

MENU FOR A DINNER PARTY (1)

Tomates aux crevettes

Potage crème de laitue

Rôti de boeuf jardinière

Pommes de terre sautées

Ananas au Kirsch

Suggested wines: Montrachet, Saint Émilion

MENU FOR A DINNER PARTY (2)

Asperges à l'huile

Bouillon de champignons

Pigeons à la Crapaudine

Pommes frites

Céleri au jus

Baba au Rhum

Suggested wine: Château Margaux

MENU FOR A DINNER PARTY (3)

Filets de sole Colbert

Canard aux cerises

Pommes de terre sautées

Salade de laitues

Mousse au chocolat

Suggested wines: Chablis, Château Laffitee

GERMAN COOKING

Nella Whitfield

To a great extent the German cuisine and style of cooking express the national characteristics of the German people. Here is a country of sturdy men, so we can expect hearty trencherman with wives who know how to prepare good substantial meals.

German delicatessen are famous, deserving a cookery book to themselves, and those who have a delicatessen store nearby will, no doubt, have sampled some of the more notable food varieties; smoked sausages, frankfurters, blood sausage, liver sausage, etc.; pickled vegetables—sauerkraut, cucumbers, etc., and smoked and pickled meats, which make delightful new dishes for the enterprising party-giver. But whether bought or home-made, these appetising savouries can be the basis of many tempting and warming meals. A speck of garlic, a pinch of herbs, or a few caraway seeds, with careful seasoning, bring out the flavours of the meat ingredients and prove to you how varied and delicious the famous German sausages can be.

Most German menus include fish from the shores and rivers of the country. They are usually smoked, salted and pickled, and served with sauces of characteristic flavour.

Fruit soups are much in favour as a prelude to the main course and are often served cold. Sometimes, they are made from the hips of wild roses, elderberries, apples or cherries. They are not at all difficult to make and, in warm weather particularly, make a pleasant change on the menu.

As for liqueurs—a wonderful ending to a good meal—there are few things to equal the delight of fresh pineapple with Kirsch, or the lingering pleasure of the pungent German Kümmel.

Americans long ago discovered the delicious flavours of the German style of cooking known as sweet and sour—and you now have the same opportunity to discover them.

PÂTÉ OF GOOSE LIVER

Gänseleberpastete

1 large goose liver	1 port wine glass cognac	½ small can truffles

Marinate the truffles in the cognac for 1 hour, then cut them into small pieces. Having removed all veins and nerves very carefully from the liver, cut that also into pieces and with a sharp pointed knife insert pieces of truffle into the pieces of liver. Put the liver into an earthenware casserole, well greased on the bottom and sides with goose fat. Pour in the cognac in which the truffles were marinated. Cover with grease-proof paper, put on the casserole lid, stand it in a large pan containing hot water, and cook slowly, for 3 hours, refilling the outer vessel with boiling water as it evaporates. Leave the pâté to get quite cold in the dish, then carefully turn it out and pour melted goose fat over it until it has a thick coating. Put away to become very cold, serve in thin slices.

ROLLED HERRING FILLETS IN VINEGAR

Rollmops

6 or more good herrings	shallots	peppercorns
sliced gherkins	white wine vinegar	tiny red chillis
		mustard seed

Remove heads and bone the fish, divide into 2 fillets each and remove the roes. Lay a line of thinly sliced gherkins and paper-thin shallots on each fillet. Roll up the fillets and fasten with tiny wooden skewers. Pack the rolls into wide-necked jars, add a pinch of mustard seed, several peppercorns and a red chilli to each jar and fill with white wine vinegar. Cover and let stand for a few days before serving. *(Illustrated in Plate 54.)*

ANCHOVY SALAD WITH BEER MAYONNAISE

Sardellensalat mit Biermayonnaise

2 small cans anchovy fillets	4 tablespoons light ale	6 small potatoes, cooked in their
1 small crisp cucumber	1 gill very thick mayonnaise (see p. 263)	skins until tender
		1 head of celery

Remove the outer stalks of the celery, cut the rest in 1 inch lengths. Peel and slice the cucumber, skin the potatoes and cut them into thin slices. Arrange the cucumber and potatoes on a large round dish, in overlapping alternate slices. Heap the celery into the centre. Arrange the anchovy strips on the celery. Beat the oil from a can and the beer, smoothly, with the mayonnaise; pour it over the salad. Serve garnished with lettuce.

ARTICHOKE SALAD

Artischockensalat

2 lb. Jerusalem artichokes	about 6 anchovy fillets	vinegar
½ pint milk	salt	thick mayonnaise (see p. 263)
½ pint water		

Wash the artichokes and scrape them, cutting off uneven pieces, dropping each into a bowl of cold water with a little vinegar in it to prevent them turning black. When all are prepared, cook until tender in milk and water, slightly salted. Cut into slices, mix with the finely minced anchovies, stir a teaspoon of the oil from the anchovy tin into the mayonnaise and pour it over the hot artichokes.

ROLLMOP SALAD

6—8 rollmops (see p. 277)	2 large cooked potatoes	2 tablespoons white wine
10—12 gherkins	few spring onions	1 teaspoon sugar
1 small cooked beetroot	few lettuce leaves	¼ teaspoon dry mustard
1 sweet apple	1 gill salad cream	

Mix the salad cream with sugar, mustard and wine. Dice the potatoes and beetroot, dress with the salad cream mixture and arrange on the lettuce leaves lying on an oval platter. Put the rollmops on top and arrange around them the apple, cut into small cubes, the gherkins sliced in half and the spring onions.

HOP SALAD

Hopfensalat

Cut a quantity of young hop shoots, wash and cook, tied in small bundles like asparagus. If eaten hot, serve with plain melted butter. If eaten cold, pour over mayonnaise (see p. 263) thinned with a little lemon juice.

HORSERADISH AND APPLE SALAD

Meerrettigsalat mit Äpfeln

½ small horseradish	¼ pint good malt vinegar	1 lb. firm eating apples
1 tablespoon salad oil		salt and pepper
1 oz. sugar		

Wash the horseradish and grate it. Mix it at once with the sugar and vinegar. Peel, core and thinly slice the apples, pour the oil over the pieces, sprinkle with salt and pepper, then mix in the horseradish. Serve with cold roast or boiled beef, or with any galantine.

RAW RED CABBAGE SALAD

Roher Rotkohlsalat

the heart of 1 small red cabbage	1 firm eating apple, peeled, cored and thinly sliced	3 tablespoons salad oil
finely chopped onion		2 tablespoons vinegar
	salt	½ teaspoon sugar

Shred the cabbage very finely, sprinkle well with salt and leave in a warm place for 1 hour. Press the cabbage well, pouring off all liquid. Beat the oil, vinegar and sugar well together, toss the shredded cabbage in it, then mix in the apple and onion.

BOUQUET SALAD

Kapuziner- oder Blumensalat

4 tablespoons olive oil	little shake of pepper	nasturtium flowers,
3 tablespoons white	nasturtium leaves,	various shades
wine vinegar	very young and	watercress
pinch sugar	tender ones	hard-boiled eggs

Mix the oil, vinegar, sugar and pepper well together in the bottom of a large bowl, then fill the bowl with alternate layers of watercress and small nasturtium leaves, using ¼ of leaves to ¾ of cress. Place a ring of little nasturtium leaves round the edge of the bowl, then a ring of variegated nasturtium flowers, then a ring of thin slices of hard-boiled egg, each slice overlapping the other. In the centre of the bowl place a tuft of flowers. Serve with rich mayonnaise (see p. 273). This salad is best with delicate cold ham and thinly sliced sausage.

BATTER FLAKE SOUP

Einlaufsuppe

3 eggs	2 pints clear beef	milk
3 tablespoons flour	stock, well flavoured	½ teaspoon salt

Beat the eggs and flour with enough milk to make a thick, smooth batter. Bring the beef stock to the boil and drop the batter by small teaspoonfuls into it, and boil for 10 minutes. Add salt. When the tiny batter balls have all risen to the top, serve soup at once.

ALMOND SOUP

Mandelsuppe

8 oz. blanched and	hot milk or thin cream	thin strips toasted
pounded almonds	1 teaspoon rose water	Vienna bread
2 eggs		sugar and cinnamon

Pound the blanched almonds very finely, using the white of one of the eggs to prevent the nuts from oiling and becoming too sticky. Heat the milk or cream and stir in enough to make about 1 pint of soup. Beat the whole egg and remaining egg white well together and stir into the soup. Add the rose water. Make quite hot or else serve quite cold, with a little sugar sprinkled with some cinnamon on top of each bowl, and with thin strips of toast. This soup is often given to convalescents as it is considered to be strengthening.

ALE SOUP

Biersuppe

2 pints mild ale	small piece cinnamon	1 tablespoon
juice ½ lemon	stick (about ½ inch)	potato flour
salt	semolina (optional)	pinch sugar

Heat the ale and lemon juice with the cinnamon, salt and sugar. Mix the potato flour to a smooth paste with a little of the ale. Stir into the ale mixture, stir and cook gently until it has thickened and is smooth. If a thicker soup is liked, scatter in 1 tablespoon of fine semolina and cook until it has been absorbed into the ale.

EGG BARLEY SOUP

Eiergerstensuppe

1 whole egg	2 pints clear beef	1 dessertspoon
1 egg yolk	soup	chopped chives
plain white flour	finely chopped parsley	1 dessertspoon dry
		grated horseradish

Mix the beaten egg and egg yolk with as much flour as will make a stiff ball. Leave for 1 hour, then grate it on a coarse grater, spreading it on a large dish. Leave to dry. When quite dry and brittle, sprinkle the pieces with the chives and horseradish into boiling beef stock and cook for about 5 minutes. Garnish with chopped parsley.

HUNTER'S SOUP

Jägersuppe

1 large carrot	1 head of celery	2 partridges
1 large onion	in season	flour
4 oz. lean ham cut in	2 pints beef stock	salt and pepper
1 thick slice	1 pint dry red wine	2 oz. butter

Roast the partridges, basting them with butter. Fry the sliced vegetables and the diced ham in the fat left from the cooked birds, lightly dredged with flour, until yellow. Carve all the meat from the birds in neat pieces, then crush the bones and put into the saucepan with the vegetables and stock. Boil briskly for 1 hour. Strain, stir in the wine and re-heat for 15 minutes. Put the meat in and serve with the soup.

FRUIT SOUPS

Obstsuppen

The basic recipe is the same for all. The fruit is cooked to a pulp with water, rubbed through a sieve, slightly thickened with potato or cornflour, and sweetened to taste. A little light red or white wine is often added to these soups in the evening, but seldom during the day. If the soups are served hot, small semolina dumplings or diced white bread from milk rolls or other breads, fried, are served with them. If the soups are cold or iced, then tiny macaroons or little lemon or almond flavoured biscuits are handed. Cherries, which grow abundantly and are usually very juicy and sweet, plums, redcurrants, raspberries, strawberries, cranberries and ripe elderberries are used and, of course, apples.

The following is an example:

APPLE AND BREAD SOUP

Äpfelbrotsuppe

6 large cooking apples	1 tablespoon well	grated rind and
4 slices pumpernickel	washed currants	strained juice of
1½ oz. sugar	or seedless raisins	1 lemon
	1½ pints water	pinch cinnamon

Peel, score and slice the apples into a pan, soak the bread in water and then squeeze it dry. Put it into the saucepan with the apples and water and simmer until the apples are tender. Put all through a sieve. Return the purée to the saucepan with the cinnamon and fruit, the sugar and lemon rind. Slowly re-heat the mixture, adding the lemon juice last. Simmer for only obout 5 minutes, then serve. The soup may be thickened even more by stirring in a teaspoonful of potato flour with enough water to mix it to a cream. Half a teacupful of white wine is sometimes added.

EELS STEWED IN BEER

Gestobter Aal mit Bier

eels as required	1 bay leaf	salt and pepper
butter	2 sage leaves	2 tablespoons wine
flour	1 clove garlic	vinegar
	1 pint light beer	

Clean and skin the required quantity of eels, cut off heads and tails and soak in salted water for 10 minutes. Cut into 3-inch lengths, melt a piece of butter in a saucepan, dredge in a little flour and stir in 1 pint of light beer. Put in the pieces of eel, with a bay leaf, 2 sage leaves, a clove of garlic, salt and pepper and 2 tablespoons of wine vinegar. Cover the pan and simmer the eels for 30 minutes. Fast cooking will break the fish. Place the pieces in a hot dish and strain the sauce over them. Serve very hot with plain boiled potatoes and rye bread with butter, or leave until quite cold and serve with sliced cucumber and rye bread and butter.

LEMON FISH STEW

Fischragout

2½ lb. cod	pinch cayenne pepper	strained juice
1 onion	½ teaspoon salt	3 lemons
1 tablespoon cooking	small pinch ginger	1 level tablespoon
oil	2 eggs	flour
3—4 tablespoons water		

Chop the onion finely and fry it in the oil, adding salt, pepper and ginger. Put the fish, cut into small cutlets or steaks, into a large shallow casserole, and pour the oil, onion and seasoning over the fish. Add 3—4 tablespoons of water. Cover closely and cook in a very moderate oven for 25 minutes. Beat the eggs, stir in the flour and lemon juice to a paste. Add a little liquid from the fish, pour back into the dish, and put back into the oven for 10 minutes to cook the sauce.

MACKEREL STEW

Makrelenragout

4 large mackerel	1 gill vinegar	chopped parsley
2 small gingerbread	1 tablespoon syrup	about ½ pint water
cakes	slices lemon	2 onions

Slice the onions very thinly and simmer them in water until quite tender in a saucepan. Put the well cleaned and gutted fish into a casserole and pour in the onion. Cook in a hot oven for 20 minutes. Crumble the gingerbread into the vinegar and syrup. Take up the fish, divide neatly and remove the back bones. Pour the gingerbread mixture on to a large dish. Arrange the mackerel on this, decorate with thin slices of lemon and chopped parsley. Serve cold.

CARP IN BROWN SAUCE

Karpfen in Brauner Sauce

Although carp is plentiful in many of the rivers of Germany and other Continental countries, it is seldom found in Britain, unless private fishermen are fortunate enough to catch one. Here are recipes for the time when this happens.

1 medium sized fish	1 gill red wine and	2 oz. butter
salt and pepper	1 gill malt vinegar	2 rashers fat bacon
1 bay leaf	1 finely minced shallot	water
2—3 thin slices lemon		flour

Cut the carp into small pieces and pack these into a dish with the lemon slices and the bay leaf, salt and pepper to season. Pour the wine and the vinegar over the fish, cover with a lid and leave to soak for 3—4 hours. Melt the butter in saucepan and dredge in enough flour to be absorbed by the butter and allow it to brown. Thin with a little water. Add the minced bacon and shallot. Drain the liquid from the fish into the pan and bring to the boil. Add a little more water if necessary; the sauce should be thick. Lay the pieces of fish in the sauce and simmer gently until the fish is tender. Serve in the sauce, with plain boiled potatoes.

CARP WITH POLISH SAUCE

Karpfen in Polnischer Sauce

1 carp	1 bay leaf	2 thick slices stale
thin slices parsnip	a little beer	gingerbread
celery and onion	thin slices lemon	2 tablespoons vinegar
1 large piece butter	1 or 2 cloves	salt and pepper

Into a large saucepan put a layer of thin slices of parsnip, celery and onion with a large knob of butter or margarine, salt, pepper, a bay leaf broken into several small pieces, several thin slices of lemon, and the cloves. Having removed the head and tail from the fish, split it open and clean it thoroughly. It must not be cut in two, only separated down the centre and held together by the back. Lay the fish, split side down, on the vegetables, and cover with the head, tail and liver. Sprinkle with the crumbled gingerbread. Pour vinegar over it and enough beer just to cover the fish. Simmer until the fish is done, but on no account cook to breaking point. Remove fish and simmer the sauce until it is thick, then strain it over the fish. The vegetables may be rubbed through a sieve and added to the sauce.

HERRING SOUSED IN WINE

Heringe in Weinsauce

6 medium sized herrings, preferably with soft roes	$\frac{1}{2}$ teaspoon peppercorns $\frac{1}{2}$ teaspoon salt	2 tablespoons dry white wine 2 tablespoons water pinch cayenne pepper

Remove head, gut and scale the fish. Roll up each herring and place in a shallow dish. Scatter peppercorns, salt and pepper over them. Mix the white wine and the water together and pour over the fish. Cover with greaseproof paper or foil and bake in a moderately hot oven for about 35 minutes. Serve cold with mustard mixed to a thin cream with the same kind of wine used for sousing the herrings.

FISH WITH PIQUANT SAUCE

Fisch in pikanter Sauce

2 lb. fresh haddock
2 oz. butter
½ oz. flour
4 oz. small mushrooms
½ teaspoon dry
  mustard

½ teaspoon meat
  extract
½ tablespoon chopped
  parsley

1 tablespoon capers
juice 1 lemon
¼ pint water
salt and pepper
2 tablespoons minced
  onion

Cut the fish into medium sized pieces, rub with salt, coat with parsley and leave for about 30 minutes. Mix the butter, flour and mustard to a stiff paste. Stir in the meat extract, water, lemon juice and pepper. Pour a little of this sauce into a casserole, lay the fish and sliced mushrooms in the sauce, sprinkle with the onion and capers, cover with the rest of sauce, place a piece of buttered paper over the casserole and put on the lid. Stand the casserole in a large saucepan of water or steamer, cook over boiling water for 30—35 minutes.

FISH BALLS

2 lb. white fish
  (bream, fresh
  haddock or cod)
2 eggs

2 onions
1 carrot
1 stick celery

1 oz. breadcrumbs
parsley
salt and pepper
1 oz. ground almonds

Remove the skin, head and bones from the fish. Cook it with one onion, sliced, half the carrot, sliced, and the celery in 1½ pints of water for 15 minutes. Strain. Mince the fish and the remaining onion, add the ground almonds, some chopped parsley and season with salt and pepper. Beat the eggs into this mixture and blend well. Add the breadcrumbs, shape into balls. Slice the rest of the carrot, add it to the strained stock. Bring the stock to the boil, simmer the fish balls in it for 15 minutes. Arrange the fish balls on a dish with a little stock strained over each. Serve cold.

FISH CAKE

Fischhackbraten

1 lb. white fish
  without bones
  or skin
2 oz. breadcrumbs
2 whole eggs and
  2 egg yolks
2 oz. butter

2 oz. chopped lean
  ham
1 thick slice fat
  bacon
1¼ oz. flour
2 teaspoons minced
  onion

1 gill sour cream or
  soured top of the
  milk
½ pint stock
salt and pepper
1 teaspoon French
  mustard

Mince the raw fish. Mix 1 oz. breadcrumbs with $\frac{1}{2}$ oz. butter and 2 eggs and stir over a low heat until thick; add the chopped onion. Put into a large basin, mix in the 2 egg yolks, 1 oz. flour, mustard, fish and ham. Season with salt and pepper. Form into a roll and coat with breadcrumbs. Put the slice of fat bacon in a baking dish, lay the fish roll on it, dot with remaining butter. Pour on stock and cook in a moderately hot oven for 20 minutes. Baste from time to time. Remove fish roll. Thicken sauce with cream, mixed with the remaining flour and pour over fish roll. Serve cold with salad.

CODLING IN BEER SAUCE

Kabeljau in Biersauce

fresh codling weighing 2—3 lb.	1 bay leaf	2 tablespoons of browned butter
1 medium onion sliced into rings	1 tablespoon vinegar	2 tablespoons flour
2 sliced carrots	1 square of ginger- bread about 2 inches	1$\frac{1}{2}$ dozen oysters
juice of 1 small lemon	by 2 inches	brown ale salt and pepper slices of toast

Remove head and tail from the fish and clean it thoroughly. Put the gingerbread, cut into small pieces, in a long casserole or oven dish, add the sliced onion and carrots and the bay leaf and lay the fish on them. Season with pepper and salt, cover with brown ale and vinegar, put on the lid and cook fast for 15 minutes in a hot oven. Reduce heat to very moderate for 10 minutes. Take up the fish carefully with two fish slices, and lay on a very hot dish. Rub the vegetables and gingerbread through a wire sieve, with the beer. Thicken with flour and butter and pour over the fish. Arrange tiny squares of toast round the fish with an oyster on each.

FRIED SALT HERRING

Gebratene Heringe

4 or 5 large salted herrings	a little milk	flour
	egg and breadcrumbs	butter
	1 gill dry red wine	

Wash the herrings and cut off fins and tails and lay them in a dish with enough milk to cover them, for 1 hour. Dry them, then cover with the wine and leave for another hour. Dredge lightly with flour, coat with egg and breadcrumbs and fry lightly in butter. Serve with hot potato salad and sauerkraut.

BLACK SAUSAGES

Schwarzwürste

4 lb. fresh pork with a fourth part solid fat	1 pint pig's blood salt and pepper allspice 8 oz. fine bread-crumbs	¼ teaspoon ground cloves 1 clove garlic, chopped

Add a little salt to the blood and keep stirring it to keep it liquid. Boil the pork and fat in as little water poslible, until tender. Cut into very small dice or chop finely. Mix with the breadcrumbs, spices, garlic and seasonings and stir in the blood. Fill the prepared skins and boil for 30 minutes. When cold, smoke them for 2 days or hang them in a cool dry place without smoking.

SMOKED SAUSAGES

Geräucherte Bratwürste

6 lb. lean pork ¼ oz. saltpetre	1 lb. fat smoked bacon	2 oz. salt ½ oz. black pepper

Mince pork finely and bacon not so finely. Mix together with the condiments, moisten with cold water. Fill skins, and hang in smoke for 6 days. To serve, grill or fry sausage and serve on a bed of sauerkraut.

FRANKFURT SAUSAGES

Frankfurter Bratwürste

Use 6 lb. pork, fat and lean as it comes, but with a slightly larger proportion of lean. Mince very finely, then season with salt, black pepper, grated nutmeg, a few ground coriander seeds and mix well. Moisten with red wine and fill the skins, not too tightly. Smoke slightly for 3 days.

LIVER SAUSAGES

Leberwürste

1 pig's liver ½ its weight in boiled pork	8 oz. fat bacon salt and pepper allspice	when possible 1 or 2 truffles (these may be canned)

Chop the liver very finely pound it and rub it through a coarse sieve. Mince the pork finely and cut the bacon fat into tiny dice. Mix all well together with the seasonings and the truffles also diced. Fill thick skins, drop them into salted boiling water and simmer them slowly for 30 minutes. Wipe and hang up to dry. Keep in a very cool place.

WHITE SAUSAGES

Weiße Bratwürste

4 lb. lean pork	1 lb. pork or bacon	½ oz. white pepper
1 lb. lean veal	fat	¼ oz. grated nutmeg
1 lb. white bread	2 oz. salt	grated rind ½ lemon

Soak the crustless bread in milk, then squeeze it dry and beat it with a fork until light. Put it, with the seasonings and all the meat and fat, through the fine cutters of the mincer until reduced almost to a pulp. Sprinkle a little water on the mixture as it goes through the mincer. Fill the skins carefully, so that no spaces are left. This is, of course, essential with all the sausages. Boil them for 30 minutes; serve cold or fry them as usual.

SWABIAN SAUSAGES

Schwäbische Würste

6 lb. pork, allowing 4 lb. lean to 2 lb. fat	2 oz. salt	a little water
	½ oz. black pepper	¼ oz. saltpetre
		¼ oz. clove garlic

Cut the meat into small pieces, scatter with the salt, pepper and saltpetre and put through the fine cutters of a mincer until reduced to a fine paste. Crush the garlic with 2 tablespoons water until it is reduced to a smooth pulp. Put this once more through the mincer with the meat. Fill sausage skins and use plain or lightly smoked.

SAUSAGES WITH APPLES

Bratwürste mit Äpfeln

8 large cooking apples	cinnamon	1½ lb. good pork
2 oz. currants	1 gill claret	sausages
1 oz. butter		sugar

Peel, core and quarter the apples, scatter a little sugar and a pinch of cinnamon over them and leave for 2—3 hours. Wash the currants and leave in warm water for 2—3 hours. Heat the butter in a saucepan and in it put the well pricked sausages. Cover with the pieces of apple and any juice that has formed. Scatter the currants over. Put on the saucepan lid and cook gently. As the pieces of apple get tender, take them up and put aside to keep hot. Turn the sausages in the fat until evenly cooked all over. Remove the sausages and pour the claret into the pan, stir carefully into the fat; boil, then strain over the sausages and apples. Serve with mashed potatoes.

BEEF SAUSAGES

Rindfleischwürste

4 lb. lean beef	2 oz. salt	⅛ teaspoon ground
1 lb. lean pork	1 teaspoon saltpetre	cloves
1 lb. bacon fat	½ oz. black pepper	clove garlic, crushed

Mince the beef and pork finely, cut the bacon fat into tiny dice, crush the garlic to a pulp with a tablespoon of cold water. Mix all the ingredients thoroughly. Fill sausage skins. Put them into cold water and bring to a gentle simmer and cook thus for 1 hour. Drop into cold water for 5 minutes, then hang in a cool airy place to dry.

PORK SAUSAGES

Bratwürste

Use lean pork for these, the proportion of meat being 6 lb. to 1 lb. of fat. Any part of the pig will do, the shoulders being considered economical for sausage making. Remove all skin and gristle from the meat and cut it into small pieces. Mix with it 2 oz. common salt, ¼ oz. saltpetre and ½ oz. black pepper. Put the meat and seasoning through a fine mincer twice. If using skins, turn and thoroughly clean them, leave them in cold water and a little salt for 4—5 hours, then wipe them dry before using. The above mixture makes a very plain and solid sausage, but every maker has her own special mixture of herbs and seasonings. To the mixture may be added 1 lb. fine breadcrumbs soaked in milk and pressed dry, half a small nutmeg grated, 2 teaspoons very finely minced fresh sage leaves, or any other herb preferred.

SWEETBREAD CROQUETTES

Kalbsmilchbälle

1 lb. sweetbreads	1 tablespoon Madeira	2 egg yolks
1 oz. powdered	6 oz. cold roast veal or	salt and pepper
gelatine	cooked calf's tongue	fine stale bread-
1 oz. butter	1 gill stock	crumbs
1 oz. flour	2 teaspoons lemon	1 whole beaten egg
4 oz. mushrooms	juice	dripping
		parsley sprigs

Boil the sweetbreads, tongue or veal and mushrooms for 15 minutes in the stock, then cut all into small dice. Make white sauce of the butter, flour and stock, season with lemon juice, salt and pepper, stir in diced mixture. Dissolve the gelatine in the Madeira and add to the sweetbread mixture with the beaten egg yolks. Scatter a large dish with some of the crumbs and spread the mixture over them, scatter more crumbs on top and leave for 1 hour. Divide into 12 croquettes, roll them in the whole beaten egg, turn in the rest of the crumbs and fry in dripping until golden brown. Serve garnished with fried parsley.

51. Marble Cake, Germany (p.315)

52. Yule Log, Britain (p.120)

53. Simnel Cake, Britain (p.120)

SAUSAGES IN BEER

Würste in Biersauce

1½ lb. good pork sausages	mashed potatoes	1 finely minced onion
½ pint brown ale	sliced carrots	1 tablespoon gravy
	2 oz. fat	thickening

Fry the sausages in fat with the onion. Take up the sausages and keep them hot. Stir the gravy thickening into the fat left in the pan, add the ale and cook to a smooth sauce. Arrange the sausages on a mound of mashed potatoes, with a border of sliced carrots. Strain the sauce and pour over the carrots.

BRAISED SWEETBREADS

Geschmorte Kalbsmilch

1 lb. sweetbreads	2 oz. butter	4 oz. mushrooms
1 tablespoon lemon juice	2 teaspoons flour	1 oz. margarine or butter
1 gill brown stock (see p. 258)	salt and pepper	chopped parsley
	green peas, cooked	

Wash the mushrooms, do not peel them, chop them roughly, and cook in the margarine or butter until just tender. Soak the sweetbreads in cold, slightly salted water for 30 minutes, cook gently for 10 minutes. Dry, remove skin and gristle and cut into ½-inch thick slices. Roll generously in seasoned flour. Brown the 2 oz. butter in a saucepan and turn the pieces of sweetbread in the hot brown butter until seared all over. Add the stock and lemon juice and stew gently for 15 minutes. Put the sweetbread slices on a hot dish. Arrange little heaps of mushrooms and peas around them. Strain a little of the gravy over and scatter with chopped parsley.

FRANKFURTERS WITH SAUERKRAUT

4 frankfurters	4 rashers bacon	bacon bones
8 oz. haricot beans	8 oz. sauerkraut	salt and pepper
2 pints water		

Soak the beans overnight. Drain and cook with the bacon bones in water until tender. Pass beans through a sieve, season with salt if necessary and pepper. Fry the bacon and remove to keep warm. Heat the sauerkraut in the bacon fat. Arrange the bean purée in the middle of a dish, surrounded by the sauerkraut, put the bacon and frankfurters on top. Put in a moderate oven until the frankfurters are hot.

HAM IN BURGUNDY

Schinken in Burgunder Wein

1 small smoked ham	2 teaspoons meat	1 pint brown sauce
1 lb. very small onions	extract	made with some of
1 oz. sugar	2 oz. butter	the liquid in which
1 pint Burgundy	seasoning	the ham was cooked,
1 tablespoon	boiled chestnuts	and the meat
redcurrant jelly	sliced carrots	extract

Have the ham boned, then tie compactly together and boil it slowly for 4 hours. Scald the onions 2—3 times and skin them. Brown the butter and sugar in a saucepan until quite a dark colour, add ½ pint of the liquid in which the ham is boiling and the meat extract. Stew the onions in this until tender. Remove onions and keep hot. When the ham is done, cool it until it is easy to remove the rind, and put it into an ovenproof baking dish and pour over it the brown sauce and half the wine, and put into a hot oven. Baste frequently until the ham takes on a brown glaze, then stir in the redcurrant jelly, the onion sauce and the rest of the wine. Season to taste. To serve, arrange slices of the ham on a large dish, pour over it enough sauce to mask it, garnish with the little onions, boiled chestnuts and sliced carrots. Hand the rest of the sauce separately.

PIGS' EARS WITH MUSTARD SAUCE

Schweinsohren mit Senfsauce

4 pigs' ears	6 peppercorns	1 tablespoon dry
2 oz. butter	3 hard-boiled eggs	mustard
2 oz. flour	½ small onion finely	salt, water
1 apple	chopped	½ teaspoon meat
½ teaspoon marjoram	3 tablespoons vinegar	extract

Scald the ears, cut each into 2 lengthways and boil until very tender in water with the onion, peppercorns, salt, marjoram and the peeled apple. Strain the liquid, cook butter and flour together until golden brown, then gradually add the liquid, the apple and onion rubbed through a sieve, the mustard, meat extract and vinegar. Cook and stir gently until the sauce is thick and smooth. Put in the pieces of ear and heat through. Just before dishing up, add the hard-boiled eggs thinly sliced. Serve with toasted rye bread and butter pats.

PORK CHOPS WITH MADEIRA SAUCE

4 large pork chops	½ tablespoon wine	1 gill Madeira
1 gill white wine	vinegar	salt and pepper
½ bay leaf	water	1 clove garlic

Rub the chops with the garlic and put them in a shallow fireproof dish, pour the wine and vinegar over them and enough water to cover the meat. Season with salt and pepper, add the bay leaf. Cover the dish and cook in a moderate oven for 1 hour. Strain the sauce and add the Madeira and simmer for 2—3 minutes. Pour it over the meat. Serve with cooked slices of apple.

SHOULDER OF LAMB WITH FRUIT SAUCE

Lammschulter mit Obstsauce

½ lean shoulder of lamb	2 tablespoons dripping	1 dessertspoon sugar salt and pepper
6 oz. mixed dried fruit: raisins, sultanas, currants, thoroughly washed	4 tablespoons white wine vinegar water	1 dessertspoon potato flour or cornflour ½ pint water 2 cloves garlic

Have the piece of lamb cut into 4 equal sized pieces. Braise them in a saucepan with the dripping and crushed garlic for about 15 minutes, barely cover with water and simmer for 45 minutes. Remove lid, skim off fat with a spoon dipped in cold water. Boil the fruit with the vinegar and sugar, add about ½ pint of the lamb stock. Thicken with the potato flour or cornflour, season with pepper and a pinch of salt. Dish up the pieces of meat and pour the sauce over them. Serve with turnips mashed smoothly with a small piece of butter and seasoned well with pepper, salt and a dash of nutmeg.

PORK PARCELS

Schweinefleisch-Rouletten

2 thin pork chops per portion	chopped apples, stoned prunes, soaked and partly cooked	fine breadcrumbs shredded lemon peel pepper
fat for frying beaten egg or eggs	boiled potatoes or red cabbage	pinch paprika lentil purée

With the cutlet bat or metal meat hammer, beat the chops until very thin. Spread half of them with a mixture of chopped prunes and apple, seasoned with lemon peel, pepper and a pinch of paprika. Cover with a second chop. Tie across with thread to keep them in pairs. Coat generously with egg and crumbs, giving each 2 covers. Fry a light golden brown in deep fat. Serve with a purée of lentils and boiled potatoes or red cabbage.

BELLY OF PORK WITH SAUERKRAUT

Schweinebauch mit Sauerkraut

2 lb. fresh belly of pork	1 sage leaf	2 medium sized
salt	1½ lb. sauerkraut	potatoes
water	1 onion	

Boil the pork with ½ teaspoon salt, the sage leaf and the onion whole, in just enough water to cover, for 30 minutes. Put the washed and drained sauerkraut into the saucepan with the liquid in which the pork was boiled, placing pork on top of cabbage. Remove the onion. Boil gently until the sauerkraut is tender, then grate the peeled raw potatoes into the pan and cook for 15 minutes, or until the liquid is quite thick.

VEAL BALLS

Kalbfleischklöße

8 oz. lean veal	1 teaspoon chopped	1 egg
3 oz. lean bacon	parsley	2 tablespoons sour
3 oz. fine white	1 teaspoon finely	cream or soured top
breadcrumbs	grated lemon peel	of the milk
	salt and pepper	

Put veal and bacon twice through the finest cutters of the mincer. Stir the breadcrumbs into the sour cream or milk. Mix with the meat, lemon rind, parsley and beaten egg and season to taste. Roll into walnut-sized balls and leave for 2 hours. Drop into boiling soup and boil for 5 minutes before serving.

ROAST PORK WITH BEER

Schweinebraten in Bier

about 2½ lb. young	1 level teaspoon dry	4 medium sized
loin of pork	mustard	onions
1 level dessertspoon	1 pink dark brown ale	8 soaked and stoned
flour		prunes

Rub the rind of the pork with the flour and mustard mixed. Put into the roasting tin and pour the beer around, but not over the joint. Cook for 20 minutes in a hot oven, then lower the oven temperature to moderate. Meanwhile skin the onions, remove centres and stuff with the prunes. Put them into the tin with the meat, then baste with the beer frequently for a further 40 minutes. Take up the meat and onions on to a very hot dish, add a sprinkling of flour or gravy thickening to the tin with the liquid. Stir and cook until the gravy is thick, strain into a gravy boat.

LEG OF MUTTON SERVED AS VENISON

Hammelkeule als Wildbret

1 leg of mutton	1 gill sour cream	1 teaspoon savoury
8 oz. fat bacon	1 teaspoon flour	meat extract
8 oz. butter	1 pint sour milk	redcurrant or
water		rowanberry jelly

Have the leg of mutton boned, lay it flat and lard it with fine strips of bacon. Leave it to soak for 3 days in the sour milk, then roll it up and roast it, allowing 15 min. to the lb., in a hot oven using 8 oz. of butter for basting, and adding a very little water to the pan occasionally. When the meat is done, take it up on a hot dish and add the sour cream to the gravy, with the meat extract mixed with the flour. Cook gently until the gravy is slightly thickened. Strain. Serve redcurrant or rowanberry jelly with the meat.

VEAL FRICASSEE

Kalbfleisch-Frikassee

about 1½ lb. knuckle of veal	1 onion	2 oz. butter
	strained juice ½ lemon	1 oz. flour
1 can asparagus tips	1 gill Rhine wine (white)	5 cardamon seeds
3 egg yolks		6 peppercorns
2 oz. chopped mushrooms	1 pint water	salt
	½ teaspoon sugar	

Boil the onion, sugar, cardamon seeds, peppercorns and salt for 15 minutes in 1 pint of water, then cut the meat into neat dice, add and boil very gently until the meat is tender. Strain off the broth. Mix the butter and flour to a smooth paste, add the broth, wine, liquid from the can of asparagus, chopped mushrooms and cook for 15 minutes. Stir in the egg yolks beaten with the lemon juice and cook, stirring very gently until the sauce is thick and creamy. Put in the meat and asparagus, heat through and serve with plain boiled potato balls.

VEAL MINCE WITH CURRANTS

Kalbsbratenwürfel mit Rosinen

about 1 lb. cold roast veal, diced	1 pint white stock	1 gill white wine
	2 oz. well washed currants	pepper
2 oz. butter		very little salt
		1 oz. breadcrumbs

Melt the butter in a saucepan and brown the crumbs in it, add the currants, stock and wine. Simmer until the currants are plump. Stir the veal, heat through and season to taste with salt and pepper. Serve with plain boiled potatoes.

STUFFED BREAST OF VEAL

Gefüllte Kalbsbrust

about 2 lb. breast of veal, boned	3 oz. fine bread-crumbs	2 tablespoons tomato purée
8 oz. finely chopped boiled belly of pork	2 eggs	1 gill stock
1 small minced onion	8 oz. part-cooked spinach, well pressed and finely chopped	salt and pepper dash grated nutmeg

Slit the piece of veal through the centre to make a pocket. Mix together the pork, crumbs, spinach, onion and eggs, season to taste with salt and pepper and nutmeg. Fill the veal bag with the stuffing and sew the ends with a large needle and stout thread. Place the meat in a large casserole lightly greased with bacon fat, mix the tomato purée and stock together and pour it into the casserole. Put on the lid and cook gently in a very moderate oven for 2 hours. Serve with a dish of leaf spinach and boiled potatoes.

SHOULDER OF MUTTON WITH STEWED CUCUMBER

Gedünstete Hammelschulter mit Gurken

1 medium-sized shoulder of lamb, not too fat	flour 2 cucumbers 1 onion	2 tablespoons vinegar salt and pepper water

Beat the shoulder well, remove skin and rub flesh well with pepper and salt. Put joint into a deep saucepan and pour in 1 pint water. Simmer over gentle heat until the water has cooked away, then brown the meat all over on a higher heat. Dredge in a little flour and add $\frac{3}{4}$ pint water, the minced onion and peeled cucumbers, quartered and seeds removed and cut in 3-inch lengths. Simmer all together until cucumbers have turned yellow, then add vinegar, and simmer again until the gravy has thickened.

BELLY OF PORK WITH PEARS

Schweinebauch mit Birnen

about 4 lb. belly of pork	2 pints water	salt
1 lb. onions	1 teaspoon potato flour	2 tablespoons vinegar
1 lb. firm cooking pears	peppercorns	1 teaspoon dry mustard 2 sage leaves

Cut the meat into a dozen neat pieces, and put into hot water with the thinly sliced onions, peppercorns, sage leaves, salt and vinegar. Bring to the boil and carefully skim. Reduce the heat and boil gently until the meat is very tender. Take it up and keep it very hot. Strain the liquid, drop the peeled, cored and quartered pears into the liquid and boil gently until tender. Arrange the pieces of pear around the pieces of pork and serve very hot with half the liquid thickened with the potato flour and mustard.

HAMBURG STEAK

1 lb. raw beef, finely chopped	1 small onion, chopped	5 eggs breadcrumbs
4 oz. raw pork, finely chopped	1 slice bread soaked in milk	fat for frying salt and pepper
	chopped parsley	

Mix the meat with the parsley, onion and soaked bread (from which the milk has been squeezed) and 1 egg, season with salt and pepper. Shape into 4 flat cakes. Roll in breadcrumbs. Fry fairly slowly on both sides. Fry remaining eggs lightly and place one on top of each meat cake.

STEAMED ROAST VEAL

Gedämpfter Kalbsbraten

about 2½ lb. loin of veal, boned, with fat and kidney removed	enough veal forcemeat to cover meat thickly	salt pepper ½ pint sour cream
butter as required	1 sliced carrot	2 tablespoons capers
	1 small bay leaf	water

Lay boned meat flat and spread thickly with the forcemeat. Roll it up firmly, tie securely with string. Slice the kidney. Brown the rolled meat and kidney in about 2 oz. butter in a deep saucepan. Put in the sliced carrot and bay leaf, pour in enough warm water to come half way up the meat roll, cover pan closely and simmer gently for 1—1½ hours. Dish up veal. Strain gravy and skim off fat. Pour the cream into the gravy, mix well, add capers and season to taste with pepper and salt. Bring these ingredients to the boil and pour a little over the meat. Put the rest in a hot sauceboat. Spinach and boiled potatoes should accompany the meat.

PORK WITH PRUNES

loin of pork weighing about 3 lb.	8 oz. prunes fat for roasting	salt 1 clove garlic

Rub the boned pork with a cut clove of garlic. Soak and stone the prunes and stuff the pork with them. Roll the meat. Roast it in a hot oven for 30 minutes per 1 lb. Sprinkle with salt after 20 minutes of cooking.

MEAT CAKES WITH SAUERKRAUT SAUCE

Meat Cakes:

8 oz. beef	1 gill milk	1 egg
8 oz. pork	1 onion chopped	1 oz. butter
2 slices bread		6 anchovy fillets

Soak the bread in the milk, squeeze it gently and mix it with the minced meat, chopped onion and minced anchovies. Season with salt and pepper. Bind with the egg. Shape into flat cakes and fry in the butter; keep hot.

Sauerkraut Sauce:

1 oz. butter	1 teaspoon capers	juice ½ lemon
1 oz. flour	1 teaspoon French	2 egg yolks
½ pint stock	mustard	salt and pepper
1 gill white wine	extra butter	1 dessertspoon sugar

Melt the butter, cook the flour in it for 1 minute, gradually add the stock and the wine. Add the capers, mustard, sugar, lemon juice, salt and pepper. Pour the sauce over the rissoles, cook slowly for 15 minutes. Mix the beaten egg yolks with a little melted butter and stir carefully into the sauce just before serving.

VEAL ASPIC

Kalbsbratensülze

about 1 lb. cold roast veal	2 oz. powdered gelatine	4 tablespoons tarragon vinegar
2 oz. lean ham	1 medium-sized	12 peppercorns
½ pint clear stock	pickled cucumber	6 cardamon seeds

Simmer the stock with the peppercorns and cardamon seeds for 20 minutes, add vinegar and gelatine, and stir until the gelatine has dissolved. Brush inside a basin with some of the liquid and leave until cold. Arrange thinly sliced veal, cucumber and diced ham in layers, each layer moistened with cooled liquid. Put away in a cold place to set. Turn out and serve with rémoulade sauce (see p. 263).

BRAISED VEAL

Geschmortes Kalbfleisch

about 3 lb. fillet of veal	flour	butter
2 oz. butter	salt and pepper	4 oz. mushrooms
¾ pint stock	strained juice 1 lemon	cooked macaroni
1 finely sliced onion		2 egg yolks

Brown the butter in a shallow saucepan, rub the meat well with pepper and salt and dust it with flour. Turn it in the butter to sear it well all over, add the onion and the stock. Simmer gently for $1\frac{1}{2}$—$1\frac{3}{4}$ hours. Take up the meat and cut it into medium thin slices and put on a large hot dish to keep hot. Boil the gravy, take it from the heat, stir in the beaten egg yolks and lemon juice, and cook without boiling until creamy. Add mushrooms previously cooked in a little butter. Surround the meat with a border of cooked macaroni, pour the sauce over the meat and macaroni and serve very hot.

BRAISED TOPSIDE

Sauerbraten

3 lb. topside	3 cloves	red wine
2 oz. lard	1 onion sliced	1 tablespoon wine
1 teaspoon dry	1 carrot sliced	vinegar
mustard	1 oz. flour	6 peppercorns
1 bay leaf	$\frac{1}{2}$ pint sour cream	salt
1 sprig thyme		1 gill stock

Put the wine, vinegar, carrots, onion, cloves, bay leaf, thyme, salt and mustard into a pan. Marinate the meat in this mixture overnight turning it 3 or 4 times. Drain the meat and fry it lightly on all sides in the lard. Pour the marinade over it and cook, covered with a lid, in a slow oven for 2 hours. Strain the sauce and thicken with the flour, add stock if necessary and the cream. Slice the meat and pour the sauce over it. Serve with noodles.

VEAL WITH TINY ONIONS

Kalbfleisch mit Zwiebeln

1 lb. thin scallop	8 oz. very small	1 tablespoon flour
of veal	white onions	$\frac{1}{2}$ teaspoon caraway
juice 1 lemon	2 tablespoons	seeds
water	margarine	

Skin the small onions, drop them into slightly salted water, and simmer gently until they are tender, but do not allow them to become mushy or broken. Drain well. Beat veal until thin, cut into strips 2 inches wide and 4 inches long. Simmer very gently in margarine until tender and faintly browned; add the onions. Put them into a casserole and sprinkle with the lemon juice. Stir the flour into the fat left in the pan after cooking the veal; gradually stir in the liquid in which the onions were cooked (not more than $\frac{1}{2}$ pint of it). Cook until smooth and creamy. Add the caraway seeds, pour the sauce over the veal and onions. Re-heat and serve with spinach.

COLD FRICANDEAU OF VEAL

Kalbsfricandeau

1 large even shaped piece of fillet of veal	1 onion and 1 carrot thinly sliced	2 small glasses dry white wine
very thin slices of ham	4 oz. streaky bacon	2 pints white stock
pieces of bacon fat, cut into thin short strips	2 calf's feet, cut into small pieces	salt and peppercorns
	very thin slices lemon	

Skin the fillet and beat it all over. With a pointed stick, the diameter of the little finger, make holes all over it, and into each hole stuff alternately a little piece of tightly rolled ham and a little piece of bacon fat. Line the bottom of a saucepan with the bacon rashers, slice vegetables including the brown onion skin and the cut up calf's feet. Lay the pieces of meat on top.

Season lightly with salt and add the peppercorns; pour in the wine and the stock.

Put on the saucepan lid and simmer all together very gently for 2 hours. Take up the meat carefully and put it on a large dish to get cold. Now boil the gravy until it has reduced to about half. Strain it, leave to get quite cold, remove all the fat then warm it sufficiently to liquify it. Then baste the meat with it until it has a thick coating of jelly all over. Pour the rest of the liquid on a cold plate and when set, chop and garnish the veal with it. Garnish also with slices of lemon.

SPICED BEEF, HAMBURG STYLE

Hamburger Rindfleisch

about 4 lb. brisket of beef	2 cloves	2 tablespoons white wine vinegar
4 slices fat back bacon	2 teaspoons powdered gelatine	1 dessertspoon brown treacle
3—4 sliced shallots	1 small bay leaf	1 gill dark brown ale
2 small red chillis	1 teaspoon peppercorns	

Have the brisket boned, rolled and securely tied with string. Put the beef into a deep saucepan, with half the bacon on it and half under it. Put in the seasonings, treacle, beer and vinegar well stirred together. Cover the saucepan closely with the lid and simmer for 3½ hours. Allow the beef to cool in the liquid, then take it out and stand it on a dish with a plate and a heavy weight on it. Meanwhile, add 2 teaspoons of powdered gelatine to the liquid, bring to the boil, strain and when the meat is quite cold, pour 2 coats of the cooling jelly over it. Chop the rest of the jelly when cold and garnish the beef with it.

HARE, BAKED WITH BEER

Hasenbraten in Bier

1 medium sized hare	butter	light ale
fine oatmeal	dripping	salt and pepper

Joint a medium sized hare, roll the joints in fine oatmeal, pepper and salt. Lightly fry them in dripping, put into a baking dish with a few shavings of butter over them and ½ pint of light ale round them. Roast slowly in a very moderate oven, baste frequently with the beer until the meat is tender. It should take about 1½ hours. Dish up, serve with gravy, which may be made with the basting beer, and redcurrant jelly, rye bread and butter.

DUCK OR GOOSE IN ASPIC

Ente oder Gans in Aspic

moderate sized goose or duck	1 onion	strips of tomato flesh without seeds
2 oz. ready-made aspic jelly	1 teaspoon tarragon vinegar	green peas
2 calf's feet	hard-boiled eggs	white stock
2—3 sage leaves	capers	salt and pepper
		pickled gherkins

Clean the bird well, put it with the chopped calf's feet, sliced onion, sage leaves, salt and pepper into a deep saucepan, cover with the stock and bring to the boil. Remove any scum, then cover the saucepan closely and simmer the bird until it is so tender that the meat will come from the bones. Cool it a little, then take all the meat from the carcass in neat slices. Lay them aside, return all the bones and skin to the saucepan with the tarragon vinegar and the aspic jelly, boil up and leave until quite cold; then remove every speck of fat from the jelly. Warm the jelly, and spoon enough into a deep oval dish to coat the bottom and sides. Leave to cool, then decorate the bottom with a pretty design of sliced hard-boiled egg, gherkins shredded into fine strips, capers, peas and strips of tomato. Carefully spoon more almost liquid jelly over and leave to set. Next arrange the meat in layers, with jelly between the layers, until all the meat has been used. Top with about ½ inch of jelly, and put away in a very cold place to set. Wrap the dish in a cloth wrung in hot water for a moment and turn out on to a large cold dish.

SPICED BEEF

Gewürztes Rindfleisch

about 3 lb. top-side of beef	1 bay leaf	1 piece dry brown crust
2 oz. bacon or fat pork	sprig each of thyme, rosemary and	1 gill sour milk
1 medium sized onion	parsley, tied together	salt and pepper
4 oz. dripping	flour	stock or water

Lard the beef with thin strips of fat bacon or fat pork. (This may be omitted.) Rub the meat with salt, pepper and flour. Heat the dripping in a saucepan and brown the meat all over in it. Add the herbs, the thinly sliced onion and the crust rolled to fine crumbs and enough water or stock to come halfway up the meat. Simmer gently for 2 hours. Take up the meat. Thicken the sauce a little more with 2 teaspoons of flour mixed smoothly with sour milk. Boil, then strain.

GERMAN SOUR CHICKEN

Saueres Hühnchen

1 medium sized chicken	1 sliced onion	1 part vinegar to 2 parts water
1 bay leaf	1 gill sour cream or curd cheese thinned	
¼ teaspoon grated nutmeg	down with olive oil and vinegar	
	3 cloves	

Joint the chicken and put pieces into a saucepan with just enough vinegar and water to cover, with the bay leaf, cloves, nutmeg and onion. Put the lid on the saucepan and cook gently until the chicken is tender. Remove bay leaf and cloves. Stir in the sour cream or the curd cheese mixture, stir with the remains of the liquid and the onion, now reduced to a pulp, and simmer for a further 10 minutes at a very low heat. Serve with plain boiled potatoes and green peas.

ROAST GOOSE, MECKLENBURG FASHION

Gebratene Gans auf mecklenburgische Art

1 goose	stock	3 tablespoons vinegar
12 oz. currants and sultanas mixed	4 oz. fine breadcrumbs	pinch cinnamon
6 small smoked sausages	½ pint water	2 beaten eggs
	butter	8 good cooking apples
		red cabbage

Draw and clean goose in the usual manner. Stuff with stuffing made this way: Peel and core apples and cut each into 8 pieces. Mix with dried fruit, crumbs, cinnamon and beaten eggs. Place the stuffed goose in a baking tin with ½ pint water and spread a little butter over it. Roast for 2 hours in a hot oven, basting frequently. Whilst goose is cooking, shred a medium sized red cabbage, wash and dry it and simmer it in a little stock until tender. Add 6 small smoked sausages, and when the cabbage is quite soft, stir in 3 tablespoons vinegar. Dish up goose and serve with the cabbage, sausages and boiled potatoes. Pour off goose fat, stir in the liquid from the cabbage, boil, strain and serve with the goose.

PIGEONS IN BACON SAUCE

Tauben in Specksauce

4 plump pigeons	finely shredded peel	about ½ pint stock,
4 oz. fat bacon	½ lemon	preferably
salt	strained juice 1 lemon	beef broth
black pepper	flour	2 oz. butter
	1 finely minced shallot	slices of toast

Quarter the pigeons, remove entrails and keep the livers. Heat the butter in a saucepan and lightly brown the pigeons in it. Dice the bacon very small and add, with the livers cut into small pieces. Dredge with flour and allow all to brown again, then put in the finely shredded lemon peel, the shallot, lemon juice, broth, salt and pepper and cover closely. Simmer gently until the pigeons are tender. Dish the portions of bird on slices of very crisp toast and pour the sauce over them.

GOOSE GIBLETS

Gänseklein

1 set goose giblets	3—4 pears, not too	fine white bread-
1 onion	ripe, or apples	crumbs
2—3 sprigs parsley	2 oz. butter	salt and pepper
1 clove		

Cut, scald and peel the inside of the gizzard, cut the neck into 4—5 pieces, slice the heart and cut the liver into several pieces. Wash them all in warm water, then stew them with the onion, stuck with the clove, and the parsley in slightly salted water until the scum rises. Remove all of this, then simmer the giblets slowly until very tender. Meanwhile peel, core and slice the pears and simmer them until tender with the butter; then mash them smoothly. When the giblets are done, remove the onion and parsley, thicken the gravy with breadcrumbs and stir in the pear purée.

ROAST GOOSE

Gänsebraten

1 prepared goose	8 oz. prunes weighed	2—3 strips lemon peel
1 tablespoon brown	when soaked and	2 lb. apples
sugar	swollen to normal	fat for roasting
	size	

Peel, core the apples and cut them into small pieces, stone the prunes and chop them finely. Mix with the sugar and lemon peel. Stuff the goose. Put the bird in a hot oven for 15 minutes, then lower temperature to moderate and roast, basting frequently, until it is done. Allow 25 minutes to the lb.

GIBLETS AS IN WESTPHALIA

Westfalisches Gänschenschwarzsauer

1 set of goose giblets	1 bay leaf	4 oz. cooked prunes
vinegar	2 cloves	1 dessertspoon flour
3 medium sized	6 peppercorns	1 oz. butter
onions	water	salt

Prepare the giblets (see p. 301), saving all the blood from the liver, and stir a little vinegar into it. Pour a tablespoon or so of vinegar over the giblets and leave overnight. Put them into a saucepan with the onions, bay leaf, cloves, peppercorns, salt and cooked prunes with stones removed. Simmer all together with enough water to cover them, until tender. Brown flour in butter, stir in vinegar and blood and the vinegar left from the giblets. Add boiling stock from giblets and boil and stir until sauce is thick. Serve the onions, prunes and giblets in this sauce, with plain boiled potatoes.

PHEASANT WITH SAUERKRAUT

Fasan mit Sauerkraut

1 plump hen pheasant	4 oz. lean streaky	3 level tablespoons
1½ lb. sauerkraut	bacon	lard or chicken fat
8 oz. smoked sausages,	1 large onion	1—2 truffles
sliced and skinned		salt and pepper

Wash and press all moisture from the sauerkraut, and place half in a casserole. Put the bacon and pheasant into a large saucepan with the thinly sliced onion and turn them together in the fat from the bacon, until the bird is lightly coloured. Arrange it on the sauerkraut and cover it with the slices of bacon and sausage and thin slices of truffle, then the remaining sauerkraut and the lard. Put on the casserole lid and cook the dish in a moderate oven for 2 hours. The truffle may be omitted, but it gives a much more delicate flavour.

GOOSE PASTY

Gänsepastete

1 medium sized goose
(with giblets)
sprig each of
marjoram, sage and
parsley, tied
together
lemon juice

1 oz. gelatine
8 oz. cooked and
peeled chestnuts
knob of butter
2 egg yolks
1 large onion stuck
with 4 cloves

½ teaspoon mixed
herbs
hot water paste
(see below)
1 teaspoon bread-
crumbs
salt and pepper
4 oz. bacon

Cut off the legs and wings of the bird close to the body and put all the pieces with the giblets, the onion and the herbs into a saucepan with enough water to cover them. Simmer for 2 hours. A little before the end of this time, put in salt and plenty of pepper. Meanwhile, pound the chestnuts with a little butter, salt and an egg yolk and roll into small balls. Cut all the meat from the leg and wing bones in thin slices, then scrape off all meat from the neck, and mince with equal quantities of bacon. Season with herbs, salt pepper, add a teaspoon or so of bread-crumbs and mix with 1 egg yolk. Form also into small balls. Return all skin and bones with feet and gizzard to the stock and boil with gelatine until reduced to a pint. Line a buttered pie dish or mould with rich hot water crust. Lay in it slices of goose, with here and there a slice of gizzard and with the two kinds of forcemeat balls tucked in among the slices. Strain the stock, season with a little lemon juice and moisten the contents of the dish with it before covering with crust. Flute the edges well together, brush with beaten egg and bake in a moderately hot oven until the crust is golden brown. When almost cold, pour in the rest of the gravy through a hole in the crust and leave to set to a jelly.

WATER CRUST FOR COLD PASTIES, RICH

Wasserteig für kalte Pasteten

3 lb. plain flour
8 oz. butter

4 egg yolks
salt

pepper
¾ pint boiling water

Put the flour into a large bowl and stir in the butter cut into very small pieces, add salt and pepper to taste.
Drop in the 4 egg yolks, stir into the flour, then gradually add the boiling water, stirring the while with a large knife.
When cool enough to handle, knead to a firm smooth dough, adding more boiling water or more flour as required.
Beat the dough with the rolling pin until it is so firm and stiff that in can be pinched up into a high border. Mould it as required and put away to get quite cold.

VENISON PASTY
Wildbretpastete

about 3 lb. haunch of
venison
2—3 sliced shallots
1 clove garlic
½ teaspoon black
pepper
1 gill vinegar

pinch ground cloves
salt
2 bay leaves
2 tablespoons port
wine
veal forcemeat balls
1 dessertspoon sugar

8 oz. mushrooms
2 oz. butter
veal bone, if no
venison bones
short crust pastry
(see p. 100)

Beat the piece of meat thoroughly with a rolling pin or cutlet bat, rub over with cut shallots, garlic, salt, pepper and sugar. Lay it in a large dish and pour over it the vinegar and port wine. Leave overnight, turning twice. Heat the butter in a large saucepan, put in the piece of meat, pour in the marinade and add 2—3 tablespoons of the liquor from boiling the venison or veal bone. Simmer until tender, cut the meat into rather thick slices and lay in the pie dish lined with crust, with forcemeat balls and sliced mushroom between. Pour in enough of the liquid in which it cooked, to moisten. Cover with crust and bake in a moderately hot oven. Serve hot or cold.

FRANKFURT KLÖSSE
Frankfurter Klöße

3 stale rolls
4 oz. ham in 1 thick
slice
butter

milk
salt and pepper
small onion finely
minced

1 tablespoon minced
parsley
3 beaten eggs
potato flour

Pare off the crusts of the rolls very thinly, cut them into tiny dice. Pour a little milk over half of them and, in butter, fry the rest golden brown with the diced ham and the onion. Mix with these ingredients the soaked and squeezed bread, salt, pepper, parsley and eggs, then stir in enough potato flour to make a mixture that will hold its shape well. Make into balls the size of tennis balls. Boil them in salted water for about 15 minutes. Crisp some crumbs in butter as before. Drain the Klösse, carefully cut them in halves, lay them in a dish cut side up, scatter with the crumbs, heat in the oven for a few minutes. Serve with spinach or cauliflower or tomato sauce.

FARMHOUSE KLÖSSE
Bauernklöße

4 or 5 rashers of fat
bacon
1 minced onion

coarse oatmeal
mashed cooked potato
salt and pepper
1 pint milk

chopped parsley
pinch powdered sage
little butter
brown gravy

54. Rollmops, Germany (p.277)

55. Caraway Soup, Czechoslovakia (p.141)

56. Hunter's Pie, Ireland (p.103)

Dice and fry the bacon with the onion but do not allow them to crisp. Pour into the pan 1 pint of milk and bring to the boil, then stir in the coarse oatmeal and the mashed potato in equal quantities sufficient to make a stiff paste; season with salt, pepper, parsley and sage; have a large dish ready buttered. With a spoon dipped in hot water, cut egg shaped pieces and lay them side by side in the dish. Bake them in a moderate oven, until they are golden brown. Pour over them a thick brown gravy and serve with a mixture of vegetables.

MEAT KLÖSSE

Fleischklöße

about 8 oz. of any pieces of cold meat or poultry	1 tablespoon each of chopped parsley and chives	2 eggs salt and pepper breadcrumbs
4 oz. stale bread butter	2 rashers of bacon, cut into little dice	rich gravy or a sauce milk

Mince the meat very finely, soak the bread in milk, press it dry and flake in with a fork. Put the diced bacon into a saucepan or frying pan and cook until crisp. Stir in the meat, bread, chives, parsley and 1 egg and cook together, stirring, for about 2 minutes. Remove from the heat, stir in the remaining egg, salt, pepper. When the mixture is quite cold, form into small balls, boil for 10 minutes in salted water, drain and roll in crumbs crisped in butter. Serve with spinach, gravy or sauce.

POTATO KLÖSSE WITH CHEESE

Kartoffelklöße mit Käse

3 oz. butter	4 oz. grated stale bread	2 oz. grated Parmesan cheese
12 oz. grated cooked potato	2 extra yolks	salt
2 whole eggs		pinch nutmeg

Put aside a knob of butter and 2 tablespoons of the bread. Cream the rest of the butter and stir in the potato, beaten eggs, cheese, bread, seasonings. Leave for 2 or more hours, then take up egg-shaped pieces with a metal spoon dipped in cold water. Poach in boiling water, salted, for 10 minutes. Meanwhile melt the knob of butter and crisp the crumbs in it. Dish up the Klösse, sprinkle with the buttered crumbs and serve with tomato sauce alone, or in a meat or vegetable stew.

BEER FRITTERS

Bierplinsen

8 oz. plain flour
2 beaten eggs
1 gill brown ale

1 tablespoon melted
lard

1 teaspoon baking
powder
1 level teaspoon salt

Mix to a smooth thick batter. Use for coating small pieces of tender
cooked meat, thick slices of smoked sausages and frying golden brown.
The batter may be used also for apple or banana fritters.

POTATO PUDDING

Kartoffelkuchen

2 lb. floury potatoes
1 lb. pork sausage
 meat
4 oz. minced ham

1 small onion
½ teaspoon powdered
 sage

butter
salt and pepper
fine breadcrumbs
tomato sauce (p. 333)

Cook the potatoes until soft, mash them to a smooth cream with butter,
pepper and salt. Mince the onion very finely. Butter a pudding basin
and coat with crumbs. Put in a layer of potato and a thin layer of sausage
meat, sprinkle with minced ham, onion and sage. Fill the basin thus
in layers with the top layer of potato. Cover with greaseproof paper
and steam for ½ hour. Turn out and serve with thick tomato sauce.

POTATO TURNOVERS

Kartoffelkrapfen

2 lb. floury potatoes
4 oz. self-raising flour
12 oz. of any minced
 meat, poultry or
 game

1 tablespoon tomato
 or mushroom
 ketchup
3 eggs
fine breadcrumbs

1 teaspoon each
 minced chives and
 parsley
salt and pepper
2 oz. butter

Boil the potatoes and while still warm, mash with the butter, knead
in the flour and 2 beaten eggs. Lay the potato paste on a board well
dredged with flour and with a floured rolling pin, roll to a thickness
of between a quarter and half an inch. Leave until quite cold. Cut
into rounds about 5 inches in diameter. Put a tablespoon of the meat
mixed with the ketchup and seasonings in the centre of each. Fold and
press the edges firmly together. Brush with the third egg well beaten,
scatter with crumbs and bake to a golden brown in a moderate oven.
Note: A fish filling, bound with cream sauce and flavoured with anchovy,
may be used instead of meat or poultry.

306

TO MAKE SAUERKRAUT
Sauerkraut

1 large or 2 medium sized white cabbages	few juniper berries (or peppercorns) 1 cup water	few caraway seeds kitchen salt

Wash cabbage or cabbages. Discard the tough outer leaves, then quarter cabbages. Cut out the stalks and large ribs. Holding the quarters of the cabbage firmly on a board, begin at the top and shred them finely, with a very sharp knife. Have a pickling tub, oak barrel or large earthenware crock ready with the bottom lined with clean cabbage leaves. As the cabbage is shredded, pack in into the tub with a few juniper berries (or peppercorns) and caraway seeds and a sprinkling of ordinary kitchen salt among the shreds. Add a cupful of water. Push the cabbage down firmly with a wooden vegetable press, cover with cabbage leaves, then with a clean linen cloth, and lay on the top a lid of wood that fits down inside the tub, with a heavy weight on top to press down the cabbage. Keep in a moderately warm place until fermentation begins, which will be shown by little white bubbles on the brine that will rise to the top of the cabbage. In 14 days' time, wash the cloth. Renew the covering of cabbage leaves with fresh ones, lay the clean cloth over them. Repeat this once a week for 3 weeks and the cabbage will be ready for use, and will keep for a year.

MARIGOLD GREENS
Schweizer Kraut

Strip marigold leaves from the stalks (this can be done while the flowers are still growing, there is no need to pick the stems). Wash the leaves, boil them in salted water, drain well and pour fresh boiling water through them, chop them roughly and add butter and pepper. Serve in the same way as spinach.

FRENCH BEANS WITH PEARS
Grüne Bohnen mit Birnen

1 lb. pears, not too juicy a variety 1½ lb. beans	¾ pint thin white stock 2 oz. butter 1 tablespoon flour	strained juice ½ lemon sugar to taste salt

String the beans and break each into 3 pieces. Boil them gently in the slightly salted stock until almost tender. Add the pears, peeled, cored and quartered, and continue to cook until the beans and pears are tender. Make a sauce with the butter, flour and stock from the bean and pears. When smooth and thickened, flavour with the lemon and sugar, re-heat the beans and pears and serve at once. Good with pork.

BAVARIAN RED CABBAGE

Rotkohl auf bayrische Art

1 red cabbage about 1—1½ lb.	3 tablespoons vinegar 1 dessertspoon flour	1 teaspoon caraway seeds
4 oz. gammon rasher or boiled bacon, cut into small dice	2 tablespoons seedless raisins pepper	1 teaspoon sugar 1 gill dry white wine 3 tablespoons water

Remove all the outer leaves of the cabbage and cut away the centre ribs. Shred the rest of the cabbage finely, pour boiling water over, and leave for 10 minutes; drain well. Put the cabbage into an earthenware or glass casserole with the raisins and diced bacon, the caraway seeds, vinegar and water. Put on a lid and cook gently for 1 hour. Pour in the wine and add the sugar; simmer for another 30 minutes, thicken the liquid with 1 dessertspoon of flour, season with pepper.

BEETROOT IN SPICED SAUCE

Rote Rüben

2 lb. small beetroots	1 gill each wine vinegar and stock	sugar
2 oz. butter		salt
1 tablespoon flour	3 tablespoons thick sour cream	2 tablespoons horseradish cream or freshly grated horseradish
½ teaspoon ground caraway seeds or whole seeds	½ small onion, finely chopped pinch ground cloves	

Wash the beetroots and boil until tender in unsalted water. Remove tops and skins and slice thinly. Heat the butter, stir in the flour to make a smooth golden paste, add the spices and onion and the boiling stock. Cook and stir to a smooth cream, then stir in the vinegar, sugar and salt to taste. Simmer for about 5 minutes; finally stir in the sour cream, horseradish and the sliced beetroot.

HARICOT BEANS OR LENTILS WITH PRUNES

Bohnen oder Linsen mit Backpflaumen

1 lb. haricot beans or lentils	1 lb. prunes	pinch bicarbonate of soda

Soak the beans or lentils overnight, then boil them for 30 minutes with a pinch of bicarbonate of soda. Wash and soak the prunes for 12 hours, stone them. Having drained the beans or lentils, add the stoned prunes, cut into pieces, with their liquor and simmer again. Serve with goose, duck or boiled pork.

ONIONS WITH CHEESE

Zwiebeln mit Käse

4—6 large onions	grated cheese of good	salt and pepper
butter	flavour	little dry mustard
	beer or red wine	

Remove the outer skin only from the onions, cut them into thick slices. Lay them on a buttered dish, smear with melted butter and put into a moderate oven until soft. Mix grated cheese with salt, pepper and a little mustard and red wine to make a thick paste. Spread on the warm onions and put beneath a hot grill to brown and melt the cheese.

BACON DRESSING

Specksauce zu Salat

4 streaky bacon	1 teaspoon French	1 gill water
rashers	mustard	pepper and salt
1 tablespoon flour	3 egg yolks	1 gill white wine
		vinegar

Dice rashers and fry until crisp. Stir in the flour, mustard, yolks beaten with water, pepper and salt. Simmer and stir over a very gentle heat, adding the vinegar as it thickens. If the sauce seems too thick, thin it with a little extra vinegar and water mixed. Serve with green salad.

FRICASSEE SAUCE

Frikasee-Sauce

To serve with veal, chicken or poached or hard-boiled eggs.

1½ pints white sauce	juice 1 lemon	2 egg yolks
(see p. 257)	2 tablespoons dry	1 oz. butter
3 anchovy strips	white wine	1 teaspoon capers
6 button mushrooms		

Chop the anchovies finely, parboil the mushrooms for 5 minutes, and chop finely. Put fish and mushrooms into the sauce and simmer gently for 15 minutes. Stir in the lemon juice, wine and capers. Just before serving, stir in the beaten egg yolks and butter, heat again, do not boil.

ONION SAUCE WITH CARAWAY SEEDS

Zwiebelsauce mit Kümmel

6 large onions	1 tablespoon flour	salt and pepper
1 teaspoon caraway	1 oz. butter	½ pint white stock
seeds		(see p. 88)

Thinly slice the onions and boil them with the caraway seeds in the stock, until quite soft. Warm the butter and mix the flour well into it, thin it with some of the stock, then add slowly to simmering stock and stir until the sauce is thick. Season with salt and pepper. Do not put this sauce through a sieve.

SALAD CREAMS

Mayonnaisen

(1) 4 oz. thick curd cheese   3 tablespoons tarragon or white wine vinegar   salt black pepper ½ clove well crushed garlic, optional
1 gill thick sour milk

Beat all the ingredients together. Serve with green salads.

(2) 1 egg
2 tablespoons salad oil   ½ teaspoon dry mustard pinch of sugar   salt and pepper 2 tablespoons white wine

Stir all together very thoroughly.

(3) yolks of 3 hard-boiled eggs, (the whites can be cut in strips and used for decorating salad)   ½ teaspoon dry mustard salt and pepper   4 tablespoons white wine or white wine vinegar strained juice 1 lemon 3 tablespoons salad oil

Rub the egg yolks very smoothly with the oil. Season with salt, pepper and mustard. When the paste is smooth, stir in the lemon juice and the wine or vinegar. If these quantities do not make sufficient sauce, add a little more oil and wine. More vinegar would make too sharp a dressing.

CHERRY FRITTERS

Kirschenküchelchen

3 eggs and 2 extra egg whites   1 tablespoon melted butter butter for frying   sugar cinnamon black cherries
4 oz. fine flour

Make a good coating batter with eggs and egg whites, flour and butter. Tie ripe black cherries in bunches of 8 by their stems and coat well in batter. Fry in butter or cooking fat until golden brown and crisp. Serve with sugar and cinnamon. Large ripe plums, small sweet apples, peeled but not cored and with the stems left on, large bunches of red, white or black currants may be cooked in the same manner. A delightful dish is made by using a mixture of fruits and serving piled on a large dish with sugar. A wine sauce may be served with the fritters.

RED GROATS PUDDING

Rote Grütze

2 lb. raspberries, red-   1 pint sweet red wine   4 oz. coarse groats
  currants or mixture   4 oz. sugar   or semolina
  of both

Cook the fruit gently until quite soft then rub through a sieve. To the purée or juice add the wine and sugar and bring to the boil; sprinkle with the groats or semolina and cook and stir until the mixture thickens. Pour into a wetted mould and when cold, turn out and serve with fresh raspberries and cream.

POTATO MOULD

Kartoffelkoch

3 eggs   grated rind 1 orange   finely grated cold
2 oz. castor sugar   or lemon   potato
                    $\frac{1}{2}$ pint cream

Beat the eggs and sugar together until frothy, add the grated lemon or orange peel and the cream. Stir in enough finely grated cold potato to make a very thick batter. Put into a buttered mould and bake in a very moderate oven for about 45 min. Serve with sugar, or with lemon or orange sauce.

CHESTNUTS WITH APPLES

Maronen mit Äpfeln

1 lb. chestnuts   sugar $\frac{1}{2}$ teaspoon vanilla
water $1\frac{1}{2}$ lb. apples

Skin chestnuts and boil gently in water until tender, with vanilla. Stew the peeled and cored apples with sugar, rub through a sieve. Add to the chestnuts. Serve with vanilla-flavoured whipped cream, or as a garnish for pork or ham, without the cream or vanilla flavouring.

HONEY CINNAMON PEARS

Birnen mit Honig und Zimt

Use canned pears, home bottled or freshly cooked
ones. They must be in halves.

Drain them from juice or syrup, and put into a cold place, preferably the refrigerator, for several hours. When ready to serve, heat 4 tablespoons thick honey with $\frac{1}{2}$ teaspoon cinnamon, when almost boiling, pour over the cold pears and serve with cinnamon biscuits.

FLAME PUDDING
Brennender Pudding

2 oz. flour
2 oz. sugar

1½ oz. blanched pounded almonds
loaf sugar

stale sponge cake
4 eggs
rum, brandy or a liqueur

Beat the sugar with the egg yolks and almonds, stir in the flour and enough stale sponge cake crumbs to make a soft dough. Fold in the egg whites well whisked. Put into a ring mould and steam for 1 hour. Dish up the moment before serving, and in the centre of the pudding place lumps of sugar soaked in brandy, rum or a liqueur. Pour a little of the spirit over the top of the pudding. Set them alight and, as the sugar burns, take to the table.

CHERRY SOUFFLÉ
Kirschenflauf

4 oz. flour
1¼ pints milk
4 oz. butter

4 oz. castor sugar
1 level teaspoon ground cinnamon

1½ lb. ripe black cherries
4 eggs

Boil the flour and milk together until very thick and smooth. Remove from the heat and stir until almost cold. Beat the butter to a cream with the sugar and cinnamon and the egg yolks. Stir with the thickened milk until well blended, then fold in the stiffly whisked egg whites, and the cherries. Put into a buttered mould and bake in a moderate oven until firm to the touch on top. Serve with a thin sauce of cherry syrup flavoured with a little kirsch.

ALMOND PUDDING
Mandelkoch

2 oz. semolina
drop of almond essence

1 gill milk
2 oz. sugar
1 gill boiling water
2 oz. ground almonds

1 tablespoon butter
5 eggs
apricot jam

Mix the semolina and milk in a double boiler and cook until thick and creamy. Stand this aside to cool. Beat into this cream the almonds, almond essence, butter and sugar, and the yolks of the eggs. Whip the egg whites separately and add these last of all. Prepare a mould by brushing with butter and have a steamer ready. Pour the mixture into the steamer and steam it for approximately 45 minutes. Heat the apricot jam and thin slightly with hot water. Serve the pudding hot with the thinned apricot jam.

BLACK BREAD
Schwarzbrot

This is the genuine rye bread; if a lighter dough is preferred, 8 oz. white flour may be added without altering the rest of the ingredients.

1½ lb. rye flour	½ teaspoon caraway	1 pint warm milk
1 oz. yeast	seeds	1 tablespoon black
1 teaspoon salt		treacle

Dissolve the yeast in a little of the milk, put one third of the flour into the bowl and mix with the yeast. Leave to ferment and rise. Stir the treacle and salt into the rest of the milk; add this, the rest of the flour and the caraway seeds to the risen yeast mixture. Knead well and leave in a warm place until double in bulk. Divide into 2 long loaves. Brush with milk and bake in a moderately hot oven for about 1½—2 hours.

PEPPERBREAD
Pfefferkuchen

1 lb. flour	1 level teaspoon	¼ teaspoon ground
8 oz. brown sugar	bicarbonate of soda	cinnamon and cloves
½ pint honey	2 tablespoons rose	4 grains cardamom
4 oz. butter	water	thin strips candied
6 ground peppercorns	4 tablespoons rum	peel
or ½ level teaspoon	4 oz. chopped candied	split blanched
black pepper	peel	almonds
	4 eggs	

Beat eggs and sugar to a thick froth, stir in spices, chopped peel and rum thoroughly. Now add the honey and butter previously warmed together, the bicarbonate of soda dissolved in the rose water, and finally the sifted flour. Put the dough into an 8-inch cake tin lined with greaseproof paper and bake for 1¼—1½ hours in a very moderate oven; 15 minutes before the cake is done, quickly arrange slices of candied peel and almonds on top.

ANISEED CAKES
Aniskuchen

4 oz. castor sugar	4 oz. flour	1 teaspoon aniseed,
3 eggs		well pounded

Beat eggs and sugar together until thick and frothy, then add the aniseed and sifted flour. Mix to a smooth dough, drop little heaps on a buttered baking sheet, leaving about 6 inches between each heap. Leave for 2 hours then bake in a hot oven for about 10 minutes.

WESTPHALIAN FRESH FRUIT CAKE

Westfalischer frischer Obstkuchen

10 oz. plain flour	8 oz. sweet cherries	2 eggs
3 oz. butter	1 teaspoon vanilla	pinch salt
3 oz. sugar	essence	milk as required
1 teaspoon cold	2 teaspoons baking	
water	powder	

Stone the cherries and drain off excess juice. Cream the sugar and butter well, add the beaten egg yolks with vanilla and cold water. Sift the flour, baking powder and salt together and add gradually, with enough milk to make a firm dough. Stir in the well whisked egg whites. Butter greaseproof paper carefully and line a deep cake tin with it; then put the prepared fruit at the bottom. Cover with the cake dough. Sprinkle the top lightly with sugar and bake in a moderately hot oven.

GINGERBREAD

Dicker Lebkuchen

1 lb. self-raising flour	4 oz. butter or	2 full teaspoons
1 lb. dark treacle	margarine	ground ginger
4 oz. brown sugar	1 level teaspoon each	1 egg beaten with
3 oz. shredded	bicarbonate of soda	a little milk
blanched almonds	and ground	almonds for
4 oz. candied peel	cinnamon	decoration

Boil the sugar and treacle together until the sugar has dissolved, take from the heat, and stir in the butter or margarine. Sift the flour into a bowl with the spices, stir in the almonds and peel. Stir the bicarbonate of soda into the hot mixture, then as it froths, pour it into the dry ingredients and mix to a soft dough. Leave all night. Next day, spread it in a buttered tin to a depth of about 1½ inches. Brush the smoothed surface over twice with the beaten egg and milk. Bake in a very moderate oven for about 1 hour. When the gingerbread has cooled, cut into squares and decorate with almonds. *(Illustrated in Plate 57.)*

ZEPHYRS

Windbeutel

1 pint water	grated lemon peel	apricot sauce or
8 oz. butter	6 eggs	sweetened straw-
8 oz. well sifted self-	sugar	berry or raspberry
raising flour		purée

Boil the water and butter together, then gradually stir in the flour and cook and stir over a very low heat until the ingredients form a clean ball that leaves the pan easily. Leave to become almost cold, then beat in the eggs one by one, with the grated lemon peel. Have a flat tin ready dusted with flour. With a spoon take up pieces of the paste the size of large walnuts and drop them on to the tin, leaving space between them for them to rise and spread. Bake at once in a hot oven, until puffed up and golden yellow. Strew sugar over the zephyrs and serve at once with a fruit sauce.

GERMAN PLUM CAKE
Rosinenkuchen

8 oz. butter	pinch salt	1 gill rum and
6 eggs	8 oz. currants,	1 tablespoon
8 oz. castor sugar	carefully washed and	extra
grated rind ½ lemon	dried	½ teaspoon each
8 oz. self-raising flour		grated nutmeg and
12 oz. large stoned		powdered cloves
raisins		

Beat the butter to a soft cream, then gradually stir in the egg yolks and the sugar, nutmeg, cloves and salt. Mix to a thick smooth cream. Stir in the lemon peel, fruit and rum, fold in the flour, then lightly stir in the whites of the eggs whisked to a stiff froth. Put the dough into a 9-inch cake tin lined with buttered paper, smooth evenly on the top and make a depression in the centre with the wooden mixing spoon. Bake in a slow oven for about 2—2½ hours. When the cake is done and is still warm, sprinkle the top with a little more rum and put away for 3 days before cutting it.

MARBLE CAKE
Marmorkuchen

8 oz. plain flour	3 tablespoons cocoa	lemon rind
6 oz. sugar	3 eggs	vanilla essence
4 oz. butter		1 gill milk

Cream the butter, add the sugar, then egg yolks, one after another. Beat into a thick cream. Alternately add the milk and flour. Stiffly whisk the egg whites and fold in a little sugar. Add to mixture. Divide the dough into two parts and lightly fold the sieved cocoa and vanilla essence into one half and the lemon rind into the other. Grease a tin mould and pile in alternate layers of light and dark dough. Bake in a moderate oven for about 45 minutes, then carefully turn out and sprinkle immediately with sugar. (Illustrated in Plate 51.)

ALMOND TUBES
Mandelhippen

2 egg whites, stiffly whisked	4 oz. sugar 4 oz. finely pounded almonds	½ level teaspoon cinnamon cream green colouring

Mix all ingredients, except cream and colouring, to a smooth dough, roll small pieces very thinly, and put on greased tins. Bake to a pale yellow colour in a slow oven. Roll each piece very quickly round the handle of a wooden spoon, leave the rolls on the cake cooling wires to dry. Fill with cream tinted a very pale green with pistachio colouring and flavouring.

BRUNSWICK CAKE
Braunschweiger Kuchen

1¼ lb. flour 1 oz. almonds pounded with a little egg white to keep them from oiling	8 oz. butter 3 eggs and 3 egg yolks 3 oz. castor sugar 4 oz. each of raisins sultanas and currants	grated rind ½ lemon 1 oz. yeast ½ pint milk 1 extra oz. butter and more castor sugar

Dissolve yeast in the lukewarm milk. Cream the butter, beat in the sugar, eggs and egg yolks, fruit, lemon rind and almonds and fold in the flour, alternately with the yeast and milk. Knead to a light dough. Flour a large flat tin that has a turned up edge all round. Roll the dough ½ inch thick, to fit the tin, and leave it in a warm place to rise a little. Make dents over the surface here and there, drop a tiny piece of butter into each and dredge thickly with sugar. Bake in a hot oven until risen and golden brown. Eat while warm.

CARAWAY STICKS
Kümmelstangen

8 oz. plain flour 3 oz. butter 1 egg 1 egg yolk	1 teaspoon caraway seeds 2 teaspoons grated Parmesan cheese	1 level teaspoon salt pinch pepper 1 tablespoon milk

Cream the butter until light and soft, stir in the whole egg, beaten, the salt, pepper, cheese and milk, and lastly the sifted flour. Blend to a smooth dough, form into little rolls about 2 inches long and ½ inch thick. Brush with the beaten egg yolk, sprinkle thickly with caraway seeds and bake in a very moderate oven for about 15 minutes.

HONEY CAKES
Honigkuchen

1 lb. flour	1 level teaspoon each	4 oz. chopped candied
8 oz. honey	ground cinnamon	peel
8 oz. sugar	and ground ginger	1 tablespoon rum
3 eggs	½ level teaspoon	1 level teaspoon
3 oz. butter	ground mace	bicarbonate of soda
grated rind ½ lemon	egg white	decorations

Warm honey and butter together, dissolve the bicarbonate of soda in the rum and stir it into the lukewarm honey and butter. Sift the flour with the spices into a bowl, make a hollow in the centre, pour into it the beaten eggs, peel, lemon rind and sugar and the warm honey and butter mixture. Knead to a firm dough. Roll out thinly and cut into fancy shapes. Put them on a greased tin and bake in a very moderate oven for about 20 minutes. The cakes may be brushed with egg white and sprinkled with hundreds and thousands or with finely minced nuts, or ornamented with tiny pieces of cherry and angelica.

BERLIN RINGS
Berliner Kränze

4 oz. each butter and	8 oz. sugar	2 eggs
margarine	grated rind ½ orange	1 lb. plain flour
For Garnish		
1 egg white	2 tablespoons castor	glacé cherry
	sugar	angelica

Cream the fats and sugar together, beat in the eggs and orange rind. Add the sifted flour and knead to a firm smooth dough. Put aside in a cold place for several hours. Break off small pieces, roll with the flat of the hand into 6 inch long pieces as thin as pencils. Form into circles and tie ends in a single knot. Place rings on ungreased baking trays. *Garnish.* Brush with thin meringue, made by beating 1 egg white stiff with 2 tablespoons castor sugar. Press small pieces of glacé cherry on the knots, with tiny pieces of angelica for leaves. Bake for 10 minutes in a moderately hot oven. Lift to cake cooling wires to become firm.

ALMOND CHIPS
Mandelspäne

4 oz. sweet almonds	1 oz. potato flour	2 egg whites
	4 oz. castor sugar	rice paper

Beat the egg whites and sugar together for about 10 minutes, then stir in the flour and almonds and mix smoothly. Spread the paste ¼ inch thick on rice paper laid on a buttered tin and bake in a very moderate oven until the mixture is firm and slightly golden. Lift from the tin and twist round a rolling pin to dry in a curve. Serve with coffee.

SOUP MACAROONS
Suppenmakronen

3 egg whites   3 oz. ground almonds   5 oz. fine white
4 oz. castor sugar   bread crumbs

Whisk the egg whites with the sugar. Mix together the crumbs and almonds and stir them into the egg and sugar until smoothly blended. Arrange small neat spoonfuls on a greased tin lined with buttered paper and bake in a very moderate oven to a light golden colour. Serve with wine, beer or fruit soups.

PRETZELS

8 oz. flour   2 egg yolks   salt and pepper
2 oz. butter   2 egg whites   coarse salt
                  milk

Work the creamed butter, beaten whites and yolks into the flour with a little salt and pepper. Roll out on a floured board, shape into figures of eight. Brush with milk, sprinkle with coarse salt. Bake in a moderately hot oven for 10 minutes.

PICKLED GOOSE
Pökel Gans

1 goose   4 oz. salt   ¼ oz. saltpetre

Cut off the legs of the goose, not too close to the body, cut the goose in two by dividing the breast from the back. Rub these 4 portions of the bird with salt and saltpetre. Pack in a dish, cover, and put away in a cool place for 5 days. The legs and back may then be stewed or made into a casserole with plenty of white beans, onions and white wine. The breast should be dried, wrapped in greaseproof paper and smoked by hanging it over the smouldering oak sawdust. When the meat is dry and no longer looks raw when cut, it is served uncooked, in very thin slices with rye bread and butter.

PICKLED SALMON
Marinierter Lachs

1 slice salmon about   best olive oil   1 sprig tarragon
    1 inch thick for each   white wine vinegar   piece lemon peel
    portion   1 bay leaf

Brush each slice of salmon with olive oil and fry a delicate brown colour, taking care the fish does not break. When fish is cold, put the slices into a deep earthenware or glass dish with a close-fitting cover. Boil white wine vinegar with bay leaf, sprig of tarragon and lemon peel. When cold, strain liquor over the salmon to cover pieces completely. Pour a little olive oil on top of liquid, cover closely and store in a cold place.

TARRAGON VINEGAR
Estragonessig

Pick fresh clean tarragon leaves from the stems before the plants flower. Push 2 to 3 oz. leaves (well pressed down) into clean bottles and fill with best wine vinegar. Cork and stand the bottles in a warm place, shaking and turning the bottles upside down frequently. The vinegar may be used in a fortnight's time but is better after a month. After that, strain off the vinegar into clean small bottles. Do not put any other ingredient, such as cloves, peppercorns, etc., in with the tarragon. This ruins the delicate flavour.

CUCUMBER PICKLE
Gurken-Essig-Mango

Choose large well grown cucumbers for this. Also required: salt, finely grated fresh horseradish, shallots, and capers in equal quantities, a good pinch of grated nutmeg, 4 bruised cloves, 1 teaspoon sugar, ½ teaspoon mustard seed. Finely mince the shallots, mix with the horseradish, cloves pounded well, the nutmeg, mustard seed and sugar. From each cucumber cut a triangular wedge the whole length, and scoop out all the seeds and pulp. Put cucumber and cut-out pieces into a china bowl and scatter generously with common salt. Leave all night with a plate on top to keep them under the salt. Next day, dry the cucumbers, fill the cavities with the spice mixture, replace the cut out pieces and tie in place with fine string. Pack upright in large preserving jars and fill with cold white vinegar.

TO PRESERVE GOOSE LARD
Gänseschmalz

1 goose	salt	few slices of apple
	cold water	

As soon as the goose is drawn, remove all the fat from the inside and around the giblets and put into cold water with a little salt. When the goose is half roasted, ladle almost all the dripping off before it begins to brown, and continue to do so, only leaving enough in the pan to baste the bird. Put the fresh fat and the goose dripping into a saucepan with a few slices of apple and a pinch of salt. Simmer until clear, then strain through a fine sieve and pot into small jars. Cover with greaseproof paper, then with covers of stout brown paper and store in a cool place.

CUCUMBER HOT PICKLE

Senfgurken

as many of the largest cucumbers as required	3 cloves	2 bay leaves broken in pieces
	1 oz. peppercorns	
	½ sliced horseradish	few sprigs tarragon
salt	8 oz. halved shallots	1 oz. root ginger
white wine vinegar	several chillis	½ clove garlic

Peel the cucumbers, cut in halves lengthways, then into chunks of about 2 inches long. Trim and shape edges to make little bolster shapes. Boil salt and water together, 1 teacup to each gallon, and in this boil the cucumber for about 1 minute. Drain the pieces on a sieve. Put the pieces into a large jar, sprinkle sparingly with salt and cover with wine vinegar. In 3 days, drain off the vinegar, boil it with the ginger, cloves, and peppercorns. Between the cucumber in the jars put the sliced horseradish, shallots, cloves, bay leaf, chopped garlic and tarragon, and one chilli to each jar. Boil the vinegar and when cold, cover the cucumber with it.

SWEET CUCUMBER

Süße Gurken

cucumbers	sugar	whole ginger
white vinegar	cinnamon stick	nutmeg

Peel as many well grown cucumbers as you wish, and cut them in halves down the centre. Scoop out the seeds and cut the cucumbers into short pieces. Put them into the preserving pan and cover with white vinegar and leave for 2 days. Pour off the vinegar and to every 3 pints allow 8 oz. of sugar, ¼ inch cinnamon stick, 1 oz. whole ginger, ¼ teaspoon grated nutmeg. Boil the vinegar and spices for 15 minutes, drop in the cucumber and bring to the boil, but scoop out the pieces before they soften at all. Put into preserving jars, pour the hot pickle over, and cover, but not finally. In a fortnight's time, take off the liquid, boil it and pour, when cold, over the cucumber. Tie down with airtight covers.

PEPPER GHERKINS

Pfeffergurken

the required quantity of tiny gherkins, about the size of a finger	peppercorns	some small pieces of bay leaf
	some small pieces of mace	vinegar
salt	2—3 sliced shallots	chillis

57. Gingerbread, Germany (p.314)

58. Swedish Scone Ring (p.522)

59. Treacle Tart, Britain (p.116)

60. St. Nicholas Day Letters, Holland (p.185)

Sprinkle the gherkins with salt and leave them for 24 hours. Wipe them free of salt and pack them neatly into jars with peppercorns, mace, sliced shallots, bay leaf and one chilli in each jar. Boil the vinegar and pour it hot over the gherkins, leave for 3 days, carefully drain off all the vinegar, boil it and when cold, re-cover the gherkins and tie down securely.

PICKLED NASTURTIUM SEEDS
Nasturzsamen in Essig

Nasturtiums make such a pleasant piquant pickle that it is a pity to waste them. They are excellent in sauces, instead of capers, with fish and mutton, they add a distinctive flavour to fish salads and mayonnaise, and they may also be included with other ingredients to make mixed pickles. Gather them while young, that is, soon after the flowers have withered. Rinse in cold water. Put them into a bowl and scatter with salt and leave for 24 hours. Boil peppercorns with vinegar, ½ oz. to 2 pints, about 1 inch sliced horseradish and ½ teaspoon allspice. When cold, strain, and pour over the seeds already wiped free from brine and packed into small bottles or little jars. Cover.

CHERRIES IN VINEGAR
Kirschen in Essig

Put a layer of cherries into a large earthenware or glass jar. Scatter with crushed loaf sugar, a few flakes of broken cinnamon stick and one or two cloves. Continue until the jar is quite full, then slowly pour in white wine vinegar that has been boiled and become cold. Slap the jar on all sides to ensure that the vinegar runs down between the layers and covers it all. Cover the jars with airtight covers and stand the jars in a warm place for 3—4 days before putting into the store cupboard.

CHERRY JAM (1)
Kirschenmarmelade

To every 4 lb. stoned sweet, ripe black cherries allow 1 lb. sugar, 1 teaspoon powdered cinnamon, 1 gill redcurrant juice made by boiling the currants without water and rubbing through a strainer. Boil fruit, sugar, juice and cinnamon until the jam thickens. Pot as before. Some cherry stone kernels added greatly improve the flavour, or add a few drops of good almond essence.

CHERRY JAM, WITHOUT SUGAR (2)

Kirschenmarmelade ohne Zucker

This jam is made in Germany and in Middle European countries when the fruit harvest is too heavy for the housewives to buy enough sugar for preserving. As many ripe cherries as required. Stone them and crush stones and kernels. Boil them in a little water. Strain the liquid over the fruit, allowing about 1 gill to 4 lb. fruit. Boil gently, stirring frequently until the jam is very thick. It takes at least 3 hours slow and constant boiling.

VIOLET VINEGAR

Veilchenessig

Gather violets (wood violets will do very well), when they are fresh and plentiful. Pull the heads from the stalks and push as many as possible into small bottles. Fill with as much white wine vinegar as can be put into the bottles. Cork securely and put the bottles in a warm place and leave for 4 weeks. Strain off the vinegar after that as the flowers will lose all their flavour. Use for flavouring cocktails, cups and sweet dishes.

TO CLARIFY SUGAR

For many of the more delicate preserves, the sugar is first clarified. Allow 12 oz. of loaf sugar to every lb. of fruit to be preserved. Moisten sugar with cold water. The quantity of water it absorbs is sufficient moisture. Put sugar into the preserving pan, bring to the boil, watching and stirring to prevent boiling over. Remove any scum, then boil very slowly until the syrup forms little beads on the back of the spoon.

FRUIT IN BRANDY

Obst in Kognak

Choose firm but ripe peaches, apricots, and large plums, preferably Victoria, not dark fruit. Large preserving jars are necessary because the fruit for this luxurious preserve must be left whole. Allow 8 oz. preserving sugar to every lb. of fruit. Wipe the fruit and prick it right to the stones with a large darning needle. Clarify the sugar as directed above, then drop in the fruit and allow it to come slowly almost to the boil, then remove from the heat and leave it until next day. Take out the fruit and drain it on a sieve. Boil the syrup to thicken it a little, then mix with an equal quantity of pale brandy. Arrange the fruit in large preserving jars and cover with the liquid. Tie down securely and store in a moderately cool place.
Note: It is very important that the fruit should not be allowed to become soft in the cooking.

UNBOILED RUM PRESERVE

Eingemachtes Rumkompott

This delicious preserve is made throughout the summer as the various fruits ripen. Put 1 pint of good rum into a deep stone jar with 1 lb. of powdered loaf sugar. Stir gently with a long spoon. Next add 1 lb. of raspberries and 1 lb. of sugar and stir up gently from the bottom. Tie the jar down with a piece of bladder until further fruits are ripe, adding 1 lb. of currants, 1 lb of black cherries, ripe greengages, large ripe plums, halved and stoned, blackberries or mulberries, always with 1 lb. of sugar to each lb. of fruit. Do not put in gooseberries as the skins will toughen. Always stir up gently from the bottom. Finally tie down securely and keep in a cool place for 2 months before using. For those who dislike the flavour of rum, a good brandy may be substituted.

CRAMBAMBOLI

Crambamboli

This used to be a favourite drink with German students. It was made with a large piece of loaf sugar, but since loaf sugar is seldom to be seen in one piece, the next best thing is to use 1 lb. made up or the largest pieces of preserving sugar. Put a bottle of rum into a china bowl and on top of the bowl arrange a piece of fine wire netting securely. Put the sugar on the netting and moisten it with rum. Set it alight and leave it to burn until it has all melted and run into the punch. Serve at once. A second method of making Crambamboli is to use a bottle of good red wine instead of rum and when the sugar is melted, pour in a pint of champagne.

FROTHED BEER

2 pints ale	½ teaspoon each	4 oz. loaf sugar
1 lemon	grated nutmeg,	4 eggs
	ground ginger and	
	powdered cinnamon	

Whisk the eggs well and strain them, then add the ale gradually, whisking all the time. Rasp all the zest from the lemon with pieces of the sugar. Put into a pan with sugar and strained juice of the lemon. Stir in the spices and the egg and beer mixture. Heat it very slowly, whisking all the time but on no account allow it to boil or it will curdle, and will be spoiled. Serve the drink as soon as it is hot and very frothy.

STRAWBERRY CARDINAL

Erdbeer-Kardinal

2 lb. ripe strawberries	1 lb. castor sugar	1 bottle seltzer
2 bottles Moselle	½ bottle light red wine	or soda water

Put strawberries into a bowl and sprinkle with the castor sugar and half
bottle of light red wine. Cover the bowl and leave for about 2 hours.
Add 2 bottles of Moselle and 1 bottle seltzer or soda water. For a special
occasion, pour in a bottle of champagne at the last minute.

ICED PEACH PUNCH

Pfirsichbowle

6 ripe peaches	8 oz. sugar	½ bottle champagne
	2 bottles Rhine wine	

Put the peeled and sliced peaches in a bowl, and sprinkle them with
sugar. Pour over them a bottle of Rhine wine and allow to stand for
two hours in the refrigerator. Immediately before serving add the rest
of the Rhine wine and the champagne. Soda water can be substituted
for the champagne, and any white wine can be used if necessary.

FROTHED WINE

Weinschaum

1 pint bottle Moselle	2 eggs	4 tablespoons water
4½ oz. castor sugar	1 slice lemon	2 extra egg yolks

Put the wine and sugar into the top of a double boiler, whisk the eggs, egg
yolks and water together, stir into the wine and sugar and, over a low
heat, begin to heat the mixture.

As it warms, begin to whisk it and continue to whisk until the liquid is
hot but not boiling, and very frothy. Put in the slice of lemon and leave for
a few minutes, then whisk again before serving.

For a more economical drink, sweet cider may be used; it makes quite
a pleasant drink, but wine is much richer.

GREEK COOKING

Elizabeth Campbell and Musia Soper

It is sometimes difficult to differentiate between Greek and Turkish cooking. A number of Greek recipes could equally well be Turkish and *vice versa*. In any case, both survive from ancient Byzantine cooking and both have had much effect on all the Balkan countries.

The ancient Greeks did not disdain to take an interest in food as is evident in their writings, and their art of cooking as well as their art, influenced the conquering Romans and all the world.

The Greeks, as all Mediterranean people, use a good deal of olive oil in their cooking. They grow vegetables, such as aubergines, ladies' fingers and peppers; fruit and honey are plentiful and many wines, such as the popular sweet Samos, are produced from their vineyards. They use a good deal of spices and herbs, dill being the herb most used from time immemorial.

CHICKEN, EGG AND LEMON SOUP
Soupa Avgolemono

2 pints chicken stock	2 eggs	salt and pepper
2 oz. rice		juice of 1 lemon

Bring the stock to the boil, throw in the rice, simmer for 20 minutes. Beat the eggs with the lemon juice. Add 4 tablespoons of the very hot stock to the eggs and lemon, stirring all the time. Remove the chicken and rice soup from the heat, pour in the egg and lemon mixture, season with salt and pepper. Serve at once. Never boil again once the eggs have been added.

GREEK FISH SOUP
Psarosoupa

2 lb. any firm white fish	1 clove garlic	2 tablespoons chopped parsley
1 cod's head	1 gill white wine	1 teaspoon chopped fennel
1 onion, chopped	3 tablespoons tomato juice	
1 leek, chopped	2 oz. flour	1 strip chopped lemon peel
4 sticks celery, chopped	½ pint milk	salt and pepper
	toast	

Put the fish, cod's head, onion, leek, garlic and celery in a large pan, season with salt and pepper, cover with cold water, bring to the boil and simmer until the fish is soft. Time cannot be accurately given as it depends on the size or sort of fish. When cooked, lift the fish out carefully. Cool, remove any bones, and break into large pieces. Simmer the stock for 20 minutes longer, strain and return to the pan. Mix the flour with the milk to a smooth paste, add the tomato juice and white wine, mix well. Add this to the fish stock, simmer and stir till it thickens. Now carefully put the cooked fish back in the soup, add the herbs. Serve with toast and one large piece of fish in each plate.

COD ROE SALAD

Taramosalata

4 oz. smoked cod roe	1 gill olive oil	2—3 tablespoons
2 large boiled potatoes	1—2 tablespoons fine	water
1 large lemon	breadcrumbs	1 small onion
	2 sprigs parsley	jellied consommé
		(optional)

Mash the potatoes and mix with the breadcrumbs and smoked roe until
well blended. Add the lemon juice mixed with the water alternately
with the olive oil, beating all the time until the mixture becomes thick
and creamy. Lay out on to a plate in the shape required and garnish
with finely chopped onion and parsley. The taramosalata may be
surrounded by small pieces of jellied consommé.

GRILLED FISH

Psari Psito

2 lb. fish	1 gill olive oil	garlic mayonnaise sauce
½ lemon	salt and pepper	(see p. 333)

Clean and wash the fish, rub inside and out with salt and pepper, and
leave in a colander for 30 minutes. Then put under a hot grill to cook
on both sides until golden brown and tender. During the grilling, dip
the lemon, on the end of a fork, into the olive oil and frequently rub
the fish with it to prevent the skin from getting too dry. Serve cold with
garlic sauce.

BAKED FISH

Psari Plaki

4 red mullets	2 cloves garlic	2 tablespoons white
8 oz. onions	12 oz. black olives	wine
8 oz. tomatoes	1 gill olive oil	salt and pepper

Clean the fish, but leave the heads and tails, rub inside and out with
a little salt and lay on a baking dish greased with olive oil. Chop the
onions finely and fry in hot oil until golden brown. Add the tomatoes,
skinned and quartered, crushed garlic, salt and pepper. Fry lightly for
a few minutes, add the white wine, cook gently for 5 minutes then pour
the mixture over the fish. Put into a medium oven and bake for 20—25
minutes. Stone the olives and put around the fish in the oven about
5 minutes before the end of cooking.

FRIED MULLET
Barbounia Tujanita

4 grey or red mullet	flour	salt
juice of 1 lemon		olive oil

Clean and fillet the mullet, removing heads and tails. Sprinkle with salt and lemon juice, inside and out and leave for a while. Cover lightly with flour and fry in hot oil on both sides until brown.

LAMB KEBAB

2 lb. leg lamb	juice 1 lemon	1 teaspoon salt
2 large tomatoes	1 teaspoon marjoram	8 skewers
1 large green pepper		¼ teaspoon pepper

Cut meat from the leg of lamb into squares of about 1 inch and moisten with lemon juice. Remove the seeds from the pepper and cut it into squares and halve the tomatoes. Thread the meat, pepper and tomato alternately on to the skewers. Sprinkle with salt, pepper and marjoram. Grill under a fierce heat and turn until all sides are cooked. Serve with rice. *(Illustrated in Plate 104.)*

LAMB WITH EGG AND LEMON SAUCE
Arni Avgolemono

2½ lb. lamb	2 medium onions,	1 dessertspoon cold
1½ pints cold water	chopped	water
8 oz. carrots, chopped	2 oz. dripping	juice 2 lemons
3 sticks celery,	2 oz. flour	salt and pepper
chopped		4 egg yolks

Cut the meat in 1½-inch squares, add the carrots, celery, onions, salt, pepper and the water. Bring to the boil, remove the scum, and simmer for 1½ hours. Strain. Put the meat and vegetables on the serving dish and keep warm. Melt the dripping, add the flour, stir for 2 minutes, pour the hot meat liquid over gradually, stir and cook for 5 minutes till it thickens. Mix the egg yolks, lemon juice and water, pour into the hot thick sauce, stir well, do NOT boil. Pour over the serving dish.

LAMB WITH COURGETTES
Arni me Kolokidia

2 lb. lamb	2 tablespoons olive oil	2—3 sprigs parsley
2 lb. courgettes	2 cloves garlic	salt and pepper
2 onions		8 oz. tomatoes

Cut the lamb into small pieces. Chop the onions and fry lightly in the oil. Add the meat and fry until brown. Add quartered tomatoes, crushed garlic cloves, chopped parsley, salt and pepper. Cover and simmer gently for 1 hour. Then peel the courgettes and put in whole, if small enough, otherwise cut in half, and cook gently for another 15 minutes.

GREEK BEEF STEW

Stiphado

2 lb. steak	6 tablespoons olive oil	1 gill red wine
4 cloves garlic,	½ pint thick tomato	salt and pepper
chopped	purée	lemon
	3 lb. small onions	parsley

Cut the steak in pieces, 3 × 2 inches. Rub well with salt and pepper. Heat the oil in a stew pan, fry the meat, onions and garlic till brown. Add the tomato purée, and the wine. Cover very tightly and simmer very slowly until the sauce is thick, like jam. Garnish with lemon and parsley. *(Illustrated in Plate 68.)*

STUFFED VINE LEAVES

Dolmades

about 40 vine leaves	1 gill olive oil	1 tablespoon chopped
8 oz. minced lamb	juice ½ lemon	parsley
4 oz. rice	1 tablespoon tomato	salt and pepper
1 pint stock	purée	water
	2 onions	

Plunge the vine leaves into boiling water for a minute then drain. Chop the onions and fry lightly in half the oil. Add the meat, rice, parsley, salt and pepper and fry for 5 minutes. Then add the stock and lemon juice and simmer gently for 15—20 minutes or until the rice has absorbed all the liquid. Fill each vine leaf with enough of the meat and rice stuffing to make small rolls about 2 inches long. Tuck in the ends and squeeze gently. Arrange a few of the remaining vine leaves at the bottom of a heavy saucepan and put in the stuffed vine leaves, closely packed together. Place more vine leaves between the layers. Blend the tomato purée with the remaining oil, add a cup of water and heat for a few minutes, mixing well. Pour into the saucepan over the dolmades, cover with a lid and cook slowly for 1 hour. Serve hot. A rice stuffing for the vine leaves, as in the Turkish recipe (see p. 586), is also a Greek way of preparing this dish, and it is best served cold.
Note: In Britain, fresh vine leaves should not be used, but leaves in 11-oz. cans are available.

MOUSSAKA

Minced Meat Pie

1 lb. minced beef or lamb or mutton	4 sliced unpeeled aubergines	1½ pints tomato sauce (see p. 333)
10 small onions, finely chopped	1 gill olive oil	1 gill cream or milk
2 tablespoons olive oil	1 bay leaf	1 egg
	butter	salt and pepper
		½ pint meat stock
		parsley

Fry the sliced aubergines till soft in hot olive oil for 3 or 4 minutes. Fry the onions in butter till transparent. Take a medium roasting dish, pour a tablespoon of oil on the bottom. Arrange a layer of aubergines, then a layer of mince, sprinkle with salt and pepper and add the bay leaf, then a layer of onions. Fill the dish with layers like this. Pour over the stock and tomato sauce. Cover the dish and cook in a slow to moderate oven for 45 minutes, or until the liquid has reduced considerably. Beat the egg in the cream or milk, season with salt and pepper and pour over the dish. Cook for 30 minutes or so more in a very slow oven, to form a custard on top of the dish. Garnish with parsley.

CHICKEN PILAFF

8 oz. cooked chicken	2 oz. butter	2 oz. chopped walnuts
8 oz. rice	2 pints chicken stock	¼ teaspoon chopped thyme
1 medium chopped onion	2 large peeled chopped tomatoes	salt and pepper

Cut the chicken meat into strips. Fry these with the onion in the butter, in a large pot until brown. Add salt, pepper, thyme. Add the rice, stir well for 5 minutes to prevent sticking. Pour in the stock, tomatoes and walnuts. Cover the pot and simmer gently till all the liquid has been absorbed and the rice is soft. With a fork stir all together. Leave covered n a warm place for 20 minutes and serve.

PINE NUT AND MEAT RISSOLES

1 lb. mince meat	1 oz. currants	½ teaspoon chopped parsley
3 medium boiled potatoes	½ teaspoon chopped thyme	salt and pepper
1 egg	½ teaspoon chopped dill	tomato sauce (see p. 333)
1 oz. pine nuts		deep fat for frying

Mash the potatoes with a fork, add the mince, stir in the beaten egg. Add the nuts, currants, herbs, salt and pepper. Mix together and form into little round flat cakes about 2 inches across. Fry in deep fat till brown. Serve with tomato sauce.

BOILED CHICKEN WITH LEMON

Kotopoulo me Lemono

1 chicken	8 oz. mushrooms, sliced	1 gill sherry
1 lemon		1 egg
8 oz. carrots, chopped	2 oz. butter	$\frac{1}{2}$ pint chicken stock
3 sticks celery, chopped	4 oz. blanched almonds	4 tablespoons cream
		8 oz. onions, chopped

Squeeze the lemon. Rub the bird with lemon juice and plenty of salt and pepper. Put half the lemon in the bird. Boil enough water to cover the bird, put it in with the vegetables. Simmer till tender. An old bird will take about 3 hours. When done, put the chicken on the serving dish and keep warm. Now cook the mushrooms in butter till soft. Pour the chicken stock into a saucepan, add the cooked mushrooms, sherry, almonds, heat slowly. Beat the egg and cream together in a basin, pour the very hot stock on gradually, stirring all the time till it thickens. Pour over the chicken and serve.

BALKAN STUFFED GREEN PEPPERS

Piperies Yemistes

4 large green peppers	salt and pepper	1 clove finely chopped garlic
8 oz. rice, cooked	4 tablespoons olive oil	
2 small finely chopped onions	2 tablespoons tomato purée	4 oz. finely chopped cooked beef, lamb, etc.
2 tablespoons currants		

Remove the stalks and slit the peppers down one side, cut out the core and seeds. Wash thoroughly under the tap to remove every fiery seed. Mix all the ingredients except the oil and tomato purée and stuff the peppers. Arrange them in a fireproof dish, pour over the oil and tomato purée, cover and bake in a moderate oven for 30 minutes.

AUBERGINES WITH PEPPERS

4 aubergines	2 large peeled sliced tomatoes	7 tablespoons olive oil
4 green peppers		salt and pepper
	2 bottles yoghourt	

Cut the aubergines in slices, salt and pepper them. Take out the core and seeds of the peppers, slice them, add salt and pepper. Salt and pepper the tomatoes. Heat the oil, first fry the aubergines till soft, remove and drain and put on the warm serving dish. Now do the same to the peppers and put on top of the aubergines. Add the yoghourt. Fry the tomatoes in the oil and put on top. Serve hot.

POTATO KEPHTIDES

1 lb. cold boiled potatoes	2 large tomatoes, chopped and peeled	salt and pepper olive oil or dripping
2 finely chopped spring onions	2 oz. flour	for frying ½ oz. melted butter

Sieve the potatoes and mix with all the ingredients. Knead slightly and roll ¾ inch thick and cut in rounds about 2½ inches across. Heat the oil or dripping till smoking hot, and fry quickly. These potato rounds can be baked on a greased oven sheet in a hot oven till golden brown. They should be crisp outside but very soft inside.

LADIES' FINGERS WITH AUBERGINES

Okra me Melitzanes

1 lb. ladies' fingers (okra)	1 onion	1 tablespoon chopped parsley
1 large aubergine	2 large tomatoes	salt and pepper
	1 gill olive oil	

Wash the ladies' fingers and cut off the stems. Peel and quarter the tomatoes and peel and dice the aubergine. Chop the onion and fry in the oil until golden brown then add the ladies' fingers, tomatoes, aubergine, parsley, salt and pepper. Mix well, cover and cook gently for about 30 minutes.

YOGHOURT AND TOMATO STEW

2 lb. leg of lamb	2 large tomatoes, peeled and chopped	2 teaspoons chopped mint
2 medium sliced carrots	1 green pepper, seeded and chopped	salt and pepper
2 bottles yoghourt		cold water

Cut the meat in 1½ inch squares. Add the carrots, salt and pepper, cover with ¾ pint cold water, simmer very gently for 1 hour. Add the tomatoes and pepper and simmer for 1 hour. Stir in the yoghourt, add the mint and serve.

BOILED CHICK-PEAS

Revidia Yahni

1 lb. chick-peas	2 tomatoes	salt and pepper
8 oz. onions	2—3 sprigs parsley	water
	2—3 cloves garlic	

Soak the chick-peas for 24 hours then drain them and put into a saucepan with plenty of water. Simmer gently for about 6 hours. Then add the salt, pepper, parsley, crushed cloves of garlic, sliced onions and skinned, quartered tomatoes and cook for a further 30 minutes. Drain and serve hot.

AUBERGINES WITH YOGHOURT

2 aubergines

4 tablespoons olive oil

2 crushed cloves garlic

salt

2 bottles yoghourt

Cut the unpeeled aubergines in ¼-inch thick slices, sprinkle the round well with salt, leave for 30 minutes. Wash and dry. Heat the oil and fry till soft. Remove and keep warm on the serving dish. Crush the garlic, stir into the yoghourt and pour over the aubergines. Serve hot.

TOMATO SAUCE OR PURÉE

2 lb. large ripe tomatoes, peeled and chopped

4 lumps sugar

1 chopped clove garlic

1 medium chopped onion

2 oz. minced beef

½ teaspoon chopped basil or fennel

salt and pepper

Put all the ingredients in a large stew pan. Cover and simmer very slowly, stirring from time to time for 30 minutes. Sieve this pulp. If the sauce is too liquid, return to the pan and reduce till thick enough.

LEMON AND EGG SAUCE

2 eggs

salt and pepper

1 gill vegetable stock

2 tablespoons lemon juice

Beat the eggs, add the lemon juice drop by drop, stirring all the time. Pour over the stock, cook in a double saucepan for 5 minutes, stirring continually, add salt and pepper.

GREEK GARLIC MAYONNAISE SAUCE

Skordalia

2 egg yolks

4 oz. ground almonds

2 oz. white bread- crumbs

6 cloves garlic

1 pint olive oil

1 tablespoon lemon juice

2 teaspoons chopped parsley

¼ teaspoon salt

¼ teaspoon pepper

Pound the garlic in a mortar, add the egg yolks, almonds, breadcrumbs, stir with a wooden spoon, add salt and pepper and the oil drop by drop stirring all the time. Lastly, stir in the lemon juice and parsley. Serve with cold fish, cold meats, cooked cold vegetables, potatoes boiled in their skins; in fact, with what you fancy.

THICK TOMATO PASTE

tomatoes   salt   olive oil

Take ½ teaspoon salt for every lb. of tomatoes. Chop the tomatoes, add the salt, cook slowly till reduced to a pulp. Sieve, then return to the pan and cook slowly to reduce the juice and make the pulp thick and fairly stiff. Spoon into bowls and put in the sun to dry out, or failing this, a warm place or cool oven will do. Pour oil over each bowl to seal and store. This paste is used in stews, rice and macaroni dishes in Greece.

HALVAS TIS RINAS

6 oz. butter	5 scant tablespoons	2 level teaspoons
6 oz. castor sugar	orange juice	baking powder
1½ level teaspoons	3 eggs	4 oz. ground almonds
finely grated orange	9 oz. fine semolina	1 tablespoon split,
rind		blanched almonds

Syrup:

6 oz. castor sugar	1½-inch piece	1 tablespoon
5 scant tablespoons	cinnamon stick	finely sliced
water	3 tablespoons	candied orange
2 dessertspoons	orange juice	peel
lemon juice		

Beat butter, sugar and orange rind to a smooth fluffly cream. Beat in orange juice. Whip eggs and beat in gradually. Stir in sifted semolina, baking powder and ground almonds. Turn into well greased and lined 7-inch square tin and sprinkle with almonds. Bake on middle shelf of a moderate oven for 1 hour 10 minutes.

A few minutes before the cake is cooked, make a syrup of sugar, water, lemon juice and cinnamon stick. Boil, without stirring, until syrup begins to thicken but do not allow it to change colour. Add the orange juice and peel and boil for a second.

Carefully turn the cake out on to a large, warm platter. Pour hot syrup over it at once. Cool and cut into squares. Serve plain or with unsweetened whipped cream. *(Illustrated in Plate 62.)*

SIPHANIAC HONEY TART

8 oz. milk cheese	4 oz. plain flour	2 eggs
2 tablespoons honey	4 oz. butter	1 teaspoon cinnamon
1½ oz. sugar		cold water

Make the pastry of the flour, sugar, butter and water. Roll out and cover a plate or shallow dish. Mix the cheese and honey together, add the beaten eggs and half the cinnamon. Spread on the pastry, sprinkle the rest of the cinnamon on top. Bake in a moderate oven for 35 minutes.

HONEY BALLS

Loukoumades

8 oz. flour	1 teaspoon lemon	warm water
1 oz. yeast	juice	pinch salt
1 gill honey	pinch cinnamon	oil for frying

Dissolve the yeast in a little warm water and mix with 2 oz. of flour. Cover and leave to sponge. Add the remaining flour and enough warm water to make a soft dough. Cover and leave for several hours and until the dough doubles its size. Heat the oil in a deep pan until it is boiling, then drop in teaspoonfuls of dough, 2 or 3 at a time. The balls will swell up, and when they are golden brown, take them out with a perforated spoon and drain them on kitchen paper. Boil the honey with lemon juice and add cinnamon and enough water to make a syrup. Serve hot with the syrup poured over the puffed balls.

NUT AND SYRUP PASTRY

Baklava

1 lb. flour	1 lb. unsalted butter	1 pint warm water
1 teaspoon baking powder	1 tablespoon cinnamon	2 teaspoons lemon juice
12 oz. chopped walnuts	2 tablespoons honey	cold water
		8 oz. sugar

Mix the flour and baking powder with enough cold water to make a stiff dough. Knead it long and well, then leave in a cool place for 1—2 hours. Then divide into equal sized pieces and roll out each one until it is paper thin. Cut into pieces which are a suitable size for a flat baking tin. Melt the butter and brush the tin with a little of it. Lay in one sheet of pastry and brush this with the melted butter. Add another sheet, brush with butter and cover with some of the walnuts, which have been blanched and chopped very finely. Sprinkle with a little cinnamon. Put on two more sheets of pastry, brushed with butter, covered with walnuts and sprinkled with cinnamon. Continue this process in the same order until all the walnuts are used up. There should be a few sheets of pastry left over. Brush these with the remaining butter and lay them on top. Then take a sharp knife, dipped in hot water, and cut the top few layers of pastry into squares, suitable for serving portions. Damp the edges at the top with water to keep them flat and put the baklava into a moderate oven to bake for about 1½ hours. Meanwhile, to prepare the syrup, boil honey, sugar, water and lemon juice together. When the baklava is cool, pour the syrup over it. Let it cool again, then cut into the portions where they were marked with a knife.

HALVA

8 oz. butter	2 pints water	cinnamon
1 lb. semolina	4 oz. blanched	1½ lb. sugar
	chopped almonds	extra butter

Boil the sugar in the water to make a syrup. Melt the butter in a saucepan, heat until it bubbles then stir in the semolina. Cook very slowly until the semolina is a pale gold. Fry half the almonds in extra butter and add to the semolina together with the syrup. Mix well, pour into a fireproof oven dish and put into a warm oven to bake slowly for about 15 minutes or until the halva is golden brown. When ready, press it down into the dish and leave to get cold. Turn out and sprinkle with cinnamon and garnish with remaining almonds.

EASTER PLAIT

1 lb. plain flour	1 oz. sugar	rind 1 small orange
½ oz. fresh yeast or	1 level teaspoon salt	or lemon
1 level teaspoon dried	1 beaten egg	7 tablespoons milk
yeast	1 oz. melted margarine	(tepid)

Glaze:

| 1 beaten egg | 1 teaspoon sugar | 1 tablespoon water |

Decoration:

| granulated sugar | split, blanched almonds | |

Make a batter using 4 oz. flour and all the milk, and crumble or sprinkle in the yeast. Cover with a greased polythene sheet and stand aside in a warm place until frothy (30—40 minutes). Sift the remaining flour into a mixing bowl, add the salt, sugar and orange or lemon rind, followed by the yeast batter, the melted and cooled margarine and the beaten egg. Work all together to make a fairly stiff dough. Knead well. Place the dough in a well greased polythene bag or plastic storage jar and put to rise in a warm place until double in size and the dough springs back when pressed with a floured finger (about 80—90 minutes).
Turn the dough on to a lightly floured board and knead well. Divide into 3 equal portions. Roll, with the hands, into long ropes, the end of which should be thinner than the middle. Plait the 3 pieces and turn the ends under, pressing them down. Place on a greased baking sheet, cover with polythene, and put aside to rise again (40—50 minutes). Brush over with egg glaze and bake on the middle shelf of a moderately hot oven for 20 minutes, re-glaze and sprinkle with granulated sugar and almonds and return to oven, reduced to moderate, for a further 30—40 minutes. Cool on a wire tray. *(Illustrated in Plate 61.)*

61. Easter Plait, Greece (p.336)

62. Halvas tis Rinas, Greece (p.334)

63. Preparing for the Casserole

HUNGARIAN COOKING

Musia Soper

Hungarian cooking is a fascinating blend of East and West. It has something of the artistry of French cooking, quite a lot in common with Austrian cooking, and it has also been influenced by Hungary's conquerors of the past, the Tartars and Turks.

Paprika, which is the Hungarian name for the sweet red pepper, is not at all hot, in spite of its appearance. It is one of the basic ingredients of Hungarian cooking, both whole and as a condiment. It is used for the many varieties of the famous goulash dishes, such as the delicious chicken paprika or pörkölt, which is like goulash, but with a thicker sauce. The sweet green peppers are also very popular, both raw and cooked. The Hungarians, like the Russians, use sour cream for many of their dishes and to enrich their sauces.

Many Hungarian dishes are characterised by their bright red colour and unique, rich flavour which go so well with the country's wild gipsy music, vivacious folk dancing and gay traditional costume.

Altogether, Hungarian cooking is a joy to look at as well as to taste; not difficult to make, although very imaginative. The recipes given here should serve as an exciting introduction to some of the best known dishes.

GOULASH SOUP

2 oz. bacon	¼ teaspoon marjoram	¼ clove garlic
8 oz. stewing beef (diced)	salt to taste (be careful if the bacon is	2 oz. flour
1 onion	rather salt)	2 pints stock
	1½ teaspoons paprika	2 cooked potatoes
		cold water

Chop bacon and fry lightly, adding *no* fat. Toss in chopped onion and continue frying. When golden, add the diced beef, and let all fry together. Keep tossing to prevent burning or sticking. Now shake in paprika, garlic (well chopped), marjoram and salt. When blended, add a little cold water, cover and simmer over low heat for 20 minutes. Now mix in flour with care, allowing no lumps to form. Add stock gradually, and simmer gently for 15 minutes. Dice the potatoes and stir in 5 minutes before serving. Here is a soup closely related to a true goulash. The ingredients are made finer and the whole, of course, thinned to a soup consistency.

FISH GOULASH SOUP

Halaszlé

1 lb. haddock or other fish	2 onions	2 pints water
1 green pepper	2 teaspoons paprika	1 tablespoon butter
		2 teaspoons salt

Fillet the fish and put the bones and head into a saucepan with the water, paprika, chopped onions and salt. Bring to the boil, cover and simmer for 30 minutes. Then cut the fish into small pieces, scoop out the inside of the pepper and cut it into thin strips and add to the strained fish stock. Simmer for about 20 minutes or until the fish is tender. Just before serving, add the butter.

SAUERKRAUT SOUP

1 lb. sauerkraut	2 oz. flour	¼ pint sour cream
1 lb. bacon bones	caraway seeds	8 oz. boiling sausage
1 onion chopped	(optional)	1 teaspoon paprika
2 pints water	1 oz. lard	

Simmer the sauerkraut with 2 pints water and the bacon bones for 30 minutes. Fry the onions in the lard until transparent, stir in the flour and cook for 1 minute. Add the paprika and caraway seeds, mix them well. Pour in the stock from the sauerkraut, stirring all the time, add the sauerkraut and the sausage cut into small pieces. Simmer for 10 minutes. Add the cream.

HARICOT BEAN SOUP

8 oz. haricot beans	1 parsnip	1 tablespoon flour
1 pint bacon stock	1 oz. bacon fat	½ pint sour cream
parsley	2 carrots	croûtons

Soak the beans overnight. Pour off the water and substitute bacon stock made by boiling bacon bones, rinds or a small knuckle. Add the sliced carrots and parsnip. Simmer until tender. Sieve the soup and mix it with the flour, cooked and slightly browned in the fat. Reheat and add cream and chopped parsley. Serve with croûtons of fried bread.

HUNGARIAN GOOSE LIVER

2 goose livers or 8 oz. chicken livers	4 oz. goose or chicken fat	2 teaspoons paprika salt
1 pint milk		2 cloves garlic

Put the livers in milk for several hours, then drain and dry with a cloth. Heat the fat in a saucepan, put in the whole livers and the garlic cloves cut into several pieces. Cover and simmer for about 30 minutes. Just before the end of cooking, add the paprika and a pinch of salt. Remove the livers, pour a little strained fat over them and serve hot. They are also good to eat chilled.

SZEKELY GOULASH

2 lb. shoulder of pork	½ pint sour cream	1 oz. butter
2 large tomatoes	2 teaspoons paprika	1 teaspoon salt
stock or water	1 lb. sauerkraut	

Peel and quarter the tomatoes and fry slowly in the butter until tender. Cut the pork into 1-inch pieces, add to the tomatoes and fry for a few minutes. Put in the sauerkraut, salt, paprika, cover with stock or water, put lid on pan and cook slowly for 1½ hours. Then stir in the sour cream and serve immediately.

ESTERHÁZY BEEF STEAK

2 lb. rump or chuck steak cut into small neat steaks and flattened	2 onions, coarsely chopped	2 teaspoons capers
	2 stalks celery, coarsely chopped	2 teaspoons paprika
		1 oz. flour
4 oz. good dripping or bacon fat	1 small green pepper, coarsely chopped	½ pint good stock
		3 tablespoons sour cream
3 tablespoons Madeira	3 carrots, coarsely chopped	salt and pepper

Melt half the dripping in a flameproof casserole, add the seasoning and vegetables, cover and sauté gently without stirring for 10 minutes. Remove the lid and raise the heat. Still without stirring, but shaking the pan, brown the vegetables, adding a little of the stock as necessary. Sprinkle in the flour. Stir gently. When blended, stir in the remaining stock and the sour cream. Heat the other half of the dripping in another pan. Sear the steaks quickly on both sides. Add the steak to the vegetables and gravy. Cover with a tightly fitting lid and cook in a moderate oven for about 30—45 minutes depending on the thickness and quality of the meat. Add the wine 5 minutes before serving.

HUNGARIAN GOULASH

1 lb. beef steak	2 tablespoons butter	1 teaspoon chopped
8 oz. lean veal	1 dessertspoon	parsley
2 onions	paprika	1 teaspoon salt
1 lb. tomatoes	stock or water	pepper

Remove any skin and fat from the meat and cut into inch cubes. Chop the onions and add these, together with the pieces of meat, to the melted butter in a thick casserole. Brown evenly. Add salt, pepper and paprika. Skin and slice the tomatoes. Lay them on top of the meat and onions. Cover with stock or water, put lid on the pan and cook slowly for about 1 hour. Serve on a flat dish surrounded by piped mashed potatoes or macaroni. Garnish with chopped parsley.

PORK GOULASH WITH PICKLED PIMENTOS

2 lb. pork fillets	3—4 pickled pimentos	salt
1 lb. onions	fat for frying	water
2 carrots		1 teaspoon paprika

Cut the meat into neat squares, fry in fat for a few minutes, then remove and put into a saucepan. Cut the onions into rings and fry in the same pan as the meat, until golden brown. Clean the carrots and cut into thin strips and add to the onions together with strips of pickled pimentos. Mix together and put into the saucepan with the meat. Season with paprika and salt, cover with water, put on a lid and simmer for 1 hour.

STUFFED VEAL FILLETS

4 veal fillets	1 onion	1 teaspoon salt
8 oz. minced ham	2 oz. butter	1 gill water
8 oz. tomatoes	1 clove garlic	1 large green pepper
	1 dozen olives	

Flatten the fillets until they are thin, cover with minced ham, roll up and tie with cotton. Heat the butter, add finely chopped onion and fry until golden brown. Add stoned chopped olives, salt and crushed garlic, and mix well. Put in the meat rolls and slices of skinned tomatoes and pour in the water. Cover and cook slowly until the meat is tender. Serve garnished with slices of pepper.

BEEF STEW

Tokany

2 lb. stewing steak	parsley chopped	stock or water
1 onion	1 teaspoon paprika	salt
3 oz. mushrooms	2 oz. butter	½ pint sour cream (optional)

Cut the meat into strips about 1 inch wide and 3 inches long. Brown them in the butter, add the finely chopped onion and fry until it is golden. Slice the mushrooms and add them to the meat. Season with paprika and salt, cover with stock or water, put lid on the pan and cook in a moderate oven for 1½ hours. Stir in the sour cream and parsley.

VEAL CUTLETS WITH LETCHO

4 veal cutlets	1 pint letcho	salt and pepper
3 tablespoons butter	(see p. 345)	boiled rice
	1 tablespoon flour	

Dip the cutlets into flour seasoned with salt and pepper and fry on both sides in the butter until light brown. Then transfer the cutlets into a baking dish, spread with the letcho, cover with a lid and cook in a moderate oven for 30 minutes. Serve with boiled rice.

BACON AND POTATO CASSEROLE

2 lb. potatoes	¼ pint milk	butter
8 rashers bacon	1 teaspoon paprika	1 onion
	salt	

Arrange alternate layers of thinly sliced potato, chopped bacon and sliced onion in a well-buttered fireproof dish, ending with a layer of potato. Mix the paprika with the milk, add a pinch of salt and pour over the potatoes. Dot with butter. Cook in a moderate oven for 1½ hours.

GOULASH WITH RUNNER BEANS

2 lb. pork	2 oz. dripping	2 lb. runner beans
1 onion	1 lb. tomatoes	salt
water	1 teaspoon paprika	

Cut the pork into cubes, brown them in the dripping, add the chopped onion and brown it with the meat. Peel and quarter the tomatoes and cook them slowly with a little water until tender, rub through a sieve. Add them and the sliced beans to the meat. Season with salt and paprika and cook slowly in a covered pan for 1½ hours. Serve with mashed potatoes.

PAPRIKA VEAL

1 lb. thin slices fillet	1 tablespoon paprika	1 tablespoon flour
veal	butter	salt and pepper
½ pint sour cream	lemon juice	very small dumplings
5 onions	1 gill stock	(see p. 347)

Marinate the slices of veal in lemon juice for 1 hour. Slice the onions and fry in butter until just turning brown. Sprinkle with paprika. Dip the slices of veal in flour and brown them separately, in butter. Lay the browned slices of meat on top of the onions. Cover the pan and cook over a low heat for 5 or 6 minutes. Meanwhile mix a tablespoon of the flour with the sour cream and stock. Add salt and pepper. Pour over the meat and cook for another 5 minutes. Serve piping hot with very small dumplings (csipetke) or other dumplings. Veal chops or steaks can be used in this recipe. Follow the same instructions but allow longer for cooking.

HUNGARIAN PORK CHOPS

4 pork chops	1 sprig parsley	1 sprig rosemary
½ bottle white wine	2 oz. butter	2 oz. breadcrumbs
2 carrots, sliced	1 oz. flour	1 teaspoon paprika
1 onion, sliced	1 clove garlic	salt and pepper
	1 bay leaf	

Put the carrots, onion, bay leaf, parsley, rosemary, garlic and wine into a shallow dish and marinate the chops in it for 12 hours. Drain the chops and brown them in the butter. Stir in the flour, cook for 1 minute and add the strained marinade. Simmer for 20 minutes. Add the paprika and simmer for another 5 minutes. Arrange the chops in a shallow dish, pour the sauce over them, cover with breadcrumbs and brown them in the oven.

VEAL WITH MUSHROOMS

1½ lb. veal	2 oz. lard	4 oz. grated Gruyère
4 oz. mushrooms	1 teaspoon paprika	cheese
4 oz. cooked rice	4 tomatoes, peeled and	1 oz. butter
water	sliced	salt

Cut the veal into slices. Brown them in the lard, stir in the paprika, add a little water and salt and simmer for 5 minutes. Slice the mushrooms and cook them slowly in the butter for 10 minutes. In a casserole, arrange alternate layers of meat, rice, mushrooms and tomatoes, ending with a layer of rice. Sprinkle with grated cheese. Bake in a moderate oven for 15 minutes. Finish under a grill if the cheese is not sufficiently brown.

HUNGARIAN CHICKEN STEW

8 SERVINGS

8 joints or portions of	2 tablespoons chopped	1 pint chicken stock
young chicken	parsley	2 tablespoons tomato
2 onions	¼ teaspoon salt	purée
2 tablespoons butter		2 teaspoons paprika
chicken giblets		

Chop the onions and fry them with the parsley in the butter, in a thick, deep saucepan. Add the chicken portions, including the giblets. Sprinkle with the salt and paprika. Cover all with the chicken stock. Put the lid on and allow to simmer very slowly until tender. Add the tomato purée and cook for another 5 minutes. Remove the chicken portions from the pan and place on a very hot dish. Strain the liquid left and serve separately. Plain noodles (or dumplings, see p. 347), are a very nice addition to this dish. Cook them with the stew.

343

VEAL CUTLETS

4 veal cutlets	1 oz flour	8 rashers streaky
2 oz. butter	1 gill sour cream	bacon
1 teaspoon paprika		salt and pepper

Season the flour with salt and pepper. Dust the cutlets with it. Fry them on both sides in the butter until golden. Remove the cutlets and keep warm. Stir the paprika into the fat in the pan, cook for 1 minute, add the cream and heat gently. Pour this sauce over the cutlets and heat in a slow oven for 5 minutes. Roll the bacon rashers and cook them separately in the oven while making the sauce. Arrange them around the cutlets.

MEAT STEW

Pörkölt

2 lb. veal or pork or	2 teaspoons paprika	1 gill sour cream
mixed veal and pork	2 tablespoons lard	1 teaspoon salt
2 onions	1 dessertspoon flour	1 gill water

Chop the onions and fry in lard until golden brown. Add the meat, cut in 2-inch cubes, and fry for a few minutes. Add paprika, water and salt and mix well. Cover and simmer until the meat is tender. Just before the end of cooking, add the flour blended with the sour cream and simmer for 5 minutes.

CHICKEN PAPRIKA

6 SERVINGS

2 young frying	5 onions	salt and pepper
chickens	3 teaspoons paprika	1 tablespoon flour
4 tablespoons butter	yolks of 2 eggs	½ pint sour cream

Quarter the chickens. Slice the onions and cook in the hot butter until a golden brown. Add the chicken quarters and allow to cook until slightly coloured. Sprinkle with the paprika. Dust with flour, salt and pepper. Beat the yolks of eggs and add to the sour cream. Cover the chicken mixture with this. Cover the pan and simmer for about 20 minutes. This can be served with noodles or rice.

GOURMAND DUCK

1 duck	8 oz. shelled peas	1 egg
2 lb. tomatoes	1 carrot	1 tablespoon sour
1 lb. onions	2—3 sprigs parsley	cream
1 aubergine	2 oz. ham	olive oil
2 green peppers	1 rasher bacon	salt and pepper
8 oz. French beans	1 tablespoon rice	

Fry 1 chopped onion in a little oil, add chopped duck's liver, chopped ham, chopped bacon rasher, grated carrot, rice and chopped parsley. Fry together for a few minutes, then remove from the heat. Cool slightly then add 1 beaten egg and sour cream and season with salt and pepper. Stuff the duck with this mixture and put into a large, greased oven dish. Sprinkle with olive oil, salt and pepper and put into a slow oven to roast gently for 3 hours. Cook vegetables separately and serve with the duck.

RABBIT PAPRIKA

8 SERVINGS

2 medium sized rabbits	1 onion	2 tablespoons butter
	1 gill water	salt
1 green pepper	1 tablespoon tomato	½ gill sour cream
1 tablespoon paprika	purée	1 tablespoon flour
		croûtons

Joint the rabbits and cut into 8 pieces, using only the best. Chop the onion, slice the pepper and fry golden brown in the butter. Sprinkle the paprika over this. Put the pieces of rabbit in it, add seasoning and let cook until the rabbit is browned slightly. Add the water. Cover tightly and let simmer slowly until the meat is tender. Sprinkle the flour over and add the tomato purée. Stir in the cream a little at a time until the sauce is thick and creamy. If too thick add a little milk or water. Place the pieces on the centre of a deep dish and pour the sauce over. Serve with croûtons of fried bread as garnish.

HAM AND PANCAKE PUDDING

12 small pancakes (see p. 114)	8 oz. minced cooked ham	½ pint béchamel sauce (see p. 256)
2 oz. grated cheese		salt and pepper

Make 12 small pancakes. Line a greased pudding basin with one of them and reserve one for the top, cut the rest into strips. Mix with the ham and sauce, season with salt and pepper, pour into the basin. Cover with the remaining pancake. Sprinkle with grated cheese. Bake in a moderate oven for 15 minutes.

LETCHO

2 large onions	2 lb. tomatoes	salt and pepper
4 large green peppers		2 tablespoons corn oil

Chop the onions finely and fry lightly in the oil. Scoop out the inside of the peppers, cut into thin strips and add to the onions. Cook slowly until soft, then add skinned, sliced tomatoes and salt and pepper to taste. Cook for another 5—10 minutes then serve hot with meat dishes.

GOURMAND PANCAKES

1 pint batter for
  pancakes (see p. 114)
1 lb. veal
2 onions

1 egg
1 tablespoon sour
  cream

1 tablespoon paprika
salt and pepper
water
fat for frying

Prepare the pancakes. Fry chopped onions in 2 tablespoons of fat, add the veal, cut into pieces, and season with paprika and a teaspoon of salt. Pour in about 1 gill water and simmer until the meat is tender. Mince the meat and mix it with an egg. Add a little ground pepper and enough of the gravy to moisten the mixture. Fill the pancakes, roll up and place close together in an oven dish. Strain the rest of the gravy, blend with the sour cream and pour over the pancakes. Put into a moderate oven and bake until the pancakes are light brown on top.

STUFFED PEPPERS

Töltött Paprika

4 large green peppers
1 small onion
1 egg

1 lb. minced beef or
  pork or a mixture
  of both

1 teaspoon salt
2 tablespoons olive oil
1 tablespoon paprika

Chop the onion finely and fry lightly in a tablespoon of oil. Mix the meat with the egg, salt and paprika, add to the onion and fry gently for 10 minutes. Scoop out and wash the inside of the pimentos and stuff with the meat mixture. Grease a baking tin with the remaining oil, arrange the pimentos in it, cover and bake in a moderate oven for 40 minutes.

HUNGARIAN MARROW

1 12-inch marrow or
  2 6-inch ones
3 onions

1 teaspoon Hungarian
  paprika

½ pint sour cream
1 dessertspoon parsley
4 oz. butter

Cut up the marrow, without peeling it, into finger-sized strips. Melt the butter in a frying pan. Peel and chop up the onions as small as possible and fry them light brown in the butter. Now add the marrow pieces. Cover the pan. Lower the heat to simmering point and cook for 15 minutes. Stir the paprika into the sour cream and mix well. Pour this over the marrow. Let it heat thoroughly. Chop the parsley and sprinkle over the marrow. It is now ready to serve.

VERY SMALL DUMPLINGS

Csipetke

| 8 oz. flour | pinch salt | water |
| | 1 egg | |

Sieve the flour and heap on a board. Make a well in the centre. Break in the egg, and stir in the flour, alternating with water until a stiff dough is formed. Roll out to a thickness of about ½ inch. Cut into strips ½ inch wide. Break off little pieces with the fingers. These are either boiled in salted water or in the sauce of the dish with which they are to be served. Generally they are served with goulash.

FLOUR PELLETS

Tarhonya

| 1 lb. flour | water | salt |
| | 3 eggs | |

Sift the flour into a bowl, make a well in the centre and break in the eggs. Add a pinch salt and just enough water to make a very stiff dough. Knead the dough until smooth, then divide into several parts and leave for a while to harden. Then chop up finely and leave until next day. Put the pastry into a large baking tin and leave in a cool oven to dry off completely. This may now be stored in jars for an indefinite period. When it is to be used as an accompaniment to dishes with paprika sauce, put into a pan of boiling, salted water and simmer for about 15 minutes. Serve hot with a little fat added, if desired.

HUNGARIAN DOUGHNUTS

8 oz. flour	4 egg yolks	1 tablespoon rum
3 tablespoons butter	1 teaspoon grated	1½ lb. lard (for frying)
½ oz. yeast	lemon rind	pinch salt
1 oz. sugar	½ gill milk	castor sugar

Mix 2 oz. flour with the yeast dissolved in the warmed milk, half the sugar and a pinch of salt. Leave in a warm place to rise. Then combine with the rest of the flour and sugar, rum, grated lemon rind and egg yolks. Mix well until the dough is smooth and fairly soft, then cover with a cloth and leave in a warm place to rise. After about an hour, turn the dough out on to a floured board, roll out to about ½ inch thick. Cut into rounds 1½ inches in diameter and leave for 30 minutes. Heat the lard in a deep pan and, when it is very hot, drop in a few doughnuts, leaving some room between them. Cover with a lid and leave the doughnuts for about 5 minutes or until they are golden brown on all sides. Drain well and roll in castor sugar.

WITCHES' FROTH

Boszorkányhab

2 lb. apples   4 oz. castor sugar   1 tablespoon apricot
2 eggs   ½ pint cream   brandy

Bake the apples until soft then remove the peel and core. Mash the
pulp with a fork, add the sugar and brandy and the stiffly whipped
egg whites. Chill and serve with whipped cream over the top.

PANCAKES WITH CHOCOLATE SAUCE

8 pancakes   vanilla   1 tablespoon strong
2 oz. ground almonds 1 oz. butter   black coffee
2 oz. seeded raisins 4 oz. cooking   ¼ pint milk
3 oz. castor sugar   chocolate

Pound the raisins with the ground almonds, 2½ oz. sugar and a drop
of vanilla. Put one pancake into a greased round fireproof dish, cover
with a layer of the almond mixture, repeat the layers until all the
pancakes have been used. Sprinkle with sugar, dot with butter and bake
in a moderate oven for 10 minutes. Serve with chocolate sauce made by
melting the chocolate in the coffee and milk.

WALNUT RÉTESH

Strudel is extensively made in Germany and Austria, where it is known
by its German name, but it originated in Hungary where it is called
rétesh.

Pastry: *Walnut Filling:*
8 oz. flour   4 oz. chopped or   1 gill seedless raisins
1 tablespoon lard   ground walnuts   1 pint milk
2 eggs   6 oz. castor sugar   few drops vanilla
1½ gills warm water   2 tablespoons apricot   essence
1 gill sour cream   jam
pinch salt

Sift the flour and make a well in the centre. Melt the fat and blend with
an egg yolk, the water, sour cream and a pinch salt, then pour into the
hollow of the flour. Knead the dough until it is smooth and elastic then
cover with a cloth and leave in a warm place for about an hour. Spread
a cloth over a wide area of kitchen table, sprinkle with flour and place
the dough in the middle. Roll it out a little, then stretch it gently in all
directions without breaking it, until it is even and as thin as paper.
Cover with the walnut filling, roll up the pastry by lifting the cloth,
then cut the rolls into the lengths required. Press the edges of the pastry
together, place the rolls, sealed side down, on a greased baking tin,

brush the top with a beaten egg and bake in a moderate oven for about 30 minutes or until the pastry is light brown and crisp. To prepare the filling, put all the ingredients except the jam into a saucepan. Bring to the boil, then simmer gently for 10 minutes, stirring constantly. Allow the mixture to cool, then add the jam. Mix well and spread over the pastry.

POPPY-SEED RÉTESH

Make the pastry in the same way as for Walnut Rétesh (see p. 348).
Poppy-Seed Filling:

4 oz. poppy-seeds	1 pint milk	2 oz. sugar
1 teaspoon grated lemon rind	1 tablespoon seedless raisins	2 tablespoons apricot jam

Crush the poppy-seeds and put into a saucepan with the sugar and milk. Add the grated lemon rind and chopped raisins, bring to the boil and simmer gently for a few minutes. Allow to cool then stir in the jam. Spread over the pastry and roll up, then proceed as for Walnut Rétesh.

HUNGARIAN SHORTBREAD BISCUITS

Pogacsa

8 oz. flour	2—3 eggs	pinch salt
5 oz. butter	about 30 salted almonds	

Sift the flour and salt and rub in the butter. Add one large egg or 2 small eggs and mix to a stiff dough. Roll out to about ½ inch thick, cut into small round shapes with a pastry-cutter, brush with an egg yolk and place a salted almond on each biscuit. Leave for a while then put into a moderate oven to bake until the biscuits are a pale golden colour.

LIPTAUER CHEESE

Although this cheese is made in Austria and Germany, its origin is Hungarian.

3 pints milk, or 8 oz. cream cheese	½ teaspoon French mustard	1 teaspoon grated onion
6 oz. butter	½ teaspoon caraway seeds	1 teaspoon chopped capers
3—4 anchovy fillets		
1 teaspoon paprika		1 teaspoon salt

Allow the milk to go sour and solidify, then put into a muslin bag for 12—15 hours to drain. Or, buy the cream cheese ready-made. Blend the cheese with the butter and add the anchovies, finely chopped, and the rest of the ingredients. Mix well, put into a mould and chill.

DOBOSH GÂTEAU

Pastry:
4 eggs
4 teaspoons castor
  sugar
4 tablespoons flour

Icing:
3 oz. castor sugar

Filling:
1 egg
2 oz. cocoa
4—5 tablespoons milk
4 oz. castor sugar
4 oz. unsalted butter

Beat the egg whites very stiff, add the sugar and go on beating. Next add the yolks, still beating the mixture with the whisk. Fold in the flour lightly and carefully. Grease and flour the inside bottom of two sandwich tins, pour a little of the cake mixture on each and spread evenly with a palette knife. Put them into a very hot oven for 3—4 minutes. Do not let them brown — they should be a pale yellow colour when ready. The cake on the higher shelf will be ready first; take it off the tin immediately, grease and flour the tin and put another portion of mixture on it and into the oven. By this time the layer on the cooler shelf will be ready, so take it out and repeat the procedure, till all is used up. With the above quantity you should be able to make 5—6 layers. Put the layers aside while you prepare the filling.

Heat milk in a saucepan, add the cocoa to it when hot, and mix it well to make a smooth paste. Add a little extra milk if you find the paste too dry. Take off the heat and let cool while you beat the egg and sugar. Add this to the paste. Add the butter to this mixture by beating in small pieces, and go on beating till the filling is light in colour, and consistency. Use this filling generously between the layers of sponge, but remember to keep a little for the sides of the cake. Do not put the top layer on till you have covered it with the caramel icing. For this you melt the sugar in a pan and heat it till it turns into a nice brown runny caramel. Pour this caramel quickly over the sponge layer, smoothing and spreading it with a buttered knife. Before it has time to cool, cut sections into it with another buttered knife. These sections in the hard caramel top make it easy to cut the cake.

ITALIAN COOKING

Dorothy Daly

Before thinking about Italian cooking, it's as well to give some thoughts to the good foods native to that sunny country. And before getting down to the food itself, give some consideration to what, in Italy, is its essential accompaniment — good wine. From north to south, whether one travels by road or by rail, one doesn't go far without seeing stretches of vineyards. From the delightful Soave, produced in the vicinity of Verona, to the slightly spicy Orvieto of the Umbrian Hills, down to the delicate Lachrima Christi with which the visitor to Naples, Pompeii and Amalfi is regaled, there's no excuse in Italy for stinting the wine with which to cook or with which to eat the finished dish. Not all Italian wines travel well enough to allow them to be sent to other countries, but a little patient exploration will result in a fairly lengthy list of Italian wines that can be purchased at a reasonable price. It is therefore not an extravagance to use them, when suggested in the recipe, for a truly Italian dish, or to form the highly agreeable habit of taking a glass or two with one's pasta or ossobuco. Not only is Italy a country of wines, it is also a country of cheeses of a staggering variety. Where cheese for cooking is concerned, we may have to substitute Bel Paese, which travels well, for Mozzarella, which doesn't, and our own cream cheese for the Italian Ricotta which again doesn't care much for transportation, but where table cheeses are concerned, there's a wide variety from which to choose. Wines, cheeses, olive oil, lemons, lemon juice and tomatoes (raw, cooked or rendered down into the purée or conserve we can now purchase in tubes), green, red, yellow and variegated peppers, purple eggplants, artichokes, and zucchini are but a few of the colourful basic foods of the Italian peninsula.

What about the fruit of the seas that wash the shores of the long, indented coastline, all the strange and lovely fish and shellfish abounding in the waters? What of the colourful fish to be seen in the fish market in Venice, to mention but one of the famous markets? In most coastal towns of Italy, fish is good and recipes for cooking it abound. Your taste won't, of course, take kindly to all of them, and the mention of octopus may bring forth a horrified shudder, but few people refuse a dish of scampi or red mullet and these are but two of a great number of piscatorial delicacies. And why, so far, no word of pasta, that ever present Italian dish? For the reason that pasta, whatever it may be to-day, is said not originally to have been a native of the country, but is alleged to be one of the many wonders brought home by the 13th century explorer, Marco Polo, from his travels in China. Nevertheless, although pasta in its many shapes and forms, may not have been a true native of Italy, to-day it seems as much a part of the country as an operatic tenor, and anyone wanting to present a truly Italian meal must perforce learn a few of the ways of preparing and cooking pasta. ANTIPASTI is the name given to the large variety of light dishes or hors-d'oeuvre, which in a truly Italian household are served as a prelude to pasta or soup.

64. Minestrone Soup, Italy (p.356)

65. Baked Gherkins, Holland (p.184)

FENNEL ANTIPASTO

head of fennel	1 tablespoon lemon	freshly ground
3 tablespoons olive oil	juice	black pepper
	salt	

Wash a head of fennel, and soak in very cold water for an hour until it is crisp. Slice thinly, and pile in a dish. Make a dressing with the remaining ingredients. Dip the fennel into this before eating.

STUFFED FENNEL OR CELERY

Wash the tender stalks of either of these, soak in cold water to allow them to become crisp, and before serving spread with cottage cheese, pounded anchovies, or a combination of the two.

OTHER WAYS WITH FENNEL

Try combining thinly sliced fennel with thinly sliced crisp red radishes, or with thinly sliced unpeeled cucumber, in each case serving with a dressing of oil, lemon juice, pepper and salt, and a sprinkling of parsley, or mint finely chopped.

PANDORATO ALLA ROMANA

Fried Bread in the Roman Fashion

For this recipe, allow 1 or 2 $\frac{1}{2}$-inch slices of bread per person, and remove the crusts so that your slices are about 3 inches square. You will need also a little warmed milk, one or two beaten eggs, depending on the number of slices, salt for seasoning, and oil for frying. An hour before starting to cook the slices, spread them in a single layer in a large flat dish and sprinkle them with warm milk, and then with sufficient beaten egg to soak the bread without making it soggy. Leave for an hour, then lift each slice gently with a spatula and fry in hot oil, first on one side then on the other until golden brown.

CHICKEN TARTLETS

Into a little rich béchamel sauce (see p. 256), say a $\frac{1}{2}$ pint, mix two tablespoons grated Parmesan, and 4 oz. or more of cold cooked chicken cut into small pieces, a few chopped mushrooms, and a slice of lean ham cut small. Mix well together and use as a filling for tartlets.

CHICKEN LIVER TARTLETS

This time, impregnate your $\frac{1}{2}$ pint of béchamel (see p. 256) with chopped chicken livers that have been cooked in a little Marsala, and to this add chopped mushrooms and seasonings. Mix well and use to fill small pastry tartlets.

FORTUNATA RUOCCO'S COLD PEPPER ANTIPASTO

For each person allow:

1 pepper (assorted colours make the finished dish more attractive)	1 small teaspoon best olive oil	½ lemon scraping of garlic

Prepare your peppers by baking them whole in a fireproof dish placed in a larger dish with water halfway up the dish containing the peppers. Cook until the skins are wrinkled — about 45 minutes — in a hot oven. Cool slightly, peel off the thin outer skin, halve and remove all the seeds. Slice thinly, and arrange on a serving dish, alternating the colours of the peppers. Sprinkle with a scraping of garlic, and marinate with olive oil. Cool thoroughly before serving, and allow ½ lemon per person when the finished dish is served.

HOT ANTIPASTO MADE WITH GREEN PEPPERS

For each person allow:

1 green pepper	2 or more anchovies	few drops oil
1 peeled tomato	suspicion of garlic	from the anchovies
	6 capers	

Remove the seeds from the pepper after having sliced off the top; stuff the cavity with one peeled tomato to each pepper, add a suspicion of garlic, two or more anchovies, half a dozen capers, and a few drops of the oil from the anchovies. Replace the top of each pepper. Place in a fire-proof deep dish, put in a hot oven, bake 45 minutes, basting at intervals with the remaining oil from the can of anchovies and a little hot water. Serve before or in place of soup, very hot. These are even more attractive if baked in individual fireproof dishes.

FRIED BREAD WITH ANCHOVIES

Allow 1 or 1½ slices of bread per person; cut the slices about ½ inch in thickness, remove the crusts and cut in two, lengthways. To each strip of bread allow a little Bel Paese and half an anchovy and for the whole dish allow one or two eggs depending on the quantity of bread to be prepared. You will need also pepper and salt, flour and oil. On half the number of strips of bread spread a layer of Bel Paese, and on that lay ½ anchovy cut into small pieces. Season with pepper, and cover with the second slice. Heat the oil in a pan, and meanwhile dip the sandwiches first of all in water or a little milk, then in flour and finally in beaten egg, and fry quickly, first on one side and then on the other until golden brown. Serve very hot.

PANDORATO ALLA CREMA DI FORMAGGIO
Fried Bread with Cheese Cream

6 slices of bread, ½ inch thick, crusts removed, cut in two lengthwise

4 oz. Gruyère cheese	olive oil for frying	2 eggs, separated
knob of butter	½ pint milk, or a little more	flour

Whip the whites of eggs. Having prepared the strips of bread, dip them first in water or a little milk, then in flour, then in the whipped egg whites; fry them in hot olive oil and, when golden brown, lay in a flat fireproof dish and cover with the following cheese cream.

Cheese cream for
pandorato alla crema di formaggio

Cut the cheese in small pieces and place in a basin. Cover with the milk and leave for quite an hour, by the end of which time the cheese will have softened. Place it in a double boiler, add the beaten egg yolks and stir with a wooden spoon until the whole is mixed well and has become a thick cream. Remove from the fire and stir in a knob of butter the size of a walnut. Spread this cream over the slices of fried bread and serve hot, garnished with sprigs of parsley.

FRIED GREEN OLIVES

3—4 large Spanish olives per person	1 anchovy to each 4 olives	salt and pepper
flour	thick slice bread with crust removed	batter
		oil for frying

Peel the olives in a spiral so that you can remove the stone without breaking the flesh; soak the bread in a little water, and when it has become saturated, squeeze it dry in the hand; one slice should be sufficient for half a dozen anchovies. Remove the bones from the anchovies and pound them in a mortar, together with the bread, a few drops of olive oil and season them with freshly ground black pepper. When they are reduced to a paste, stuff the cavities of the olives with the mixture, then dip in flour, and after that into a thin batter, and fry in hot olive oil. Drain well before serving.

PARMA HAM AND FIGS
6 SERVINGS

6 slices Parma ham	12 ripe figs

Place the slices of Parma ham on a serving dish. Surround them with ripe little black figs and serve.

CROSTINI ALLA NAPOLITANA

For each person allow 2 slices of bread, ½ inch thick, with crusts removed and cut in two lengthwise, and for each slice of bread allow one anchovy, a little Bel Paese and ½ tomato skinned and with the seeds removed. Allow a little oregano and pepper for seasoning. Fry the pieces of bread in hot oil on one side only, then arrange in a single layer in a greased flat fireproof dish, fried side uppermost. On each slice spread a layer of Bel Paese, ½ anchovy cut small and a thin slice or two of tomato, and finally sprinkle with oregano and black pepper and a few drops of olive oil. Cook in a hot oven for 10 minutes to allow the cheese to melt. Serve very hot.

PARMA HAM AND MELON

6 SERVINGS

| 1 melon | 6 slices Parma ham | 12 black olives |

Cut the melon into six slices, scrape off the pips. Roll the slices of ham and place them on the upturned melon slices. Decorate with black olives and serve.

HARICOT BEAN SOUP

| 8 oz. haricot beans, soaked in water overnight | 3 pints water
1 tablespoon olive oil
salt and pepper to taste | 4 heaped tablespoons chopped parsley
1 clove garlic, crushed |

Cover the beans with water, bring to the boil and cook slowly for at least 3 hours. Towards the end of the cooking time, heat the olive oil, and to it add the crushed garlic and parsley and cook together for 5 minutes. Pass beans and the water in which they have cooked through a sieve or food mill, return to the saucepan, and stir in the garlic mixture. Serve hot with snippets of toast, and if liked, hand with the soup a dish of grated Parmesan.

MINESTRONE (1)

4 oz. salt pork cut in small pieces	½ lettuce	2 oz. of small macaroni—elbow
1 large or 2 small onions	8 oz. tomatoes	macaroni, pastina
4 pints water	handful French beans, cut in pieces	(rice-shaped
1 large carrot	8 oz. shelled green	macaroni) or alpha-
1 head celery	peas	bet macaroni, small
½ small spring cabbage	1 small can sweet corn	stars, or any of the
	salt and pepper to taste	small types

Fry the pork in a little lard until it is slightly brown; add onion cut small and cook till golden brown; add water and bring to the boil add carrots and celery cut into small pieces; add shredded cabbage and lettuce, beans, peas, peeled and sliced tomatoes, and corn, and salt and pepper to taste. Cover and allow to cook gently for about 1½ hours. Twenty minutes before serving add the macaroni. Serve hot with hand-grated Parmesan to be added at will. *(Illustrated in Plate 64).*

MINESTRONE (2)

1 lb. salt pork cut small	1 clove crushed garlic, (optional)	8 oz. peas, shelled few French beans
4 pints water, or beef stock	1 tablespoon butter small cabbage	4 tablespoons rice grated Parmesan
2 tablespoons finely chopped parsley	8 oz. haricot beans, soaked overnight	salt and pepper 2 carrots, diced

Place cut up pork in water or stock and bring to the boil before adding parsley, garlic and chopped vegetables, peas and beans. Allow to boil gently for 2½ hours, then add rice and cook for a further quarter of an hour. Season to taste. Serve with a layer of Parmesan cheese sprinkled over the soup.

ZUPPA PAVESE

For this really nourishing 'meal in itself' soup, you need a quart of clear chicken broth, into which at the end of its cooking time, while still boiling, one egg at a time is thrown for each person, stirred rapidly while it 'poaches', and removed to its individual soup bowl while the other eggs are similarly treated.

ALTERNATIVE METHOD FOR ZUPPA PAVESE

If you do not mind your eggs very lightly poached, place ½-inch slice of toasted French bread in each individual soup bowl, and on to it break an egg very carefully so as not to break the yolk. Over this pour the boiling soup, and serve immediately.

CHESTNUT SOUP

2 pints stock, or mixed stock and water	8 oz. chestnuts 1 bay leaf	2 cloves 1 slice lean ham

Score the chestnuts across the pointed end, and bake in a moderate oven 10 to 15 minutes, after which it should be simple to remove the outer and inner skins. Peel and put to cook slowly with the water and ham and seasonings, for 40 minutes or slightly longer. Pass through a sieve or food mill and serve with snippets of fried bread.

ZUPPA PARADISO

6 SERVINGS

This recipe, given in Rose L. Sorce's *La Cucina*, is just too good not to be ncluded.

4 pints good soup stock	nutmeg	4 tablespoons grated Parmesan
4 eggs, separated	4 tablespoons bread- crumbs	salt and pepper

Beat the egg whites till stiff, add beaten yolks and beat till well blended. Add cheese and breadcrumbs. Bring stock to a boil, slowly add mixture a spoonful at a time, boil 5 to 8 minutes and serve.

ZUPPA ALLA MARINARA

about 2 lb. fish, including heads and tails and some shell- fish	parsley 2 pints water 2 tablespoons white wine	1 stalk celery, chopped 4 tomatoes, peeled and chopped
bay leaf peppercorns	1 small onion, chopped	1 oz. butter salt and pepper

Chop fish in pieces. Make stock by combining heads, skins and a couple of pieces of the cheaper fish with bay leaf, peppercorns, parsley, and water. Boil for about 20 minutes. Meanwhile melt the butter in a sauce-pan and sauté onion until golden brown, add celery, tomatoes and seasoning, sauté a few minutes longer, add wine. Strain stock, bring to boil and gently poach remainder of fish until cooked. Combine with onion, tomatoes, celery and wine and serve with snippets of toast or fried bread.

ZUPPA DI PESCE DEI PESCATORI DI POZZÙOLI

Fish Soup Made by the Fishermen of Pozzuoli

From Pozzuoli, once one of the chief commercial ports of the Mediter-ranean in the days of Roman domination, and previously one of the most important Greek cities of the region, and now not much more than a fishing village, the fishing fleet goes out each year for a fishing season in the waters of Santa Marinella. The villagers help the fishermen with their nets and it is the custom for the fishermen to prepare, at sea, a delicious fish soup, which they share with the villagers. This is a soup you won't be able to make at home, one you won't be able to taste, unless you happen one day to be lucky enough to join this fishing fleet during their summer migration from Pozzuoli to Santa Marinella. But imagine the scene, the rough old-fashioned stove on board the boat, the earthenware pot in which, with plenty of water, an assortment of freshly caught and cleaned fish is placed, with a few tomatoes, a clove or two of garlic, a few spoonfuls of oil, and a coarsely chopped red pepper; cooked together for twenty minutes or so, then served in earthenware soup plates, with lumps of home-baked bread brought by the villagers to the fishing fleet.

ZUPPA DI PESCE ALLA GENOVESE

Genoese Fish Soup

2 lb. of assorted flat and shell fish, cut in pieces; use heads, skins and bones to make stock with 2 pints of water,	bay leaf and a few peppercorns 2 tablespoons oil 1 or 2 stalks celery 2 tablespoons dry white wine	2 anchovies 1 clove garlic 1 medium sized onion 1 tablespoon chopped parsley 1 pint cleaned mussels

Heat the oil and in it brown the chopped onion, add the chopped celery and parsley, and the anchovies cut small, the crushed clove of garlic and the wine and cook together 2 or 3 minutes; add the prepared fish, with the exception of the mussels and the stock, and cook together for 20 minutes; about 12 minutes before serving, add strained stock, bring to boil, add cleaned mussels and continue to cook until all are opened, then serve the soup immediately with slices of crisp toast or freshly fried bread.

ZUPPA DI PESCE ALLA SIRACUSANA

Fish Soup as Prepared in Syracuse

2 lb. assorted fish, using heads, skins and bones to make 2 pints stock 1 medium sized onion	1 clove crushed garlic 1 stalk celery 2 tablespoons oil salt and pepper	1 tablespoon chopped parsley 1 bay leaf 4 or 6 tomatoes 1 gill white wine

This is a dish cooked in the oven. Boil heads skins and bones in 2 pints water to make stock. Strain. Then in a fireproof casserole, large enough to hold the entire mixture, place your prepared fish, cut small, together with the chopped onion, parsley, bay leaf, celery cut small, tomatoes skinned and cut up, crushed garlic, oil, wine and sufficient of the prepared fish stock to cover well. Season with salt and pepper, put the lid of the casserole on, weight it down if necessary to ensure a tight fit, and place in a moderate oven for 40 minutes. Before serving, remove the bay leaf. Serve with toasted or fried bread.

STRACCIATELLA

2 eggs	2 teaspoons fine semo-	1 tablespoon grated
1½ pints chicken broth	lina	Parmesan

Beat eggs, and blend with semolina and cheese, add a cup of cold broth, and beat well. Bring the remainder of the broth to the boil, and slowly add the egg mixture, beating with a fork or whisk; allow to cook slowly for 4 or 5 minutes before serving. The eggs will appear as little flakes or 'rags' in the soup.

PASTA

The Italian term pasta covers a multitude of various shapes and forms of what we in England tend to lump together in our minds under the heading of macaroni or spaghetti.

A word first of all about the various types of pasta to be met with in Italy. Starting with the fine string-like vermicelli, too fine to have a bore through its centre, the tubular types come in all widths, from the regular and familiar macaroni and spaghetti, to the 3-inch lengths of cannelloni, ¾ inch in diameter which, after a preliminary cooking in boiling water are stuffed and re-cooked in various ways, and served with sauce or cheese and butter.

There are the fancy shapes of pasta: shells, elbows, cartwheels, twists, even alphabet letters, and there are the various flat types: the narrow noodles, the broader tagliatelli, progressing to the broad lasagne, and there are also the tiny rice-type grains known as pastina, and small star-shapes used as a garnish for soups. The variety is infinite and the possibilities of cooking the various types into tempting dishes are endless.

HOME-MADE PASTA

Although there are excellent commercial brands of pasta in the various shapes and sizes, if you are a good pastry maker and have time to experiment, you may care to try your hand at making pasta. If you do, remember that the cooking time for the home-made variety is considerably less than that required for the packaged types — 5 to 7 minutes is all that is necessary.

You will need a fairly large pastry board, and a longer than usual rolling pin.

The following quantities will give you sufficient tagliatelle, the most usual type of home-made pasta, for six people:

1 lb. flour	pinch salt	lukewarm water
	3 eggs	

Pile flour in a mound on your pastry board, making a well in the middle into which break the eggs, adding salt, and a couple of tablespoons o lukewarm water. Fold the flour over the eggs and water and knead until the liquid is used up. If the paste is too stiff, add a little more water, but be careful not to 'drown' it. When the paste can be formed into a fairly solid ball, its consistency is right. Now knead it for at least 10 minutes flouring your hands lightly from time to time, and flouring the board, then, divide it into 2 portions. Each will need quite 10 rollings and the board and roller should be lightly floured each time. Finally it should be thin enough. Spread a floured cloth over the back of a chair and lay the pasta over it while you proceed similarly with the other half. When both sheets are rolled thin, leave them to dry out for 30 minutes, after which roll them up as you would a Swiss roll, or pinwheel biscuit mixture. With a sharp knife cut across the roll at intervals of a quarter of an inch or less. Lay them on a floured cloth until you are ready to cook your tagliatelle and remember, 5 to 7 minutes in boiling salted water will be ample.

SPAGHETTI CON SALSA DI VONGOLE
Spaghetti with Clam Sauce

1 lb. spaghetti. When cooked and drained pour over it hot clam sauce (see p. 395) and serve with or without grated Parmesan cheese.

SOUFFLÉ OF TAGLIATELLE

1 lb. tagliatelle	salt and pepper	¾ pint milk
1½ teaspoons flour	pinch nutmeg	6 tablespoons grated
3 oz. butter	3—4 eggs	Parmesan

The home-made pasta made with eggs is preferable for this, though the commercially made spaghetti may be used. Cook in boiling salted water in the approved manner, remembering that the bought variety will need 10 to 12 minutes, the home-made only 5 minutes.

Melt butter in a saucepan, and before it begins to turn brown, blend in the flour and add milk slowly. Stir until it thickens and allow to cook over boiling water for a further 12 to 15 minutes, season with salt, pepper, nutmeg and the grated Parmesan, mix well and remove from the heat. Separate eggs, beat yolks lightly and add to the sauce when it has cooled a little, otherwise the yolks may curdle. Whip egg whites stiff and fold into the sauce. Combine the cooked and drained tagliatelle with the sauce, slowly, to ensure it is really well mixed. Place in a buttered soufflé dish and cook in moderate oven for 20 minutes. Serve in the dish in which it is cooked.

TAGLIATELLE ALLA CREMA

1 lb. tagliatelle	2 tablespoons flour	pinch nutmeg
8 tablespoons grated Parmesan	3 eggs	pinch salt
	4 oz. butter	1 pint milk

Place 4 tablespoons of the grated cheese with the flour in a saucepan and mix slowly with the milk and a pinch of salt and nutmeg. Place on a slow heat and stir with a wooden spoon until it thickens, add a nut of butter and blend well, then remove from the fire, add the remainder of the butter and the balance of the grated cheese and finally, when it has cooled a trifle, the beaten yolks of the 3 eggs. Whip the egg whites separately and fold in. Add the cooked and drained tagliatelle to the sauce, place in a greased earthenware or oven-glass dish, and allow to cook in a medium oven for 15 minutes.

SPAGHETTI WITH BUTTER AND CHEESE

One of the simplest and at the same time one of the most delicious macaroni dishes this, and one for which any of the various forms of pasta may be employed.

For each person allow:

1 tablespoon or more of grated Parmesan cheese	3 to 4 oz. pasta	1 really generous lump good butter

When pasta is cooked, blanched and drained, stir the butter and cheese into it, allow to melt and serve immediately, handing at the same time a dish of the grated cheese so that more may be added at will.

SPAGHETTI WITH MEAT BALLS

1 lb. spaghetti or macaroni	1 tablespoon brown sugar	2 thick slices white bread
1 small onion	good pinch oregano or pinch dried thyme	1 small onion
1 or 2 cloves garlic, crushed		1 tablespoon chopped parsley
3 tablespoons olive oil	salt and pepper	3 oz. grated Parmesan
1 large can tomatoes		1 egg
1 tablespoon tomato purée	*Meat Balls:*	salt and pepper
½ pint water	1 lb. minced lean beef	fat for frying

Soak the bread in water, squeeze dry and mash with a fork, and to it add the onion chopped finely, the parsley, minced beef, cheese and seasoning. Beat the egg lightly and combine with the mixture; shape into small balls — this amount should make about 12 — and fry in hot fat. Drain and set aside. Heat the oil in a heavy pan, add chopped onion and crushed garlic and cook till golden; add strained tomatoes, tomato purée thinned down with a little water, the balance of the ½ pint water, sugar, oregano, pepper and salt; lower heat, cover and cook slowly for an hour. At the end of an hour, add the meat balls, cover the pan once more and allow to cook slowly for another 30 minutes before serving over the freshly cooked spaghetti. With this dish hand a bowl of freshly grated Parmesan.

Two Typically Sicilian Recipes

SPAGHETTI WITH ANCHOVIES

1 lb. spaghetti or 'shells'	1 small can anchovies (about a dozen fillets)	8 tablespoons grated Parmesan cheese
just under 1 gill good olive oil		salt and pepper
		1 clove garlic

Heat oil in a heavy frying pan, and when hot add garlic, crushed, and fry until it is brown, then remove. Chop anchovies into short lengths, add to hot oil and cook for a couple of minutes, stirring with a wooden spoon. Add plenty of black pepper, but add salt with caution, remembering the saltiness of anchovies. Add this to a dish of cooked and drained spaghetti, topping with the grated Parmesan cheese, and serve immediately.

SPAGHETTI WITH OIL AND GARLIC

2 SERVINGS

8 oz. spaghetti	at least 2 cloves garlic, crushed	generous pinch basil
4 tablespoons best olive oil	grated Parmesan	salt and pepper

While spaghetti is cooking, heat the oil in a heavy pan, add crushed garlic and basil, and cook for two or three minutes to allow the oil to become thoroughly impregnated with the flavour of the garlic. When the spaghetti has been cooked and drained, pile in a heated dish, add the oil and garlic mixture, blend well, and serve with freshly ground black pepper, salt and generous helpings of freshly grated Parmesan.

Note. It is possible to purchase a garlic crusher, made on the principle of a potato ricer, which enables a few drops of garlic juice to be added to a dish rather than a too coarsely chopped clove. These presses are not cheap, but in labour-saving and flavour refinement are a worthwhile investment.

MACARONI WITH BROCCOLI

1 lb. elbow macaroni	grated Parmesan	salt
1 gill olive oil	1 lb. young broccoli	

While the macaroni is cooking, clean the broccoli, break into small pieces, and cook 10 minutes in boiling salted water. Heat oil, in a heavy frying pan, add drained broccoli, and fry lightly for 3 or 4 minutes. Grease a casserole, sprinkle with grated Parmesan. Pile into this the cooked and drained macaroni, and over it pour the broccoli and oil. Mix well. Sprinkle with more grated Parmesan, and place in a hot oven for 5 minutes. Serve very hot.

SPAGHETTI WITH FRESH FENNEL SAUCE

1 lb. spaghetti	1 tablespoon pine nuts	1 lb. fresh sardines,
4 tablespoons olive oil	or blanched almonds	pilchards or sprats
½ pint cold water	1 lb. fennel	1 tablespoon sultanas
6 oz. dried bread-	1 large or 2 small	or seedless raisins
crumbs	onions	salt and pepper

Clean and bone fish. Clean fennel and cook for 15 minutes in about 2 pints of boiling water. Drain and chop small. Heat olive oil in a saucepan and cook in it the chopped onion until it is a golden colour, add fish, cook gently for 10 minutes, stirring frequently; add fennel sultanas and nuts, cold water and seasoning and allow to simmer gently for 10 minutes. Place breadcrumbs on a fireproof plate below a hot grill for a few seconds to brown. Meanwhile cook the spaghetti. When cooked and drained, place in deep, warmed dish, pour over half the fish and fennel sauce and half the breadcrumbs and mix well. Then pile on balance of fennel mixture and top with remainder of bread-crumbs and serve very hot.

SPAGHETTI BOLOGNESE

12 oz. spaghetti	4 oz. minced beef	1 gill white wine
1 onion, sliced	2 rashers streaky	½ pint stock
1 carrot, sliced	bacon	1 clove garlic
1 stick celery, chopped	2 oz. chicken liver,	3 oz. butter
1 dessertspoon concen-	chopped	4 oz. grated cheese
trated tomato purée		salt and pepper

Melt 1 oz. butter, cook the onion in it until soft, add the bacon cut into small pieces, the carrot and the celery. When these are brown put in the beef and stir so that all the pieces are coated with fat. Add the liver, stirring in the same way. Put in the tomato purée, the wine and the stock. Season with salt, pepper and crushed garlic. Simmer for 40 minutes. Cook the spaghetti. Stir the sauce into it with 2 oz. butter and the grated cheese.

BAKED MACARONI WITH SOUR CREAM

8 oz. elbow macaroni	½ pint sour cream	salt and pepper to
4 eggs	12 oz. finely chopped	taste
	cooked ham	

Cook and drain macaroni. Separate eggs. Beat yolks and to them add cream, salt and chopped ham. Add drained macaroni. Pile into buttered casserole. Whip egg whites stiffly and fold into mixture. Bake 30 minutes in moderate oven.

SPAGHETTI WITH TOMATO SAUCE

12 oz. spaghetti	1 lb. tomatoes, peeled	1 clove garlic, chopped
1 tablespoon olive oil	and quartered	basil (fresh or dried)
1 onion, sliced	4 oz. Parmesan cheese	salt and pepper

Cook the spaghetti. Mix with the sauce just before serving, stirring in 2 oz. melted butter and the grated cheese.

The Sauce:

Cook the onion with the garlic in the olive oil. When it is soft and transparent, add the tomatoes, a little basil, salt and pepper. Simmer for 30 minutes, sieve. Add sugar if the tomatoes are not very ripe.

ELBOW MACARONI PIE

12 oz. elbow macaroni	8 oz. cooked meat,	short crust pastry
¾ pint tomato sauce	chopped finely	(see p. 100),
(see above)	4 tablespoons grated	enough to line and
2 eggs	Parmesan	cover casserole

Grease an earthenware or oven-glass casserole and line with pastry. Mix together cooked macaroni, tomato sauce, cheese and chopped meat and lay on top of pastry. Beat eggs lightly and pour over the mixture. Cover with pastry, and bake in moderate oven for half an hour, or until crust is brown. Serve hot. This, with a simple salad, makes a sustaining meal.

RAVIOLI

Once you have become expert in the art of making tagliatelle at home, (see p. 360) you may use the same recipe for ravioli, agnolotti, anolini, tortellini, or cappelletti, to give a few of the various names given to the many types of filled pasta. But when the paste has been rolled as thin as possible (remember, thin enough for you to be able to read the newspaper—or at least the headlines—through it), instead of rolling it into a roll, as when making tagliatelle, keep it in two large, flat sheets, or, if the pastry board is on the small size, a greater number of small sheets of thin pasta.

As each sheet is rolled to the desired thinness, spread it on a clean cloth, and keep it covered with another cloth, to prevent it going crusty and becoming too breakable to handle.

When the pasta is made and the filling you intend using is prepared, spread a sheet of the pasta on to a floured pastry board, and dot with the filling at regular intervals of about 1½ to 2 inches. Cover lightly with the second sheet of pasta, after having brushed the 'walks' between the lines of filling with beaten egg so that the second sheet of pasta will close down over the filling. Then use either a small round cutter, or run a pastry wheel between the fillings, so that there is a series of little filled envelopes of pasta. Transfer these to a floured dish, being careful not to let them overlap and cover with a floured cloth or paper until they are needed.

Ravioli Fillings:

SPINACH FILLING

8 oz. each of cooked puréed spinach and chopped chicken or veal (cooked)	4 tablespoons grated Parmesan cheese	1 heaped tablespoon finely chopped parsley
2 oz. breadcrumbs	2 eggs	salt and freshly
	½ clove garlic, crushed	ground black pepper

Mix dry ingredients and blend together with lightly beaten eggs. Drop in teaspoonfuls at regular intervals on one sheet of pasta, cover with second sheet and press together gently around each mound of filling. Cut into squares with pastry cutter, and cook in boiling salted water in deep saucepan for 5 or 6 minutes, or until the envelopes of pasta rise to the top of the boiling water. Transfer carefully with perforated spoon to a hot dish, serve with tomato sauce (see p. 365), and a bowl of freshly grated Parmesan cheese.

CHEESE FILLING

5 oz. each grated Parmesan and Gruyère	2 eggs	pinch thyme
	pinch nutmeg	salt and pepper
	½ pint milk	

Blend all together, place in spoonfuls on a sheet of pasta as directed in previous recipe, cover with second sheet, press down, cut with pastry cutter and cook in boiling, salted water as previously directed. Serve with melted butter and additional grated Parmesan.

MEAT FILLING

8 oz. each raw minced beef and raw minced veal
2 tablespoons olive oil
1 oz. grated Parmesan

1 tablespoon finely chopped parsley
1 gill cooking sherry, or preferably Marsala

1 egg
salt and pepper
clove crushed garlic, (optional)

Heat oil in a heavy pan, add garlic and chopped meat, and allow to cook for 5 or 6 minutes, add the wine, and cook for another 20 minutes. Cool, then add the beaten egg, Parmesan and seasonings; blend well, and use as a filling for ravioli, or for capelletti (little hats), which are 2½-inch rounds of ravioli pasta, in the centre of which is placed a teaspoon of filling, after which the pasta is folded over and sealed at the edges with a fork.

CREAM CHEESE FILLING

1 lb. cottage cheese
4 oz. grated Parmesan
1 whole egg

1 egg yolk
2 tablespoons finely chopped parsley

freshly grated black pepper and salt
pinch nutmeg

Blend well together and use as directed for previous ravioli fillings. Serve with melted butter.

CHICKEN FILLING

4 oz. cold boiled chicken, chopped finely
4 oz. finely chopped cold cooked veal or pork
nutmeg

1 egg
½ clove crushed garlic (optional)
salt and pepper to taste

8 oz. spinach purée
4 tablespoons bread-crumbs
2 tablespoons grated Parmesan

Mix ingredients together, blend with the beaten egg and use as directed for previous ravioli fillings.

CANNELLONI (TO PREPARE)

Although it is possible to buy the large 'channel' macaroni and, after a preliminary cooking, to fill them with the filling mixture, the home-made variety is far preferable, and once again the recipe for pasta given under Tagliatelle may be used (see p. 360). But when it has had its final rolling, it must be cut into oblongs about 4 inches by 3 inches, and cooked, a few at a time, in boiling salted water for 4 or 5 minutes, removed gently with a perforated spoon, and allowed to cool. For four people, allow 20 to 24 cannelloni.

CANNELLONI

| tagliatelle pasta | béchamel sauce | grated Parmesan |
| (see p. 360) | (see p. 256) | meat or spinach filling |

Make a spinach or meat filling, as for Ravioli (see p. 366, 367.) Place a tablespoonful in the centre of each piece of pasta, and roll up into a tube. Grease a fireproof dish well and put the cannelloni in it, side by side. Cover with béchamel sauce and bake in a moderate oven for 15 minutes. Serve with the grated Parmesan cheese.

LASAGNE VERDI

These are the pale green strips of pasta, cut in oblongs as large as 3 inches by 2 inches, and although it is possible and permissible to use in their place the green ribbon noodles obtainable in most shops that sell pasta, you may, if you are successful with your home-made tagliatelle, wish to experiment with this refinement of pasta.

For six people, the quantities are the same as those for tagliatelle, except that instead of lukewarm water for mixing, you need 3 oz. puréed spinach (weighed after, not before, cooking).

Start with 1 lb. of flour heaped on a board, with a well in the centre into which you break 3 eggs. After blending these with the flour, work in the spinach, and proceed with kneading, rolling, drying and cutting as for the tagliatelle, except that instead of cutting the pasta into strips, it is cut into rather large, flat oblongs. Using either home-made oblongs of lasagne, or 1 lb. of bought green noodles, you can make one of the most famous pasta dishes of all:

LASAGNE AL FORNO

2 tablespoons olive oil	salt and pepper	12 oz. to 1 lb. Mozza-
1 lb. minced beef	1 tablespoon tomato	rella or Bel Paese
1 medium sized onion,	purée	cheese
chopped finely	1 lb. lasagne or green	3 tablespoons grated
1 crushed clove garlic	noodles	Parmesan
	1 pint water	

Heat oil in a heavy frying pan, add the onion and garlic, and when slightly browned, add and brown the minced meat. Blend the tomato purée with a little water, pepper and salt, dilute with the balance of the water and pour slowly over the meat; cover and allow to simmer gently for 1½ hours. Take 1 lb. lasagne and cook in rapidly boiling salted water, 5 to 7 minutes if lasagne is home-made, 15 minutes if commercially packaged. Blanch and drain. Grease an oven-glass or earthenware casserole, and in it lay a layer of the cooked lasagne, a layer of meat sauce and a layer of Mozzarella or of Bel Paese. Continue filling the dish

66. Pizza, Italy (p.376)

67. Christmas Ham, Sweden (p.514)

68. Greek Beef Stew (p.329)

69. Smoked Sausages, Germany (p.286)

in layers until all the ingredients are used up, finishing with the balance of the sauce poured over the finished dish, topped with grated Parmesan. Bake for 20 minutes in a moderately hot oven.

LASAGNE IMBOTTITE

Stuffed Noodles

1 medium sized can tomatoes	6 tablespoons grated Parmesan	12 oz. cottage cheese
4 tablespoons hot water	1 tablespoon tomato purée	8 oz. Bel Paese
1 clove garlic, crushed	2 tablespoons olive oil	8 oz. sausages
salt and pepper	1 stick celery, diced	12 oz. lasagne

Heat olive oil in heavy pan and brown garlic for about 3 minutes; blend the tomato purée with hot water, and add to garlic, together with diced celery and tomatoes; after about 3 minutes, lower heat and allow to simmer for 1 hour. Season with pepper and salt. Fry sausages in separate pan until brown, and cut into small pieces. Boil lasagne in boiling salted water as previously directed (see p. 368). Drain. Into a greased casserole place alternate layers of lasagne, tomato sauce, Parmesan, more sauce, Bel Paese, sausage and more sauce, finishing with a layer of sauce topped with grated cheese. Bake in moderate oven 20 minutes. Serve the balance of tomato sauce and grated Parmesan separately.

GNOCCHI

Although Gnocchi is placed at the end of the various forms of pasta it is about the easiest form to make at home, for it requires neither rolling nor filling and consists merely of little rolls, croquettes or circles of pasta, various recipes for which follow.

SEMOLINA GNOCCHI

1¼ pints milk	3 or 4 oz. grated	1½ oz. butter
yolks of 2 eggs	Parmesan	pinch nutmeg
	8 oz. semolina	

Heat milk, and add semolina slowly, stirring constantly and cooking slowly until thick. Remove from fire, add beaten yolks of eggs, grated cheese and butter and seasoning and mix well. Rinse a flat dish with cold water and on it spread the semolina to a thickness of ½ inch. Leave for an hour, and when cold, cut with a knife rinsed under the tap, into squares or rounds.

GNOCCHI ALLA ROMANA

Having prepared your gnocchi according to the foregoing instructions, butter a fireproof dish and in it lay a layer of gnocchi, sprinkled with grated Parmesan and dotted with butter. Add a second and a third layer, with Parmesan and dots of butter between each. When the last of the gnocchi are used up, sprinkle with more Parmesan and over the whole pour 1 oz. melted butter. Place dish in moderate oven for 20 minutes or until the gnocchi have taken on a golden colour. Serve in the dish in which they were cooked. Garnish with parsley. *(Illustrated in Plate 71.)*

PLAIN RISOTTO

12 to 15 tablespoons Piedmont or Patna rice, quantity depending on number of servings

2 medium sized onions, chopped small

2 tablespoons best olive oil, or a mixture of oil and butter or 2 oz. of butter

about 1½ pints stock, preferably chicken or substitute a gill white wine for equal quantity of stock

pinch saffron

Heat the oil or butter in a heavy pan, add the onion, chopped small, and allow to cook until it is a golden yellow but *not* brown. Add the rice *dry*, and cook slowly together for a few minutes, stirring with a wooden spoon, until the grains are almost transparent. Now begin adding your stock which is added in very small quantities a few tablespoons at a time, and the risotto is stirred frequently to prevent sticking. When the first instalment of the stock is absorbed, add the next and so on until the rice has finished cooking, and most if not all of the stock has been used. This should take from 25 to 30 minutes. Test the rice and when it is tender and the dish looks creamy but is not sticky, the risotto is ready for the table. The grains, though tender, should still be separate. To give your risotto a truly Milanese appearance it should be coloured a primrose yellow with saffron, at the end of the cooking time. If you are using the filaments—take 2 or 3 of these, and having pounded them to a powder and allowed them to steep 5 minutes or so in a little warmed stock, strain and add them to the rice. If it is powdered, add it, small pinch by small pinch, until the desired colour is obtained.

PLAIN RISOTTO
A somewhat richer version

Proceed as before, but with the addition of white wine, and if you can procure about an ounce of marrow from marrow bones, you will have a really rich dish.

You may also substitute for the white wine a glass of Marsala, but in this case, I would advise against the marrow, as that and the Marsala combined would make the dish over-rich for most palates.

PRAWN RISOTTO

2 dozen prawns or 1 lobster	3 oz. butter 1 small onion salt and pepper	8 oz. rice 4 oz. grated cheese

Cook the rice as for plain risotto. Melt 1 oz. butter and heat the cooked prawns in it. Add them to the rice. Stir in 2 oz. melted butter and the grated cheese. Season with salt and pepper.

RISOTTO WITH SHELLFISH

Make a perfectly plain risotto, but instead of stock made from meat or chicken, use fish stock, or plain water plus a wineglass of white wine. Meanwhile, allowing 5 or 6 scampi or Dublin Bay prawns, or the equivalent quantity of lobster or peeled shrimps per person, sauté the shelled and cut up fish in a little butter to which a little crushed garlic has been added. Towards the end of the cooking of the risotto, add the fish, together with the butter in which it has been cooked. Finally stir in butter and grated Parmesan. *(Illustrated in Plate 78.)*

RISOTTO WITH BRAINS

12 oz. lean veal little beef marrow 12 tablespoons Piedmont rice	4 oz. butter 1½ pints stock 4 tablespoons grated Parmesan	1 calf's brain 1 medium-sized onion 1 tablespoon parsley salt and pepper saffron

Wash the brains in salt and water, remove the skin and fibres and soak brains in salt and water till ready to use. Heat butter in a heavy pan, add chopped onion and allow to cook a few minutes until the onion is golden yellow, add the chopped parsley, chopped veal and marrow and allow to brown for 8 to 10 minutes; add the rice and the stock, little by little. Drain the brains and cut into small pieces, and, when the dish has been cooking for 15 or 20 minutes, add to the risotto and continue cooking until the rice is tender. Just before serving, add the seasonings and the grated Parmesan.

MUSHROOM RISOTTO

2 SERVINGS

1 rasher streaky bacon	12 oz. mushrooms	nutmeg
2 oz. butter	6 medium sized	salt and pepper
2 medium sized	tomatoes	4 to 6 oz cold, lean
onions	¾ pint stock	meat
6 oz. rice	grated Parmesan	1 tablespoon sultanas

Cut the bacon small and fry lightly in the butter, remove from pan, and add to the pan the chopped onions, frying them for 2 or 3 minutes. Add the rice and cook gently until it is transparent — about 5 minutes — add all the mushrooms except about 2 tablespoons for garnishing; add sliced and peeled tomatoes, pepper, salt and a little grated nutmeg and replace bacon in pan. Add the stock in small instalments, stirring the risotto from time to time to prevent the rice sticking to the bottom of the pan. 10 minutes before serving, add the cold meat, chopped small, and the sultanas, together with the remainder of the mushrooms which have been cut in small pieces and sautéed in a little butter. The rice should be cooked in about 30 minutes from the time it was added to the dish. Serve with grated Parmesan.

RISOTTO GENOVESE

Rice in the Genoese Style

For this dish the rice is first of all parboiled. Cook 12 oz. of rice in boiling, salted water in a large pan but remove and drain a few minutes before it is completely cooked, and when drained, turn it into a clean saucepan. To it add the following sauce, plus a generous lump of butter, cooking together and stirring to avoid sticking, for 5 minutes or until the rice has finished cooking. Serve with a bowlful of freshly grated Parmesan cheese.

Sauce for Risotto Genovese

8 oz. raw lean meat, beef or veal, minced	butter for frying	chopped parsley
	2 or 3 carrots, washed and diced	pinch oregano or thyme
2 or 3 stalks celery, washed and cut fine	1 medium onion, chopped	1 gill white wine
		salt and pepper

Sauté the vegetables in butter until a golden colour; add the meat and allow to brown, stirring to prevent sticking. Add the wine, and cook fairly rapidly until the liquid has diminished by half, then cover and simmer for an hour, when the sauce should have the consistency of syrup.

CHICKEN RISOTTO

If you have some left-over boiled chicken, remove any skin, and cut the meat into small pieces.

1 lb. chopped chicken
1 medium sized onion
1 clove garlic, crushed
4 oz. mushrooms
¼ pint chicken stock; and 1 extra pint

1 oz. butter
chopped parsley
12 oz. rice
2 peeled tomatoes
1 small carrot
1 stalk celery

2 tablespoons chopped lean ham or gammon
1 gill white wine
salt and pepper
grated Parmesan
extra butter

Sauté the chopped onion, garlic, celery and chopped carrot in butter. After 5 minutes add the chopped mushrooms, and the tomatoes cut small; allow to cook together for a couple of minutes, then stir in the chopped chicken, chopped ham and the wine. Increase the heat for a couple of minutes more; add the seasonings; stir in the stock, cover the pan and allow to cook slowly for 30 minutes before adding the rice. Proceed as for an ordinary risotto, using chicken stock or water for further moistening during the cooking of the rice. Finally stir in grated Parmesan and a generous portion of butter.

RICE AND PEAS AS SERVED IN VENICE

'Risi e Bisi'

2 SERVINGS

3 lb. peas weighed before shelling
1 lb. rice
2 tablespoons butter

2½ to 3 pints hot meat stock
1 tablespoon olive oil
2 tablespoons Parmesan

1 tablespoon lard
2 tablespoons finely chopped parsley
2 spring onions
extra Parmesan

Shell and wash peas. Heat oil, half the butter and the lard in heavy pan add finely chopped onions and parsley and cook gently. Add peas and allow to cook long enough to absorb fat. Then add just enough hot meat stock to cover and allow to bubble before adding rice, having done this, add a further ¾ pint heated stock and cook gently without stirring for 25 or 30 minutes until rice is cooked. Then stir in remaining butter and 2 tablespoons of grated Parmesan and serve with grated Parmesan. This dish should not be allowed to become too dry in the cooking.

RICE SOUFFLÉ WITH CHICKEN LIVERS

8 oz. rice	4 eggs	2 tablespoons grated
4 oz. butter	2 pints chicken stock	Parmesan
8 oz. chicken livers		1 gill Marsala

Cook the rice for 20 minutes in the chicken stock, then stir in the cheese, butter and the chicken livers which have been cut in strips, floured lightly and fried in a little butter and the Marsala. Allow the mixture to cool, and then stir in the beaten yolks of the eggs and mix well. Beat the egg whites stiff, and fold into the mixture. Grease a soufflé dish, line it with buttered paper, and pour in soufflé mixture. Cook in a moderate oven for about 15 minutes.

ARANGINI

Often when a train has stopped at a small station in Italy or Sicily, the attendant wheeling the *Tavola Calda,* the trolley containing hot food to be consumed on the train, makes his way down the platform to the accompaniment of the cry *Aran-g-e-e-e-e-ni.* The hardy traveller who takes a chance on this typically Italian tit-bit is handed a piece of brown paper, containing a warm mound of rice, the colour of a pale orange. The best way of eating it is out of the paper, using the paper later as a napkin to wipe mouth and hands.

To make 8 of these 'delicacies', you will need the following ingredients:

1 lb. rice	pinch salt	2 hard-boiled eggs
4 tablespoons grated	12 oz. lean minced	breadcrumbs
Parmesan	beef	oil for deep frying
1 beaten egg	2 tablespoons chopped	
1 tablespoon olive oil	parsley	

Cook the rice in boiling, salted water, drain and mix with half the beaten egg. Heat the olive oil in a heavy pan, brown the minced meat in this, remove from the heat and mix with grated cheese, parsley and chopped hard-boiled eggs. Rinse the hands in cold water, take a handful of cooked rice, and in the centre of this place a generous portion of the mixture, closing the rice up to encase it and form a ball. Repeat this until all the rice and all the filling is used up. Dip the balls in the balance of the beaten egg, coat with fine breadcrumbs and fry in deep, hot oil until they have taken on a light golden brown colour. A few left-over cooked spring peas are a welcome addition to the other ingredients. The above recipe makes a delicious dish for home consumption, that is good with hot tomato sauce (see p. 365).

POLENTA

One more of the farinaceous foods beloved by Italians is the yellow maize flour, known as polenta, which can be obtained in Italian provision shops in this country. It can be bought either finely or coarsely ground. To cook sufficient polenta for four people, take 6—8 oz. of the finely ground variety. Bring a pint of water to the boil in a fairly large saucepan, and to this add the polenta and cook slowly for about 20 minutes, stirring all the time. At the end of this time it should be thick and smooth.

Spread it on a large plate that has been rinsed with cold water, allow to cool, and then either cut it into slices, or with floured hands form it into little dumplings the size of a small egg.

The following are one or two ways in which the cooked product may be used.

BATUFFOLI AL SUGO

Prepare 8 oz. finely ground polenta as directed, and when cool form into little dumplings. Butter a fireproof dish, and in it place a layer of these dumplings. When the first layer is completed, cover with a meat sauce (see p. 395), sprinkle generously with grated Parmesan; on top place a second layer, continuing the layers until the dumplings are all used. Sprinkle little dabs of butter on the top layer, and a generous sprinkling of grated Parmesan; place in a hot oven for a few moments to allow the cheese to melt and serve very hot.

POLENTA AND CHEESE

Cook 8 oz. polenta as previously directed, spreading on a moistened dish or a marble slab to cool. Cut into slices and lay these in a buttered fireproof dish, sprinkling generous helpings of grated Parmesan between the layers, and seasoning with salt and a little cayenne. Cover top layer with grated cheese and a little butter, and bake in a hot oven until brown. Serve very hot.

POLENTA WITH TOMATO SAUCE

½ pint hot water	oil for frying	salt and pepper to
½ pint milk	1 egg	taste
8 oz. finely ground	fine breadcrumbs	8 tablespoons grated
polenta		Parmesan

Cook the polenta for 30 minutes in a double boiler in the hot water and milk which have been mixed and brought to the boil. At the last minute stir in cheese and seasonings, and stir until thoroughly mixed. Spread on a moistened dish to cool.

Beat the egg and when the polenta is cold, cut into slices, dip in egg and breadcrumbs and fry in hot olive oil until brown. Serve hot with tomato sauce (see p. 365).

SARTÙ

Rice does not appear on the Neapolitan menu nearly as frequently as do the various types of pasta, but there is one rice dish that is a speciality of Naples, and that, in spite of the length of time required for its preparation, is well worth trying. For six people you will need the following:

12 oz. of rice
8 oz. minced lean beef
1 egg plus 1 egg yolk
1 clove garlic, crushed
salt and pepper
chopped parsley
2 1-inch crustless slices
  bread
flour

oil or lard for frying
about 8 oz. cooked
  green peas
4 oz. Bel Paese cheese
little milk
4 oz. fresh mushrooms
cut in small pieces or
½ oz. of dried
  mushrooms, soaked
  in warm water for
  few minutes

turkey or chicken
  giblets
1 small onion
1 chopped carrot
8 oz. Italian sausage
meat sauce
  (see p. 395)
5 tablespoons grated
  Parmesan
crisp breadcrumbs
1 bay leaf (optional)

Combine minced lean beef, the bread — soaked in a little milk and squeezed dry — the garlic and chopped parsley with the beaten egg and egg yolk, together with the seasonings. Form into small balls or rissoles, and fry in hot oil until brown on both sides. Meanwhile cook rice in boiling, salted water and drain well. Cook the giblets with the exception of the liver, in a little water, with the chopped carrot and onion, for at least 2 hours, adding a bay leaf. 10 or 15 minutes before the end of this time, add the liver and the sliced mushrooms. Butter a fireproof soufflé dish, and sprinkle crisp breadcrumbs over the bottom and sides. Arrange about ¾ of the boiled rice in a layer covering the bottom and the sides of the soufflé dish, and in it put the meat balls, the giblets cut into pieces, the mushrooms, peas and the sausage cut in pieces. Over this pour the gravy from the giblets and sufficient meat sauce to moisten. Cut the cheese in small pieces and arrange on top, and finally cover with the balance of the boiled rice, and pour over a little more of the meat and tomato sauce, so that the dish is moist but not 'mushy'. Sprinkle with a fairly heavy layer of crisp breadcrumbs and the grated Parmesan cheese. Bake in a moderate oven for 30 minutes.

PIZZA

4 oz. flour
½ oz. yeast
4 tomatoes

6 anchovy fillets
3 oz. Bel Paese cheese
basil

1 tablespoon olive oil
salt
water

Put the flour in a bowl, add a pinch of salt. Mix the yeast with a little warm water. Put the yeast into the flour and mix well. Add enough warm water (about a gill) to make a stiff dough. Knead it thoroughly, until the dough becomes elastic. Put it in a warm place, covered with a cloth until it has doubled its size. Roll the dough out on a floured board. It should be ¼-inch thick. Peel the tomatoes, and chop them into small pieces, cut the cheese into thin slices, halve the anchovies. Put the pizza dough on to a baking tin, cover it with tomatoes, sprinkle with basil and a little oil and put into a hot oven to bake for 25 minutes. Lav the cheese over the top, arrange the anchovies in a criss-cross fashion and bake for another 5 minutes. (*Illustrated in Plate 66.*)

PIZZA ALLA CAMPOFRANCO

8 SERVINGS

8 oz. plain flour	5 oz. butter	8 oz. Bel Paese cheese
5 eggs	1 teaspoon chopped	1 lb. tomatoes
½ tablespoon sugar	basil	1 tablespoon olive oil
4 oz. ham	½ oz. brewers' yeast	pepper
	3 tablespoons grated	
	Parmesan	

Pile the flour on to pastry board or cooking table, make a hollow in it and in this put the butter, two eggs, a pinch of salt and the yeast diluted with a little water or milk. Work the flour with the hands until the ingredients are absorbed, then blend in the next two eggs, and work the dough until it is elastic to the touch; then add the sugar; work the dough a little more; then place in a warmed basin. Cover with a cloth and leave in a fairly warm place for a couple of hours, or until it has doubled in size.

For the filling; slice the cheese, and the ham; peel the tomatoes and remove the seeds and cook very quickly in oil so they retain their firmness.

When the dough has risen, flour pastry board; divide the dough in two pieces, one slightly larger than the other and roll out into two circles. With the larger one, line a greased pie plate or flan tin, and on it lay first of all a layer of the cheese, then a layer of the cooked tomatoes. Season with salt and pepper and a little basil, and on this place a layer of strips of ham; continue in this way till the filling is all used up, and finish off with a layer of the grated Parmesan. Now beat the fifth egg, and with a brush paint the edges of the dough, and over it place the smaller circle of dough, pressing the edges together so that they remain closed; leave it to rise again in a warm place, for about an hour, then paint the top with the balance of the beaten egg, and cook for 20—25 minutes in a hot oven. Serve hot.

ROAST TUNNY FISH

After our own brief acquaintance with beige-coloured tunny fish in small tins, it is a startling thing to behold one's first piece of 'tunny in the raw', a huge, liver coloured piece of fish on a fishmonger's slab in Naples or the towns of Sicily.

For roast tunny take a fairly thick slice of fresh tunny and place it in an earthenware vessel with 2 tablespoons oil, some chopped parsley, chopped onion, the juice of a lemon, one or two cloves and salt and pepper to taste. Allow it to remain in this marinade for a couple of hours, turning from time to time. Drain, sprinkle with breadcrumbs and bake in the oven for 1 hour or a little longer, basting from time to time with the marinading mixture.

TUNNY AS COOKED IN LIGURIA

1 lb. tunny 'ventresca' cut in thin slices	1 clove garlic, crushed	½ oz. dried mushrooms,
2 anchovies	1 heaped tablespoon chopped fresh	reconstituted by soaking in warm
2 tablespoon olive oil	parsley	water for 10 minutes
½ pint white wine	1 tablespoon flour	juice of ½ lemon
knob butter	salt and pepper	

Heat the oil, add the flour, then slowly add the wine, the anchovies pounded to a paste and the other ingredients, except for the fish; allow to cook together for 10 minutes, stirring frequently. Add the tunny fish, and pepper and salt to taste; cover the pan, and lower the heat, allowing to cook slowly for 45 minutes. Remove the fish to a hot dish, and to the sauce add a piece of butter the size of a walnut, and the juice of ½ lemon; bring this to boiling point and pour over the fish and serve hot.

ANGUILLA ALLA FERRARESE

Eels as Served in Ferrara

1½ lb. eels, cleaned and cut into 1-inch slices	1 bay leaf butter	1 egg, lightly beaten breadcrumbs
1 gill white wine	pinch mixed spice pinch thyme	salt and pepper nutmeg (optional)

Having prepared the eels, place in a casserole and over them pour the wine mixed with the spices and herbs; add the bay leaf. Cover and cook in a moderate oven for 45 minutes. At the end of that time, lift the eels from the sauce, drain, dip in oiled butter, then in beaten egg and breadcrumbs flavoured with a little nutmeg, and fry brown on both sides in hot butter.

GRILLED SCALLOPS

4 scallops
2 tablespoons olive oil

1 tablespoon chopped
  parsley
½ onion, chopped

1 clove garlic
salt and pepper

Remove the coral and grill the lightly oiled scallops under a hot flame for 5—10 minutes. Slice the coral, mix it with the remaining oil, onion, parsley and crushed garlic. Simmer gently until onion is tender. Pour over the scallops. Season with salt and pepper, and re-heat.

TRIGLIE ALLA LIGURE

Red Mullet as Cooked in Liguria

4 medium sized red
  mullet
1 tablespoon chopped
  parsley
2 anchovies cut in
  small pieces

1 tablespoon olive oil
½ pint tomato sauce
  (see p. 365)
1 chopped onion

½ oz. dried mushrooms
  soaked
in warm water
1 gill white wine
little chopped
  fennel

Heat the oil in a heavy pan and in it place the onion, parsley, fennel and chopped mushrooms and anchovies, and allow to cook together for 5 minutes, then add the tomato sauce and white wine and cook for a further 20 minutes, stirring frequently. Meanwhile clean and prepare the fish and lay them side by side in a flat earthenware dish. Pour sauce over the fish, and cook in a hot oven for 20 minutes.

TRIGLIE ALLA TRIESTINA

Red Mullet as Cooked in Trieste

4 red mullet, medium
  sized

1 gill white wine
1 tablespoon olive oil
juice ½ lemon

1 tablespoon chopped
  capers

Heat together in a heavy pan the oil, lemon juice, capers and wine, and after 10 minutes add the cleaned fish and allow to cook for 20 minutes, turning the fish carefully after 10 minutes. Serve hot.

FRIED SCAMPI

For this you may suit your own particular fancy; allowing 10 or a dozen per person, remove the shells, and fry the fish in any of these three ways:

Dust lightly with flour and fry in hot olive oil, serve with sections of lemon.

Dip first in beaten egg and then in crisp breadcrumbs and fry in hot oil or hot butter and serve with sections of lemon.

Dip in a light frying batter and fry in hot butter, serve with sections of lemon, or with sauce tartare (see p. 256).

SCAMPI ALLA LOMBARDA

Scampi as Cooked in Lombardy

36 to 40 scampi or Dublin Bay prawns	1 clove garlic, crushed 4 cloves	1 tablespoon chopped parsley
1 gill white wine vinegar	½ small onion, chopped small 1 bay leaf	little chopped fennel salt

Mix together all the ingredients except the fish, and cook together for 5 minutes; then add the shelled fish, cover, and cook over a medium heat for 15 or 20 minutes, stirring from time to time. Serve very hot. Shrimps may be substituted for the scampi.

A GENOESE WAY OF COOKING FISH

This method may be used to advantage when cooking cod, trout, carp, eels, mackerel, etc.

After preparing the fish for cooking, lay it in a pan, and cover with the following sauce, allowing it to cook gently for 20 or 30 minutes or until tender.

Fish sauce

1 tablespoon olive oil	salt and pepper	1 tablespoon tomato sauce (see p. 365)
1 chopped onion	1 tablespoon flour	
2 tablespoons white wine	½ pint water or fish stock	1 or 2 anchovies cut small
½ oz. dried mushrooms	juice of ½ lemon	2 oz. butter

Heat the oil and in it brown the onion. Then add the butter, and stir in the flour; slowly add the wine, water and tomato sauce, stirring all the time to make sure the mixture does not stick to the bottom of the pan; add the dried mushrooms, reconstituted in a little warm water and cut small, and the anchovies and seasonings. Cook together for 10 minutes, then pass through a sieve, and use as directed above. Just before serving, remove the fish and keep hot, and add to the sauce the juice of ½ lemon; cook the sauce for a further 2 or 3 minutes and when serving, pour over the cooked fish.

OSTRICHE ALLA VENEZIANA

Oysters, Venetian Style

Allow half a dozen oysters per person; open the fish, loosen them in their shells, and to each add a little of the following mixture, and a few drops of olive oil before grilling under a hot grill. Serve with sections of lemon.

Mixture for oysters

1 tablespoon chopped fresh parsley	1 clove garlic, crushed pinch chopped fresh thyme	pepper to taste 1 tablespoon crisp breadcrumbs
1 stalk celery, chopped finely	olive oil	

PIGS IN BLANKETS

Allow 6 oysters per person, remove from the shells, wrap each oyster in a strip of ham or streaky bacon, and fry in hot butter.

OR WITHOUT BLANKETS

Omitting the wrapping of ham or bacon, dip the shelled oysters first in beaten egg and then in breadcrumbs and fry in hot butter. Serve with sections of lemon.

FRITTO MISTO MARE

Mixed Fried Fish

If you go to Italy and having visited a town on the coast and come away without having eaten at least one dish of Fritto Misto Mare, then you might almost as well have stayed at home. In Venice you will probably be served with a mixture of tiny octopus, not much larger than a hefty house spider, scampi, and minute mullet, all dipped in a light batter and fried in hot oil, drained and served with sections of lemon.

Farther south you may meet some peculiar white circles in your Fritto Misto Mare that have a more than slight resemblance in texture to the pencil eraser of school days. Rubber it isn't, but inkfish it is, and it should previously have undergone a fairly lengthy operation of skinning, having its insides removed, its eyes and ink-bag removed also, and the balance boiled until tender, and this may take up to an hour if you want to avoid that too-great resemblance to pencil eraser texture. When tender, and not before, the inkfish should be cut into rings, and if you're frying your own Fritto Misto Mare, allow 6 of these per person, with the same number of scampi and one or two tiny mullet.

CALAMARI

1 lb. calamari	flour	marjoram
(inkfish, cuttlefish)	oil	salt and pepper
	lemon juice	

Clean the cavities of the inkfish by turning them inside out and washing under running water. Remove the ink bags and the skin and cut the body into narrow rings and the tentacles into strips. Sprinkle with salt, pepper and marjoram and dust lightly with flour. Fry in hot oil for about 10 minutes. If the fish is large and inclined to be tough, it may have to be boiled first; stew gently with tomatoes, onions and garlic.

CALAMARETTI

A dish met with along the Adriatic coast, where baby inkfish are fried whole in butter and are often accompanied by scampi.

CLAMS OR MUSSELS COOKED WITH EGGS

Allow about 1½ pints per person. Before cooking, leave clams in slightly salted water for 2 hours so that they may open and the sand may come out of them. Meanwhile prepare in a heavy pan a *soffritto* of two table-spoons of oil in which you have browned a small chopped onion and a teaspoon of chopped parsley; add the fish and add the beaten yolks of 2 or 3 eggs, depending on the quantity of fish, and the juice of ½ lemon. Stir the mixture, and keep it just below boiling point, and serve as soon as it is well mixed.

CACCIUCCO ALLA TOSCANA

This dish is interesting if an assortment of fish is used. Try the combination of sole with red mullet. Wash and clean fish and wipe dry. In a pan heat a couple of tablespoons of olive oil and in it brown a chopped onion, a crushed clove of garlic and a little chopped parsley; add rather more than 8 oz. fresh tomatoes, peeled and cut in small pieces, pepper and salt; when the tomatoes are cooked, add the juice of ½ lemon, boil for a few minutes longer and then pass through a sieve or a food mill. Return the strained sauce to the pan, and in it cook the fish for 30 minutes or until tender; finally add a further tablespoon of oil. Serve the fish on a heated dish with the sauce poured over and fingers of toast with which to soak up the sauce.

CAPPON MAGRO

If you are expecting guests for a buffet supper, and know them to be lovers of fish, you could prepare few things more appetising than this famous fish salad, originating in Genoa, but likely to be found in any seaside town in Italy. The recipe given below should prove sufficient for a party of eight. First of all, look out your handsomest round or oval serving dish, for this is a 'dressed up' dish. Next, procure 8 oz. ships' biscuits, break them up, and soak them overnight in a tablespoon of olive oil mixed with an equal quantity of vinegar. Or dry half a dozen slices of bread in the oven, and when crisp, treat them as suggested for the ships' biscuits. Next, prepare a selection of vegetables in season, say 8 oz. or more of small new potatoes, and similar quantities of shelled fresh green peas, French beans, young carrots, cauliflower. Cook separately in boiling, salted water—don't overcook—drain and set on one side. Prepare a head of celery, 8 oz. button mushrooms, 2 oz. black olives, a similar quantity of green olives, and 4 hard-boiled eggs; a small jar of preserved artichoke hearts would add interest to the dish; one or two small cooked beetroots would be colourful — and this is a dish where colour matters. Cut the mushrooms in pieces and marinate with a little oil and vinegar, pepper and salt.

Prepare a boiled lobster; $\frac{1}{2}$ pint of shrimps or prawns; 6 scallops and 2 lb. white fish, turbot, sole or halibut. Poach the white fish and the scallops for 7 minutes, lift from the water, flake and season with oil, lemon juice, pepper and salt. Shell the shrimps, and lobster, and season with oil, lemon juice and pepper and salt.

Next prepare the special sauce:

1 teaspoon chopped parsley	1 tablespoon grated fennel root	2 tablespoons vinegar
6 anchovies	1 clove garlic	6 stoned green olives
1 tablespoon chopped nuts	2 tablespoons capers	1 thick slice bread, soaked in vinegar
pinch oregano	2 or 3 gherkins	and squeezed dry
1 gill olive oil		4 egg yolks (2 raw, 2 hard-boiled)

Place the parsley and garlic in a mortar and pound to a paste, add capers, olives, gherkins, fennel, hard-boiled egg yolks, bread, nuts and oregano; when all are pounded to a paste, slowly add the oil, the vinegar and the two raw egg yolks, stirring with a wooden spoon; the finished sauce should have the consistency of mayonnaise. Arrange a platform of the ships' biscuits or bread and on it spread a little of the sauce; next arrange the various ingredients attractively in pyramid fashion on the platform, a layer of flaked fish, a layer of assorted vegetables, a layer of the sauce and so on until all are used up. The bright coloured vegetables, the sliced beetroot, peas and small or diced carrots, may be used as garnishes, as may a few unshelled prawns, the lobster claws, cracked for easy eating, and the quartered hard-boiled eggs. This dish should, of course, be served very cold, and the prettier it is in appearance the better.

COSTOLETTE OR SCALOPPE MILANESE

Either a cutlet or an escalope of veal may be cooked *alla Milanese*. In either case allow 1 or 1½ per person, depending upon the size, and before starting to cook, either flatten the meat yourself with a cutlet bat, or have the butcher flatten it for you. Allow your meat to marinate in a bath of milk for an hour or so before starting to cook it. Remove all fat and gristle. Coat cutlets or escalopes in beaten egg which has been seasoned with salt and pepper; allow surplus egg to drip off, then dip the meat in fine toasted breadcrumbs before frying it on both sides in a generous amount of hot butter. Cook quickly on one side until golden, then turn and cook the other, and lift out of the pan with a perforated slice. Serve with quartered lemons and a garnish of parsley. Serve these hot, with a green salad, or having drained them well, they are equally delicious served cold.

SCALOPPE ALLA MODENESE

Allow 1 or 1½ escalopes per person; flatten them with a cutlet bat, coat with egg and breadcrumbs and fry in hot butter. Then place the escalopes side by side in a flat fireproof dish, and on top of each place a slice of ham, and on top of that a thin slice of Gruyère cheese. Place in a hot oven, and serve immediately the cheese has melted.

VITELLO TONNATO
Veal with Tunny Fish

Remove the skin and fat from a piece of leg of veal; remove the bone, and stick the meat with small fillets of anchovy. Tie it firmly and allow it to boil for 1½ hours in a saucepan, covered completely with water in which have been placed a small onion, two cloves, a bay leaf, a little chopped celery, parsley and salt. At the end of this time, lift the meat from the water — reserving the broth to form the basis of a minestrone. Untie the meat, cut it in slices and place in a dish covered with the following sauce, in which it should be left overnight in a refrigerator after which it should be served cold, with the sauce served in a separate vessel.

Sauce

Mince the contents of a 4 oz. can of tunny fish with two anchovies, and pass through a sieve or a food mill, adding olive oil and lemon juice in the proportions of 3 parts of oil to 1 of lemon juice, and finally adding a few chopped capers. Garnish with slices of lemon, capers and curled anchovy fillets. *(Illustrated in Plate 112.)*

70. Gouda Asparagus Rolls, Holland (p.181)

71. Gnocchi alla Romana, Italy (p.370)

72. Coquilles Saint-Jacques, France (p.220)

SCALOPPINE AL MARSALA

The combination of thin, crisply fried pieces of veal with Marsala is an experiment well worth trying. Scaloppine, known sometimes by the name of *piccate* are much smaller than escalopes; they are cut very thin and should not be much more than 2 inches square. 3 or 4 per person is the usual allowance. Beat scaloppine flat, and flour them with flour that has been seasoned with pepper and salt. In a frying pan heat a fairly generous knob of butter, and when it is really hot, brown the scaloppine very quickly on each side. While they are still in the pan, add about a tablespoon of Marsala for every 4 scaloppine, and bring to a bubbling boil; add a teaspoon of chicken stock for each tablespoon of Marsala; stir well, and allow to cook for a few moments under a lower heat. One essential of this dish is quick cooking; altogether the process should take under 10 minutes. Serve very hot.

VITELLO IN UMIDO CON PISELLI

Veal Stew with Peas

2 lb. lean veal	meat stock and/or	8 oz. fresh green peas
butter or oil	tomato sauce	(weighed after
	(see p. 365)	shelling)

Heat a little butter or oil in a pan, and in it brown the veal, which has been cut into 2-inch pieces. Add several tablespoons of hot stock and/or tomato sauce, cover and cook gently for 30 minutes, adding a little more stock if necessary; add the peas, and simmer gently for a further ½ hour.

BRACIUOLE DI VITELLO
ALLA VERONESE

Veal Chops in the Veronese Style

Allow one chop per person, and while these are being grilled, prepare the following sauce:

1 tablespoon chopped	2 or 3 anchovies	2 oz. butter
parsley	(bones removed)	2 cloves garlic

Pound together all the ingredients, except the butter, in a mortar until a paste is formed, then add the butter and cream well together. Serve on hot chops.

STUFATO ALLA FIORENTINA

Stew as Cooked in Florence

2 lb. stewing beef, cut in pieces	1 teaspoon chopped rosemary	2 tablespoons red wine
2 tablespoons olive oil	3 cloves garlic,	1 tablespoon tomato purée
potatoes (optional)	crushed	meat stock or water

Heat the oil and in it allow the garlic and rosemary to brown before adding the meat; allow the meat also to brown, then reduce heat and add wine, and the tomato purée diluted with meat stock or water. Cover the pan and cook slowly for $2\frac{1}{2}$ hours, adding more hot stock or boiling water from time to time, if necessary. Potatoes peeled and cut in pieces may be added an hour before serving.

AGNELLO O CAPRETTO IN CASSERUOLA

Lamb or Kid Pot Roast

Kid is eaten a great deal in Italy and the flesh of young goats makes excellent eating. Try a leg of either kid or lamb stuck at intervals with rosemary, salted, and then browned on all sides in a pan in which two tablespoons of olive oil have been heated. Cover the pan when the flesh is browned on all sides, and allow it to cook slowly, 15 minutes to the pound, in a covered pan.

OSSOBUCO ALLA MILANESE

allow one small knuckle of veal per person, and it should be sawn nearly through in sections about $1\frac{1}{2}$ or 2 inches long, so that there	are a number of sections of bone, each surrounded by a circle of muscle 2 or 3 oz. butter flour 1 gill dry white wine	1 tablespoon chopped parsley 1 anchovy grated rind $\frac{1}{2}$ lemon stock or water clove garlic salt and pepper

Heat the butter in a heavy pan large enough to accommodate the veal knuckles in one layer; flour the knuckles and brown on both sides in the hot butter, seasoning with salt and pepper; add the wine, and continue cooking until the wine has almost evaporated, then add stock or water just to cover the meat; cover closely, and cook slowly for at least an hour, adding more stock if necessary. Meanwhile pound together in a mortar the garlic, anchovy, lemon rind and parsley, and, 5 minutes before serving, add to the gravy and bring to the boil, stirring with a wooden spoon. It is customary to serve ossobuco with a plain risotto coloured with saffron.

PORK COOKED IN MILK
'ALLA BOLOGNESE'

For this you need a piece of loin of pork, boned and with some of its fat removed. Prepare it overnight by sprinkling with salt and pepper and leaving till morning, but this is not essential if time is at a premium.

If you are preparing the meat the day you are cooking, sprinkle it with salt and black pepper before rolling it up, and it is an improvement if a clove of garlic is sliced thin and rolled up in the centre of the meat, together with a few seeds of coriander or fennel.

Use a saucepan that is more or less the size of the rolled joint, and when the pork is ready for the pan, heat a little butter in it and brown the pork all over.

Heat the milk, allowing roughly 1 pint milk to 1 lb. pork, and pour over the meat. Cover the saucepan and allow to simmer gently for an hour or a little longer; uncover, and allow to cook for another 30 minutes, by which time the quantity of liquid will be reduced considerably and it should be a golden brown in colour. Take care that the saucepan does not go dry; if there is any danger of this, add a little more hot milk. The joint is excellent hot, served with the sauce from the cooking, and if you are able to add a few sliced truffles to this it is all the better. Another addition is that of a chopped onion and a rasher of bacon cut in small pieces, and cooked in the butter before the pork is browned.

PORK CHOPS
'ALLA NAPOLITANA'

6 SERVINGS

The Neapolitans use a lot of green and red and yellow peppers in their cooking, and these 'marry' well with pork. For this recipe take:

6 pork chops	8 oz. mushrooms	oil for cooking
2 red or yellow peppers	1 tablespoon tomato purée	salt and pepper
		1 clove garlic, crushed

Heat oil in a heavy pan, fry garlic in it till pale brown, add the chops and brown on both sides; add salt and pepper. Remove from the pan and keep warm. Meanwhile, dilute the tomato purée with a little water and add to the pan in which the chops have been cooked, remove the seeds and stem from the peppers and chop them finely, and add these to the pan together with the chopped mushrooms; cover and cook slowly for about 15 minutes, then replace the chops, cooking together for another 20 minutes or so. Serve very hot.

PORK CHOPS WITH PRUNES

6 SERVINGS

6 pork chops	oil or butter for frying	2 tablespoons white
salt and pepper		wine

Heat the oil with the pepper and salt in a pan and in it fry the chops first on one side and then on the other until brown, add the wine and cook over slightly lowered heat until the wine has evaporated, then remove the chops to a hot dish and cover with the following sauce:

Prune Sauce

10 or 12 prunes,	2 slices lean ham	salt
soaked in water	2 tablespoons wine	chopped thyme
until softened	vinegar	bay leaf
	1 onion	water
	1 oz. butter	

Soak the prunes, and when soft remove the stones. Fry the chopped onion and ham cut in small pieces in butter until light brown, add the vinegar, and cook until the sauce is reduced by one half. Place the prunes in a small saucepan, with barely enough water to cover them, a pinch of chopped thyme and a bay leaf and cook slowly till soft. Pass through a sieve or food mill and add to the chopped onion and ham; mix well and pour over the pork chops.

FEGATO ALLA MILANESE

6 SERVINGS

1½ lb. calf's liver, cut	a beaten egg	butter for frying
into thin slices	breadcrumbs	1 lemon
flour	tablespoon chopped	salt and pepper
	parsley	

Start preparations 1¼ hours before you wish to serve the dish, for the slices of liver are spread on a flat dish, seasoned with salt, pepper and the chopped parsley and left for a good hour. At the end of this time, heat the butter in a heavy pan; flour the liver, then dip in beaten egg, and then into crisp breadcrumbs, and fry quickly first on one side and then on the other. Arrange on a flat, heated dish, pour over the liver the remainder of the butter in which it was fried, and garnish with sections of lemon and sprigs of parsley.

AGNELLO ARROSTO
Roast Lamb

Try roasting a leg of lamb Italian fashion. Before putting it in the oven, make a slit in the flesh near the bone and into this place 1 or 2 cloves of garlic and a sprig of rosemary. Oil the meat lightly all over, and place in a hot oven, allowing 15 minutes to the pound and 15 minutes over, basting from time to time with oil. To make it even more delicious, 15 minutes before serving, pour over it a gill of white wine and baste finally with the juices that have run into the roasting pan.

LIVER WITH ARTICHOKES

For each person allow 6 oz. calf's liver, and 1 or 2 artichokes. In a heavy pan fry a chopped onion in a little oil until it is golden brown; lower the heat and add the artichokes divided into sections, and cook slowly for 20 minutes or so until the artichokes are tender; increase the heat, add the floured liver and cook quickly on first one side then the other; remove from the heat, season with salt, pepper and 1 tablespoon of finely chopped parsley; sprinkle with lemon juice, and shake the pan well so that liver and artichokes are impregnated with the seasonings and lemon juice. Serve on a hot dish.

TESTA DI VITELLO ALLA TOSCANA
Brains as Cooked in Tuscany

calf's brains	juice ½ lemon	salt and pepper
1 oz. butter	1 carrot	piquant sauce
1 tablespoon parsley,	1 stalk celery	(see p. 256)
chopped		1 small onion

Wash the brains in salt and water, removing the skin and fibres and allow to remain in salt and water for 30 minutes or longer. Wrap in a piece of muslin and tie with string and put on to cook with water to cover and the chopped vegetables, seasoning and lemon juice, and cook for a further 15 or 20 minutes, or until the brains are firm; remove, untie, and serve on a hot dish with a piquant sauce.

BRAIN RISSOLES

calf's brains	fine breadcrumbs	lemon
2 eggs	oil or butter	salt and pepper

Having prepared the brains as in the preceding recipe, cook and then chop fine and bind together with 1 beaten egg; stir over the fire in a small pan until the mixture thickens but does not boil; then form into small rissoles; fry in hot oil or butter after coating with egg and fine breadcrumbs. Serve with sections of lemon.

TUSCANY LIVER

Here is an excellent way of serving pig's liver as prepared in Tuscany. There it is customary to serve the liver thus treated on a skewer, interspersed with small sections of toast, and bay leaves, but you can omit the toast and the bay leaves, and having dipped your thin slices of pig's liver in beaten egg, dip them in the following mixture so that they are completely coated with it, fry quickly in hot oil, then serve with sections of lemon.

Mixture for coating

A good handful of crisp breadcrumbs; a clove of garlic, crushed or cut very fine, a teaspoon of fennel seeds, salt and pepper. Mix well together and when the liver has been dipped in beaten egg, coat with breadcrumb mixture before frying in hot oil.

LINGUA ALLA SALSA
Tongue with Sauce

8 SERVINGS

1 calf's tongue	½ pint stock	1 bay leaf
1 lb. rump steak	2 slices streaky bacon	4 oz. mushrooms
1 teaspoon chopped basil	1 medium sized onion	salt and pepper
	1 teaspoon chopped parsley	

Cover the tongue with salted water and bring to the boil, then simmer gently for at least 1½ hours. Drain, cool and remove the skin; puncture it here and there and into the holes introduce slivers of the streaky bacon. Grease a pan and in it place half the steak, well beaten with a cutlet bat, then the chopped onion, basil, parsley, bay leaf and mushrooms cut small; on this lay the tongue, and cover with the other half of the steak, well beaten, and over it pour the stock. Cover the saucepan and allow to cook very slowly for about 3 hours, adding more stock if necessary during that time, but allowing the broth to reduce almost to nothing by the end of the cooking period. Serve hot with a piquant sauce, or if preferred, lift on to a dish, allow to cool and serve cold with a green salad.

LINGUA CON OLIVE
Tongue with Olives

1 calf's tongue	½ pint boiling stock	6 large green olives
1 carrot, chopped	1 small chopped onion	salt
	1 oz. butter	

Put the tongue in a pan, cover with cold water to which a little salt has been added; boil for 1½ hours, then drain, cool and skin. Melt the butter in a pan and in it brown the chopped vegetables; add the tongue and brown all over, then add the stock and the olives cut in small pieces, cover and allow to cook gently for a further 1½ hours, adding a little more stock from time to time if necessary.

TRIPPA ALL'ITALIANA
Tripe, Italian Fashion

1 lb. tripe
1 clove garlic
1 dessertspoon flour
1 teaspoon chopped basil

large onion
bay leaf
4 tablespoons olive oil
2 medium tomatoes, peeled
1 pint stock

1 carrot
1 stalk celery
1 teaspoon chopped parsley
salt and pepper

Heat the oil and in it fry the chopped onion and crushed garlic until golden brown and then stir in the flour. Cut the washed tripe into squares, and add to the mixture together with the tomatoes peeled and cut small. Slowly add the stock, stirring to prevent sticking to bottom of pan; add diced celery and carrot and seasoning. Allow to simmer gently for 1½ hours. Serve hot, removing the bay leaf before serving.

VITELLO RIPIENO AL PASTICCIO
Stuffed Veal Pie

For the Stuffing:

about 4 oz. lean veal
4 oz. veal sweetbreads
4 oz. lean ham
1 small onion, chopped small

2 oz. uncooked green peas
pinch marjoram
1 egg and 3 extra yolks

1 oz. butter
1 tablespoon chopped parsley
4 oz. mushrooms, cut small

Heat the butter, and in it cook the onion until it is a golden colour; then add the veal, sweetbreads and ham, cut small, and cook together for 10 or 12 minutes; remove from the stove and chop finely, then add the other ingredients.

For the Pie:

Take about 1½ lb. of lean veal, cut in thin slices and pounded with a cutlet bat. Place a layer in a greased fireproof casserole, and on this place a layer of the stuffing, then a further layer of veal, and continue in this way till all is used up, finishing with a layer of veal; dot with butter, and bake in a moderate oven for 45 minutes, basting from time to time with a little good stock or strained tomato sauce. This may be eaten hot or cold.

TRIPPA ALLA FIORENTINA
Tripe, Florentine Style

1 lb. tripe	½ pint tomato sauce	salt and pepper
2 tablespoons Parmesan	(see p. 365)	1 teaspoon chopped marjoram

Cut the tripe into squares and boil for 30 minutes in boiling, salted water. Drain, then place in a pan with the tomato sauce and allow to simmer gently for a further hour; 15 minutes before serving, sprinkle in the marjoram, and when dished up, scatter the grated cheese over it, or serve cheese separately.

ROGNONI ALLA BOLOGNESE
Kidneys as Cooked in Bologna

1 lb. calf's or pig's kidneys	juice ½ lemon	1 tablespoon chopped parsley
2 oz. butter	2 medium sized onions vinegar	1 gill stock

Skin the kidneys, cut in half, removing the core, then plunge in boiling water to which a little vinegar or lemon juice has been added and leave for 2 or 3 minutes. Drain and cut in slices. Heat the butter in a stewpan and in it fry chopped onion until golden brown and add the parsley; add the chopped kidneys and cook for 5 or 6 minutes, shaking the pan so that they are cooked on all sides and do not stick; finally, add the stock and a little lemon juice and cook gently for a further 10 minutes, but do not allow to boil.

PETTI DI POLLO ALLA LOMBARDA
Chicken Breast Lombardy Style

alow half a breast of chicken for each person	livers of 1 or 2 chickens	2 oz. butter
1 small onion	1 teaspoon chopped parsley	½ pint hot stock or water
1 tablespoon chopped fennel	1 lb. shelled green peas	juice ½ lemon
		2 egg yolks
		salt and pepper

Heat the butter in a pan and in it brown the chopped onion and parsley; add the chicken, lightly floured, and brown on all sides, add the chopped fennel and the hot stock, cover and allow to cook for 25 minutes. Meanwhile cook the peas in boiling salted water for 10 minutes, drain and add to the pan together with the chicken livers and seasoning; cook for a further 10 minutes, then remove from the stove and stir in the beaten egg yolks mixed with the lemon juice. Serve immediately.

73. Dishes from Brittany

74. Pork and Cranberry Patties, Britain (p.103)

75. Rabbit with Prunes, Belgium (p.85)

76. Dutch Fondue (Bier Kaass) (p.184)

77. Moussaka, Greece (p.330)

78. Risotto with Shellfish, Italy (p.371)

POLLO ALLA CREMA

Chicken with Cream

1 medium sized roasting fowl	1 gill cream or 'top of the milk'	2 tablespoons butter
1 small onion		seasoned flour

Prepare the fowl, cut in pieces for serving. Heat the butter and in it brown the onion; then flour the pieces of chicken and brown on all sides in the butter, adding more if necessary. Add the cream and allow to cook to boiling point; remove from the stove and serve sprinkled with chopped parsley.

CHICKEN AS SERVED IN ROME

1 medium sized boiling fowl	1 tablespoon tomato purée	little chopped parsley
4 tablespoons olive oil	2 oz. flour	1 pint stock
1 sliced leek	4 cloves	4 oz. macaroni
	pinch thyme	salt and pepper

Heat the oil in a large pan, and having prepared the chicken, add it with the chopped leek, cloves, herbs; allow it to brown thoroughly on all sides. Pour off half the oil. Add the stock and the tomato purée diluted with a little stock or water; cover and allow to finish cooking — at least another 1½ to 2 hours until the chicken is tender. Meanwhile cook and drain the macaroni, and when the chicken has finished cooking, remove it from the sauce and keep hot; add the macaroni to the sauce, mix well and serve around the chicken as a garnish.

PERNICIOTTE ALLA MILANESE

Young Partridges as cooked in Milan

Pluck and draw the birds and cut in two, lengthwise, and flatten slightly with a cutlet bat. Allow them to marinate for an hour before cooking, in oil seasoned with salt, pepper, a little parsley and a crushed bay leaf. Then, one half at a time, dip in crisp breadcrumbs and fry on both sides in hot olive oil. Arrange on a heated dish and serve with anchovy sauce (see p. 397).

FAGIOANO AL MADERA

Pheasant cooked in Madeira

Pluck and draw a pheasant, and place in a pan with 4 slices of fat bacon, and 2 slices of ham cut small, half an onion cut small, a stick of celery chopped fine, a teaspoon of chopped parsley, a diced carrot and 1 oz. butter, with pepper and salt and a dash of nutmeg. Cook together slowly until the pheasant begins to brown, then add a gill of Madeira, and an equal quantity of stock; cover and allow the bird to finish cooking — about 45 minutes. Then place the bird in a hot dish, strain the fat from the sauce, sieve it and pour over the bird. Send it to the table, garnished with croûtons of fried bread.

CARCIOFI

Artichokes

Globe artichokes, a luxury everywhere, are one of Italy's staple vegetables. In Sicily one can pass acres and acres of land planted with these delicious vegetables; small wonder that they make frequent appearances on the Italian menu.

To prepare them for cooking, remove the outer leaves, cut off half of the top, or point of the artichoke, cut in halves and then in quarters, and allow to remain for about 30 minutes in water to which you have added a little lemon juice or vinegar. Drain and place in a saucepan with a little oil, a little lemon juice, salt, pepper, a clove of garlic, crushed, and a pinch of oregano, allow the artichokes to cook for 15 minutes, turning them frequently so that they become golden brown all over; remove to a hot dish and keep warm and to the sauce add one or two anchovies cut in small pieces, and cook together for a few minutes then pour over the artichokes and serve hot.

CARCIOFI IN FRICASSEA

Fricassee of Artichokes

Prepare the artichokes by removing the outer leaves, and cutting off half or a little more of the pointed end; leave for 30 minutes in water to which you have added a little lemon juice. Drain, and place in a saucepan with a little butter, chopped parsley, a crushed clove of garlic, and salt to taste. Allow to cook slowly for 45 minutes, then remove the pan from the heat, and add one or two egg yolks (depending on the quantity of artichokes) beaten lightly with a teaspoon of water per egg yolk, the juice of $\frac{1}{2}$ lemon, and a tablespoon of grated Parmesan cheese. Serve very hot.

TUNNY FISH SAUCE

FOR 1 POUND OF SPAGHETTI

1 6-oz. can tunny fish	3 anchovies	1 tablespoon chopped
1 tablespoon chopped	3 tablespoons olive oil	capers
parsley	1 clove garlic, crushed	1 lb. (or 1 medium
salt and pepper		sized can) tomatoes

Heat the oil and in it allow the capers and crushed garlic to cook a few minutes, but not to brown; add tomatoes (cut up, skinned and seeded if raw — strained through a sieve if canned), and cook for a further 30 minutes. Flake tunny fish small, and chop anchovies finely and add with parsley to the tomato sauce, together with salt and pepper. Cook uncovered until it is thick.

CLAM SAUCE

Substituting a medium sized can of clams (drained) for the tunny fish and anchovies of the preceding recipe, you have a favourite sauce for spaghetti, frequently met with in and around Naples, except that there the clams come direct out of the sea.

SHRIMP SAUCE

1 pint (before shelling)	1 tablespoon chopped	2 tablespoons olive oil
shrimps or prawns	parsley	1 small onion
warm water		almonds (optional)

Chop onion and cook without browning in the heated oil, adding a tablespoon of chopped parsley, and the shelled shrimps, together with warm water to cover and simmer 20 minutes. The addition of a few finely chopped toasted almonds is interesting.

MEAT SAUCE

FOR SERVING OVER SPAGHETTI

2 tablespoons tomato	1 bay leaf	2 tablespoons olive oil
purée	8 oz. lean beef,	¾ pint warm water
1 clove garlic, crushed	minced twice	1 onion, chopped fine
½ pint dry white wine		salt and pepper

Heat oil and in it brown onion and garlic and meat, add tomato purée and cook for a further 5 minutes before adding pepper, salt, bay leaf water and wine. Cover and allow to cook slowly for 1 hour, stirring from time to time; remove bay leaf and cook a few minutes longer before serving with spaghetti, or with sartù (see p. 376).

'SOFFRITTO' OR 'BATTUTO'

This is the name given to the foundation from which stews and soups are often started; in its simplest form it consists of hot oil, butter or dripping, in which has been browned a chopped onion or a clove of garlic crushed, but it can be elaborated by the addition of chopped carrot, parsley and celery, but all very finely chopped and browned before adding the meat or game which is to form the stew or soup.

CHICKEN SAUCE

½ pint cream	2 oz. butter	4 oz. mushrooms
2 oz. Bel Paese cheese	6 oz. cooked breast of chicken, diced	4 oz. cream cheese grated Parmesan (optional)

Place cream and cheese in a double boiler and cook slowly over hot water, stirring constantly until the mixture is smooth and creamy. Meanwhile, sauté the chopped mushrooms in the butter, add these and the chopped chicken to the sauce; mix well and serve hot over any kind of pasta asciutta. Grated Parmesan cheese sprinkled over the finished dish is an improvement.

PEA SAUCE

To Serve with Macaroni or with Rice

1 onion, chopped finely	½ pint chicken stock salt and pepper to taste	1 lb. peas (before shelling)
1 rasher of streaky bacon	3 tablespoons olive oil	1 tablespoon parsley, chopped fine

Heat olive oil in heavy pan, and in it cook the onion until it is golden colour; cut bacon small and add, allowing it to cook for 3 or 4 minutes. Add stock, peas and seasoning, and cook slowly for 15 or 20 minutes. Serve sprinkled with parsley.

MARINARA SAUCE

1 medium sized onion	1 pint shrimps	½ teaspoon brown sugar
4 tablespoons olive oil	1 clove garlic, crushed	
½ pint white wine	salt and pepper	6 tomatoes, peeled basil or parsley

Heat the oil in a heavy pan and in it cook the chopped onion and crushed garlic until golden colour; add tomatoes, cut small, together with sugar and pepper and salt. Lower heat and allow to cook gently for 20 minutes. While this is cooking, peel shrimps and add them, together with the wine, to the tomato mixture, cooking gently together for 15 minutes. A little chopped fresh basil may be added 4 minutes before the end of the cooking time, or failing this, chopped parsley. Serve hot over pasta of any type.

HAM SAUCE WITH CREAM

| 2 oz. butter | 4 oz. lean ham or cooked gammon cut small | ½ pint cream |

Melt the butter in a heavy pan, add the ham or gammon and allow to brown slightly before adding the cream. Lower heat, and cook together until the mixture begins to bubble. This sauce is delicious served over freshly cooked pasta of any variety.

ANCHOVY SAUCE

| 10 to 12 anchovy fillets pounded to a paste | 2 tablespoons tarragon vinegar | 2 tablespoons best olive oil |
| yolks of 4 hard-boiled eggs | 1 clove garlic, crushed | 4 tablespoons parsley, chopped fine |

Heat oil in a heavy pan, add pounded anchovies and crushed garlic, and cook slowly for 5 minutes; add parsley, vinegar and pounded egg yolks, stirring constantly until well blended. Remove from fire and serve very cold. A good sauce to serve with cold meats or fish.

RAGÙ BOLOGNESE

No book on Italian cookery would be complete without a recipe for this, one of Italy's most famous sauces.

8 oz. beef or veal, or mixture of both, minced twice	3 oz. streaky bacon	clove garlic, crushed
1½ oz. butter	2 or 3 cloves or pinch powdered cloves	2 teaspoon tomato purée
onion, carrot, stick of celery minced	¾ pint stock or water, or	3 tablespoons cream
	½ pint stock plus 1 gill white wine	salt and pepper

A few chopped mushrooms may be added if liked, and if you have three or four chicken livers available, these, chopped, are a great improvement. Place meat in a pan with the heated butter, add chopped bacon, onion, carrot and celery. Add two or three dried cloves or a pinch of powdered cloves, and allow to cook until the meat has browned and the vegetables are a golden colour. Add the stock and/or wine little by little, add tomato purée moistened with a little stock, stir well; add salt and pepper. Cover meat with the liquid, lower heat and allow the mixture to cook gently for another 15 minutes. In one of the traditional recipes milk is used instead of stock, which results in a richer tasting sauce, but this is purely a matter of personal preference. At the end of the cooking time add the cream and mix well. Excellent with spaghetti.

PESTO

2 SERVINGS

Pesto is a sauce of Genoese origin that finds its ways into many dishes; it is excellent with spaghetti, for instance, and a tablespoon added to minestrone greatly enhances the flavour. Any left-over pesto may be placed in a small jar, covered with olive oil and kept for some days.

3 cloves garlic, or fresh basil (3 table-spoons when stalks removed)	8 oz. grated Sardo cheese, this is a Sardinian cheese made of ewe's milk; if unobtainable use Parmesan	about 2 tablespoons fresh olive oil almonds, pine nuts or walnuts (optional)

Pound the garlic and basil to a paste in a mortar, add the cheese and continue pounding until a thick paste results, then slowly add oil until the mixture is the consistency of mayonnaise. A few almonds, pine nuts or even walnuts pounded into the paste make an interesting variation.

SALZA ALLA PIZZAIOLA

1 tablespoon olive oil	1 tablespoon fresh	salt and pepper
2 or 3 crushed cloves garlic	oregano, basil or parsley	6 good sized tomatoes 1 clove garlic, chopped fine

Heat the oil and allow crushed garlic to cook gently in it, but do not allow it to brown. Add peeled and cut up tomatoes, pepper and salt and cook fairly fast until tomatoes are cooked through but not reduced to a pulp. Add a good tablespoon of oregano, basil or parsley, and before serving add another clove of garlic cut very, very fine. Canned tomatoes may be used if fresh are not available, but for this sauce the fresh are infinitely preferable. An excellent sauce to serve with beefsteak.

SALSA RÉMOULADE

To ¾ pint mayonnaise (see p. 263) add the following:

1 tablespoon made mustard	2 tablespoon finely chopped capers 1 tablespoon finely chopped parsley	2 or 3 chopped gherkins

Excellent to serve with cold meat or with shellfish.

MEAT SAUCE WITH MUSHROOMS

8 oz. lean beef, minced twice
2 tablespoons olive oil

pinch cayenne pepper
4 oz. mushrooms, washed and sliced thinly
1 tablespoon tomato purée

1 clove garlic, crushed
1 medium sized can tomatoes
salt and pepper

Heat oil in heavy pan, add mushrooms, garlic, cayenne, meat and simmer for 5 minutes; strain tomatoes and add, simmer gently for 45 minutes, blend tomato purée with a little water, add to first mixture, together with salt, cover and cook slowly a further 30 minutes, stirring from time to time. Serve hot.

MUSHROOM AND TOMATO SAUCE

SUFFICIENT FOR 6 PEOPLE

1 lb. mushrooms
1 medium sized can tomatoes
3 tablespoons olive oil

pinch chopped thyme
pinch salt
cayenne pepper
1 clove garlic, crushed

1 tablespoon chopped basil, or finely chopped mint or parsley

Heat oil and in it allow the crushed garlic to brown; add mushrooms, sliced finely, and simmer for 10 minutes; pass tomatoes through a sieve, and add to the sauce together with the remaining ingredients. Cover and allow to cook very slowly for an hour, stirring from time to time. Serve very hot as a sauce with any type of pasta.

ALMOND SAUCE

2 tablespoons butter

2 oz. blanched chopped almonds

juice 2 lemons

Brown butter slightly, and slowly add chopped almonds and lemon juice. Serve hot or cold with fish.

LIVER SAUCE FOR GNOCCHI

8 oz. liver (preferably chicken liver)
½ pint chicken stock

2 oz. butter
4 oz. button mushrooms

1 gill white wine
1 tablespoon flour
salt and pepper

Chop and flour liver, chop mushrooms small, and sauté both in butter in a heavy pan for 10 to 20 minutes, season with salt and pepper, stir in any balance of flour, and slowly add the wine; allow to cook 7 or 8 minutes longer before adding the stock. Simmer until thick.

TOMATO SAUCE ALLA NAPOLITANA

1 lb. tomatoes	few leaves fresh basil	1 carrot
2 sticks celery	1 onion	salt and pepper

Wash tomatoes, cut in pieces and place in saucepan with other vegetables cut coarsely. Allow to cook slowly for 30 minutes or until the vegetables are tender. Remove from heat and pass through a sieve. Season with pepper and salt. Usually in Naples a knob of fresh lard is added at the end of the cooking and mixed with the sauce, and just before serving a little freshly chopped basil makes an excellent finishing touch.

ZABAGLIONE OR ZABAIONE

When talking of sweets in the Italian menu, this airy-fairy refinement of egg punch is the one that springs first to the mind, and it is worth knowing how to make it to perfection.

For each person allow 2 egg yolks, 2 tablespoons castor sugar, and 2 tablespoons of Marsala, or good sherry.

Beat together the egg yolks and sugar until they are pale and creamy, then slowly add the Marsala. Place the mixture over hot water in a double boiler, and stir slowly until it thickens, taking care not to overcook it, otherwise it will curdle. Serve immediately in warmed sherbet glasses. There is a school of thought that dictates 'serve hot or cold', but this to most Italian palates is heresy — serve your zabaglione hot.

CHESTNUT FRITTERS

To 8 oz. chestnut flour, add sufficient water to make a thick paste; add a pinch of salt, a few seedless raisins, and a few chopped pistachio nuts; mix together well and drop spoonfuls into deep hot oil, cooking till golden brown. Drain and serve hot, sprinkled with castor sugar.

MONT BLANC

1 lb. chestnuts	8 oz. castor sugar	salt
	1 gill double cream	

Cut a slit in the chestnuts at the pointed end, and place them a dozen at a time in a very hot oven for 10 minutes, after which they will peel easily. When all are peeled, place in boiling water and allow to simmer for an hour or until they are tender. Strain, and mash the nuts, adding the sugar and a pinch of salt. Pass them then through a potato ricer, allowing them to pile up in pyramid form on a dish. The less you touch them with your hands the better, otherwise the light appearance of the finished dish is apt to be spoiled. Whip the cream, flavouring it if you like with a little good liqueur, and pile it lightly on the top of the mound of chestnuts, rather like snow on a mountain top.

79. Cod with Cheese Sauce, Sweden (p.492)

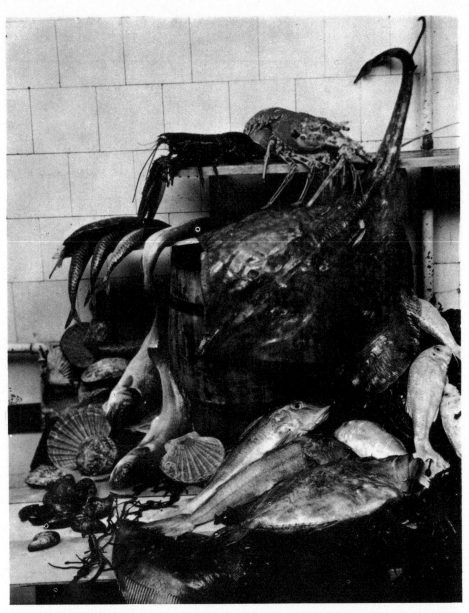

80. Fruits of the Sea

POLISH COOKING

Elizabeth Campbell

The Poles have had the stormiest and most struggling career as a nation and, as often happens, this resulted in a very high achievement in all their arts — including the art of cookery. They have always taken an intelligent and lively interest in good food and the large peasant population had a slavonic gusto in producing original and tasty dishes from the simplest and cheapest ingredients.

Soups play an important part in the diet of a Polish family. They have adopted the Russian Borshch and transformed it into their own national soup. The basis of Borshch is beetroot, a cheap enough vegetable, but don't be misguided into thinking that it is a flimsy little soup. It is not only a wholesome nourishing soup, it also has fragrance and colour to make it attractive.

Bigos is an excellent one-course meal — most useful and economical for using up left-over meat without spending a long time in the kitchen. All the Polish cakes and pastries are delightful, but among the best are the Cheese Pastries. They take a few minutes to prepare, they are economical and they put the best cheese straws to shame.

For a summer dish of salad, or for picnics, the Polish way of making a Cream Cheese Spread is slightly unusual, and very pleasant.

SALT CUCUMBER SOUP

Chlodnik

½ pint pickled cucumber juice	4 oz. cooked veal	2 hard-boiled eggs
2 pints sour cream	8 oz. prawns	1 oz. chives
8 oz. beetroot	1 fresh cucumber	1 oz. dill
	1 pickled cucumber	salt and pepper

Cook the beetroot in water until tender then peel and rub through a sieve. Add the beetroot tops, finely chopped, and the cucumber juice. Mix with chopped dill and chives, the sour cream, cooked prawns and diced pickled cucumber. Peel and slice the fresh cucumber and add to the soup together with sliced hard-boiled eggs. Season with salt and pepper and leave the soup in a very cold place. Serve well chilled.

DRIED MUSHROOM SOUP

Zupa Grzybowa

2 oz. dried mushrooms	1 oz. flour	3 tablespoons sour cream
2 pints stock	1 oz. butter	
	salt and pepper	

Blanch the mushrooms. Simmer in the seasoned stock until tender. Melt the butter, add the flour, cook for 1 minute. Gradually add the stock and the mushrooms. Stir in the sour cream before serving.

CHRISTMAS EVE BORSHCH
Barszczyk

8 oz. beetroot, sliced	parsley, chopped	½ pint kvass (optional)
½ celeriac, sliced	1 clove garlic	(see p. 473)
1 small carrot, sliced	2½ pints stock	1 teaspoon salt
½ oz. dried mushrooms		½ oz. butter

Simmer all the vegetables and the garlic in the stock, until the beetroot is cooked. Remove the mushrooms to make mushroom patties (see p. 405). Pour the hot soup over the patties.

HERRINGS WITH SOUR CREAM
Sledz Marynowany ze Smietana

4 herrings	1 clove garlic	½ teaspoon paprika
1 gill milk	¼ teaspoon mustard	½ teaspoon chopped
1 gill white wine	2 egg yolks	parsley and thyme
2 tablespoons wine	2 tablespoons sour	½ bay leaf
vinegar	cream	½ teaspoon salt
1 onion, sliced		6 peppercorns

Soak the herrings in milk for 1 hour. Strain. Cook them for 7 minutes in the vinegar and wine, with the onion, garlic, peppercorns, and salt; add water if necessary. Strain off the juice, cool and mix with the beaten egg yolks, paprika, sour cream and mustard. Cover the herrings with the sauce. Serve chilled.

TRIPE
Flaki

2 lb. tripe	1 onion	grated cheese
3 tablespoons butter	2 celery stalks	salt and pepper
2 tablespoons flour	2 sprigs parsley	water
3 pints bone stock	1 teaspoon marjoram	
1 carrot	½ teaspoon ground	
	ginger	

Clean the tripe and wash thoroughly. Blanch in boiling, salted water and then rinse in cold water. Put into a saucepan of cold water and simmer until the tripe is soft. Then drain and cut into 2-inch lengths. Meanwhile, melt the butter, blend with the flour and dilute with a little of the stock. Put into a large saucepan with the rest of the stock and add the vegetables, cut into small pieces, the marjoram, chopped parsley, ground ginger, salt and pepper. Bring to the boil and simmer for 10 minutes. Put in the prepared tripe, cover and simmer for another 15 minutes. Serve hot with grated cheese.

SAUERKRAUT STEW

Bigos

1 lb. left-over beef or poultry	1 onion, sliced	1 pint stock
1½ lb. sauerkraut	1 oz. flour	pinch paprika
	1 oz. butter	salt to taste
		1 gill white wine

Simmer the sauerkraut in the stock for ½ hour. Cook the onion in 1 oz. butter, add the flour, cook for 1 minute. Chop the sauerkraut and add the onion mixture to it. Cut the meat into small pieces. Put the meat and the sauerkraut mixture into a casserole, add the wine, season with salt and paprika, mix well. Cook in a slow oven with the lid on for 1 hour. White cabbage may be used instead of sauerkraut, in which case add a grated sour apple and 2 tablespoons of vinegar.

HUSSAR'S ROAST

Pieczen Huarska

2 lb. sirloin	½ oz. flour	1 egg yolk
1 onion, chopped	1 tablespoon brown breadcrumbs	salt
juice ½ lemon		3 oz. butter

Beat the meat, sprinkle with salt, dredge with flour. Melt 2 oz. butter, brown the meat in it on both sides. Add the lemon juice and a little water. Simmer. Cook half the chopped onion in the rest of the butter until transparent, add the breadcrumbs, season with salt and pepper. Mix with the egg. Make crosswise incisions in the meat. Fill with the stuffing. Fry the rest of the onion in a casserole, add the meat and about ½ pint water. Cook covered, in a moderate oven for 1 hour or more, until the meat is tender. Serve with the following sauce:

Sauce for roast beef

2 onions	½ bay leaf	½ pint vegetable stock
1 clove garlic	2 oz. ham	1 teaspoon sugar
1 slice carrot	2 gills red wine	salt
1 tomato	2 tablespoons grated horseradish	parsley
juice ½ lemon	basil	2 oz. butter
		2 oz. flour

Melt the butter. Chop the onions, garlic, carrot, parsley. Cook in the butter with the bay leaf and a pinch of basil until browned. Stir in the flour, add the stock. Simmer for 20 minutes and sieve. Return to pan, add wine and lemon juice. Cut ham into strips. Peel tomato, remove seeds, cut flesh into slices. Add ham, tomato and horseradish. Serve hot.

POTATO PANCAKES
Racuszki z Kartofli

6 medium potatoes	2 oz. butter	nutmeg
½ pint milk	3 eggs	salt

Boil the potatoes in salted water until cooked. Mash. Mix with the egg yolks, beat in the milk. Flavour with nutmeg. Fold in the stiffly beaten egg whites. Cook as ordinary pancakes, in the butter.

BACON ROLLS
Kromeskies

8 oz. cooked minced meat	1 teaspoon chopped onion	1 egg
1 tablespoon breadcrumbs	½ pint batter (see pancakes, p. 114)	pinch mixed herbs salt and pepper fat for frying
1 teaspoon chopped parsley		8 slices bacon

Combine the minced meat, onion, parsley and breadcrumbs. Season with salt, pepper and herbs and add the egg. Mix well and then divide into 8 portions. Roll each one in a rasher of bacon and put aside in a cool place for about 30 minutes. Then dip each one in batter and fry in hot fat until golden brown on all sides.

MUSHROOM PATTIES
Pierozki Grzybowe

3 oz. flour	1 oz. dried mushrooms	1 egg white
1 egg yolk	1 oz. butter	½ teaspoon chopped parsley
Filling:	1 tablespoon breadcrumbs	
1 onion, chopped		salt and pepper

Mix the egg yolk with the flour. Add a little water if necessary. Knead until smooth, roll out and cut into 2-inch squares. Put a little of the filling into each square. Pinch the edges together to form a triangle, and cook in boiling water for 5 minutes. To make the filling, simmer mushrooms until tender. Melt the butter, add the mushrooms and the onion and cook until the onion is transparent. Mix with the beaten egg, crumbs and salt.

CREAM CHEESE SPREAD

4 oz. cottage cheese	12 slices cucumber	1 tablespoon cream
3 radishes	chives	salt

Add the cream to the cheese, beat until light. Peel and dice the cucumber, sprinkle with salt, leave to drain. Cut the radishes into thin slices, chop the chives. Mix cucumber, chives and radishes with the cheese. Season.

RUM BUCKWHEAT

Kaszka Manna z Rumem

4 oz. buckwheat	4 oz. sugar	strip of lemon peel
or ground rice	1 gill rum	icing sugar and
1 pint cream	¼ teaspoon salt	cherries to decorate

Put the buckwheat and sugar in a bowl and pound it. Add the other ingredients, pour into a pie dish and cook in a slow oven for 2 hours. Turn out, cover with icing sugar and decorate with cherries.

POLISH BABA

8 egg yolks	4 oz. melted butter	saffron
4 oz. castor sugar	vanilla	½ teaspoon salt
1 gill milk	1 lb. flour	1 oz. yeast

Beat the egg yolks and sugar over hot water until white and thick. Dissolve the yeast in a little warm milk. Add it and all the other ingredients, except the butter, to the eggs. Beat until thoroughly blended. Pour in the butter and beat again. Fill a greased tin with the mixture to one third of its depth. Cover and leave to rise in a warm place. Bake in a moderate oven for 1 hour.

CHEESE PASTRIES

Serniki

2 oz. flour	2 oz. Parmesan cheese,	paprika
2 oz. butter, cut into	grated	salt
pieces		1 egg

Put the flour, butter, cheese, paprika and salt into a bowl. Mix with a spoon until the dough is smooth and firm. Leave for an hour. Roll out thin. Cut into fancy shapes, glaze with the egg, bake in a hot oven for 10 minutes.

TO MAKE CHEESE STRAWS

Roll out the pastry on a board and cut out an oblong about 3 to 4 inches wide. Put piece of pastry on the baking sheet and cut it into narrow strips about ¼ inch wide and then separate them slightly so that they do not stick together while baking. This method prevents the straws becoming twisted and broken while transferring them from the board to the baking sheet. As a variation to the basic recipe the straws may be rolled in caraway seeds or chopped nuts. They can also be spread with Marmite or made into twists with strips of anchovy. *(Illustrated in Plate 98.)*

PORTUGUESE COOKING

Musia Soper

Portugal has the advantage of a beautiful situation and a lovely climate, with the warm sun helping to produce the many good things to eat — and drink. Fruit, fish, olives, olive oil and the grapes which produce the famous port and other wines, are plentiful.

Although in many ways the cooking resembles that of Spain, Portugal has many of her own regional specialities, and it was her adventurous voyagers of the old days who first brought back spices and rice from far away to be introduced to their home kitchens.

Tunny fish and sardines are the main fishing hauls. Salted cod is much used, but it is not monotonous to eat because it is prepared in so many different and pleasant ways. Eggs too are used a good deal in soups and sauces, as an addition to other dishes and on their own. Tomatoes, onions, olive oil and wine are also very much part of Portuguese cookery.

As far back as the 17th century there was a Portuguese cookery book called 'The Art of the Kitchen', which shows there must always have been a great interest in cooking in Portugal.

TOMATOES WITH SARDINE STUFFING

1 small can	2 hard-boiled eggs	mayonnaise
Portuguese sardines	4 tomatoes	(see p. 263)
		salt and pepper

Cut a thin slice off the top of each tomato, scoop out and sprinkle the insides with salt and pepper. Drain the contents of a can of boneless sardines, dice the sardines, chop the eggs and stir into some mayonnaise. Fill the tomatoes with the mixture, put back the top slices of tomatoes, and serve as an hors-d'oeuvre.

PORTUGUESE EGGS

Ovos à Portuguesa

4 large tomatoes	4 tablespoons	2 sprigs parsley
4 eggs	breadcrumbs	salt and pepper
	2 tablespoons butter	

Cut off the tops of the tomatoes, scoop out the interior and break an egg into each one. Season with salt and pepper, cover with breadcrumbs, sprinkle with chopped parsley and put pats of butter on top. Place on a buttered oven dish and put into a moderate oven to bake for about 15 minutes.

POTATO AND WATERCRESS SOUP

Sopa de Batata e Agriao

| 1 lb. potatoes | 1 tablespoon butter | 2 pints water |
| 1 bunch watercress | ½ cup milk | salt and pepper |

Peel the potatoes and boil in the water until done. Strain off the water into a saucepan, rub the potatoes through a sieve and put back into the water. Add finely chopped watercress and cook for a further 5 minutes. Then put in the milk and butter and heat for a few minutes. Serve the soup sprinkled with chopped, uncooked watercress.

PORTUGUESE HARD-BOILED EGGS

Ovos Duros à Portuguesa

2 large tomatoes	3 tablespoons olive oil	1 small onion
4 hard-boiled eggs	1 small clove garlic	salt and pepper

Cut the tomatoes in half and scoop out the insides. Sprinkle with salt and pepper and fry for a few minutes in a tablespoon of oil. Then place a peeled, hard-boiled egg into each half tomato. To make the sauce to pour over the eggs, chop the onion finely and fry until golden brown in a tablespoon of oil. Add the tomato pulp, crushed garlic, salt and pepper and the remaining oil and simmer gently for 10 minutes. Serve as a hot hors-d'oeuvre.

PORTUGUESE COD

Bacalhau Fresco à Portuguesa

2 lb. cod	4 oz. rice	2—3 sprigs parsley
8 oz. onions	½ gill olive oil	salt and pepper
1 lb. tomatoes	2 oz. butter	water
½ gill white wine		1 clove garlic

Chop the onions and fry in butter until golden brown. Boil the rice in salted water for 10 minutes and strain. Cut the fish into 4 cutlets and put into a pan with hot oil. Add the onions, rice, skinned sliced tomatoes, crushed clove of garlic, salt and pepper. Cover the pan and simmer for 10 minutes. Then add chopped parsley and cook gently for another 10 minutes. Serve the cod in its own sauce.

PORTUGUESE SALT COD

Bacalhau à Portuguesa

1 lb. salt cod	8 oz. tomatoes	2 tablespoons olive oil
1 lb. potatoes	8 oz. peppers	salt and pepper
	1 lb. onions	

Soak the cod for 12 hours then remove the bones and slice the fish. Peel the potatoes and onions, skin the tomatoes and remove the seeds from the peppers, then slice and put into an oven dish in alternate layers with the fish. Finish at the top with a layer of potatoes. Add the olive oil, season with salt and pepper, cover with a lid and put into a moderate oven to cook for 1—1½ hours.

COD WITH 'PODRE' SAUCE

2 lb. salt cod	2 tablespoons butter	2 tablespoons grated
3 eggs and	breadcrumbs	cheese
2 yolks	1½ cups olive oil	salt and pepper
8 oz. flour	1 lb. potatoes	water
1 pint milk		

Soak the salt cod in cold water overnight and then scald with boiling water to soften. Remove skin and bones and cut the fish into small pieces. Make a batter with 3 egg yolks, flour, milk and stiffly whipped whites of 3 eggs. Dip the pieces of cod into the batter, fry in 1 cup of hot oil and drain.

Add a cup of water to the pan in which the cod was fried, put in 2 egg yolks and 2 tablespoons of butter. Cook gently for 5 minutes, stirring continuously to prevent the eggs from curdling. Add 1 tablespoon of grated cheese and heat until melted.

Parboil the potatoes, drain, slice and fry in the remaining oil. Place at the bottom of a baking dish, lay the fried fish over them and cover with a layer of breadcrumbs and the remaining grated cheese. Pour in the sauce and bake in a moderate oven until the top is a golden brown colour. Serve very hot.

LOBSTER À PORTUGUESA

1 large or 2 small	4 oz. onions	4 cloves garlic
boiled lobsters	1 tablespoon flour	salt and pepper
3 oz. butter	2 tablespoons brandy	boiled rice
	2 lb. tomatoes	

Remove the lobster meat from the shell, cut into 8 slices and put into a wide pan. Chop the onions and fry lightly in the butter. Skin and chop the tomatoes, add to the onions and cook until soft. Add crushed garlic, sprinkle with salt, pepper and flour, mix well and simmer for a few minutes. Sieve the sauce and stir in the brandy. Pour over the lobster meat, cover, and simmer for 5 minutes. Remove from the heat and leave until the next day in the refrigerator. Before serving, heat and serve with boiled rice.

CLAMS À MARINEIRA

2 pints clams	1 gill olive oil	¼ teaspoon pepper
4 large tomatoes	2 teaspoons chopped	1 teaspoon salt
2 large onions	parsley	water
2 cloves garlic		1 tablespoon flour

Wash the clams well, then put into a saucepan with 1 pint of water. Cover and put on a moderate heat until the shells open. Take out the fish and cut into small pieces. Chop the onions and fry in the oil until golden brown, then add the tomatoes, skinned and quartered, crushed garlic, flour, salt and pepper. Cook until the tomatoes and onions are done then add the parsley and clams and cook for another 2—3 minutes. Clams prepared this way go well served with fried pork or a plain omelette.

LIVER À TRANSMONTANA

1 lb. calf's liver	1 onion	1 clove garlic
5 eggs	juice ½ lemon	3 tablespoons water
4 oz. lean ham	sprig parsley	salt and pepper
	2 tablespoons butter	juice of ½ lemon

Cut the liver into 4 slices. Hard-boil 2 eggs, shell and chop. Chop the parsley and ham, crush the garlic and combine with the chopped eggs. Season with salt and pepper and place equal portions on each slice of liver. Roll up the liver slices, tie with cotton, and put into a baking dish. Chop the onions and fry lightly in the butter. Add the water and pour over the liver rolls. Put into a moderate oven to bake for about 20 minutes. On removing from the oven, cover with scrambled eggs prepared with 3 eggs and the juice of ½ lemon.

CHICKEN À PORTUGUESA

1 chicken	2 oz. button	salt and pepper
1 onion	mushrooms	water
8 oz. tomatoes	2 cloves garlic	cooked rice
	3 tablespoons olive oil	2 tablespoons water

Divide the chicken into 8 portions and fry in hot oil until slightly brown. Chop the onions and fry until golden coloured. Add quartered tomatoes, crushed garlic, sliced mushrooms, salt, pepper and 2 tablespoons of water. Fry for a few minutes then put into a large saucepan together with the chicken. Cover with a lid and simmer gently for 1 hour. Serve with boiled rice.

CHICKEN À CASTELO VIDE

1 boiling chicken	2 eggs	salt and pepper
8 oz. rice	2 tablespoons butter	water

Boil the chicken in 3 pints of water until tender. Boil the rice in the chicken stock for 20 minutes, then strain. Put the chicken into a deep casserole, covered with the butter and rice, and season with salt and pepper. Beat 2 eggs, pour over the chicken and rice, cover with a lid and put into a moderate oven to bake until the eggs are set.

HUNTER'S PARTRIDGE

Alentejo

2 partridges	2 small onions	2—3 sprigs parsley
½ pint olive oil	2 cloves garlic	salt and pepper
¼ pint vinegar	*bouquet garni*	4 slices bread
1 gill dry white wine	1 bay leaf	

Clean and prepare the partridges and put into a large pan with the olive oil, vinegar, wine, salt and pepper. Cover with a lid and cook very slowly for 2 hours. To prevent the birds catching at the bottom, shake the pan well now and again, without removing the lid. Then add the onions, roughly chopped parsley, crushed garlic, the *bouquet garni* and the bay leaf and cook very slowly for another hour. Serve halves of the birds on slices of fried bread.

NUT PUDDING

Pudim de Noses

8 oz. shelled walnuts	¼ teaspoon mixed	3 eggs and 3 whites
8 oz. castor sugar	spice	butter

Crush the nuts, or use ground walnuts, and mix with the spice. Beat the egg yolks and sugar, add to the nuts and mix well. Whisk 3 of the egg whites and fold into the nut mixture. Pour into a buttered mould, leaving space at the top, cover with greaseproof paper and put into a saucepan of water to steam for about 1 hour. Keep the water simmering until the pudding is set, adding a little more water when necessary. When ready, turn out of the mould and leave to get cold. Serve with whipped cream, if desired.

RUMANIAN COOKING

Musia Soper

Rumania reaches to the shores of the Black Sea and the Danube flows through the land into the sea. The fishermen catch many kinds of fish including, at the mouth of the river, the sturgeon from which they, like the Russians, prepare caviar. The farmer grows chiefly maize and sugar-beet in the flat land of the Danube valley and the shepherd takes his flock into the hills beyond, to over 5000 feet up.

Rumania, the historians believe, fell under the Hungarian rule towards the end of the 19th century and perhaps that is why some of their gypsy music and songs share an affinity with Hungarian gypsy music. In the 15th century Rumania was conquered by the Turks and in the 19th century they came under the influence of the Russians. Rumanian cooking shows the influence of her conquerors and also of her neighbours, Yugoslavia, Bulgaria and the Ukraine.

The usual, staple food is black bread, aubergines, fish, plenty of garlic and olive oil and enormous water melons which are grown all over the Balkans.

In some parts of Rumania tea is still made in a samovar, as in Russia, but that habit is not common now in either country.

SOUP WITH MEAT BALLS

Ciorba de Perisoare

1 marrow bone	2—3 tomatoes	salt and black pepper
8 oz. beef	1 tablespoon rice	1 gill sour cream
2 carrots	1 tablespoon fine	2—3 sprigs parsley
2 parsnips	breadcrumbs	water
2 onions		

Simmer the bone in water with a carrot, parsnip and onion for 2—3 hours. Strain off the stock into a saucepan and add quartered tomatoes and the rest of the vegetables, finely chopped. Season with salt, bring to the boil and simmer gently until the vegetables are tender. Meanwhile, prepare the meat balls. Mince the beef, add rice, breadcrumbs, 1 egg, salt and pepper. Mix well, then, with wet hands, make small balls about the size of walnuts. When all are made, drop into the simmering soup and cook slowly for about an hour or until the meat is done. Before serving, add a beaten egg to the soup and put sour cream and chopped parsley into each plate.

STUFFED CARP

Umplut

1 carp 2—3 lb.	1 tablespoon chopped	cayenne pepper
8 oz. olives	chives	1 teaspoon salt
2 cloves garlic	1 tablespoon	1 tablespoon olive oil
1 lemon	breadcrumbs	1 gill water
	2 sprigs parsley	

Scale, clean and rinse the fish, and rub with salt. Stone the olives and chop finely. Add juice of a lemon, chopped parsley, chives, pinch of cayenne pepper, salt and a tablespoon of olive oil. Stuff the carp with the mixture, put into an oiled baking dish, sprinkle on top with bread-crumbs and put into a moderate oven to bake for about 40 minutes. About half way through the cooking, add a little hot water and then baste occasionally with the hot stock. Serve hot or cold.

RUMANIAN BAKED FISH

4 cutlets any firm, white fish	1 onion	1 teaspoon cummin seeds
4 oz. French beans	1 tablespoon sultanas	salt and pepper
4 oz. carrots	2—3 tomatoes	frying oil
2 tablespoons cooked peas	2—3 cloves garlic	1 gill water
	few sprigs parsley	1 gill sherry

Place the fish into a deep oven dish, greased with oil. Chop the onion and fry for a few minutes in hot oil, then add sliced French beans and diced carrots. Fry for 5 minutes then mix with the tomatoes, cut in quarters, the peas, sultanas, chopped garlic, cummin seeds, salt and pepper. Add the sherry and water, stir well then pour over the fish. Cover with a lid and cook in a moderate oven for 30 minutes. Then take off the lid and cook for another 5—10 minutes.

MEAT WITH CABBAGE

2 lb. pork or beef	½ pint tomato purée	1 teaspoon sugar
1 cabbage—about 2 lb.	3 tablespoons oil or fat	salt and pepper
	8 oz. sauerkraut	1 gill water
	1 large onion	

Cut the meat into 2-inch pieces. Slice the onion and fry lightly in hot oil or fat. Shred the cabbage, sprinkle liberally with salt and leave for about 20 minutes. Then squeeze with the hands to get rid of the moisture. Line a large oven dish with the onion, then put in a layer of meat and a layer of cabbage. Use alternate layers of meat and cabbage until used up. Spread the sauerkraut in between and finish with a layer of cabbage. Mix the tomato purée with 1 gill of warm water, add the sugar and a pinch of salt and pepper and pour into the oven dish. Cover with a lid and cook in a slow oven for 2 hours.

GRILLED SAUSAGES
Mititei

¼ teaspoon mixed spices	½ teaspoon bicarbonate soda	1 clove garlic
¼ teaspoon black pepper	olive oil	3 tablespoons warm water
	1 lb. best beef	1 teaspoon salt

Mince the meat twice. Combine the salt, pepper, spices, crushed garlic clove and bicarbonate of soda in the water, add to the minced meat and mix well. Using wet hands, roll portions of meat into thin sausages 2 inches long. Brush them with oil and put under a hot grill until brown. Serve hot.

TRIPE À LA ROUMAINE
Tuzlama

1½ lb. tripe	1 onion	1 tablespoon butter
1 calf's foot	1 celery stick	6 peppercorns
1 egg	1 tablespoon lemon	1 bay leaf
1 carrot	juice	salt and pepper
1 parsnip	1 teaspoon flour	water

Put the tripe into a pan of cold water with the calf's foot and bring to the boil. Remove the scum and add peppercorns, salt, sliced onion, parsnip and celery stick and simmer for 2 hours. Meanwhile, grate the carrot coarsely and fry lightly in the butter. Add the flour and a little of the stock and simmer gently for 15 minutes. Strain off the stock. Cut the tripe into 2-inch squares, remove the meat from the calf's foot and put into another saucepan. Add the yolk of an egg and lemon juice to the carrot mixture and pour over the meat and tripe. Simmer very slowly for 10—15 minutes. Serve very hot.

DUCK VINAIGRETTE
Ostropel

1 duckling	2 tablespoons tomato	1 bay leaf
2 tablespoons olive oil or fat from duck	purée	4 tablespoons wine vinegar
2—3 medium sized onions	½ tablespoon flour	salt
	2 cloves garlic	1 gill water or stock
	6—8 peppercorns	

Cut the duckling into suitable portions and brown in hot oil or fat. Slice the onions thinly, fry until golden brown, add the flour and mix well. Add 1 gill of stock or water, the tomato purée, crushed garlic, bay

81. Stuffed Onions, Rumania (p.417)

82. Herrings Soused in Wine, Germany (p.283)

83. Muesli, Switzerland (p.582)

leaf, peppercorns and salt to taste. Stir well and pour this sauce over the duck in a saucepan. Cover with a lid and cook slowly until the duck is tender. Add extra stock or hot water if necessary and stir frequently. When almost ready, add the vinegar and cook for another 10—15 minutes. The same dish can be prepared with chicken or goose.

AUBERGINE SALAD

2 medium sized aubergines	½ pint olive oil 1 small onion	salt and pepper small red pepper

Put the aubergines under a hot grill and cook all round them until the skin is charred almost black. Then rinse with cold water and remove the skin carefully. Put the pulp into a bowl and mash with a wooden spoon. Then add the olive oil, drop by drop, stirring vigorously, until the mixture is a smooth, thick purée. Add salt and pepper and very finely chopped onion. Garnish with thin slices of red pepper and serve cold.

STUFFED ONIONS

4 large onions	1 tablespoon olive oil	2 sprigs parsley
4 lamb's kidneys	2 tablespoons butter	salt and pepper
4 cloves	½ teaspoon mixed herbs	water

Peel the onions and scoop out the centres. Skin and trim the kidneys and chop finely. Add finely chopped parsley, herbs, salt and pepper and mix well. Stuff the onions with the mixture, stick a clove into each onion, and put a pat of butter on top of each one. Stand the stuffed onions in a buttered oven dish, close together, pour on the olive oil, sprinkle with salt and pepper, cover and put into a moderate oven to bake for 40—50 minutes. *(Illustrated in Plate 81.)*

POTATO DISH

Iahnie de Cartofi

1½ lb. potatoes	1 bay leaf	2—3 sprigs parsley
2 tablespoons tomato purée	2 tablespoons fat or oil	salt and pepper ½ pint hot water
	2 onions	

Chop the onions finely and fry in fat or oil until golden brown. Peel the potatoes, cut lengthwise and add to the onions. Mix the tomato purée with hot water, add salt and pepper to taste and pour over the potatoes. Put in a bay leaf, cover with a lid and cook gently until the potatoes are done. Serve the potatoes, sprinkled with chopped parsley, as an accompaniment to meat dishes or fried eggs.

CORNFLOUR PORRIDGE

Mamaliga

4 oz. cornflour	1 teaspoon salt	sour cream or grated
1 pint water		cheese

Put the water into a saucepan, add the salt and bring to the boil. Gradually add the cornflour and simmer gently, stirring frequently, until the mixture is thick and smooth. Serve hot accompanied by sour cream or grated cheese.

CORNFLOUR PUDDING

4 oz. cornflour	1 tablespoon	1 teaspoon salt
1½ pints water	breadcrumbs	1 tablespoon grated
	1 teaspoon butter	cheese

Prepare in the same way as for mamaliga. Then pour into a buttered baking tin, sprinkle with breadcrumbs and grated cheese and bake in a moderate oven for about 30 minutes, or until there is a golden brown crust on top. Serve hot.

CORNFLOUR FRITTER

4 oz. cornflour	1 egg	1 teaspoon salt
1 pint water	8 oz. grated cheese	oil for frying

Prepare in the same way as for mamaliga. Leave to cool then cut into slices, dip into beaten egg, cover with grated cheese and fry in hot oil until golden brown.

RUSSIAN COOKING

Musia Soper

As the U.S.S.R. covers so vast an area, a sixth of the world's surface, stretching from the icy north to the sunny south, over mountains and endless steppes, through crowded cities and many small villages, it naturally has within its bounds a considerable variety of climate, customs and cooking. In the extreme south, the U.S.S.R. touches northern India, in the east, China; countries in Europe and Asia are close neighbours, and each of these countries has had its own particular effect, one way or another.

In the Caucasus alone, there can be found a fascinating mixture of races. In the northern part they are chiefly Cossacks, in the southern regions principally Turco-Tartars, Georgians and Armenians, but there were many tribes amongst the different races, each with their own customs, costumes and language. The Arabs called the Caucasus *Jebel Assuni* — 'The Mountain of Languages'. Some of the tribes were nomadic at one time, some were Christians, others Moslems, but now, after being invaded through the centuries by the Persians, Arabs, Mongols, Tartars and Turks, they are united and a part of the U.S.S.R. though keeping their own languages, and a traditional way of life where it affects music, art and cooking, and they occupy themselves in the peaceful cultivation of their rich land.

Peter the Great, who reigned in the latter part of the seventeenth century and the early part of the eighteenth century, formed a close association with the Prussian Court, and German Barons from the Baltic provinces came to serve in Russia. Because of that, many German military terms came to be used in Russia, and from the same sources, no doubt, came the introduction of sausages, sauerkraut and schnitzel. Some food, such as salami, noodles and macaroni, came from the Italians at a time, probably, when their influence was most potent in music and ballet, before the Russian Ballet emerged in its full glory. That part of Russia next to Poland called the Ukraine had much in common with the Poles in language, dance and dishes.

The French influence was very strong in Russia during the reign of Catherine II in the eighteenth century. She enthusiastically adopted the culture, the language, and, of course, the cuisine of France—consequently everything had to be French with the aristocracy.

Needless to say, the poor Russian peasants of those days had little to do with all these fads and fashions; they lived as best they could on soup, kasha (a kind of porridge) and black bread. They had a saying then: 'Shchy da kasha pishcha nasha,' which means, 'Cabbage soup and kasha is our fare.' Their main dish, perhaps a soup such as *shchy* or *pokhlyobka*, a typical countryside soup, would be served in a brightly coloured wooden bowl and put in the centre of the table. Everyone would sit around it, ready with a painted wooden spoon to help themselves from the big bowl. Each would consume a spoonful in turn, then put the spoon down with a bang and wait for the next round. The meal was thus accompanied by the rhythmic castanet of sound until the bowl was empty.

Out of all this, Russian cooking emerged and was transformed into something entirely its own, with *smetana* (sour cream) being, as it were, a common denominator for many of the dishes, giving them their unique flavour. It is sometimes said that too much *smetana* is used in Russian dishes, but when one considers a superb soup like Borshch served with it, or the internationally popular Beef Stroganoff made with it, or hot *bliny* (Russian pancakes) covered in it, much may be forgiven. The Russian custom of consuming sour milk is a very pleasant and healthy one, and is shared by the Balkan countries and other regions. Bulgarians, who eat a great deal of their own special kind of sour milk, maintain that their well known longevity is due to this habit. The cheese obtained from sour milk is called *tvorog* in Russian and is used by them in many ways. It has been referred to as cream cheese as that is usually its name in shops, but for most dishes mentioned here, a plain, dry cottage type of cheese, without the addition of any cream, would be best to use.

Eating habits, however, are changing in Russia as in so many other places. A good deal of Russian food is now being canned both for export and home consumption. Varied canned food is now obtainable there such as crab, Beef Stroganoff, tomato purée, Borshch and many other soups, and many kinds of fish, fruit and vegetables. Caviar is usually exported in small jars but it is sold in bulk for home use. A good variety of all food is available in the shops which stay open until quite late and on Sundays, on a rota system. Eating out is catered for in canteens at places of work, at schools and at ordinary restaurants. Snack bars are gradually making their appearance, and at the moment, there is talk of opening serve-yourself supermarkets. A high standard of hygiene is maintained wherever food is handled, and only dummy food is shown in shop windows.

There is less of mother's home cooking now, as she is probably busy with a job, but there are still quite a few *babushkas* (grannies) left who carry on the traditional, old-time cooking. Not for her baking powder or bicarbonate of soda; she uses yeast for her pastry and bakes her own bread. *Piroshky* (small pies) or a *pirog* (pie) can be made with either puff pastry or yeast dough.

The most popular restaurants for an evening out are the Caucasian ones providing dishes such as shashlik and other exotic dishes from South Russia. There are also special shops from these regions selling their own particular type of food for cooking.

All the ingredients mentioned can be obtained in the food departments of the large stores in London and other large cities. Salted herrings and cucumbers, buckwheat for kasha, various spices and herbs and many other items can be found in most Continental shops. Not only is it quite easy to get the necessary ingredients for Russian cooking, but the dishes are not difficult to prepare, not even where yeast is used. The flour mentioned here is always plain; the baking powder occasionally referred to is a concession to hurried modern times.

421

Nevertheless, Russian cooking, in spite of changes, remains uniquely itself with much to offer. Every country has its specialities which have become famous. Among the Russian dishes you are sure to find many which you will return to again and again and which will become great favourites in your family.

CAVIAR

The Russians have a word for it, which is *ikra* and it is the choicest of their hors-d'oeuvre delicacies.

Caviar is the roe obtained from various types of sturgeon. Preparing this roe is an elaborate process which explains why it is such an expensive luxury. The best is considered to be the grey, loose-grained type from the Beluga which is the largest of the sturgeon fish family. The pressed, black caviar is the kind usually obtainable here, probably because it travels better.

Red caviar is the prepared roe of salmon and is not nearly as expensive as the sturgeon product. It has a pleasant flavour, though, and its pink colour makes a decorative addition to hors-d'oeuvre.

CAVIAR WITH EGGS

4 eggs	1 teaspoon lemon juice	1—2 tablespoons
1 oz. caviar	salt and pepper	mayonnaise
1 cucumber		(see p. 263)

Hard-boil the eggs and, when cold, peel and slice off the tops at the broad ends. Remove the yolks, fill the spaces with caviar and sprinkle with lemon juice. Wash the cucumber, but do not peel. Cut into thin slices and arrange around the stuffed eggs. Rub the yolks through a sieve, blend with mayonnaise, add salt and pepper to taste and cover each egg with the dressing.

SALTED HERRING

Salted herring are extensively used in Russia as an hors-d'oeuvre. They are very popular as an accompaniment to a glass of vodka. Filleted salted herring can be bought from most Continental or Delicatessen shops. However, if they are not filleted, soak them first in cold water for about 6 hours, then remove the skin, heads and tails and cut the fillets from the bones, lengthwise. Arrange the fillets on a dish to reproduce the shape of a herring, with its head and tail put back into place. Garnish with onion rings, slices of hard-boiled eggs and fresh or pickled cucumbers. Pour on vinegar or a mixture of two parts of olive oil to one part of vinegar.

Salted herring are also used in salads or served, to make a meal, with potatoes baked in their jackets.

CHOPPED HERRING

2 fillets salted herring
1 tablespoon butter
1 small apple
sprig parsley
1 hard-boiled egg

Chop the herring very finely and mix well with creamy, unsalted butter. Peel and core the apple, chop finely, mix with the herring and put through a sieve. Shape the mixture like a herring, using the head and tail at the ends, and garnish with slices of hard-boiled egg and chopped parsley.

FISH IN ASPIC

2 lb. carp or other suitable fish
2 eggs
1 onion
1 parsnip
1 carrot
1 oz. gelatine
1 gill white wine
1 bay leaf
6 peppercorns
sprigs parsley
1 lemon
1 cucumber
few olives
salt and pepper
2 pints water
beetroot and horseradish sauce (see p. 448)

Cook the fish in water with a bay leaf, peppercorns and ½ teaspoon of salt, and sliced onion, parsnip and carrot. Strain off the stock and boil down to 1 pint. Dissolve the gelatine in a little water, add to the stock, bring to the boil and simmer, stirring constantly, until well mixed. Strain through a cloth, add wine and allow to cool but not to set. Pour some of the aspic over a long, flat dish, lay the fish on it and decorate with the slices of the cooked carrot, hard-boiled eggs and washed, unpeeled cucumber. Cover with the rest of the aspic and leave to set in a cold place. Serve well chilled, surrounded by olives, sprigs of parsley and slices of lemon, and accompanied by beetroot and horseradish sauce.

SUCKING PIG IN ASPIC

small sucking pig
2 hard-boiled eggs
1½ oz. gelatine
2 lemons
water
2 cloves
12 peppercorns
2 bay leaves
1 cooked carrot
sprig parsley
salt
horseradish and smetana sauce (p. 450)

Boil the pig in water to cover and, when ready, leave to cool in the stock. Strip meat from the bones and slice it. Put the bones into the stock with the peppercorns, cloves, bay leaves, juice of 1 lemon, salt to taste and the gelatine dissolved in 1 gill water. Bring to the boil and simmer until the liquid is reduced to 1½ pints. Then strain and leave to cool but not to set. Arrange the meat on a dish or in a mould, decorate with parsley and slices of carrot, lemon and eggs. Pour on the aspic and leave to get cold. Serve with horseradish and smetana sauce. Sometimes the sucking pig is cooked whole and served that way in aspic.

FORSHMAK

1 lb. cooked meat or poultry	2 eggs	1 tablespoon breadcrumbs
1 filleted salted herring	1 onion	tomato sauce (see p. 451)
2 tablespoons butter	4 tablespoons mashed potatoes	salt and pepper
	½ pint smetana (sour cream)	

Mince the meat and herring together and combine with beaten eggs, the smetana and mashed potatoes. Chop the onion and fry in half the butter. Add to the minced mixture, together with the remaining butter, season with salt and pepper and pass through the mincer. Butter a baking dish, put in the mixture, sprinkle with breadcrumbs and bake in a moderate oven for about 30 minutes. Serve with tomato sauce.

STUFFED MUSHROOMS WITH SMETANA

1 lb. large mushrooms	1 small onion	2 tablespoons butter
2 oz. butter	4 oz. cooked rice	salt and pepper
	½ pint smetana (sour cream)	

The large, high-domed type of mushrooms are needed for this dish. Wash and peel the mushrooms and remove the stalks. Chop and fry the onion in 1 tablespoon of butter, add chopped stalks, sprinkle with salt and pepper and mix with the rice. Fill mushrooms with the rice stuffing. Butter a baking pan, put in the mushrooms, stuffed side up, sprinkle with melted butter and a little salt and bake in a slow oven until the mushrooms are soft. Just before removing them from the oven, add the smetana. Serve as a hot hors-d'oeuvre.

STUDEN

Calf's Foot Jelly

4 calf's feet	3—4 sprigs parsley	about 8 pints water
4—6 eggs	1 lemon	beetroot and horse- radish sauce
2 carrots	6 peppercorns	(see p. 448)
2 onions	salt	
	2—3 bay leaves	

Singe and scald the calf's feet, split them lengthwise, separate the bones from the meat and chop them into several sections. Put the meat and bones into a saucepan with the water, making sure there is enough to cover, with 2 or 3 inches to spare, add carrots, onions, bay leaves, parsley, peppercorns and 1 teaspoon of salt, and simmer, covered, for 2½ to 3 hours. Strain, skim off the fat, remove all the meat and chop it. Put the bones back into the stock, add the juice of a lemon and more

424

seasoning, if required, and continue cooking until about 2 pints of liquid are left. Then mix with the meat and pour into moulds. Hard-boil and slice the eggs and space in the jelly before it has set. When ready, stand the mould in hot water for a few minutes, then turn out on to a dish. Serve with beetroot and horseradish sauce.

CUCUMBER WITH SMETANA

1 gill smetana (sour cream)	1 cucumber 1 teaspoon salt ¼ teaspoon pepper	2 teaspoons lemon juice

Peel the cucumber, slice thinly, sprinkle with salt and leave for about an hour. Then strain off the liquid. Mix the smetana with lemon juice and pour over the cucumber slices. Serve chilled.

VINAIGRETTE
Russian Salad

1 lb. boiled potatoes	1 salted cucumber	1 tablespoon vinegar
4 oz. pickled cabbage	2 cooked beetroots	2 teaspoons sugar
1 onion or 6 spring onions	1 cooked carrot *Dressing:* 3 tablespoons salad oil	1 teaspoon mustard salt and pepper

Dice the potatoes, beetroot, carrot and cucumber. Put into a large salad bowl and add chopped onion and chopped cabbage. Mix the oil, vinegar, mustard, sugar, salt and pepper together and pour into the bowl. Mix well and decorate with slices of beetroot. Fillets of salted herring, cut into small strips, may be added to this salad, or slices of hard-boiled eggs, or diced cooked ham or other cooked meat.

CAUCASIAN SALAD

2 large potatoes	1 cucumber	2 tablespoons
8 oz. peas	2 eggs	mayonnaise
2 carrots	2 sweet apples	(see p. 263)
4 oz. cold meat (beef or lamb)	1 gill smetana (sour cream)	salt and pepper 2—3 sprigs dill

Cook the potatoes, carrots and peas separately and leave to cool. Dice the peeled cucumber, potatoes, carrots and peeled, cored apples and put into a large salad bowl with peas. Make a stiff, firm omelette with the 2 eggs and let it cool. Cut the meat into small squares and the omelette into small strips and put into the salad bowl. Make a dressing with a mixture of mayonnaise, smetana, salt and pepper, pour over the salad and mix well. Serve chilled, sprinkled with chopped dill.

FISH SALAD

8 oz. sturgeon	2 oz. smoked salmon	1 tablespoon vinegar
1 crayfish	8 oz. black olives	2 large potatoes
1 small crab	2 eggs	1 lettuce
2 oz. prawns	1 salted cucumber	salt and pepper
2 oz. caviar	4 tablespoons olive oil	water

Boil separately the sturgeon, crayfish, prawns, crab and potatoes. Hard-boil the eggs. When cold, cut the sturgeon into small pieces and put into a large, shallow bowl lined with lettuce leaves. Add diced potatoes, and cucumber, small pieces of crayfish and crab meat, 4 oz. stoned, chopped olives and some chopped lettuce. Mix well with a dressing of the olive oil and vinegar seasoned with salt and pepper, and surround with peeled prawns, slices of hard-boiled eggs and the rest of the olives. Put over the top of the salad small rolls of caviar wrapped in very thin slices of smoked salmon. Serve well chilled.

HERRING SALAD

1 lb. potatoes	1 dozen black olives	1 small eating apple
2 pickled herrings	1 gill smetana (sour	2 teaspoons vinegar
1 hard-boiled egg	cream)	pepper

Boil the potatoes, preferably new ones, and cut them into rounds. Arrange in a salad bowl with slices of filleted herring and egg, stoned olives and grated apple. Mix smetana with vinegar and a dash of pepper and pour over the salad.

BORSHCH

Beetroot Soup

There are many kinds of this famous Russian soup, but this one is one of the best known.

1 lb. meat	4 oz. tomatoes	1 teaspoon salt
2½ lb. beetroot	1 tablespoon butter	½ teaspoon pepper
2 carrots	2 tablespoons vinegar	½ pint smetana (sour
1 large onion	1 bay leaf	cream)
8 oz. cabbage	1 tablespoon sugar	4 pints water

Prepare the stock from the meat cooked in 4 pints of water, remove the scum and fat and strain. Peel the beetroot, shred finely and put 8 oz. aside to give the borshch colour at the end of cooking. Peel the carrots and onion and cut into thin strips, skin the tomatoes and chop. Put all these prepared ingredients into a saucepan, pour in enough stock to cover, add a tablespoon of butter, put on a lid and simmer for 20 minutes. Then add finely shredded cabbage, a bay leaf, 1 tablespoon vinegar, sugar, salt, pepper and the rest of the stock. Mix well, cover and simmer for a further 20 minutes. Take the beetroot, which was put aside, bring to the boil with a cup of stock and a tablespoon of vinegar, simmer for a few minutes and strain the red liquid into the borshch. Serve with smetana in each plate.

POKHLYOBKA

This is a Russian country soup made without meat, and it is very good and warming, especially in the winter.

4 oz. dried mushrooms	2 large potatoes	½ tablespoon flour
2 tablespoons pearl barley	2 tablespoons butter	4 peppercorns
	2 sprigs dill	2 bay leaves
2 onions	2 tablespoons smetana	about 4 pints water
2 leeks	(sour cream)	1 teaspoon salt
	2 carrots	

Soak the mushrooms in a pint of water for at least 2 hours. Chop the onions and fry lightly in the butter. Slice the leeks and carrots, add to the onions, fry together for a few minutes then put into a large saucepan. Pour in 3 pints water and the water in which the mushrooms were soaked. Slice the mushrooms, dice the potatoes and put into saucepan together with the bay leaves, peppercorns, pearl barley and salt. Simmer, covered, stirring occasionally, until the mushrooms, potatoes and pearl barley are tender. Thicken the soup with a mixture of flour and smetana about 5 minutes before removing from the stove. Serve sprinkled with chopped dill.

LAZY SHCHY

1 lb. beef	1 onion	1 bay leaf
1 lb. cabbage	8 oz. tomatoes	4 pints water
1 celery stick	1 tablespoon butter	1 teaspoon salt
1 turnip	1 tablespoon flour	2—3 sprigs dill or
1 carrot	6 peppercorns	parsley

This is supposed to be an easier way of making cabbage soup, hence the name, no doubt. Put the meat into a large saucepan with the water, peppercorns, bay leaf and salt and add prepared, sliced celery, carrot, turnip and onion. Cover, and simmer for 2 hours. Strain the stock into a saucepan and bring to the boil. Have ready a washed cabbage, cut into large sections and plunge it into the boiling stock. Add skinned, sliced tomatoes, cover and simmer for another 10 minutes. Brown the flour in butter, pour in a cup of warm stock, mix well and blend with the soup. Simmer for a further 15 minutes. Serve sprinkled with chopped dill or parsley.

BOTVINIA

12 oz. cooked fish	2 fresh cucumbers	1 teaspoon sugar
2 pints kvass	4 oz. spring onions	2—3 sprigs of dill
(see p. 473)	2 oz. horseradish	salt and pepper
8 oz. spinach and	mustard	water
sorrel		

Sort out the spinach and sorrel and wash thoroughly. Cook them separately in ¼ cup boiling, salted water in a covered saucepan. Rub both the spinach and the sorrel through a sieve, put into a saucepan, stir in salt, sugar and a pinch of mustard and add diced cucumber, chopped spring onions and dill. Dilute with kvass and mix well. Grate horseradish into each plate of soup and put in small pieces of cooked fish. The fish may be served separately. Sometimes young nettles are used instead of the spinach.

OKROSHKA

A Summer Soup

2 pints kvass	1 salted cucumber	1 teaspoon prepared
(see p. 473)	8 oz. cooked beef or	mustard
1 gill smetana (sour	poultry	1 teaspoon sugar
cream)	2 oz. spring onions	few sprigs dill
1 fresh cucumber	2 hard-boiled eggs	salt and pepper

Cut the meat into small cubes. Peel and dice the fresh cucumber and dice the salted cucumber. Chop the spring onions and mix with the smetana together with sugar, mustard, chopped eggs, salt and pepper. Put all the ingredients into the kvass and mix well. Serve ice-cold, sprinkled with chopped dill.

ARMENIAN SOUP

1 lb. beef	1 onion	1 bay leaf
4 oz. rice	2 egg yolks	salt and pepper
1 tablespoon flour	2½ pints water	parsley or dill
1 tablespoon butter		sprig thyme

Wash the meat and cut into fairly small pieces. Put into a saucepan with cold water and a teaspoon of salt and bring to the boil. Cover, and simmer for 1 hour, removing the scum when it appears. Strain the soup then return the pieces of meat to it, together with the rice, previously well rinsed in cold water. Add chopped onions, fried lightly in butter, a sprig of thyme, a bay leaf and salt and pepper to taste. Cook gently for 30 minutes, occasionally stirring the rice. Remove the soup from the stove, add 2 egg yolks beaten in a little stock and mix well. The soup should be very thick. Serve with pieces of meat and chopped parsley or dill.

MEAT SOLIANKA SOUP

1 lb. meat (for 3 pints of stock)	2 tablespoons tomato purée	1 gill smetana (sour cream)
8 oz. cooked meat or sausage	2 tablespoons butter	½ lemon
4 salted cucumbers	4 oz. tomatoes	2 sprigs parsley or dill
2 onions	1 tablespoon capers	salt and pepper
	12 olives	

Prepare the meat stock. Chop the onions, fry lightly in butter, blend with tomato purée and 1 pint of stock and simmer for 5 minutes. Add thin strips of meat or sausage, diced cucumbers, capers, a bay leaf, skinned sliced tomatoes, remaining 2 pints of stock, salt and pepper and simmer for 10 minutes. Serve with smetana, stoned olives, thin slices of peeled lemon and chopped parsley or dill, in each plate.

SHURPA

An Uzbek Soup

1 lb. mutton	8 oz. mutton bones	few sprigs of dill
2 onions	1 lb. potatoes	1 teaspoon salt
8 oz. tomatoes	2½ pints water	½ teaspoon pepper
	1 tablespoon butter	

Cut the meat into small pieces and put into a saucepan with the bones and salt. Cover with cold water, put on the lid and simmer for 1½ hours. Strain off the stock and return the pieces of meat to it. Chop one onion, fry in butter and add to the stock, together with diced potatoes and the tomatoes skinned and cut into quarters. Cook slowly for a further 20 minutes. In the meantime, chop the remaining onion and crush with a spoon. Put a portion of onion into each plate, sprinkle with freshly ground pepper and pour in the soup. Serve with chopped dill.

MOLDAVIAN CHICKEN SOUP

1 boiling fowl—about 2½ lb.	1 celery stick	4 pints water
1 carrot	1 lb. potatoes	1 dessertspoon vinegar
1 parsnip	1 tablespoon butter	1 teaspoon salt
1 onion	1 tablespoon smetana (sour cream)	cayenne pepper
		sprig parsley or dill

Put a cleaned chicken and the giblets into a saucepan with cold water and bring to the boil. Slice the parsnip, onion, celery and carrot, fry lightly in butter and add to the chicken together with the vinegar and salt. Simmer gently with the lid on for 2 hours. The chicken should then be tender. Strain the stock, let it cool, then remove the fat. Dice the potatoes and cook in the stock until ready, then add a dash of cayenne pepper and the smetana. Serve a quarter portion of the chicken in each plate of soup, sprinkled with chopped parsley or dill.

MOSCOW RASSOLNIK

Salted Cucumber Soup

3 pints meat stock	1 celery stick	salt and pepper
1 lb. ox kidneys	1 parsnip	1 gill smetana (sour
2 salted cucumbers	2 large potatoes	cream)
8 oz. sorrel or lettuce	2 tablespoons butter	sprig parsley or dill
1 onion	1 tablespoon vinegar	water
	1 leek	

The stock may be prepared from meat bones, chicken or meat. Trim the kidneys, cut into several pieces, put into a saucepan of cold water and bring to the boil. Strain, rinse the kidneys and put back into fresh cold water. Bring to the boil again, simmer for 1 hour then strain. Meanwhile, dice the potatoes and cucumbers and put into the meat stock. Chop the onion, slice the vegetables, fry lightly in butter and also add to the meat stock. Season with salt and pepper, bring to the boil and simmer for 20 minutes. Shred the sorrel or lettuce leaves, put into the soup, together with the vinegar, to cook for another 5—10 minutes. Serve with smetana, thin slices of kidney and chopped dill or parsley n each plate.

KHARCHO

A Georgian Soup

1 lb. mutton	8 oz. sour plums	1 tablespoon butter
8 oz. rice	1 tablespoon flour	3 pints water
1 onion	2 tablespoons tomato	salt and pepper
3 cloves garlic	purée or 8 oz.	sprig dill
	tomatoes	

Wash the meat and cut into portions, allowing about three pieces for each person. Put into a saucepan with water and one teaspoon of salt and simmer for 1½ hours, removing scum when it appears. Chop the onion finely and fry in butter. Blend in the flour and stir in the tomato purée or skinned, quartered tomatoes. Add to the meat stock together with the crushed garlic, plums and rice, previously washed in cold water. Bring to the boil, then simmer for 20 minutes. Stir occasionally to prevent the rice from sticking to the bottom of the pan. Serve with the pieces of meat in each plate and sprinkled with chopped dill.

SUMMER BORSHCH

1½ pints kvass	4 oz. spring onions	1 teaspoon sugar
(see p. 473)	2 tablespoons smetana	1 cucumber
1 lb. young beetroot	(sour cream)	1½ pints water
with leaves	2 eggs	salt and pepper

Peel and wash beetroot, put into a saucepan with water, and boil for 20—30 minutes. About 10 minutes before the end of cooking, add the beetroot leaves. Strain off the stock, chop the beetroot and leaves finely and put back into the stock. Set aside to cool. Then add thinly sliced cucumber, slices of hard-boiled eggs, chopped spring onions, sugar, smetana and salt and pepper to taste. Pour in kvass and serve the soup very cold with crushed ice.

FISH SOLIANKA SOUP

1½ lb. fish	1 lemon	2 oz. olives
4 salted cucumbers	few sprigs parsley or	3 pints water
2 onions	dill	4 oz. fresh tomatoes
2 tablespoons butter	salt and pepper	or 2 tablespoons
1 tablespoon capers		tomato purée

Most fish are suitable for this dish except the very small kind or those, with many bones. Clean and prepare the fish and cut into portions, allowing 2 or 3 pieces per person. Prepare a stock from the head and the bones cooked in water with seasoning. Chop the onions finely, fry lightly in butter, add ½ pint of strained stock, tomato purée or chopped tomatoes and simmer for 5 minutes. Then add the pieces of fish, diced cucumber, capers, remainder of stock, salt and pepper to taste and simmer for 10—15 minutes. Serve with stoned olives, finely chopped parsley or dill, thin slices of peeled lemon and portions of fish in each plate.

OUKHA

Fish Soup

This dish may be made with an assortment of fish or from perch, turbot, halibut, bream, etc.

2½ lb. fish	4 oz. spring onions or	2 sprigs parsley
4 pints water	chives	1 bay leaf
2 onions	6 peppercorns	2 tablespoons butter
1 celery stick		2 teaspoons salt

Fillet the fish and put 2 lb. into a saucepan with the fish bones and water and bring to the boil. Slice the onions and celery and add to the fish stock together with bay leaf, peppercorns, parsley and salt and simmer for 1 hour. Strain before using. Cut the rest of the fish into small pieces, sprinkle with salt and fry in butter. Serve the soup with the pieces of fried fish and chopped spring onions or chives. Fish pie usually accompanies oukha.

431

EGGS WITH CREAM CHEESE

8 eggs	2 tablespoons butter	½ teaspoon salt
3 oz. cream cheese	2 tablespoons cream	chives
½ pint milk	pinch paprika	

Put the cream cheese and butter into a double saucepan and heat until well blended. Add milk gradually, stirring well, then the cream, salt and paprika. Beat the eggs and add slowly to the mixture, stirring with a fork. Continue until the mixture has thickened but is not too solid. Serve sprinkled with chopped chives.

EGGS WITH RYE BREAD

4 eggs	2 oz. butter	salt
dark rye bread		

Cut the bread into small squares or strips and fry in hot butter on both sides. Break the eggs into the frying pan over the bread, sprinkle with salt and fry until eggs are ready.

EGGS WITH YOGHOURT

4 eggs	4 slices bread	salt and pepper
½ pint yoghourt	2 tablespoons butter	sprig parsley

Take four slices of bread about 1 inch thick and cut each slice into a round with a pastry cutter. From the centre of each round, cut a small circle. Fry the rings of bread in hot butter until golden brown then lay them on a buttered baking dish. Drop a raw egg into the centre of each ring of bread, cover each egg with yoghourt, season with salt and pepper and bake in a moderate oven until the eggs are set. Decorate with chopped parsley.

STURGEON

The sturgeon deserves special mention on its own, being a very splendid fish with a fine flavour and the additional merit of producing the roe for caviar.

It can, however, be somewhat hard, at times, so it is a good idea to marinate it first in white wine, before cooking. To prepare a boiled sturgeon, put it in a pan together with the marinade and a few pepper-corns, 1 or 2 bay leaves, sliced onion, celery stalk and parsnip and salt to taste. Add water, if necessary, so that all the ingredients are covered completely, put on a lid and simmer until the fish is tender.

To bake a sturgeon, wash it in boiling water and remove its skin. Then dry the fish, rub in salt and butter, put into a well buttered oven dish and bake in a moderate oven, allowing 15 minutes to each pound of fish.

84. Lobster for lunch in France

85. Nasi Goreng, Holland (p.182)

86. Fish Kulebiak, Russia (p.457)

STURGEON WITH SHRIMP SAUCE

2 lb. sturgeon	½ pint shrimps	½ pint water
4 oz. mushrooms	1 tablespoon flour	salt and pepper
2 gills white wine		1 tablespoon butter

Remove the skin from the sturgeon and put the fish into a china dish. Sprinkle with salt, pour on the white wine and leave in a cool place for several hours. Then put the sturgeon, with the wine, into a saucepan, add the cold water, cover and simmer gently until the fish is tender. Melt butter in a pan, blend with flour and dilute with some of the fish stock. Add thinly sliced mushrooms, small boiled peeled shrimps, salt and pepper to taste and cook for 5 minutes. Serve the sturgeon with the hot shrimp sauce poured over it.

BAKED FISH IN SMETANA SAUCE

2 lb. fish	2 tablespoons flour	6 oz. butter
½ pint smetana sauce	8 oz. white	salt and pepper
(see p. 450)	mushrooms	4 tablespoons grated
2 hard-boiled eggs	1½ lb. potatoes	cheese

Any fish suitable for baking, such as cod or halibut will do. Clean and skin the fish, cut into 4 portions, cover with flour and fry on both sides for a few minutes in 2 oz. of butter. Put into a buttered oven dish and lay slices of half an egg on each portion. Slice the mushrooms, fry lightly in 2 oz. butter and pile over the eggs. Peel and slice the potatoes, fry in the rest of the butter until golden brown, and put around the fish. Sprinkle all over with salt and pepper, pour smetana sauce over the fish, cover all the ingredients with grated cheese and bake in a moderate oven for 20 minutes.

BREAM STUFFED WITH KASHA

2 lb. bream	mixed herbs	3 tablespoons butter
1 lb. baked kasha	salt and pepper	1 gill smetana (sour
(see p. 451)	1 onion	cream)
	1 hard-boiled egg	breadcrumbs
		melted butter

Cut off the head and clean the inside of the fish. Chop the onion and fry in butter until soft then mix with kasha, salt, pepper, a pinch of herbs and chopped egg. Stuff the bream with the mixture, sprinkle with salt, pepper and breadcrumbs and pour on melted butter. Grease an oven dish with butter, put in the fish and bake in a moderate oven for about 35 minutes or until tender. Add a little warm water to the dish when it gets hot. Before serving, stir smetana into the dish in which the fish was cooked, heat for a few minutes and pour over the bream.

BREAM WITH HORSERADISH AND APPLES

2 lb. bream
1 lb. cooking apples
2 celery stalks
1 leek
2 onions

1 tablespoon sugar
about ½ pint vinegar
3 tablespoons grated
  horseradish

6 peppercorns
mixed herbs
1 teaspoon salt
1 lemon
2 bay leaves

Skin the fish and cut it into 4 portions. Put them into a saucepan, cover with vinegar and bring to the boil. Slice the vegetables and put into a saucepan with enough boiling water to cover them. Drain the fish and put into the saucepan with the vegetables, adding salt, peppercorns, bay leaves and a pinch of mixed herbs. Cook slowly until the fish is tender. Mix the horseradish with peeled, cored and grated apples, add sugar and dilute with enough vinegar to make a creamy sauce. Serve with the fish garnished with slices of lemon.

LENINGRAD PIKE

2 lb. pike (in 4 slices)
1 onion
1 tablespoon butter
½ pint milk

2 hard-boiled eggs
2 tablespoons bread-
  crumbs

2 sprigs parsley
flour
salt and pepper
4 oz. bread

Remove the bone and skin from the pike and flatten out slices. Soak the bread in the milk and squeeze out the excess moisture. Chop the eggs and the onion and combine with the bread, salt and freshly ground pepper. Put the filling into the centre of each piece of fish and fold over. Sprinkle the stuffed fish with salt and flour and fry in butter for 5 minutes. Place in an oven dish, sprinkle with breadcrumbs and bake in a moderate oven for 20 minutes. Serve the fish sprinkled with chopped parsley.

FISH SOLIANKA

1½ lb. filleted fish
2 lb. pickled cabbage
4 oz. butter
2 onions
1 tablespoon bread-
  crumbs

1 oz. capers
½ lemon
2 sprigs dill
olives
salt and pepper
2 tablespoons
  tomato purée

2 salted cucumbers
1 tablespoon sugar
½ pint fish stock or
  water
2 tablespoons vinegar
2 bay leaves

Chop the onions and fry lightly in 3 oz. of butter. Add the cabbage, tomato purée, vinegar and sugar, and cook for 10 minutes. Cut the fish into small sections, put into a saucepan with bay leaves, sliced salted cucumbers, capers, salt and pepper and cover with stock or water. Put on the lid and simmer for 15 minutes. Lay half the cabbage in a buttered baking dish, put the fish and its sauce on top, cover with the remaining cabbage, sprinkle with breadcrumbs, dot with butter and bake in a moderate oven for 10 minutes. Serve garnished with olives, slices of lemon and chopped dill.

STUFFED FISH

2½ lb. fish (preferably bream)	2 beetroots	1 egg
8 oz. white bread	1 tablespoon olive oil	½ pint milk
1 lb. onions	3 carrots	salt and pepper
		1 tablespoon sugar

Remove the head and gills, wash the fish in cold water and cut into 4 thick steaks. Cut out a small portion of fish from each steak, taking care not to break the skin. For the stuffing, take the bread, previously soaked in milk, onions and the cut-out pieces of fish and put them through a mincer. Then add a raw egg, sugar, olive oil, pepper and salt and mix well. Stuff the fish steaks, filling the spaces where the pieces have been cut out, and flatten out the stuffing with a wet knife. Take a large saucepan, cover the bottom of it with a layer of peeled sliced beetroot, carrots and well-washed onion skins and lay the fish steaks over the vegetables. Continue with alternate layers of fish and vegetables, finishing with the vegetables. Add sufficient water to cover, put a lid on the saucepan and simmer gently for 1½—2 hours. Take care that the fish does not burn, and, if necessary, add a little water from time to time. Serve with the liquid in which the fish was cooked.

COD WITH HORSERADISH

2 lb. cod	2 tablespoons butter	1 gill smetana (sour cream)
4 oz. horseradish	1 dessertspoon flour	salt and pepper
½ pint fish stock	1 tablespoon vinegar	

Fillet the cod but do not remove the skin. Cut the fish into small pieces and put into a saucepan with a tablespoon of butter. Add finely grated horseradish, fish stock made from the bones, vinegar, salt and pepper. Cover, and cook very slowly for 25 minutes. Then put 1 gill fish stock into another saucepan, add smetana and bring to the boil. Melt a tablespoon of butter, blend with flour and add to the smetana mixture. Stir until smooth, pour over the fish and cook slowly for another 15 minutes.

STUFFED PLAICE

4 fillets plaice	1 whole egg	1 tablespoon flour
2 onions	1 gill milk	1 tablespoon butter
4 slices bread	1 yolk	salt and pepper
	1 pint frying oil	

Chop the onions and fry in the butter until golden coloured. Soak the bread in the milk then squeeze out the surplus liquid. Mix the fried onions with the bread, add salt and pepper and bind with 1 egg. Fill each fillet with the stuffing and roll up. Cover with flour, dip into a beaten egg yolk, roll in breadcrumbs and fry in deep, hot oil.

FISH CUTLETS WITH RAISIN SAUCE

1½ lb. filleted fish
1 egg
4 slices white bread
4 oz. raisins

1 gill white wine
1 tablespoon flour
2 tablespoons bread-
  crumbs
4 oz. butter

1 teaspoon sugar
1 teaspoon lemon juice
½ pint water
salt and pepper
1 tablespoon extra
  butter

Soak the bread in milk and squeeze out the excess liquid. Mince the fish, mix with the bread, season with salt and pepper and put through the mincer together. Shape the mixture into cutlets, cover with bread-crumbs, and fry in butter, on both sides, until brown and crisp. Soak the raisins in hot water and strain. Melt a tablespoon of butter, blend it with flour and dilute with a cup of warm water. Add the raisins, lemon juice, sugar and a pinch of salt, bring to the boil and simmer, stirring frequently, for 15 minutes. Add the wine in the last 5 minutes. Serve the fish cutlets and sauce separately.

CRAB IN EGG SAUCE

3 lb. boiled crab
1 gill white wine

salt and pepper
½ pint egg sauce
  (see p. 260)

green salad
½ pint vegetable stock

Remove the crab meat from the shells and cut into pieces. Put into a saucepan, pour in the wine and the stock—which should be enough to cover the crab meat—and season with salt and freshly ground pepper. Cover and cook for 10 minutes. Drain off the liquid and use for making the sauce. Serve the crab with the egg sauce and a green salad.

PIKE-PERCH WITH FENNEL

2 lb. pike-perch
4 sprigs of dried fennel

1 gill white wine

salt and pepper
1 tablespoon butter

Clean and wash the fish, sprinkle with salt and pepper and put the sprigs of fennel inside. Rub all over with butter and grill for 10 minutes on each side. Add the wine to the liquid obtained from the cooking, heat and pour over the fish when served.

COD WITH CABBAGE

2 lb. cod
1 dessertspoon flour

1 lb. cabbage
½ pint vinegar
1 tablespoon butter

4 oz. spring onions
salt and pepper

Fillet the cod but leave the skin. Cut the fish into small pieces, sprinkle with salt and pepper, roll in flour and fry lightly in hot butter. Shred and wash the cabbage, lay half in a shallow baking pan, sprinkle with salt, pour in 1 gill vinegar and cover with the fish. Put the remaining cabbage on top, sprinkle on a little more salt, and pour on the rest of the vinegar. Cook in a slow oven for 1 hour.

FISH WITH RICE

1 lb. filleted fish	3 oz. butter	salt and pepper
(cod, bream or hake)	8 oz. tomatoes	2 onions
	4 oz. rice	

Cut fish into small pieces and season with salt and pepper. Chop onions finely and fry in butter. Partly boil the rice, strain it and put half into a saucepan greased at the bottom with butter. Place the fish and onions over the rice in the saucepan then add a layer of sliced tomatoes. Put the remainder of the rice on top with a knob of butter. Simmer with the lid on until the rice is cooked.

PLAICE WITH MUSHROOMS AND GHERKINS

4 small plaice	8 oz. mushrooms	4 oz. gherkins
1 tablespoon flour	1 onion	salt and pepper
	2 tablespoons butter	extra butter

Wash the fish, dry it and sprinkle with salt and pepper. Cover with flour and fry lightly on both sides in hot butter. Put into a moderate oven to finish cooking. Chop the onion finely and fry in extra butter, until golden, slice the mushrooms, add to the onions and fry for 5 minutes. Cut the gherkins into thin strips, mix with the onion, mushrooms and a little liquid obtained from the fish and spread over the plaice. Leave in the oven for another 5 minutes, then serve.

TEFTELY IN TOMATO SAUCE

Meat Balls in Tomato Sauce

1 lb. meat (preferably veal)	2 tablespoons butter	2 cloves garlic
	4 slices white bread	5 peppercorns
1 gill tomato purée	1 onion	salt
4 oz. tomatoes	½ pint meat stock	cooked rice or kasha
	2 bay leaves	(see p. 451)
	2 tablespoons flour	

Soak the bread in milk then squeeze out the excess moisture. Mince the meat, mix with the bread and pass through the mincer together. Chop the onion finely, fry in a tablespoon of butter and add to the meat mixture. Season with salt and pepper, mix well, roll into balls and cover with flour. Fry lightly on all sides in hot butter then add the tomato purée, peppercorns, bay leaves, crushed garlic and sliced tomatoes. Sprinkle with flour, dilute with stock, cover and cook gently for 15 minutes. Serve with rice or kasha.

PLAICE WITH APPLES AND ONIONS

4 small plaice or	4 oz. spring onions	lemon
1½ lb. filleted plaice	1 tablespoon fish stock	salt and pepper
2 apples	or water	1 gill white wine

Peel and core the apples and cut into thin slices. Place the fish in a shallow pan with the apple slices and the heads of the spring onions. Add salt, freshly ground pepper, fish stock or water and the wine. Cover firmly and cook gently for 15 minutes. Serve with a garnish of lemon slices.

BEEF STROGANOFF

This famous Russian dish has had the honour of being adopted by the French *haute cuisine* and is now often served in many restaurants.

1½ lb. fillet of beef	1 tablespoon tomato	1 dessertspoon flour
1—2 small onions	purée (optional)	1 teaspoon salt
4 oz. mushrooms	½ pint smetana (sour	¼ teaspoon pepper
3 oz. butter	cream)	pinch mustard

Cut the meat into thin strips, about 2 inches long, and sprinkle with salt and pepper. Chop the onions very finely and fry in hot butter until golden coloured. Wash, peel and slice the mushrooms and add to the onions. Make room in the pan, put in the meat and fry for 5 minutes. Blend the smetana with the flour, mustard and tomato purée, mix well and pour into the pan. Stir the contents of the pan, cover and simmer gently for about 10 minutes, or until the meat is tender. Add a little more smetana just before the end of cooking. (*Illustrated in Plate 88.*)

GOLUBTSY

Stuffed Cabbage Leaves

1 lb. minced beef	2 tablespoons vinegar,	2 tablespoons tomato
4 oz. cooked rice	juice ½ lemon	purée or
3 tablespoons butter	1 white cabbage —	8 oz. tomatoes
½ pint smetana	medium size	½ pint stock
(sour cream)	1 tablespoon flour	salt and pepper
2 teaspoons sugar	2 onions	

Chop the onions and fry lightly in one tablespoon of butter. Add the minced meat, salt and pepper and fry together for a few minutes. Remove from the stove and mix in the cooked rice and a little of the stock. In the meantime, put the whole cabbage into boiling, salted water and cook it until the leaves are just soft enough not to break when bent. Strain, separate the leaves, flatten them out and cut away the thick stalks. Put a heaped tablespoon of meat stuffing on each leaf and roll up, turning in the ends. Fry in 1 tablespoon butter, browning them slightly on all sides. Put the stuffed cabbage leaves, closely packed, into a casserole or baking dish. Melt the remaining butter, blend in the flour and dilute with the rest of the stock. Sprinkle with salt, add the smetana, tomato purée (or tomatoes) and sugar and bring to the boil. Mix well and remove them from the stove. Add the lemon juice or vinegar and pour over the stuffed cabbage. Cook in a slow oven for 1 hour.

SUCKING PIG WITH HORSERADISH AND SMETANA SAUCE

small sucking pig	horseradish and smetana sauce (see p. 450)	1 tablespoon salt

Cut the prepared sucking pig into sections and put into a large pan with enough cold water to cover. Bring to the boil, then reduce the heat and simmer very gently for about 2 hours or until the meat is white and tender. When ready, add salt and leave the sucking pig in water until cold. Then take out and serve with horseradish and smetana sauce.

STUFFED MEAT LOAF

1 lb. minced beef	2 tablespoons butter	4 oz. rice
1 egg	2 oz. breadcrumbs	tomato sauce
1 onion	salt and pepper	(see p. 451)
	1 gill water	

The Russian name for this dish is Blind Hare, presumably because there is no opening to it. Boil the rice in salted water until tender and strain. Hard-boil the egg, chop and mix with the rice. Chop the onion and fry lightly in butter. Soak the breadcrumbs in 1 gill of water, and squeeze out the moisture. Mix the minced meat, breadcrumbs and fried onion together, add salt and pepper and lay out flat. Pile the rice and egg mixture in the centre and push the meat mixture up over it, covering it completely, to make a pyramid shape. Dot with butter and bake in a moderate oven for 45 minutes. Serve with tomato sauce.

GEORGIAN SOLIANKA

1 lb. lamb or mutton	2 tablespoons tomato purée	2 cloves garlic
2 onions	1 gill red wine	1 gill stock
	3 tablespoons oil	sprig parsley
		salt and pepper

Cut the meat into small squares, chop the onions and fry together in oil in a shallow pan. Add the tomato purée, slices of salted cucumbers, crushed garlic cloves, salt and pepper. Pour in the meat stock and wine, cover with a lid and simmer gently for 30 minutes. Serve sprinkled with chopped parsley.

CHICKEN À LA KIEV

4 lb. roasting chicken	2 oz. mushrooms	cayenne pepper
8 oz. butter	2 oz. breadcrumbs	1 lemon
1 egg	1 teaspoon salt	¼ pint frying oil

Skin the chicken and remove the legs and wings. Take a very sharp pointed knife and carefully cut away the meat from each side of the breast-bone. Flatten the two fillets of chicken breast into thin slices, then divide each piece into half. Place on each of the four portions 1 oz. of cold, firm, finger-shaped butter and finely chopped mushrooms. Sprinkle with salt and a small pinch of cayenne pepper. Then roll up the fillets over the butter into the shape of tubes, tucking in the ends so that the butter is well enclosed, and put into a cold place. Before cooking, dip the rolled chicken fillets into a beaten egg and into the breadcrumbs, then fry in deep hot fat, which can cut a mixture of frying oil and the remaining butter. Fry for 5 minutes, turning the chicken fillets over until they are golden brown on all sides. Make one or two small slits in each portion before serving, to prevent butter squirting out. Garnish with lemon and serve with rice or potatoes.

CHICKEN WITH WALNUT SAUCE

1 cooked chicken	1 teaspoon paprika	walnut sauce
8 oz. cooked rice	2—3 sprigs dill	(see p. 449)

Put the rice in the centre of a dish and sprinkle with paprika. Cut thin slices of chicken breast, arrange round the rice and sprinkle with chopped dill. Serve with walnut sauce.

POZHARSKY CHICKEN CUTLETS

1 chicken, 2 lb.	4 tablespoons	4 tablespoons butter
1½ gills milk	breadcrumbs	salt and pepper
	4 oz. white bread	

Clean the chicken, separate the meat from the bones and mince. Soak the bread in milk, press out some of the excess moisture, add to the minced chicken and put through the mincer together. Add a tablespoon of melted butter, season with salt and pepper, mix well and shape into cutlets. Cover with breadcrumbs and fry in hot butter on both sides until golden brown. This should take about 5 minutes. Then cover with a lid and leave on a low heat for another 5 minutes. Serve with melted butter poured over the cutlets.

CHICKEN WITH CHERRY SAUCE

1 boiling chicken,	4 oz. raisins	1 teaspoon salt
about 2½ lb.	1 tablespoon sugar	water
	8 oz. cherries	

Put the chicken into a saucepan with salt and enough water to cover. Simmer until tender, then strain off the stock. Cut the chicken into four portions, put into a pan with enough stock to cover and add the sugar, raisins and stoned cherries. Simmer for 10—15 minutes.

CHICKEN IN SMETANA

1 chicken, 2½ lb.	3 oz. butter	salt and pepper
½ dessertspoon flour	½ pint smetana (sour cream)	4 slices toast

Cut the chicken into 4 portions, dip into flour, sprinkle with salt and pepper, fry in 2 oz. of hot butter until almost done, then drain off most of the fat. Blend the smetana with flour, pour over the chicken in the pan, reduce the heat, cover, and simmer for 10 minutes. Arrange the chicken on four slices of buttered toast and pour the sauce over all the portions.

CHICKEN STUFFED WITH RAISINS

1 chicken, 2½ lb.	2 tablespoons butter	salt and pepper
½ pint milk	8 oz. seedless raisins	1 gill chicken stock or water
4 slices white bread		

Soak the bread in the milk, then squeeze out the surplus liquid. Soak the raisins in water and when they are soft enough, drain and mix them with the bread. Wash and dry the chicken, sprinkle with salt and pepper, inside and out, rub with butter and stuff with the raisin mixture. Place in a roasting pan, greased with butter, and put into a hot oven for 15 minutes; then reduce the heat to very moderate, cover the chicken with buttered greaseproof paper and roast for about an hour. A few minutes before removing the chicken from the oven, add 1 gill of stock or water and baste. If greaseproof paper is not used, baste frequently.

CHAKHOKHBILY

A Caucasian Chicken Dish

1 chicken, 2½ lb.	1 gill stock	1 bay leaf
2 tablespoons tomato purée	8 oz. tomatoes	1 lemon
	2 onions	salt and pepper
1 tablespoon vinegar	2—3 tablespoons oil	parsley or watercress

Divide the chicken into four portions and put into a saucepan with hot oil. Brown lightly, then add chopped onions, bay leaf, tomato purée, vinegar, stock, salt and pepper. Cover and simmer gently for 1½ hours. 15 minutes before the end of the cooking, skin the tomatoes, cut into quarters, and add to the chicken. Serve with slices of lemon and decorate with watercress or parsley.

441

MEAT ROLLS WITH KASHA

1 lb. beef	½ pint stock	1 gill smetana
4 oz. baked kasha	2 onions	(sour cream)
(see p. 451)	2 tablespoons butter	salt and pepper

Cut the meat into four slices and flatten them out. Chop the onions, fry in butter and then mix with the kasha. Spread a quarter portion on each slice of meat, sprinkle with salt and pepper, roll up and tie with cotton. Fry the meat rolls in butter in a shallow pan until slightly brown, then add enough stock to cover, put on a lid and simmer very slowly for 1 hour. Use some of the juice from the cooked meat to heat up with the smetana. Serve the smetana sauce separately.

BITKY
Minced Meat Cutlets

1½ lb. lean steak	3—4 oz. butter	¼ teaspoon pepper
2 slices white bread	4 teaspoons bread-	1 gill smetana (sour
1 gill milk	crumbs	cream)
1 small onion	1 egg	1 teaspoon salt

Soak the bread, without crusts, in the milk, then squeeze out the excess moisture. Mince the meat, mix with the bread and put through the mincer together. Add a grated onion, egg, salt and pepper and mix well. Form into small balls, push a knob of butter into the centre of each one and press down into round, flat shapes. Cover lightly in fine breadcrumbs and fry over a low heat in very hot butter for 3—4 minutes each side. Cover while cooking. The bitky should be golden brown, when ready, but not crusty. Put the smetana into the pan used for the frying, heat gently for a few minutes, pour over the bitky and serve.

PORK WITH PLUM SAUCE

leg of young pork	8 oz. plums	pinch cinnamon
1 carrot	1 bay leaf	1 oz. butter
1 onion	2 cloves	1 tablespoon sugar
1 celery stalk	½ lemon	salt
1 turnip		6 peppercorns

Plunge the pork into boiling water, sufficient in quantity to cover it. Let the water boil again, then skim the surface. Add all the vegetables, crushed cloves, bay leaf, juice of ½ lemon, peppercorns and salt and simmer for 1½—2 hours. Stew the plums in just enough water to cover, adding sugar and a pinch of cinnamon. When cooked, remove the stones and rub the plums through a sieve. Mix with the butter and a little plum juice and serve separately with the leg of pork.

SHASHLIK

Shashlik is the Caucasian name for food cooked on skewers. This way of doing it is known all over the Near and Middle East under other names. In the Caucasus, in the old days, the meat was often grilled on a sword over an open fire.

LAMB SHASHLIK

1½ lb. of lamb	1 lemon	1 teaspoon salt
2 shallots	juice 1 lemon	ground pepper
4 oz. spring onions	1 tablespoon olive oil	1 lb. cooked rice
	8 oz. tomatoes	

Wash the meat and cut into small squares. Put into a dish and season with salt and ground pepper, add finely chopped onion and the lemon juice and mix well. Cover the dish and leave in a cool place for 2 or 3 hours. Put the pieces of lamb on skewers, alternating with slices of onion. Cook on charcoal, if possible, otherwise grill, for 15 or 20 minutes, turning the skewer so that the meat is cooked on all sides. Garnish with spring onions, slices of tomatoes and lemon. Serve with rice.

SPRING CHICKEN ON A SKEWER

2 spring chickens, about 1½ lb. each	1 salted cucumber	tkemaly sauce (see p. 449)
2 tablespoons butter	2 tomatoes	salt

Wash the chickens and sprinkle with salt. Place them on a skewer that is at an angle from the feet to the wings, and grill over glowing charcoal, if possible, otherwise under a grill for 20—30 minutes. Turn the chickens during the grilling , and pour melted butter over them from time to time. When ready, the chickens should be golden brown. Serve half a chicken to each person and garnish with slices of salted cucumber and tomatoes. Tkemaly sauce should accompany this dish.

SPRING CHICKEN WITH APPLES

1 chicken, 2½ lb.	1 lb. apples	½ pint chicken stock
2 tablespoons butter	1 tablespoon flour	salt and pepper
	1 gill white wine	

Wash the chicken, divide it into four portions, cover in flour and fry in butter for 5 minutes. Add chicken stock, made from the giblets, heat and then transfer the chicken and the liquid to a casserole. Surround the chicken with peeled, cored and sliced apples, pour in the wine and cook until tender. Serve in the casserole dish.

MUSHROOM SOLIANKA

1 lb. mushrooms	1 tablespoon vinegar	1 bay leaf
2 salted cucumbers	1 lb. cabbage	salt and pepper
2 tablespoons tomato	1 tablespoon sugar	1 lemon
purée	2 tablespoons butter	olives
1 onion		3 tablespoons water

Wash and shred the cabbage and put into a saucepan. Add a tablespoon of butter, water and vinegar, cook slowly for 15 minutes. About 5 minutes before the cabbage is ready, add the tomato purée, diced cucumbers, sugar, salt, pepper and a bay leaf. Clean and wash the mushrooms and leave in hot water for 15 minutes, then slice and fry in butter. Remove the mushrooms, fry the chopped onion in the same pan and mix together. Lay half the cabbage in an oven dish and put the mushrooms on top. Cover with the rest of the cabbage, sprinkle with breadcrumbs, dab with butter and put into the oven to bake until brown on top. Serve with olives and slices of lemon. This dish may be prepared with sauerkraut, in which case do not add any vinegar to the cabbage. Dried or salted mushrooms may also be used, but they will need soaking for 2 hours beforehand.

MUSHROOMS WITH SMETANA

8 oz. small white	1 tablespoon butter	juice $\frac{1}{2}$ lemon
mushrooms	1 gill smetana (sour	$\frac{1}{2}$ pint meat stock
1 tablespoon flour	cream)	$\frac{1}{2}$ teaspoon salt

Wash and peel the mushrooms and boil whole in the stock for 5 minutes. Melt the butter, blend with the flour and dilute with a little of the stock. Stir well and add the mushrooms, the rest of the stock, lemon juice and salt. Simmer for 10 minutes, stirring occasionally, then add the smetana. Serve hot with potato dishes, vegetables, rissoles or omelettes.

MUSHROOMS WITH CHEESE

1 lb. mushrooms	1 teaspoon flour	$\frac{1}{2}$ teaspoon salt
$\frac{1}{2}$ pint smetana	2 tablespoons grated	few sprigs dill or
(sour cream)	cheese	parsley
	2 tablespoons butter	

Wash and slice the mushrooms. There is no need always to peel them unless they are old and tough as they often have a better flavour with their skins. Fry the mushrooms lightly in butter, stir in the flour and salt and remove from the heat. Blend in the smetana, sprinkle with grated cheese and brown under a grill. Serve sprinkled with chopped dill or parsley.

MUSHROOMS WITH ONIONS

1 lb. mushrooms	2 onions	salt
3 tablespoons butter	1 gill Madeira	sprig parsley or dill

Clean and wash the mushrooms and pour boiling water over them. Cut into thin slices, season with salt and fry in butter. Fry finely chopped onions, mix with the mushrooms, add the wine and cook for 5 minutes. Serve sprinkled with chopped parsley or dill. Fried potatoes go well with this dish.

FRENCH BEANS WITH MUSHROOMS

1½ lb. French beans	1 gill smetana	1 gill water
8 oz. mushrooms	(sour cream)	½ teaspoon salt
2 tablespoons butter		parsley

Wash and slice the beans, put into boiling, salted water, cover with a lid and cook until tender. Wash and slice the mushrooms, fry lightly in butter, sprinkle with salt, add 2 tablespoons of the water in which the beans were cooked and simmer for 5 minutes. Add the beans, stir in the smetana and heat for another few minutes. Serve sprinkled with chopped parsley

MUSHROOMS IN WHITE SAUCE

1 lb. mushrooms	1 tablespoon butter	salt and pepper
1 gill cream	1 gill white sauce (see p. 257)	squeeze lemon juice

Peel, wash and slice the mushrooms. Put into a saucepan with white sauce, cream, butter, salt and pepper. Simmer gently until the mushrooms are tender. Before serving, add a squeeze of lemon.

POTATO PATTIES WITH MUSHROOMS

2 lb. potatoes	4 oz. dried	2 eggs
2 onions	mushrooms	salt and pepper
2 oz. fine bread-crumbs	4 tablespoons butter or oil	tomato sauce (see p. 451)

Peel the potatoes and boil in salted water. Drain, dry off and rub them through a sieve while they are still hot. Chop the onions finely, fry in butter, add sliced mushrooms, previously soaked for 2 hours, and season with salt and pepper. Divide the potato purée into small, flat rounds. Put some of the mushroom filling in the centre of each potato round, then fold each one over, making the shape of a half moon. Press the edges firmly together. Brush the patties with beaten egg, cover in breadcrumbs and fry in hot butter or oil until crisp. Serve with tomato sauce.

POTATO ROLL WITH VEGETABLES

2 lb. potatoes	½ pint milk	water
1 lb. mixed vegetables	2 eggs	smetana sauce
4 oz. butter	salt and pepper	(see p. 450)

Peel and boil the potatoes. When cooked, mash them with milk, add beaten eggs, 3 oz. butter, salt and pepper. Lay out the potato purée on a damp cloth and flatten out to about 1 inch thick. Chop the vegetables, fry lightly in butter, spread down the centre of the potato purée and roll up in the cloth. Take the roll out, press the ends together, brush with a little milk and put into a baking pan, greased with butter. Bake for 25—30 minutes and serve with smetana sauce.

FRIED CUCUMBERS IN SMETANA

1 large cucumber	½ pint smetana sauce	2 oz. spring onions
1 tablespoon butter	(see p. 450)	salt

Peel and slice the cucumber. Chop the onions, fry in hot butter, add the cucumber, sprinkle with salt and fry until soft. Stir in the smetana sauce and simmer for 2 minutes. Serve with hot meat dishes.

CABBAGE SOLIANKA

2 lb. white cabbage	2 onions	1 tablespoon vinegar
2 salted cucumbers	8 oz. frankfurter	1 bay leaf
1 tablespoon flour	sausages	olives
3 tablespoons butter	3 tablespoons tomato	salt and pepper
1 teaspoon sugar	purée	
½ pint stock		

Shred the cabbage, put into a saucepan with 1 tablespoon butter and 1 gill stock, cover and cook slowly for 20 minutes. Then add finely chopped onion, tomato purée, vinegar, sugar, a bay leaf, salt and pepper, mix well and cook for another 10 minutes. Add the flour, browned in butter, bring to the boil and stir for 5 minutes. Cut the sausages into small slices, fry lightly with chopped onion, and add diced cucumber, the capers and the rest of stock. Cover and boil for several minutes. Take half the cooked cabbage, lay out evenly in a pan and place over it the sausages and ingredients cooked with it. Cover with the rest of the cabbage, flatten the top, sprinkle with breadcrumbs, dot with butter and bake in moderate oven for 15 minutes. Serve garnished with olives.

NEW POTATOES IN SMETANA

2 lb. new potatoes	1 gill smetana	1 teaspoon salt
1 tablespoon butter	(sour cream)	2 sprigs parsley

Scrape the potatoes and boil in salted water until ready. Drain well, add smetana and butter to the potatoes, heat for a few minutes, shaking the pan frequently, and serve sprinkled with chopped parsley.

BEETROOT SAUCE

2 lb. beetroot	½ lemon	salt
	2 tablespoons cream	

Boil the beetroot in plenty of water until tender. Skin them and, when cool, pass through a mincer or grate finely. Then put them into a saucepan with cream, juice of ½ lemon, and a pinch of salt. Heat for 5 minutes, stirring well. Serve with meat dishes.

MUSHROOM SAUCE

2 oz. dried mushrooms	1 tablespoon flour	salt, pepper
	2 tablespoons butter	¾ pint water
	1 onion	

Wash the mushrooms in warm water and soak in cold water for 2—3 hours. Then cook the mushrooms until tender in the same water in which they were soaked, without using salt. Brown the flour in butter, dilute with ½ pint of hot mushrooms stock and simmer for 15—20 minutes. In the meantime, chop the onion finely and fry lightly in butter. Add the mushrooms, finely chopped, and fry together with the onions for a few minutes. Mix with the mushroom stock, season to taste and cook gently for 5—10 minutes. Serve with potato cakes, rissoles or vegetables.

SWEET AND SOUR WALNUT SAUCE

2 oz. shelled walnuts	2 oz. butter	6 peppercorns
2 oz. seedless raisins	1 tablespoon sugar	3 tablespoons vinegar
2 oz. grated horseradish	1 bay leaf	1 gill water
	4 oz. prunes	½ teaspoon salt

Stew prunes in water until soft. Strain the juice into a saucepan and add the raisins, peppercorns, bay leaf, sugar, salt, vinegar, chopped walnuts and finely grated horseradish. Stone the prunes, rub them through a sieve and add to the mixture. Stir well and simmer for 10—15 minutes. The sauce should be the consistency of thick cream. Serve with boiled ham, game or cold meat.

SWEET AND SOUR RAISIN SAUCE

4 oz. seedless raisins
2 tablespoons flour
2½ tablespoons butter
½ pint fish stock
1 teaspoon burnt sugar

2 oz. chopped
  almonds
1 clove
grated nutmeg
2 teaspoons castor
  sugar

1 gill dry white wine
1 bay leaf
2 teaspoons lemon
  juice
salt and pepper

Soak the raisins in hot water. Melt the butter, blend with flour and dilute
with stock. Add burnt sugar, clove, a little grated nutmeg, salt and pepper
to taste and bring to the boil, two or three times. Strain off the liquid
and add to it wine, lemon juice, almonds and raisins. Boil again and
simmer for 5 minutes. Serve hot with boiled fish or fish rissoles.

BEETROOT AND HORSERADISH SAUCE

8 oz. grated horse-
  radish
4 oz. grated cooked
  beetroot

2 tablespoons butter
1 teaspoon dry
  mustard
1 gill vinegar

1 pint stock
3 tablespoons flour
1 teaspoon sugar
1 teaspoon salt

Melt the butter, blend with the flour, dilute with stock and bring to
the boil. Add horseradish, mustard, vinegar, sugar, salt and simmer
for 10 minutes, stirring constantly. Add the cooked beetroot and heat
for another 5 minutes. Serve the sauce with calf's foot jelly, aspic dishes,
roast pork, cold beef and cold fish.

CAVIAR SAUCE

2 tablespoons caviar
2 teaspoons butter

2 tablespoons water

2 teaspoons lemon
  juice

Stir hot water into the caviar and add butter. When mixture is well
blended, add the lemon juice and let the sauce cool. Serve with roast
veal or baked fish.

SMETANA AND ONION SAUCE

1 gill smetana
  (sour cream)
2 onions

1 tablespoon flour
1 gill stock
2 tablespoons butter

¼ teaspoon mustard
1 teaspoon vinegar
½ teaspoon salt

Melt 1 tablespoon of butter, blend in with flour and gradually dilute
with meat or vegetable stock. Chop the onions finely, fry lightly in the
remaining butter and mix with the sauce. Add salt, vinegar and mustard,
mix well, bring to the boil and simmer for 10 minutes. Pass through
a sieve and heat again when required. Serve with boiled mutton, potato
rissoles or cauliflower.

87. Cornish Pasties, Britain (p.102)

88. Beef Stroganoff, Russia (p.438)

89. Crown Roast of Lamb, Britain (p.96)

DILL SAUCE

4 tablespoons chopped dill	3 tablespoons flour	2 teaspoons sugar
3 tablespoons butter	1 pint vegetable stock	1 tablespoon vinegar
	1 tablespoon cream	salt and pepper

Melt the butter and gradually blend with flour over a low heat. Dilute with stock, stirring well, then add the dill, vinegar, sugar and salt and pepper to taste. Bring to the boil and simmer gently, for 10 minutes, stirring occasionally. Remove from the stove and add the cream. Serve hot with fish, boiled meat or vegetables.

SWEET AND SOUR MUSHROOM SAUCE

4 oz. mushrooms	½ pint stock	½ teaspoon salt
1 tablespoon lemon juice	½ tablespoon butter	pepper
	2 teaspoons sugar	½ tablespoon flour

Wash, peel and slice the mushrooms and simmer in stock until tender. Melt the butter, blend in the flour and dilute with a little of the stock. When well mixed, add the mushrooms and the rest of the stock, sugar, lemon juice, salt and pepper. Bring to the boil and cook for 5 minutes, stirring constantly. Serve with liver, rissoles or fried meat.

WALNUT SAUCE

4 oz. shelled walnuts	pinch cayenne pepper	4 oz. spring onions
1 clove garlic	½ teaspoon salt	2 tablespoons chopped parsley
1 gill vinegar		

Crush the walnuts and garlic together. Add salt, pepper and finely chopped onions. Mix well with vinegar and sprinkle with parsley. Serve with vegetables, fish or poultry.

SAUCE TKEMALY

8 oz. plums	½ pint smetana	cayenne pepper
2 cloves garlic	(sour cream)	pinch basil
sprig parsley or dill	1 gill water	½ teaspoon salt

Tkemaly is the Georgian name for the wild plums which grow in the Caucasus. They are used for making a piquant sauce for shashlik, chicken on a skewer, or other dishes. Stew the plums in water until they are soft. Remove the stones, rub the plums through a sieve, mix with smetana and cook over a low heat. While the sauce is thickening, add salt, cayenne pepper, crushed garlic, basil and chopped dill. Dilute with enough plum juice to give the sauce the consistency of thick cream.

SMETANA SAUCE

| 1 gill smetana | 2 tablespoons butter | 1 gill stock |
| (sour cream) | 1 tablespoon flour | salt |

Melt the butter. blend it with flour and gradually dilute with warmed meat or vegetable stock. Add smetana, salt to taste, mix well and simmer gently for 5—10 minutes. Serve with liver, rissoles, roast game, fish or vegetables.

HORSERADISH AND SMETANA SAUCE

2 tablespoons grated	1 gill smetana	1 tablespoon flour
horseradish	(sour cream)	3 peppercorns or
2 tablespoons vinegar	3 tablespoons butter	pinch cayenne
1 bay leaf	2 tablespoons water	½ teaspoon salt
extra butter		½ pint stock

Melt a tablespoon of butter, blend with flour and dilute with hot stock. Add smetana and cook slowly for 5—10 minutes. Grate the horseradish and fry lightly in a small saucepan in 2 tablespoons of melted butter. Pour in vinegar and an equal quantity of water, add bay leaf, salt and peppercorns, or a pinch of cayenne pepper, and cook gently for 10 minutes. Combine with the smetana mixture and heat for 5 minutes. Add a knob of butter and stir well. Serve with boiled beef, lamb, pork or tongue.

RUSSIAN SALAD DRESSING

| 1 gill smetana | 2 yolks hard-boiled | pinch pepper |
| (sour cream) | eggs | ¼ teaspoon salt |

Rub the egg yolks through a sieve and blend with smetana. Sprinkle with salt and pepper and stir until the sauce is creamy. Add a little fresh cream or top of the milk if a thinner consistency is required.

KIZIL SAUCE

Cherry Sauce

8 oz. cherries	2 teaspoons butter	1 gill water
½ pint chicken stock	1 teaspoon sugar	pinch salt
2 oz. seedless raisins		4 teaspoons flour

Steam and stone the cherries, cook gently in water until soft, strain off the juice and put aside. Rub the cherries through a sieve, put back into the juice, together with raisins, sugar, salt and stock. Blend the butter with flour, dilute with a little liquid and add to the cherry sauce. Mix well, bring to the boil and simmer for 10 minutes, stirring frequently. Serve with poultry, game or shashlik.

RUSSIAN TOMATO SAUCE

1 pint fish stock	½ tablespoon capers	1 gill Madeira
2 tablespoons tomato purée	6 olives	sprig parsley
	1 tablespoon flour	1 teaspoon salt
2 oz. mushrooms	1 carrot	pinch cayenne pepper
3 tablespoons butter	1 onion	pinch pepper
1 salted cucumber		

Melt 1 tablespoon of butter, blend with flour and dilute with stock. Stir until thickened. Slice the onion and carrot, brown slightly in 1 table-spoon of butter and add to the white sauce together with tomato purée, salt, pepper and a bay leaf. Simmer for 15 minutes then strain through a sieve. Meanwhile, peel and dice the cucumber, stone the olives and chop with the parsley and put into the tomato sauce together with the capers. Peel and slice the mushrooms and add to the sauce with a dash of cayenne pepper. Mix well and simmer for 10 minutes. In the last few minutes of cooking, add the Madeira. Serve with fish dishes.

BAKED KASHA

8 oz. buckwheat	½ teaspoon salt	1 tablespoon butter
water		

Put the buckwheat into an earthenware oven dish and pour in enough water to cover, but leaving sufficient space for the grains to swell. Add butter and salt, cover with a lid and put into a moderate oven for 15 minutes. Reduce the heat to very moderate and cook for 2½—3 hours. When the kasha is ready it should be soft, and all the water should have been absorbed. Kasha is served with various soup and meat dishes or eaten on its own with butter or milk. Also, it can be made into puddings.

KASHA WITH CREAM CHEESE

8 oz. buckwheat	½ pint smetana	1 tablespoon
1 pint milk	(sour cream)	breadcrumbs
8 oz. cream cheese	2 tablespoons butter	½ teaspoon salt
	2 beaten eggs	

Put the milk into a double saucepan and heat. Stir in the buckwheat and cook until it thickens. Remove from the stove and add cream cheese, eggs, and salt. Grease a baking tin with butter, sprinkle with breadcrumbs and put in the kasha mixture. Flatten out the top, brush with smetana, pour on melted butter and bake in a moderate oven for about 45 minutes. When it is ready, a brown crust will form on top. Cut into slices and serve hot with melted butter and smetana. Some-times this dish is served with soups such as borshch or shchy.

GRECHNEVAYA KASHA

Buckwheat Kasha

1 lb. buckwheat	1 teaspoon salt	2 oz. butter
water		

Wash the buckwheat with cold water and put into a double saucepan. Add the salt and enough water to cover. Bring to the boil, stir well, then cover and cook very slowly for 3 hours.

KASHA WITH MUSHROOMS AND ONIONS

1 lb. buckwheat	2 oz. dried	1 teaspoon salt
2 onions	mushrooms	1½ pints water
	3 tablespoons butter	

Wash the mushrooms and leave in cold water for about an hour. When the mushrooms are swollen, take out and chop finely. Put the mushrooms back into the same water, add salt and boil for 10—15 minutes. Fry the buckwheat in 2 tablespoons of butter, add to the mushrooms in water and continue cooking, stirring well, until the kasha thickens. Chop the onions finely, fry in butter and add to the mixture. Put into a slow oven, cover, and cook for 1½ hours.

KASHA CUTLETS

8 oz. buckwheat	2 tablespoons butter	¾ pint water
2 eggs	4 oz. cream cheese	½ pint smetana
2 oz. fine	1 teaspoon sugar	(sour cream)
breadcrumbs		½ teaspoon salt

Combine water and salt, bring to boil. Sprinkle in the buckwheat and cook for 30—35 minutes. When it has thickened, remove from the stove and mix with the cream cheese. Rub the mixture through a sieve, then add the eggs and sugar. Mix well, shape into cutlets, cover with breadcrumbs and fry on both sides until golden brown. Serve with smetana on each cutlet. They may also be served without smetana and added to soups such as borshch or rassolnik.

UZBEK PLOV

An Uzbek Rice Dish

6 oz. rice	2 tablespoons lamb	2 onions
4 oz. lamb	dripping	salt and pepper
8 oz. carrots	pinch aniseed	2 oz. spring onions

Cut the meat into small squares and fry in hot fat until a crust has formed. Add thin slices of onions and carrots, fry for 5 minutes, sprinkle with salt, pepper and aniseed. Rinse the rice in cold water, lay it over the meat and vegetables and pour in enough water to cover. Simmer until all the water is absorbed, then make two holes in the rice and fill them both with a tablespoon of boiling water. Continue cooking until the rice is soft. Serve garnished with spring onions.

CHICKEN PLOV

An Azerbaijan Rice Dish

1 spring chicken	2 oz. seedless raisins	pinch saffron
4 oz. rice	or sultanas	salt and pepper
6 oz. butter	2 oz. dried apricots	water

Soak the apricots and raisins or sultanas in hot water for about 2 hours. Then strain, dry and fry in 1 oz. of butter until soft. Boil the rice in salted water for 20 minutes, or until tender, strain and rinse with cold water. Put into a double saucepan with 1 oz. butter and the saffron, mix well and cook until hot. Cut the prepared chicken into 4 portions, rub all over with salt and pepper and fry in the remaining butter until tender and golden brown on all sides. Serve the chicken with the rice and fruit heaped around each portion.

CAUCASIAN PLOV

1 lb. rice	4 oz. melted butter	salt and pepper
1 lb. lamb	2 pomegranates,	2 onions
	medium size	water

Cut the lamb into small pieces, season with salt and pepper, and brown in butter, or other fat, with finely chopped onions. Peel the pomegranates, cut out the pith, chop the pulp and add to the lamb. Pour on enough water to cover, put on a lid and cook until the meat is tender. Cook the rice and serve with the meat and gravy on top.

CABBAGE PIROG

Cabbage Pie

rough puff pastry	1 onion	1 tablespoon stock
1 egg for glazing	2 hard-boiled eggs	salt and pepper
	1 cabbage about 1 lb.	3 tablespoons butter

Shred the cabbage, pour boiling water over it, sprinkle with salt and leave for about 15 minutes to drain. Chop the onion and fry lightly in butter. Add the cabbage, sprinkle with pepper and cook over a low heat until soft. Then add chopped eggs and mix well. Prepare the pastry as for chicken pirog (see p. 455) and proceed in the same way, but using the cabbage filling.

VARENIKY WITH CREAM CHEESE

Cream Cheese Dumplings

8 oz. flour	1 tablespoon butter	1 gill smetana
1 tablespoon sugar	2 eggs	(sour cream)
4 tablespoons water	1 egg yolk	salt
	1 lb. cream cheese	

Mix the flour with 2 eggs, a pinch of salt and the water. Knead the dough until it is firm and elastic, then roll out thinly and cut out circles with a tumbler or pastry cutter. Mix the cream cheese with sugar, yolk of 1 egg and butter and put a spoonful on each round of pastry. Fold the circles of pastry over, press the edges together firmly and put into a large saucepan of boiling water containing $\frac{1}{2}$ teaspoon of salt. Cook for 10 minutes or until the vareniky float to the surface. Serve hot with smetana.

SIBERIAN PELMENY

Meat Dumplings

6 oz. beef	1 onion	salt and pepper
6 oz. lean pork	1 egg	butter
8 oz. flour	cold water	smetana (sour cream)

Prepare the pastry by breaking an egg into the flour, adding $\frac{1}{2}$ teaspoon of salt and mixing with 2 or 3 tablespoons of cold water. Knead into a stiff dough and leave in a cool place for about 30 minutes. In the meantime, mince the meat together with an onion, season with salt and pepper and moisten with 1 or 2 tablespoons of water. Roll out the dough until very thin then cut into small circles with a glass about 2 inches across or a pastry cutter. Put a little meat filling on to each round, fold over, press the edges together firmly and roll them up slightly to prevent meat coming out. Drop into boiling water and when they rise to the surface they are ready. Serve with melted butter and smetana, or in clear soup.

UKRAINIAN GALUSHKY

8 oz. flour	1 gill smetana	1 gill water
2 eggs	(sour cream)	salt
		4 oz. butter

Sieve the flour into a large bowl. Make a hollow in the centre of the flour and pour in 1 gill water, 2 tablespoons of melted butter, 2 beaten eggs and a flat teaspoon of salt. Mix well until the dough is smooth but not too stiff. Roll out until it is about $\frac{1}{4}$-inch thick and then cut into a variety of small shapes. Dip these shapes (called galushky) into boiling, salted water and cook for about 10 minutes. When they float to the surface, they are ready. Strain the galushky and fry in the rest of the butter until golden brown. Serve with the butter in which the galushky were fried. Smetana may be added if desired.

FISH PELMENY

Fish Dumplings

1 lb. filleted fish,	1 gill milk	salt and pepper
cod or haddock	2 eggs	½ pint smetana
8 oz. pork	8 oz. flour	(sour cream)
1 onion	2 tablespoons water	sprig parsley

Mince the fish, pork and onion, mix together and season with 1 teaspoon of salt and a dash of freshly ground pepper. Pass the mixture through the mincer again, then add milk and 1 egg and mix well. For the pastry, sieve the flour with a pinch of salt, and add 1 egg and enough water to make a stiff dough. Knead the dough until smooth and firm and leave in a cool place for a while. Then roll out thinly and divide into two equal parts. Lay out balls of the fish mixture, about the size of walnuts, over one half of the pastry. Moisten the other half with a little milk and cover the fillings. Press down the pastry around all the fillings and cut around each one until they are all separated. Put the dumplings into boiling, salted water for about 10 minutes. When they rise to the top, they are ready. Serve with chopped parsley and smetana. These dumplings may also be put into clear fish soup.

CHICKEN PIROG

Chicken Pie

1 small boiling chicken	4 oz. rice	1 carrot
1 lb. flour	1 teaspoon lemon	1 celery stalk
1 lb. butter	juice	salt and pepper
5 eggs	3¼ pints water	1 onion

Cook the chicken in 3 pints water with prepared, sliced carrot, celery and onion. When it is tender, strain off the stock, strip the meat from the chicken and cut into small pieces. Rinse the rice in cold water and boil in the chicken stock, seasoned with salt and pepper. When cooked, strain and mix with 2 oz. butter. Hard-boil and chop 4 eggs, mix with the rice and combine with the chicken meat.

To make the rough puff pastry, sift the flour and ½ teaspoon salt into a basin, cut 14 oz. cold butter into small squares and work into the flour with a knife. Make a hollow in the centre and gradually pour in 1 gill very cold water and the lemon juice. Knead into a fairly stiff dough and leave in a cold place for about an hour. Then roll out the pastry, fold in three and leave in a cold place again for about 30 minutes. Repeat this process three times and finish up with rolling out the pastry to ¼-inch thick. Divide in half, lay one part in a buttered baking dish and trim the edges. Spread with the chicken filling, cover with the other half of the pastry, press the edges together firmly, prick in a few places on top and brush with a beaten egg. Bake in a hot oven for the first 10 minutes, then reduce the heat gradually to moderate during the last 25 minutes of baking.

RICE AND MUSHROOM PIROG

Rice and Mushroom Pie

rough puff pastry	2 oz. dried	2 teaspoons chopped
1 egg for glazing	mushrooms	parsley
8 oz. rice	1 onion	salt and pepper
	2 tablespoons butter	

Soak the mushrooms in cold water for 2 hours. Then boil in the same water until tender, strain and chop finely. Boil the rice in salted water until cooked, then strain. Chop the onion and fry in butter until slightly brown, add the rice, mushrooms and parsley, season with salt and pepper and mix well. Prepare the pastry as for chicken pirog (see p. 455) and proceed in the same way, but using the rice and mushroom filling.

MEAT PANCAKE PIE

8 oz. flour	1 pint milk	1 tablespoon
1 lb. cooked meat	1 hard-boiled egg	breadcrumbs
2 eggs	3 tablespoons butter	salt and pepper
1 onion		1—2 tablespoons stock

Sift the flour with ½ teaspoon of salt into a basin, break in 2 eggs, pour in half the milk and mix well. Add the rest of the milk and beat until the batter is smooth. Pour into a jug and leave for 30 minutes in a cool place. Meanwhile, mince the cooked meat, preferably beef, with an onion. Add chopped, hard-boiled egg, season with salt and pepper, moisten with a little stock and mix well.

Pour 1 tablespoon of batter at a time into a small, greased, heated frying pan and brown lightly on both sides. When all the pancakes are ready, butter a suitable shaped baking tin, line with pancakes and cover with a layer of minced meat. Continue filling the tin with these alternate layers until used up, finishing at the top with pancakes. Sprinkle with breadcrumbs, and bake in a moderate oven for 15 minutes, or until the top of the pie is brown and crisp. Alternatively, a cream cheese mixture, such as prepared for vareniky (see p. 454), may be used as a filling instead of the meat.

MEAT KULEBIAK

rough puff pastry	1 onion	1 tablespoon stock
1 egg for glazing	2 hard-boiled eggs	salt and pepper
1 lb. cooked beef		2 tablespoons butter

Chop the onion and fry lightly in butter. Mince the meat and mix with the onion. Add chopped eggs, season with salt and pepper and moisten with a little stock. Prepare the pastry as for chicken pirog (see p. 455) and proceed in the same way, using the meat filling, but with a kulebiak the shape should be rectangular and flat.

FISH KULEBIAK

rough puff pastry	2 oz. butter or	1 onion
1 egg for glazing	margarine	salt and pepper
1 lb. salmon	8 oz. cooked rice	2 oz. mushrooms

Prepare the pastry as for chicken pirog (see p. 455). Divide into equal parts and lay one half in a rectangular, buttered tin. Chop the onion and fry lightly in butter or margarine. Wash, peel and slice the mushrooms and add to the onion together with the cooked rice. Mix well and spread half over the pastry in the tin. Cover with thin slices of salmon, sprinkle with salt and pepper and spread the remaining rice mixture over the fish. Put the second half of the pastry on top, press the edges of both parts together, puncture with a fork and brush with a beaten egg. Bake in a hot oven for about 35 minutes or until the crust is brown and crisp, as with chicken pirog. *(Illustrated in Plate 86.)*

FISH PIROZHKY

Small Fish Pies

rough puff pastry	4 oz. rice	2 teaspoons chopped
1 egg for glazing	2 hard-boiled eggs	parsley
8 oz. filleted fish	2 tablespoons butter	salt and pepper

Cook the rice in salted water, and strain. Cut fish into very small pieces and fry lightly in butter. Add the rice, chopped eggs and parsley, season with salt and pepper and mix well. Prepare the pastry as for chicken pirog (see p. 455) and roll out to less than ¼-inch thick. Cut into circles with a 3-inch pastry cutter or tumbler and moisten with water. Place a spoonful of fish mixture on a round of pastry, cover with another round and press the edges together firmly. Puncture the top, brush with a beaten egg, place on a greased tin and bake in a hot oven for 10—15 minutes. Serve as a hot hors-d'oeuvre or as an accompaniment to fish soups. Pirozhky may also have the fillings used for a pirog, such as cabbage, meat, mushrooms and so on.

CREAM CHEESE AND POTATO FRITTERS

2 large potatoes	4 oz. flour	1 gill smetana
1 lb. cream cheese	2 tablespoons milk	(sour cream)
2 eggs	2 oz. butter	salt and pepper

Peel the potatoes, boil in salted water, strain and mash with the milk. Add the cream cheese, eggs, 2 oz. flour, ½ teaspoon salt and a dash of pepper and mix well. Put on a floured board, flatten out to about 1-inch thick and roll up into a sausage shape. Cut into 1 inch slices, dip in flour and fry in butter on both sides, until golden brown. Serve with melted butter and smetana.

BLINY

Russian Pancakes

1 lb. flour	½ oz. yeast	2 oz. butter
1 pint milk	1 tablespoon sugar	½ teaspoon salt
	2 eggs	

Dissolve the yeast in warm milk, stir in the sugar and half the flour, mix until smooth, cover with a cloth and leave in a warm place for an hour. When the batter has risen, add salt, sugar, 2 egg yolks, 1 oz. melted butter and the rest of the flour. Mix until the batter is well blended, then cover with a cloth and leave to rise again. Whisk the egg whites until stiff, fold into the batter and leave for 15 minutes. Grease a small frying pan lightly with butter, heat it and spread with a thin layer of batter. As the pancake fries, sprinkle with melted butter, then turn it over to fry the other side. They should be paper-thin when done. Bliny are served very hot with plenty of melted butter and accompanied by caviar, thin slices of smoked salmon or smetana.

BLINCHIKY WITH CREAM CHEESE

Pancakes with Cream Cheese

8 oz. cream cheese	3 oz. butter	pinch ground cin-
8 oz. flour	3 tablespoons sugar	namon
½ pint milk	1 gill smetana	½ teaspoon salt
3 eggs	(sour cream)	

Sift the flour and salt into a basin, make a hollow in the centre, break in 2 eggs and pour in half the milk. Beat until smooth, add the rest of the milk, beat again then stand in a cool place for 30 minutes. Mix the cream cheese with 1 egg yolk, 1 tablespoon sugar, pinch of cinnamon and 1 tablespoon soft butter. Heat a small frying pan greased with butter and pour in just enough batter to cover the bottom of the pan thinly. Fry the batter on one side only, until brown, tilting it over in different directions to make it even. When all the pancakes have been prepared this way, put a spoonful of cream cheese mixture on each brown side, fold over so that one side overlaps the other, brush under each flap with egg white to seal, and fry on both sides in hot butter until golden brown. Sprinkle with sugar and serve with smetana.

MUSHROOM FRITTERS

8 oz. mushrooms	2 eggs	½ teaspoon salt
4 oz. flour	2 tablespoons milk	frying oil
1 teaspoon baking	1 tablespoon butter	smetana sauce
powder	pinch paprika	(see p. 450)

Peel, wash and chop the mushrooms and fry lightly in butter. Beat 2 yolks with milk and blend with flour, baking powder, salt and paprika. Beat the mixture until smooth then add the mushrooms. Whisk the egg whites until stiff and fold into the batter. Drop spoonfuls into hot oil and fry on both sides until golden brown. Serve with smetana sauce.

VATRUSHKY WITH CREAM CHEESE
Cream Cheese Tartlets

1 lb. flour	8 oz. butter	2 teaspoons sugar
½ pint water	2 eggs	½ teaspoon salt
	1 lb. cream cheese	

Use very cold butter; cut into small squares and rub into the flour until the mixture is of the consistency of breadcrumbs. Add cold water, salt and 1 egg and mix well. Leave in a cool place for 30 minutes. Mix the cream cheese with 1 egg, a pinch of salt and the sugar. Roll out the pastry to about ¼-inch thick and cut into rounds, with a 3-inch pastry cutter. Shape the rounds into the form of tartlets, fill each one with cream cheese and put them on a buttered baking tin. Bake in a hot oven for 10—15 minutes. Serve the tartlets as an accompaniment to borshch and other soups.

MEAT PANCAKES

8 oz. flour	1 lb. cooked beef	1 egg white
½ pint milk	1 hard-boiled egg	4 oz. butter
2 eggs	1 onion	salt and pepper
	sprig dill or parsley	

Mix the flour with ½ teaspoon of salt and sift into a bowl. Make a hollow in the flour and put in 2 eggs with half the milk. Beat until the batter is smooth, gradually add the rest of the milk and beat the mixture for 5 minutes. Pour into a jug and stand in a cool place for 30 minutes. Chop the onion and fry lightly in butter. Mince the meat, chop the hard-boiled egg and dill, and add to the onion. Sprinkle with salt and pepper and fry together for a few minutes. Fry all the pancakes in butter on one side only, using a small pan. Lay a heaped tablespoon of the meat mixture on the cooked side of each pancake, fold over, so that one side overlaps the other, and brush under each flap with the white of an egg, to seal it. Fry the stuffed pancakes on both sides until light brown. Serve as a separate dish or as an accompaniment to soups.

CHEBOUREKY

Meat Pasties

1 lb. lamb	1 dessertspoon	8 oz. dripping for
2 eggs	chopped parsley	frying
2 oz. flour	4 oz. lamb fat	salt and pepper
4 oz. cooked rice	water	1 onion

Bone the lamb and put it through a mincer together with the lamb fat and the onion. Season with salt and pepper, add chopped parsley and the cooked rice. Mix well with 2 or 3 tablespoons of cold water. Mix the flour with 1 egg and ½ teaspoon of salt, and add sufficient water to make a stiff dough. Roll out the pastry, paper thin, and then cut into rounds of about 4 inches across the centre. Fill half of each round with some of the lamb stuffing, turn the other half over and press the edges of the pastry together. Brush with a beaten egg and fry in deep, hot fat.

POTATO BABKA

A Byelorussian Dish

2 lb. potatoes	1 large onion	½ teaspoon
2 tablespoons flour	2 tablespoons butter	baking powder
	salt and pepper	

Peel the potatoes and grate them. Chop the onion, fry lightly in 1 table-spoon of butter, and add to the grated potatoes. Season with salt and pepper, add the flour sieved with baking powder and mix well. Butter a pie dish, put in the potato mixture and bake in a moderate oven for 1 hour.

KISSEL

This dessert is very popular in Russia and can be made from a variety of fruit, such as apples, cherries, redcurrants and so on. Juice left over from canned or stewed fruit can be used too. The consistency of kissel may vary from a firm, cold jelly, to a thick, creamy liquid. The soft kissel may be served warm as an accompaniment to other dishes.

FRUIT JUICE KISSEL

1 pint fruit juice	1 tablespoon potato	4 oz. sugar
	flour	

Strain the juice, mix a little with the flour until well blended, then gradually add the rest. Put into a saucepan, add the sugar and slowly bring to the boil, stirring all the time. Pour into little dishes to be served individually.

APPLE KISSEL

2 lb. apples	1 lemon	1½ pints water
4 oz. sugar	2 tablespoons potato	nutmeg
	flour	

Core and peel the apples, slice them and stew in water until soft. Pass the apples through a sieve and put into a saucepan with the juice of a lemon, a little grated nutmeg and the peel of ½ a lemon. Blend the flour with a little water, add to the apple purée, bring to the boil and simmer for 5 minutes, stirring constantly. Remove the lemon peel, pour the kissel into a wet mould and leave to cool.

COFFEE KISSEL

2 tablespoons ground	1 pint milk	1 pint water
coffee	2 oz. potato flour	cream
	4 oz. sugar	

Add 1 pint boiling water to the coffee, let it stand for 5 minutes and strain. Blend the flour with 1 cup milk and add the coffee. Heat the mixture in a saucepan with the sugar and the rest of the milk, stir well and bring to the boil. Leave to get cold then serve with cream.

STRAWBERRY OR RASPBERRY KISSEL

| 1 lb. berries | 1½ pints water | 2 tablespoons potato |
| 10 oz. sugar | | flour |

Remove the stalks, wash the fruit and rub through a sieve. Put the water and sugar into a saucepan and bring to the boil. Blend the flour with a little of the hot syrup, bring to the boil again and remove from the stove. Add the fruit purée, put into a dish and leave to get cold.

KHVOROST

The word 'khvorost' means twig.

1 lb. flour	1 gill smetana	1 tablespoon vanilla
1 gill milk	(sour cream)	sugar (see p. 73)
3 egg yolks	1 gill brandy or vodka	or icing sugar
2 tablespoons sugar	butter or oil for frying	pinch salt

Mix flour, sugar and salt and blend with the milk, smetana, brandy or vodka, and beaten yolks. Stir until the mixture is smooth then roll out very thinly and cut into strips about 4 inches long and 1 inch wide. Slit the centre of each strip and push one end of the pastry through it, or make rings with a pastry cutter and twist them into various shapes. Fry in plenty of hot fat until golden brown then drain on greaseproof paper and sprinkle with vanilla sugar or icing sugar.

461

PASKHA

The word 'Paskha' means Easter in Russian and this dessert is tradition-ally served at Easter with kulich (see p. 467). Surrounded by gaily coloured hard-boiled eggs, paskha takes the place of honour on a table laden with cold ham, roast veal, fish in aspic, salads, and many other dishes waiting for the family and guests to celebrate Easter together.

1 lb. cream cheese	¼ teaspoon vanilla	4 oz. candied fruit
1 gill smetana	essence	4 oz. shelled walnuts
(sour cream)	¼ teaspoon almond	or almonds
4 oz. butter	essence	pinch salt
8 oz. castor sugar	8 oz. seedless raisins	2 oz. glacé cherries

Strain the cheese through butter muslin to get rid of excess moisture, put into a large bowl and mix with smetana and butter until smooth. Soak the raisins in hot water until they are soft and chop the candied fruit and nuts. Add these and all the other ingredients to the bowl of cream cheese and mix together until well blended and smooth. The mixture should be firm but if it is too soft, add a little more cream cheese and sugar. Put into a clean flower-pot or mould perforated at the bottom, lined with butter muslin, and place a weight on top. If possible, stand the mould on a wire tray with a basin underneath to collect the liquid as it comes out. Leave in a cool place for 12 hours. Turn the paskha out on to a dish and decorate with glacé cherries.

GOGOL-MOGOL

A Ukranian Dish

6 tablespoons brown	4 egg yolks	¼ teaspoon vanilla
sugar	2 oz. shelled walnuts	essence

Beat the egg yolks with the sugar until creamy. Then put into a double saucepan, add the vanilla essence and heat until the mixture thickens, beating continuously. Pour into a bowl and leave to get cold. Serve decorated with chopped walnuts.

CREAM CHEESE PUDDING

1 lb. cream cheese	1 tablespoon	2 teaspoons grated
1 egg	breadcrumbs	orange or lemon
3 tablespoons sugar	1 gill smetana	rind
2 tablespoons flour	(sour cream)	pinch salt
2 tablespoons butter	few drops vanilla	smetana or fruit syrup
	essence	

Mix the cheese with 1 tablespoon of melted butter, an egg, sugar and salt. Add the flour gradually, mixing well, then the vanilla essence and grated rind. Put the mixture into a buttered baking tin and sprinkle with breadcrumbs. Flatten the surface of the pudding, brush with smetana and bake in a hot oven for 30 minutes. Serve with smetana or fruit syrup.

KARAKOT

An Uzbek Sweetmeat

2 lb. apples, prunes or cherries	2 oz. ground almonds	¼ teaspoon vanilla essence
1½ lb. sugar	2 egg whites	1 pint water
	½ tablespoon butter	

Prepare the fruit chosen, stone if necessary, and stew in water until soft. Strain off the juice and rub the fruit through a fine sieve. Mix the purée with sugar, ground almonds and vanilla essence and cook gently until the mixture thickens. Fold in 2 whipped egg whites and whisk the mixture until stiff. Put into a shallow tin lined with greaseproof paper and leave in a cool oven to get firm. This will take several hours, as it is a matter of drying off the mixture rather than baking it. When set, cut into slices and leave to get cold. Serve as a sweetmeat to accompany tea with lemon.

RUSSIAN RICE PUDDING

4 oz. rice	1 tablespoon seedless raisins	2 oz. butter
1 pint milk		few drops vanilla essence
3 oz. sugar	2 eggs	
1 oz. candied peel		cherry jam

Wash the rice well and put into a saucepan with milk and 1 oz. butter. Cook gently for 15 minutes, stirring occasionally, then set aside to cool a little. Beat the yolks of the eggs with the sugar and add to the rice together with a few drops of vanilla essence, the candied peel and the raisins, previously soaked in water for 10 minutes. Whisk the whites of the eggs until stiff and fold into the rice. Butter a pudding dish, put in the rice and bake in a slow oven for 45 minutes. Serve with cherry jam.

ALMOND DESSERT

A Kirgiz Sweetmeat

4 oz. shelled almonds	8 oz. honey	4 oz. butter
4 oz. yellow maize flour	3 tablespoons sugar	pinch cream of tartar
	1 egg	pinch salt

Cream the butter with sugar, add a well beaten egg, maize flour, cream of tartar and salt and mix well. Bring the honey to the boil, pour over the mixture and stir until well blended. Mix in blanched, chopped almonds, pour into a shallow, square, buttered tin and bake in a slow oven for about 30 minutes. When ready, cut into squares and leave to cool.

VARENIKY WITH CHERRIES

Cherry Dumplings

8 oz. flour	2 eggs	1 lb. cherries
4 tablespoons water	1 gill smetana	pinch salt
4 oz. sugar	(sour cream)	water

Blend the eggs and flour, add a pinch of salt and 2 tablespoons of water, knead into a stiff dough and leave for 1—2 hours. Then roll out the pastry very thinly and cut into circles with a tumbler or pastry cutter. In the meantime, cover the cherries with sugar and let them stand for several hours. Then strain off the juice and set aside. Stone the cherries and cook them with a cup of water for 5 minutes. Put a few cherries into each circle of pastry, fold, press the edges together and put into a large pan of boiling water to cook for 10 minutes. Use both kinds of juice obtained from the cherries and mix with smetana to make a sauce to serve with the vareniky.

HONEY MOUSSE

8 oz. honey	4 eggs

Separate the yolks from the eggs and blend with the honey. Simmer on a very low heat, stirring constantly, until the mixture thickens then remove from the stove and leave to cool. Whisk the egg whites until stiff and fold into the honey mixture. Pour into individual glass dishes and chill.

RICE FRITTERS

8 oz. rice	3 oz. butter	2 oz. candied fruit
1 pint milk	2 tablespoons sugar	nutmeg
2 eggs		strip of lemon rind

Rinse the rice and cook slowly in milk, with the lemon rind, until the mixture is thick and the rice soft. Remove the rind put in sugar and set aside to cool slightly. Then add 2 egg yolks and a sprinkling of grated nutmeg and mix well. Whip the egg whites until stiff and fold into the mixture. Shape into flat, oval cakes and brown on both sides in hot butter. Serve hot, decorated with candied fruit.

TVOROZHNIKY

Cream Cheese Fritters

1 lb. cream cheese	3 tablespoons sugar	2 eggs
2 oz. flour	pinch salt	1 gill smetana
3 oz. butter		(sour cream)

90. Spinach Soup, Holland (p.181)

91. Roast Chicken with Bread Sauce, Britain (p.98)

If the cheese is too moist, wrap in a muslin cloth and leave in a colander with a weight on top until some of the liquid has been pressed out. Mix the cheese with flour, eggs, salt and a tablespoon of sugar and roll out on to a floured board. Shape into round, flat cakes, about ½ inch thick and 3 inches wide, and fry in hot butter, on both sides, until golden brown. Sprinkle with sugar and serve hot with smetana. Slices of lemon go well with this dish.

DRACHONA

A Russian Batter Pudding

8 oz. flour	3 oz. butter	1 pint milk
1 gill smetana	2 tablespoons sugar	pinch salt
(sour cream)		3 eggs

Make a hollow in a mound of flour, break in the eggs and mix well. Blend with smetana, add a pinch of salt and beat until smooth and light. Warm the milk, pour it in gradually and continue beating for a few minutes. Pass the mixture through a sieve, pour into a buttered baking dish and put into a moderate oven for 30 minutes. Sprinkle with sugar and serve hot with melted butter. Drachona is rather like Yorkshire Pudding, and if the sugar is omitted, it can be served as a supper dish or as an accompaniment to other dishes.

GURYEVSKAYA KASHA

2 oz. semolina	4 oz. cherry jam, or	2 oz. shelled almonds
½ pint clotted cream	any other full fruit	3 oz. sugar
8 oz. shelled walnuts	jam	few drops vanilla
2 oz. crystallized fruit	1 tablespoon	essence
1 pint milk	breadcrumbs	

Warm the milk, sprinkle in the semolina and cook slowly until it thickens, then stir in 2 oz. sugar, chopped walnuts and vanilla essence. Butter a pie dish and spread in it a layer of the semolina, a layer of clotted cream, then cherry jam, another layer of semolina, then small, diced crystallised fruit and so on until all these ingredients are used up. Finish off the top with semolina decorated with chopped almonds. Sprinkle with breadcrumbs and bake in a moderate oven for about 25 minutes or until a golden brown crust has formed. Sprinkle with remaining sugar and bake for a further 5 minutes.

KISH MISH
An Armenian Dish

4 oz. dried apricots	4 oz. dried figs	1 teaspoon mixture of
4 oz. prunes	1 lb. sugar	grated nutmeg
4 oz. dried apple rings	1 strip of lemon rind	cinnamon,
4 oz. sultanas	water	and allspice

Kish Mish is the Armenian for dried fruits, but the expression has been
adopted to mean a hash or a mixup in colloquial Russian.

Wash the fruits and soak overnight in enough water to cover. Next
day, strain off the water and boil it with the sugar, lemon rind and
spices, for 10 minutes. Put in the fruit, simmer until tender and leave
to get cold. Remove the lemon rind before serving.

CREAM CHEESE DESSERT

1 lb. cream cheese	1 tablespoon candied	1 egg yolk
2 tablespoons cream	peel	½ teaspoon grated
2 tablespoons nuts	few drops vanilla	lemon rind
4 tablespoons sugar	essence	pinch salt
2 oz. butter		

Rub the cream cheese through a sieve and mix with chopped candied
peel, grated lemon rind, vanilla essence and a pinch of salt. Blend the
egg yolk, butter and sugar together, beat until smooth and combine
with the cream cheese mixture. Whip the cream until stiff, fold in until
well blended. Leave in a cold place until chilled. Serve the dessert
individually in pyramid shapes covered with roughly chopped nuts.

SWEET VATRUSHKY WITH CREAM CHEESE
Sweet Cream Cheese Tartlets

1 lb. flour	1 gill smetana	4 oz. seedless raisins
1 egg, 1 egg yolk	(sour cream)	½ pint water
4 tablespoons sugar	8 oz. butter	melted butter or
1 lb. cream cheese		smetana

Cut small pieces of cold butter into the flour and rub lightly with finger
tips until the mixture resembles breadcrumbs. Add a pinch of salt,
1 egg and water and mix well. Leave in a cold place for 30 minutes.
Mix the cream cheese with the yolk of 1 egg, smetana, sugar and raisins,
previously soaked in warm water. Roll out the pastry to about ¼ inch
thick and cut into rounds about 3 inches across. Shape the rounds into
the form of tartlets, fill with the cream cheese mixture and put on to
a buttered baking tin. Bake in a hot oven for 10—15 minutes, or until
the tartlets are golden brown. Serve with melted butter or smetana.

KULICH

Russian Easter Cake

2 lb. flour	¾ pint milk	½ teaspoon saffron
8 oz. butter	5 eggs	pinch salt
4 oz. currants	½ teaspoon vanilla	2 oz. candied peel or
2 oz. almonds	essence	glacé cherries
4 oz. sugar	1 oz. yeast	icing *(see page 471)*

Make a dough with half the flour and the yeast dissolved in warm milk. Cover, and leave in a warm place, where the temperature is between 70°F and 80°F., to rise. Cream the butter and sugar, mix in the yolks of 4 eggs, salt, vanilla esssence, saffron and the rest of the flour and add to the yeast dough. Fold in 5 egg whites whisked until stiff and leave the mixture in a warm place to rise again. Chop the candied peel and almonds, wash the currants and dry them and add these ingredients to the dough, mixing well. Kulich is usually baked in tall round tins, rather like chimneys, but a deep bread tin will do. Grease the inside of a tin with butter, sprinkle with flour and line the bottom with grease-proof paper. Fill half way up with the pastry, cover with a cloth, and leave in a warm place to rise to three-quarters of the way up. Then brush the top of the cake with the remaining egg yolk and put in a moderate oven for 1 hour. The dough will rise over the top during baking and, to prevent it burning after it turns golden brown, cover with damp greaseproof paper. The cake may need turning round in the oven to bake evenly. When the cake has cooled, ice the top and decorate with glacé cherries or candied peel.

KRENDEL

A Russian Birthday Cake

1 lb. flour	1 oz. yeast	1 tablespoon castor
8 oz. sugar	½ pint milk	sugar
4 oz. seedless raisins	4 oz. butter	vanilla essence
or sultanas	2 oz. almonds	pinch salt
	6 egg yolks	egg for glazing

Dissolve the yeast in warm milk, add half the flour and leave in a warm place to rise. Blend the rest of the flour with the butter, stir in the egg yolks, sugar, a few drops of vanilla essence and a pinch of salt and add to the dough when it has doubled its size. Knead the mixture, add the raisins and leave in a warm place to rise again. Turn out the dough on to a floured board and shape into a long, narrow roll. Twist into the shape of a letter B and place in a buttered baking tin. Brush with an egg, sprinkle with chopped almonds and leave for a little while. Then put into a hot oven and bake for 35—40 minutes. When ready, cool on a wire cake tray and sprinkle with castor sugar.

SMETANA CAKES

1 gill smetana (sour cream)	4 oz. butter	1 oz. shelled nuts
8 oz. sugar	4 oz. flour	½ teaspoon baking powder
1 egg	1 teaspoon grated orange rind	pinch salt

Cream butter and sugar and blend with the egg and smetana. Sift in flour, mixed with baking powder and salt, add grated orange rind and beat the mixture until it is quite smooth. Grease a tartlet tin with butter, fill with the pastry, sprinkle with sugar, decorate each cake with a nut and bake in a hot oven for 10—15 minutes.

CREAM CHEESE LAYER CAKE

4 oz. cream cheese	3 eggs	2 tablespoons water
4 oz. flour	1 teaspoon grated lemon rind	few drops vanilla essence
4 oz. castor sugar	6 oz. icing sugar	pinch salt
1 teaspoon baking powder	2 tablespoons cream	powdered sugar

Sift the flour, baking powder and salt into a bowl and mix with castor sugar. Make a hollow in the centre and put in 3 lightly beaten eggs, water and the lemon rind. Stir until the mixture is smooth, put into a buttered cake tin and bake in a moderate oven for 20 minutes or until the cake is a light golden brown.

To prepare the filling, beat the cream cheese with the icing sugar until the mixture is smooth and blend with the cream and vanilla essence. Let the cake cool on a wire cake tray then slice it crosswise into two equal parts and spread the filling between the layers. Sprinkle the top with powdered sugar.

TARTE EVGENIA

6 eggs	4 oz. ground almonds	1 teaspoon grated orange rind
8 oz. sugar	1 teaspoon candied peel	2 oz. butter
4 oz. shelled pistachio nuts	3 oz. potato flour icing or jam	pinch salt

Mince the pistachio nuts and mix with the ground almonds, sugar, finely grated orange rind and chopped candied peel. Add 3 eggs and 3 egg yolks, the potato flour and a pinch of salt and mix all the ingredients together well. Whisk the remaining 3 egg whites until stiff and fold into the mixture. Put into a buttered tin and bake in very moderate oven for about 30 minutes.

Leave in the tin to cool. The top may be covered with icing or jam.

CREAM CHEESE CAKE

The Pastry:
4 oz. flour
1 tablespoon sugar
1 egg
1 tablespoon lemon
  juice
½ tablespoon water

½ teaspoon salt
2 oz. butter

The Cheese Filling:
2 lb. cream cheese
8 oz. sugar
4 eggs

2 oz. flour
3 tablespoons smetana
  (sour cream)
2 oz. seedless raisins
1 teaspoon vanilla
  essence
pinch salt

To make the pastry, sift the flour and combine with sugar, salt and cold butter cut into small pieces. Work the mixture with the finger tips until it feels like breadcrumbs, add water, lemon juice and a beaten egg and knead into a smooth, firm dough. Roll out to less than ¼ inch thick, line a buttered baking tin with it and leave in a cold place. To make the filling, mix the cream cheese with sugar, flour, smetana, raisins, vanilla essence and a pinch of salt. Beat the eggs until frothy and fold into the cheese mixture. Put into the baking tin lined with pastry, flatten out, smooth the top and bake in a moderate oven for about 1 hour.

BUBLINKY

Ring Rolls

8 oz. flour
4 oz. butter

9 eggs
½ pint water

1 teaspoon sugar
½ teaspoon salt

Put the water and butter into a saucepan, bring to the boil then remove from the stove. Add salt to the flour, sift and pour all at once into the hot liquid. Mix well, put the saucepan back on to the stove and cook for 5 minutes, stirring constantly. By then, the mixture should be a firm ball in the centre of the pan, leaving the sides quite clean. Set aside for about 10 minutes to cool. Then add 8 eggs, one at a time, beating the mixture until it is quite smooth and of the right consistency for piping. Use a pastry forcing-tube of ½-inch diameter to squeeze out the dough into about 6-inch lengths. Join the ends together to form rings, brush with a beaten egg and put them on to a greased baking tray. The shapes can also be obtained by filling buttered, individual ring moulds. Put into a moderately hot oven and bake for 30—35 minutes.

PROSTOKVASHA

Thick Sour Milk

Prostokvasha is very popular in Russia. Before the pasteurisation of milk, it was possible to let it go sour naturally, but now in order to thicken the milk it is usually better to add pure cultures of lactic acid bacteria. The simplest way to make *prostokvasha* is to mix a quantity of fresh

469

milk with a very little yoghourt or soured milk and to leave it in a warm place until it thickens.

This thick sour milk is considered a very healthy food, and is used extensively in Russia for making cream cheese as well as being eaten on its own. It is very good served chilled, sprinkled with sugar, cinnamon and some breadcrumbs made from rye bread or black bread.

VARENETZ

| ½ pint smetana (sour cream) | 4 pints creamy milk castor sugar | cinnamon rye breadcrumbs |

This is an old Russian countryside dish. Pour the milk into a wide, earthenware pan and put into a very slow oven and cook until a skin forms and the milk takes on a faintly golden colour. Push the skin down to the bottom of the pan and repeat this 5 or 6 times as the skin forms. By then, the milk will be a peach colour. Take out the pan and let the milk cool until it is tepid. Add smetana, mix well and leave in a warm place for 24 hours. Then keep in a cold place until required. Serve sprinkled with sugar, rye breadcrumbs and cinnamon.

TVOROG
Cream Cheese

Tvorog, the Russian name for cream cheese, is very much used in Russia, either eaten on its own or to make a variety of dishes. It can be bought as a cottage or cream cheese in Continental shops here and at some grocers and dairies, but it is easy to produce at home and is a good way of using up milk which has gone sour. At least 4 pints of solidified sour milk are needed to make a worthwhile quantity of cheese. Put the sour milk into a muslin bag and hang it over a basin to strain off the whey. Leave there until the curd is firm but not too dry. Then mash it until it is smooth and creamy. It is very good mixed with chopped chives and a pinch of salt, spread on rye bread and butter.

SMETANA
Sour Cream

Smetana is extensively used in Russia for many dishes, both sweet and savoury. It is put into sauces, cakes, puddings and soups and served with meat, fish and vegetables. It can be bought here in Continental shops and some dairies, but it can easily be made at home. Simply leave a quantity of thick, double cream in a warm place until it is sour. This usually takes 2 or 3 days, but do not let the cream go 'cheesy'. A teaspoon of sour milk or a few drops of lemon juice will speed up the process. When it is ready, it will keep in a very cold place or refrigerator for about a week.

RUSSIAN EASTER EGGS

It has always been the custom in Russia to use gaily decorated hard-boiled eggs at Easter.

Cover the eggs in onion skins and wrap them round with pieces of cloth to keep them in position. Boil in plenty of water for 10 minutes. The egg shells will be a beautiful golden colour. Other harmless colouring substances can be obtained from chemists or Continental shops to decorate the eggs in many bright colours.

SMETANA ICING

1 gill smetana (sour cream)	6 oz. icing sugar	few drops vanilla essence
	4 oz. butter	
	pinch salt	

Cream the butter with sugar and add the vanilla essence, salt and smetana. Beat the mixture until well blended and smooth. Then, after icing a cake, put into a very slightly heated oven to dry.

CANDIED CRANBERRIES

1 lb. cranberries	8 oz. icing sugar	1 egg white

Beat the white of an egg with icing sugar until very stiff. Coat the cranberries with the mixture, place them on a baking dish and put into a very low oven for 10—15 minutes to dry.

CRANBERRY JAM

2 lb. cranberries	4 lb. sugar	½ pint water

Remove the berries from the stalks and rinse several times. Put into hot water for 10 minutes to soften the somewhat tough skins. Boil the sugar with water until dissolved, pour over the cranberries and boil until they are soft. Pour into warm jars and cover. 2 small peeled and chopped apples and a pinch of cinnamon may be added to the cranberries while they are cooking, if desired.

PICKLED GRAPES

2 lb. grapes	1 pint water	¼ oz. stick cinnamon
½ pint vinegar	2 cloves	¼ teaspoon allspice
8 oz. sugar		¼ teaspoon mace

Remove the grapes from the stalks, wash them and put into jars. Boil the water, vinegar, sugar and spices together and allow to cool. Then pour over the grapes, cover and store the jars in a cool place.

PICKLED CHERRIES

2 lb. Morello cherries	½ pint vinegar	3 cloves
1 lb. sugar	1-inch cinnamon stick	¼ oz. root ginger

Stem, stone and wash the cherries. Put the sugar, cloves, cinnamon stick and ginger into the vinegar, bring to the boil and simmer until the sugar dissolves. Strain the mixture into a saucepan, put in the cherries and simmer until they are tender. Strain off the liquid and put the cherries into warm jars. Continue heating the liquid until it thickens, then pour into the jars of cherries, filling them to the top, and cover. Store for several weeks before using.

PICKLED HERRINGS

The Ukrainian Way

12 herrings	2 bay leaves	½ oz. allspice
2 onions	2 pints vinegar	¼ oz. cinnamon
1 lemon	½ oz. peppercorns	¼ oz. mace
2 cloves	1 tablespoon sunflower oil (or olive oil)	1 teaspoon salt

Soak the herrings for 3 hours. Cut into fillets, lengthwise, and put into a jar in layers with thin slices of onion and lemon lying between. Boil the vinegar with cloves, salt, bay leaves, peppercorns, and spices then put aside to cool. Mix the oil and spiced vinegar and pour over the herring. Cover the jar and put in a cool place. The herrings will be ready after 2 weeks.

SALTED CUCUMBERS

6 lb. cucumbers	2 tablespoons grated horseradish	12 sprigs dill
24 peppercorns		6 cloves garlic
2 cloves garlic		6 tarragon leaves
8 oz. cooking salt		vine or oak leaves

Choose cucumbers about 4 inches long and fresh green in colour. Line a large stone jar with washed vine or oak leaves and distribute over them a layer of dill, peppercorns, horseradish, garlic and tarragon leaves. Put in a tightly packed layer of cucumbers, standing upright, and cover with the same ingredients as underneath. Repeat this process until all the cucumbers are in the jar. Dissolve the salt in boiling water and leave to cool. Then pour it into the jar, covering to 2 inches above the cucumbers, put on a firm lid, weighed down if necessary but not resting on the cucumbers. Store in a cool place. The cucumbers should be ready after 1—2 weeks.

PICKLED MUSHROOMS

| 1 lb. mushrooms | 1 gill vinegar | 6 peppercorns |
| 1 clove | salt | 1 bay leaf |

Peel the mushrooms, wash thoroughly and remove the stalks. Put the heads into hot, salted water, simmer until tender and strain. Pour the vinegar into a saucepan, add peppercorns, bay leaf, clove and ½ teaspoon salt and bring to the boil. Simmer for 5 minutes and set aside to cool. Pack the mushrooms into jars, pour in the spiced vinegar and cover.

DRIED MUSHROOMS

Mushrooms for drying must be fresh and firm. Skin the mushrooms and if some are large, cut them into suitable sizes. Make holes in the centre of each mushroom or section of mushroom, and thread on to a string. Dry in a very slow oven and then store, covered, in a dry place.

VODKA

Vodka is to Russia what whisky is to Scotland. It is usually made of wheat, but potatoes and maize can also be used to make it.
Vodka is served in small glasses and usually accompanies 'zakuska', the Russian for hors-d'oeuvre, and it should not be sipped but drunk at a gulp. Vodka is colourless and looks like water, but its effects can be marked as it is a very strong drink.

KVASS

| 2 lb. dark rye bread | 8 oz. sugar | 2 oz. raisins |
| 1 oz. yeast | 1 oz. mint | 16 pints water |

Cut the bread into slices and put into a moderate oven to bake until they become rusks. Put them into a large saucepan, pour boiling water on them and leave for 3—4 hours. Strain off the liquid and combine with the yeast, sugar and mint. Cover with a cloth and leave to ferment in a warm place for about 6 hours. When the first froth appears, strain the liquid again and pour into bottles containing 1 or 2 raisins at the bottom. Cork the bottles firmly and store in a cool place. It is advisable to soak the corks in boiling water before using them, or it would be a good idea to use beer bottles with screw tops. The kvass will be ready in 3 day's time. It is a refreshing drink, as well as a basis for some soups.

RUSSIAN TEA

Russians drink a great deal of tea, much more than coffee. China tea is often used, sometimes served in glasses, without milk and often with a thin slice of lemon floating in the pale amber liquid. Jam, in small individual glass dishes, accompanies the tea in the evenings.

The samovar, an urn providing hot water for making the tea, and on which the tea-pot stands, used to be seen in most Russian homes. It is a feature of many a Russian book or play, standing on the table, probably near a lamp, with talks and discussions going on around it endlessly.

VISHNYOVKA

Cherry Vodka

6 lb. Morello cherries	5 lb. castor sugar	about ½ pint vodka or brandy

Stem and stone the cherries and put into a stone jar with alternate layers of sugar, finishing up with sugar at the top. Crush about 3 dozen cherry stones, tie up in a muslin bag, put into the jar with cherries and cover with a loose top. Stir the cherries every day until the sugar is dissolved, then stop up firmly, but not too tightly, and leave in a warm place to ferment.

Morello cherries are usually available in England towards the end of July and if the drink is prepared then, it will be ready for Christmas. Add the vodka (or brandy) after the liquid stops fermenting, seal firmly and leave for at least 1 month — but the longer the better. When ready to use, strain the cherry vodka through a muslin cloth into bottles and cork firmly. But leave enough liquid to preserve the cherries, which are delicious rolled in sugar or served with coffee ice cream. When they are finished, strain the rest of the cherry vodka left in the jar.

CHERRY VODKA COCKTAIL

1 tumbler cherry vodka (see above)	1 tablespoon red Caucasian wine	1 tablespoon sugar
1 tumbler sherry	2 tablespoons lemon juice	1 tablespoon water
2 teaspoons cognac		cherries
		crushed ice

Make a syrup by boiling the sugar in water. Let it cool and shake with all the ingredients, except cherries and ice. These should be served separately with each drink.

SCANDINAVIAN COOKING

Elna Adlerbert

There was a time when Scandinavian food habits were largely conditioned by the climate, which limited the supply of fresh food to a few months of the year. As a result, meals tended to be rather monotonous, and salted fish or meat with potatoes was served most of the time. But things are very different to-day, and Scandinavian specialities like smörgasbord and Swedish meatballs are popular all over the world. The smörgasbord plays an important role in Scandinavian food culture. It is known all the world over and is often the first thing that comes to people's minds when thinking of Scandinavian cooking. The word actually means sandwich table, and bread and butter are of course provided, but there is a great variety of cold dishes to choose from, and a selection of these is set out as an introduction to the main meal.

Scandinavian cooking as we know it to-day really began to develop in the eighteenth century. At that time France exerted a great influence on Scandinavia, and its culture even penetrated to the kitchens. At first, this influence was felt only in the upper strata of society, which could afford to experiment with more exotic dishes and sometimes even went so far as to import French cooks. But in time, better communications and methods of food preservation made it possible for the general public to take advantage of this widened scope, and the French influence is still present in Scandinavian cuisine.

The Scandinavians are a rather taciturn and formal people, and have preserved a ritualistic tradition round their eating habits in spite of being progressive in many other spheres. Thus almost every festivity has its own traditional menu, which will be faithfully adhered to in every home. On each Tuesday during Lent there is a standard dessert of buns with almond cream and milk. Easter Eve is celebrated with smörgasbord and boiled eggs, at which time there is usually a competition in the family to see which child can eat the most eggs.

The Name Day for Martin Luther is on the 11th November. This day is celebrated by southern Swedes and Danes with a roast goose dinner.

Christmas is the main festival of the year, and it has a special significance for Scandinavians. In pagan days there was a mid-winter festival at this time, which is the darkest period of the year. There is, in the northern parts, no daylight at all, and even as far south as Denmark the days are very short indeed. To relieve this dreary period, an atmosphere of light and gaiety is created, a custom which must stem from a deeply rooted need in our nature. The season is ushered in by the Lucia festival, which celebrates the Queen of Light. Although this is Christian in origin, as St. Lucia brought light in a spiritual sense to Scandinavia, there is very little in this festival to remind us of anything associated with the Church. Scandinavians are not particularly religious, and for most of them, these celebrations are more important for traditional reasons than as reminders of religious faith.

The Lucia festival occurs on the 13th December. A female member of each family then dresses in a white gown, wears a crown of lighted candles, and wakes the family in the early morning with the Lucia song, carrying a tray with coffee and Lucia buns. It is celebrated in the same way in schools and various institutions, where the prettiest girl is selected to be Lucia. It has in fact developed into a major beauty contest in Sweden, where each district selects a Lucia, and from them the national Queen of Light is chosen. It is after this festival that in most families the real preparation for Christmas begins.

Christmas Eve is most important, as it is then that the presents are given out. After the evening meal the tree is lighted, Christmas songs are sung and everyone joins hands to dance round the tree. Then the presents are given out by someone dressed up as Santa Claus. In some parts it is believed that little gnomes live about the house. In order to please them and ensure their help for the coming year, many people set plates of porridge in the attic or cellar on Christmas Eve, hoping that the gnomes will partake joyfully of the meal.

On Christmas Day ham is always served, but the garnishing varies. After that, New Year's Day is usually celebrated with parties, when the Christmas menu is repeated.

Though most countries have their traditional and seasonal meals, the Scandinavians go a bit further. For it is not only in this way that their adherence to table ritual is manifest. An individual meal has its special formalities, mainly to do with drinking. The traditional drink is 'schnapps' or aquavit, which is served with the smörgasbord. One must however not start drinking until the word 'skol' is spoken in response to the host's 'skol', whereupon the glass is drained in one gulp. It is a tremendous faux pas to drink in a haphazard manner, and there are strict rules about who may invite whom to a 'skol'. These rules, oddly enough, do not apply to beer, which is served with smörgasbord also. They do however apply to wine, served with the other courses.

There are also rules about thanking the hostess for the meal. On formal occasions, this is done by the guest seated on the left side of the hostess, who makes a little speech of appreciation on the part of all present. But on all occasions, each guest must go up to the hostess on leaving the table, and thank her for the food.

You will gather from this that the Scandinavian takes the pleasures of eating very seriously. He believes that the gathering together of friends and family for a festive meal is an occasion to be marked by dignity and ceremony. Perhaps the climate and the relative isolation of Scandinavia engenders this attitude. The customs may seem strange to the foreigner, but one must remember that they have developed as an expression of the pleasures to be derived from entertaining. The rituals serve to enhance the festive mood and their enactment forms a bond between the participants.

MACKEREL FOR THE SMÖRGASBORD
Swedish

2 lb. mackerel	lettuce	2 tablespoons chopped
1 tablespoon salt	5 tablespoons	parsley
2 tablespoons vinegar	mayonnaise (see	2 tablespoons chopped
10 white peppercorns	p. 263)	chives
¼ lemon	5 tablespoons whipped	2 hard-boiled eggs
1 onion	cream	2 tablespoons chopped
sprigs dill	2 tomatoes	dill

Clean the mackerel and place in a fish kettle with sufficient water to cover. Add salt, vinegar, peppercorns, lemon, onion and a few sprigs of dill. Bring to boil and simmer for about 15 minutes, when flesh should come free from the bone. Let it cool in the stock overnight. Shortly before serving, mackerel should be filleted and skin removed. Arrange some lettuce leaves on a serving dish and place filleted mackerel on top. Mix mayonnaise and cream and spread over mackerel. Mix chopped parsley, dill and chives and sprinkle on top. Quarter eggs and tomatoes and arrange nicely around fish. Serve on smörgasbord with little, new, boiled potatoes.

STUFFED EGGS WITH CURRY
Danish

hard-boiled eggs	mayonnaise	salt
curry powder		lettuce

Shell hard-boiled eggs and cut in halves. Remove yolk and mix with mayonnaise and curry powder to taste. Season with salt. Stuff egg halves with the mixture and arrange on a plate with other cold dishes at the smörgasbord. *(Illustrated in Plate 35.)*

STUFFED EGGS WITH SARDINES
Danish

hard-boiled eggs	mayonnaise	lettuce
sardines in oil	(see p. 263)	French mustard

Wash and drain lettuce. Spread leaves over serving dish. Shell eggs and cut in halves. Mix egg yolks with equal amount of boned, drained sardines. Stir in mayonnaise and a little French mustard to taste, blending until smooth. Pile high in egg halves, place on lettuce and serve on smörgasbord.

MARINATED SALMON

Swedish

8 SERVINGS

2 lb. fresh salmon	3 oz. sugar	fresh dill
5 oz. salt		20 white peppercorns

Prepare piece of salmon in fillets, removing bone but leaving the skin on. Do not wash unless necessary, in which case it should be done quickly and then dried by wrapping in a clean cloth. Place a thick layer of fresh dill in a deep bowl. Crush peppercorns and mix with salt and sugar. Rub salmon with some of this mixture, and sprinkle some on top of the dill. Place one fillet with skin side down on top of dill. Place a layer of dill on top and sprinkle some salt mixture on it. Place other fillet on top, skin side up, so that the thicker part on one fillet meets the thinner part of the other. Place another layer of dill on this and sprinkle rest of salt mixture over it. Cover fish with a plate that fits upside down into the bowl, and place something heavy on it so that fish is pressed down. Stand in a cool place for 6—24 hours, during which time fish should be turned over a few times, but without moving its relative position. When ready to be served, scrape off seasoning, slice slantwise towards the skin, place on a cold serving dish and garnish with sprigs of fresh dill.

MARINATED SPRATS

Swedish

1½ lb. sprats	1 teaspoon French	5 tablespoons oil
2 tablespoons chopped	mustard	½ teaspoon pepper
fresh dill	½ tablespoon sugar	2 tablespoons vinegar
	½ tablespoon salt	

Clean sprats and wash them carefully. Open and remove bone. Skin and soak for a few minutes in cold, salted water (3 tablespoons salt to 2 pints water). Remove and dry well, discarding water. Place a little chopped dill in the bottom of a bowl. Put in sprats and rest of dill in layers. Mix other ingredients together and pour over fish. Take a fork and lift up layers of sprats a little so that marinade can penetrate. Let it stand in a cold place for 3 hours. Chill well before placing on a serving dish, garnish with sprigs of dill and serve at the smörgasbord. This dish can also be made with fresh mackerel, in which case mackerel fillets are sliced thinly, slant-wise towards the skin.

GLASMÄSTARSILL

Glassblowers Herring

Swedish

6 SERVINGS

2 salt herring	½ teaspoon mustard	2 onions, sliced
1 tablespoon crushed	seed	½ carrot, sliced
allspice	1 teaspoon grated	4 tablespoons water
2 bay leaves	horseradish	½ pint vinegar
	3 oz. sugar	

Clean fish and remove heads. Wash and put to soak in cold water for about 12 hours. Drain and dry. Slice across, in ½-inch pieces, leaving in bone. Place in glass jar in layers with spices, horseradish, onions and carrot. Put vinegar, water and sugar in saucepan and bring to the boil. Chill and pour into jar. It should cover the herring completely. Cover jar and place in refrigerator for at least 12 hours, but the longer the better. Serve directly in own jar on the smörgasbord.

PICKLED SALTED HERRING

1 large salted herring	2 tablespoons chopped	2 sprigs fresh dill
¼ pint vinegar	onions	sliced onion and
2 tablespoons water	5 crushed peppercorns	chopped dill for
2 oz. sugar	10 crushed allspice	garnish

Wash, clean and fillet herring. Then soak in cold water for about 12 hours. Remove skin and any bones that may be left. Dry carefully and arrange neatly in serving dish. Mix all ingredients in saucepan, bring to the boil and simmer for 5 minutes. Leave to cool, strain and pour over fillets of herring. Garnish with dill and onion rings. *(Illustrated in Plate 103.)*

GRAPEFRUIT WITH SHRIMPS

Danish

2 grapefruit	castor sugar	1 small tomato
4 oz. peeled, cooked	pinch salt	mayonnaise
shrimps		(see p. 263)

Cut the grapefruit in half and divide into segments, leaving them in the skin. Sprinkle very lightly with castor sugar. Put a portion of shrimps on to each half grapefruit, sprinkle with a little salt and cover with mayonnaise. Decorate with a slice of tomato on each one and serve chilled.

92. Zarzuela de Pescado, Spain (p.551)

93. Fricassée of Veal, Sweden (p.507)

FÅGELBO

Bird's Nest

Swedish

12 anchovy fillets
2 raw egg yolks
2 tablespoons chopped
  raw onion

capers
chopped chives

chopped cold boiled
  potatoes
chopped pickled
  beetroot

Place in 2 circles piles of chopped anchovy, capers, chopped chives, chopped beetroot and chopped cold boiled potatoes. Place a raw egg yolk carefully in the centre of each circle. Season with very little salt and freshly ground pepper to taste. Chill and serve on smörgasbord.

DANISH LIVER PÂTÉ

8 oz. liver
  (calf's or pig's)
4 oz. lard
½ oz. butter

½ oz. flour
½ pint milk
1 egg
a little grated onion

1—2 teaspoons sherry
  (optional)
½ teaspoon salt
½ teaspoon pepper

Wash the liver. Take away sinews and veins, cut liver finely and mince three times, then mince lard with liver. Make a thick sauce of butter, flour and milk. Mix the liver, lard, sauce and egg well, then season the mixture with salt and pepper. Add grated onion and sherry. Place mixture in a greased baking tin; place baking tin in meat pan filled with water and steam for an hour in a moderate oven. (*Illustrated in Plate 13.*)

RAW BEEF

Swedish

1 lb. fillet steak
4 egg yolks

2 medium onions
1 large boiled beetroot

1 tablespoon vinegar
salt and pepper

Mince fillet steak finely and form into 4 cakes. Season with salt and a generous amount of freshly ground pepper. Place on serving dish. Chop beetroot finely and soak in vinegar for 30 minutes. Drain and place on serving dish and make 4 piles. Chop onion finely and place in 4 piles on serving dish. Place the raw egg yolks in their halved eggshells in the centre of the dish. Serve chilled on smörgasbord. This dish can also be arranged to form 4 eyes, in which case egg yolks are placed in the middle, each one surrounded by rings of steak, onion and beetroot.

MEAT BALLS FOR SMÖRGASBORD

Swedish

1 lb. minced beef
1 oz. butter
3 tablespoons chopped
  onion

4 tablespoons
  breadcrumbs
½ pint water
2 teaspoons salt

½ teaspoon pepper
3 tablespoons
  thin cream
margarine for frying

Place breadcrumbs in large mixing bowl, add cream and water. Let stand to swell. Fry finely chopped onions in butter until golden brown and add to bowl. Mix in meat, stirring very well until smooth and creamy in texture. Stir in seasoning. Form mixture into small round balls ¾-inch in diameter and fry in margarine until evenly brown. This is best achieved by gently shaking pan, so that meat balls roll, which also helps to maintain their shape. Serve cold on smörgasbord.

WHITE COLE SLAW

Danish

white cabbage
oil

vinegar
chopped parsley

chopped chives
salt and pepper

Remove coarse leaves and stalk from cabbage. Shred it finely. Make salad dressing with 3 parts oil to 1 part vinegar. Season to taste with salt and pepper. Mix cabbage well with generous amount of dressing. Let it stand for 2 hours. Sprinkle with equal portions chopped chives and parsley and serve. *(Illustrated in Plate 95.)*

DANISH HERRING SALAD

1 pickled herring or
  rollmop (see p. 277)
4 oz. cooked meat
  (tongue, ham or
  veal)
½ small onion or 2 oz.
  chopped pickled
  gherkins

2 oz. pickled beetroots
4 oz. uncooked apples
Sauce
little mustard
sugar to taste
1 oz. flour
1 oz. butter

½ pint beetroot
  vinegar (use the
  liquid from pickled
  beets or vinegar and
  some of the juice
  from canned
  beetroots)

Melt the butter in a saucepan and add the flour. Then add the beetroot vinegar gradually to make a thick sauce. Allow to simmer for 10 minutes. When sauce is cold, add the mustard and sugar to taste. Peel the apples. Dice the meat, apples, gherkins, beetroots and herrings. Blend them gently into the sauce. Serve on Danish open sandwiches with slices of hard-boiled eggs.

SHRIMP SALAD

Norwegian

6 SERVINGS

6 oz. peeled shrimps	6 tablespoons	2 tomatoes
1 small can fine peas	mayonnaise	2 tablespoons chopped
3 tablespoons diced	(see p. 263)	parsley
cucumbers	3 tablespoons whipped	lettuce leaves
1 hard-boiled egg	cream	salt and pepper

Mix the shrimps, cucumber and well drained peas together and season to taste. Mix cream and mayonnaise and stir carefully into the salad. Spread the lettuce leaves on a serving dish and heap salad on top. Chop hard-boiled egg finely and sprinkle over salad, together with chopped parsley. Quarter the tomatoes and place decoratively around the salad.

BIRGITTE SALAD

Norwegian

8 oz. boiled white fish	1 orange	3 tablespoons sugar
4 oz. boiled peas	2 gherkins	½ teaspoon salt
4 oz. raw grated	2 tablespoons vinegar	pepper or paprika to
carrots	2 tablespoons oil	taste
1 grated apple	3 tablespoons water	lettuce leaves

Bone the fish carefully and divide into nice pieces. Chop gherkins and cut up orange finely. Mix the fish and vegetables carefully in a bowl, using two forks. Mix all other ingredients into a sauce and pour over the salad. Spread lettuce leaves over a serving dish and pile the salad on top.

POTATO SALAD

Swedish

8 medium potatoes	freshly ground pepper	1 teaspoon chopped
1 small onion	2 teaspoons chopped	chives
2 tablespoons vinegar	parsley	1 teaspoon salt
	6 tablespoons oil	

Boil potatoes in their skins. Test with a fork to see they are done. Pour off water and hold pot over flame to dry them a little. Place in dish and cool. Peel and cut into slices. Mix vinegar, oil, salt and pepper in and stir well. Let the salad stand for 30 minutes, stirring occasionally in a salad bowl. Chop onion finely and stir into salad sauce. Add potatoes so that sauce is absorbed by potatoes. When ready to serve, mix in chopped chives and parsley and add a little fresh pepper to taste. (*Illustrated in Plate 16.*)

CHICKEN SALAD

Danish

cold diced chicken (about 12 oz.)	1 tablespoon grated horseradish	1 tablespoon chopped parsley
3 hard-boiled eggs	5 tablespoons whipped cream	salt and pepper
1 tablespoon vinegar		

Mash 3 hard-boiled eggs and mix in horseradish and vinegar. Stir in whipped cream. Mix in diced chicken. Season to taste with salt and pepper. Place in salad bowl and sprinkle parsley on top.

CABBAGE AND APPLE SALAD

Swedish

10 oz. shredded white cabbage	2 apples juice 1 orange	1 gill double cream sugar

Wash apples but do not peel them. Shred coarsely and mix with shredded cabbage. Mix cream and orange juice, adding a little sugar to taste. Pour over salad and serve slightly chilled.

DANISH OPEN SANDWICHES

(Illustrated in Plate 96.)

SANDWICH WITH CHEESE, SHRIMPS AND MAYONNAISE

Danish

shrimps, peeled	mayonnaise (see p. 263) white bread	butter parsley
sliced cheese		

Butter the bread and remove crusts. Cut cheese into strips and place 3 on each piece of bread, running from edge to edge. Place 2 rows of shrimps between cheese strips. Place dabs of mayonnaise on the shrimps and decorate with small sprigs of parsley.

SALT BEEF SANDWICH

Danish

slices salted beef	gherkins	butter
rye bread		French mustard

Mix 1 teaspoon French mustard with each 2 oz. butter. Spread on each slice of bread. Cover the entire sandwich with slices of salted beef. Slice gherkins thinly across and place an overlapping row of gherkin slices diagonally across the sandwich.

SALMON BUTTER AND ASPARAGUS SANDWICH
Danish

2 oz. smoked salmon	canned asparagus tips	pepper
3 oz. butter		white bread

Remove crusts of bread and cut each slice in half so that 2 rectangles remain. Chop salmon finely. Pass salmon and butter through a fine sieve, using a wooden spoon. Season with pepper to taste. Spread salmon butter fairly generously on bread. Let asparagus drain well and place one piece lengthwise on each sandwich.

ANCHOVY AND CHOPPED EGG SANDWICH
Danish

anchovy	dark bread	capers
hard-boiled eggs		butter

About 1 egg and 4 fillets of anchovy will be needed for each slice of bread. Butter bread and remove crusts so that a square remains. Chop egg whites and yolks separately and finely. Place anchovy in squares or strips across the bread. Fill in spaces with alternating egg white and yolk, so that it makes a nice design. Dot the chopped egg with capers.

SMOKED SALMON AND EGG SANDWICH
Danish

smoked salmon	white bread	fresh dill
hard-boiled egg		

Cut each slice of bread into a nice round shape, removing edges. Butter each slice and cover neatly with smoked salmon, cut to size. Slice hard-boiled egg and place one piece in centre of each sandwich. Garnish with a small sprig of dill.

HERRING SANDWICH
Danish

canned herring	lettuce	chopped chives
(gaffelbitar)	sour cream	butter
	rye bread	

Sliced rye bread will do well for this sandwich. Butter each slice carefully. Cover it with a washed and dried lettuce leaf. Place a row of herring pieces diagonally across the sandwich. Put a teaspoon of whipped sour cream in the other 2 corners. Sprinkle all over with chopped chives.

LAMB AND VEGETABLE SOUP

Swedish

2 lb. neck end of lamb	2 oz. butter	1 small packet frozen
3 pints water	1 carrot	peas
1 tablespoon salt	1 parsnip	2 tablespoons flour
6 white peppercorns	½ celeriac	chopped parsley
1 bay leaf		1 small leek

Put water and spices in soup pot and bring to the boil. Cut meat into convenient pieces and brown in butter. Take out meat and place in boiling water, leaving butter in frying pan. Allow meat to simmer for about 2 hours. In the meantime, clean root vegetables and cut into ½-inch cubes or slice. Brown them in remaining butter. Sprinkle flour on top and brown too, stirring when necessary. Take ½ pint stock and add to vegetables, cover and simmer in frying pan for 30 minutes. De-frost peas and chop parsley. When meat is tender, remove from soup, take out bones, cut into smaller pieces. Skim off excess fat from soup, add meat and vegetables with their stock, peas and parsley. Bring to the boil, season to taste and serve.

TUESDAY SOUP

Swedish

1 lb. pickled pork	1 large carrot	3 medium potatoes
2½ pints water	¾ pint milk	2½ tablespoons flour
3 tablespoons barley	1 parsnip	salt and pepper
½ celeriac		¼ swede

Rinse pork and place in water. Bring to the boil and skim off any foam. Simmer for 1½ hours. Clean vegetables and cut into pieces. Rinse barley in cold water and add to soup. Boil for about 10 minutes. Add vegetables and simmer for about 30 minutes, or until they are soft. Pour off stock and strain it. Put meat and vegetables to the side and re-heat stock. Stir milk and flour until smooth and add gradually to boiling stock. Cut up meat and place back in soup together with vegetables. Simmer for another 10 minutes, season to taste and serve.

CLEAR TOMATO SOUP

Swedish

2½ lb. ripe tomatoes	2 sticks celery	2 tablespoons dry
1 pint chicken stock	2 oz. butter	sherry
2 tablespoons dripping	2 tablespoons flour	2 tablespoons chopped
2 chopped onions	1 bouillon cube	parsley
1 clove garlic		salt and pepper

Melt dripping in cast iron pot and sauté onion and garlic, for 5 minutes. Wash tomatoes and celery, cut up and add to pot. Pour in stock and simmer, covered, for 40 minutes. Pass through fine sieve. Melt butter in pot and stir in flour. Add tomato purée and bouillon cube and stir until well blended. Season to taste and stir in sherry. Sprinkle with chopped parsley and serve.

SPRING SOUP

Swedish

5 new carrots	2½ tablespoons flour	2 egg yolks
2 leeks	2 oz. butter	6 tablespoons cream
6 oz. spinach	2½ pints water	salt and pepper
	1 bunch radishes	

Wash carrots, leeks, spinach and radishes. Melt butter in saucepan and add sliced leeks and carrots. Season with salt and pepper and simmer for 5 minutes. Add water and bring to the boil. Simmer for 10 minutes. Add chopped spinach and sliced radishes. Mix flour in a little cold water and add while stirring. Simmer until carrots are soft. Remove from heat, stir in yolks mixed with cream. Serve immediately with little cheese sandwiches, plain or toasted.

CAULIFLOWER SOUP

Swedish

2 lb. cauliflower	2 oz. butter	3 tablespoons chopped
1 pint stock	2 egg yolks	parsley
1 pint water		salt and pepper

Wash cauliflower and break it into sections, removing tough stem. Place in a large saucepan with boiling water and 1 teaspoon salt, simmer until soft, about 15 minutes. Take a wire whisk and beat vigorously until cauliflower is minced. Add stock, bring to boil and season to taste with salt and pepper. Stir in butter. Beat egg yolks, cream and parsley, beat quickly into soup and remove from heat. Serve immediately.

AEG OFG FLOESK

Danish Egg and Bacon Cake

4 rashers streaky	4 eggs	knob of butter
bacon		½ pint milk

Fry or grill the rashers of bacon and keep them hot. Break the eggs into a bowl, add the milk, and salt and pepper to taste. Beat well with a whisk. Heat an omelette pan and melt the butter in it. When hot, pour in the egg mixture and cook gently until nearly set, shaking the pan from time to time. Turn out with a palette knife on to a hot dish and arrange the grilled bacon on the top. Serve with a green salad.

ROLLED HAM WITH SAMSOE CHEESE FILLING AND TOMATO SAUCE

Danish

8 slices ham	6 oz. Samsoe cheese	2 tablespoons tomato
1 oz. butter	2 egg yolks	purée mixed with
1 oz. flour	pinch black pepper	4 tablespoons milk
	¼ pint milk	

Melt the butter, gradually mix in the flour and cook for 1 minute. Pour in the milk slowly, stirring all the time and cook for 3 minutes. Let the sauce cool, mix in the egg yolks, salt and pepper to taste. Cut the cheese into cubes, first setting aside sufficient thinly sliced or grated cheese to garnish the finished dish. Add cubed cheese to the sauce and heat until mixture is well blended. Put a dessertspoon of the cheese filling on each slice of ham, roll up and place in an ovenproof dish. Cover the rolls with tomato purée and place the thin slices of cheese on the top. Cook for approximately 15 minutes in a moderate oven.

EGG AND ONION CASSEROLE

Swedish

6-hard-boiled eggs	3 tablespoons flour	2 tablespoons grated
2 large onions	¾ pint milk	cheese
2½ oz. butter		salt and pepper

Peel, slice and fry onions in 1 oz. butter. Place in a casserole so that the bottom is covered. Peel and slice eggs and spread over onions. Melt rest of butter in saucepan and stir in flour. Gradually add milk, while continuing to stir. Let sauce simmer for 10 minutes. Stir in grated cheese and season to taste with salt and pepper. Pour sauce into casserole and place high in a very hot oven or under grill until slightly browned on top. Serve with fried potatoes.

MEAT CAKES WITH BACON AND CHEESE

Swedish

1 lb. minced beef	6 tablespoons	6 slices cheese
4 oz. minced veal	breadcrumbs	1 oz. butter
1 egg	½ pint milk	salt and pepper
	6 slices back bacon	

Mix egg, milk and breadcrumbs. Add minced meat and stir well until smooth and creamy. Season to taste with salt and pepper. Form into 6 cakes and wind a slice of bacon around each one, securing it with a toothpick. Melt butter in an oven pan and place meat cakes in it. Bake in a very hot oven for 20—25 minutes, basting with fat from time to time. After 15 minutes, place a thick slice of cheese over each one and replace in oven. Serve when cheese is almost melted, with green salad.

DANISH HAM BALLS

4 oz. flour	1 egg	*Filling:*
1 oz. butter	4 dessertspoons milk	2 oz. butter
½ teaspoon salt	½ oz. yeast	8 oz. chopped ham

Mix the butter, flour and salt together with the fingertips and add half the beaten egg. Warm the milk to blood heat and mix a little with the yeast. Pour this into the flour and butter with the rest of the milk and mix into a dough. Divide the dough into 8—10 even balls and put on a greased tray in a warm place until they are double in size. Brush them with the rest of the egg and bake in a hot oven for about 8 minutes. When the balls are cool, cut them almost in half and remove the centres. Mix together the chopped ham and butter and put this in the balls. Place in a warm oven for 5 minutes before serving.

TOMATOES STUFFED WITH MUSHROOMS

Swedish

8 medium tomatoes	2 oz. butter	2 tablespoons flour
8 oz. mushrooms	6 strips bacon	salt and pepper

Wash and dry tomatoes. Slice off top of each one and remove pulp. Season inside with a little salt and pepper. Clean and chop mushrooms. Fry them in 1½ oz. butter. Season with salt and pepper and when browned a little, sprinkle in flour. Stir well and add fried, chopped bacon and tomato pulp. Simmer for 5 minutes then cool before filling tomatoes. Replace tops and put tomatoes close together in shallow buttered oven dish. Dot with rest of butter and bake in moderate oven for 20 minutes. Serve hot. *(Illustrated in Plate 30.)*

MORMORS SILL

Grandmother's Herring

Swedish

6 salted herring	2 hard-boiled eggs	2 tablespoons chopped
fillets	2 oz. butter	parsley
	2 leeks, finely chopped	

Soak herring fillets overnight in cold water. Remove skin and dice rather finely. Place herrings in saucepan and add sufficient water barely to cover them. Bring to the boil. Chop eggs finely and add to fish, together with butter. Allow to simmer for a few minutes and add parsley and chopped leeks. When leeks are cooked dish is ready to serve with boiled, potatoes.

HOT MINCED MEAT SANDWICH

Swedish

10 oz. minced beef	1 tablespoon chopped	2½ oz. butter
3 tablespoons	capers	4 large slices white
breadcrumbs	2 tablespoons	bread
2 tablespoons chopped	chopped, pickled	salt and pepper
onions	beets	¼ pint milk

Place breadcrumbs and milk in a bowl and mix in meat until smooth., Add chopped onions, beets and capers, mixing well. Season to taste with salt and pepper. Brown about a third of butter and fry bread slices on one side. Take them out and spread a quarter of the mince on fried side of each slice. Brown another third of butter and place sandwiches with meat side down in frying pan. Fry until evenly brown. Add rest of butter and fry other side of bread. Place on heated dish and serve.

FILLED PANCAKES

Swedish

3 eggs	*Filling:*	1 small can evaporated
5½ oz. self-raising	8 oz. mushrooms	milk (equivalent to
flour	4 oz. peeled shrimps	¾ pint diluted)
1½ pints milk	2 tablespoons chopped	1 tablespoon dry
2 oz. butter	onion	sherry
½ teaspoon salt	3 oz. butter	salt and pepper
butter for frying	2 tablespoons flour	water
	grated cheese	

Beat eggs in large bowl. Add flour and salt while stirring, then add milk gradually. Beat until well blended. Melt butter and stir in. Stand batter for 1 hour. Melt a little butter in frying pan, pour in enough batter to cover pan and fry golden brown on both sides. Repeat until all batter is used up. Melt butter in saucepan, add chopped mushrooms and onion and sauté until starting to colour. Season with salt and pepper. Sprinkle flour over and stir in. Dilute evaporated milk with water to make ½ pint in all, which is gradually added whilst stirring. Add shrimps and sherry. Season to taste. Divide mixture between pancakes, placing it in middle and rolling each one up. Place side by side in buttered oven dish, sprinkle with grated cheese and dot with butter. They can now stand until 15 minutes before required, when they are heated in hot oven until cheese melts. Filling can be varied according to taste.

BACON CASSEROLE

Swedish

1 lb. leeks	¾ pint milk	1 egg yolk
1½ oz. butter	4 tablespoons grated	8 strips bacon
2 tablespoons flour	cheese	salt and pepper

Clean leeks well and slice. Place in saucepan with 1 oz. butter, cover and simmer until soft. Season lightly and place in a shallow, buttered oven dish. Melt rest of butter in same saucepan, stir in flour and gradually add milk while continuing, to stir until sauce is thick and smooth. Season lightly with salt and pepper. Remove from heat and stir in 3 tablespoons cheese and egg yolk. Pour sauce over leeks so that they are completely covered. Sprinkle rest of cheese on top. Cut bacon across grain to make short strips. Place these over top so that it is completely covered. Bake in a very hot oven or put under grill until bacon is crisp. Serve with boiled or fried potatoes.

FISH FILLETS WITH MUSHROOMS AND VEGETABLES

Swedish

2 lb. fish fillets	3½ oz. butter	1 small can
¾ pint fish stock	1½ tablespoons flour	evaporated milk
6 tablespoons carrots	4 oz. mushrooms	(equivalent to
2 egg yolks	3 tablespoons leek,	¾ pint diluted)
	sliced	2 tablespoons top of
		milk or cream
		2 firm tomatoes
		salt and pepper

Soak fish in cold, salted water (3 tablespoons salt to 2 pints water) for 10 minutes. Make fish stock from fish scraps, and strain. Slice mushrooms and fry in 2½ oz. butter, together with leek and carrots. Season with a little salt and pepper, add 3 tablespoons of fish stock, cover and allow to simmer until vegetables are soft. Remove fish from cold water and poach in fish stock for 5—10 minutes. Melt remainder of butter in a saucepan and stir in flour. Add ½ pint of fish stock gradually while stirring, letting sauce thicken each time before more stock is added. Stir in evaporated milk, season to taste, and allow to simmer for a few minutes. Mix egg yolks and cream together and add to sauce while stirring vigorously. Add vegetable mixture to sauce. Place fish fillets on hot serving dish and pour sauce on top. Garnish with quartered tomatoes and serve with boiled potatoes.

KNUTS SILLADA

Knut's Herring Casserole
Swedish

4 herrings	5 tablespoons cream	3 tablespoons
3 oz. butter	2 tablespoons tomato	breadcrumbs
2 tablespoons grated	purée	salt
horseradish		3 tablespoons water

Clean and fillet herrings. Season with a little salt. Mix butter and grated horseradish to a paste and divide between fillets, putting a little on each. Roll fillets up and place in buttered oven dish. Mix tomato purée, water and cream together and pour over fish. Sprinkle breadcrumbs on top and bake in a moderately hot oven for about 30 minutes. Serve with boiled potatoes.

HALIBUT ON BACON AND VEGETABLE BED

Swedish

2 lb. slice halibut	2 tablespoons chopped	1 teaspoon chopped
8 slices bacon	parsley	dill
8 oz. carrots	½ pint dry white wine	2 teaspoons salt
1 large onion	2 tablespoons sliced	4 slices lemon
4 oz. mushrooms	celery	2 oz. butter
	pepper	

Wash carrots, scrape if necessary and slice rather thinly. Place bacon slices in shallow casserole. Spread carrots over. Chop onion and mushrooms and spread over carrots. Sprinkle with parsley, celery, dill, 1 teaspoon salt and a little pepper. Place fish slice on this bed and sprinkle with rest of salt. Place lemon slices on top, dot with butter and pour wine over. Cover tightly with foil and bake in a moderately hot oven for 20 minutes. Remove foil and bake for another 20 minutes. Serve with mashed potatoes and green salad.

COD WITH CHEESE SAUCE

Swedish

2 lb. cod steaks	2 tablespoons salt	cheese sauce
2 pints water	1 slice onion	(see p. 257)

Make cheese sauce before boiling fish. Place fish steaks in cold, salted water (3 tablespoons salt to 2 pints water) for 10 minutes. Meantime, bring water, salt and onion slice to the boil in fish kettle. Take fish out of cold water, which is discarded, place steaks carefully on grating and sink into water. There should be just enough to cover fish. Bring to the boil again and skim off any foam. Cover and simmer for about 5 minutes, when flesh should just have loosened from bone. Be careful not to overcook fish as it then loses its flavour. As water in which fish is boiled is very salty, it should not be used as stock for sauce. Place fish steaks on hot dish and serve with cheese sauce. (*Illustrated in Plate 79.*)

SMOKED COD WITH GRATED CARROTS

Norwegian

1½ lb. smoked cod fillet	2 tablespoons chopped parsley	4 oz. butter
3 tablespoons oil	2 teaspoons French mustard	1 tablespoon lemon juice

Wash and dry smoked cod fillets. Cut them into suitable portions. Put oil in frying pan and turn fillets in it. Fry on low heat, shaking pan from time to time. Heat should be low enough to cook fillets through without browning them. When ready, place them on a hot serving dish and spread a little mustard on each piece. This is best done with a brush, to get it evenly spread in a thin layer. While fish is still frying, mix butter, lemon juice and parsley together into a smooth paste. Dot each piece of cod with this before serving with raw grated carrots and mashed potatoes.

FISH BALLS

Swedish

1 lb. fillet of cod or haddock	2 eggs	3 tablespoons thick cream
4 oz. butter	3 tablespoons thin cream	1 pint fish stock
1½ tablespoons flour		salt and pepper

Soak fish fillets for 10—15 minutes in cold, salted water (3 tablespoons salt to 2 pints water). Remove and drain fish, discarding water. Place fillets with skin down on a wooden board and scrape fish until all flesh is minced. Place flesh in bowl and pound together with butter. Pass it through a sieve to get smooth even texture. Season lightly with salt and pepper. Beat egg yolks, flour and single cream together. Add cream mixture to fish, a little at a time, while stirring vigorously. Then add double cream in same manner. Beat egg whites stiff and stir in carefully. Bring fish stock to the boil. Use teaspoons to form the mixture into round balls. Dip spoons in hot stock to prevent sticking. As fishballs are formed, place in boiling stock. Allow to boil for about 10 minutes. Make a sauce from the stock, pour over fish balls and serve with boiled potatoes and vegetable of choice.

COD STEW

Norwegian

1 lb. cod fillet	4 medium potatoes	2 tablespoons flour
8 oz. Brussels sprouts	4 medium carrots	4 tablespoons chopped
½ celeriac	1 pint milk	parsley
1 leek		1 oz. butter

Clean, peel and dice all vegetables into about ½-inch cubes. Place in a saucepan, season and boil in milk. Wash cod fillets and place in a colander that fits into saucepan. Cover tightly and leave to steam until vegetables are cooked. Strain off milk. Cut cod into pieces and mix with vegetables. Melt butter in another saucepan and stir in flour. Add milk gradually, stirring until sauce is smooth. Allow to simmer for 10 minutes. Season with salt and pepper and stir in chopped parsley. Pour sauce over fish and vegetables. Mix all together and allow to come to the boil again, after which it is ready to be served.

COD WITH RICE AND TOMATO SAUCE

1½ lb. boiled cod	2 oz. margarine or	2 tablespoons
(left-over)	corn oil	grated cheese
12 oz. rice (cooked)	½ pint milk	sugar
1 tablespoon flour	2 tablespoons tomato	salt and pepper
	purée	

Shred and bone fish carefully. Place fish and rice in layers in a casserole. Melt half the margarine in saucepan and stir in flour. Add milk gradually while stirring until sauce is smooth. Stir in tomato purée. Season to taste with salt, pepper and a little sugar. Pour sauce over fish. Sprinkle cheese on top and dot with rest of butter. Place in pre-heated moderately hot oven for about 30 minutes. Serve with green salad.

COD BAKED IN MAYONNAISE

Norwegian

1½ lb. cod fillet	1 onion	salt and pepper
2 tablespoons chopped	10 tablespoons	3 tablespoons
parsley	mayonnaise	breadcrumbs
	(see p. 263)	

Wash and dry cod fillets. Place in a buttered casserole and season with salt and pepper. Sprinkle parsley over and then cover with mayonnaise. Bake in pre-heated hot oven for 20 minutes. Sprinkle breadcrumbs over and bake another 5 minutes. Serve with mashed potatoes.

FISK TURBANER

Fish Turbans

Swedish

1 lb. fillet of sole or plaice	1½ tablespoons flour	breadcrumbs
1 can crab meat	¼ pint fish stock	2 tablespoons grated
8 oz. mushrooms	1 can evaporated milk	Parmesan cheese
3 oz. butter	(equivalent to	salt
	¾ pint diluted)	paprika

Fish Turbans are baked in small individual oven dishes. Soak fish fillets for 5—10 minutes, in cold, salted water (3 tablespoons salt to 2 pints water). Remove, dry carefully on a clean cloth and discard water. Slice mushrooms (do not wash or peel them as this destroys some of the flavour) and fry lightly in 2 oz. of butter. Chop crab meat and add to mushrooms. Save liquid to make up part of fish stock which is made from boiling a few fish scraps. Sprinkle flour on top of mushrooms and crab meat, and stir in. Add fish stock and canned milk gradually, stirring gently until sauce has thickened. Season to taste. Wipe oven dishes with buttered paper. Stand a fish fillet on its side, inside edge of each dish, so that it forms a circle. Divide sauce mixture between each dish, placing it in the middle. Bake in a moderately hot oven for about 10 minutes. Sprinkle cheese, breadcrumbs and a dash of paprika on top of each one. Distribute remainder of butter on top of this. Place under grill until they turn golden and cheese is melted. Serve with boiled or mashed potatoes and green salad.

BOILED COD WITH MUSTARD SAUCE

Norwegian

1½ lb. cod fillets	2 tablespoons cornflour	3 teaspoons French mustard
2 pints water	½ pint milk	lemon slices
2 tablespoons salt	½ pint fish stock	salt and pepper
1 tablespoon vinegar	1 oz. butter	

Allow cod fillets to rinse in running water while sauce is prepared. Make stock by boiling some fish scraps. Stir cornflour in a little milk. Bring remainder of milk and fish stock to the boil and stir in flour mixture. Let sauce simmer for 10 minutes. Add butter and mustard and season to taste with salt and pepper. While sauce is simmering, put on water for cod and bring to the boil with salt and vinegar added. Put in cod steaks and when it comes to the boil again, skim off any foam. Allow to simmer for about 10 minutes, when cod should be ready to be served. Decorate with lemon slices; serve sauce separately. Boiled potatoes and a cooked vegetable go well with this.

BAKED MARINATED MACKEREL

Swedish

4 mackerels	1 packet saffron	2 medium onions
12 tablespoons oil	(5 grains)	4 medium tomatoes
4 tablespoons lemon	2 tablespoons chopped	2 tablespoons chopped
juice	chives	dill
½ teaspoon pepper		salt

Clean and fillet mackerels. Wash and dry them. Mix oil, lemon juice, saffron, pepper and chopped chives and marinate the mackerel fillets in this mixture for at least 1 hour. Wipe casserole with buttered paper, peel and slice onions and place in bottom. Take fillets out of marinade and place in casserole. Sprinkle with a little salt. Slice tomatoes and place on top. Sprinkle with chopped dill. Bake in a hot oven for about 30 minutes. Serve with green salad and potatoes.

BAKED HERRING WITH MUSSELS

Swedish

4 fresh herrings	2 tablespoons bread-	1 carton thin cream
1 can mussels (5 oz.)	crumbs	(3 tablespoons)
chopped dill	2 oz. butter	salt and pepper

Clean and fillet herrings. Butter an oven dish and place 4 fillets side by side in it, skin side down. Season with salt and pepper. Fry mussels lightly in half the butter and spread on top of herrings. Sprinkle generously with chopped dill. Place remaining 4 fillets on top, skin side up. Sprinkle breadcrumbs over them and dot with rest of butter. Bake in a hot oven for 15 minutes. Pour cream over and bake for another 10 minutes. Serve with mashed or boiled potatoes and green vegetable.

COD AND POTATO CASSEROLE

Norwegian

1½ lb. cod fillet	2 tablespoons chopped	2 oz. butter
6 medium potatoes	parsley	salt and pepper
1 medium onion	3 tablespoons	lemon juice
	breadcrumbs	

Wash and dry cod fillets. Butter a shallow oven dish and place fillets side by side in it. Sprinkle with lemon juice, salt and pepper to taste. Peel and slice potatoes, place in a layer over cod. Dot with butter and bake in a hot oven for 15 minutes. Peel and chop onion. Sprinkle over potatoes together with parsley and breadcrumbs. Bake for another 15 minutes. Serve with green vegetables or salad.

94. Toad-in-the-Hole, Britain (p.93)

95. White Cole Slaw, Denmark (p.482)

96. Danish Open Sandwiches (pp.484, 485)

COD Á LA TRONDHEIM

Norwegian

1½ lb. cod fillet	3 tablespoons chopped	3 oz. butter
2 carrots	parsley	3 tablespoons
½ celeriac (or 4 oz.	1 medium onion	breadcrumbs
diced celery)	6 slices white bread	salt and pepper

Peel and grate carrots and celeriac. Chop onion finely. Remove crusts from bread and cube it. Melt butter. Mix vegetables, bread and parsley in a bowl with melted butter, and season to taste with salt and pepper. Wash cod fillets and dry them. Place in shallow, buttered oven dish and season with salt. Spread vegetable mixture over fish and sprinkle breadcrumbs on top. Bake in a hot oven for about 30 minutes. Serve with potatoes.

MORS MAKRIL LÅDA

Mother's Mackerel Casserole

Swedish

4 mackerel	2 tablespoons chopped	1 carton sour cream
4 medium tomatoes	dill	(6 tablespoons)
2 medium leeks	½ teaspoon paprika	salt
	juice of ½ lemon	

Clean and fillet mackerel. Wash and dry fillets. Wipe casserole with buttered paper and place fillets in it, with meaty side up. Sprinkle with a little salt. Clean leeks, cut them finely and place on fish. Add chopped tomatoes and dill. Sprinkle paprika on top and add lemon juice and sour cream. Cover and bake in a hot oven for about 30 minutes. Serve with boiled potatoes.

BAKED HERRING WITH ANCHOVY SAUCE

Swedish

4 herrings	3 tablespoons	salt, pepper
1 carton thin cream	breadcrumbs	lemon juice
(3 tablespoons)	1 oz. butter	8 anchovy fillets

Clean and fillet herrings. Butter shallow oven dish and place fillets in it, skin side down. Season with salt, pepper and a little lemon juice. Chop anchovy fillets finely and mix into cream. Spread this over herring. Sprinkle with breadcrumbs and dot butter on top. Bake in a hot oven for about 30 minutes. Serve with mashed potatoes.

STUFFED FILLET OF MACKEREL
Swedish

4 medium mackerel, filleted	1 tablespoon Worcester sauce (see p. 108)	½ tablespoon chopped chives
6 oz. mushrooms		tomatoes and parsley
1 oz. butter	½ tablespoon chopped, fresh dill	for garnish

Soak fish fillets in cold, salted water (3 tablespoons to 2 pints water) for 10—15 minutes; remove fish, dry it, discarding water. Chop mushrooms finely, but do not wash and peel them. Melt butter in saucepan and let mushrooms sauté slowly for a few minutes until soft. Remove from heat and allow to cool a little before mixing in other ingredients. Divide mixture in 4 portions and spread over 4 of the fillets. Place other 4 fillets on top, pressing them together in pairs. Wrap each pair in tin foil, place in oven dish and bake in a hot oven for 20—25 minutes. Remove fish from wrapping, place on hot serving dish and pour juice over them. Garnish with quartered tomatoes and chopped parsley and serve with boiled potatoes and green salad.

POACHED COD
Norwegian

1½ lb. cod steaks	slices lemon	salt and pepper
1 oz. butter		chopped parsley

Wash and dry cod steaks. Melt butter in wide saucepan and place cod steaks in it, side by side. Season with salt and pepper. Place lemon slice on each cod steak and sprinkle chopped parsley on top. Cover tightly and allow to poach on low heat for 15 minutes. Shake saucepan from time to time, to make sure fish does not stick to bottom. Serve with its natural sauce and mashed potatoes.

MOCK LOBSTER COCKTAIL
Norwegian

6 oz. boiled white fish	2 tablespoons oil	1 tablespoon chopped parsley
2 oz. shrimps, peeled	1 tablespoon vinegar	
1 medium celeriac (or diced celery)	1 teaspoon salt	lobster colouring
	½ teaspoon pepper	lettuce leaves

Bone the fish carefully and divide into nice pieces. Scrub the celeriac and boil it, peel and cut into small dice. Mix the fish and diced celeriac carefully, using 2 forks. Make a salad dressing of oil, vinegar and spices and pour over slowly while mixing the salad. Sprinkle parsley over it, add the colouring and mix all together. Place lettuce leaves in cocktail glasses and heap the salad on top. Decorate with shrimps and serve chilled.

HERRING OR MACKEREL CASSEROLE

Swedish

2 lb. herring or mackerel
1 teaspoon salt
¼ teaspoon pepper

½ teaspoon crushed cloves
1 tablespoon chopped parsley
breadcrumbs

½ tablespoon chopped chives
5 tablespoons vinegar
1 tablespoon butter

Prepare casserole by wiping it with buttered paper and coating with breadcrumbs. Fillet fish and let it soak in cold, salted water (3 tablespoons salt to 2 pints water) for 10 minutes. Remove fillets, discarding water, and let them drain well. Score skin of each fillet a couple of times. Roll each fillet up and place in casserole so that they stand close together. Sprinkle spices on top. Pour vinegar over and dot with butter. Place in a very hot oven and bake for 10 minutes. Take out casserole and sprinkle top with breadcrumbs. Then bake for another 10 minutes, when it should be ready to be served with fried or new, boiled potatoes.

BAKED MACKEREL WITH STUFFING

Swedish

4 mackerel
2 tablespoons lemon juice
2 tablespoons chopped dill

4 tablespoons water
4 tablespoons chopped parsley
4 slices white bread

2 tablespoons chopped chives
3 medium onions
2 tablespoons oil
salt

Clean and fillet mackerel. Wash and dry them and sprinkle with lemon juice and a little salt. Remove crusts from bread slices and let them soak in water. Peel and chop onions and mix with bread. Stir in chopped dill, parsley and chives and then work in oil. Divide this stuffing into 4 parts and place between each pair of fillets. Wrap the pairs in foil and place in a hot oven for about 30 minutes. Serve with potatoes boiled with fresh dill.

SMOKED BUCKLING WITH EGGS

Swedish

4 smoked buckling
2 hard-boiled eggs
1½ oz. butter

2 tablespoons chopped chives (or parsley)

3 tablespoons flour
¾ pint milk
salt and pepper

Remove all skin and bones from fish and divide into pieces. Peel and chop eggs. Melt butter in a saucepan and stir in flour. Add milk gradually while stirring, until smooth. Simmer for at least 5 minutes. Season with salt and pepper. Stir in smoked fish, eggs and chives (or parsley). Bring to the boil again and serve with fried potatoes.

MACKEREL BAKED IN WINE

Swedish

4 mackerel	2 tablespoons chopped	6 tablespoons dry
2 medium onions	dill	white wine
3 medium tomatoes	2 oz. butter	salt and pepper

Clean and fillet mackerel. Wash and dry fillets, sprinkle with a little salt and pepper. Peel onions, slice thinly and fry golden brown in a little of the butter. Place in casserole, covering the bottom. Place mackerel fillets on top, then layer of sliced tomatoes. Sprinkle with chopped dill and dot with remainder of butter. Bake in a very hot oven for 15 minutes. Pour wine over it and let it bake for another 10 minutes. Serve with potatoes baked in their jackets.

FRIED MACKEREL WITH TOMATO AND MUSHROOM SAUCE

Swedish

4 mackerel	4 oz. butter	4 tablespoons
4 peeled tomatoes	1 clove garlic	breadcrumbs
4 oz. mushrooms	4 tablespoons flour	margarine for frying
1 medium onion		salt and pepper

Clean and fillet mackerel, wash and dry and sprinkle with a little salt and pepper. Peel and chop onion and sauté in 2 oz. butter, together with sliced mushrooms, chopped tomatoes and crushed garlic. Season to taste, cover and let it simmer. Mix flour and breadcrumbs and coat fillets in this. Fry them golden brown in remaining 2 oz. butter and place on hot serving dish. When mackerel is done, the tomato and mushroom sauce will also be ready. It is then poured over fish. Serve with mashed potatoes.

COBBLER'S HERRING

Swedish

8 salted herring	2 bay leaves	3 oz. butter
fillets	1 tablespoon chopped	1 teaspoon lemon
2 tablespoons vinegar	parsley	juice

Soak herring fillets overnight in cold water. Remove skins and roll each fillet up, securing with a tooth pick. Boil in water to which vinegar and bay leaves are added for 10—15 minutes. Melt butter and add lemon juice. Place herrings on warm dish, sprinkle parsley over them and pour melted butter on top. Serve steaming hot with boiled potatoes.

FRIED HERRING WITH ONION SAUCE

4 herrings, filleted	2 tablespoons flour	1 teaspoon cold
rye or wholemeal flour	1 pint milk	butter
margarine for frying	2 medium onions	salt and pepper
	1 oz. butter	

Soak fish fillets in cold, salted water (3 tablespoons salt to 2 pints water) for 10—15 minutes. Drain them and discard water. Coat fillets in wholemeal flour and fry golden brown on each side. Place on a serving dish and keep warm in oven. Peel and chop onions. Brown the butter in frying pan and fry onions golden brown. Sprinkle flour on top and stir in. Add milk gradually, stirring constantly and letting sauce thicken before adding more milk, until it is all worked in. Season to taste, cover and let sauce simmer for 10 minutes. Remove from heat and stir in cold butter. Pour sauce over fish and serve with potatoes baked in their jackets.

FRIED MACKEREL WITH CAPERS

Swedish

4 mackerel	1½ teaspoons soya	margarine for frying
1 tablespoon capers	sauce	salt
top of milk	breadcrumbs	1 lemon

Clean and fillet mackerel. Wash and dry fillets. Sprinkle with a little salt, coat them in breadcrumbs and fry golden brown in margarine. Place on serving dish and keep warm. Add capers, soya sauce and top of the milk to margarine that is left in pan and bring to boil. Pour sauce over mackerel. Chop lemon peel and sprinkle on top. Serve with mashed potatoes and green salad.

WEST COAST HERRING CASSEROLE

Swedish

6 salted herring fillets	1 carton sour cream	2 tablespoons
8 oz. carrots	(6 tablespoons)	breadcrumbs
2 medium leeks		2 oz. butter

Soak herring fillets in cold water overnight. Remove skins. Butter a casserole. Dry herring fillets and cut them diagonally across into inch wide strips. Place in casserole. Clean and slice carrots, place on top of herrings. Clean leeks and slice crosswise. Place in layer on top of carrots. Dot butter on top of this and pour cream over. Sprinkle with breadcrumbs, and bake in a moderately hot oven for about 45 minutes. Serve with mashed potatoes.

BAKED MACKEREL WITH LEEKS

Swedish

4 mackerel	sprigs dill	2 tablespoons chopped
2 medium onions	3 tablespoons vinegar	dill
2 leeks	9 tablespoons oil	salt

Clean and fillet mackerel. Wash and dry fillets, sprinkle with a little salt. Wipe casserole with buttered paper and place fillets in it, meaty side up. Peel and chop onions and leeks. Mix together and place in layer over fish. Put a few sprigs of dill on top of this. Mix oil and vinegar and pour over. Cover dish and bake in a hot oven for about 30 minutes. When dish is ready, remove sprigs of dill and sprinkle with freshly chopped dill instead. Serve with potatoes baked in their jackets.

FRIED MACKEREL WITH ANCHOVY STUFFING

Swedish

4 mackerel	margarine for frying	1 tablespoon chopped
juice ½ lemon	2 hard-boiled eggs	parsley
1 teaspoon ground	10 anchovy fillets	½ oz. butter
allspice	1 tablespoon chopped	sliced lemon for
1 egg	chives	garnish
breadcrumbs		salt

Clean and fillet mackerel. Wash and dry fillets. Sprinkle allspice and a little salt over fillets and let them stand for 10 minutes. Beat egg, dip in fillets, coat them in breadcrumbs and fry golden brown in margarine. Place in pairs on serving dish and keep warm. Chop anchovy fillets finely and mash together with hard-boiled eggs, using a fork. Mix in chopped parsley and chives and lightly fry in butter. Spread filling on 4 of the fillets, placing other 4 on top. Garnish with lemon slices and serve with mashed potatoes and creamed spinach.

BAKED COD WITH APPLES AND CELERIAC

Norwegian

1½ lb. cod fillet	4 medium cooking	4 tablespoons tomato
½ celeriac (or 3 oz.	apples	purée
diced celery)	1 medium onion	¼ pint top of milk
	salt and pepper	

Peel onion, apples and celeriac and chop finely. Mix together and spread in bottom of a shallow, buttered oven dish. Wash and dry cod fillets and place on top. Season with salt and pepper to taste. Mix milk and tomato purée into a sauce and pour over fish. Bake in a hot oven for about 30 minutes. Serve with boiled potatoes.

FISH SOUFFLÉ

Swedish

1 lb. boiled fish	4 eggs	salt and pepper
2 oz. butter	2 tablespoons	mushroom or shrimp
3 tablespoons flour	breadcrumbs	sauce (see p. 447, 395)
	¾ pint milk	

Melt butter in saucepan and stir in flour. Add milk gradually, stirring until smooth and creamy. Remove from heat. Beat egg yolks and add to sauce, beating vigorously. Divide fish into small flakes and add to sauce. Season to taste with salt and pepper and allow to cool. Beat egg whites until very stiff and fold into sauce. Butter soufflé tin and pour mixture in. Sprinkle with breadcrumbs and bake in a moderate oven for 1 hour or until set. Serve immediately with either mushroom or shrimp sauce.

WHITING BAKED WITH VEGETABLES

Norwegian

2 lb. whiting	6 tablespoons sour	2 tablespoons grated
3 leeks	cream	cheese
2 carrots	6 tablespoons white	2 tablespoons
juice 1 lemon	wine	breadcrumbs
3 oz. margarine		salt and pepper

Fillet the whiting, wash and dry it. Clean the vegetables and slice them. Butter a casserole and put the fish and vegetables in alternate layers in it. Season between the layers with salt, pepper and lemon juice. Pour the white wine and sour cream over and sprinkle the cheese and breadcrumbs on top. Dot with the margarine and bake in a hot oven for about 35 minutes. Serve with potatoes.

MARGARETA SILL

Margareta Herring

Swedish

4 large herrings	4 tablespoons tomato	4 tablespoons cream
4 tablespoons French	purée	salt
mustard		2 oz. butter

Clean, wash and fillet herrings. Divide butter equally between 8 fillets, place some on each one and roll them up separately, with skin side out. Pack into casserole and sprinkle with a little salt. Mix mustard, tomato purée and cream to a smooth sauce and spread over fish. Bake in a moderately hot oven for about 30 minutes. Serve with mashed potatoes.

JANSONS FRESTELSE

Janson's Temptation

Swedish

10 canned Swedish anchovies or 4 fillets of pickled herring	5 medium potatoes 2 medium onions 4 oz. butter	6 tablespoons thin cream

Clean and fillet anchovies. If herring is used, cut each fillet into strips. Cut onions into slices and sauté in some of the butter until transparent. Peel potatoes and slice fairly thinly. Butter a casserole and place half the sliced potatoes in it. Spread onions on top and then anchovies or herring, finishing with the rest of the potatoes. Dot remainder of butter on top and place in a moderately hot oven for about 10 minutes. Then pour half the cream over it and replace in oven, letting it cook for another 10 minutes. Add rest of cream and continue cooking until potatoes are done. Serve immediately with green salad.

MARSTRANDS SILL

Marstrand's Herring

Swedish

4 large herrings 8 small onions ½ oz. butter ¼ pint water	4 tablespoons chopped dill 4 tablespoons cream juice of ½ lemon	4 crushed cloves 1 crushed bay leaf salt

Clean, wash and fillet herrings. Peel onions and put in saucepan with ¼ pint water and the butter. Allow to simmer until onions are soft. Place herring fillets in wide saucepan, with a little salt, and add onions with their water. Add lemon juice and cream, sprinkle dill, cloves and bay leaf on top. Liquid should come about half-way up contents. Cover tightly and bring to the boil. Turn heat down and allow to simmer for 15 minutes. Serve with mashed potatoes.

VEAL POT-ROAST

Swedish

6 TO 8 SERVINGS

4½—5 lb. leg of veal 2 oz. butter 1 bouillon cube ¼ pint boiling water	2 sliced onions ½ teaspoon allspice 2 tablespoons flour 2 sliced carrots gherkins for garnish	1 small can evaporated milk (equivalent to ¾ pint diluted) salt and pepper

Rub meat with salt and pepper. Melt butter in large cast iron pot and brown meat on all sides. Dissolve bouillon cube in boiling water and pour over meat. Add carrots, onions and allspice, cover and simmer gently for 1½—2 hours, when meat should be tender. Remove meat from stock and keep warm. Strain stock and return to pot. There should be about ¾ pint stock but if not, add water to make up quantity. Mix flour in 3 tablespoons cold water and add stock gradually, while on low heat. Stir until smooth, then add evaporated milk and simmer while stirring until sauce is smooth and thick. Season to taste. Serve sauce from separate bowl. Slice meat and place on hot serving dish, garnished with sliced gherkins.

MINCED VEAL CUTLET

Swedish

13 oz. minced veal	1 egg	1 oz. butter
3 oz. minced pork	anchovy paste	2½ oz. margarine
3 cold boiled potatoes	½ pint milk	salt and pepper

Place potatoes in mixing bowl and mash them, using wooden spoon. Mix in veal and pork and stir in egg. Add milk gradually and stir in. Season to taste with salt and pepper. Form into cakes and fry slowly in margarine until nicely brown. Place on hot serving dish and pour fat from pan over. Mix butter with anchovy paste to taste. Form into little balls, placing one on each veal cutlet and serve with potatoes.

ROAST LEG OF LAMB

Swedish

6 SERVINGS

4 lb. leg of lamb	1 teaspoon sugar	½ pint milk
2 teaspoons salt	½ pint made coffee	1 teaspoon redcurrant
¼ teaspoon pepper	1 tablespoon cream	jelly
2 tablespoons flour		

Rub meat with salt and pepper, place in oven pan and roast in a moderate oven for ¾ hour. Mix coffee with sugar and cream and pour over roast. Continue to roast, while basting from time to time, for another hour, when meat should be done. Remove on to serving dish and keep warm. Strain liquid from pan and skim off fat. Add milk to stock to make 1 pint in all. Put 2 tablespoons of fat back in pan and place on low heat. Stir in flour and add stock gradually while stirring until thick and smooth. Pour into saucebowl and add redcurrant jelly. Serve with potatoes and green vegetables.

SWEDISH POT-ROAST

6 SERVINGS

3 lb. silverside or chuck steak	¾ pint water	2½ tablespoon flour
suet	1 bouillon cube	1 small can evaporated
1 oz. butter	salt and pepper	milk
1 small carrot		¾ pint stock
1 medium onion	*Sauce:*	parsley
	2 tablespoons fat	gherkins

Clean meat with damp cloth and cover with suet. Heat a large cast iron pot and brown butter. Brown meat on all sides, turning it gently with 2 wooden spoons. Cut onion and carrot in quarters and brown together with meat. Dissolve bouillon cube in water using a small saucepan. When meat is brown, remove from heat and pour some of the stock around it. Cover with tight fitting lid and place in a very moderate oven cooking for about 2 hours. Keep adding rest of stock, basting meat occasionally. When roast is tender, remove from pot, keeping it warm while sauce is prepared. Strain stock into saucepan and skim off 2 tablespoons of fat. Heat this in cast iron pot and work in flour to a smooth paste. Add warm stock slowly, stirring vigorously to prevent lumps forming, or burning. Simmer for a few minutes while stirring in milk. Season with salt and pepper to taste. Slice meat across the grain, place on warm serving dish garnished with parsley and sliced gherkins, serve with sauce and boiled or mashed potatoes.

FINE STEAK SAUCE

Swedish

4 SERVINGS

¼ teaspoon freshly ground pepper	2 tablespoons vinegar	2 tablespoons chopped parsley
1 tablespoon chopped onion	4 tablespoons cold water	cayenne pepper and salt
	5½ oz. butter	
	3 egg yolks	

Place chopped onion, pepper, vinegar and water in a small cast iron pot and simmer until the liquid is reduced to about 2 tablespoons. Remove from heat and strain. Rinse pot and replace liquid. Stir in egg yolks and 1 oz. butter. Place pot over saucepan of hot water. Beat constantly whilst water heats, but do not let it get too hot, as sauce will then curdle. When sauce begins to thicken the butter should be added a little at a time, while continuing to beat. Add parsley and season to taste with cayenne pepper and salt. The sauce should be thick and smooth. It is best to serve sauce immediately, but if it must be kept a while, let it stand in water bath and stir from time to time. This sauce is delicious with steak, roast beef or veal fillet.

BOILED LAMB OR VEAL WITH DILL SAUCE

Swedish

6 SERVINGS

3 lb. shoulder of lamb or 3 lb. best neck end of veal	¾ tablespoon salt	1½ tablespoons vinegar
	1 oz. butter	1 egg yolk
	2 tablespoons flour	1½ tablespoons sugar
2 pints water	2 tablespoons chopped dill	1 tablespoon cold stock
4 white peppercorns		
fresh dill	hot stock	

Rinse meat and place in boiling water, which should be just enough to cover it. Bring to the boil and skim off any foam. Add peppercorns, salt and a few sprigs of dill. Boil gently for about 1 hour, skimming again if necessary. To make sauce, melt butter in a small saucepan. Add flour, stirring continuously until smooth. Stir in 1 pint hot stock and boil for a few minutes. Add chopped dill, vinegar and sugar. Mix egg yolk and cold stock together and add to the sauce, stirring vigorously until it comes to the boil again, when it is ready. Slice meat and place in a casserole, pour sauce over and garnish with a few sprigs of dill. Serve with boiled potatoes.

FRICASSÉE OF VEAL

Swedish

6 SERVINGS

3 lb. shoulder of lamb or	1 clove, 1 bay leaf	2 tablespoons cream
	1 medium onion	lemon and parsley for
3 lb. best neck end of veal	1 large can condensed mushroom soup	garnish
2 pints water	1 oz. butter	1 teaspoon salt
4 white peppercorns	2 tablespoons flour	1 teaspoon lemon juice
4 oz. mushrooms	1 egg yolk	½ teaspoon sugar

Rinse meat and place in just enough boiling water to cover. Bring to the boil and skim off any foam. Stick clove in onion and add this together with peppercorns, bay leaf and salt. Boil gently for about 1 hour, skimming again if necessary. To make sauce, melt butter in a small saucepan. Add flour, stirring continuously until smooth. Stir in hot soup and boil for a few minutes. Add lemon juice, mushrooms and sugar. Mix cream and egg yolk together and add to sauce, stirring vigorously until it comes to the boil again. Slice the meat and place on a serving dish, pour sauce over and garnish with lemon slices and parsley. Serve with boiled rice.
(Illustrated in Plate 93.)

MEAT LOAF IN TOMATO SAUCE

Swedish

1 lb. minced beef	1 large chopped onion	1 leek
3 large slices white	1 egg	1 can tomato soup
bread	¼ pint water	salt and pepper

Remove crusts from bread. Beat egg and water lightly and crumble bread into it. Add chopped onion, meat and 4 tablespoons tomato soup. Mix together thoroughly. Season to taste with salt and pepper. Form into loaf and place in buttered oven pan. Clean leek and slice across thinly. Sprinkle over meat and pour on rest of tomato soup. Bake in a hot oven for 45 minutes. Serve with mashed potatoes.

SAVOURY PORK CHOPS

Swedish

6 SERVINGS

6 lean pork chops	4 slices bacon	2 tablespoons ketchup
½ pint water	2 chopped onions	1 gill cream
1 bouillon cube	2 tablespoons flour	salt and pepper
8 oz. mushrooms	1½ teaspoon paprika	little fat for frying

Sprinkle chops with salt and pepper and fry until golden brown on both sides, using just enough fat to avoid sticking. Place pork chops in shallow oven dish. Pour water into frying pan and dissolve bouillon cube in it whilst stirring. Pour into bowl and keep. Slice mushrooms and place over chops. Cut bacon into fairly small pieces and fry slowly together with chopped onion for about 10 minutes. Sprinkle with paprika and flour. Add cream and bouillon gradually, stirring until smooth. Simmer for 5 minutes. Stir in ketchup and season to taste with additional salt and pepper, as sauce should be rich and spicy. Pour over chops and mushrooms and bake in a moderate oven for about 30 minutes. Serve with boiled rice and green salad.

PORK POT-ROAST

Swedish

6 SERVINGS

3 lb. leg of pork	1½ tablespoons	1 tablespoon salt
2 tablespoons	vinegar	4 onions
margarine	2 tablespoons tomato	4 carrots
¾ pint water	purée	2 tablespoons flour
1 teaspoon marjoram	2 bay leaves	pepper

Have meat cut into thick slices. Melt margarine in frying pan and brown meat well on both sides. Place in large cast iron pot. Rinse out frying pan with a little water and pour over meat. Mix rest of water with vinegar and tomato purée and pour over meat. Add marjoram and bay leaves, cover and simmer for about 1½ hous. Cut carrots into strips, peel and slice onions. Add vegetables and simmer for another 30 minutes. Mix flour in a little cold water and stir in to thicken gravy. Simmer for a few minutes, season to taste and serve with boiled potatoes.

STUFFED PORK ROLLS
Swedish

1½ lb. neck end of pork, boned	1 oz. butter	2 tablespoons cream
	½ pint water	salt and pepper
1 apple	1 bouillon cube	¼ teaspoon ground
4 prunes	1 tablespoon flour	ginger

Cut meat into 4 equal portions and pound them flat. Sprinkle with ginger, salt and pepper. Peel, core and quarter the apple. Rinse prunes carefully in lukewarm water, halve them and remove stones. Place 1 piece apple and 1 prune on each slice of meat, roll up and secure with toothpicks. Brown in butter, using cast iron pot. Sprinkle with a little salt and pepper. Melt bouillon cube in water and pour over meat. Cover tightly and cook gently 45 minutes, basting occasionally. Remove toothpicks and place meat in casserole, keeping it warm. Stir flour into a little cold water, add boiling stock and stir vigorously to prevent lumps forming. When sauce is smooth and thick add cream and simmer for a minute or so. Pour sauce over meat and serve with fried potatoes.

ROLLED PORK WITH RED CABBAGE
Swedish

1½ lb. neck end of pork, boned	¼ teaspoon pepper	¼ pint water
	2 oz. margarine	4 cloves
1 apple	1 lb. red cabbage	3 tablespoons black-
1½ teaspoons salt	1 large onion	currant juice
	4 prunes	

Pour some boiling water over prunes and stand for few hours to soften. Remove from water, cut in half and take out stones. Peel, core and quarter apple. Cut meat into 4 equal slices and pound each one flat. Sprinkle with salt and pepper. Place ¼ apple and 1 prune on each slice, roll up and secure with toothpick. Brown in margarine. Cut cabbage into small dice and brown in remaining fat. Slice and brown onion. (If pork is very lean, some more margarine may be needed.) Mix onion and cabbage in cast iron pot. Place pork rolls on top. Add cloves, water and blackcurrant juice. Cover tightly and simmer for 45 minutes. Serve with boiled or mashed potatoes.

ROLLED BEEF WITH ANCHOVY STUFFING

Swedish

1½ lb. skirt of beef
8 anchovy fillets
2 tablespoons chopped parsley

3 tablespoons chopped onion
2 oz. butter

½ pint water
1 bouillon cube
salt and pepper
1 tablespoon flour

Cut meat into 4 equal portions and pound flat. Season with pepper and very little salt. Chop anchovy finely and mix with parsley and onion. Divide mixture equally and spread on meat. Roll each piece and secure with toothpicks. Warm a cast iron pot and brown the rolled meat in half the butter, taking care all sides are evenly browned. Sprinkle with flour, pepper and pinch of salt. Melt bouillon cube in water and pour on meat. Cover tightly and cook slowly for 1½ hours, basting from time to time. Remove toothpicks and serve in its own sauce with fried potatoes and a green vegetable.

BRAISED BEEF ROLLS WITH BACON

Swedish

4 TO 6 SERVINGS

2 lb. skirt of beef
8 slices bacon
4 frankfurters
2 teaspoons mustard

2 tablespoons flour
2 oz. butter
1 bouillon cube

3 tablespoons top of the milk
salt and pepper
¼ pint water

Pound meat thin and flat. Cut into 8 strips about 4 inches by 2½ inches and sprinkle both sides with salt and pepper. Spread one side with mustard and place a strip of bacon and ½ frankfurter on each slice. Roll up and secure with toothpicks. Roll in flour and fry in butter, using a cast iron frying pan, until nicely browned on all sides. Bring water to boil in saucepan and dissolve bouillon cube. Pour over meat, cover and simmer until tender, about 1 hour. Remove beef rolls to a casserole, take out toothpicks and keep warm. Add cream to frying pan whilst stirring, simmer for few minutes and pour over meat. Serve with fried potatoes and vegetable to choice.

SWEDISH MEATBALLS

1½ lb. minced beef
1 egg
1 large onion
3 slices white bread

¼ pint water
3 oz. butter
2 tablespoons flour
1 pint water
salt and pepper

1 can evaporated milk (equivalent ¾ pint diluted)
½ teaspoon soya sauce

Mix egg and ¼ pint water in a bowl. Crumble bread into it, letting it soak until thoroughly broken up. Remove any hard crusts. Chop onion finely and fry lightly in a little butter. Add to mixture together with minced beef. Mix all thoroughly, using wooden spoon, until it is smooth and holds together. Moisten a wooden board with cold water. Form mince into round balls, about 1 inch in diameter, and place on the board. Brown rest of butter and fry meatballs evenly on all sides, placing them in a saucepan as they are finished. Stir flour into butter left in frying pan, working to a smooth paste. Heat water and add gradually, stirring all the time. Let it come to the boil and thicken before more is added. Stir in canned milk and soya sauce. Pour sauce over meatballs and simmer together for about 15 minutes. Season to taste and serve with mashed or boiled potatoes and tomato ketchup, if desired. (*Illustrated in Plate 97.*)

VEAL BIRDS

Swedish

1½ lb. veal fillet	2 tablespoons oil	¼ pint boiling water
8 slices boiled ham	3 tablespoons top of	3 tablespoons flour
8 slices cheese	the milk	salt and pepper

Have butcher cut meat into 8 slices and pound very thin. Mix flour with a little salt and pepper and turn meat slices in this. Place 1 slice ham and 1 slice cheese on each piece of meat and fold up, securing with toothpicks. Heat oil in cast iron frying pan and brown meat quickly on all sides. Pour boiling water over meat, cover and simmer for about 30 minutes. Place meat in hot serving dish, remove toothpicks and keep warm. Add cream to stock while stirring over low heat. Simmer for a few minutes, season to taste and pour over meat. Serve with fried potatoes and vegetable to choice or green salad.

MEAT LOAF

Danish

8 oz. minced veal	3 tablespoons flour	breadcrumbs
8 oz. minced pork	1 pint boiled milk	salt and pepper
1 egg		1 grated onion

Butter a suitable mould and sprinkle with breadcrumbs. Place meat and egg in bowl and mix well. Work in flour and add milk very gradually, stirring until it is all absorbed. Mix in grated onion and season to taste with salt and pepper. Put mixture into prepared mould and bake in a baking tin half-filled with water in a moderately hot oven for about 1 hour. Turn out on to warm serving dish, decorate with mixed vegetables and serve with macaroni and melted butter.

ROLLED VEAL WITH MUSHROOM STUFFING

Swedish

1½ lb. boneless stewing veal	½ pint water	1 small carrot
8 oz. mushrooms	1 bouillon cube	1 medium onion
3 oz. butter	1 tablespoon flour	salt and pepper
		2 tablespoons cream

Cut meat into 4 equal portions and pound them flat. Season with salt and pepper on one side. Slice mushrooms, leaving peel on, and fry in 1 oz. butter. Season to taste. Place 2 oz. fried mushrooms on each slice of meat, roll up and secure with toothpicks. Brown together with carrot and onion in 1 oz. butter, using cast iron pot. Melt bouillon cube in water and pour over meat. Cover tightly and cook gently for 1 hour, basting occasionally. Remove toothpicks and place meat in a casserole, keeping it warm. Pour stock into a container, discarding carrot and onion. Brown remaining butter in cast iron pot, stir in flour to a smooth paste, add warm stock stirring continuously and simmer for a few minutes. Then add cream and bring to the boil again. Season to taste. Pour sauce over meat and serve with mashed potatoes and a vegetable.

FRIED SWEETBREADS WITH MUSHROOMS AND BACON

Swedish

2 lb. sweetbreads	1 tablespoon salt	12 oz. button
2 pints water	8 slices bacon	mushrooms
1 tablespoon lemon juice	4 tablespoons breadcrumbs	4 oz. butter
		salt and pepper

Soak sweetbreads for 1 hour in cold water, then drain well. Bring water to the boil and add salt and lemon juice. Add sweetbreads and simmer for 18 minutes. Remove sweetbreads and let stock cool. Replace sweetbreads in cold stock. Melt 1 oz. butter in saucepan. Cut mushrooms in half and sauté, covered, for 6 minutes. Season with salt and pepper and keep warm. Grill bacon slices until crisp and keep warm. Drain sweetbreads and cut into ¾-inch slices. Mix breadcrumbs with a little salt and pepper and turn sweetbreads in this. Melt rest of butter in frying pan until golden brown, add sweetbread slices and fry for 4 minutes on each side on fairly high heat, so that they become crisp and golden. Arrange sweetbreads in middle of large hot serving dish. Place bacon on one side and mushrooms on the other. Serve immediately with grilled tomatoes, buttered toast and green salad.

97. Swedish Meat Balls (p.510)

98. Cheese Straws, Poland (p.406)

99. Fine Lamb Stew, Sweden (p.513)

FINARE LAMMRAGU

Fine Lamb Stew

Swedish

2 lb. shoulder lamb boned	¾ pint water	8 oz. new carrots
3 tablespoons flour	2 bouillon cubes	1 tablespoon chopped parsley
1 tablespoon meat dripping	4 oz. shelled peas	1 tablespoon salt
3 cloves garlic	8 oz. tomatoes	¼ teaspoon pepper
	2 bay leaves	1 lb. small onions
	2 sticks celery	

Cut meat into 1-inch cubes and turn in mixture of flour, salt and pepper. Melt dripping in large cast iron pot, add meat and brown on all sides. Dissolve bouillon cubes in boiling water and add to pot together with chopped garlic, tomatoes, bay leaves and celery. Bring to the boil, cover and simmer for 30 minutes. Clean and slice carrots. Peel onions and, if very small, leave whole. Peel potatoes and add these vegetables to pot, stirring to mix with meat and stock. Cover and continue to simmer for another 40 minutes when meat and vegetables should be tender. Sprinkle with parsley and serve. *(Illustrated in Plate 99.)*

MINCED BEEF À LA LINDSTROM

Swedish

1½ lb. minced beef (lean)	4 oz. boiled beetroots	3 oz. butter
2 egg yolks	2 tablespoons grated onion	parsley
4 oz. cold boiled potatoes	2 tablespoons vinegar	salt and pepper
	sliced beetroot for garnish	2 tablespoons chopped capers

Slice beetroots and let them marinate in the vinegar for 20 minutes. Remove from vinegar and chop finely. Mince potatoes or chop very finely. Place meat in bowl and mix in egg yolks. Season lightly with salt and pepper. Work mixture until it is smooth, using a wooden spoon. Stir in potatoes, beetroots, grated onion and capers. Taste and season again if necessary. Form into 12 cakes, about ¾-inch thick. Brown 1 oz. butter in a large frying pan, preferably of cast iron, and place 4 meat cakes in it, frying them quickly on both sides on a high heat. Keep warm while remainder are fried in the same manner. Place on a warm serving dish and pour browned butter over. Garnish with parsley and sliced beetroots. Serve immediately with fried potatoes.

ROASTED SPARERIBS

Swedish

6 SERVINGS

4 lb. spareribs	4 sour apples	1 bouillon cube
1 tablespoon salt	½ teaspoon pepper	¾ pint water
½ teaspoon ginger		20 prunes

Have bones in spareribs cracked. Rub with mixture of salt, ginger and pepper. Place spareribs on grid in oven pan and bake in a moderate oven for 45 minutes. Remove spareribs and pour off fat. Peel, core and slice apples. Wash prunes in warm water, halve, and remove stones. Spread apples and prunes in bottom of oven pan and place spareribs on top with inner side up. Dissolve bouillon cube in water and pour over meat. Replace in oven and bake for another 30 minutes. Turn ribs and put oven up to moderately hot. Bake for another 20 minutes, when spareribs should be nicely brown. Remove meat, cut into portions and place on hot serving dish. Drain fruit and arrange around meat. Strain dripping into saucebowl and serve with red cabbage.

CHRISTMAS HAM

Swedish

ABOUT 20 SERVINGS

1 unsmoked gammon (10—12 lb.)	½ teaspoon allspice	1 tablespoon sugar
2 bay leaves	1 chopped carrot	breadcrumbs
½ teaspoon peppercorns	1 egg white	*For garnish*
1 chopped onion	1 tablespoon dry mustard	glacé cherries
		orange slices

Place gammon in large saucepan, fat side up, and cover with cold water. Bring to the boil and skim off any foam. Add bay leaves, peppercorns, allspice, onion and carrot. Cover and simmer gently for 2 hours. Turn over and simmer for another 1½ hours, when ham should be cooked through. Remove from stock. Skin ham and remove loose fat. Return to stock and leave overnight to cool. Remove ham from stock and wipe dry. Mix egg white, mustard and sugar. Brush this over ham so that it covers all fat. Sprinkle generously with breadcrumbs, place in large oven pan fat side up and bake in a very moderate oven for about 50 minutes, when it should be golden brown. Garnish with glacé cherries and orange slices. Serve either cold on smörgasbord, or hot with red cabbage and potatoes.

STEWED PIG'S HEART

Danish

2 lb. pig's hearts
5 oz. butter

4 tablespoons chopped parsley
2 tablespoons flour

½ pint cream
salt and pepper

Open pig's hearts, remove sinews and vessels, wash well. Mix 4 oz. butter with parsley, divide between hearts and stuff into centre cavity. Sew hearts up. Season flour with salt and pepper. Turn hearts in this, so that they are well coated. Melt rest of butter in cast iron pot and allow to darken. Add hearts and brown well on all sides. Heat cream and pour over meat. Cover tightly and simmer for 2 hours. Season to taste with salt and pepper and serve with boiled potatoes.

DANISH PARSLEY CHICKEN

2 spring chickens (about 1½ lb. each)
8 oz. butter

1 pint stock
2 tablespoons cream or top of milk
flour

4 oz. bacon rolls
4 sprigs parsley
salt and pepper
bacon rolls for garnish

Rub the outside of the chickens with salt and pepper. Remove the stalks from the parsley but do not chop. Mix parsley with half the butter, and stuff the chickens with this mixture. Melt remaining butter in a heavy saucepan. Brown the chickens well in the butter, starting with the breasts (this takes about 10 minutes). When browned all over, place the chickens on their backs and add the heated stock. Cover tightly and simmer for 1½ hours. Add the cream to the sauce during the last ten minutes of cooking time. Remove the chickens to a hot dish and garnish them with crisply fried bacon rolls. Strain the sauce, thicken slightly with flour, and add a little browning for colour, if liked.

RABBIT IN CREAM SAUCE

Swedish

6 SERVINGS

6 large rabbit pieces (preferably leg and breast)
4 oz. butter

1 small can evaporated milk (equivalent to ¾ pint diluted)

1 teaspoon soya sauce
3 tablespoons flour
salt and pepper
1 pint milk

Brown rabbit pieces in 2 oz. butter, using a large cast iron pot. Season with salt and pepper. Warm the milk and pour over. Cover and cook slowly for 1½ hours. Brown the rest of the butter slightly in a frying pan. Stir in flour to a smooth paste. Add milk from the rabbit, stirring constantly until texture is smooth and creamy. Add canned milk and soya sauce. Season to taste with salt and pepper. Pour sauce over rabbit pieces, simmer for 5 minutes. Serve with boiled potatoes and cranberries.

ROAST GOOSE

Swedish

8 TO 10 SERVINGS

1 12 lb. goose	6 cooking apples	2 teaspoons potato
½ lemon	½ teaspoon pepper	flour
1 tablespoon salt		20 prunes

Wash and dry goose well. Rub outside with lemon. Rinse prunes carefully in lukewarm water. Boil them in water until soft. Drain and stone them. Wash, peel, core and slice apples. Put mixture of apples and prunes inside goose and sew up at both ends. Rub goose with salt and pepper. Place in oven pan and cover tightly with tin foil. Roast in a moderately hot oven for about 2 hours. The exact time depends on age of goose. Remove tin foil and pour off stock which has collected. Replace goose in oven for 5—10 minutes to get crisp and brown. Mix flour in a little cold water and add to stock. If necessary add a little water to make desired quantity of sauce. Serve with roast potatoes and red cabbage.

ROAST VENISON

Swedish

½ leg venison (3—4 lb.)	1 pint water	1 small can evaporated
2 oz. fatty bacon	salt and pepper	milk (equivalent to
	3 tablespoons flour	¾ pint diluted)

Wash meat carefully and dry in a clean cloth. Place meat in oven pan and cover with strips of bacon. Brown meat for 30 minutes in hot oven. Cover pan carefully with tin foil. Let it roast in moderately hot oven for about 2 hours. When meat is tender, remove from pan, discard bacon and keep meat warm. Pour dripping into large cast iron frying pan and heat. Stir in the flour to a smooth paste, taking care to prevent burning or lumps forming. Rinse out oven pan with water, heat and gradually add to the frying pan. Let the sauce simmer for a few minutes. Stir in evaporated milk and season to taste. Colour should be light brown. Slice meat and place it in a large casserole. Pour sauce over, cover and simmer together for 5 minutes. Serve with boiled potatoes and Swedish cranberries.

DANISH BLUE SALAD DRESSING

1 gill salad oil	1 teaspoon salt	4 oz. Danish Blue
1 gill lemon juice	1 teaspoon paprika	cheese
	1 tablespoon sugar	

Crumble the cheese with a fork. Then add all other ingredients and put them together in a bottle or jar. Cover tightly and shake well. Chill and shake before serving. Serve with egg, cheese or fish salads.

KRISTINE'S FRUIT SALAD

Danish

Danish mayonnaise	fresh fruit and nuts in season	whipped cream

Fold two-thirds of whipped cream into one-third of mayonnaise very gently. Prepare and dice fresh fruits in season, bananas, apples, oranges, grapes, melons, grapefruits, etc., or use canned fruit, well drained. Blend this into the cream and mayonnaise mixture after draining off all excess moisture. Add chopped walnuts or hazel nuts. Serve in a bowl decorated with walnuts and whole pieces of fruits. If serving as a Danish open sandwich place fruit salad on a lettuce leaf on pieces of well buttered white bread.

CHOCOLATE CHIFFON PUDDING

Swedish

5 tablespoons cocoa	3 tablespoons cold water	1 teaspoon vanilla essence
1 teaspoon instant coffee	2 eggs	almonds or chopped nuts
3 tablespoons gelatine	3½ oz. sugar	
¼ pint thick cream	½ pint milk	

Soften gelatine in cold water. Beat egg yolks and sugar until light and creamy. Stir in cocoa and milk. Pour into saucepan and bring to the boil while stirring. Add coffee, vanilla and gelatine and remove from fire. Cool until starting to set. Beat egg whites stiff and fold in. Whip cream and stir in, saving a little for garnish. Rinse mould in cold water and pour mixture into it. Chill until completely set. Turn out on to cold serving dish and garnish with nuts or almonds.

LAYER PANCAKE

Swedish

3 eggs	4 teaspoons sugar	1 gill double cream
7 oz. self-raising flour	1¾ pints milk	5 almonds
	1 oz. butter	margarine for frying
1 teaspoon salt		jam

Place flour, salt and sugar in a bowl. Add milk gradually while beating. Let batter stand for 1—2 hours. Beat eggs and stir in together with melted butter. Melt some margarine in a large frying pan and pour in just enough batter to cover the pan. Fry golden brown on both sides and place on a hot dish. Spread jam on pancake and continue in this way until all the batter is fried, and piled in layers with jam in between. Whip cream and decorate top with cream, jam, and strips of almonds. Serve immediately, slicing like a cake.

FATTIGA RIDDARE

Poor Knights

Swedish

1 pint milk	1½ tablespoons sugar	margarine for frying
12 slices white bread	5 tablespoons flour	½ teaspoon cinnamon
1 egg		½ oz. butter

Place flour, cinnamon, salt and sugar in a bowl. Mix ½ pint milk and egg together. Add this gradually to the flour, stirring constantly until smooth. Melt butter and stir into mixture. Let batter stand for 2 hours. Trim off crusts of bread slices and soak in ½ pint milk, being careful they do not break. Dip in batter and fry golden brown on each side in margarine. Serve with jam or sugar.

STUFFED BAKED APPLES

Swedish

8 medium cooking apples	5 tablespoons sugar	4 tablespoons breadcrumbs
2 tablespoons water	4 tablespoons ground almonds	1½ oz. melted butter

Mix 3 tablespoons sugar with almonds and water. Wash and dry apples. Remove cores but leave apples whole. Puncture skin all over apples with a fork. Stuff almond mixture in the centre of apples, dividing equally between them. Coat with melted, slightly cooled butter. Mix breadcrumbs with remainder of sugar and roll apples therein. Place in buttered shallow oven dish. Bake in moderately hot oven for about

1 hour or until they are soft. As the exact time depends on their size, it is best to test them with a fork. Serve warm with whipped cream or vanilla custard (see p. 267).

BEER BREAD

Norwegian

1 pint light beer	½ pint cream	croûtons or diced fried
½ pint water	sugar to taste	bread
	2 egg yolks	

Pour liquids into saucepan and add yolks. Heat slowly while whipping. Add sugar to taste. Remove from heat just before it comes to the boil. Serve immediately with croûtons or diced fried bread.

BIBA'S APPLE CAKE

Danish

1 lb. cooking apples	1 tablespoon brown	1 dessertspon lemon
4 oz. castor sugar	sugar	juice
4 oz. plain flour	1 teaspoon cinnamon	1 tablespoon chopped
2 tablespoons	1 teaspoon ginger	nuts
sultanas	4 oz. butter	1 egg

Core, peel and slice the apples thinly. Melt the butter and mix with the sugar then gradually add the flour, stirring thoroughly, and lastly add the egg. Spread two-thirds of the mixture on the bottom of a well greased cake tin, place half the sliced apples on top, and sprinkle with the cinnamon, ginger, lemon juice and brown sugar. Cover with the remainder of the apples, and sprinkle with chopped nuts. Place the remainder of the mixture on top and cook in a moderate oven for approximately 20 minutes.

DANISH PASTRY DOUGH

33 TO 35 PASTRIES

1 lb. plain flour	2¼ oz. yeast	1 egg
1 teaspoon salt	½ pint milk	12 oz. butter
	4 tablespoons sugar	

Sift flour and mix with sugar and salt. Mix yeast with a little cold milk and stir into flour, together with beaten egg, sugar and rest of milk. Stir with wooden spoon until well mixed. Sprinkle a little flour on baking board and roll out dough until about ¾ inch thick. Stir butter until it has softened sufficiently to spread. Put a little on to dough and spread over two-thirds of surface. Fold in plain part, then butter part, so that it is in three layers. Roll out again and repeat until all the butter is folded in. Leave in cold place for 30 minutes.

COCK'S COMB PASTRY

Danish

basic dough (see p. 519)	egg white	almond paste
butter	chopped almonds	(see below)
	sugar	

Roll out dough until ¼ inch thick. Mix equal portions of sugar and butter and spread over dough. Cut dough into 4 inch squares. Place about 1 tablespoon almond paste across middle and fold over. Press edges together and make 4 cuts in the outer edge. Place on buttered baking sheet and leave in cold place for 20 minutes. Brush with egg white, sprinkle with chopped almonds and sugar. Bake in a hot oven until golden.

SPANDAUER PASTRY

Danish

basic dough (see p. 519)	butter	almond paste filling
sugar		egg white

Roll out dough to ¼ inch thick. Mix equal portions of sugar and butter and spread over dough. Cut into 4 inch squares. Place 1 tablespoon filling in the centre. Fold in all four corners so that they meet the middle and press down. Place on buttered baking sheet and leave in cold place for 20 minutes. Brush with egg white and bake in a hot oven until golden.

ALMOND PASTE

Danish

4 oz. butter	4 oz. sugar	3 oz. ground almonds

Mix all ingredients until well blended.

LUSSE KATTOR

Lucia Cats

Swedish

½ pint milk	2 oz. yeast	*Garnish:*
6 oz. butter	2 lb. flour	1 beaten egg
6 oz. sugar	25 almonds	castor sugar
1 egg	5 bitter almonds	10 chopped almonds
1 envelope saffron (5 grains)	10 tablespoons raisins	

Warm milk and saffron. Stir yeast with a little sugar. Mix flour, yeast, milk and egg to smooth dough. Stir sugar and butter until light and creamy and work into dough. Allow to rise for 30 minutes. Scald and chop almonds finely and work into dough together with raisins. Place dough on floured baking board and shape into buns. Make cuts on 2 opposite sides of each bun, elongate corners a little and curl outwards. Place on buttered baking sheet and allow to rise for 20 minutes. Brush with egg and sprinkle with sugar and chopped almonds. Bake in a hot oven until golden brown.

BRUNE KAGER

Brown Biscuits

Danish

6 oz. flour	½ teaspoon ground	pinch bicarbonate
4 oz. treacle	cloves	soda
2 oz. brown sugar	1 teaspoon cinnamon	chopped almonds
1 oz. margarine	½ teaspoon ground	chopped mixed peel
or cooking fat	ginger	little water or milk
	grated rind ½ orange	

Put the treacle, sugar, fat, cloves, cinnamon, ginger and orange rind into a saucepan and stir over a low heat. When just warm, add the bicarbonate of soda. Sieve the flour into a bowl and pour in the mixture from the saucepan. Knead into a dough, turn out on to a floured board and roll out thinly to the shape of a square. Cut into rectangular pieces about 3½ by 1¼ inches and place in a greased shallow baking tin. Brush with a little milk or water and decorate with chopped almonds and peel. Put into a moderate oven near the top, and bake for 8—10 minutes. Remove and cool on a cake rack.

SWEDISH PASTRIES

8 oz. butter	1 oz. yeast	*For garnish:*
½ pint milk	¼ teaspoon salt	1 beaten egg
1 egg	1 lb. flour	10 chopped almonds
2 tablespoons sugar		

Soften yeast in little milk. Beat eggs, salt and sugar. Work in flour, milk and yeast and knead dough until smooth. Place on floured baking board and roll out to ½ inch thick. Place butter in little lumps on dough and fold in 3 parts. Flatten by patting gently with roller. Fold dough again and roll out. Keep folding until butter is well worked into dough. Roll out until ½ inch thick, cut into narrow strips and form into figures of eight or other interesting shapes. Place on buttered baking tray and allow to rise for 30 minutes. Brush with beaten egg and sprinkle with chopped almonds. Bake in a very hot oven until golden.

DEEP FRIED SAILOR RINGS

Swedish

10 oz. self-raising flour	2 eggs 6 oz. sugar oil for frying	4 tablespoons thin cream

Beat eggs, 4½ oz. sugar and cream until light. Stir in flour. Form into rings and deep fry in oil until golden. Drain and coat in remaining sugar.

SHROVE TUESDAY BUNS

Swedish

5 tablespoons thick cream	1 oz. yeast	2 tablespoons sugar
5 tablespoons water	1 teaspoon sugar	2 tablespoons ground almonds
2½ oz. butter	1 lb. flour	icing sugar
1 egg	*Filling:*	
2 tablespoons sugar	1 gill thick cream	

Place cream, water and butter in saucepan and warm, allowing butter to melt. Mix yeast with 1 teaspoon sugar. Beat egg and sugar until light and creamy. Work in liquid, yeast and flour to a smooth dough and allow to rise for 30 minutes. Place on floured baking board and knead thoroughly. Form into 10 buns, place on buttered baking sheet and allow to rise for 20 minutes. Bake in a very hot oven for 6—10 minutes. When cool, slice off tops. Beat cream until stiff and mix in sugar and ground almonds. Divide between buns, place filling on cut part. Replace lid, sprinkle with icing sugar and serve in deep plates with hot milk.

SWEDISH SCONE RING

4 oz. butter or margarine	1 egg	3 oz. chopped dates
8 oz. self-raising flour	3 tablespoons milk	glacé icing
2 oz. fine semolina	3 tablespoons marmalade	(see p. 120)
2 oz. castor sugar		chopped nuts
		3 oz. mixed fruit

Rub fat into the flour until it resembles fine breadcrumbs. Add semolina and sugar and mix well, then put in the egg and 2 tablespoons of milk and knead to a soft but not sticky dough. Turn out on to a lightly floured board and roll to a rectangular shape. Cover with a mixture of marmalade, fruit and dates, roll up and shape into a ring. Place on a greased baking sheet, and put a small round tin or mould in the centre so that the cake keeps its shape. Make dents around the edge of the cake at regular intervals and glaze with the remaining milk. Put into a hot oven to bake for about 30 minutes. Leave to cool. Then run a little glacé icing over the surface and sprinkle with chopped nuts. Serve freshly baked, with or without butter. *(Illustrated in Plate 58.)*

SPANISH COOKING

Elsa Behrens

This is a collection of dishes I have enjoyed during my sojourn in Spain and, more recently, during my travels as a courier conducting tourists through the country. I will give you a culinary sample of just a few days of our tour, and you will realise what a dramatic variation of characteristics and scenery awaits you. For, though I only deal with the food of Spain, it proves once again that the cooking of a country reflects the life and the character of its people.

Olive oil, garlic, rice, peppers, mussels and saffron are some of the ingredients that come to mind when thinking of Spain. Quite right — but many other things too, and it is a fallacy to believe that Spanish cooking need be heavier than French or Italian cooking. Only bad cooking is heavy, and food is only greasy if the oil in which it is fried is not sufficiently hot. Spanish cooks often fry a piece of bread in the oil just before using it, to eliminate some of the grease. It is a proven fact that if olive is used correctly, the results are less greasy than frying with fat or lard, more commonly used in this country. However most of the recipes here can be made with fat or lard instead of olive oil, and most of the ingredients are obtainable in other countries, particularly in the delicatessen stores which are to be found in any large city.

We enter Spain by crossing the Pyrenees into the Basque country. Then we drive along the banks of the Bidasoa river, past the paper mills and the green pastures of Navarre, and stop to have a drink in the little town of Vitoria, before entering the more austere plateau of Castilla la Vieja, Old Castile. Our supper in the dining-room of our Burgos hotel is served by sturdy waitresses with beautiful faces under their starched white caps.

> Melón con Jamón Serrano
> Sopa Crema de Yema
> Tournedo à la Crema con Patas Fritas
> Alcachofas con Salsa Tartara
> Flan y Fruta

Next day, after visiting the Gothic Cathedral of Santa Maria, we drive through rolling hills and dramatic isolation to the very top of the Somosierra Pass, and there we suddenly come upon a delightful Fonda, where they give us the following succulent meal:

> Entremeses, comprised of
>   Albondigas, Buñuelitos de Queso, as well as
>   the usual sardines, salads, etc.
> Tortilla de Patatas
> Ternera Rellena con Judias verdes
> Crema de Chocolate
>   and a nice hot coffee which is most welcome
>   on this cold and misty summit

Next morning we take a day excursion to the ancient Moorish city of Toledo, once capital of Spain and, after a morning's enthralling sightseeing, we go to a restaurant outside the old city walls and enjoy a truly typical meal:

> Tomates Rellenos
> Chuletas de Ternera à la Zingara
> Esparragos Mimosa
> Queso y Fruta

By the evening we are back in Madrid. Once again we sit on the roof garden, sipping Tio Pepe and talking about the wonderful El Grecos we have seen and the souvenirs we have bought, till they bring our supper:

> Sopa de Queso
> Camarones Fritos
> Rosca de Carne con patatas y espinaca
> Granizado de Café

In the morning we leave Madrid via Jetafe, the geographic centre of Spain. We lunch at one of the motels in that desolate and arid New Castile. It is delightfully cool inside and the dining room is large and shaded. They give us:

> Canalones con Jamón
> Chuletas de Cordero con patatas Vilareal
> Queso y Fruta

We leave the Parador at Manzanares and drive through the valley of the Guadalquivir River and the increasing heat of Andalusia, past heavily laden little donkeys trotting for miles towards a distant white-washed village where they are anxiously awaited. We are very happy to find the 'patio' in our hotel in Córdoba cool, hung with flowers, and the dining room most colourful with its brilliantly hued tiles. Here we start our supper with the cold and tasty Andalusian soup:

> Gazpacho
> Pastelitos de Pollo con Hojaldre
> Escalopas de Ternera Rellenas
> Legumbres variadas
> Crema de Malaga

After a couple of days in Córdoba, the cultural centre of ancient Moorish Spain with its wonderful Mosque, we leave for Seville; it is not very far from Córdoba, so we arrive in time for lunch:

> Pastel de Tortilla
> Alcachofas à la Vinagreta
> Fabada
> Melocotones en Almibar

In the afternoon we wander through the narrow little streets and admire the flowers which we see in profusion in every window and every tiny patio.

After two days in Seville we leave very early in the morning for Granada through miles and miles of olive groves. Suddenly in the evening light we see the Alhambra on the mountainside, with the Sierra Nevada mountains in the background. That fabulous Moorish Palace was the last stronghold of those strange, cultured people in Spain. Our hotel is on the mountain and we enjoy a lovely view while eating our last meal on this tour, for our six days are up. We continue towards the Mediterranean Coast through Cataluña and then through France. But your own personal culinary expedition to Spain is only just beginning—so HASTA LA VISTA! Till we meet again!

ALCACHOFAS CON JAMÓN

Artichokes with Ham

Wash the artichokes, cut off the tops and soak in lemon water for 1 hour. Cook in salted boiling water till tender. Remove the leaves and take out the hearts, sprinkle with lemon juice and fill with a mixture of finely chopped ham and hard-boiled egg bound with mayonnaise. Serve chilled.

MELON CON TOCINO

Melon with Bacon

Fry the bacon slices till crisp, take out of the fat and drain well, then curl around strips of melon. Fry little slices of bread in the bacon fat and drain. Serve the melon and bacon rolls on the fried bread. This dish is delicious both hot and cold. It is important to drain off the fat so it is not greasy.

TOMATES RELLENOS

Stuffed Tomatoes

Take large, firm tomatoes. In Spain they are very often used while still green. Cut in half horizontally or just take off the top if they are not very large. Take out the soft centre pulp, leaving some of the hard flesh around the sides. Mix the pulp with chopped hard-boiled egg and chopped onion, or with anything left over that is suitable. For instance, rice and chopped ham make a very delicious filling and can be served either hot or cold. A finely chopped salad makes a nice filling for tomatoes. When served cold, sprinkle with French salad dressing.

BOLITAS DE ORO
Golden Balls

8 eggs	2 sticks celery	1 leaf gelatine
½ pint mayonnaise (see p. 263)	8 rounds of bread or toast	1 crisp head of lettuce
a little liver pâté	salt	1 lemon
		olive oil

This is a very tasty hors-d'oeuvre and, if carefully made, looks very elegant.

Boil the eggs for exactly 10 minutes, plunge into cold water and peel. Cut the whites away very carefully, leaving the yolks whole. Place these on a flat dish. While the eggs are boiling, dissolve a leaf of gelatine in the mayonnaise. Pour some of this over the eggs and when it has begun to set, place the yolks on the rounds of toast or bread, which have been spread with liver pâté and laid on a bed of shredded lettuce and celery. In between the rounds place rings of white of egg with some mayonnaise in the centre. Season the lettuce with salt, lemon and a little olive oil. Keep in cool place till served.

SON LAS DOCE Y CUARTO
It Is 12.15

This name describes the dish of mixed hors-d'oeuvre which is arranged to look like a clock.

In the centre of a large round dish put a rounded mound of potato salad, into which chopped ham, little peas and chopped olives have been mixed together with mayonnaise. Cut 6 hard-boiled eggs in half and place all around the edge of the salad like a clock. The figures of the clock can either be cut out of truffles and fixed to the egg with gelatine, or an easier and tasty way is to take a tube of anchovy paste and carefully press the paste out, making the face of the clock. The hands can be cut out of truffles or red peppers, fixed in the centre with a toothpick through a stoned olive. Garnish the edge of the dish with sliced radishes, olives and sliced tomato.

CROQUETITAS DE CAMARONES
Little Shrimp Croquettes

1 lb. shrimps or prawns	2 egg yolks	salt and pepper
1 gill thick Béchamel sauce (see p. 256)	1 tablespoon fresh white breadcrumbs	nutmeg
		oil for frying

Shell and clean the shrimps or prawns and chop up finely, mix with the Béchamel sauce, one egg yolk and the breadcrumbs, season with salt and pepper and a little nutmeg. Roll into tiny croquettes, coat with egg and breadcrumbs and deep fry. Serve hot on toothpicks as a cocktail savoury.

AGUACATE CON CANGREJO

Crab in Avocado

1½ lb. fresh crab meat
juice 1 lemon
3 sticks celery,
  chopped

1 gill French dressing
2 large ripe avocados

crisp lettuce leaves
4 olives
cayenne pepper
salt

Cut the avocados in half, lengthwise. Remove large stone. Carefully loosen pulp from peel without breaking and sprinkle with lemon juice and salt to prevent discoloration.

In a separate bowl flake the crab meat, blend with salt and a dash of cayenne. Fill the avocado halves with crab mixture, chill, and when ready to serve place each avocado half on a bed of lettuce leaves and chopped celery, prepared on individual plates. Pour the French dressing over and garnish with olives.

AGUACATE

Avocado Pear

Cut the avocado in half, take out the stone and place on a bed of crisp lettuce leaves. Garnish with grapefruit sections and serve with salad dressing (salt, pepper, vinegar and oil).

POMELOS CALIENTES CON CREMA

Hot Grapefruit With Cream

Cut the grapefruit in half, release the flesh from the skin and dust with brown sugar. Pour a little thick cream over each half and place in a hot oven for a few minutes.

CANAPÉS CALIENTES DE QUESO Y JAMÓN

Hot Cheese and Ham Canapés

white bread
butter
2 egg yolks

creamy cheese
juice ½ lemon
olive oil

salt and pepper
1 teaspoon mustard
slices smoked ham

Cut thick slices of white bread into rounds with a glass, butter and toast lightly. Prepare a hot mayonnaise by beating up the yolks with a metal whisk in a double saucepan (*bain-marie*). Continue to beat while gradually adding the olive oil till the sauce thickens. Take off the fire, add salt and pepper, mustard and lemon juice to taste, beating up well all the time. Spread the mayonnaise on to the buttered toast and on this lay a slice of ham. Spread with cheese and put into a hot oven for a few minutes. Serve hot.

100. Churros on the Streets of Madrid

101. Grilled Bacon Chops, Britain (p.107)

ALBONDIGAS

Little Meat Balls

8 oz. minced meat	oil for frying	4 oz. breadcrumbs
2 oz. minced bacon	1 onion	salt and pepper
1 clove garlic		1 egg

Chop the onion and garlic very finely and fry till golden. Drain well and mix with minced meat and minced bacon and half the egg beaten up. Season and roll into small balls. Dip into rest of the egg and roll in breadcrumbs. Fry in deep hot oil. Strain and serve.

BUÑUELITOS DE JAMÓN

Little Ham Puffs

2 oz. flour	8 oz. finely chopped	salt and pepper
2 eggs	ham	olive oil

Separate the whites from the yolks and beat until stiff. Mix the flour with the egg yolks to a smooth paste. Fold in the whites, season and beat in the finely chopped ham. Drop a teaspoonful at a time into smoking hot oil. Drain well and serve either hot or cold as one of the many dishes of 'entremeses'.

BUÑUELITOS DE QUESO

Little Cheese Puffs

These are made in the same way as the Ham Puffs, but instead of chopped ham, add 8 oz. grated cheese.

DELICIAS CON QUESO

Cheese Patties

6 egg whites	4 oz. grated cheese	1 egg yolk
breadcrumbs	(either Gruyère or	butter or oil for frying
	Cheshire)	

Beat the egg whites till stiff. Fold in the grated cheese. Season and roll into small balls or croquettes, dip into breadcrumbs, then into the beaten yolk and again into the breadcrumbs. Deep fry in oil or butter and serve very hot. (If butter is used for frying it is wise to put in a drop of oil to prevent burning.)

DELICIAS Á LA PIGNATELLI

Almond Patties

Exactly as preceding recipe, but instead of cheese fold in ground almonds or coconut.

Chicken Filling

Instead of cheese, left-over chicken and chicken livers can be used. Mince the chicken, chicken livers and a little ham if available and fold in this mixture in place of the cheese.

Lobster Filling

As above, with minced lobster instead of chicken.

Mushroom Filling

As above, with chopped mushrooms.

CIRUELAS RELLENAS

Stuffed Prunes

prunes	oil for frying	breadcrumbs
ham	1 egg	toothpicks

Soak the dried prunes in water for 1 hour, dry well and remove the stone without breaking the prune too much. Fill with chopped ham and dip in beaten egg and breadcrumbs. Fry in deep, hot oil, drain well and serve hot on toothpicks.

PASTELITOS DE POLLO CON HOJALDRE FRITA

Fried Chicken Patties

Pastry:

1 lb. flour	cold water	salt
	7 oz. fat or margarine	

Sift the flour into a basin with a pinch of salt. Rub in 5 oz. fat, and add sufficient cold water to make a smooth paste, which is not too firm. Leave for 5 minutes before adding one more oz. fat, fold and roll out, sprinkle lightly with flour and add remaining fat. Roll out to required thickness and cut into squares.

Filling:

½ boiled chicken	8 olives	1 teaspoon granulated
3½ oz. margarine or fat	1 tablespoon seedless	sugar
1 onion	raisins	salt and pepper
1 tomato	1 hard-boiled egg	oil for frying

Cut the chicken into small pieces. Fry the onion till golden, add the chicken and the chopped, peeled tomato, simmer for a few moments and add the sugar, salt and pepper, chopped olives and seedless raisins. Cut up the hard-boiled egg and fold in. Put 1 tablespoon of this filling into the centre of the little pastry squares. Place another square over as a lid, moistening at the edge to stick. Heat the oil in a deep pan (not to boiling point), simmer patties over a low heat till the pastry rises, then turn up the heat and fry till golden on both sides. Drain well and serve hot.

FRITOS DE CAMARONES

Prawn Pancakes

4 oz. flour	pinch salt	Béchamel sauce
1 egg	½ pint milk	(see p. 256)
8 oz. prawns	1 teaspoon baking	grated cheese
	powder	

Make some very thin pancakes by beating the egg with the flour, milk, baking powder and salt. Allow the batter to stand for at least an hour before using. In the meanwhile shell and cut up the prawns (or lobster) and bind with a thick Béchamel. Spread some of this mixture on each pancake and roll up. Arrange side by side in a dish and sprinkle with grated cheese. Keep warm in the oven or under the grill till all the pancakes are ready.

CONCHAS DE POLLO CON MAYONESA À LA ANDALUZA

Chicken in Shells with Mayonnaise, Andalusian Style

8 oz. cooked breast of	3 hard-boiled eggs	parsley
chicken or left-overs	a few radishes	3 shells or individual
4 tomatoes	crisp lettuce leaves	dishes
3 sour-sweet gherkins		½ pint mayonnaise
		(see p. 263)

Chop up the chicken, the gherkins, 2 eggs, parsley and 2 tomatoes. Mix with the mayonnaise. Line the shells with crisp lettuce leaves, lay thin slices of tomato over the lettuce and pour in the mayonnaise mixture. Garnish with finely sliced egg, radishes and tomato.

ENSALADILLA DE TOMATES Y PIMENTOS VERDES À LA ANDALUZA

Tomato and Sweet Pepper Salad, Andalusian Style

Boil the sweet peppers for 5 minutes, cool and cut in strips. Dip the tomatoes in boiling water, peel and cut into fine slices. Arrange in a salad bowl and garnish with a vinaigrette sauce with plenty of grated onion, apple, parsley, a hard-boiled egg and cucumber.

ENSALADA DE ACHICORIA

Chicory Salad

Wash several crisp heads of chicory in lemon water and chop into small rounds. Rub a salad bowl with garlic, put the chicory in with some chopped green olives and a finely chopped pimento. Season with the following dressing:

½ clove garlic	2 tablespoons olive oil	1 teaspoon French
salt and pepper	1 teaspoon chopped	mustard
sugar	tarragon or mint	1 lemon

Pound the garlic, add the mustard, salt, pepper and a pinch of sugar. Stir in gradually the lemon juice. Into this slowly blend in olive oil and chopped mint. Pour over the salad.

ENSALADA DE ESCAROLA À LA ALMORAIMA

Endive Salad Almoraima

endives	1 hard-boiled egg	3 tablespoons olive oil
1 lemon	red pepper	1 tomato
1 clove garlic	salt and sugar	2 tablespoons vinegar
	green and black olives	

Choose tender, white endives. Chop every leaf in two and immerse in water with lemon juice. Crush garlic clove, a red pepper, salt and a pinch of sugar with a couple of drops of olive oil into a smooth paste, add peeled tomato. Mix vinegar with olive oil and mix all this well together. Add chopped green and black olives. Drain the endives well, pour the sauce over and garnish with hard-boiled egg. Serve very cold.

SOPA CATALANA

Catalan Soup

3 large onions	3 potatoes	3 pints stock or water
1 gill white wine	2 oz. chopped ham or	thyme and parsley
1 stick celery	bacon	pinch nutmeg
3 tomatoes	olive oil or	2 egg yolks
	bacon fat	salt and pepper

Slice the onions and fry in olive oil or bacon fat till golden in the saucepan in which you are going to make the soup. Stir to prevent catching and add the diced ham or bacon, then the tomatoes, cut in quarters, and the chopped celery. After a few minutes pour in the wine, let it almost come to the boil and then add the stock or water. Finally put in the finely diced potatoes, herbs, spice and egg yolks and season.

UN BUEN CALDO GALLEGO

Gallego Soup

6 SERVINGS

8 oz. white beans	8 oz. boiling beef	3—4 potatoes
knuckle bone bacon	1 white cabbage	salt and pepper
	veal bone	7 pints water

This is a nourishing, filling soup for a cold day. Soak beans overnight in cold water. Put 7 pints water to boil in a large saucepan, add beans, bacon and veal bones and beef. Bring to boil and take off the scum, then simmer for 2—3 hours. Add shredded cabbage and diced potatoes, season to taste, remove bones and serve.

ESCUDELLA À LA CATALANA

Catalan Thick Soup

4 lb. potatoes	clove garlic	2 carrots
4 oz. rice	saffron	2 turnips
1 oz. short, thick	4 oz. bacon	1 stick celery
spaghetti	1 onion	2½ pints stock
	small piece cabbage	

Wash and cut the vegetables into small pieces, boil in the stock for 30 minutes. Add the chopped bacon, the rice and the spaghetti. Mix the saffron with a little of the stock and add. Boil for another 10—15 minutes. Season to taste and serve.

PORRU-SALDA

Basque Soup

2 lb. dried cod	3 potatoes	1 clove garlic
2 leeks	2 teaspoons oil	salt and pepper
water	1 onion	

Soak the cod overnight, put in cold water with an onion and boil for about 15 minutes. Flake the cod with a fork. In the meanwhile fry the garlic and the leeks in a little oil, and the peeled, diced potatoes. Add the cod and a little of the fish stock and bring to boil. Mash everything up together, slowly adding the rest of the fish stock. Season. Simmer for an hour and serve hot.

CREMA DE LANGOSTINOS

Cream of Lobster Soup

4 oz. lobster, prawns or shrimps	2 pints milk	2 tablespoons cream
4 oz. butter	1 liqueur glass cognac or sherry	salt and cayenne pepper
water	2 oz. ground rice	

Cook the lobster or shrimps in boiling water and salt. Keep the water. Take off the claws, tails, etc. and pound part of the meat well in a mortar. Mix this together with the ground rice and make a smooth paste with a little cold milk and butter. Simmer slowly, stirring well with a wooden spoon. Take off the fire and pass through a sieve. Put the lobster cream into a saucepan with the rest of the lobster or shrimp meat, adding sufficient stock and milk to make a creamy soup. Simmer, add the sherry and just before serving stir in the cream and a little cayenne pepper.

SOPA CREMA DE YEMAS

Egg Cream Soup

8 SERVINGS

4 pints consommé	6 egg yolks	4 tablespoons chopped ham or chicken
1 gill cream	croûtons	salt and pepper

Separate the yolks, taking care that no white remains. Beat the yolks up well, add the cream and heat together. Add the consommé and cook slowly in double saucepan *(bain-marie)* beating all the while. When the soup starts to thicken add salt and pepper. Pour through a sieve straight into a heated tureen. Add chopped ham or chicken and fried bread croûtons.

SOPA DE QUESO

Cheese Soup

1 oz. fat	1 onion	salt and pepper
2 oz. butter	8 oz. grated cheese	pinch nutmeg
4 slices white bread		1 pint stock or water

Remove crusts from slices of bread. Heat the butter and fat in a pan and cook the finely chopped onion till tender. Put 2 slices of white bread in a saucepan, over this pour half of the fat and the onion from the pan; over this sprinkle half the grated cheese. Repeat this with the rest of the bread, fat, onions and cheese. Season and pour in the stock. Simmer or put into the oven till the bread has dissolved. This is a tasty, thick soup.

SOPA REAL

Royal Soup

4 oz. smoked ham	3 hard-boiled eggs	salt and pepper
1 cooked chicken	1 gill sherry	croûtons
breast	3 pints stock	

Chop the chicken, ham and hard-boiled eggs and put into a warmed soup tureen. Add the sherry to the stock, bring to the boil and pour into the tureen. Serve with croûtons.

POTAJE DE HABICHUELAS ALFONSINAS

Broad Bean Soup Alfonsina

8 oz. white beans	2 tomatoes	1 onion
2 cloves garlic	4 oz. Butifarra	1 hard-boiled egg
olive oil	(boiling sausage)	3 pints water

Soak the beans in cold water for several hours and boil. Into a saucepan pour some olive oil and heat, cook the garlic, chopped onion and tomato, add the Butifarra and the drained beans (keep the water), fry all together slightly and add the water from the beans. Boil for a few minutes and when ready to serve add the chopped hard-boiled egg.

SOPA DE AJO À LA CASTELLANA

Garlic Soup Castilian Style

2 cloves garlic	2 tablespoons olive oil	salt and pepper
2 pints water	4 slices white bread	

This very tasty soup is made in every Spanish household, whether rich or poor. It is made with practically nothing and is consequently not very nourishing, but for many poor families it means 'something in the stomach'.

Remove crusts from bread. Pound the garlic cloves and fry in oil. When they are golden, add the bread and fry slightly, season and pour in 2 pints cold water. Bring to the boil and simmer for about 10 minutes.

SOPA DE AJO CON HUEVOS

Garlic Soup with Egg

Make a garlic soup as above, but when frying the bread, add 4 tomatoes and fry, then add the water and boil in the usual way. Just before serving beat up the yolks of 3 eggs and add to the soup.

POTAJE DE GARBANZOS Y ESPINACAS
À LA ESPAÑOLA

Spanish Pea and Spinach Soup

1 lb. chick peas	4 oz. spinach purée	1 bouquet herbs
olive oil	parsley	(bay leaf, parsley
2 onions	1 carrot	etc.)
small piece dried	water	2 tomatoes
cod		1 clove garlic

Soak the chick peas in cold water overnight. Then put them into a large saucepan of boiling water, add a tablespoon of olive oil, 1 onion, carrot, garlic and herbs and the small piece of dried cod. Boil till the chick peas are tender (about 1½ hours). Pass the mixture through a sieve and add cooked spinach purée. Put on one side while frying the other onion (chopped), the garlic clove and a little chopped parsley. Add a little of the soup, simmer for a moment and add to the rest of the soup. Continue to simmer for another 45 minutes. A chopped boiled egg can be added if required. It is important that this soup should be creamy without being too thick, which would make it stodgy.

GAZPACHO

Cold Soup As Made In Andalusia

There are many ways of making this refreshing cold soup but the result is always delicious. For those who have a liquidizer here is a good recipe:

2 lb. tomatoes	2 green peppers	2 tablespoons vinegar
1 onion	2 tablespoons oil	salt and pepper
1 lemon	1 clove garlic	cucumber
bread or toast	pinch sugar	extra onion

Wash the tomatoes, peel the onion and garlic, wash the lemon and cut in half to extract the pips. Clean the peppers of all the inner seeds. Put all this in the liquidizer with the oil and vinegar. Season to taste with salt and pepper and a pinch of sugar. Put in the refrigerator to cool. Serve with finely diced cucumber, tiny pieces of white bread or toast and finely chopped onion.

A Simple Gazpacho

1 can tomato juice	2 tablespoons oil	salt and pepper
juice 1 lemon		2 tablespoons vinegar

Mix this well, cool in the refrigerator and serve with finely diced peppers, onions, cucumber and bread.

SOPA AL CUARTO DE HORA

The Quarter of an Hour Soup

8 clams	6 oz. rice	4 oz. white fish
8 shrimps (peeled)	1 can small peas	(cod or turbot etc.)
2 hard-boiled eggs	a dash of saffron	salt and pepper
4 oz. chopped ham		2 pints stock

This is a good meal in itself. Boil the clams until they open; keep the water and add to stock, bringing it up to required quantity. Take the clams out of their shells and return to simmering stock. Cut the white fish to small pieces and add together with the rice, chopped ham, peas and chopped hard-boiled egg. Meanwhile pound the shrimps in a mortar with the saffron, salt and pepper and add. In a quarter of an hour it will be a delicious soup.

HUEVOS EN CAMISA

Eggs in Shirts

as many eggs as required	butter	salt and pepper
		a little parsley

Grease a baking dish well with butter. Separate the yolks and place in the greased dish. Beat the whites till stiff, adding a little finely chopped parsley or grated cheese. Cover the yolks and bake for 5 minutes. This very easy and quick dish is delicious.

PASTEL DE TORTILLAS ESPECIAL

Special Omelette Cake

8 eggs	fresh tomato sauce	1 onion
4 oz. mushrooms	(see p. 333)	fat or oil for frying
(or mushroom	4 oz. mixed cooked	salt and pepper
stalks)	vegetables (*petits pois*	2 cooked potatoes
	and carrots)	
	4 oz. shrimps	

Dice the mushrooms, shrimps, potatoes and mixed vegetables separately. The dish is composed of four small, round omelettes of 2 eggs each—one mushroom, one shrimp, one potato, and one mixed vegetable placed one on top of the other and garnished with tomato sauce. When serving, cut like a cake and the different colours and tastes blend to make an outstandingly attractive dish.

HUEVOS À LA FLAMENCA

Eggs Flamenca Style

6 SERVINGS

6 eggs (or 2 each if
  required)
2 lb. tomatoes
8 oz. small peas
  (petits pois)
8 oz. asparagus tips
olive oil

8 oz. green beans
6 slices ham
4 oz. chopped ham
4 oz. chorizo (garlic
  sausage)
1 onion
2 cloves garlic

1 teaspoon chopped
  parsley
½ pint stock
3 pimentos, canned
fried bread
pinch sugar
salt and pepper

Heat the oil in a saucepan and slightly fry the onion and garlic, but do
not allow to brown, add the chopped ham, and the tomatoes cut into
slices, season with salt and pepper and a dash of sugar (the latter to
modify the acidity of the tomatoes). Add the stock (or water), add the
green beans and the peas. (If canned *petits pois* are used do not add till
everything else is tender. This also applies to asparagus tips.) Cook slowly,
till tender. Place the cooked vegetables in a baking dish, break the eggs
over them, spacing them well, garnish with the chorizo and strips of ham
and pimentos. Place at the bottom of a hot oven so the whites set quickly,
leaving the yolks liquid. Serve immediately with strips of fried bread.
Garnish with parsley. The Huevos Flamenca are suitable for little
individual dishes.

HUEVOS COCOTTE À LA CASTELLANA

Castilian Eggs in Cocotte

6 SERVINGS

6 eggs
4 oz. minced meat

2 tablespoons grated
  cheese
1 pint Béchamel sauce
  (see p. 256)

1 onion
olive oil

The eggs should be very fresh for this dish. Fry the chopped onion, add
the minced meat and fry till brown. Line individual baking dishes with
a drop of oil and the minced meat. On to this carefully break an egg.
Put into a hot oven till the white has set, then add the Béchamel sauce.
Sprinkle with grated cheese and replace in oven for a couple of minutes.
Serve immediately.

HUEVOS EN SALSA AGRIA

Eggs in Sweet-Sour Sauce

6 SERVINGS

6 eggs	bay leaf	butter or margarine
1 gill white wine	2 cloves	1 tablespoon flour
½ pint stock	1 tablespoon sugar	salt and pepper
1 onion	3 tablespoons vinegar	croûtons

Boil the eggs for 6 minutes and plunge into cold water to peel more easily. Melt the butter and simmer the chopped onion till soft; stir in flour till smooth and add the stock, salt and pepper, cloves and bay leaf. Simmer for 15 minutes. Strain and reheat with the sugar and white wine. Put the eggs in the sauce and simmer for a few minutes. Garnish with fried bread croûtons and serve hot.

HUEVOS ESCALFADOS À LA ESPAÑOLA

Spanish Poached Eggs

6 SERVINGS

6 poached eggs	2 green peppers	1 clove garlic
2 onions	1 small marrow	salt and pepper
4 tomatoes	olive oil	pinch sugar

Chop the onions, peel and chop the tomatoes and peppers (taking care to extract the seeds); also peel and chop the marrow. Heat the oil and fry the onions and garlic till golden, then add the peppers and marrow and finally the tomatoes, salt and pepper. Add a dash of sugar. Fry till quite tender. Line a baking dish or individual dishes with this. Place the poached eggs on top, garnish with small triangles of bread, fried crisp in oil.

TORTILLA DE PATATAS À LA ESPAÑOLA

Spanish Potato Omelette

6 eggs	salt and pepper	oil for frying
1 onion	water	1 lb. potatoes

Chop the onion and fry till golden. Peel and dice the potatoes. Slowly fry these till tender, but not crisp (boiled potatoes can also be used). Beat the eggs well with a few drops of water. Take care not to leave too much oil in the pan. Place the potatoes and onion in and pour the eggs over. When done on one side, carefully turn over by slipping on to a saucepan lid and, putting a little more oil into the pan, return to pan. Serve immediately. All Spanish omelettes are served flat, not rolled over like French omelettes.

HUEVOS ESCONDIDOS
Hidden Eggs

Make four, fine, large pancakes. Scramble 6 eggs in the usual way and divide into four portions. Wrap the scrambled egg into slices of ham, and roll and enclose the ham roll in a pancake. This makes a delicious luncheon dish or a first course for dinner.

HUEVOS PRESIDENCIA
Presidential Eggs
6 SERVINGS

7 eggs	1 lb. chopped spinach	½ pint milk
4 oz. liver pâté	2 oz. flour	salt and pepper

Hard-boil 6 eggs, plunge in cold water and peel. Cut in half and take out the yolks; mix these with the liver pâté and replace in the white halves. Keep in a warm place till the spinach is boiled and strained. Line a dish with the spinach to make a nest for the eggs; then make a Béchamel sauce with the yolk of an egg, flour and milk and pour over the eggs. Heat quickly in the oven and serve immediately.

TORTILLA MADRILEÑA
Madrid Omelette

3 sweetbreads	2 tomatoes or small	1 gill dry sherry or
6 eggs	can of tomatoes	white wine
2 onions	4 oz. chopped ham	chopped parsley
8 oz. butter		salt and pepper

Fry 1 chopped onion in butter; before it colours add the sweetbreads, a little chopped parsley and when almost done add the sherry or white wine. Keep warm while making the omelette. Fry 1 finely chopped onion in butter; as soon as it starts to turn golden add the chopped ham and 6 eggs well beaten up. Season and make a flat round omelette, cooked on both sides. Place on serving dish and garnish with the sweetbread mixture and fried tomatoes.

SOUFFLÉ DE PATATAS
Potato Soufflé
8 SERVINGS

3—4 large potatoes	4 oz. lean smoked ham	salt and pepper
8 oz. butter	4 egg yolks	2 tablespoons melted
1 gill cream	6 egg whites	butter

Boil the potatoes in their skins. Peel and mash well while hot, season, add the butter over a low heat, beating well. Add the cream little by little and season. Remove from the heat and add the finely chopped ham and the yolks. Beat well. Exactly 20 minutes before required, add the stiffly beaten whites of egg, pour into buttered dish and bake in the usual way. Serve immediately.

TO MAKE CANALONES AT HOME

2 lb. flour	salt	a little water
	4 eggs	

This quantity will make about 12 servings and it is economical to make plenty as the canalones can be kept for later use. Put flour and salt on to pastry board, make a well in the centre into which you pour the beaten eggs, add a teaspoon of lukewarm water and knead till all the liquid is absorbed; add another teaspoon of lukewarm water if the dough is too firm. Knead well for a few minutes and roll into a ball on to a well floured board. Cut the ball into several slices, flour the rolling pin and carefully roll into very fine paste. When one piece is almost as thin as paper, hang a clean cloth or serviette over the back of a chair, flour to prevent sticking and hang the 'sheets' of paste over it, flouring each slightly. When the sheets of paste are dry, cut them into 4-inch squares and wrap in a floured cloth till ready to use. Home-made canalones take less time to cook than the ready-made (about 5 minutes is enough).

CANALONES CON JAMÓN

Ham Canalones

canalones	2 teaspoons tomato	1 egg
8 oz. chopped ham	purée	butter
1 onion	1 teaspoon chopped	salt and pepper
1 teaspoon flour	parsley	Parmesan cheese
	1 dash nutmeg	

Fry the chopped onion and the chopped ham in a little fat, sprinkle with the flour, add the tomato purée and simmer, stirring to make it smooth. Beat the egg together with the chopped parsley and add. Season with salt and pepper and a dash of nutmeg. Simmer for a few moments until firm. Allow to cool before filling the boiled canalones. Roll up, sprinkle with butter and grated Parmesan and heat in a hot oven.

541

CANALONES CON ESPINACA

Canalones with Spinach

1 lb. spinach purée (or 1 large packet frozen spinach)	canalones 1 egg yolk	2 anchovies 1 gill thick Béchamel sauce (see p. 256)

Pound the anchovies in a mortar (a teaspoonful of anchovy paste can be used instead). Beat the egg yolk, mix with the anchovy and the Béchamel sauce and into this beat the spinach purée until it thickens. Season and allow to cool before filling the canalones in the usual way. When filled and placed in a buttered baking dish, pour a little Béchamel over the canalones. Bake in a hot oven for a short while. Serve as an entrée.

CANALONES CON PESCADO

Canalones with Fish Fillings

canalones butter 2 tablespoons milk	2 hard-boiled eggs 8 oz. of any white fish such as cod, turbot, etc. or any left-overs	4 oz. mushrooms or mushroom stalks salt and pepper

Flake the boiled fish with a fork, chop the hard-boiled eggs and the mushrooms very finely. Bind all this with 2 tablespoons milk and a little creamed butter, season and allow to cool before filling the canalones. Roll up, dot with butter and place in a hot oven or under the grill for a short time. This fish filling can also be made with a Béchamel or if preferred tomato sauce; in short, with a little imagination, delicious fillings can be made of any left-overs.

PAELLA

Spanish Rice

6 SERVINGS

1 pint mussels 1 pint prawns 1 small cooked lobster few chicken livers 12 black olives	few pieces of cooked white fish 1 clove garlic 12 oz. rice 2 onions 4 tomatoes	2 red or green peppers olive oil few crawfish or canned clams saffron ½ pint boiling water

Heat the oil in a Paella or large iron frying pan, fry the sliced onions till golden, add the chopped garlic, peppers, stoned olives and chicken livers. Over this, which should be liquid with oil, pour the rice. Fry till the oil is absorbed, then add the lobster, clams, white fish, prawns, boiled mussels and tomatoes. Add $\frac{1}{2}$ pint boiling water into which a little saffron has been dissolved. Simmer over a low fire till rice is tender; this should be when all the liquid has evaporated. Serve immediately.

ARROZ ABANDA DE VALENCIA

Valencia Rice with Fish

8 oz. fresh cod	1 onion	$\frac{1}{2}$ teaspoon saffron
8 oz. hake	1 lb. Patna rice	salt and pepper
1 clove garlic	8 oz. shrimps or cray-	oil for frying
	fish	water

Boil all the fish together. In the meanwhile fry the chopped onion and garlic clove in a little oil, add the rice and fry till golden. Add the fish stock and saffron, and simmer. Keep the fish warm till required. When the rice is tender serve, either together with the fish or put the fish in another dish and serve with piquant or tomato sauce (see pp. 256, 333).

ARROZ CON POLLO

Rice with Chicken

6 SERVINGS

1 boiling fowl	1 pint Béchamel sauce	nutmeg
1 lb. rice	(see p. 256)	salt and pepper
1 onion		

Boil the chicken till tender, but be careful not to overcook. Boil the rice in the usual way. Make a fairly liquid Béchamel with the chicken broth, milk and 1 egg yolk. Line a large serving bowl with the rice, carve the chicken into reasonable pieces, place on top of the rice, pour the Béchamel over and serve hot.

ARROZ À LA PAMPLONESA

Rice Pamplona Style

1 onion	olive oil	2 pints boiling water
2 chilli peppers	8 oz. tomatoes or	sweet peppers
8 oz. cod	1 small can	salt and pepper
1 teaspoon saffron		1 lb. rice

Fry in olive oil chopped onion, red peppers and a piece of cod; season with salt and pepper. When this is well done, add tomatoes and then the rice. Continue to fry till the rice is golden, add sliced sweet peppers, boiling water (double the amount of that of the rice) and saffron. Boil for 15 minutes and finish by placing for 5 minutes in a hot oven.

ARROZ À LA CRIOLLA
Argentinian Rice

3 tomatoes or 1 can tomatoes or tomato purée	12 oz. Patna rice	1 onion
	8 oz. minced meat	oil or lard for frying
	2 pints boiling water	1 clove garlic

Slowly pour rice into 2 pints boiling water. Boil fiercely for 20 minutes. Drain the rice through a colander and rinse with boiling water. Place in a large dish with a well in the centre for the meat sauce. For this, fry a chopped onion and garlic clove and tomatoes or tomato purée and minced meat. When the meat is brown and well done, add a table-spoon of water if the sauce is too thick.

ARROZ ESTILO BARCELONÉS
Rice Barcelona Style

8 oz. margarine	2 tomatoes or 1 small can	4 oz. *petits pois* (or 1 small can)
1 onion	nutmeg	chopped parsley
4 oz. ham	1 pint stock or water	salt and pepper
8 oz. rice		

Melt the margarine in a large saucepan and fry the chopped onion till golden; add the ham and sliced tomatoes. Put in the rice and fry till it changes colour then add 1 pint boiling water or stock. Boil rapidly for 7 minutes, when the liquid will be almost all absorbed. Add the peas, season and finish cooking in a moderate oven for about 10 minutes.

ARROZ CON ALMEJAS
Rice with Mussels (or Clams)

6 SERVINGS

1 lb. rice	1 head or piece of cod	1 carrot
1 lb. mussels or clams	1 tablespoon chopped parsley	1 teaspoon saffron
2 tablespoons oil	water	salt and pepper
2 cloves garlic		1 onion

Boil the cod's head, the carrot and the onion in sufficient water to make the stock. Simmer for 1½ hours. Finely chop the parsley and the garlic cloves and fry in oil with the saffron. To open the mussels put in boiling water, take out of shells and add to the fried garlic and saffron. Add the fish stock and bring to boil, then turn heat down and simmer for a little while. Bring to boil again and add the rice, gradually, so it continues to boil. There should be double the amount of liquid to rice. Boil for 15 minutes, then put into a warm oven and leave there for about 10 minutes before serving, to dry the rice completely.

102. Strawberry Shortcake, Holland (p.185)

103. Pickled Salted Herring, Sweden (p.480)

104. Lamb Kebab, Greece (p.328)

ARROZ CON MENUDILLAS
Rice with Giblets

1 lb. rice	1 onion	1 gill wine
2 oz. ham	salt and pepper	oil for frying
1 small can tomato	butter	sweet herbs
purée	giblets or chicken livers	grated cheese

Boil the rice in the usual way. Meanwhile, chop and fry the onion, giblets and ham in the oil with salt and pepper and sweet herbs. When done, add the tomato purée mixed with a teaspoon of butter and the wine. Simmer for a few minutes. Make a circle of the boiled rice on the serving dish, put the giblets in the centre and serve with grated cheese.

ARROZ FRITO
Fried Rice

8 oz. rice	2 oz. margarine or olive oil	1 onion
		1 pint boiling water

Fry the chopped onion till tender, but do not let it turn brown. Add the rice and fry, shaking well so it does not catch. When the rice has absorbed the fat add 1 pint boiling water. Season and simmer slowly for 20 minutes. The water will be absorbed and the rice will be tender with each grain separate. Serve with fish or chicken.

PAELLA VALENCIANA
Valencian Rice
6 SERVINGS

1 tender chicken	1 small can tomato	1 lb. rice
1 dozen snails or clams	purée	2 pints water
1 dozen mussels	8 oz. garlic sausage	olive oil
1 can artichoke hearts	(chorizo)	1 small can *pimentos*
1 can small peas (*petits pois*)	2 cloves garlic	*morrones* (sweet
	2 teaspoons saffron	peppers)

Cut the chicken into 6 or 8 pieces. Heat about ½ pint best olive oil in a Paella or large iron frying pan. Add the chopped garlic and cook the chicken slowly, basting all the time till golden; then gradually add the rice and cook for 15 minutes. By this time the rice will have turned slightly golden. Add the boiling water in which the saffron has been dissolved. Add the tomato purée and then the snails or clams and the mussels. Cook for about 15 minutes and then add the artichokes and peas. Cook for 5 minutes and then garnish with strips of pimentos and garlic sausage. Cook for another few minutes till the rice is tender and the liquid is absorbed. The secret of the Paella is to serve immediately, before the rice gets too dry.

HIGADO CON ARROZ

Liver with Rice

1 lb. calves' liver	5—6 tablespoons oil	a little sage
2 onions	or fat	salt
1 gill red wine	1 gill water	3 tablespoons flour

Cut the liver into thick slices and coat with salted flour. Fry in heated oil or fat with a little sage. When the liver is cooked, remove from the pan and cut into very small pieces. Fry the chopped onions till golden, thicken with flour and add the wine and water to make the sauce. Simmer for a few moments and return the liver to the sauce to heat. Serve hot with boiled rice.

RAPE À LA MONISTROL

Rock Cod Monistrol

2 lb. rock cod	1 onion	1 coffee spoon saffron
½ pint milk	1 tablespoon flour	salt and pepper
1 clove garlic		2 tablespoons olive oil

Chop the onion and the garlic up very finely and pound in a mortar with the saffron and a pinch of salt, then mix well with the flour and milk till smooth. Pour this over the fish and simmer till tender. Turbot or hake can be used instead of cod for this dish.

CAZUELITAS DE LANGOSTINOS SAN RAFAEL

Casserole of Clams San Rafael

1 lb. shrimps	2 tablespoons flour	6 shallots or 1 onion
12 clams	bouquet of herbs	1 clove garlic
4 oz. rice	½ pint white wine	1 gill cream
10 oz. butter	1 tablespoon tomato	salt and pepper
8 oz. grated Parmesan	purée	pinch cayenne pepper
cheese	½ pint water	1 gill cognac

This is rice with clams in individual baking dishes with aurora sauce and garnished with shrimps, sprinkled with grated cheese and baked in the oven au gratin. In a saucepan put 4 oz. butter, fry the chopped garlic and chopped shallots or onion till golden, add the shrimps and then the cognac. Light this and when the flame dies down, add the wine and ½ pint water, the herbs, salt and pepper; cover and simmer for 10 minutes, then take out the shrimps, shell and put on one side. To make the sauce, first grind the shrimp shells in a mortar, replace in the liquid, adding the tomato purée. After first mixing the flour with 4 oz. butter and the cream to a smooth paste, add to the saucepan and boil for 10 minutes, stirring all the while with a wooden spoon. Take the pan from the fire and strain the liquid through a sieve. The sauce should be thick, and if it is not sufficiently thick, continue to simmer, stirring all the time. Add a dash of cayenne. In the meanwhile, boil the rice until cooked, drain. Wash the clams well and boil for 5 minutes. When they have opened, take out of shells. Put the rest of the butter into a pan, heat and fry the rice together with the clams for a few minutes. Then put two clams with rice into each dish, garnish with shrimps, pour the sauce over, sprinkle with grated cheese and bake in a hot oven until brown.

MERLUZA À LA CATALANA
Catalan Hake

4 thick fillets hake	1 pint tomato sauce	1 dessertspoon
4 pieces fried bread	anchovy butter	chopped parsley
	oil for frying	

Clean and dry the fillets of fish. Fry in oil four pieces of bread, the same size as the fillets. Grill the fillets and place each one on a piece of fried bread spread with anchovy butter. Serve on individual plates with tomato sauce. Sprinkle with parsley. Any white fish can be used for this recipe.

PESCADILLAS CECILIA
Small Hake Cecilia

1 small hake or	olive oil	1 hard-boiled egg
4 fillets of hake	salt and pepper	½ pint white sauce
juice 2 lemons	1 can asparagus tips	(see p. 257)
	flour	

This dish can be made with the whole small fish or a large fish, filleted. Sprinkle with lemon juice, season and coat with flour, fry in olive oil and garnish with chopped boiled egg. Serve in a flat dish with asparagus tips and white sauce.

MEJILLÓNES
Mussels

3 pints mussels	1 chopped onion	bouquet of herbs
½ pint water	1 tablespoon flour	(bay leaf, thyme
½ pint white wine		and parsley)

Clean the mussels thoroughly and put them into a pan. Cover with white wine and water, adding the chopped onion and bouquet of herbs. Simmer till the shells are open; when they have opened, the mussels are cooked. Take the mussels out and reduce the liquid if less is required. Remove half a shell from each mussel. Thicken remaining liquid with the flour. Flavour, adding a little more wine if necessary. Pour this sauce over the mussels immediately before serving.

BACALAO À LA VIZCAINA

Dried Cod from Vizaya

2 lb. dried cod	1 can *pimentos*	3 cloves garlic
½ pint olive oil	*morrones*	½ pint stock
2 onions	1 bouquet herbs	salt and pepper
8 tomatoes or 1 can tomatoes		water

Cut the cod in pieces and soak overnight in cold water. Skin and take
out the bones. Fry the chopped onions and garlic. Add the cod, the
peeled tomatoes, the peppers and herbs; add the stock and simmer, then
add sufficient water to cover. Cook slowly over a low heat for about
1½ hours.

No Spanish cookery book would be complete without this tasty national
dish from the North of Spain.

BACALAO À LA NAVARRA

2 lb. dried cod	6 tomatoes*	2 cloves garlic
½ pint olive oil	3 red or green sweet	3 red chilli peppers
6 onions	peppers	water

* (or a large can *pimentos morrones* and 2 cans tomatoes)

Soak the cod in cold water for 24 hours, changing the water two to three
times. Dice the onions and the sweet peppers together with the chilli
peppers. Heat the oil in a large pan and fry the onions till golden, add
the peppers. Put the tomatoes in boiling water for a few minutes to
make peeling easier. Peel and cut in quarters, add to the fried onions
and finally add the chopped garlic cloves. The vegetables should not
be fried until they dissolve, as this is not a sauce.

Keep warm till ready to use. Cut the cod into strips and bring slowly
to the boil, taking care that the pieces remain whole. Take the fish out
of the water and place in a flat baking dish in which it can be served,
Throw half the stock away and add the rest to the fried vegetables.
Mix this well and pour over the fish; leave in hot oven for about 10
minutes. Serve immediately.

SALMON À LA ALICANTINA

Alicante Salmon

4 thick slices fresh	olive oil	parsley
salmon	2 sliced red chilli	salt and pepper
1 lemon	peppers	1 onion

Wash and dry the salmon and soak for 2 to 3 hours in a sauce made
of 1 gill olive oil, the lemon juice, sliced onion, salt and pepper, red
peppers and a sprig of parsley. 20 minutes before serving take the salmon

out of this pickling sauce, dry, and grill till tender. Serve garnished with slices of lemon and hollandaise sauce (see p. 258). This should be served separately.

TRUCHAS RELLENAS À LA JIRONESA
Stuffed Trout in the Style of Jiron

Clean and cut open 4 trout, season with salt and lemon juice, stuff with the following mixture: chopped olives, onions, canned pimentos, almonds, peeled mushrooms, salt and pepper and a little oil and vinegar. Tie the fish up with thread, dip into oil or butter, and breadcrumbs. Encase each fish in brown or greaseproof paper, which has been slightly greased on the inside. Tie again and place in the oven or under a slow grill, taking care the paper does not burn. Serve in the paper.

PULPETAS DE LENGUADO
Stuffed Sole

2 large Dover soles	1 egg	1 gill milk ⎫ for
½ pint shrimps,	breadcrumbs	2 oz. butter ⎬ Béchamel
prawns or a piece of	oil or fat for frying	2 oz. flour ⎭ sauce
lobster		

This is an elegant dish for special occasions. Wash the filleted soles. Cut the fillets in half, so you have 8 long strips of fish. For the filling, first make the Béchamel sauce in the usual way; this should be firm enough not to run. Into the Béchamel mix the finely chopped peeled shrimps or prawns, season to taste and fill the fillets. Roll these up and tie with white thread or string. Beat the egg and first dip the fillet rolls in egg, then into breadcrumbs and fry in deep fat or oil till golden. Snip off the thread and serve with tomato or tartare sauce (see pp. 333, 256).

LENGUADO AL VINO TINTO
Sole in Red Wine

4 filleted soles	4 oz. chopped	1 lemon
4 oz. shrimps	mushrooms	salt and pepper
	½ pint red wine	oil for frying
	2 chopped onions or	
	shallots	

Slightly fry the chopped onions and mushrooms in oil. Place the fillets in a large, flat baking dish, garnish with the onions and mushrooms, add the wine, salt and pepper, and cook slowly under a medium grill or in the oven till the fish is tender. Garnish with hot shelled shrimps and slices of lemon.

LENGUADOS AL PLATO

Plaice in Casserole

4 fresh plaice	salt and pepper	breadcrumbs
4 oz. mushrooms or	1 gill white wine	6 oz. butter
mushroom stalks	½ pint stock or water	2 onions

Grease a casserole with butter, make a bed of finely chopped onions and mushrooms. On to this lay the plaice, which has been washed and dried. Pour the white wine and the stock (or water) over the fish, cover with the rest of the onions and mushrooms and sprinkle lightly with breadcrumb Season. Finally melt the remaining butter and pour over. Bake in a moderate oven till tender (this should take about 15 minutes). Serve immediately with boiled potatoes.

BUDÍN DE MERLUZA CON MAYONESA

Hake Pudding with Mayonnaise

8 SERVINGS

2 lb. hake	¼ stale white loaf	salt and pepper
1 lb. tomatoes or	(6 slices)	1 lemon
1 large can	½ pint hot milk	1 clove garlic
4 onions	4 eggs	3 teaspoons oil
4 oz. butter		parsley

Boil 2 sliced onions, parsley, salt and pepper in 1 pint of water with lemon juice for a little while before putting in the hake. Simmer the fish slowly in a covered saucepan. In the meanwhile soak the bread in hot milk. Fry 2 onions (chopped) in oil till golden, add the garlic clove and tomatoes, stirring till it thickens. Sieve and season. Take the fish out of the stock, skin and take out the bones, flake with a fork and beat with melted butter and the bread, which has been squeezed out, then add the tomato sauce. Beat up the egg yolks and add. Finally beat the whites stiffly and add. Pour the whole into a buttered ovenproof dish, which fits into a saucepan. Boil this in *bain-marie*. This pudding is also good baked in the oven. Serve with a hot mayonnaise sauce if the pudding is served hot, or cold sauce if the pudding is served cold. Both are equally nice. The pudding can be garnished with shrimps or prawns. This pudding can be made with any white fish.

SARDINAS FRITAS

Fresh Fried Sardines (or Sprats)

26 fresh sardines or	flour, salt	1 lemon
32 sprats	oil or fat for frying	parsley

Clean and take the fish heads off. Dry well and salt. Dip in flour, then deep fry. Drain and serve with slices of lemon and garnished with parsley.

CORVINA À LA VASCA

Basque Eel

1 lb. eel	1 bay leaf	1 gill oil
1 clove garlic	4 tablespoons vinegar	salt and pepper

Wash and cut the eel into pieces. Grill for a few moments, then fry in oil, adding the crushed garlic and bay leaf. Fry till brown, take off the fire and add the vinegar. Continue to simmer till the eel is tender. Serve in its own sauce, with boiled potatoes.

CAMARONES FRITOS

Fried Prawns

1 lb. large prawns	3 tablespoons	oil for frying
1 egg	breadcrumbs	
	3 tablespoons flour	

After shelling and cleaning carefully, coat the prawns in flour and then in beaten egg and breadcrumbs. Heat the oil and fry the prawns to a golden brown. Serve with boiled potatoes and mayonnaise.

ZARZUELA DE PESCADO

Fish Stew

6 SERVINGS

4 thick slices turbot or hake	12 shrimps or prawns or some slices of	parsley
6 tomatoes	lobster	1 lemon
1 clove garlic	12 mussels	1 gill dry white wine
4 oz. mushrooms	2 onions	oil for frying
		cooked sweetcorn

Cut the turbot or hake into fairly small pieces. Shell the shrimps or prawns and the mussels. Fry the chopped onions with a little chopped garlic in oil till golden. Add the mussels, chopped tomatoes and mushrooms. When these are fairly tender add the rest of the fish together with the wine. While this is simmering, add the juice of a lemon, salt and pepper. Garnish with sweetcorn and serve immediately with boiled potatoes or rice.

551

FILETES DE RODABALLO À LA ANDALUZA

Fillets of Turbot Andalusian Style

6 SERVINGS

6 fillets of turbot	4 oz. mushrooms	1 clove garlic
1 piece of fish	2 sweet peppers	chopped parsley
(for stock)	2 tablespoons	salt and pepper
2 onions	breadcrumbs	1 gill white wine
8 oz. tomatoes	lemon juice, water	4 oz. butter

Flatten the fillets of turbot with a wooden spoon, place in baking dish, spread with butter and keep in cool place till ready to use. Boil piece of fish (or fish head for economy) with one onion and salt in sufficient water to cover. While boiling add white wine. To make good stock simmer for about 20 minutes. In the meanwhile chop the onion and garlic clove, clean and chop the sweet peppers; peel and cut the mushrooms; wash and cut the tomatoes into small pieces. Fry the onion till golden, then add the peppers and mushrooms; when these are tender add the tomatoes. Pour the stock, of which there should be about two full tumblers, over the turbot and over this lay the fried vegetables. Bake in a fairly hot oven for 25 minutes. The fish will be tender and the stock absorbed, but the dish will not be dry. Add lemon juice before serving.

ENSALADA DE LANGOSTA

Lobster Salad

1 small lobster	4 chopped olives	mayonnaise
(or piece left-over)	½ tablespoon capers	(see p. 263)
3 hard-boiled eggs		2 sticks celery

Cut the lobster into small pieces, add chopped hard-boiled eggs, stoned, chopped olives, chopped celery and capers. Pour in mayonnaise, mix gently with a wooden spoon and serve chilled.

LOMO DE CERDO ENVUELTO EN COL

Ribs of Pork in Cabbage

1 white cabbage	fat for frying	8 oz. tomatoes
1 lb. pork ribs	1 onion	a little flour

Fry the meat till almost done, take off the bone. In the meanwhile put the cabbage to boil in salt water until almost tender, but taking care that the leaves remain whole. Drain and wrap the pieces of meat in a cabbage leaf, tying with cotton. Sprinkle with flour and fry. Serve with fried tomatoes and onion.

CALAMARES À LA BILBAINA

Bilbao Calamares Squids (Ink Fish)

24 small squids	salt and pepper	2 oz. breadcrumbs
2 onions	1 tablespoon olive oil	1 teaspoon parsley
2 tomatoes	1 clove garlic	water

Clean the squids in several waters, separate the ink-bags carefully and place the liquid in a cup. Heat the oil in a saucepan and slightly fry the chopped onions, chopped garlic, tomatoes (previously peeled) and chopped parsley. Put the squids in this, adding sufficient water to cover; simmer till tender. In the meanwhile stir the ink with the breadcrumbs, salt and pepper, adding a little of the stock from the saucepan. When the squids are cooked add the ink, stir well while slowly bringing to the boil. Serve with slices of fried bread and boiled rice.

CHULETAS DE CERDO À LA MADRILEÑA

Madrid Pork Chops

4 pork chops	2 cloves garlic	1 chilli pepper
4 tablespoons olive oil	1 bay leaf	salt and pepper
parsley		marjoram

Chop the garlic and parsley, add the oil, bay leaf, marjoram, sliced pepper and salt and pepper. Put the chops in this and cover the dish. Turn the chops from time to time so the herbs can penetrate both sides. Bake till done, basting so the chops do not get dry. Serve with fried potatoes.

COCIDO À LA MADRILEÑA

Madrid Stew

1 lb. stewing steak	2 leeks, water	2 carrots
2 marrow bones	6 oz. Continental	2 onions
2 oz. bacon	smoked boiling	2—3 potatoes
8 oz. chick peas	sausage	salt and pepper

Soak the chick peas overnight in plenty of cold water. Put the meat, marrow bones and bacon in cold water, salt and bring to boil. Skim the scum and add the peas. Simmer for 30 minutes. Now add the finely cut vegetables and diced potatoes. Cover the pan and simmer over a low fire for at least 1½ hours. Cut the sausage into small pieces and put into the stew. Flavour to taste. Pieces of chicken or any leftovers can be added to the cocido.

CHULETAS DE TOCINO CON SALSA DE TOMATE

Pork Chops With Tomato Sauce

4 pork chops or cutlets	3 oz. oil or fat	1 small can tomato purée
2 oz. flour	1 clove garlic	salt and pepper
	1 gill water	sherry or white wine

Remove most of the fat from the meat and pound gently with the back of a wooden spoon or knife. Season with salt and pepper, dip both sides in flour, rub with garlic clove. Heat the oil in frying pan and brown the meat until it is tender. Keep hot while making the sauce. Dilute the tomato purée in 1 gill boiling water, sherry or white wine. Drain half the fat off, mix the rest with tomato purée and serve separately. This dish is good with boiled rice.

ESTOFADO MONTAÑESA

Montañesa Stew

2 lb. stewing steak	2 carrots	2 tablespoons cocoa
2 oz. flour	fat or olive oil	bay leaf, water
2 chopped onions	French mustard	salt and pepper

Cut the steak into 1-inch pieces, roll in the flour. Fry 2 onions till golden, add the steak and fry till brown. Add sufficient boiling water almost to cover, together with the sliced carrots and bay leaf. Simmer for 30 minutes, add 1 teaspoon French mustard to the sauce. Continue to simmer. When almost ready to serve, take out half a cup of the liquid, mix with the cocoa and return to the stew, which should be rich and delicious. Serve with boiled potatoes, spaghetti or boiled rice.

LOMO DE CERDO À LA BATURRA

Fillets of Pork Batura

2 fillets of pork	1 onion	1 tablespoon tomato purée
flour	4 oz. smoked ham	2 hard-boiled eggs
oil or fat for frying	2 dozen olives	
	1 gill red wine	

Flour the fillets of pork and fry in hot oil till golden and well done all through. Drain well and keep hot. In the same oil, fry the chopped onion and ham; mix the tomato purée with the wine and a little flour to thicken the sauce, add and stir while simmering. Add the meat again and at the last moment the chopped olives. These should not boil as they would get hard. Garnish with finely sliced hard-boiled egg.

Chocolate Sauce.

Good ½ pint H_2O.   6 oz dessert or bitter choc.
                                          olate
4 oz gran sug.

Method

1. Break up choc, put in pan c H_2O.
2. Dissolve slowly, add sugar
3. When melted bring to boil c̄ lid on + allow
   to simmer to a rich syrupy consistency
   — takes about 10 - 15 mins.

Advanced Cookery
Margary Rhys.
Hilda M Ferris
[J. Smith + Son (Glasgow) Ltd]

Crème à la Greaque

½ lb smoked cod's roe.

4-6 oz unsalted butter

juice of 1 lemon

Tomato juice

Method.

1. Skin the cod's roe.

2. Cream the butter. Pound the roe adding the butter, lemon juice tomato juice & pulp.

3. When ʋ light & creamy serve w. black olives & hot toast or H_2O biscuits

Caramel Sauce.

½ lb loaf sugar

lemon juice

½ pint hot H_2O.

Method.

1. Put loaf sugar in heavy pan & cover w a little H_2O. Dissolve gently & boil steadily to rich brown caramel

2. Cover hand w. thick cloth & pour on rest of hot H_2O. Boil up, add lemon juice to flavour. pour of & cool.

CHULETAS DE CORDERO VILAREAL

Lamb Chops Vilareal

5 SERVINGS

10 lamb chops	bouquet of herbs	2 tablespoons stock
4 rashers bacon	1 lb. parboiled sliced	salt and pepper
2 onions	potatoes	oil for frying

Wash chops and flatten well with the back of a wooden spoon; fry over high heat till brown on both sides. In another saucepan, fry the rashers of bacon; when brown, fry the sliced onions in the bacon fat with a bouquet of herbs. Pour this together with the chops into a casserole, place the lid on firmly and bake in a medium oven. When almost ready, add the sliced, parboiled potatoes. When these are tender, serve very hot. If necessary a little stock can be added to this hot-pot.

CHULETAS DE CORDERO BRASEADAS À LA PAYESANA

Lamb Cutlets Payesana

As above, using lamb cutlets instead of chops. When adding the sliced potatoes, also add boiled carrots and turnips. Serve very hot.

PIMENTOS RELLENOS CON CARNE À LA BILBAINA

Stuffed Peppers Bilbaina

6 SERVINGS

6 large sweet peppers	2 egg yolks	1 gill white wine
4 oz. minced pork	2 onions	salt and pepper
4 oz. minced veal	1 carrot	olive oil for frying
4 oz. smoked ham	1 small can tomato	1 chopped clove garlic
2 slices white bread	purée	flour

Prepare the peppers by washing them and carefully cutting off the top with the stem. Extract all the seeds. To prepare the sauce put some oil in a pan, dry 1 chopped onion and carrot and thicken with 2 tablespoons flour. Add the tomato purée, diluted with the glass of wine. Keep warm till required. To make the filling, fry 1 onion in oil, with the garlic till golden. Add the bread, which has been soaked in milk and squeezed out, mix well till a smooth paste is formed, take off the heat and add 1 egg yolk, salt and pepper, and the meat. Fry till light brown and remove from the heat. Fill the peppers and tie the tops on with thread. Put into flour and egg yolk and flour again. Deep fry in oil till tender. Drain and place in heated serving dish. Pour the sauce over and serve.

HIGADO À LA FAVORITA

Braised Liver

1 lb. liver	pepper	lemon
1 onion	sage and cloves	oil for frying bread
1 carrot	1 clove garlic	1 tablespoon bread-
8 oz. tomatoes	chopped parsley	crumbs
	4 slices bread	

Scald the liver in boiling water, drain and cut in slices. Heat the oil and fry the breadcrumbs and sliced onion and carrot until a light brown. Then add the liver, piercing a clove into each slice. Simmer and add a little sage, the tomatoes, garlic, salt and pepper. Almost cover with cold water and bring to boil, then lower the heat, cover the pan and simmer till the liver is tender. In the meanwhile fry four slices of bread till crisp. When the liver is ready, take out the cloves and the garlic and serve, garnished with the fried bread, slices of lemon and parsley.

MANITAS DE CORDERO À LA CATALANA

Calf's Trotters à la Catalana

4 trotters	bouquet of herbs	oil or fat for frying
1 onion	1 egg	salt
1 clove garlic		breadcrumbs

Boil the trotters in salt water, after washing thoroughly, for 15 minutes. Throw the water away and put into fresh boiling water, salt, garlic clove and a bouquet of herbs. Simmer until tender. Drain, remove the bones and cut into pieces. Dip in egg and breadcrumbs, deep fry in oil or fat and serve with fried potatoes.

ROSCA DE CARNE

Meat Loaf

1 lb. minced beef	1 onion	1 clove garlic
4 rashers streaky	breadcrumbs	lard or dripping
bacon	mixed herbs	salt and pepper
	2 eggs	

Fry the chopped onion and garlic in fat, till golden. Remove garlic and mix the onion with meat. Beat 1 egg and fold into the meat, with mixed herbs, salt and pepper. Roll the meat into a loaf and dip in egg and breadcrumbs. Place in baking pan, wrap the bacon over the roll and bake in a hot oven for 1 hour (add a tablespoon of fat to the pan). Serve with tomato sauce (see p. 333).

JAMÓN AL JEREZ CON ESPINACAS

Ham With Sherry and Spinach

As much boiled ham and spinach as required, with sauce as follows:

2 carrots	1½ gills sherry	1 tablespoons tomato
2 onions	4 oz. butter	purée
2 rashers bacon	2 tablespoons flour	½ pint stock
bouquet of herbs		salt and pepper

Chop the onions and carrots and put into a saucepan with the butter. Put in the herbs and simmer. Add the flour to thicken, then add the tomato purée and the stock. Season. Simmer, take out the herbs and add the sherry. Sieve and put into a double saucepan to keep hot, for once the sherry has been added the sauce should not boil again. Make spinach purée in the usual way and serve with bread croûtons.

REDONDO DE TERNERA AL HORNO

Roast Round of Veal

2 lb. best veal	bay leaf	1 gill white wine
4 oz. lard	1 small can tomato	parsley
2 onions	purée or 4 tomatoes	salt and pepper
2 carrots		2 rashers bacon

Wrap the bacon rashers around the veal, place in a roasting tin, add the sliced onions, carrots and the lard, and roast in a moderately hot oven. When half done, add the wine, bay leaf, sliced tomatoes or purée. Cover the roasting tin and return to a moderate oven, finish cooking, sieve the sauce. Season and re-heat. Carve the meat and place on a serving dish, garnish with fried potatoes and parsley and serve the sauce separately.

TERNERA ENCEBOLLADA

Veal With Onions

2 lb. veal	1 clove garlic	3 cloves
3 oz. margarine or	2 onions	salt and pepper
lard		1 gill white wine

Melt the fat in a saucepan. Brown the veal a little on all sides; add the whole onions, cloves, garlic and the wine. Season. Cover and cook on a slow heat till tender. Then take the garlic, cloves and onions out of the sauce, which should be thick and tasty. Serve with boiled potatoes.

TERNERA EN CAZUELA CON BERENJENAS

Veal Casserole with Aubergines

2 lb. veal	2 oz. ham or bacon	herbs (thyme, bay
1 onion	4 aubergines (egg	leaf, marjoram)
2 tomatoes	plant)	1 gill white wine
1 can little peas	olive oil	salt and pepper
(*petits pois*)	flour	pinch cinnamon

Fry chopped veal in oil, with chopped ham or bacon, add chopped onion and the herbs. When well done, add the tomatoes, cinnamon, salt and pepper and the white wine. Simmer and if necessary add a little water. Add the *petits pois* when almost ready to serve. In the meanwhile wash and slice the aubergines, dip in flour and fry in oil. Serve separately as the veal is served in the casserole in which it is cooked. Of course, other vegetables can replace the aubergines if they are out of season. Serve with boiled rice.

CHULETAS DE TERNERA À LA ZINGARA

Veal Cutlets Zingara

6 SERVINGS

6 veal cutlets	6 slices boiled ham	olive oil
butter	1 pint Spanish sauce	salt and pepper
1 pint stock	(see p. 568)	

Fry the cutlets in butter and 1 tablespoon of olive oil. This mixture prevents the meat from sticking to the pan. When brown on both sides, strain off the fat. Add stock and the Spanish sauce and simmer for 30 minutes. In the meanwhile, fry the ham in the butter and oil, take the cutlets out of the sauce, roll in the slices of ham. Place on serving dish, pour the sauce over and serve immediately.

GIUSADO DE TERNERA

Veal Ragoût

1 lb. lean veal	bunch of herbs	½ pint stock
lard or margarine	1 onion	1 gill white wine
4 rashers bacon	4 oz. mushrooms	nutmeg

Cut the veal into little squares. Fry the bacon, onion and herbs in fat, add more fat and cook the meat slightly to seal. Add the wine, the mushrooms, the stock and a little grated nutmeg and simmer with the lid on till the meat is tender (about 1 hour). Serve with new potatoes and *petits pois*.

ESCALOPAS DE TERNERA RELLENAS

Stuffed Veal Cutlets

4 large veal cutlets	breadcrumbs	oil or fat for frying
1 egg, beaten		4 large slices cheese

Slice the veal cutlets open, leaving one end uncut. Choose a cheese that melts (like American cheese). Open the cutlet and slip a piece of cheese inside. Coat with egg and breadcrumbs and deep fry till golden. This dish, so simple to make, is very tasty. Serve with fried potatoes and vegetables.

LOMO DE CERDO RELLENO

Stuffed Pork Cutlets

As above, only use lean pork instead of veal.

PIERNA DE CARNERO CON GUISANTES
À LA ESPAÑOLA

Leg of Lamb with Peas, Spanish Style

Rub the leg of lamb over with garlic, olive oil and rosemary. Put into the roasting pan with a little oil, salt and pepper and roast, first in a hot oven, then somewhat lower. Make a sauce with the liquid in the pan, mixed with a little tomato sauce, chopped smoked ham and tender *petits pois*. Serve very hot with roast potatoes.

TOURNEDOS CON DELICIAS DE QUESO

Tournedos Steaks with Cheese Balls

6 SERVINGS

6 tournedos steaks	3 eggs	olive oil
1 gill Spanish sauce	3½ oz. grated cheese	salt and pepper
(see p. 568)	breadcrumbs	6 slices white bread

Rub the steaks with oil and grill in the usual way; place each on a slice of fried bread (this should be well drained and not greasy). For the cheese balls; beat the white of eggs stiffly, add the grated cheese, salt and pepper. Roll into little balls, which are first dipped into the beaten egg yolks and then into breadcrumbs. Deep fry. Make a little heap o these golden balls in the centre of the platter with the tournedos steaks all around. Pour a little Spanish sauce over the meat and serve immediately.

TERNERA RELLENA

Stuffed Veal

6 SERVINGS

3 lb. breast of veal	1 clove garlic	½ pint sherry or white
2 lb. minced pork	1 onion	wine
8 oz. minced smoked	1 egg	salt and pepper
ham	1 tablespoon chopped	olive oil or butter
4 oz. soft breadcrumbs	parsley	1 gill milk
	½ pint stock	

Soak the bread in milk and squeeze, then beat together with egg and chopped parsley, salt and pepper. Put into a large bowl and mix with wine or sherry; fold in the minced pork and ham. The best way to mix this filling is with your hands. Lay the breast of veal flat on the table. Spread the filling evenly, not too near the edges. Roll tightly and tie in the centre and at both ends with white string or thread. Into a large saucepan put the oil or butter and slightly fry a chopped onion and garlic clove. Put the meat roll into the hot fat and slightly brown on each side, then add the stock and white wine and slowly simmer for 2 hours. Watch to make sure there is sufficient liquid, otherwise add more stock, wine and some butter. Snip the string off and serve in its sauce.

BISTECS À LA ANDALUZA

Andalusian Beefsteaks

4 lean steaks for	3 tomatoes or 1 small	4 large tomatoes
grilling	can purée	4 oz. cooked rice
2 aubergines	olive oil	butter
4 oz. ham		2 onions

Rub the steaks with olive oil on both sides. Grill and season. Garnish with baked aubergines stuffed with ham, large tomatoes stuffed with rice and a sauce made with fried onions and tomatoes and the gravy from the steaks mixed with a little butter.

TOURNEDOS À LA CREMA

Creamed Tournedos

6 SERVINGS

6 beef tournedos	salt and pepper	1 teaspoon chopped
4 tablespoons oil	1 gill milk	parsley
1 onion	1 egg yolk	juice 1 lemon
1 tablespoon flour		butter

105. Lancashire Hot Pot, Britain (p.97)

106. Fat Rascals, Britain (p.123)

107. Swiss Apple Sponge (p.581)

Fry the tournedos in oil, season and keep warm while preparing the sauce. Fry the finely chopped onion in butter, add the flour and the milk, stir till thick and add the beaten yolk, the parsley and the lemon juice, season and pour over the tournedos. Serve with boiled potatoes.

ESTOFADO DE VACA À LA CATALANA

Catalan Beef Stew

2 lb. stewing steak	1 small can tomato	garlic sausage or
1 onion	purée	smoked ham
8 new potatoes	½ pint red wine	salt and pepper
lard or oil	bouquet of herbs	1 clove garlic

Fry the sliced onion and the garlic in lard or oil. When the onion is golden, remove the garlic, put in the meat, cut into 1-inch squares, fry till well browned, then pour the whole into a deep casserole or saucepan with a lid, add the herbs, the wine and the tomato purée, diluted with a few tablespoons of boiling water and simmer for 30 minutes. Add more wine and continue to simmer, adding 8 new potatoes, a few pieces of garlic sausage or smoked ham and simmer till done. Serve hot in the same casserole.

FIDEOS À LA CAZUELA

Chops and Spaghetti in Casserole

8 SERVINGS

2 lb. thick, short	2 oz. cheese	1 chilli pepper
spaghetti	½ coffee spoon saffron	2 cloves garlic
1 lb. Butifarra	1 pint stock	1 teaspoon parsley
(garlic sausage)	2 onions	2 tablespoons cocoa
2 lb. pork chops	2 tomatoes	salt and pepper
2 lb. pork sausages	grated cheese	2 oz. toasted hazel
2 oz. fat or butter		nuts

In a large casserole melt the fat or butter, fry the chopped onions and garlic with the pork chops and the pork sausages; when brown add the sliced pepper (taking care to extract the seed), the chopped tomatoes and the garlic sausage. Add stock, salt and the chopped parsley. Dilute the saffron in a little of the liquid and add. Simmer for 20 minutes, then add the spaghetti. Pound the hazel nuts in a mortar, mix in the cocoa and add (this addition might seem strange, but it gives a delicious taste to the sauce and neutralises the fat). Boil till the spaghetti is tender and serve in the same casserole. Garnish with grated cheese.

GUISO DE VACA CON COÑAC

Beef Stew with Brandy

6 SERVINGS

2 lb. best fillet of beef	4 oz. mushrooms	1 gill cream
2 tablespoons butter	1 small can tomato	salt and pepper
2 tablespoons brandy	purée	paprika
	2 pints stock	

Melt the butter in a large casserole and brown the meat quickly on all sides. Pour in the brandy, set alight and shake the pan till the flame dies out. Pour in the stock, mixed with the tomato purée and chopped mushrooms. Stir, season and simmer for a few minutes, then add the cream, stir and put on the lid. Cook gently for 2 hours. Make sure from time to time that the stew is not dry, in which case add a little more stock.

FABADA

Pork and Beans

4 pork chops	tomato sauce	1 lb. haricot beans
2 large slices cooked	(see p. 333)	4 slices black pudding
ham	olive oil for frying	1 clove garlic
	4 slices Spanish	
	sausage	

Heat the olive oil in the pan with the garlic clove. When golden, remove the garlic and quickly fry the chops until they are golden on both sides. Boil the haricot beans (previously soaked overnight) and put them into a deep casserole, moistened with a little tomato sauce. Add the chops, ham, black pudding and sausage. Cover and cook in a moderate oven for about 15 minutes.

LENGUAS CON SALSA DE ALMENDRAS

Tongue with Almond Sauce

6 small lamb's tongues	juice 1 lemon	2 oz. chopped or
1 onion	2 large tablespoons	ground almonds
1 carrot	flour	1 oz. seedless raisins
1 bay leaf	stock from the tongues	salt and pepper
	2 oz. butter or lard	

Clean the tongues well, boil in salt water with onion, bay leaf and carrot. When they are tender, melt the fat in a casserole and stir in the flour, stir and simmer, add the stock from the tongues and bring to boil, stirring to avoid lumps. Add the ground almonds and the raisins and season with lemon juice, salt and pepper. Cut the tongues in half lengthwise, place them in a warm serving dish, pour the sauce over them and serve with boiled potatoes and vegetables.

PATO À LA ANDALUZA

Andalusian Duck

6 SERVINGS

1 duck	pinch black pepper	1 tablespoon vinegar
8 oz. chick peas	butter	or 2—3 tablespoons
2 onions	4 tomatoes	wine
1 clove garlic		1 chilli pepper

Soak and boil the chick peas in the usual way. Separately boil the duck, with a sliced onion, in water. Carve when done. In the meanwhile crush 1 onion, garlic clove, tomatoes, chilli pepper and a little black pepper in a mortar. Put some butter into a large saucepan and fry the crushed onion etc., pour in the chick peas with half their water and the vinegar or white wine, simmer, and season to taste. Add the duck and simmer for 1 minute. Serve with vegetables prepared separately.

PATO CON ACEITUNAS

Duck with Olives

5 TO 6 SERVINGS

1 tender duckling	1 pint stock or water	4 dozen olives
8 oz. butter	½ pint white wine or	chopped parsley
2 oz. flour	Madeira	salt and pepper
4 onions	1 large can tomato	oil
6 carrots	purée	

Melt the butter with a spoonful of oil in a large saucepan, put in the duck, well cleaned and washed, together with sliced onions and carrots. Cook till golden on all sides (about 20 minutes). Take care not to break the skin, so the duck does not lose its juice, and that the butter does not burn. When golden, take the duck out and put aside. Slowly add the flour to the butter, stirring to smooth paste, add the wine and the tomato purée (the purée can be diluted with a tablespoon of hot water or stock), stir well and replace the duck in the pan. Add parsley and season, add the stock, but do not make the sauce too liquid. Simmer for about 1 hour. Before serving, add the stoned olives to the sauce. These should first be immersed in hot water for a few minutes so they are not cold, but they must not boil.

PATO ALCAPARRADA

Duck With Caper Sauce

6 SERVINGS

1 duck	3 oz. stoned olives	2 oz. blanched
2 onions	and raisins	almonds
4 oz. butter	1 oz. capers	4 tomatoes
water	salt	

Wash duck well and boil in water, with an onion and salt. Carve into pieces and take off the bone. Melt the butter in a saucepan, chop an onion and fry with peeled tomatoes. When done, add the pieces of duck and simmer. Add the almonds, capers, stoned olives and stoned raisins. Add sufficient hot stock from the duck just to cover. Simmer till most of the stock has evaporated and the remaining sauce is thick. Serve hot.

JUDIAS VERDES À LA LIONESA

Green Beans Lionesa

2 lb. green beans	3 oz. butter	chopped parsley
	2 small onions	salt and pepper
	4 oz. smoked ham	

String, cut and wash the beans well. Boil in salt water for 20 minutes, drain and dry. Chop the onions and ham, fry gently in butter till golden. Add the beans, shaking in the pan so they do not stick. Sprinkle with chopped parsley, serve in a heated dish.

COLIFLOR CON MAYONESA

Cauliflower with Mayonnaise

1 cauliflower	6 olives	mayonnaise
2 hard-boiled eggs		(see p. 263)

Cook and drain the cauliflower. Cool and place in a serving dish in small pieces. Garnish with chopped stoned olives, chopped hard-boiled eggs and cover with mayonnaise.

ALCACHOFAS GUISADAS À LA ESPAÑOLA

Artichokes Cooked in the Spanish Style

6 TO 8 SERVINGS

6 to 8 artichokes	1 gill (scant) vinegar	salt and pepper
3 tablespoons oil	1 gill stock	lemon juice
1 gill (scant) white	½ tablespoon flour	1 clove garlic
wine	bay leaf	3 onions

If the artichokes are big, take off all the leaves, and if they are small and tender only take off the outer leaves, and cut off the ends. Rinse well in water and lemon juice, drain and dry. Slightly fry finely chopped onions in the oil and put in the artichokes, but do not allow the onion to get brown. Add vinegar and wine and simmer till the liquid has almost evaporated, leaving only about 3 tablespoons. Add the stock, garlic clove and a bay leaf, cover and simmer till the artichokes are tender (about 30 minutes). Thicken the sauce with a little flour, stirring well to avoid lumps. Cook for another 2 minutes. Take out the bay leaf and the garlic and serve immediately.

ALCACHOFAS À LA CUSSY

Artichokes Stuffed and Fried

6 SERVINGS

6 large artichokes	1¼ oz. butter	breadcrumbs
2 chicken livers	water, with lemon	oil
2 eggs	juice added	nutmeg
1 tablespoon flour	1 gill milk	salt and pepper

Take the outer leaves off the artichokes, leaving the heart and a few of the tender leaves encircling it. Immediately submerge in the lemon water to retain colour. Boil in the lemon water with salt. Make a Béchamel sauce with 1 oz. butter and milk (see p. 256). Season with salt, pepper and nutmeg and add the chopped chicken livers; simmer and add the yolk of 1 egg; simmer until sufficiently thick, then season. Fill the artichokes with the mixture. Sprinkle the artichokes with flour, dip into beaten egg and then into breadcrumbs. Deep fry in oil. Drain well and serve with slices of lemon.

ALCACHOFAS DE JERUSALEM AL GRATIN

Jerusalem Artichokes Au Gratin

4 cups diced boiled Jerusalem artichokes	mushroom sauce (Béchamel with mushrooms added see p. 256)	6 oz. breadcrumbs 2 oz. melted butter

Butter a baking dish. Place the artichokes in it. Pour the sauce over the artichokes. Fry the breadcrumbs in butter till golden and sprinkle over. Heat in a moderate oven.

ALCACHOFAS À LA SEVILLANA

Seville Artichokes

12 artichokes	½ teaspoon saffron	1 lemon
8 oz. new potatoes	½ tablespoon flour	dash of vinegar
oil for frying	stock	salt
	3 cloves garlic	

Peel the leaves off the artichokes leaving the hearts only; submerge in lemon juice and water to keep white. Fry the garlic in oil till golden; take out of oil. In the meanwhile peel the potatoes. Toast the saffron by putting it into a hot oven for a few minutes. Pound the garlic and the saffron in a mortar with salt, a few drops of water or stock and vinegar. Take the artichokes out of the lemon water and drain. Put them into the oil in which the garlic has been fried, together with the new potatoes, and simmer; add the flour mixed with 1 tablespoon stock and the garlic and saffron paste. Mix well and cover to simmer slowly till tender, but taking care that the artichokes and potatoes remain whole.

BERENJENAS SALTEADAS

Aubergines Sautés

6 SERVINGS

1 gill oil	1 tablespoon stock	2 tomatoes or 1 small
1 onion	salt and pepper	can
	6 aubergines	

Fry the chopped onion in oil; when golden add the aubergines sliced into large rounds, simmer for 5 minutes, then add the stock and the tomatoes. Season, cover and simmer very slowly until done.

CALABACINES AL HORNO

Baked Courgettes

6 SERVINGS

6 courgettes	1 clove garlic	salt and pepper
olive oil		breadcrumbs

Take 6 medium-sized courgettes: clean carefully and cut off stem end. Cut in half. Rub round a baking dish with the garlic clove, then place courgettes in a dish with 2 tablespoons oil. Season with salt and pepper and sprinkle a little oil over the top. Bake in a medium oven till tender. Baste with the oil, sprinkle with breadcrumbs and brown in oven. Serve hot.

ESPARRAGOS SEVILLANOS

Asparagus Seville Style

Clean the asparagus and cut off the hard ends. Fry a garlic clove in oil together with a slice of bread. Take the garlic and the bread out of the oil and put in the asparagus with a little hot water. Simmer till tender. Season with salt. In the meantime crush the garlic and the bread with a little vinegar. Add a chopped hard-boiled egg and serve with the asparagus.

ESPARRAGOS MIMOSA

Asparagus Mimosa

2 lb. asparagus	1 pint vinaigrette	salt
3 hard-boiled eggs	dressing (see p. 425)	chopped parsley

Cook the asparagus in salted water till tender (canned asparagus can also be used). Drain well and arrange on a serving dish. Cut the whites of egg into thin strips and sprinkle over the tips of the asparagus. Mince or mash the yolks and sprinkle over the whites. Keep cool till required. Mix chopped parsley with the dressing and serve together.

JUDIAS VERDES À LA CASTELLANA

Castilian Green Beans

green beans	olive oil	parsley
sweet red peppers	garlic clove	salt and pepper

Cook the green beans in boiling salt water till tender. Cut up and fry the peppers in oil, together with a chopped garlic clove and chopped parsley. Drain the beans and mix with the fried peppers.

GUISANTES CON JAMÓN À LA ESPAÑOLA

Ham and Peas in the Spanish Style

8 SERVINGS

2 lb. peas	1 onion	oil
(petits pois)	1 lettuce	salt and pepper
2½ lb. ham		1 carrot

Fry the finely chopped onion and the carrot till golden; add the chopped ham and the chopped lettuce and the peas. If canned or frozen peas are used not much cooking time is required. If fresh peas, cook for about 20 minutes. Simmer till all the vegetables are tender and serve separately with meat or eggs.

567

SALSA ESPAÑOLA

Spanish Sauce

3 pints stock	salt and pepper	2 oz. butter
4 oz. ham	2 onions	1 tablespoon chopped
4 oz. beef	2 tomatoes, or 1 small	parsley
1 gill sherry	can	1 tablespoon flour
1 sweet red pepper		bay leaf

Melt the butter and gradually add the flour, stir with a wooden spoon, add the chopped onions, chopped parsley, bay leaf, pepper and stock. Put the beef and ham in and cook slowly for 2 hours. Add the sherry and the tomatoes. Simmer for a little while and serve hot.

SALSA CHAUD-FROID

Chaud-froid Sauce

There are quite a number of sauces that come under the category 'chaud-froid' and the story goes that a famous chef put a cold sauce on a hot dish, thus combining the hot and the cold. Pleased with the originality and success of this new experiment, he put hot sauces on a cold dish—it was still 'chaud-froid'. Here are the two most famous of these sauces:

CHAUD-FROID BLANCO

White Chaud-froid

1 gill good stock	1 gill white wine	salt and pepper
	$\frac{1}{4}$ pint thick cream	

Boil the stock with the wine for a few minutes, allow to cool and beat in the cream. Season. Serve with chicken or veal.

CHAUD-FROID VERDE

Green Chaud-froid

$\frac{1}{2}$ pint rich stock	1 tablespoon capers	salt and pepper
8 oz. spinach purée	1 gill thick cream	1 sour-sweet gherkin

Cook the capers, the gherkin and the spinach in a little water, season with salt and pepper and mash well together. Add the stock, put through a sieve and add the cream.

TARTA DE CEBOLLA

Onion Tart

8 oz. flour	3 oz. fat	¼ pint milk
1 teaspoon baking powder	lemon juice	3 rashers streaky bacon
pinch salt	6 large onions	2 eggs

Make a short pastry with the flour sieved with baking powder, fat, cold water and a few drops of lemon juice. Cut the bacon into pieces and fry. Finely mince the onions and fry in the bacon without browning, then cool and drain. Mix well with the eggs beaten up in the milk, and season. Line a baking dish with the pastry and pour in the onion filling. Bake in a hot oven about 30 minutes, when the pastry will be done and the onion mixture golden brown.

TARTA DE LEGUMBRES

Mixed Vegetable Tart

pastry as above	chopped cooked leeks or onions	sliced cooked potatoes
spinach purée	margarine or butter	grated cheese

Line a baking dish with pastry as above and fill with a layer of spinach purée, then a layer of chopped cooked leeks or onions and finally a layer of sliced, cooked potatoes. Dot with a little margarine or butter and sprinkle a thin layer of grated cheese. Bake in a quick oven until the pastry is done and the top nicely browned.

PASTEL DE TOMATE

Tomato Flan

2 SERVINGS

2 lb. tomatoes or 1 large can	1 egg	short pastry (see p. 100)
2 onions	parsley	salt and pepper
4 rashers streaky bacon	2 courgettes or small marrows	mixed herbs
	1 clove garlic	sugar
	grated cheese	

Line a baking dish with short pastry and bake for 5 minutes. In the meanwhile fry the bacon and the chopped onions and garlic in the bacon fat. Remove the bacon when crisp. Add the peeled and sliced tomatoes, 1 tablespoon chopped parsley, the sliced courgettes, a pinch of mixed herbs, salt and pepper and a pinch of sugar. Simmer until soft, add the chopped bacon, pour the mixture into the pastry. Beat the egg and pour on top, sprinkle with grated cheese and bake in a hot oven till the pastry is done. Serve hot.

CHURROS

Fried Batter

½ pint water	pinch salt	sugar
1 oz. butter	2 eggs	icing sugar
8 oz. flour		fat or oil for frying

Put the water into a large saucepan and when warm add the butter, a pinch of salt and a little sugar. Stir and when it comes to the boil carefully add the flour, stirring all the time with a wooden spoon to a smooth batter. Remove from the heat and beat in the eggs, stir till smooth. Heat the oil till it smokes, force the mixture through a funnel into the hot oil and deep fry till golden. Cut the churros with scissors into sticks and drain. Sprinkle with icing sugar and eat hot or cold. Churros at fairs and in the streets are usually made without eggs.

SOUFFLÉ FRIO DE FRESA

Cold Strawberry Soufflé

3 heaped dessert-spoons castor sugar	1 dessertspoon kirsch	greased soufflé mould
	3 egg whites	6 oz. strawberries

Whisk the egg whites until very stiff. Rub the strawberries through a sieve and stir with the sugar and kirsch. Fold the egg whites into this mixture and beat gently until blended. Tip into the buttered mould. Bake for 3½ minutes in a moderate oven. This soufflé should not drop when cold.

SPANISH FRITTERS

4 slices white bread	cinnamon	butter for frying
1 pint thin cream	1 oz castor sugar	apricot jam
	1 blade mace	

Cut the crusts off the bread and cut into fingers 1 inch wide. Soak the fingers in the cream flavoured with mace, cinnamon and sugar for 10 minutes. Drain and fry quickly in the butter. Serve with hot sauce made by heating the jam with a little water and sieving it.

BUÑUELITOS DE SAN JOSÉ

St. Joseph's Day Fritters

4 oz. rice	1 gill sweet sherry	breadcrumbs
1 pint milk	1 lemon	fat or oil for frying
vanilla or vanilla essence	3 eggs	icing sugar
		2 oz. flour

Boil the rice in sweetened milk and vanilla for about 20 minutes, when it should be tender and have absorbed all the milk. Flavour with grated lemon rind. When cool, beat in 2 whole eggs, the juice of ½ lemon and the flour. Add sweet sherry. Mix well and leave for several hours in a cool place, preferably the refrigerator. Roll into little balls or croquettes. Cover in beaten egg and breadcrumbs and deep fry in hot fat or oil. Drain well and sprinkle with icing sugar.

PASTELITOS DE MIEL

Honey Fritters

8 oz. flour	1 coffee spoon baking	oil for frying
3 tablespoons sweet	powder	honey
wine	2 eggs	3 tablespoons sugar

Pour the flour into a bowl leaving a well in the centre for the beaten eggs, sugar and baking powder. Mix these ingredients well into the flour, add wine and knead into a smooth dough. Roll out thinly and cut into 3-inch strips about 1 inch wide. Deep fry these biscuits, drain well and dip into honey. Leave to cool.

CHOCOLATE CREAMS

8 oz. sugar	6 egg yolks	4 oz. plain chocolate
	¼ pint water	

Melt the sugar in the water, boil to a thick syrup. Cool and add to the beaten egg yolks. Pour into small greased fireproof dishes, bake in a slow oven until set (about 45 minutes). Cool the dishes and pour the melted chocolate over. Serve chilled.

CHESTNUT CAKES

3 eggs	3½ oz. butter	2 tablespoons apricot
4 oz. sugar	4 oz. almonds	jam
3 oz. flour		8 oz. chestnut purée

Beat the eggs and the sugar together over a pan of hot water until they are white, add the sifted flour. Melt 3 oz. butter and fold it into the mixture. Bake in a greased Swiss roll tin in a moderately hot oven for 25 minutes. Put on a rack and when cool cut into rounds with a pastry cutter. Chop the almonds, put in a frying pan with ½ oz. butter, stir them about over a low flame until browned. Spread the jam over the sponge cake rounds, cover with chopped almonds. Pipe chestnut purée on the top.

QUINCE SQUARES

quinces   sugar

Wash the quinces. Cut into pieces and remove the stones. Steam until tender, then sieve them. Boil the purée with the same weight of sugar in a preserving pan, stirring continuously until it thickens and comes away from the sides. Pour into shallow tins and leave in a very cool oven to harden. Cut into 1-inch squares and keep in a tin, wrapped in greaseproof paper.

TARTA VALENCIANA

Valencia Pudding

3 eggs   4 oz. toasted almonds   8 oz. boiled, mashed
5 oz. sugar   (ground)   potatoes
                       1½ tablespoons butter

Beat the egg yolks with the sugar, mix with the potato purée and ground almonds and knead to a dough. Beat the whites stiffly and fold in. Pour the batter into a greased baking dish and bake in a very hot oven for 10—15 minutes.

POSTRE DE NARANJA

Orange Cups

4 oranges   1 dessertspoon   ¾ pint thick cream
½ pint orange juice   cornflour   4 candied cherries or
2 egg yolks   4 oz. granulated   peel
                         sugar

Cut the top off the oranges about a third of the way down, leaving a nice cup. Extract the flesh and juice. Blend cornflour with juice, add egg yolks and sugar. Beat over double saucepan *(bain-marie)* until it thickens. Pour into orange cups. Chill and decorate with whipped cream and candied peel.

NOUGAT

1 lb. almonds   12 oz. castor sugar   butter

Blanch, skin and chop the almonds. Melt a little butter, fry the almonds in it until brown. Pound the almonds with half of the sugar, add the rest of the sugar gradually. Cook slowly in a heavy saucepan, stirring all the time, until the mixture thickens. Pour into shallow tins lined with rice paper. Cut into small rectangular pieces when set.

TORTA DE MIEL Y NUECES

Honey and Nut Roll

8 oz. flour	1 tablespoon	chopped walnuts
4 oz. butter	castor sugar	and hazelnuts
pinch salt	1 egg	juice ½ lemon
honey		2 tablespoons sherry

Make a rich short pastry as follows. Rub the butter into the flour, add salt and castor sugar. Add the beaten egg yolk, lemon juice and sherry to make into a stiff paste. If necessary add a little cold water. Roll into a strip. Brush with honey and sprinkle with the chopped nuts (chopped candied peel can also be added). Roll and sprinkle with a little more castor sugar. Bake in a moderate oven for about 20 minutes.

VISITAS

Little Cakes for Visitors

2 DOZEN

7 oz. icing sugar	3 oz. butter	4 egg whites
½ oz. flour	2½ oz. ground almonds	sugar for caramel

Cream the butter and the sugar. Beat whites stiffly, fold in, beat well and add the ground almonds and the flour. Bake in individual shapes or paper cups in a moderate oven. When cold, glaze with caramel (boiled sugar).

BIZCOCHO DE ALMENDRA

Almond Cake

½ oz. butter	5 oz. ground almonds	6 eggs
5 oz. sugar		3 oz. biscuit crumbs

Beat the yolks with the sugar till firm and frothy. Beat the whites to a stiff snow and fold in. Add the biscuit crumbs and ground almonds and beat well. Pour the mixture into a well buttered baking tin and bake in a moderate oven for 15 minutes.

BIZCOCHOS DE AVELLANA

Hazelnut Biscuits

8 oz. ground	juice ½ lemon	2 oz. flour
hazelnuts	3 oz. castor sugar	1 tablespoon grated
1 egg		lemon rind

Pound the hazelnuts with the sugar in a mortar to a fine paste, add the flour and lemon rind. Beat the egg and lemon juice together and add to the mixture; place teaspoonfuls on a greased baking sheet and bake in a moderate oven until the little biscuits are brown and crisp.

TORTA DE QUESO

Spanish Cheese Cake

short pastry (see p. 100)   vanilla essence   icing sugar
3 eggs   1 lb. cottage cheese   2 tablespoons
4 oz. sugar   1 tablespoon candied   seedless raisins
   peel

Beat the eggs till they are frothy, separately whisk the cheese until creamy and mix; add vanilla essence and the sugar. Beat everything well together and finally add the seedless raisins and chopped peel. Grease a cake dish, line with the short pastry and fill with the mixture. Bake in a very hot oven for about 10 minutes, then reduce the heat to moderate and continue to bake for about 20 minutes until the cheese filling has set. When done, leave inside the open oven to cool gradually. Serve when cold.

MANZANAS RELLENAS

Stuffed Apples

6 SERVINGS

6 large cooking apples   4 oz. sugar   2 tablespoons icing
   2 eggs   sugar

Scoop out the core and some of the flesh of the apples, sprinkle with a little sugar and put 2 tablespoons water in the pan so they do not catch. Bake until half done. Cook the sugar in 1 cup water till brown. Beat up the yolks and add. Pour this custard into the apples and bake in a medium hot oven till the custard has set. Beat the whites stiffly, cover the apples with this and sprinkle with icing sugar. Put back in the oven till slightly golden and serve hot.

VOL-AU-VENT CON CREMA

Cream Vol-au-Vent

8 vol-au-vent cases   4 eggs   7 oz. sugar
   (see p. 200)   2 oz. flour   vanilla
   1 pint milk

Whisk the eggs lightly, beat in the flour and sugar until thoroughly blended. Bring the milk to the boil, add a drop of vanilla, gradually beat into egg mixture. Pour into a double saucepan and cook slowly, stirring continuously until the custard thickens. When cold, but not set, pour into the vol-au-vent cases.

CREMA DE MALAGA

Malaga Cream

5 SERVINGS

12 egg yolks	4 glasses Malaga	6 oz. sugar
	(or sweet white wine)	1 teaspoon cinnamon

Beat the yolks till frothy, beat in the Malaga wine, together with the sugar and the cinnamon. Continue to beat over a low fire till the froth has risen considerably. Serve immediately in individual glasses.

CREMA DE COCO

Coconut Cream

1 coconut	4 oz. sugar	4 sponge cakes
	4 egg yolks	

Drain the milk from the coconut. Grate the coconut flesh. Cook the milk and the grated coconut in a double saucepan for 30 minutes. Strain through fine muslin. Beat the egg yolks until thick, whisk in the strained coconut. Cook in a double saucepan until the mixture thickens. Pour over the sponge cakes and leave to cool.

BORRACHITOS

Tipsy Cakes

3½ oz. butter	1 teaspoon vanilla	1 teaspoon baking
2 oz. sugar	essence	powder
3 eggs	5 oz. flour	sugar to glaze

Cream the butter with the sugar, add the vanilla essence. Beat the yolks and mix with the flour and baking powder. Beat the whites stiffly and add, mixing well. Pour the batter into small greased tins or paper cups. Bake in a hot oven. Allow to cool and pour melted sugar over them.

SABAYON DE NARANJA

Orange Cream

6 SERVINGS

2 oz. sugar	½ pint orange juice	½ pint milk
5 eggs	with juice ½ lemon	

Put the sugar in a double saucepan *bain-marie*, beat up the yolks of 4 eggs together with the orange juice and add to the sugar. Beat 1 whole egg with the milk and add. Beat all the time over the fire till it has turned into a thick, frothy cream.

GRANIZADO DE CAFÉ

Coffee Sorbet

1 tablespoon Benedictine or other sweet liqueur	sugar	1 small pot black coffee

Sweeten the coffee while it is hot. Allow to get cold, mix with the liqueur, and pour into the freezing tray in the refrigerator. Allow to freeze, 1 hour will suffice. Beat up with a fork and serve in individual glasses.

BLANCO Y NEGRO

Black and White

As above, leaving room in the glass for a tablespoon of vanilla ice or frozen milk.

GRANIZADO DE LIMON

Lemon Sorbet

As coffee sorbet, but add lemon juice and sugar and a dash of syrup.

JEREZ

Sherry

No book on Spanish cooking would be complete without a mention of sherry—and what better way of ending a Spanish meal than with one of the rich, sweet varieties?

Sherry is made from the white grapes that grow in the south of Spain. The name is taken from the Andalusian town of *Jerez*, the centre of the sherry distilleries. There are many wines called sherry, but there is no other wine in the world quite like the real Jerez. It is made from the very best of the good wine of each vintage and kept for many years to mature in huge barrels and blended with the best wines from other years. There is the dry sherry, a pale amber colour, the medium dry, slightly darker and the very sweet which is dark and rich, known as Oloroso or Amoroso.

And the Spanish toast is: SALUD Y PESETAS!

108. Omelette with Ham, Potatoes and Cheese, Britain (p.107)

109. Ingredients for Fondue, Switzerland (p.578)

SWISS COOKING

Musia Soper

You can spend many a happy holiday in Switzerland and enjoy the capacity of the Swiss for looking after you magnificently in all classes of hotels, without realising that there is a typical Swiss cuisine with its own specialities. In the hotels and restaurants you will get an even mixture of French, German and Italian dishes cooked to perfection. Naturally enough, as this lovely little country draws its population from these three language groups. On top of that it draws tourists from all over the world and caters for them in the most masterly manner.

Behind the international hotels and the large tourist industry there beats the normal rhythm of a home-loving and industrious people. Hard-working families in small villages, isolated farmers on deserted mountain slopes have to cook substantial and down-to-earth meals. Spring Chicken prepared in the Swiss way is just this kind of a meal. Its ingredients are all the kind which every Swiss housewife would find in her larder, once she bought or killed her two chickens. It makes a tasty and satisfying Sunday meal for the family—it neither costs more, nor is it more trouble to prepare than a Sunday roast and it makes a simply luscious meal.

As the Swiss are well known for their wonderful cheeses, it is only natural that they also specialise in exquisite cheese dishes and pastries. The best known among these is their fondue. Fondue in Switzerland is eaten as a communal dish, and there is no equivalent to it as an 'ice-breaker' for any party. Put a large bowl of fondue on your dining room table on a plate warmer, hand out large slices of French bread and let your guests dip into the bowl with them. In less than no time, you will find you need no further stimulants to give the party a swing, especially if you serve a little kirsch with the fondue, like the Swiss do.

FONDUE

1½ lb. grated Gruyère cheese	2 teaspoons cornflour	pepper
	4 tablespoons kirsch	nutmeg
1 pint dry white wine	1 clove garlic	French bread

In Switzerland the cheese is prepared in a special fireproof earthenware dish with a handle, called a *Caquelon*. Also, a long fondue fork is supplied for each person. Rub the inside of a chafing dish or suitable pan with garlic. Heat the wine in it then add the cheese, stirring constantly. As soon as bubbles begin to appear add the cornflour blended with the kirsch and season with a little pepper and grated nutmeg. Serve the fondue in the pan in which it was cooked, and keep it hot and slightly bubbling on a small spirit stove. Cut the bread into cubes: then everyone spears a piece of the bread on to a long fork, dips it into the fondue, turns it once or twice and eats it. The custom is that anyone who loses a piece of bread in the dish must supply the company with a bottle of wine. *(Illustrated in Plate 109.)*

FONDUE BOURGUIGNONNE

This fondue is not like the traditional Swiss fondue, but the same utensils are used. The same type of earthenware casserole or chafing dish, the spirit stove and the long fondue forks. Each person is served with 6 oz. of raw filleted steak on a plate and two long forks. A fireproof dish, half-filled with hot oil, is put on to a spirit stove set in the middle of the table. A small crust of bread is put in to prevent splashing. Everyone spears a piece of meat with a fork and fries it in the bubbling oil as long as desired. Then the piece of meat is transferred to another fork, as the first one becomes too hot, and eaten with various sauces and seasonings. This kind of fondue can have a variety of accompaniments such as: mustard, horseradish, salt and pepper, tomato sauce, cayenne pepper, béarnaise sauce, pickled onions or cucumber mixed pickles and so on.

EGGS FLORENTINE

1 lb. spinach	2 tablespoons thin	salt and pepper
4 eggs	cream	water
4 slices Swiss cheese		4 black olives

Remove the spinach leaves from the thick stalks and wash thoroughly. Do not dry them, but put into a heavy saucepan, cover with a lid and cook until soft. Drain well and chop finely or rub through a sieve. Stir in the cream, or top of the milk, add salt and pepper to taste and put into an oven dish. Poach the eggs in boiling, salted water for 5 minutes then arrange them on the spinach purée. Place a slice of cheese on each egg and put into a hot oven or under a grill until the cheese melts and turns golden brown. Garnish with olives. Serve immediately.

SWISS CHEESE SOUFFLÉ

4 oz. Gruyère cheese	1 oz. flour	3 eggs
3 tablespoons butter	¼ pint milk	salt and pepper

Grease a 7-inch soufflé dish with 1 tablespoon butter. Melt the remaining butter, stir in the flour and add the milk and a pinch of salt and pepper. Cook for 2—3 minutes, stirring constantly. Allow to cool slightly then add the yolks of the eggs and 3 oz. cheese, grated, and mix well. Whisk the egg whites until stiff, fold into the mixture and pour into the soufflé dish. Bake in a moderate oven for about 30 minutes or until the soufflé is well risen and golden brown. Just before serving, cut the rest of the cheese into very thin slices and place on top of the soufflé, and they will just begin to melt when ready. Serve the soufflé immediately, in the dish in which it was baked.

SWISS EGGS

4 eggs	salt and pepper	2½ tablespoons grated
2 tablespoons butter		cheese

Butter 4 small fireproof dishes. Put ½ tablespoon grated cheese into each dish and carefully break an egg into each one. Season with salt and pepper and put into a hot oven to bake for 10 minutes. Serve sprinkled with the remainder of the grated cheese.

BAKED BREAD AND CHEESE

Croûte Fromage

6 oz. grated Gruyère	1 egg	lemon juice
cheese	½ pint milk	½ oz. butter
	4 slices bread	salt and pepper

Beat the egg in the milk. Season with salt and pepper and a little lemon juice. Dip the bread slices in this mixture one at a time. Put alternate layers of soaked bread and grated cheese into a greased pie dish, ending with a layer of cheese. Pour the remaining milk over the dish, dot with butter and bake in a moderate oven for 20 minutes.

BERNESE DISH

Berner-Platte

2 lb. sauerkraut	1 Bernese tongue	1 onion
2 oz. beef	sausage	1 gill white wine
8 oz. bacon		1 pig's trotter

Remove the fat from the bacon, cut it into small cubes and fry with the finely chopped onion until they are lightly browned. Slice the meat. Put a layer of sauerkraut in a pan, then a layer of meat, and repeat until you have used all the ingredients, with the pig's trotter, bacon cubes and onion on top. Pour on the wine, and add enough water to cover two-thirds of the ingredients. Simmer with a tight lid on the pan for 1—2 hours. Now add the sliced sausage and cook for a further 20 minutes without the lid. Arrange the sauerkraut in a big dish and garnish with the sliced meat and sausage. Serve with potatoes.

VEAL SLICES

Piccata

8 small veal fillets	1 tablespoon lemon	1 tablespoon flour
4 oz. grated Swiss	juice	2 oz. butter
cheese	2 tablespoons milk	salt and pepper
	2 eggs	

Beat the meat into thin slices and cut round the edges. Sprinkle with lemon juice, salt and pepper and cover with flour. Mix the eggs with milk and cheese and season. Dip the veal slices into this batter and fry in butter on both sides until golden brown. Serve with spaghetti.

SPRING CHICKEN

2 spring chickens	6 oz. butter	4 medium potatoes
2 thick slices bread	8 oz. streaky bacon rashers	salt

Split the chickens into halves. Cover with bacon fat and 2 oz. butter and roast in a hot oven until tender (about 15 to 20 minutes). Cut the potatoes as for chips and fry in the rest of the butter. Fry the rest of the bacon and the bread cut into fingers in the bacon fat. Serve the chicken garnished with the potatoes, bacon and fried bread. Pour surplus bacon fat and butter over the potatoes.

SWISS APPLE SPONGE

8 oz. dessert apples	½ pint milk	3 eggs
2½ oz. blanched almonds	1½ oz. semolina	1 teaspoon cinnamon
2 oz. raisins	4 oz. butter	fine breadcrumbs
		4 oz. sugar

Heat the milk, put in the semolina, simmer for 3 minutes, stirring constantly, and then set aside to cool. Cream butter and sugar, beat the yolks of the eggs, chop 2 oz. of the almonds finely and add to the semolina mixture together with the raisins and cinnamon. Peel, core and slice apples and add to the mixture. Whisk the egg whites until stiff and fold in. Pour into a buttered 8-inch cake tin and bake in a moderate oven for 1 hour 15 minutes. Serve hot or cold, garnished with the remaining almonds. *(Illustrated in Plate 107.)*

MARZIPAN SHAPES

8 oz. ground almonds	2 egg yolks	3 tablespoons orange
8 oz. castor sugar	3 oz. icing sugar	flower water
1 egg white	butter for greasing	

Put sugar, ground almonds and 1 tablespoon orange flower water into a double saucepan and cook until the paste comes away from the sides of the pan. Cool slightly add beaten egg yolks, mix well and roll out on to a slab. Cut into squares or various shapes, sprinkle with icing sugar, put on to a well buttered baking tin and leave until next day in a warm room. Then bake in a moderate oven for 10—15 minutes. To prepare the icing, beat together the icing sugar, 1 egg white and 2 tablespoons of orange water. Spread over the marzipan shapes as soon as they are taken out of the oven. Other colours and flavours can be used according to taste.

SWISS APPLE FLAN

4 oz. margarine	6 oz. plain flour,	1 tablespoon
1 level tablespoon	sieved	water
castor sugar		

Filling:

1 lb. apples,	1 red and	little lemon juice
sweetened, cooked	1 green eating	1 tablespoon sieved
and sieved	apple	apricot jam
1 glacé cherry		

To make pastry, put margarine, sugar, 2 tablespoons flour and water in a bowl. Cream together with a fork about half a minute, until well mixed. Stir in remaining flour to form a firm dough. Knead lightly on a floured board. Roll out thinly and line a 7-inch fluted flan ring. Trim surplus pastry. Place the apple purée in the flan case. Divide the eating apples into quarters. Remove the cores but not the skins. Cut into thin slices, dipping them in lemon juice to prevent discoloration. Arrange overlapping on top of the purée, alternating red and green skins. Bake near the top of a moderately hot oven for 30—35 minutes. Brush with sieved apricot jam and decorate the centre with slices of glacé cherry. Serve hot or cold. *(Illustrated in Plate 10.)*

MUESLI

4 tablespoons rolled	4 tablespoons sweet	juice 1 lemon
oats	condensed milk	1½ gills water
4 oz. shelled walnuts	2 bananas	4 sweet apples

Soak the oats in the water overnight. Next day, wash the apples and grate into the oats. Add lemon juice and the condensed milk and mix well. Decorate each of four plates with sliced bananas and walnuts. Other fruit, such as grapes, raspberries or anything else in season, may be added. This makes a good breakfast dish. *(Illustrated in Plate 83.)*

TURKISH COOKING

Elizabeth Campbell and Musia Soper

In Turkey much of the cooking survives from Byzantine times. So when you enjoy any particular Turkish delicacy, you may think of your self as eating in the style of Byzantium!

From time immemorial, the Turks have been grilling pieces of meat on skewers. They are also said to have introduced rice from Persia, the basis for their famous pilaffs. They make imaginative use of many vegetables, such as aubergines, courgettes, peppers and beans, and also of the great variety of fish which exist in the seas around them. Garlic, spices, herbs, nuts and currants add taste and colour to many of the dishes.

In their fierce conquests of the past the Turks always managed to have a considerable effect upon the customs and cuisines of the countries they invaded. And for such a warlike people they seem to have had an exceptionally sweet tooth! The popularity of Turkish Delight in other European countries is undoubtedly a memento of one of their earlier conquests. Even today they are still very partial to extremely sweet delicacies. You will enjoy trying another of their particular favourites, the fragrantly delicious Rose Petal Jam.

ROE SAVOURY

Tarama

4 oz. dried grey mullet eggs or 8 oz. smoked cod's roe	juice 1 large lemon 1 gill olive oil	black pepper

If smoked cod's roe is being used, scoop the roe out of skin. Put this or the mullet eggs into a mortar, pound very slowly with the lemon juice and pepper, add the olive oil very slowly and pound till it forms a thick smooth paste. Serve very cold on bread and butter or hot toast.

ISTANBUL EGGS

olive oil	outside skins of onions eggs	Turkish coffee

Take as many eggs as are required, cover with an equal quantity of olive oil and Turkish coffee and add the brown skins of 2 large onions. Cover the pan and simmer very gently for ½ hour. The egg whites will be coffee coloured when done and the yolks brilliant saffron yellow. The eggs will taste like chestnuts.

PLAIN TURKISH OR GREEK PILAFF

8 oz. rice	3 oz. dripping or	1 teaspoon black
2 pints meat stock	butter	pepper
1 teaspoon salt		2 oz. melted butter

110. Lemon Meringue Pie, Britain (p.115)

111. Dutch Ring Cake (p.186)

112. Vitello Tonnato, Italy (p.384)

113. Hot Cross Buns, Britain (p.123)

114. Poulet en Casserole, France (p.237)

115. Bread and Butter Pudding, Britain (p.115)

116. Dundee Cake, Britain (p.122)

Melt the fat in a large pot, add the rice and fry for 5 minutes. Boil the stock and when boiling pour on to the frying rice; add salt and pepper. Cover the pot with a clean cloth and then clamp on the lid. Cook on a very low heat until there is no liquid left (about 50 minutes). Remove from heat, still covered, and stand for 20 minutes. Pour the melted butter over and mix well before eating.

LAMB PILAFF

10 oz. rice
1½ lb. lamb
4 oz. butter
2 onions
2 tomatoes
1 tablespoon sugar

2 oz. currants
1 oz. pine kernels
1 teaspoon chopped parsley
1 teaspoon chopped sage

½ teaspoon mixed spice
2 pints stock
1 teaspoon black pepper
2 teaspoons salt

Bone the lamb, cut the meat into small cubes and fry in half the butter until brown. Chop the onions and fry lightly in the rest of the butter. Add the rice and nuts and fry for 5 minutes, stirring all the time, then put in the currants, salt and pepper and chopped tomatoes. Pour on hot stock, put in the meat, sage, parsley and spice and mix well. Cover the pot with a clean cloth then clamp on the lid. Cook very slowly for 1 hour. When the lamb pilaff is ready, all the liquid should have been absorbed. Serve piled on a hot dish.

TURKISH LAMB STEW

2 lb. lamb, cut in 3-inch pieces
1 lb. potatoes, peeled and quartered
3 large tomatoes, peeled and sliced

1 teaspoon chopped sage
1 teaspoon chopped fennel
1 teaspoon dill
2 bay leaves
3 large onions, sliced

1 green pepper, sliced and seeded
2 cloves garlic, chopped
1½ pints meat stock
salt and pepper

Put all the ingredients in a large pot. Simmer for 2½ hours.

SKEWERED LAMB

Shish Kebab

2 lb. leg of lamb
1 large onion, grated
2 large onions sliced

4 tablespoons olive oil
1 teaspoon salt

¼ teaspoon black pepper
1 bay leaf

Beat the lamb, rub with the salt, pepper and grated onion. Cut into 1¼-inch squares. Put into a bowl and pour on the olive oil and the bay leaf; leave for 2 hours, turning occasionally. Slice the onions thinly and cut the bay leaf into pieces. Impale the meat on skewers with a slice of onion and bay leaf between each piece. Grill under a fierce heat, watching carefully.

STUFFED VINE LEAVES

Dolma

3 dozen vine leaves	2 oz. rice (cooked)	½ pint tomato juice
1 medium onion,	1½ tablespoons	salt and pepper
finely chopped	olive oil	juice 3 lemons

Throw the leaves into boiling salted water and boil for 3 minutes. Drain. Heat the oil and fry the onions till golden brown. Remove from heat. Mix the onions and the oil with the cooked rice; add salt and pepper. Put 1 teaspoon of this mixture on the smooth side of each leaf, fold up into a little parcel, squeeze in the palm of the hand. Pack the stuffed leaves tightly in a shallow fireproof dish, sprinkle with the lemon juice and pour in the tomato juice. Put a plate on top to prevent them moving about and simmer for 30 minutes. Eat cold.

THE IMAM SWOONED

Aubergines Imam Bayeldi

4 medium aubergines	2 green or red sweet	2 oz. white fresh
2 large tomatoes	peppers, seeded and	breadcrumbs
2 medium onions	finely chopped	1 gill olive oil
finely chopped	2 oz. pine kernels	salt and pepper
3 chopped cloves		2 tablespoons chopped
garlic		parsley

Do not peel the aubergines, cut off the stalks. Heat the oil in a large frying pan, cook the aubergines gently for 10 minutes. Lift them one by one out of the oil. Put the chopped onion and peppers into the oil and cook very gently for 10 minutes. Meanwhile cut the aubergines in half, longways, and scoop out the flesh without breaking the skins. Add the onions, peppers, garlic, parsley, pine kernels, breadcrumbs and quartered tomatoes to the aubergine flesh, season with salt and pepper and mix well. Fill the aubergine skins with the mixture, arrange in a shallow fireproof dish, pour over them the remaining oil in the frying pan and cook in a slow oven for 1 hour. Serve cold. It is said that the Imam (or priest) found this dish so delicious that the first time he tasted it he swooned!

PASTRY WITH CHEESE AND MEAT
Börek

8 oz. plain flour	2 tablespoons cold	3 oz. cooked minced
3 oz. melted butter	water	meat
2 eggs	2 oz. cream cheese	salt

Make a dough with the flour, a third of the butter, 1 egg and the water. Roll into 2 balls and leave for 15 minutes in a cold place. Roll each piece very thinly, spread with melted butter. Repeat until all the butter is used up. Roll out as thinly as possible into 2 rounds—paper thin is perfect. Grease a round shallow baking tin and spread one round on the bottom. Pinch it with the finger tips to crumple it. Mix the cheese, minced meat and salt well together, place on the pastry, put the other round on top, damp and seal the edges. Beat the second egg, brush the top and bake in a moderate oven for 35 minutes.

MILK PUDDING
Muhallebi

1½ pints milk	4 oz. sugar	1 oz. ground rice
1 gill water		2 oz. rice

Bring the milk and water to the boil, throw in the rice, simmer for 10 minutes. Mix the ground rice to a paste with enough milk from the pan. Add to the cooked rice and simmer for 10 minutes more. Eat cold, sprinkled with cinnamon or coarsely ground mixed nuts.

PALACE BREAD
Saray Ekmek

8 oz. honey	1 lb. crustless stale	4 oz. butter
4 oz. sugar	bread	cream

Dice the bread. Mix with the honey, sugar and butter in a saucepan over a low heat, stirring into a moist paste. Press into a shallow round dish. When cold cut like a cake. Serve with the cream.

HONEY SOUFFLÉ

6 tablespoons honey	4 eggs	1 gill cream

Separate the eggs, whip whites till stiff. Whip cream till thick. Beat the egg yolks and honey. Put in double saucepan, stir until the mixture thickens: do *NOT* boil. Cool. Fold in the whites and the cream. Serve very cold.

TURKISH DELIGHT

Rahat Lokum

2½ lb. sugar
1¼ pints water
½ teaspoon tartaric
  acid

4 oz. cornflour mixed
  to a paste in cold
  water
icing sugar

1 tablespoon rose
  water
2 oz. chopped
  pistachio nuts
almond oil

Mix the tartaric acid, rose water and cornflour paste together. Boil the sugar and water together to a thick syrup. Stir the cornflour mixture into the syrup, add the nuts. Pour into a shallow tin, greased with almond oil. Cool, dust well with icing sugar. Ease from the tin, dust with more icing sugar, cut into squares. Roll each piece in icing sugar.

ROSE PETAL JAM

Gül Receli

2 dozen roses
1 lb. castor sugar

1 tablespoon lemon
  juice

1 gill water
½ pint rose water

Choose fresh red or pink roses, pull off the petals and cut off the hard, white bases. Put the sugar into a saucepan with the lemon juice, water and rose water, bring to the boil and simmer until the sugar has dissolved. Pour over the rose petals and leave covered overnight. Next day, put into a saucepan and simmer gently, stirring all the time, for about 30 minutes or until the jam thickens. Pour into small, warmed jars and seal.

TURKISH COFFEE

coffee

sugar

water

Turkish coffee should be made in a Turkish coffee pot, one to each person. However, it can be made for 4 people in a lipped saucepan. The secret is that it must be strong, sweet and frothy.

For 4 people, take 4 teaspoons coffee, 4 teaspoons sugar and 4 coffee cups cold water. Bring to the boil, remove from the heat and stir. Bring to the boil again, remove and stir. Repeat once more, three times in all. Serve immediately while still frothy. If more cups are wanted, boil a fresh brew.

YUGOSLAV COOKING

Gordana Žunić

Yugoslavia is a South European country, part of the Balkan Peninsula, with Greece, Hungary, Austria, Rumania, Bulgaria, Albania and Italy on her borders. Here is a land of mountains, lakes, rivers and forests, with areas of rich agricultural country; her coast of Dalmatia is bounded by the Adriatic Sea and her climate is warm and sunny. This is a fascinating country of contrasts, untouched in some ways by modern living and the countries around her, but in others, affected by her neighbours and the march of time. Turkish influence from the past mingles with modern progress.

In remote villages in Yugoslavia, old customs still survive; national costumes can still be seen and time-honoured ceremonies still take place. Cooking is sometimes done out of doors over an open fire, especially for weddings and other festivities, when whole sucking-pigs and young lambs are roasted on spits.

Yugoslav cooking tends to be rich and rather highly flavoured, showing influences from the East as well as the countries around her. The representative Yugoslav dish which is bound to be met with in that country is Djuveć. Village women may be seen balancing big dishes gracefully on their heads as they take the family dinner to the bakehouse. This ancient Yugoslav dish is very simple to prepare and makes an excellent meal on its own as it contains meat, vegetables and rice all cooked together.

SERBIAN SOUR SOUP

Srpska Kisela Čorba

1 chicken	2 tomatoes	pinch paprika
1 carrot	2—3 bay leaves	2—3 sprigs parsley
1 turnip	2 tablespoons cream	1 tablespoon oil
1 parsnip	juice 1 lemon	salt and pepper
1 green pepper	1 teaspoon flour	3 pints water
	1 egg yolk	

Clean and wash chicken and cut into joints. Put into a saucepan with the water and a teaspoon of salt, cover and simmer for 1 hour. Then put into the chicken stock the vegetables and bay leaves and continue cooking until the chicken is tender. Strain the stock. Heat the oil in a pan and blend with flour and the paprika. Dilute with a little of the stock then add to the rest of the stock, stirring well. Add the juice of a lemon, heat for a few minutes, then remove from the stove. Beat the egg yolk with the cream and put into the soup. Serve sprinkled with chopped parsley.

ROE SOUP

Čorba od Ikre

8 oz. roe	1 egg yolk	1—2 bay leaves
2 tablespoons olive oil	1 parsnip	juice ½ lemon
2 tablespoons sour	1 turnip	2 tablespoons vinegar
milk	1 carrot	salt and pepper
2 teaspoons flour	1 onion	3 pints water

Put prepared vegetables into a saucepan with the water and a teaspoon of salt, and simmer for 30 minutes Meanwhile, remove the skin from the roe and leave to soak in vinegar. Heat the oil and brown the flour in it. Strain off the vegetable stock, pour on to the browned flour, and bring to the boil. Add the roe, mix well and leave to simmer for 10 minutes. Beat the egg yolk with the sour milk and lemon juice and pour into the soup before serving.

DALMATIAN EELS

Jegulje na Dalmatinski Način

2 lb. eels	2—3 cloves garlic	salt and pepper
½ lemon	3—4 sprigs parsley	water
	1 gill olive oil	

Using a sharp knife, make deep cuts to the bone along the backs of the eels. Salt and place in a fireproof dish. Sprinkle with chopped parsley, crushed garlic and pepper, and garnish with lemon slices. Add enough water to cover the eels and bake slowly for 30 minutes. Serve with boiled potatoes.

BREAM IN GARLIC

Šaran na Belom Luku

1 river bream —	1 celery stalk	2 teaspoons lemon
about 2 lb.	celery leaves	juice
1½ gills olive oil	4—5 cloves garlic	salt and pepper
3 sprigs parsley		1 gill water

Chop the parsley, the celery stalk and leaves and combine with crushed garlic, olive oil, lemon juice, 1 teaspoon of salt and ¼ teaspoon of pepper. Clean the bream and make deep, diagonal cuts to the bone on one side of the fish. Stuff the fish with some of the chopped mixture, place cut-side uppermost into a greased fireproof dish and sprinkle with the rest of the mixture. Pour in water, put into a moderate oven and bake for 30 minutes. Serve from the same dish.

PORK STUFFED WITH SAUERKRAUT

Uvijene Švinjske Šnicle s Miselim Kupusom

8 pork fillets	1 onion	salt and pepper
1 lb. sauerkraut	1 gill oil	

Chop the onion and fry lightly in 2—3 tablespoons of hot oil. Add chopped sauerkraut and fry until golden coloured. Lay out the pork fillets, flatten, sprinkle with salt and pepper, and spread with sauerkraut mixture. Roll up and tie with cotton. Heat the rest of the oil and fry the meat rolls all round until brown and tender. Put them on to a hot dish and pour over them some of the oil in which they were fried. Serve hot with mashed potatoes.

VEAL ESCALOPES WITH GARLIC

Teleče Šnicle sa Belim Lukom

4 veal escalopes	flour	salt
4 cloves garlic		oil

Salt the meat and cover in flour. Fry in hot oil on both sides until cooked, then place on a hot dish and garnish with finely chopped garlic. Pour 1 gill water into the frying pan, bring to the boil, then pour over the escalopes. Serve with salad.

MOUSAKA WITH CAULIFLOWER

Mousaka od Karfiola

2 large cauliflowers	3 eggs	flour
8 oz. minced pork	½ gill milk	salt and pepper
8 oz. minced steak	½ pint oil	water
3—4 onions		breadcrumbs

Boil the cauliflowers together with the leaves in salted water until cooked but not overdone. When drained, set aside the leaves and divide the cauliflowers into segments. Beat 1 egg and dip each segment into it, roll in breadcrumbs and fry in some of the oil until light brown. Meanwhile, chop the onions and fry lightly in the rest of the oil. Add the minced meat, season with salt and pepper and fry for 5 minutes. Arrange alternate layers of the fried cauliflower and meat in a baking dish, finishing with the cauliflower. Beat the eggs and milk, pour over the top of the cauliflower layer and put into a slow oven to bake for 30 minutes or until the top is well set. A salad may be made from the cauliflower leaves. Cut them up and add salt, pepper, olive oil, vinegar and crushed garlic.

117. Stuffed Herrings, Britain (p.92)

118. Moules à la Marinière, France (p.219)

119. Haarlem Celebration Cake, Holland (p.186)

120. Macaroons, Britain (p.127)

VEAL WITH SPINACH

Teleća Janija od Spanaca

1 lb. veal	2 tablespoons oil	salt and pepper
1 lb. spinach	2 onions	water
1 green pepper	1 tablespoon flour	½ pint sour milk

Cut the veal into neat pieces, put into a pan with enough water to cover and simmer gently until the meat is tender. Meanwhile, wash the spinach, chop finely, sprinkle with salt and leave in a strainer for the liquid to run out. Heat the oil in a frying pan, put in chopped onions and fry until golden coloured. Gradually add flour and then spinach, fry for a few minutes and add to the meat. Clean out the seeds from the pepper, cut it into slices and put in with the meat. Season with salt and pepper to taste and simmer gently until very little liquid is left. Serve with sour milk.

SERBIAN MEAT BALLS

Srpske Ćufte na Luku

8 oz. minced pork	1 egg	breadcrumbs
8 oz. minced steak	2 tablespoons oil	salt and pepper
1 lb. onions	2 slices white bread	½ pint water
8 oz. tomatoes		½ teaspoon paprika

Mix together the minced meat, egg, salt, and the bread, without crusts, previously soaked in water. Add one chopped, lightly fried onion, mix well, then make the meat balls about the size of eggs and roll in breadcrumbs. Chop the rest of the onions, fry in oil, add a little salt and pepper and the paprika and put into a casserole. Arrange the meat balls on top and place a slice of tomato on each one. Pour in a ½ pint of water, put on a cover and cook in a moderate oven for 30 minutes.

SOUTH SERBIAN LAMB

Jogurt Tava

1 large shoulder lamb	5 eggs	1 teaspoon paprika
1½ pints yoghourt	2 tablespoons fat	salt and pepper

Season the shoulder of lamb with salt and pepper and put into a baking dish greased with fat. Roast the meat until tender, basting frequently. In the meantime, beat the egg yolks then blend with the yoghourt, salt, pinch of pepper and the paprika. Whisk the egg whites until stiff and fold into the mixture. Pour over the meat and cook in the oven until the sauce thickens. Serve from the same dish.

LAMB WITH VEGETABLES AND MUSHROOMS
Jagnjetina sa Povrčem i Pečurkama

1½ lb. lamb	8 oz. mushrooms	1 chilli pepper
8 oz. rice	2 oz. grated cheese	1 teaspoon salt
1 lb. asparagus	1 tablespoon butter	1—1½ pints water

Cut lamb in 1-inch squares, put into a large saucepan and cover with the rice. Wash and prepare the asparagus and mushrooms and put into the saucepan over the rice. Add salt, butter and the chilli and pour in enough water to cover all the contents of the saucepan. Put on a lid and simmer for 40 minutes. Serve very hot.

BOSNIAN MEAT DISH
Bosanski Ionac

8 oz. beef	3—4 green peppers	2 sprigs parsley
8 oz. lamb	3—4 carrots	1 teaspoon paprika
8 oz. pork	1½ pints cooked	10—15 peppercorns
8 oz. potatoes	tomatoes or tomato	2 tablespoons vinegar
8 oz. onions	juice	1 teaspoon salt
4 cloves garlic	2 chilli peppers	water
	1 small cabbage	

Cut the meat into 1-inch squares and clean and slice the vegetables. Cut the onions into large rings and the cabbage into fairly large slices. Leave the cleaned garlic cloves whole. Lay the vegetables in a large saucepan with the meat, add the tomatoes or tomato juice, vinegar, peppercorns, garlic cloves, parsley, paprika, chillies and a teaspoon of salt. Cover completely with water, put greaseproof paper over the pan and tie it down with string or an elastic band and cook very slowly for 3½ hours.

MEAT AND VEGETABLE STEW
Djuvće

1 lb. pork or beef	1 carrot	1 teaspoon paprika
1 lb. onions	8 oz. rice	1 teaspoon chopped
3—4 sweet peppers	2 potatoes	parsley
4 oz. runner beans	2 tablespoons olive oil	salt and pepper
4 oz. peas	1 clove garlic	water
	1—2 tomatoes	

Heat oil in a large pan and put in sliced onions and the meat cut into cubes. Fry until the meat is slightly brown then add a cup of water and simmer until the meat is tender. Then add sliced runner beans, tomatoes and peppers (with seeds removed), diced potatoes and carrot, and the peas, parsley, rice and crushed garlic. Season with salt, pepper and paprika, mix well, add enough water to cover completely, put on a lid and simmer gently for 1½—2 hours. When ready, all the water should have been absorbed.

CHICKEN WITH SAUCE

Pača

1 chicken	2 tablespoons olive oil	chicken stock
4 eggs	1 clove garlic	water
3 pints sour milk	½ teaspoon paprika	salt and pepper
	2 tablespoons flour	

Cut the chicken into joints, put into a saucepan with enough water to cover, add a little salt and pepper and cook until tender but not too soft. To make the sauce, mix the flour and eggs together, blend with the sour milk and heat, stirring until smooth. Add a tablespoon of warmed olive oil and ½ pint chicken stock and cook gently, stirring with a wooden spoon, until the sauce thickens. Add more stock and crushed garlic, and continue stirring over a low heat until the sauce is the consistency of thick cream. Place the chicken on a hot dish and cover with the sauce. Dissolve the paprika in the remaining oil and sprinkle over the chicken just before serving.

GOOSE ON SAUERKRAUT

Guska na Podvarku

young goose	1 onion	1 teaspoon paprika
2 lb. sauerkraut	2 tablespoons oil	salt and pepper

Clean and dry goose, rub with salt and goose fat inside and out, and roast until nearly cooked—for about 2 hours or according to size—basting frequently. Fry chopped onion lightly in oil, then add the sauerkraut, a little salt and pepper to taste, and the paprika, and continue frying until the sauerkraut is golden. Put the sauerkraut into an oven dish, pour some goose gravy over it and place the goose on top. Roast in the oven for another 15—20 minutes.

SERBIAN SALAD

Srpska Salata

1 lb. tomatoes	1 green pepper	2 tablespoons olive oil
½ cucumber	1 onion	salt

Peel and slice cucumber and chop the onion. Sprinkle with salt and leave for about 10 minutes, then squeeze the liquid out of the cucumber with your hands. Combine the cucumber, chopped onion, sliced tomatoes and pepper. Add olive oil and mix well.

LIKA SAUERKRAUT

Lički Kupus Ribanac

2 lb. sauerkraut	1 tablespoon fat	salt and pepper
8 small pork chops	few slices bacon	1½ pints water
	1 lb. potatoes	

Lay alternate layers of sauerkraut and chops in a fireproof dish, sprinkle with salt and pepper and finish up with a top layer of sauerkraut. Place the fat and slices of bacon over the sauerkraut, pour in the water, cover and cook slowly in the oven for 1½ hours. Meanwhile, boil the potatoes in their skins, and when cooked, peel. Put the meat and sauerkraut on a dish surrounded by the potatoes.

STUFFED AUBERGINES WITH CHEESE

Modri Patlidjan Punjen Sirom

4 aubergines	1 egg	salt
8 oz. grated cheese	1 teaspoon chopped	water
4 oz. butter	parsley	
	1 onion	

Peel aubergines and boil in salted water for 10 minutes. Then strain off the water, and, when cool, cut the aubergines in half. Scoop out the inside, chop finely and mix well with grated cheese, 2 oz. butter, chopped onion, chopped parsley, an egg and salt to taste. Stuff the aubergines with this mixture and place, stuffed side up, in a baking dish greased with the remaining butter. Put into a moderate oven and bake for 20 minutes.

CORN BREAD WITH CHEESE

Razlevusa

8 oz. cottage cheese	4 eggs	¾ pint milk
4 oz. cream cheese	1 tablespoon melted	½ teaspoon salt
4 oz. Gruyère cheese	butter	
	8 oz. flour	

Cut the Gruyère cheese into small pieces and combine with the cream cheese and cottage chesee. Add milk, salt and the yolks of the 4 eggs and mix well. Add the flour gradually and when smooth blend with melted butter. Whisk the egg whites until stiff and fold into the batter. Pour into a well-greased baking tin, put into a hot oven and bake until the top is a golden brown. Slice and serve hot.

DALMATIAN RICE WITH CHEESE

Dalmatinski Pirinač sa Sirom

4 oz. rice	2—3 onions	chicken stock
6 oz. grated cheese	2 tablespoons oil	salt and pepper

Chop the onions and fry in oil. Add rice and enough chicken stock to cover. Season with salt and pepper, put on a lid simmer until the rice is tender but not overcooked. Drain the rice and mould in a bowl. Then turn out on to a hot plate and sprinkle with cheese. Serve hot.

SPINACH PIE

Pita od Spanača

strudel pastry, using	4 oz. cream cheese	1 oz. butter
8 oz. flour etc.	1 lb. spinach	1 tablespoon oil
(see p. 62)	2 eggs	salt and pepper
8 oz. cottage cheese	2 tablespoons milk	

Roll out the strudel pastry thinly and cut into 8 slices the same size as the pie-dish to be used. Wash the spinach well and cook until tender. Drain and chop finely or mince. Then add the cottage cheese and cream cheese, the eggs, milk, butter, salt and pepper and mix well. Oil a pie-dish, arrange alternate layers of the mixture and the slices of pastry, finishing with pastry. Bake in a moderate oven until the top is crisp and light golden brown. Cut into slices and serve hot.

CHEESE PIE

Pita od Sira

strudel pastry	4 oz. cream cheese	1 pint milk
(see p. 62)	4 oz. Swiss cheese	4 oz. butter
8 oz. cottage cheese	5 eggs	salt

Cut the Swiss cheese into small pieces and combine with the cottage and cream cheeses. Add the eggs, milk, a tablespoon of melted butter and ½ teaspoon of salt and mix well. Roll out the pastry very thinly and cut 12 slices, the shape and size of the baking tin to be used. Melt the rest of the butter, use a little to grease the baking tin, then place 2 or 3 thin sheets of the pastry at the bottom. Sprinkle with melted butter and place a layer of cheese mixture on top. Place layers of pastry and cheese mixture alternately, finishing with a covering of pastry. Sprinkle the top with the remaining melted butter and bake in a moderately hot oven until the pastry is crisp and golden. Serve hot.

ACKNOWLEDGMENTS

Illustrations by courtesy of the following:

Angel Studios: Plates 1, 4, 6, 19, 26, 44, 56, 68, 90, 92, 97, 105, 109, 112
Atora Suet: Plate 20
Bacon Information Council: Plates 42, 101
Batchelors Foods Ltd: Plates 49, 66, 114
Bird's Eye Foods Ltd: Plate 17
Blue Band Bureau: Plates 10, 59
British Egg Information Service: Plates 12, 46
Brown & Polson Ltd: Plate 108
Cheese Bureau, The: Plates 36, 40, 79
Colmans Semolina: Plates 62, 71, 107
Cookeen Test Kitchen: Plate 87
Country Life: Plate 72
Dutch Dairy Bureau: Plates 33, 60, 65, 70, 76, 85, 102, 119
Eden Vale Ltd: Plate 88
Farmer & Stockbreeder: Plates 5, 8, 21, 22, 24, 27, 28, 30, 34, 41, 63,
                       75, 80, 81, 103, 116
Flour Advisory Bureau: Plates 7, 58, 61
French Government Tourist Office: Plates 14, 38, 48, 50, 73, 84
H. J. Heinz Company Ltd., Editorial Service: Plates 25, 35, 54, 95,
Herring Industry: Plate 82
Kraft Foods Ltd: Plates 9, 11, 31, 39, 55
Mac Fisheries Ltd: Plates 91, 117, 118
McDougall: Plate 110
Pig Industry Development Council, Home Service: Plates 3, 13, 23, 69,
                                                74, 94

The Potato Desk: Plates 16, 29
Quaker Oats Ltd: Plates 18, 83
Spanish National Tourist Office: Plate 100
Spry Cookery Centre: Plates 43, 45, 57, 111
Stork Cookery Service: Plates 2, 52, 53, 86, 106, 113
Syndication International: Plates 15, 32, 37, 64, 67, 78, 93, 98, 99, 104
J. Walter Thompson Ltd: Plate 115

INDEX

Salt Rolls	59
Salty Yeast Dough for Rolls	
or Salt Sticks	166
Salzstangerln	59
Swarzbrot	313
Scottish Soda Scones	126
Striezel	60
Stuffed Bread Rolls	184
Sweet Scones	125
Vánochka	171
Yeast Dough	64
Bream:	
Baked Bream with Sauerkraut	134
Bela Riba sas Kiselo Zele	134
Bream in Garlic	591
Bream Stuffed with Kasha	433
Bream with Horseradish and	
Apples	434
Saran na Belom Luku	591
Stuffed Fish	435
Breast of Fattened Goose with	
Garlic	158
Breast of Pork Stuffed	152
Brennender Pudding	312
Breton Entrecôtes	230
Breton Salmon	221
Brill Saint-Germain	222
Brioches	273
Brittany Eggs	216
Broad Bean Soup Alfonsina	535
Broth with Rice	209
Brown Bean Soup	180
Brown Biscuits	521
Brown Sauce	258
Brunswick Cake	316
Brussels Pâté	78
Brussels Sprouts, Sauté	85
Bücklinge Herrings with Egg	29
Buckling, Smoked, with Eggs	499
Buckwheat Kasha	452
BUNS AND SMALL CAKES:	
Almond Tubes	316
Aniseed Cakes	313
Aniskuchen	313
Baked Batter Balls	168
Baklava	335
Banbury Cakes	121
Billets Doux	273
Borrachitos	575
Boter Letters	185
Buchteln	65
Bukhty	170
Buns with Filling	170
Caraway Sticks	316
Celestial Favours	176
Chelsea Buns	124
Chestnut Cakes	571
Chocolate Éclairs	270
Choux à la Crème	271
Cornish Splits	124
Cream Buns	271
Deep Fried Sailor Rings	522
Dicken Lebkuchen	314
Eccles Cakes	119
Fat Rascals	123
Gingerbread	314
Gypsy Slices	176
Honey and Nut Roll	573
Honey Balls	335
Honey Cakes	317
Honigkuchen	317
Hot Cross Buns	123
Hungarian Doughnuts	347
Indiánky	173
Kümmelstangen	316
Little Cakes for Visitors	573
Lomnice Rings	170
Loukoumades	335
Lucia Cats	520
Lusse Kattor	520
Macaroons	127
Madeleines	272
Maids of Honour	122
Mandelhippen	316
Meringues	272
Muffins	127
Nut and Syrup Pastry	335
Rich Potato Slices	177
Rozpeky	168
Rum Doughnuts	64
Saint Nicholas Day Letters	185
Scotch Shortbread	126
Shrove Tueasday Buns	522
Smetana Cakes	468
Swedish Pastries	521
Tipsy Cakes	575
Torta die Miel y Nueces	573
Visitas	573
Welsh Griddle Cakes	123
Windbeutel	314
Zephyrs	314
Burgundian Cheese Loaf	264
Burnt Sugar Icing	76
Butter Dumplings	24
Butter Icing	59
Butter Sauce, Austrian	53
Butter Sauce, French	263

C

Cabbage:	
Bavarian Red Cabbage	308
Beef Soup with Cabbage and	
Rice	143
Blauer Kohl	47
Cabbage and Apple Salad	484
Cabbage Pie	453
Cabbage Pirog	453
Cabbage Solianka	446
Cabbage Soup	207
Chou Farci	249
Fresh Cabbage Soup with Bacon	133
Garbure	207
Golubtsy	438
Kraut auf Wiener Art	46
Liha ja Kaalilaatikko	190
Meat with Cabbage	415
Minced Meat and Cabbage	190
Moravian Cabbage	162
Partridges with Cabbage	242

INDEX

INDEX

INDEX

INDEX

INDEX